SECOND EDITION

CASES IN
LEADERSHIP

THE IVEY CASEBOOK SERIES

A SAGE Publications Series

Series Editor

Paul W. Beamish
Richard Ivey School of Business
The University of Western Ontario

Books in This Series

SECOND EDITION

CASES IN LEADERSHIP

W. GLENN ROWE
The University of Western Ontario

LAURA GUERRERO
The University of Texas at El Paso

Los Angeles | London | New Delhi
Singapore | Washington DC

For information:

SAGE Publications, Inc.
2455 Teller Road
Thousand Oaks, California 91320
E-mail: order@sagepub.com

SAGE Publications Ltd.
1 Oliver's Yard
55 City Road
London EC1Y 1SP
United Kingdom

SAGE Publications India Pvt. Ltd.
B 1/I 1 Mohan Cooperative Industrial Area
Mathura Road, New Delhi 110 044
India

SAGE Publications Asia-Pacific Pte. Ltd.
33 Pekin Street #02-01
Far East Square
Singapore 048763

Printed in the United States of America.

Library of Congress Cataloging-in-Publication Data

Rowe, W. Glenn.
Cases in leadership / authored by W. Glenn Rowe, Laura Guerrero. — 2nd ed.
    p. cm.
Includes bibliographical references.
ISBN 978-1-4129-8019-7 (pbk.)
    1. Leadership—Case studies. 2. Management—Case studies. I. Guerrero, Laura K. II. Title.

HD57.7.R6895 2011
658.4'092—dc22   2009051845

This book is printed on acid-free paper.

10   11   12   13   10   9   8   7   6   5   4   3   2

Acquisitions Editor:	Lisa Cuevas Shaw
Editorial Assistant:	MaryAnn Vail
Production Editor:	Catherine M. Chilton
Copy Editor:	Kim Husband
Typesetter:	C&M Digitals (P) Ltd.
Proofreader:	Sue Irwin
Cover Designer:	Janet Kiesel
Marketing Manager:	Christy Guilbault

Contents

Introduction to the SAGE–Ivey Casebook Series

As the title of this series suggests, these books all draw from the Ivey Business School's case collection. Ivey has long had the world's second largest collection of decision-oriented, field-based business cases. Well over 1 million copies of Ivey cases are studied every year. There are more than 3,000 cases in Ivey's current collection, with more than 8,000 in the total collection. Each year approximately 200 new titles are registered at Ivey Publishing (www.iveycases.com), and a similar number are retired. Nearly all Ivey cases have teaching notes available to qualified instructors. The cases included in this volume are all from the current collection.

The vision for the original series was a result of conversations I had with SAGE's then–Senior Editor, the late Al Bruckner, starting in September 2002. Over the subsequent months, we were able to shape a model for the books in the series that we felt would meet a market need. Each volume in the original series contained text and cases. "Some" text was deemed essential in order to provide a basic overview of the particular field and to place the selected cases in an appropriate context. We made a conscious decision to not include hundreds of pages of text material in each volume in recognition of the fact that many professors prefer to supplement basic text material with readings or lectures customized to their interests and to those of their students.

In early 2010, Lisa Shaw, Executive Editor at Sage, contacted me about extending our publishing partnership. This present volume is a result.

The editors of the books in this new series are all highly qualified experts in their respective fields. I was delighted when each agreed to prepare a volume. We very much welcome your comments on this book.

Paul W. Beamish
Series Editor
and
Director, Ivey Publishing

Preface

The purpose of this leadership casebook is to expose MBA and undergraduate business students to cases that help them gain a better understanding of leadership. It is expected that this understanding will better enable them to be effective leader/managers and to more effectively lead their organizations given the opportunities and challenges they will face throughout their careers. This casebook may be used alone or serve as a supplement to a leadership textbook such as Northouse's (2010) *Leadership: Theory and Practice* (5th ed.). The cases selected for this casebook describe complex leadership issues that require the attention of the decision maker in the case.

In addition, the cases will generate much discussion in the classroom as students grapple with difficult real-world decisions that have grabbed the attention of real-world managers already. The casebook contains 29 cases (11 of which are new to this edition) from Ivey Publishing and 15 readings (7 of which are new to this edition) related to leadership issues from the *Ivey Business Journal*. In addition, we have added a new chapter on authentic leadership in accordance with the new chapter in Northouse (2010). Each chapter begins with a quotation (all of which are new) from a real-world CEO/former CEO or recognized leadership expert selected to introduce the concepts and theories in that chapter. For each chapter, we briefly summarize leadership concepts and theories and describe the relevance of the issues/problems in the case. As a whole, the cases provide students with the opportunity to practice and hone several skills. Some of these skills are the ability to analyze, to make decisions, to apply lessons learned, and to plan and engage in oral communication.

Kotter (1998) argued that business organizations are overmanaged and underled. Mintzberg (1998) suggested that as organizations become more diversified, those in leadership positions rely more on managerial skills and less on leadership skills. Rowe (2001) argued that large, overdiversified business organizations will lead to those with leadership skills only exercising managerial skills, using their leadership energy to fight the system, or leaving the organization. All these scenarios leave many organizations without strategic or visionary leadership and with only managerial leadership. This casebook is designed to help students grapple with leadership issues so that they can more effectively exercise leadership as well as exercise effective managerial skills. Leading is different from managing (Kotter, 1998; Mintzberg, 1998; Rowe, 2001; Zaleznik, 1977), and most, if not all, business schools teach their undergraduate and graduate students to be effective managers. Few business schools do as well at giving their students the opportunity to develop leadership skills. This casebook is designed to help leadership professors facilitate a discussion on leadership concepts among business students and to engage students in that discussion.

The cases are selected for their integrative issues. These include globalization, diversity, ethical dilemmas, and motivation. These issues will surface in several cases and are not emphasized in only one case. There is opportunity for professors to refer to previous cases and to integrate learning from one case into another case. Of course, all of the cases have leadership implications—whether they concern leading within the organization, leading teams, and/or leading oneself.

▧ References

Kotter, J. P. (1998). What leaders really do. In *Harvard Business Review on leadership* (pp. 37–60). Boston: Harvard Business School Press.

Mintzberg, H. (1998). Retrospective commentary on the manager's job: Folklore and fact. In *Harvard Business Review on leadership* (pp. 29–32). Boston: Harvard Business School Press.

Northouse, P. G. (2010). *Leadership: Theory and practice* (5th ed.). Thousand Oaks, CA: Sage.

Rowe, W. G. (2001). Creating wealth in organizations: The role of strategic leadership. *Academy of Management Executive, 15*, 81–94.

Zaleznik, A. (1977). Managers and leaders: Are they different? *Harvard Business Review, 55*, 67–78.

▧ Acknowledgments

We want to acknowledge and thank all of those involved in the writing of this book. First, we want to thank the staff at Ivey Publishing, the case writers, and the *Ivey Business Journal* authors, without whom this casebook would not have been possible. Second, this project would not have happened without the initiative, encouragement, and support of Paul Beamish and the late Al Bruckner. Without Al's support and encouragement, this book would not have been written. Third, MaryAnn Vail, Laureen Gleason, and Lisa Shaw displayed the nicest ability to encourage us to get done what needed to be done when it needed to be done. Fourth, we want to thank Daina Mazutis for writing the new chapter on authentic leadership. Finally, Kim Husband did a wonderful job as our copy editor—thank you.

▧ Dedications

Glenn Rowe

To Fay, Gillian, and Ryan—I love you very much.

Laura Guerrero

To my friends new and old—thank you for being there.

CHAPTER

1

Leadership: What Is It?

Leadership is, most fundamentally, about changes. What leaders do is create the systems and organizations that managers need, and, eventually, elevate them up to a whole new level or . . . change in some basic ways to take advantage of new opportunities.

—John P. Kotter[1]

Gary Yukl (2006) defines leadership as "the process of influencing others to understand and agree about what needs to be done and how to do it, and the process of facilitating individual and collective efforts to accomplish shared objectives" (p. 8). Peter Northouse (2010) defines leadership as "a process whereby an individual influences a group of individuals to achieve a common goal" (p. 3). These definitions suggest several components central to the phenomenon of leadership. Some of them are as follows: (a) Leadership is a process, (b) leadership involves influencing others, (c) leadership happens within the context of a group, (d) leadership involves goal attainment, and (e) these goals are shared by leaders and their followers. The very act of defining leadership as a process suggests that leadership is not a characteristic or trait with which only a few certain people are endowed at birth. Defining leadership as a process means that leadership is a transactional event that happens between leaders and their followers.

Viewing leadership as a process means that leaders affect and are affected by their followers either positively or negatively. It stresses that leadership is a two-way, interactive event between leaders and followers rather than a linear, one-way event in which the leader affects the followers but not vice versa. Defining leadership as a process makes it available to everyone—not just a select few who *are born with it*. More important, it means that leadership is not restricted to just the one person in a group who has formal position power (i.e., the formally appointed leader).

---

[1]John P. Kotter is the retired Konosuke Matsushita Professor of Leadership at Harvard Business School.

Leadership is about influence—the ability to influence your subordinates, your peers, and your bosses in a work or organizational context. Without influence, it is impossible to be a leader. Of course, having influence means that there is a greater need on the part of leaders to exercise their influence ethically.

Leadership operates in groups. This means that leadership is about influencing a group of people who are engaged in a common goal or purpose. This can be a small center for management development in a business school with a staff of 4, a naval ship with a ship's company of 300 (a destroyer) or 6,000 (an aircraft carrier), or a multinational enterprise such as Starbucks with more than 10,500 stores worldwide and in excess of 100,000 partners (employees). This definition of leadership precludes the inclusion of leadership training programs that teach people to lead themselves.

Leadership includes the achievement of goals. Therefore, leadership is about directing a group of people toward the accomplishment of a task or the reaching of an endpoint through various ethically based means. Leaders direct their energies and the energies of their followers to the achievement of something together—for example, hockey coaches working with their players to win a championship, to win their conference, to have a winning (better than 0.500) season, or to have a better won–lost percentage than last season. Thus, leadership occurs in, as well as affects, contexts where people are moving in the direction of a goal.

Leaders and followers share objectives. Leadership means that leaders work with their followers to achieve objectives that they all share. Establishing shared objectives that leaders and followers can coalesce around is difficult but worth the effort. Leaders who are willing to expend time and effort in determining appropriate goals will find these goals achieved more effectively and easily if followers and leaders work together. Leader-imposed goals are generally harder and less effectively achieved than goals developed together.

In this casebook, those who exercise leadership will be referred to as leaders, while those toward whom leadership is exercised will be referred to as followers. Both are required for there to be a leadership process. Within this process, both leaders and followers have an ethical responsibility to attend to the needs and concerns of each other; however, because this casebook is about leadership, we will focus more on the ethical responsibility of leaders toward their followers. Finally, it needs to be said that leaders are not better than followers, nor are they above followers. On the contrary, leaders and followers are intertwined in a way that requires them to be understood in their relationship with each other and as a collective body of two or more people (Burns, 1978; Dubrin, 2007; Hollander, 1992).

In the previous paragraphs, leadership has been defined and the definitional aspects of leadership have been discussed. In the next few paragraphs, several other issues related to the nature of leadership will be discussed: how trait leadership is different from leadership as a process, how emergent and appointed leadership are different, and how coercion, power, and management are different from leadership.

Trait Versus Process

Statements such as "She is a born leader" and "He was born to lead" imply a perspective toward leadership that is trait based. Yukl (2006) states that the trait approach "emphasizes leaders' attributes such as personality, motives, values, and skills. Underlying this approach was the assumption that some people are natural leaders, endowed with certain traits not possessed by other people" (p. 13). This is very different from describing leadership as a process. In essence, the trait viewpoint suggests that leadership is inherent in a few select people and that leadership is restricted to only those few who have special talents with which they are born (Yukl, 2006). Some examples of traits are the ability to speak well, an extroverted personality, or unique physical characteristics such as height (Bryman, 1992). Viewing leadership as a process implies that leadership is a phenomenon that is contextual and suggests that everyone is capable of exercising leadership. This suggests that leadership can be learned and that leadership is observable through what leaders do or how they behave (Daft, 2005; Jago, 1982; Northouse, 2010).

Assigned Versus Emergent

Assigned leadership is the appointment of people to formal positions of authority within an organization. Emergent leadership is the exercise of leadership by one group member because of the manner in which other group members react to him or her. Examples of assigned leadership are general managers of sports teams, vice presidents of universities, plant managers, the CEOs of hospitals, and the executive directors of nonprofit organizations. In some settings, it is possible that the person assigned to a formal leadership position may not be the person to whom others in the group look for leadership.

Emergent leadership is exhibited when others perceive a person to be the most influential member of their group or organization, regardless of the person's assigned formal position. Emergent leadership is exercised when other people in the organization support, accept, and encourage that person's behavior. This way of leading does not occur when a person is appointed to a formal position but emerges over time through positive communication behaviors. Fisher (1974) suggested that some communication behaviors that explain emergent leadership are verbal involvement, keeping well informed, asking other group members for their opinions, being firm but not rigid, and the initiation of new and compelling ideas (Fisher, 1974; Northouse, 2010).

The material in this casebook is designed to apply equally to emergent and assigned leadership. This is appropriate since whether a person emerged as a leader or was assigned to be a leader, that person is exercising leadership. Consequently, this casebook uses cases that focus on the leader's "ability to inspire confidence and support among the people who are needed to achieve organizational goals" (Dubrin, 2007, p. 2).

Leadership and Power

Power is related to but different from leadership. It is related to leadership because it is an integral part of the ability to influence others. Power is defined as the potential or capacity to influence others to bring about desired outcomes. We have influence when we can affect others' beliefs, attitudes, and behavior. While there are different kinds of power, in organizations, we consider two kinds of power—position power and personal power. Position power is that power that comes from holding a particular office, position, or rank in an organization (Daft, 2005). A university president has more power than a dean of a business school, but they both have formal power.

Personal power is the capacity to influence that comes from being viewed as knowledgeable and likable by followers. It is power that derives from the interpersonal relationships that leaders develop with followers (Yukl, 2006). We would argue that when leaders have both position and personal power, they should use personal power a vast majority of the time. Overuse of position power may erode the ability of a leader to influence people. Of course, it is important to know when it is most appropriate to use position power and to be able and willing to use it (Daft, 2005).

Power can be two-faced. One face is the use of power within an organization to achieve one's personal goals to the detriment of others in the organization. The other face is that power that works to achieve the collective goals of all members of the organization, sometimes even at the expense of the leader's personal goals.

Leadership and Coercion

Related to power is a specific kind of power called coercion. Coercive leaders use force to cause change. These leaders influence others through the use of penalties, rewards, threats, punishment, and negative reward schedules (Daft, 2005). Coercion is different from leadership, and it is important to distinguish between the two. In this casebook, it is important for you to distinguish between those who are being coercive versus those who are influencing a group of people toward a common goal. Using coercion is counter to influencing others to achieve a shared goal and may have unintended, negative consequences (Dubrin, 2007; Yukl, 2006).

Leadership and Management

Leadership is similar to, and different from, management. They both involve influencing people. They both require working with people. Both are concerned with the achievement of common goals. However, leadership and management are different on more dimensions than they are similar.

Zaleznik (1977) believes that managers and leaders are very distinct, and being one precludes being the other. He argues that managers are reactive, and while they are willing to work with people to solve problems, they do so with minimal emotional involvement. On the other hand, leaders are emotionally involved and seek to shape ideas instead of reacting to others' ideas. Managers limit choice, while leaders work to expand the number of alternatives to problems that have plagued an organization for a long period of time. Leaders change people's attitudes, while managers only change their behavior.

Mintzberg (1998) contends that managers lead by using a cerebral face. This face stresses calculation, views an organization as components of a portfolio, and operates with words and numbers of rationality. He suggests that leaders lead by using an insightful face. This face stresses commitment, views organizations with an integrative perspective, and is rooted in the images and feel of integrity. He argues that managers need to be two faced. They need to simultaneously be managers and leaders.

Kotter (1998) argues that organizations are overmanaged and underled. However, strong leadership with weak management is no better and may be worse. He suggests that organizations need strong leadership and strong management. Managers are needed to handle complexity by instituting planning and budgeting, organizing and staffing, and controlling and problem solving. Leaders are needed to handle change through setting a direction, aligning people, and motivating and inspiring people. He argues that organizations need people who can do both—they need leader-managers.

Rowe (2001) contends that leaders and managers are different and suggests that one aspect of the difference may be philosophical. Managers believe that the decisions they make are determined for them by the organizations they work for and that the organizations they work for conduct themselves in a manner that is determined by the industry or environment in which they operate. In other words, managers are deterministic in their belief system. Leaders believe that the choices they make will affect their organizations and that their organizations will affect or shape the industries or environments in which they operate. In other words, the belief systems of leaders are more aligned with a philosophical perspective of free will.

Organizations with strong management but weak or no leadership will stifle creativity and innovation and be very bureaucratic. Conversely, an organization with strong leadership and weak or nonexistent management can become involved in change for the sake of change—change that is misdirected or meaningless and has a negative effect on the organization. Bennis and Nanus (1985) expressed the differences between managers and leaders very clearly in their often quoted phrase: "Managers are people who do things right and leaders are people who do the right thing" (p. 221). Implicit in this statement is that organizations need people who do the right thing and who do the "right things right."

▧ References

Ashby, M. D., & Miles, S. A. (2002). *Leaders talk leadership: Top executives speak their minds.* Oxford: Oxford University Press.

Bennis, W. G., & Nanus, B. (1985). *Leaders: The strategies for taking charge.* New York: Harper & Row.

Bryman, A. (1992). *Charisma and leadership in organizations.* London: Sage.

Burns, J. M. (1978). *Leadership.* New York: Harper & Row.

Daft, R. L. (2005). *The leadership experience* (3rd ed.). Mason, OH: Thomson, South-Western.

Dubrin, A. (2007). *Leadership: Research findings, practice, and skills.* New York: Houghton Mifflin.

Fisher, B. A. (1974). *Small group decision-making: Communication and the group process.* New York: McGraw-Hill.

Hollander, E. P. (1992). Leadership, followership, self, and others. *Leadership Quarterly, 3*(1), 43–54.

Jago, A. G. (1982). Leadership: Perspectives in theory and research. *Management Science, 28*(3), 315–336.

Kotter, J. P. (1998). What leaders really do. In *Harvard Business Review on leadership* (pp. 37–60). Boston: Harvard Business School Press.

Mintzberg, H. (1998). Retrospective commentary on the manager's job: Folklore and fact. In *Harvard Business Review on leadership* (pp. 29–32). Boston: Harvard Business School Press.

Northouse, P. G. (2010). *Leadership: Theory and practice* (5th ed.). Thousand Oaks, CA: Sage.

Rowe, W. G. (2001). Creating wealth in organizations: The role of strategic leadership. *Academy of Management Executive, 15*(1), 81–94.

Yukl, G. (2006). *Leadership in organizations* (6th ed.). Upper Saddle River, NJ: Pearson-Prentice Hall.

Zaleznik, A. (1977). Managers and leaders: Are they different? *Harvard Business Review, 55,* 67–78.

▧ The Cases

Food Terminal (A)

In this case, a recently appointed store manager at a wholesale food company must make some decisions regarding management and leadership. The store is losing $10,000 per week, sales are spiraling downward, the key people in the company do not want him there, and employee morale is terrible.

Dickinson College: Inspiration for a Leadership Story (In the Vision of a Founding Father)

In January 1999, William Durden became the 27th president of his alma mater, Dickinson College. He quickly realized that for much of the 20th century, Dickinson had lacked a strong sense of organizational purpose. By autumn, Durden had turned to the life and writings of Dr. Benjamin Rush, who had secured the college charter in 1783, as the inspiration for the story. After introducing Durden and the challenges confronting Dickinson, the case describes the early history of the college and the ideas and accomplishments of Rush. It then provides students with a brief overview of the strategic challenges that had surfaced for Dickinson by the mid-1990s. The conclusion indicates that Durden still had to resolve many issues associated with the identity story.

▧ The Reading

Great Leadership Is Good Leadership

Look into the soul of any great leader and you will find a good leader. But if only that were the case! Some leaders, those who crave and bathe in the spotlight, are in fact not so great. Others, who are highly effective (and modest) and possess the five key characteristics this author describes, are good leaders first and foremost—which is what, in the end, makes them great!

The Food Terminal (A)

Prepared by Leo J. Klus, under the supervision of John F. Graham

In July 1991, three months after graduating from the Western Business School, 23-year-old Mike Bellafacia knew that he was in for a rough ride.

> When I arrived at the store, the staff morale was terrible. The previous manager had made a mess of things, the recession was hitting home, sales were spiralling downward quickly, and my store was losing $10,000 per week. To make matters worse, most of the key people in the company felt that I didn't deserve the store manager's position.

As the recently appointed store manager of the newest Foodco location in St. Catharines, Ontario, Mike knew that he had to turn the store around by improving its financial performance and the employee morale. He also knew that

something had to be done immediately because the losses at this store were seriously affecting the entire company.

▧ Foodco Ltd

Foodco Ltd. (FC), with its head office located in St. Catharines, Ontario, was a large player in the Niagara Peninsula grocery retailing industry. FC, a retailer in this market since 1962, was currently made up of seven stores: three St. Catharines locations, one Welland location, one Port Colborne location, and two Lincoln locations. Most of the ownership and key management positions were held by Frank Bellafacia, Tony Bellafacia, and Rocco Bellafacia, as shown in Exhibit 1. Selected financial ratios for FC are shown in Exhibit 2.

Version: (A) 2001-08-10

Exhibit I Personnel Organization Chart

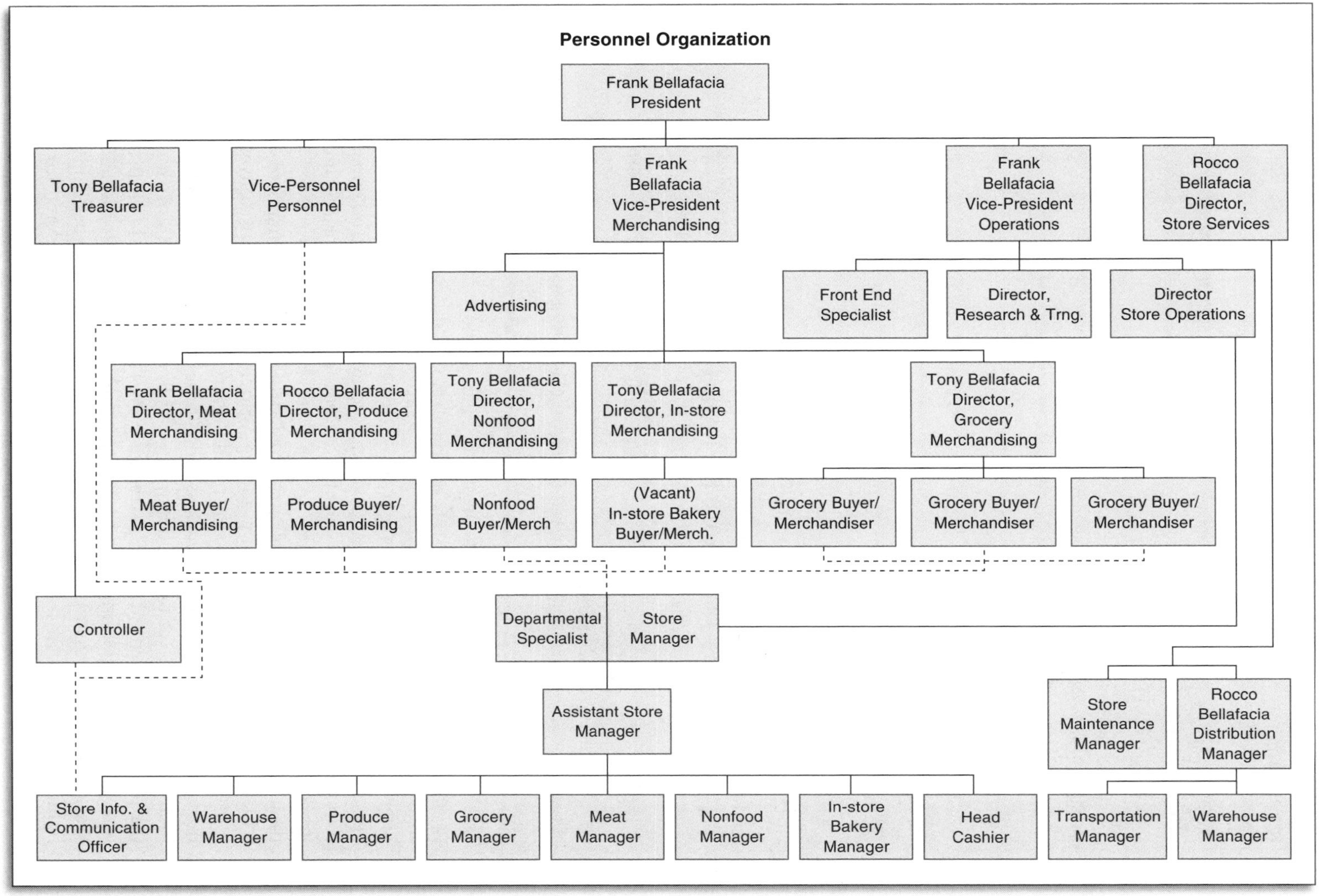

Personnel Organization

```
                                    Frank Bellafacia
                                       President

    Tony Bellafacia          Frank Bellafacia          Frank Bellafacia          Rocco Bellafacia
       Treasurer             Vice-President            Vice-President           Director, Store Services
                             Merchandising              Operations

    Vice-Personnel
       Personnel

                                                         Director,
                                                      Research & Trng.          Director Store Operations

                             Advertising                Front End
                                                        Specialist

    Frank Bellafacia        Rocco Bellafacia         Tony Bellafacia          Tony Bellafacia          Grocery Buyer/
    Director, Meat          Director, Produce        Director, Nonfood        Director, Grocery        Merchandiser
    Merchandising           Merchandising            Merchandising            Merchandising

                                                                                                       Grocery Buyer/
                                                                                                       Merchandiser

    Meat Buyer/             Produce Buyer/           Nonfood                  (Vacant)                 Grocery Buyer/
    Merchandising           Merchandising            Buyer/Merch              In-store Bakery          Merchandiser
                                                                              Buyer/Merch.
                                                                                                       Grocery Buyer/
                                                                                                       Merchandiser

    Controller                                       Departmental                                      Store Maintenance       Rocco Bellafacia
                                                     Specialist                                        Manager                 Distribution Manager

    Store Info. &                                    Assistant Store                                   Transportation          Warehouse
    Communication                                    Manager                                           Manager                 Manager
    Officer

    Warehouse    Produce      Grocery    Meat      Nonfood    In-store    Head
    Manager      Manager      Manager    Manager   Manager    Bakery      Cashier
                                                              Manager
```

Exhibit 2	Selected Financial Ratios				
	1986	**1987**	**1988**	**1989**	**1990**
PROFITABILITY					
Cost of goods sold	81.2%	80.2%	79.7%	78.7%	78.3%
Operating expenses	19.4%	18.7%	19.1%	19.6%	19.8%
Net income before tax	−1.1%	0.5%	0.3%	0.7%	0.7%
RETURN					
After-tax return on equity	0.0%	715.0%	n/a	725.0%	94.2%
STABILITY					
Interest coverage*	1.28x	1.36x	1.05x	1.19x	2.37x
LIQUIDITY					
Net working capital ($000)*	(1,447)	(2,051)	(13)	(316)	(243)
GROWTH					
Sales		26.0%	10.7%	14.1%	15.5%
Assets*		16.7%	3.8%	11.2%	9.6%
Equity*		−0.3%	1.2%	4.9%	19.5%

*Denotes a ratio calculated from the statements of Bellafacia's Consolidated Holdings Inc.

FC had created a powerful presence in this industry by developing and refining a strategy that worked. Their product offering was that of any typical supermarket: groceries, meats, bakery and dairy items, packaged foods, and nonfood items. Each store carried eight to ten thousand different items. FC planned to widen the selection available by adding more lines and to follow a general trend in consumer preferences toward an increased percentage of nonfood items in the product mix. Central to FC's strategy was a well-managed marketing effort. Weekly flyers were distributed that highlighted five or six items. FC priced these items below cost to draw customers. The rest of the flyer's products were representative of all the product groups. FC's ability to differentiate itself from the other competitors centred on its corporate vision: low food prices and fast, friendly service. Central to the FC competitive strategy was the mandate to be the low-price leader among conventional supermarkets, during good and bad economic times. Mike Bellafacia stated: "This is a no frills and low price store for a no frills and low price clientele. Most markets are shifting in this direction." FC had developed aggressive expansion plans with six stores being considered for development.

Exhibit 3 Front Page of the Weekly Flyer

✠ The Retail Grocery Industry

The job of managing the store and the staff became crucial to the overall success of FC given the demanding challenges in the industry. The industry was shifting from a simple mass market to a spectrum of distinct, serviceable segments. A recent statistic stated that 30 per cent of consumers switch stores every year. Moreover, a new Food Marketing Institute study found that consumers buy on the basis of the following criteria (ranked in decreasing priority): service, quality products, variety, and low prices. Thus, there was now more opportunity for competitive differentiation based on service and on quality than on price alone.

There were tremendous opportunities for niche players to enter the market, and such entrants had been observed. Health and organic food stores, fruit markets, and independent single-commodity stores (i.e., pet food stores) emerged and were servicing their target segments more effectively than the supermarkets were willing or able to do. Consumer demands varied from region to region, and many small independent retail grocers emerged to meet these demands both in the Niagara Peninsula and across all of Ontario. These independents managed not only to survive, but to take sizable portions of market share from the major chains. This shift toward niche marketing and catering to the local market outlined the need to employ store managers who understood how to please and retain the local customer.

✠ The Role of the Store Manager

The success of FC depended upon each of the seven store managers operating his/her store consistently with the corporate strategy. Traditionally, the road to store manager (SM) began within one of the stores at a lower management position. The family culture within each Food Terminal location was very important to FC management. Thus, store managers were selected from within the company to ensure a leader who understood the FC vision and values. Five managers reported directly to the SM, as shown in Exhibit 4, and their development was an important job for the SM. The SM position became increasingly more important at FC. Many of the current SM functions that used to be handled by the head office were delegated downward to the store level to allow head office to focus on overall company strategy. The stores were now more attuned to the local market they serve. An SM was responsible for the following:

1. Ensuring that merchandising skills were strong among all department managers;

2. Monitoring local market information;

3. Focusing staff on organizational goals (such as sales, gross margin, and profit goals);

4. Organizing weekly staff meetings;

5. Developing all employees and encouraging staff training;

6. Generating and producing sales, gross margin, and profit objectives;

7. Meeting cost objectives (motivating the staff to be cost conscious);

8. Analyzing the performance of each inter-store department; and

9. Attending FC "Top Management Meetings" (TMMs).

| Exhibit 4 | Scott & Vine Organizational Chart |

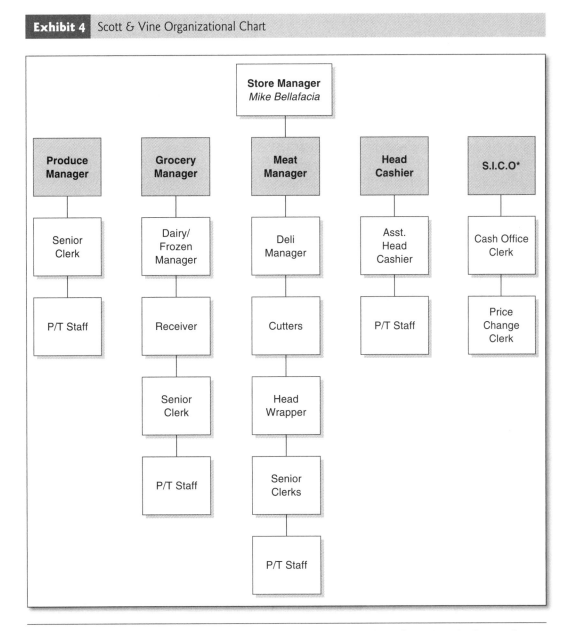

*Store Information and Communications Officer. Responsible for maintaining the lines of communication between the store and head office.

⌧ Mike Bellafacia's Background

Mike Bellafacia graduated from The University of Western Ontario with an Honors Business Administration degree (HBA). During his summers at university, he was assigned special projects from his father that focused on a variety of company problems. Mike would combine the analytical skills developed in the business school with his knowledge of the family business to address these issues. In his last year in the HBA program, Mike and a team of student consultants spent the year focusing on the long-term strategy and competitive advantage of FC. They examined every aspect of the company and developed many strategic recommendations for the top management at FC.

Upon graduation, Mike decided to work for FC. He planned to start off working in some of the various departments (i.e., the produce department) and at different stores within FC to work his way up in order to get the experience he needed to manage a store. This would have allowed him the opportunity to work under some of the most knowledgeable managers in the company. He didn't expect to be store manager so soon.

◼ The Scott & Vine Location: The First Month

Mike's career at FC was supposed to begin in one of the departments in the company. Both Mike and FC management felt strongly about that. However, while Mike was on vacation in May, FC management made a chancy decision. As of June 1, 1991, Mike Bellafacia would take over the SM position at the Scott & Vine location from the existing SM. The store's performance was deteriorating, and Mike was expected to change things. Mike reflected on the first week at the three-month old location:

> When I first started I was extremely nervous. The district supervisor brought me to the store to have a meeting with the department managers, and I could see the look of disappointment in their eyes. Most of these managers had been forced to move to this new store from other locations. The staff morale was definitely low to begin with. Combined with the fact that I am the boss's son,

they probably assumed that I was sent to check on them.

After getting settled in, Mike began to realize that something was terribly wrong at the Scott & Vine food terminal. The store was not producing a bottom line, and many of the 95 employees were not performing well. Mike commented:

> This building used to be a Food City that was on the verge of closing down. We acquired it and picked up where they left off. The task I had was to get above average performance from an average staff. They were just not driven to succeed, were poorly trained, and many of them, especially the managers, didn't want to be there.

The previous manager had performed poorly by FC standards. Although he had been an SM at other grocery stores, he was unable to create a productive atmosphere at this one. When this location opened, the sales level was $160,000 per week, but by Mike's first month it had dropped by 17 per cent. FC management expected this location to be operating at over $200,000 per week. The other St. Catharines stores were operating at over $350,000 per week. They had a long way to go.

What took place at the Scott & Vine location was a symptom of a more serious problem: the performance of FC as a whole. Mike explained the situation:

> Some of what was happening here can be attributed to FC. They became fat cats and, in the process, they lost touch with the customers. Pricing had gone way out of line, cross-border shopping was cutting into our bottom line, and our marketing efforts were poor. The weekly ads that are developed by head office for all the stores were not drawing in customers like they used to. As a result, we had no word-of-mouth advertising which is

so essential to a retail outlet. When our sales across the board went down, we had only ourselves to blame.

⬛ Sorting Through the Disorder

The job of managing the Food Terminal was overwhelming, and the problems were endless. Some of the more prevalent problems are listed below:

1. Product rotation (a job monitored by department managers and very important for customer satisfaction) was handled improperly.

2. It was not uncommon to find empty counters and shelves.

3. The staff paid very little attention to cleanliness. (Customers complained about this.)

4. Customers were not treated with respect by those employees who had frequent contact with them.

5. Department managers were doing a poor job of managing and motivating the employees in their departments.

6. Department sales and gross profit results were poor. (See Exhibit 5 for a breakdown of departmental sales and gross profit figures.)

Exhibit 5	Selected Financial Indicators, Scott & Vine Location, for the Week Ending June 9, 1991

Departmental Performance			
DEPARTMENT	SALES ($)	GROSS PROFIT ($)	% OF SALES
Produce	22,677	4,602	20.3
Grocery	77,363	12,467	16.1
Meat	32,963	7,629	23.1
Non-Food	4,784	1,228	25.7
IS-Bakery	2,337	934	40.0
TOTAL	140,124	28,860	19.2

Overall Store Performance (One Week)		
WEEKLY INDICATORS	BUDGET ($)	ACTUAL ($)
SALES	155,000	140,124
GROSS PROFIT	33,683	26,860
EXPENSES:		
Wages	16,483	19,600
Supplies	1,895	1,410
Other Expenses	17,091	16,257
TOTAL EXPENSES	35,469	37,267
NET INCOME	(1,786)	(10,407)
# OF CUSTOMERS	7,723/WEEK	

Difficulties arose within the staff that made the SM job even more strenuous. Mike described the situation:

There were a lot of people problems that I had to face. The weekly staff meetings we had together were a joke. Instead of a time to interact and solve problems together, it was just a waste of time. As well, the entire staff was demoralized due to the continual failure to meet monthly performance goals since the store opened. We had the worst performance in the FC organization. The controller of the company told me that the Scott & Vine location was hurting the entire company. I felt as though head office was blaming me for the store's poor performance, and I knew that I had to set some goals that we could all rally behind.

For the first month I was very auto-cratic. I had to be! I replaced all the cashiers that month, because of the numerous customer complaints about their attitude, but that was just the beginning of my problems. The part-time staff were continually standing around doing nothing. The receiver was not handling the deliveries very well. I found it tough to get along with the department managers. My worst employee problems came from the produce and meat managers. They just were not doing their jobs well. I tried going over the product orders with them, developing schedules, and assisting with their product display plans. I even brought in some of FC's department experts to go over things with them. They would not listen to any of my suggestions. Even though I had some problems with my grocery manager, I began to see that he had real potential for managing. There was some resentment toward me for

being a family member and getting the SM position so young, and as a result, people would not open up to me. I also knew that some of the other SMs at other locations didn't want me to succeed, and I found myself conve-niently left out of important SM meetings. To make matters worse, after two months here, the general manager of FC made it known that I should be pulled out of this job.

◪ Facing the Future

It was a tough season to compete in the retail grocery business. Mike Bellafacia found this out after only two months at the Food Terminal and the situation was now grave. The Scott & Vine location was losing over $10,000 per week and the sales level was stag-nant. The staff morale had changed very little. Customers were not responding to advertise-ment efforts, and things looked as if they were going to worsen. Mike reflected on what had happened during these last two months and where things were going. He wondered if he was responsible for the mess the store was in—had he mismanaged his managers, thereby making the situation worse? Had FC made a big mistake putting him in the posi-tion of SM? Thinking back on his education, Mike commented:

The business school helped me under-stand the decision-making process. I'm not afraid to make decisions, do analysis and pin-point problem areas. But it didn't teach me how to get the job done, the execution of a decision. More importantly, I was not prepared to deal with people who didn't have the training I did, or the desire to suc-ceed as I did.

Although he was unsure about these issues, he focused on what he should do to get the Scott & Vine food terminal operating profitably, with good management and with a growing customer base. As he looked over the financial data, he wondered if he should lay off some employees to bring the wages expense down. Mike reflected on this: "We didn't have the sales to support the exorbitant number of employees we had at the store." He was concerned about how he would handle these layoffs. He also thought about the serious morale problem. Many of the employees were lazy and demotivated, and customers complained regularly about cleanliness and service. He wondered if there was a way to use the weekly meetings to his advantage. Things seemed just as complicated as they did in June.

Dickinson College

Inspiration for a Leadership Story (in the Vision of a Founding Father)

By Michael J. Fratantuono

On a mid-October morning in 1999, William G. (Bill) Durden got up from his desk and looked out his window onto the main green of the campus. Many thoughts filled his mind. The prior January, the board of trustees had named him the 27th president of his alma mater, Dickinson College. In a few weeks, on October 30, during the autumn board meeting, he would be officially instated and deliver his inaugural address.

In both personal and professional terms, the appointment represented a dramatic turn of events. When contacted by the Dickinson search committee in late autumn of 1998, Durden was not initially interested in the position. Yes, he had graduated from Dickinson in 1971, was certainly grateful for the education he had received and was mindful of the opportunities that had flowed from that experience.[2] However, he was serving as the president of a division of the Sylvan Learning Systems, Inc. and the vice-president of academic affairs for the Caliber Learning Network, positions that he found challenging and rewarding. Furthermore, as an alumnus, he had become increasingly angry and frustrated that over the past few decades, the school had not realized its potential; sometimes he had even been embarrassed that the name Dickinson did not command more respect in academic and professional circles. He only agreed to take the job after talks with trustees, alumni, faculty and students convinced him there was a genuine, broad-based desire for fundamental change at the college.[3]

Once he decided to accept and was named by the board, Durden began the process of

---

Version: (A) 2008-04-16

[2]For example, Durden won a Fulbright Scholarship, studied in Switzerland and Germany, and earned a Ph.D. in German language and literature from Johns Hopkins University. He had stayed on at Johns Hopkins, taught in the German department for 16 years, and had become the executive director of the well known Center for Talented Youth (CTY). He had acted as a consultant and advisor to numerous government agencies, non-profit organizations, and foundations in the field of education. "President William G. Durden, Biography," Dickinson College web site, http://www.dickinson.edu/about/president/bio.html, accessed July 28, 2007.

[3]Bill Durden, "Comments as Guest Lecturer for the Dickinson College course, Financial Transformation of Dickinson College, February 6, 2007," Dickinson College, Carlisle, PA.

transition. In the spring, he had visited the college several times. On July 1, at the start of the academic year, he had moved into the president's office in West College, Dickinson's most historically significant building. In the final days of August, as the semester started, he had mingled with students and their families, and prepared his convocation speech. Over the past nine months, Durden had uncovered what he regarded as two shortcomings at the college. The first quickly surfaced. For its entire 216-year history, the college had never had a fully articulated strategy. That realization had informed Durden's first major goal: the college would have a strategic plan by the spring of 2000. Towards that end, in the spring of 1999 he had asked the dean and other administrators to invite respected members of the college to serve on a special committee. During the summer, he and the group read more than 1,200 pages of white papers, reports, self-studies, and other documents that had been written in recent years about Dickinson. Informed by that background material, with the start of the semester, the committee began to meet each week to start the process of writing a first draft of a high-level strategic plan, one that would identify a vision and mission, defining attributes, and priorities for the college. Their objective was to complete a first draft by late autumn, so that the document could be vetted by faculty, students, administrators and trustees; redrafted over the winter; re-circulated; and then released in final form to the community by the end of the academic year. Later that day, he would be attending another such meeting, participating not as a convener or facilitator, but as a contributor to the conversation. While the work was tough going, the attitude among committee members was upbeat and they had started to make some good progress.

The second shortcoming, more subtle and deeply embedded, involved the culture of the college. For much of the 20th century, the Dickinson community had lacked the sense of organizational pride and purpose one typically encountered at a college with a national reputation for excellence. Previous leaders had been comfortable with the status quo and had not conveyed a sense of urgency with respect to the internal and external challenges that confronted the school. Dickinson had remained relatively anonymous in the field of higher education, had failed to establish a strong and clear identity—the type of identity that could help distinguish the college from rivals and contribute to the experience of students, the sense of purpose of the faculty, and the affinity of alumni. That insight had come to Durden some two months earlier. During orientation week, he had gone on a day-hike with a group of students, and engaged in a lengthy conversation with a rising senior who had earned good grades and been deeply involved in campus life before spending time abroad during her junior year. The same evening, she sent him an e-mail and confessed that despite all that she had accomplished and experienced, she still did not have a clear sense of what it meant to be a Dickinsonian. That troubled Durden: if such an accomplished student could not explain what a Dickinson education stood for, then who could?[4]

The disturbing, albeit important, exchange with the young lady gave Durden a new purpose. That is, while Durden had—in addition to reading college documents for the special committee—also spent time throughout the summer studying the history of the college, the exchange had prompted him to revisit the circumstances associated with the college being granted a charter from the Assembly of Pennsylvania in 1783. Durden had become particularly intrigued by the life and writings of Dr. Benjamin Rush, the man responsible for founding the college. During a period of American history characterized by dramatic

---

[4]Bill Durden, "Leadership, Language Study, and Global Sensibility," keynote address delivered at the East Asia Regional Council of Overseas Schools (EARCOS), Ho Chi Minh City, Vietnam, November 2, 2004, http://www.dickinson.edu/about/president/earcos.html.

change in political, social, and economic affairs, Rush had articulated a clear and compelling vision for Dic kinson. Unfortunately, in rather short order, those managing college affairs chose to disregard Rush and dismiss some of the central elements of his plan. Soon thereafter, Rush and his vision faded as guiding lights: by the 1900s, new generations of Dickinson faculty and students—including Durden when he was an undergraduate—never heard much at all from old hands about the man, his efforts, or his ideas.

Through his various life experiences, Durden had developed a somewhat non-traditional view about leadership. First, while he was a voracious reader, he did not spend much time with popular books about business management. Instead, he far preferred to read works of literature and visit museums for insights about human nature and group dynamics. Second, he had come to appreciate the power of a leadership story for motivating and channeling the energies of members of an organization. In his various posts, he always asked himself and those around him, "What is our story?" and given the story, "How are we doing?"[5] Durden now wondered, could Rush's vision and the history surrounding the college's origin be translated into a leadership story that informed the strategic plan and helped establish a strong sense of identity among members of the Dickinson community?

Turbulent Events; Clear Vision (1681–1783)

Early History of Pennsylvania and of Carlisle[6]

William Penn was born in London in 1644 to a family of wealth and status—his father was Admiral Sir William Penn. He gradually gravitated to the beliefs of the Society of Friends, or Quakers, then a persecuted sect. Despite his conversion, he retained the trust of the Duke of York (later King James II) and thus good social standing at the King's Court. Given his beliefs, Penn petitioned the Crown for land in the Americas that might serve as a haven for those of all religious persuasions. Ultimately—and at least in part due to an outstanding debt of £16,000 owed to the estate of the admiral, who had passed away in 1670—King Charles II signed the Charter of Pennsylvania, named in honor of the elder Penn, in March of 1681. Later that year, Penn visited the colony and summoned a general assembly. Under the charter, while officials bearing the title lieutenant-governor would represent the interests of the Penn family, the assembly would concentrate on matters of concern to residents.

During the 1700s, immigrants to the colony tended to cluster according to their heritage. English Quakers and Anglicans gathered in the southeast, in and around Philadelphia, which became a vibrant center for commercial, political, and intellectual life. Germans, many among them followers of the Lutheran faith, tended to move to the central part of the colony and take up farming. Scottish and Irish settled further west and were primarily frontiersmen and practitioners of Presbyterianism.

To help shape development, in 1750 the Assembly established Cumberland County, which included all of Pennsylvania west of the Susquehanna River. In 1751, Carlisle, a community of between 500 and 1,000 people, who were mostly of Scottish-Irish descent, was designated as the county seat.[7]

In the 1750s, hostilities broke out between settlers and Indian tribes, and then between

---

[5]Bill Durden, comments as guest lecturer, February 6, 2007.

[6]Most of this section is based on information found at the web site of the Pennsylvania Historical and Museum Commission: http://www.phmc.state.pa.us/bah/pahist/quaker.asp, accessed July 2, 2007.

[7]Charles Coleman Sellers provides a nice sketch of the history of Carlisle and the town's most prominent citizens in *Dickinson College: A History*, Wesleyan University Press, Middletown, CT, 1973, chapter 2. A digital version of the book is available at http://chronicles.dickinson.edu/histories/sellers/toc_frame.html.

the British and the French over lands in the Allegheny Mountains and the Ohio River Valley. Carlisle served as an outpost for royal and provincial militias heading west, a place "where the wagon roads ended and the pack horse trails began."[8] By 1756, when the French and Indian War was officially declared, defenses in Carlisle had been fortified. By 1758, Carlisle was a boom town, with some speculating it might grow into a metropolis.[9]

In the 1750s and 1760s, Carlisle was also witness to a power struggle between two factions of Presbyterians, one that was being waged on a larger scale in congregations, grammar schools, and colleges throughout the colonies. Generally speaking, the Old Side (conservatives) displayed the two defining characteristics of the religion: they organized themselves into a traditional governance structure, under which congregations belonged to presbyteries, and presbyteries to synods; and they accepted traditional Calvinist theology, which asserted that God had to intervene in order for an individual to achieve salvation—essentially, a form of predestination that dismissed the relevance of human volition and self-reliance in shaping one's spiritual destiny. The New Side (progressives) had no quarrel with governance structure, but influenced by the Enlightenment, they saw a greater role for the individual: a person could evaluate scripture, attempt moral self-improvement, and in a moment of transformation be touched by God's grace and experience a personal "revival."[10] In Carlisle, while members of the Old Side maintained a dominant position in the local congregation, advocates of New Side principles established a foothold.

By the late 1760s, a Carlisle minister had begun to offer lessons to the boys living in the town. In 1772, construction of a church, under the leadership of an Old Side clergyman was completed, and it afforded space for regular school lessons. In keeping with the practices found in grammar schools of the day, boys 10 years of age and older studied moral philosophy ("the application of sound doctrine to right living"), Latin, Greek, and other topics. Schools such as this were only a step below and in some cases were an adjunct to the handful of colleges that had been established in the colonies.[11] In 1773, the Assembly granted a deed to a plot of land for a grammar school in Carlisle. Nine of Carlisle's most prominent residents, men who had achieved their status through their military, church, or commercial activities, were named to the school board.[12] While the school was immediately successful, the outbreak of the American Revolutionary War distracted all parties from the task of constructing a schoolhouse. Lessons continued to be held in the Presbyterian Church.

In 1781, the trustees were finally able to initiate construction of a new building. They also were intent on requesting a formal charter from the assembly, a document that would give the school status as a permanent corporation. In 1782, Colonel John Montgomery, one of the trustees, shared news of those developments with Dr. Benjamin Rush. Rush, who believed that an educated citizenry was the key to preserving liberties that had been earned during the American War for Independence, became intrigued—and a bit obsessed—by

---

[8]Ibid, p. 22.

[9]Ibid, p. 22 and p. 31.

[10]D. G. Hart and John R. Muether, "Turning Points in American Presbyterian History Part 3: Old Side versus New Side, 1741-1758," New Horizons, web site of the Orthodox Presbyterian Church, http://www.opc.org/nh.html?article_id=46 and The American Presbyterian Church, History of American Presbyterianism, http://www.americanpresbyterianchurch.org/htm.

[11]Charles Coleman Sellers, *Dickinson College: A History*, Wesleyan University Press, Middletown, CT, 1973, p. 3.

[12]James Henry Morgan, *Dickinson College: The History of One Hundred and Fifty Years 1783-1933*, Mount Pleasant Press, Carlisle, PA, 1933, Chapter 1. The book is also available in digital form at http://chronicles.dickinson.edu/histories/morgan/chapter_1.html.

the prospect of establishing a college in Carlisle.[13] Within a year Rush, in consultation with Montgomery and in conjunction with his compatriot and friend John Dickinson, would see his vision become a reality.

John Dickinson and Benjamin Rush: Founding Fathers of a New Country[14]

John Dickinson was born in 1732 and was raised as a Quaker, on his family's Maryland wheat and tobacco plantation. He received his higher education in London. Upon his return to the colonies, he settled in Philadelphia, began the practice of law, and was elected to the Pennsylvania Assembly. Dickinson became more deeply involved in public affairs when parliament levied the Stamp Act of 1765. Under the pen name A Farmer, he wrote 12 powerful essays that were published in newspapers throughout the colonies. Therein, he criticized the act on the grounds that it contradicted traditional English liberties, citing legal authorities and the works of antiquity to buttress his arguments. He was elected to the First Continental Congress of 1774 and made a significant contribution by drafting declarations in the name of that body. He was also elected to the Second Continental Congress.

On June 7, 1776, Richard Henry Lee of Virginia introduced a resolution in the Second Congress declaring the union with Great Britain dissolved, proposing the formation of foreign alliances, and suggesting the drafting of a plan of confederation to be submitted to the respective states. Dickinson stood in opposition, believing the colonies should first form a confederation before declaring independence from Great Britain.

One month later, on July 4, 1776, Dickinson held to his principles and in an act of moral courage, did not sign the Declaration of Independence. Given Dickinson's opposition to the declaration, he was assigned to a committee to draw up Articles of Confederation. The Congress was unable to reach agreement on the articles until November 17, 1777, at which time the articles were forwarded to each of the thirteen states. The articles were finally approved by a sufficient number to become operative on July 9, 1778.

At the conclusion of the Congress, Dickinson took a position as a colonel in the Continental Army. However, he eventually resigned his commission, due to what he interpreted as a series of insults stemming from the public stance he had taken. While there is a mixed record, some accounts suggest he subsequently served as a private soldier at the Battle of Brandywine. Following that service, he remained centrally involved in political affairs. In 1782, Dickinson was elected president of the Supreme Executive Council of Pennsylvania, a post equivalent to a modern day governor. In 1786 he participated in and was elected president of a convention at Annapolis to revise the Articles of Confederation. The brief session was soon adjourned, in favor of a constitutional convention held in Philadelphia from May to September, 1787. In the latter gathering, Dickinson drafted passages that dealt with the election of and powers for the President of the United States. The constitution was completed in 1787. To promote ratification, Dickinson wrote nine widely read essays under the pen name Fabius. The constitution was adopted in 1788 and took effect in 1789, thereby replacing the Articles of Confederation. While amended over time, it is the oldest, operative, written

---

[13]Charles Coleman Sellers**,** *Dickinson College: A History*, Wesleyan University Press, Middletown, CT, 1973, chapter 3 provides a history of the grammar school.

[14]This section is based on a range of sources, including the respective entries for Benjamin Rush and John Dickinson found in the Chronicles of Dickinson College, *Encyclopedia Dickinsonia*, http://chronicles.dickinson.edu/encyclo/r/ed_rushB.html and http://chronicles.dickinson.edu/encyclo/d/ed_dickinsonJ.html, as well as a variety of other web sites dealing with John Dickinson, Richard Henry Lee and the Second Continental Congress.

constitution in the world. Given his patriotic efforts, Dickinson earned a spot in U.S. history as the "Penman of the Revolution."

Benjamin Rush was born in 1745 on a farm near Philadelphia. He was raised in the Calvinist tradition. He earned his bachelor's degree in 1760 from the University of New Jersey (subsequently renamed Princeton), returned to Philadelphia and studied medicine from 1761 until 1766, and then moved abroad and earned a degree in medicine from the University of Edinburgh (Scotland) in June 1768. He returned once again to Philadelphia in 1769 and started a private practice while also serving as the professor of chemistry at the College of Philadelphia. He wrote essays on a range of subjects. His commentary about the emerging crisis between the colonies and Britain brought him into association with men such as John Adams and Thomas Jefferson. When the American Revolutionary War broke out in 1775, Rush joined the Continental Army as a surgeon and physician. In June 1776, he was appointed to the Second Continental Congress. Unlike Dickinson, when the time came, he chose to sign the declaration.

In April 1777, Rush was appointed surgeon-general of the Continental Army. However, he soon became embroiled in a dispute with Dr. William Shippen, Jr., director of hospitals for the Continental Army, about medical conditions for the troops. He wrote letters about his concerns to key persons, including Commander in Chief George Washington.[15] When he received no answers, Rush wrote a letter to Patrick Henry: therein, he repeated his concerns and expressed doubts about Washington's leadership.[16] After Henry disclosed the contents of the letter to Washington, Rush was asked to appear before a congressional committee. The committee sided with Shippen, prompting Rush to resign his

commission. Nonetheless, Rush would not let the matter drop. He continued to write letters to Washington and other leaders, claiming that Shippen was guilty not only of mismanagement, but also of selling supplies intended for patients for his own profit. In one such letter to Nathaniel Greene, he unleashed his scathing wit.

> I find from examining Dr. Shippen's return of the numbers who die in the hospitals that I was mistaken in the accounts I gave of that matter in my letters to you. . . . All I can say in apology for this mistake is that I was deceived by counting the number of coffins that were daily put under ground. From their weight and smell I am persuaded they contained hospital patients in them, and if they were not dead I hope some steps will be taken for the future to prevent and punish the crime of burying Continental soldiers alive.[17]

In January of 1780, Shippen was arrested. In what was regarded as an "irregular trial," which included Shippen wining and dining members of the hearing board, he was acquitted by one vote.[18] Rush eventually repaired his private relationship with Washington, but given that Washington had already started his rise to god-like status at the time of Rush's letter to Patrick Henry, the incident undermined Rush's public reputation for a number of years to come.

Rush returned to his practice in Philadelphia in 1778. In 1780, he began to lecture at the new University of the State of Pennsylvania. In 1783, Rush joined the staff of the Pennsylvania Hospital. He was relentless in his efforts to help battle the yellow fever epidemics which repeatedly surfaced in Philadelphia between 1793 and

---

[15]*Letters of Benjamin Rush*, Princeton University Press, Princeton, NJ, 1951, Volume 1, p. 180–182.

[16]Ibid, p. 182–183.

[17]Ibid, p. 195.

[18]"William Shippen, Jr.," University of Pennsylvania Archives, http://www.archives.upenn.edu/histy/features/1700s/people/shippen_wm_jr.html, accessed September 23, 2007.

1800; however, he was excoriated by some contemporaries for his aggressive advocacy and use of purging (bleeding) as proper treatment for the disease. Ultimately, he gained the reputation as a pioneer, credited with writing the first textbook published in the United States in the field of chemistry and the first major treatise on psychiatry. At the time of his death in 1813, he was regarded as the preeminent physician in the United States.

In 1787, Rush briefly reentered politics: he actively advocated ratification of the constitution and was appointed to the ratifying convention for the state. Of greater significance, Rush was an ardent social activist—he helped found the Pennsylvania Society for Promoting the Abolition of Slavery—and a prolific writer, advocating prison reform, abolition of capital punishment, temperance, better treatment of mental illness, universal health care, and a robust system of education. In 1797, he was appointed by President John Adams to be treasurer of the United States Mint, a post he occupied until he passed away.

Rush's Values and World View

Rush was a complex character. He accumulated an enormous breadth of formal knowledge, was a keen observer of everyday events, and was able to engage in either detailed analysis or sweeping generalization. He was a man of principle who would not back down in the face of pressure. At times, he was charming and persuasive, at others, nasty and domineering. While he could be a loyal, devoted, and caring friend, he sometimes abruptly turned on those who did not share his sentiments or opinions, and only later sought reconciliation.

All of Rush's efforts to institute social reforms and promote the cause of education in the new country were informed by his assertion that the struggle for independence was a never ending process, illustrated for example by a public statement he made in 1787.

> There is nothing more common than to confound the terms of American Revolution with those of the late American war. The American war is over; but this is far from being the case with the American Revolution. On the contrary, nothing but the first act of the great drama is closed.[19]

Rush was the type of man who, as the years passed by, could be found arguing positions he had previously rejected—at times he even appeared to be self-contradictory.[20] Despite that tendency, at the most fundamental level he was concerned with two sets of relations: the configuration of social institutions such as family, church, school, and state; and the role of the individual within the context of those institutions.

Rush was informed by and contributed to three major intellectual movements of his time. First was the Scottish Enlightenment.[21] The University of Edinburgh, where Rush received his medical training, was an important center of the movement. Like their French counterparts, Scotsmen wrote about the power of the human mind to uncover the logic of natural laws, and celebrated the scientific achievements of the 17th century. However, they had an additional point of emphasis: they were concerned that Scotland, which in 1707 had been unified with an economically superior England, risked becoming a poverty-stricken backwater. Thus, men such as David Hume and Adam Smith investigated moral philosophy, history, and political economy in order to better understand the process of economic growth and development, in hope of applying insights and keeping Scotland economically vibrant.

---

[19] *Letters of Benjamin Rush*, Princeton University Press, Princeton, NJ, 1951, Volume 1, p. lxviii.

[20] Ibid, introduction.

[21] Department of Economics, New School for Social Research, "Scottish Enlightenment," The History of Economic Thought http://cepa.newschool.edu/het/schools/scottish.htm.

Second, Rush was raised as a Calvinist. He gradually became sympathetic to the teachings of the New Side Presbyterians. The College of New Jersey was decidedly Presbyterian in its affiliation. While at Edinburgh, Rush, acting at the behest of some of the College of New Jersey Trustees, wrote to and visited with the progressive Scottish clergyman John Witherspoon, and convinced Witherspoon and his wife that Witherspoon should accept the presidency of the college. That was a maneuver important in the ongoing struggle being waged at the school between Old Side and New Side factions. Nonetheless, in later years, Rush became frustrated with Presbyterian elders and began to attend services of various Christian faiths. Even later in life, he withdrew to his own private reflections on religious matters.

Third, in terms of political philosophy, Rush's position also changed. In the years preceding the American Revolution, he was radical in his beliefs, calling for an overthrow of existing authority. As the prospect of independence became more certain, Rush became more conservative. For example, in the early 1780s, he asserted that democracy "meant rule by an elite drawn from the whole," with the elite reflecting the influence of God's grace.[22] A few years later, in the debate regarding the need for a bill of rights in the U.S. Constitution, Rush was sympathetic to the conservative views associated with the Federalist Party of John Adams, and stood in opposition to the Democrat-Republicans and Thomas Jefferson, who favored a more egalitarian concept of democracy.

> There can be only two securities for liberty in any government . . . representation and checks. By the first the rights of the people, and by the second the rights of representation, are effectively secured. Every part of a free constitution hangs upon these two points; and these form the two capital features of the proposed Constitution of the United States. Without them, a volume of rights would avail nothing; and with them, a declaration of rights is absurd and unnecessary.[23]

In the presidential election of 1796, however, he favored Jefferson, who was defeated by Adams. In the early 1800s, he maintained a steady correspondence with Jefferson, who by that time had been elected president, as well as with Adams.

In 1797, when Rush was seeking the position at the U.S. Mint, Judge Richard Peters, a long-time Philadelphia Federalist, was asked by Secretary of State Pickering to provide a written evaluation of Rush. Peters suggested that Rush had made a series of bad political choices over time—he had after all, gravitated to the Democrat-Republicans—and had suffered from the Shippen affair. But he went on to say the following.

> I lament his Want of Stability, for he certainly has great Merit, unshaken Integrity & eminent Talents. . . . I admire his Abilities, lament his Foibles, & with them all sincerely love him, therefore I cannot but wish him gratified.[24]

⬛ Securing a College Charter[25]

Rush imagined that the college in Carlisle would be part of a larger system that also included a handful of colleges located throughout the state and a university in Philadelphia. At the outset, it would be located at the site of the grammar school. He initially asserted that it should be affiliated with one religion—in this case the Presbyterian Church—and that a symbiotic relationship existed between religion and learning.

---

[22]Charles Coleman Sellers, *Dickinson College: A History*, Wesleyan University Press, Middletown, CT, 1973, p. 53.

[23]*Letters of Benjamin Rush*, Princeton University Press, Princeton, NJ, 1951, Volume 1, p. 453.

[24]Ibid, p. 1210.

[25]The following paragraph is based on James Henry Morgan, *Dickinson College: The History of One Hundred and Fifty Years 1783–1933*, Mount Pleasant Press, Carlisle, PA, 1933, chapter 2.

Religion is best supported under the patronage of particular societies. Instead of encouraging bigotry, I believe it prevents it by removing young men from those opportunities of controversy which a variety of sects mixed together are apt to create and which are the certain fuel of bigotry. Religion is necessary to correct the effects of learning. Without religion I believe learning does real mischief to the morals and principles of mankind; a mode of worship is necessary to support religion; and education is the surest way of producing a preference and constant attachment to a mode of worship.[26]

Rush soon realized that in order to achieve his objective of founding a college, he would have to win the support of three groups of constituents. First were the leaders of Carlisle, for although Montgomery endorsed the idea, others who were on the board of the grammar school were resistant. Second was the Doneg al Presbytery, composed of elders from congregations located in communities throughout the region. Third was the Assembly of Pennsylvania. The need to win over the last group led him to retreat from the notion of an exclusive affiliation with the Presbyterian Church, and to consider a non-sectarian school, one that could be endorsed by clergymen of other Christian faiths including the Lutherans, and could eventually win financial support from the assembly.

Thus, during the first eight months of 1783, Rush adapted four sets of tactics. First, he contacted influential and wealthy friends from Philadelphia to elicit political support and financial commitments for the college. Among those he visited was John Dickinson, who was by that time the president of the Supreme Executive Council of Pennsylvania. Dickinson rejected Rush's first proposal to name the school John

and Mary's College after Dickinson and his wife, on grounds that it sounded too much like the College of William and Mary, which had been named for British royalty; however, he gradually warmed to the idea of a college that would bear his family name.[27] Second, Rush wrote letters to those he knew objected to the plan, and made his case for a school: it would obviate the need for young men from the Carlisle region to travel to Philadelphia or New Jersey for an education; and it would contribute to the emergence of a new commercial center in Carlisle, thereby raising land prices and creating better economic balance with Philadelphia, which dominated the eastern part of the state.[28] Third, in light of the heavy Scottish-Irish presence in the region, Rush argued that the college would provide a sound educational foundation to young men who aspired to be ministers in the Presbyterian Church. Fourth, he told those he contacted about the pledges of money and support he had already earned from others, and held out the promise of positions on the board of trustees of the college to people representing different professions, religions, and parts of Pennsylvania. As Rush acknowledged, the going was not easy.

[One group of opponents] accuse us of an attempt to divide the Presbyterians . . . [To some groups] they say our college is to be a nursery . . . of the Old Lights [Old Side]—with the Old Lights they accuse us of a design to spread the enthusiasm of the New Lights [New Side] through the state. . . . In some of their letters and conversations I am considered as a fool and a madman. In others I am considered as a sly, persevering, and dangerous kind of fellow. Almost every epithet of ridicule and resentment in our language has been exhausted upon me in public newspapers and in private cabals since the

---

[26]*Letters of Benjamin Rush*, Princeton University Press, Princeton, NJ, 1951, Volume 1, p. 294–295.

[27]Charles Coleman Sellers, *Dickinson College: A History*, Wesleyan University Press, Middletown, CT, 1973, p. 55.

[28]*Letters of Benjamin Rush*, Princeton University Press, Princeton, NJ, 1951, Volume 1, p. 294–296.

humble part I have acted in endeavoring to found a college at Carlisle.[29]

Nonetheless, his methods worked. He successfully neutralized critics in Carlisle. In spring of 1783, the Donegal Presbytery endorsed the idea of a college. And, on September 9, 1783, by a margin of only four votes, the General Assembly of Pennsylvania approved the Dickinson College charter, entitled "An act for the establishment of a college at the borough of Carlisle, in the county of Cumberland, in the state of Pennsylvania."[30]

The date of the charter fell only six days after the September 3, 1783, signing of the Treaty of Paris, an event that formally ended the American Revolutionary War and included recognition by the United Kingdom and by France of the thirteen colonies as independent states.

Rush's Vision for the New College

Rush's philosophical leanings informed his vision of a Dickinson education. At the third Carlisle meeting of August 1785, Rush shared his "Plan of Education for Dickinson College." The original document, which survived, is filled with notations, suggesting Rush's plan was modified during conversations with other board members. The initial curriculum actually approved by the board included instruction in six major areas of study: (1) philosophy of the mind, moral philosophy and belles lettres (the translation from French is "fine letters" or "fine literature"), economics, and sociology; (2) Greek and Latin; (3) history and chronology; (4) mathematics; (5) English; and (6) natural philosophy (science).

As far as Rush was concerned, the curriculum was not ideal. For example, in his plan,

Rush had placed chemistry in the same cluster of courses as mathematics and natural philosophy; but it was lined through. Given that Rush was one of the leading experts in the field in the United States, and that he believed that chemistry was fundamental to other sciences and could be applied to fields of practical importance in the new nation, such as agriculture and manufacturing, the omission of chemistry as a stand-alone topic in the initial Dickinson curriculum had to be a source of frustration to him: indeed, the first professor in that field did not arrive at Dickinson until 1810.[31] Furthermore, while Rush believed that history and government were critical courses, he downplayed the significance of moral philosophy. Finally, despite his low opinion regarding the study of Greek and Latin, he had made a strong concession: in light of the central place those languages held in the education of the times, they should be included in Dickinson's program. But he did expect that modern languages such as French and German should also be taught.[32] However, as was the case with chemistry, the first faculty member who was expert in Spanish, Italian and French did not arrive on the scene until 25 years had passed. It took even longer for a professor of German to come to Dickinson.

Rush's disappointment with the shape of the initial Dickinson curriculum did not stop him from speaking out and staying involved in educational reforms. In 1786, Rush wrote the first version of an essay entitled, "Upon the spirit of education proper for the College in a Republican State," in which he more clearly and fully articulated his view of the purpose, principles, and content of the education that should be provided at Dickinson College (see Exhibit 1).

---

[29]Ibid, p. 299–300.

[30]A digital copy of the original charter is available at the Chronicles of Dickinson College, http://chronicles.dickinson.edu/archives/charter_orig/. A digital copy of the original plus subsequent amendments through 1966 is available at http://chronicles.dickinson.edu/archives/charter_1966/charter.html#amendments.

[31]Charles Coleman Sellers, *Dickinson College: A History,* Wesleyan University Press, Middletown, CT, 1973, Appendix A, p. 507–508.

[32]Ibid, p. 81–82.

Exhibit 1

Selected Passages From Benjamin Rush, "Of the Mode of Education Proper in a Republic"

The business of education has acquired a new complexion by the independence of our country....

An education in our own, is to be preferred to an education in a foreign country. The principle of patriotism stands in need of the reinforcement of prejudice ... formed in the first one and twenty years of our lives.

Our schools of learning, by producing one general, and uniform system of education, will render the mass of the people more homogenous, and thereby fit them more easily for uniform and peaceable government.

The only foundation for a useful education in a republic is to be laid in Religion. Without this there can be no virtue, and without virtue there can be no liberty, and liberty is the object and life of all republican governments....

Next to the duty which young men owe to their Creator, I wish to see a regard to their country, inculcated upon them. [Our student] ... must love private life, but he must decline no station ... when called to it by the suffrages of his fellow citizens.... He must avoid neutrality in all questions that divide the state, but he must shun the rage, and acrimony of party spirit.

[To improve students' ability to absorb their lessons] it will be necessary to subject their bodies to physical discipline.... [T]hey should live upon a temperate diet ... should avoid tasting Spirituous liquors. They should also be accustomed occasionally to work with their hands.... [They should receive guidance on] those great principles in human conduct—sensibility, habit, imitations and association.

[Students should not be crowded] together under one roof for the purpose of education. The practice is ... unfavorable to the improvements of the mind in useful learning.... [If we require them to separately live in private households] we improve their manners, by subjecting them to those restraints which the difference of age and sex, naturally produce in private families.

A knowledge of [the American language is essential] ... to young men intended for the professions of law, physic, or divinity ... [and] in a state which boasts of the first commercial city in America.

The French and German languages should ... be ... taught in all our Colleges. They abound with useful books upon all subjects.

Eloquence ... is the first accomplishment in a republic ... We do not extol it too highly when we attribute as much to the power of eloquence as to the sword, in bringing about the American Revolution.

History and Chronology [are important because the] ... science of government, whether ... related to constitutions or laws, can only be advanced by a careful selection of facts, [especially those related to the] ... history of the ancient republics, and the progress of liberty and tyranny in the different states of Europe.

(Continued)

(Continued)

Commerce . . . [is] . . . the best security against the influence of hereditary monopolies of land, and, therefore, the surest protection against aristocracy. I consider its effects as next to those of religion in humanizing mankind, and lastly, I view it as the means of uniting the different nations of the world together by the ties of mutual wants and obligations.

Chemistry by unfolding to us the effects of heat and mixture, enlarges our acquaintance with the wonders of nature and the mysteries of art . . . [and is particularly important] [i]n a young country, where improvements in agriculture and manufactures are so much to be desired.

[T]he general principles of legislation, whether they relate to revenue, or to the preservation of liberty or property . . . [should be examined, and towards this end, a student should] be directed frequently to attend the courts of justice . . . [and for this reason] colleges [should be] established only in county towns.

[T]he prerogatives of the national government . . . [should be studied, including] those laws and forms, which unite the sovereigns of the earth, or separate them from each other.

[W]omen in a republic . . . should be taught the principles of liberty and government; and the obligations of patriotism should be inculcated upon them.

SOURCE: Selected by the case author from Benjamin Rush, "Of the Mode of Education Proper in a Republic," *Essays, Literary, Moral & Philosophical*, printed by Thomas and Samuel F. Bradford, Philadelphia 1798: (available in digital form at http://deila.dickinson.edu/theirownwords/title/0021.htm; accessed July 23, 2007).

He asserted that a liberal education should be informed by the core values associated with religious doctrine—especially that of the New Testament—in order to cultivate virtue; in turn, virtue was essential to liberty, and liberty to a republican form of government. An education should promote a sense of homogeneity, civic duty, and patriotism among young men and women who had a critical role to play in shaping the new nation. With respect to the residential experience, students should live with host families rather than in dormitories, in order to learn civility and to develop an appreciation of family values. In terms of life style, students should have a balanced diet, avoid consuming liquor, and be exposed to rigorous physical activity and manual labor, all for the purpose of learning discipline and achieving balance in the conduct of life and affairs. A college should be located in a county seat, so that students could leave the classroom, visit the courthouse and witness government in action. The curriculum should not be preoccupied with the classics, but instead should include subjects—from history, to contemporary foreign languages such as French and German, to mathematics and chemistry—that were useful, that would help strengthen the intellectual, economic, political, and technical foundations of the new republic.

In "Thoughts on Female Education" written in 1787, he argued that in America, which had fewer class distinctions and a lower prevalence of servants than did England, a woman needed an education so she could be a partner to her husband in managing household property and affairs.[33] In "Observations on the Study of Greek and Latin," written in 1791, Rush posited that because useful knowledge was

---

[33]Benjamin Rush, "Thoughts Upon Female Education, Accommodated to the Present State of Society, Manners, and Government in the United States of America—July 28, 1787," *Essays Literary, Moral, and Philosophical*, Thomas & Samuel F. Bradford, Philadelphia, 1798, available in digital form at http://deila.dickinson.edu/cdm4/document.php?CISOROOT=/ownwords&CISOPTR=19843.

disseminated in contemporary languages, time spent studying Greek and Latin crowded out topics more relevant to a republic.[34] He also pointed to the instrumental and intrinsic nature of a liberal education.

The great design of a liberal education is to prepare youth for usefulness here, and happiness hereafter.[35]

Citing rationales similar to those he cited when founding Dickinson, Rush continued to endorse other educational initiatives. For example— and perhaps a reflection of his disappointment about the absence of German language at Dickinson[36]—he helped found in 1787, in Lancaster, Pennsylvania—located only 55 miles from Carlisle—the German College, which was subsequently named Franklin College and even later Franklin and Marshall College. Since instruction would be in English, he believed the school would help German-speaking citizens in that part of the state be more quickly assimilated and eliminate barriers between them and English speaking inhabitants. Meanwhile, he felt that capability in German could be preserved, and employed to understand books and articles from the sciences and other fields written in that language. He also believed the school would help unite the Calvinists and Lutherans among the German population.[37]

As another illustration of his thinking, in 1788, Rush publicly advocated a federal university to help prepare youth for civil and professional life, one which students would attend after completing a college education in their respective home states.[38] A promising handful

should be deployed to Europe, and others selected to travel the United States, to collect insights on the latest innovations in agriculture, manufacturing, commerce, the art of war, and practical government, in order to report these to their faculty. The purpose of the curriculum for the University was much like that he had proposed for Dickinson College: it should be forward looking and practical in its orientation.

> While the business of doing education in Europe consists in lectures upon the ruins of Palmyra and the antiquities of Herculaneum, or in disputes about Hebrew points, Greek particles, or the accent and quantity of the Roman language, the youth of America will be employed in acquiring those branches of knowledge which increase the conveniences of life, lessen human misery, improve our country, promote population, exalt the human understanding, and establish domestic social, and political happiness.[39]

Rush and Nisbet[40]

On the important question of who should serve as the first headmaster, Rush strongly endorsed a well renowned scholar Dr. Charles Nisbet of Montrose, Scotland, who had completed his studies at Edinburgh in 1754—twelve years prior to the time when Rush started his studies—and was also deeply influenced by the Scottish

---

[34]Benjamin Rush, "Observations on the Study of Latin and Greek Languages, As a Branch of Liberal Education, With Hints of a Plan of Liberal Instruction, Without Them, Accommodated to the Present State of Society, Manners, and Government in the United States—August 24, 1791," *Essays Literary, Moral, and Philosophical*, Thomas & Samuel F. Bradford, Philadelphia, 1798, p. 21, available in digital form at http://deila.dickinson.edu/cdm4/document.php?CISOROOT=/ownwords&CISOPTR=19843.

[35]Ibid, p. 27.

[36]This possibility was suggested by Bill Durden, interview with the case author, October 23, 2007.

[37]*Letters of Benjamin Rush*, Princeton University Press, Princeton, NJ, 1951, Volume 1, p. 420–429.

[38]Ibid, p. 491–495.

[39]Ibid, p. 494.

[40]This section is primarily based on James Henry Morgan, *Dickinson College: The History of One Hundred and Fifty Years 1783–1933*, Mount Pleasant Press, Carlisle, PA, 1933, chapter 4.

Enlightenment. Rush had first heard of Nisbet when John Witherspoon, who had initially declined the invitation to become president of the College of New Jersey, had suggested Nisbet as a worthy candidate. At their April 1784 meeting, the board unanimously elected Nisbet the first principal of the college. Following that meeting, John Dickins on, as chairman of the board of trustees, wrote to Nisbet, informing him about the position. Nisbet was not initially eager for the job. Thus, from December 1783 to June 1784, Rush took it upon himself to write letters to Nisbet, describing in enthusiastic if not hyperbolic terms the prospects for the college.

> The trustees of Dickinson College are to meet at Carlisle on the 6th of next April to choose a principal for the College. I have taken great pains to direct their attention and votes to you. From the situation and other advantages of that College, it must soon be the first in America. It is the key to our western world.[41]

> [T]he public is more filled than ever with expectations from your character. They destine our College to be the FIRST IN AMERICA under your direction and government. [Rush provided the emphasis in his original letter].[42]

> Our prospects . . . brighten daily. . . . Indeed, Sir, every finger of the hand of Heaven has been visible in our behalf. . . . Dickinson College, with Dr. Nisbet at its head, bids fair for being the first literary institution in America.[43]

Rush's repetition of the phrase "first in America" in his series of letters was provocative,

for it had two possible meanings: Dickinson would become the foremost college in the new country, in terms of quality; and, in light of the date September 9, 1783, coming as it did only six days after the signing of the Treaty of Paris, Dickinson had been the first college to receive a charter in the newly recognized country.

Nisbet ultimately succumbed to Rush's persuasiveness and accepted the post. His first months in America were filled with highs and lows. He arrived with his family in Philadelphia, on June 9, 1785. They stayed with Rush for three weeks before departing for Carlisle on June 30. Rush wrote to a friend, "The more I see of him, the more I love and admire him."[44] Nisbet reached Carlisle on July 4, 1785, took the oath of office the next day, and got to work. Ten days later, July 15, he wrote his first letter to Rush, and was somewhat critical of conditions in Carlisle—for example, he pointed to the need for a new building, describing the grammar school as shabby, dirty, and too small to accommodate all the students. Soon thereafter, he and his entire family contracted malaria. He became demoralized, and in August informed Rush that he had experienced a change of heart, would relinquish the position of principal and return to Scotland as soon as feasible.

Perhaps Rush, like an overly protective parent, was offended by Nisbet's early criticism of the college. Perhaps he was disappointed with Nisbet's lack of resolve. Perhaps he was beginning to get a different read on the man. For whatever reason, by the time of the August 9, 1785, board meeting in Carlisle, Rush had soured on Charles Nisbet. He ignored a note delivered to him on Nisbet's behalf, and did not visit the Nisbet family, who were still convalescing. Nisbet, at first perplexed, grew angry. In the ensuing years, the relationship between the two men remained strained.

---

[41] *Letters of Benjamin Rush*, Princeton University Press, Princeton, NJ, 1951, Volume 1, p. 316.

[42] Ibid, p. 334.

[43] James Henry Morgan, *Dickinson College: The History of One Hundred and Fifty Years 1783–1933*, Mount Pleasant Press, Carlisle, PA, 1933, chapter 1, p. 31–32.

[44] James Henry Morgan, *Dickinson College: The History of One Hundred and Fifty Years 1783-1933*, Mount Pleasant Press, Carlisle, PA, 1933, p. 34.

▨ Glorious Intentions; Disappointing Outcome (1785–1816)

In summer 1785, the board accepted Nisbet's resignation and appointed faculty member Robert Davidson as acting principal for the first year of classes. At the outset, the attributes of the school bore little resemblance to a modern liberal arts college. The school was in session year round, except for one month breaks in October and May, with commencement occurring on the last Wednesday of September. Fees ranged from $15 to $25 per year. The campus consisted of one building, the original Carlisle Grammar School, which had been ceded to the college in 1783. In 1786, the building was enlarged from its original two-story, two-room dimensions. The original faculty consisted of only four professors, including the head of the Grammar School. Enrollment in the classes of 1787 to 1816 fluctuated between zero and 60. Students found it relatively hard to earn an undergraduate degree, as the average number who actually received a diploma during that period was often less than 75 per cent of each class.[45] In terms of scale, Dickinson was typical of the times: for example, in the 1780s, while Columbia College had two professors and some two dozen students, the College of New Jersey had two professors, a provost, and roughly 60 students.[46]

Meanwhile, Nisbet decided he and his family would wait until spring of 1786 to return to Scotland. Over the winter months, the weather cooled, Nisbet and family recovered their health, and he had a change of heart. By February of 1786, he expressed in writing his desire to be reinstated. While Rush was opposed, the Carlisle-based members of the board rallied to the idea, and in May of 1786 reelected him as first principal of Dickinson College. His performance as principal was influenced by a range of factors, including his own character traits, the structure in place for governing the college, financial pressures, and efforts to construct the first major building on the college campus.[47]

Nisbet was a relentless worker and generally regarded as a brilliant scholar, a man who possessed deep knowledge about an extraordinary range of subjects. In addition to serving as principal, Nisbet carried a full-time teaching load, responsible for lectures in philosophy of the mind, moral philosophy and belles lettres, economics, and sociology. His lectures—which the students wrote verbatim in their notebooks—were remarkable for their breadth and insights. Nisbet was extremely well-liked and admired by his students. Although Nisbet tended to place a higher value on the classics than did Rush, intellectually speaking the two men appeared to be in fundamental agreement about the purpose of a liberal education.[48] Unlike Rush, however, Nisbet remained politically conservative throughout his life. Ultimately, he was not able to sympathize with the dominant values and institutions of the new country

---

[45]Author's computations, based on information found in "Alumni 1787–1900," *Encyclopedia Dickinsonia*, Dickinson Chronicles, http://chronicles.dickinson.edu/encyclo/a/alumni/.

[46]Charles F. Himes, *A Sketch of Dickinson College*, Lane S. Hart, Harrisburg, 1879, Chapter 1, page 3. A digital version of this book is available at the Chronicles of Dickinson College, http://chronicles.dickinson.edu/histories/himes, accessed July 23, 2007.

[47]This section is based on James Henry Morgan, *Dickinson College: The History of One Hundred and Fifty Years 1783–1933*, Mount Pleasant Press, Carlisle, PA, 1933, chapters 5–10 and on Charles Coleman Sellers, *Dickinson College: A History*, Wesleyan University Press, Middletown, CT, 1973, chapters 5 and 6.

[48]Dickinson College History Professor John Osborne, interview, September 6, 2007, and Dickinson College Archivist Jim Gerencser, interview, September 7, 2007, each suggested that Rush and Nisbet were actually closer in their way of thinking than one might expect, given the tension in their personal relationship.

and he regarded himself an outsider in his community.[49]

Throughout his administration, Nisbet—who was quite good at being critical of events but quite ineffective at being persuasive[50]—was constrained by his formal relationship with the board of trustees. Under the original charter, neither the principal nor any faculty member could serve on the board, and by 1786, the board had adopted an even more stringent policy—the principal and faculty were prohibited from attending board meetings.

When the charter for Dickinson was being drafted, Rush had endorsed the idea that the president of the college should be subservient to the board of trustees. He based his opinion on what he had observed at the College of Philadelphia: he believed that a controlling and rigid-minded president had dominated the board to the detriment of the school.[51] Nevertheless, Rush objected to this new development at Dickinson on both philosophical and practical grounds. In a letter written to the trustees in October of 1786, Rush wondered why his plan, which had been agreed by the board in August of 1785, had not been adopted. He was particularly concerned that the behavior of the boys was "irregular" and that the faculty was not imposing discipline.

> I beg leave to recommend that the trustees would exercise a watchful eye over their own authority, and that they would divide the government of the College among every branch of the faculty agreeably to the spirit and letter of our charter. Unless this be the case, the dignity and usefulness of our teachers will be lessened and destroyed, and the republican constitution of the College will be reduced to the despotism of a private school. When our professors cease to be qualified to share in the power of the College, it will be proper to dismiss them, for government and instruction are inseparably connected.[52]

However, the situation did not change. Given that making the journey to Carlisle from any of the cities to the east was a difficult undertaking; that seven of the nine Carlisle men who had been on the board of the grammar school were also members of the board of the college; and that only nine people were needed for a quorum, the Carlisle contingent of the board were in a position to dominate college governance and micromanage daily affairs.

In its early history, the endowment of the college never exceeded $20,200, an amount achieved in 1784. Thus, the endowment did not generate large annual returns. Furthermore, the small number of students paying tuition caused the college to experience budget deficits. Given those difficulties, the trustees repeatedly appealed to the Assembly for assistance; in turn, the Assembly responded with modest annual grants that averaged about $550 per year. However, budget pressures continued, the college took out loans, and overall debts began to rise.

Furthermore, the college had some difficulties in raising contributions. Rush assigned some of the blame to Nisbet. He believed that when Nisbet announced his decision to retire that first year, and when he continued to publicly complain about the treatment he had received at the hands of Rush and more generally about the state of affairs in America, he did harm to the reputation of the college.[53] By 1799, Rush—who had become

---

[49]James Henry Morgan, *Dickinson College: The History of One Hundred and Fifty Years 1783-1933*, Mount Pleasant Press, Carlisle, PA, 1933, p. 66.

[50]Charles Coleman Sellers, *Dickinson College: A History*, Wesleyan University Press, Middletown, CT, 1973, p. 79.

[51]Ibid, p. 139–140.

[52]*Letters of Benjamin Rush*, Princeton University Press, Princeton, NJ, 1951, Volume 1, p. 397.

[53]*Letters of Benjamin Rush*, Princeton University Press, Princeton, NJ, 1951, Volume 1, p. 537.

a supporter of Jefferson—was even more distressed that Nisbet was expressing pro-federalist sentiments in his classroom, thus undermining the college's ability to raise contributions from Democratic-Republicans.[54]

In 1800, the board voted to reduce Nisbet's salary from $1,200 to $800 per year, to reduce those of the other faculty as well, and to borrow $2,000. In 1801, the board sold stock worth another $2,000. In spring 1802, the board stopped making full payment of faculty salaries. Those developments impacted the morale of Nisbet and his faculty.

Meanwhile, in 1799 the college purchased a seven acre parcel of land on the then-existing western boundary of Carlisle, for $151. The board began to solicit contributions, and on June 20, the cornerstone for a building called New College was set in place. The board hoped construction would be finished by winter, but progress was slow. That fact, along with the college's mounting financial difficulties, fueled speculation that Dickinson would have to close its doors. Finally, in the winter of 1802–1803, New College was receiving final touches: sadly, on February 3, 1803, the building burned to the ground.

In the aftermath of the disaster, the trustees demonstrated their determination. They appealed to the presbytery for financial assistance. They visited Philadelphia, Baltimore, New York and Norfolk to raise funds, and met with success. In Washington DC, they won a personal contribution of $100 from President Thomas Jefferson, as well as contributions from other important political figures. Buoyed by the inflow of funds, the board solicited help from one of the foremost architects and engineers of the time, Benjamin Latrobe, who graciously agreed to contribute a design for a replacement building larger than the first. The new building—which became known in later decades, when other buildings were added to the campus, as

West College—would be constructed of limestone with brown sandstone accents, and would be multipurpose in nature, providing dormitory, dining hall, chapel, and classroom space for the students and living quarters for the faculty. Once again, Rush had to accept a compromise, as the plan to house students in the building, rather than to have them board with local families, ran counter to his philosophy of education. The cornerstone of the building was laid on August 8, 1803. It was first used for academic purposes in November of 1805.

Charles Nisbet died from complications associated with pneumonia, on January 18, 1804. While they had been at odds for the better part of 20 years, at the last it appears that Rush and Nisbet managed to find some common ground, judging by a letter Rush wrote to Montgomery when Nisbet died.

> He has carried out of our world an uncommon stock of every kind of knowledge. Few such men have lived and died in any country. I shall long, long remember with pleasure his last visit to Philadelphia, at which time he dined with me in the company [of two friends]. His conversation was unusually instructing and brilliant, and his anecdotes full of original humor and satire.[55]

Following Nisbet's death, the board once again turned to Robert Davidson[56] to serve as acting principal, a position he held for the next five years. While never formally elected as such, he came to be recognized as the second principal of Dickinson College. Financial pressures were a reality throughout Davidson's tenure. Although Davidson was an outstanding churchman, he was not a successful college president. Of note, John Dickinson, still serving as a trustee of the college, died on February 14, 1808.

---

[54]Ibid, p. 812.

[55]Ibid, p. 878.

[56]This section is based on James Henry Morgan, *Dickinson College: The History of One Hundred and Fifty Years 1783–1933*, Mount Pleasant Press, Carlisle, PA, 1933, chapter 14.

Davidson was succeeded by Jeremiah Atwater,[57] a Presbyterian who was serving as the first president of Middlebury College when informed of the post at Dickinson. A devout, conservative Presbyterian, he hoped to create a culture at Dickinson based on religious principles, and in this sense was in step with Rush. However, upon his arrival, he was aghast at the state of affairs in Carlisle, complaining in correspondence to Rush that the boys were prone to "drunkenness, swearing, lewdness, & dueling" and the faculty did not take responsibility for imposing discipline.[58] Atwater quickly took steps to introduce the type of discipline typical of that found in the colleges of New England.

During Atwater's tenure, financial pressures continued to plague the college, especially given efforts to add dining rooms and other features to the interior of the college building. Given the small scale of the college and the relatively low standard of living at the time, the ongoing construction drained resources, consumed the entire endowment, and forced the college into debt. In light of developments, Rush wrote in 1810 about raising tuition, which he understood would limit access to a liberal education.

> I wish very much the price of tuition be raised in our College. Let a *learned* education become a luxury in our country. The great increase of wealth among all classes of our citizens will enable them to pay for it with more ease than in former years when wealth was confined chiefly to cities and to the learned professions. Besides, it will check the increasing disproportion of

learning to labor in our country. This suggestion is not intended to lessen the diffusion of knowledge by means of reading, writing, and arithmetic. Let those be as common and as cheap as air. In a republic no man should be a voter or juror without a knowledge of them. They should be a kind of sixth or civil sense. Not so with *learning*. Should it become *universal*, it would be as destructive to civilization as universal barbarism. [Emphasis provided by Rush.][59]

During the first three years of Atwater's term, the number of students at the college nearly tripled. But the War of 1812 had a negative impact on student attendance and graduation rates. As time passed, Atwater became increasingly discouraged by the unyielding financial difficulties, and by internal dissention among his faculty. On April 19, 1813, Atwater lost a sympathizer when Benjamin Rush died rather suddenly at his home.

In early 1815, the trustees ordered Atwater and each professor to submit a weekly written report to the secretary of the board that identified all student absences or transgressions. In a corrosive environment of friction among the faculty and hostility between the faculty and the board, that proved to be the last straw. Within the year, Atwater retired from the college, as did the other faculty. The college was in shambles.

In November of 1815, the board elected John McKnight,[60] a professor and member of the board of trustees at Columbia University and influential Presbyterian, to serve as fourth principal of

---

[57]This section is based on James Henry Morgan, *Dickinson College: The History of One Hundred and Fifty Years 1783–1933*, Mount Pleasant Press, Carlisle, PA, 1933, chapter 15 and Charles Coleman Sellers, *Dickinson College: A History*, Wesleyan University Press, Middletown, CT, 1973, chapter 7.

[58]James Henry Morgan, *Dickinson College: The History of One Hundred and Fifty Years 1783–1933*, Mount Pleasant Press, Carlisle, PA, 1933, p. 183.

[59]*Letters of Benjamin Rush*, Princeton University Press, Princeton, NJ, 1951, Volume 1, p. 1053.

[60]This section and the next are based on James Henry Morgan, *Dickinson College: The History of One Hundred and Fifty Years 1783–1933*, Mount Pleasant Press, Carlisle, PA, 1933, chapter 16.

Dickinson. In December 1815, a Dickinson student was killed in a duel. The incident further undermined the college's reputation. In 1816, the board of trustees closed down the college.

Dickinson remained closed for five years, resumed operations in 1822, and then closed its doors again in 1832.

Despite the enormous strains of the first 50 years and the sad circumstances associated with the closing of the college, many of the young men who attended Dickinson during the era 1785 to 1832 went on to highly successful careers. Their number included ministers; college professors and presidents; secondary school teachers and principals; representatives and senators at the state and national level of government; a U.S. president and members of the executive branches of various administrations; military officers; lawyers and judges; physicians; civil servants; and businessmen.[61]

In order to reopen the college yet again, the board of trustees realized they had to end their loose affiliation with the Presbyterian Church and accept the invitation of the Methodist Episcopal Church to establish an alliance. In 1834, the college was reopened. Over the next 130 years, Dickinson experienced eras of growth and decline. The college's fortunes were influenced by external events, such as wars, economic fluctuations, and shifts in social norms. They were also influenced by internal factors, including the governance structure, the culture and the financial health of the college. Finally, they were influenced by the leadership and management abilities of individual presidents and the relationships each man had been able to forge with various constituents. Throughout that period, Dickinson remained a school with a relatively conservative and parochial culture.

In the 1960s, the college began the lengthy process of separation from the Methodist Church. By the 1970s, the college was characterized by a culture based on cooperation and collegiality. In that environment, the faculty greatly enhanced the curriculum, as reflected in more breadth in the foreign languages and opportunities for international education; innovative teaching methods in the sciences; interdisciplinary programs of study; and more faculty-student interaction. Dickinson had an enrollment of approximately 1600 students. By the mid-1990s, the relationship between the Methodist Church and Dickinson was cordial—the church continued to hold approximately $2 million in trust on behalf of the college and conducted its own decennial review of the college's performance. However, the church had no substantive influence on matters related to college policy or strategy.

Mounting Frustrations

In the early 1980s, the external environment confronting colleges became more challenging: costs of providing an education continued to rise; families were becoming less willing and able to pay higher tuition fees; and the public increasingly questioned the relevance of a liberal arts education. In that competitive environment, Dickinson made two strategic choices. First, given the dominant, egalitarian culture of the 1960s and 1970s, the college did not celebrate the accomplishments of any single department over others and continued to describe itself as a pure liberal arts college. Second, the college opted to award aid to incoming students on a loan-first rather than grant-first basis, and to award less overall aid than other colleges— to illustrate, through the mid-1990s, Dickinson had an average discount rate[62] of 24 per cent, compared to a discount rate of 33 per cent of

[61]A matrix that describes professions pursued by alumni graduating during the administrations of various presidents is provided in James Henry Morgan, *Dickinson College: The History of One Hundred and Fifty Years 1783–1933*, Mount Pleasant Press, Carlisle, PA, 1933, p. 396–397.

[62]The discount rate states, in percentage terms, the reduction from the full tuition price paid by the average student. To say this in another way, a 24 per cent discount rate implied that Dickinson realized $.76 for each $1.00 of the posted tuition price.

most rivals.[63] Between 1988 and 1996, applications for first year admissions dropped from 4,438 to 2,829, the acceptance rate rose from 40 per cent to 84 per cent, enrollment dropped from 2,079 to 1,824, and average SAT scores for admitted students dropped from 1,216 to 1,150.

To combat that trend, in the mid-1990s, the college moved to a grant-first aid approach, and aggressively elevated average aid awards. At one level, the tactic worked. From 1996 to 1999, applications rose from 2,829 to 3,434; the acceptance rate fell from 84 per cent to 64 per cent; and average SAT scores rose from 1,150 to 1,193. At another level, it was a serious mistake. By 1999, the discount rate had risen to 52 per cent, and the college was experiencing an operational deficit of roughly $5 million with an even larger deficit forecasted for the following year. Those deficits could only be covered in the short term by drawing down the endowment, and were clearly unsustainable in the long run.

More broadly, there was gnawing concerns among various members of the college community that successive administrations had been ineffective relative to those at rival schools in terms of managing admissions and raising funds. For example, while there were certainly many highly motivated and talented students entering the college, Dickinson remained a school with regional appeal that primarily received applications from students living in the Mid-Atlantic States. By the early 1990s, some among that group regarded Dickinson as a "safety" school rather than as a first choice. Furthermore, while Dickinson prided itself on admitting students who were the first in their family to receive a college education, and while it had good socio-economic diversity, it had very low representation from students of color or from international students. With respect to financial profile, although Dickinson's endowment was experiencing relatively high returns,

by the end of 1998, it stood at only $143 million, an amount that did not measure up well to the endowments of other colleges.

Those circumstances prompted Dickinson's Committee on Planning and Budget to release a white paper in the spring of 1996 to the entire faculty. The paper asserted that Dickinson had to develop a "grounding vision."

> Dickinson must be able to show . . . that a liberal education is simultaneously the most humanly fulfilling and ennobling *and* the most practical education. And it must be able to show that the liberal arts education offered *by this College* is superior to one offered elsewhere. (Emphasis included in original.)[64]

In response, college President A. Lee Fritschler formed a task force on the future of the college, consisting of a student and six senior faculty and administrators, to convene in early summer of 1997, for the purpose of identifying problems and proposing general solutions. Their report was released to the faculty, under the cover letter and signature of President Fritschler, on June 18. The telling language contained in the preface echoed the themes of the white paper.

> We want Dickinson to be generally recognized as one of the twenty-five most prestigious liberal arts colleges in the United States within the next ten years. . . . [We envision] Dickinson as a living and learning community that embraces change, that regards diversity as an essential feature of an educational community, and that declares liberal education to be the most humanly liberating and practical preparation for citizenship in an interdependent, competitive, culturally-complex world.[65]

---

[63]The data included in this paragraph and the next is based on the PowerPoint presentation, "Dickinson College: A Case Study in Financial Transformation," created by Annette S. Parker (Class of 1973), vice-president and treasurer of the college, spring 2007.

[64]Planning and Budget Committee, April 29, 1996, "A White Paper," Dickinson College internal document, p. 2.

[65]"Report for the President's Task Force on the Future of the College," June 18, 1997, Dickinson College internal document, p. 1–2

The report offered the following diagnosis: "The College's greatest external challenge is visibility, the greatest internal challenge is communication." To address the former, the college had to stop describing itself as a "pure liberal arts college" with "balance across all departments" and start celebrating core competencies, such as "excellence in international education." To address the latter—which involved concerns that in light of growing difficulties, the administration was becoming insular and less than transparent—steps had to be taken to reopen communication channels among administration, faculty, students and trustees.

In late 1997, President Fritschler indicated to the community he would resign his position in June of 1999. In January of 1998, a search committee was named to find a new president.

The Challenge of Creating an Identity Story

When Bill Durden agreed to be president of Dickinson College, he was aware that the board of trustees wanted to improve the reputation and the financial foundation of the college, but did not have a detailed blue-print on how to proceed; instead, they hoped they could establish high expectations and grant a new president a broad mandate to engineer a transformation. He was aware that the program of study was first-rate and the internal governance system was sound.

Durden also knew that there was an intense desire for change and progress among the faculty and some members of the administration: he had come to appreciate that desire via conversations during the spring and from his extensive review of previously written white papers and self-studies during the summer months.

Of all the documents he had read, a passage included in the 1997 Report of the President's Task Force—"We want Dickinson to be generally recognized as one of the 25 most prestigious liberal arts colleges in the United States within the next ten years"—was most provocative. While he would certainly give it more thought, his initial reaction was that such an externally focused objective—based on rankings produced by for-profit organizations such as *U.S. News and World Report*—might be a distraction from what he saw as the appropriate areas of concentration: the organizational culture and capabilities and the financial foundation of the college. Furthermore, he believed those rankings were based on a set of flawed metrics that did not properly capture the relative strengths of various institutions, including Dickinson. Finally, he was also troubled by what he saw as an emerging tendency in America to regard higher education as a standardized commodity: he believed that the increased attention being paid by the public to the rankings were a manifestation of that tendency.

Via his various experiences, Durden had come to believe in the power of a leadership story. He acknowledged that he had been influenced by the work of psychologist and leadership theorist Howard Gardner (see Exhibit 2).[66] Given his general assessment of the situation at Dickinson and prompted by his conversation with the rising senior who had expressed her concerns about what it meant to be a Dickinsonian, Durden had over the past several weeks started to imagine a story based on Rush and the founding of the college that he believed would help create a unique Dickinson identify. But several issues and questions remained unresolved. Durden knew that he had to achieve greater clarity regarding the story's purpose and target audience and its structure and content. He also had to think more about the tactics and timing he would employ in introducing the story to the Dickinson community.

[66]Bill Durden, interview with case author, August 31, 2007, Dickinson College, Carlisle, PA.

Exhibit 2

Role of a Leader and the Relevance of an Indentity Story

Leaders are "persons who, by word and/or personal example, markedly influence the behaviors, thoughts, and/or feelings of a significant number of their fellow human beings."

Leaders influence other people either *directly*, through the stories they communicate to others; or *indirectly*, through the ideas they create. Examples of these two types include Winston Churchill, a direct leader who sits at one end of a spectrum, and Albert Einstein, an indirect leader who sits at the other. Other leaders would fall somewhere between those two, with most corporate and political leaders closer to the spot occupied by Churchill, and most artists and researchers closer to the spot occupied by Einstein.

Direct leaders achieve their effectiveness in one of two ways: they *relate* stories to others, and they *embody* those stories, thereby serving as an example which inspires others. The ability to embody stories is much more relevant to direct leaders than indirect leaders.

While it may be hard to draw precise lines between categories, leaders can be ranked as *ordinary*, *innovative*, or *visionary*. An

> ordinary leader . . . simply relates the traditional story of his or her group as effectively as possible. . . . The innovative leader takes a story that has been latent in the population, or among the members of his or her chosen domain, and brings new attention or a fresh twist to that story. . . . [T]he visionary leader . . . [is not] content to relate a current story or to reactivate a story drawn from a remote or recent past . . . [and therefore] actually creates a new story.

> The ultimate impact of the leader depends most significantly on the particular story that he or she relates or embodies, and the receptions to that story on the part of audiences. . . . [A]udience members come equipped with many stories that have already been told and retold. . . . The stories of the leader . . . must compete with many other extant stories; and if the new stories are to succeed, they must transplant, suppress, complement, or in some measure outweigh the earlier stories, as well as contemporary counterstories.

> [L]eaders present a *dynamic* perspective to their followers: not just a headline or snapshot, but a drama that unfolds over time, in which they—the leader and followers—are the principal characters or heroes. Together, they have embarked on a journey in pursuit of certain goals, and along the way and into the future, they can expect to encounter certain obstacles or resistances that must be overcome. Leaders and audiences traffic in many stories, but the most basic story has to do with issues of *identity*. And so it is the leader who succeeds in conveying a new version of a given group's story who is likely to be effective. Effectiveness here involves fit—the story needs to make sense to audience members at this particular historical moment, in terms of where they have been and where they would like to go.

SOURCE: Howard Gardner, in collaboration with Emma Laskin, *Leading Minds: An Anatomy of Leadership*, Basic Books, a Division of Harper Collins Publishers, New York, NY, 1995.

Great Leadership Is Good Leadership

By Jeffrey Gandz

Look into the soul of any great leader and you will find a good leader. But, if only that were the case. Some leaders, those who crave and bathe in the spotlight, are in fact not so great. Others, who are highly effective (and modest) and possess the five key characteristics this author describes, are good leaders first and foremost. Which is what, in the end, makes them great.

The extraordinarily successful book *From Good to Great*[67] focused attention on the kind of leadership that was required to achieve enduring high performance. While it has been one of the best-selling management books of all time, it tends to focus on the effectiveness dimension of leadership to the virtual exclusion of other important dimensions. In my view, you cannot have truly great leadership without considering the broader challenges that face organizational leaders today. Great leadership must be good leadership too.

The word "good" is an interesting word in the English language because of the many meanings that it has. No more so is this true

| **Exhibit I** | Great Leadership |

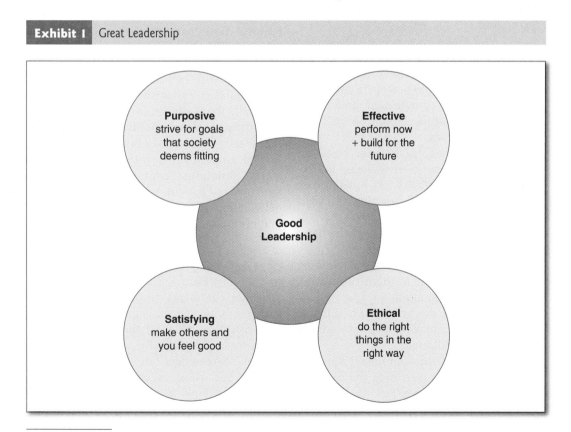

Purposive
strive for goals
that society
deems fitting

Effective
perform now
+ build for the
future

Good
Leadership

Satisfying
make others and
you feel good

Ethical
do the right
things in the
right way

Reprint# 9B07TC07

[67]Collins, J. C. (2001). *Good to great: why some companies make the leap—and others don't.* New York, NY, HarperBusiness.

than when it is used in conjunction with the words "leader" or "leadership." Good leadership can, indeed, refer to *effective* leadership—getting followers to pursue and attain goals. But it can also refer to the *purpose* or goals that leaders pursue and whether those are deemed fitting by the societies within which they operate; it can refer to the *ethics* of leaders—doing the right things in the right ways. It can also refer to the ways in which leaders make followers *feel* good and, indeed, the way they feel about themselves as leaders.

▧ Good as Effective

It goes without saying that good business leaders must be highly effective in getting people to follow them in pursuit of selected goals. Highly effective leaders:

- Recognize and analyze the driving forces in the political, economic, societal and technological environments in which they operate and understand the impact of these forces on their current strategies;
- Develop winning strategies based on sound competitive analysis, understanding buyer-behaviors, building core competencies and selecting the right domains in which to compete that will satisfy the expectations of their shareholders and other stakeholders;
- Execute those strategies brilliantly by involving people in their formulation and implementation;
- Evaluate the execution and results systematically, making strategic adjustments as indicated;
- Beyond this, they continually build for the future by increasing the capabilities of their organizations, divisions, departments, teams and themselves.

Really effective leaders drive for results *now* while *simultaneously* building for the future. It is simply not acceptable to view these as trade-offs, as perhaps used to be done by coaches of perpetually losing sports teams. The performance bar is continually being raised and to be three, four, six percent or more than last year is baked into the expectations that we have of leaders of organizations today.[68]

Much has been written about effective leadership. Suffice it to say that we expect our leaders to: work with their followers to develop a compelling future vision; enlist the support of others—inside and outside their organizations—in achieving this vision; energize, enable, and encourage high performance; empower people to act within an agreed-upon vision; and to be exemplars of the values of the organizations they lead. To do this requires both competencies and character. Competencies determine *what* leaders are able to do; character determines what they *will* do, how they will exercise those competencies under various circumstances. Good leaders, especially those who endure, are seldom one-dimensional, simple individuals. They are often complex, contradictory and multifaceted, especially in how they respond to different situations: confident *and* humble, assertive *and* patient, analytical *and* intuitive, deliberate *and* decisive, principled *and* pragmatic, among others.

▧ Good Purpose

When the character Gordon Gecko uttered his famous phrase "Greed is good" in the movie *Wall Street,* he reflected the view that managers, by single-mindedly pursuing the interests of shareholders, are fulfilling the true purpose of the business entity. The late Milton Friedman, the Nobel prize winner and high-priest of free-market economics, held that this

---

[68]Gandz, J. (2005). "The Leadership Role." *Ivey Business Journal* 66(1): 5.

approach by business produces the most good for the most people since other institutions—government agencies, trade unions, consumer protection associations, etc.—will curb the excesses of business and that the maximum aggregate benefits come from the tension between these forces. Leaders of businesses must then pursue shareholder interests exclusively and should be compensated for so doing. They should eschew the role of social arbiters attempting to balance competing interests, a role with which they are neither charged nor competent to perform. This is not an immoral or amoral argument on the part of Friedman. Indeed, it holds to the precept that the moral action is the one that brings the most good to the most people. Attempts to demonize Friedman for this argument are misguided.

Such a philosophy does not negate the importance of other stakeholders in the business enterprise. Indeed, customers, suppliers, employees, governments—national, regional and local—and the broader societies within which these businesses operate are also very important. Businesses benefit suppliers but also depend on excellent service and quality from those suppliers; they pay wages to employees but depend on their engagement and commitment; they provide value to customers but also benefit from the dependence of customers on them; they provide employment to members of communities but also depend on getting planning permission from a local government when they want to put up a new building, and they pay taxes to governments but also seek subsidies and other protections. But it subordinates their importance to the fundamental primacy of shareholders. They are to be considered only to the extent that they may be instrumental in creating a return to shareholders.

The alternate perspective is that shareholders are but one group of stakeholders in the business enterprise and that there are other stakeholders such as customers, suppliers, employees, community groups, pensioners,

etc. to whom the business enterprise has obligations.

These obligations stem from the reciprocal social and moral obligations between the parties. Businesses owe senior employees job security and a rising standard of living because employees who have worked for the organization for many years have been committed and involved in the business; they should not pollute or degrade their environments because they are responsible moral actors in the societies within which they operate; they should not outsource work to countries with poor labor or environmental standards because to do so is morally wrong for employees in those countries since it perpetuates those poor standards while damaging the livelihoods of those on the countries from which products were outsourced; they should not deplete natural resources because it will make the societies in which they operate unable to sustain economic and social life for generations to come.

Leaders of businesses, as viewed from this perspective, must seek a fitting balance between the interests of various stakeholders both when they coincide and when they differ, constantly seeking "win-win" or compromise resolutions when conflict occurs between stakeholders' interests. If this balance or integration sub-optimizes profit and reduces shareholder value, good business leaders should take the high road of "balance of interests." As leaders, business people cannot avoid the requirement to seek this balance even 'though—as the protagonists of shareholder primacy point out—they may be ill equipped to do so. They can seek advice, sift arguments, reflect and consider different interests and endeavor to find creative solutions that either satisfy all parties' demands or compromise between them, sub-optimizing shareholder value in favor of some broader, societal contribution.

This debate is ongoing. Sometimes it is trivialized by those who seek to make the case that striving for good purpose is axiomatic with shareholder value creation, and that in the long-run business does well by doing good. This negates the reality that by consolidating plants, profits are increased and communities are destroyed; by pursuing minimally legal environmental compliance, costs are minimized; that by selling legal products that may be harmful, profits are generated for years or even decades. Recent hard-edged research indicates that the financial returns to corporate social responsibility are dubious but, despite this, there are increasing demands on business leaders to expand their horizons to embrace this ethic.

Ethical Goodness

The excesses of business and business leaders have been a pervasive if not dominant theme in the popular business literature in the last decade, leading not only to new legislation but to a widespread revulsion with the ways in which some managers have been proven to have ripped off shareholders, customers, employees, creditors, and other stakeholders. Unlike the broader issue of corporate social responsibility, this does not address the fundamental purpose of business but, rather, the ways in which business people act. It recognizes that many decisions made by managers and executives benefit some people at the expense of others. Whenever someone may be hurt by an action of management, there is an ethical decision involved.

Business ethicists recognize three distinct forms of unethical behavior.[69] The first of these are actions that are clearly not within the scope of the role. Chief Financial Officers should not fiddle the books, senior executives should not pad their expense accounts or charge personal expenses to the corporation, corporate directors should not trade stock based on inside information; companies should not conspire to rig bids; defense contractors should

not charge unrelated expenses to cost-plus government contracts; and so on. In many cases we have laws and regulations that expressly prohibit these behaviors and, in most cases, breaking laws or evading regulations is *prima facie* unethical.

The second type of unethical action is one that serves the purpose of the role but pushes beyond the types of behavior that society would consider morally right. So, we expect marketers to emphasize the benefits of their products but they should not lie about the performance of their products or conceal dangers that might be associated with their use; human resource managers should not mislead people about terms and conditions of employment to induce them to accept a job; salespeople should not spread false rumors about the financial health of their competitors in order to deter customers from doing business with them; financial advisors should not tailor their advice to meet their rewards to the detriment of their clients. Clearly, different societies have different tolerance levels for these behaviors and what is considered ethical in one society might be considered beyond the pale in another.

The third type of unethical action is one that describes something that should be done but which is not done—an act of *omission* rather than commission. These non-actions that many people consider unethical include a failure to recognize the talent that exists in minority groups, failure to give people regular performance reviews and candid feedback that would help them improve, failure to point out to people that their choice of products and services may not be in their best long-term interests, and failure to review a client's financial portfolio to ensure that it is appropriately balanced for their investment objectives. This type of unethical action is often fiercely debated since it clashes with other philosophies such as "buyer-beware," or "you get what you negotiate" that appear to put the onus on

[69]Bird, F. B., and J. Gandz (1991). *Good management: Business ethics in action.* Scarborough, Ont., Prentice-Hall Canada.

the customer, employee, or other party. Unlike the more black-and-white non-role acts, this type of unethical behavior is also more subject to gradations, with some people expecting minimal compliance and others expecting standards of excellence.

When businesses meet or exceed the expectations of the societies within which they operate, they will be free to operate. When they cease to meet those expectations they will be regulated, controlled and, perhaps, even be put out of business.

The issue of what "society" condones and what is right is not trivial. At the extreme, the anti-Semitic laws of National Socialist Germany were both popular and passed by parliament as, indeed, were the anti-apartheid laws of South Africa. Petty bribery—and some that is not so petty—is commonplace in some societies yet frowned upon in others. Some societies protect intellectual property rights whereas others either have no protection or, if a law does exist, may not bother to police it. The extent to which something is criminal or not, widely or narrowly accepted, or considered a civil tort may vary widely from place to place.

Quite often, people make an assumption that "if it's widely done, it must be okay!" With this assumption, there would have been very little if any progress made over the years to deal with the blatant discrimination against racial minorities, gender-based discrimination, or indeed ANY act of discrimination by a powerful group imposed on a less powerful one. Even if something is widely practiced, people may not think that it is right. For example, while corruption is widespread in business in many parts of the world, it may be expressly forbidden by both legal and moral authorities but, because the powerful can escape the sanctions associated with the disapproval, they may perpetuate the practice.

◪ Feel-Goodness

It's a leap from thinking about "good" as effective, purposive and ethical, to thinking about the importance of making people *feel* good or feeling good about your leadership. Yet it is a critical leap. The sociologist Amitai Etzioni proposed that people comply with leadership if they are *forced* to do so, if they are *paid* to do so or if they are moved by ideas and ideals so that they *want* to do so.[70] When people are forced to follow, they feel alienated; when they are paid to follow, their followership can be bought by others or will cease when the money stops flowing. When they buy into ideas or ideals and when they realize them through effective leadership, then the positive feelings generate their own energy and momentum and wanting to be led is more likely to result in extraordinary and sustained support for those shared goals. The leaders of slave or mercenary armies were never as durable as those whose armies were fired up by ideals and values.

The great leader described by Jim Collins is one who through "level-5" leadership embraces fierce determination and humility that leads to involvement and commitment by his or her followers.[71] They develop a sense of self-efficacy, of value, of worth. They want to be led by such leaders, not because they are sheep but because they understand that they can achieve their goals through those leaders. And they are prepared to exercise leadership themselves within the umbrella of the organizational leader who makes them feel good about themselves.

None of this is intended to suggest that the good leader should always adjust to the surface wants and desires of those who are to be led. Indeed, panderers generally make poor leaders since they end up promising too much to too many and cannot deliver the goods.

---

[70]Etzioni, A. (1961). *A comparative analysis of complex organizations; on power, involvement, and their correlates.* New York, Free Press of Glencoe.

[71]Collins, J. (2001). "Level 5 leadership: The triumph of humility and fierce resolve." *Harvard Business Review* 79(1): 66–76.

A cynical perspective on leadership suggests that leaders find out which way the parade is heading and scramble to the front of it, or that leaders take people where they really want to go anyway. Some have proposed, judgmentally or paternalistically, that leaders take people not to where they want to go but, rather, to where they really need to be. Perhaps it is more accurate to suggest that great leaders satisfy people's deep needs rather than their surface wants, even if they may not immediately realize their needs.

The ability of leaders to understand their potential followers' needs has been associated with great religious, military, political and, yes, even business leaders. Sometimes this has resulted in great good and sometimes in great evil. Sadly, not all effective leaders who tap into their followers' needs and motivate them to action do so with good purpose in mind. Genocides, persecutions, and the unrelenting pursuit of corporate greed through fraud, misrepresentation, or even callous indifference of the impact of their actions on others have left their scars.

However, the good leader never ignores how his or her followers feel about their leadership. They know that short-term pain must be followed by long-term gain, that efforts must lead to rewards, that sacrifices will be made but not forever. And they nurture their followers through these tough times. They draw on wellsprings of optimism when things are not going well, without losing their grip on reality.

Leadership is also hard work, especially when times are tough, when things are not working the way they were planned and people are beginning to question the credibility of leadership. Often the only thing that leaders have to draw on at those times is their own self-confidence, their sense that they are doing the right things for their people. The borderline between self-confidence and arrogance, between steadfastness and hubris may be very narrow and the leader treads it all the time. If they are to cope with the stresses and strains of leadership, it is essential that they feel good about what they are doing to make it worth the effort.

◪ The "Good" Leader

There will always be debates about what constitutes good or great leadership in a business context, and each generation will yield its crop of candidates. Creation of shareholder value will always be high among the criteria considered, as indeed it should be. But as societal values embrace broader concerns, as we judge not only what these leaders appear to have achieved but also how they have done it, as we assess leaders not just in terms of their achievements but on their contributions to the societies within which they operate, I suspect that the emphasis will shift toward the goodness of leadership as described in this article as a necessary condition for leadership greatness.

There is an argument to be made that, given a long enough time frame, "Goodness" as I mean it and "Greatness" as suggested by Jim Collins converge into one and the same thing. That may turn out to be the case but there is too much press given to leaders who have yet to achieve either. Perhaps it is we—the public, who look to our business leaders to drive the prosperity of this and future generations—who need to be more restrained in granting this ultimate accolade and granting someone the title a "good leader."

Leadership Trait Approach

I usually look first for character. Do they have stamina and dedication? Do they have the physical and mental balance to be leaders? Not everybody makes the same choice in weighing work and personal life, and that is legitimate. But for leaders you need people who are willing to work hard and get results. . . . Leadership also demands an open mind and the willingness to engage with different points of view.

—Alain Gomez[1]

Leadership trait research was developed to ascertain why certain people were great leaders. This research led to the development of the "great person" theory as it focused on the inherent characteristics and qualities of leaders who were considered to be great. This research also led to the nature argument, which said that only certain people were born with these traits and, consequently, only those certain people became great leaders. The research focused on finding those traits that discriminated between followers and leaders (Bass, 1990; Dubrin, 2007; Jago, 1982).

Eventually, researchers questioned the universality of leadership traits. It was argued that no one set of traits was appropriate in all situations. This led to the reconceptualization of leadership as relationships among individuals in social situations. Recently, researchers have returned to the trait approach. The nature of this research is different in that it now emphasizes the importance of traits in effective leadership.

Traits are attributes that include aspects such as values, needs, motives, and personality (Yukl, 2006). One very prominent leadership researcher (Stogdill, 1948, 1974) demonstrated that average leaders were different from average group members in several ways. In his first study (Stogdill, 1948), he identified the following traits: (1) intelligence, (2) alertness,

---

[1]Alain Gomez is the former chairman and CEO of Thomson S. A.

(3) insight, (4) responsibility, (5) initiative, (6) persistence, (7) self-confidence, and (8) sociability. This study also identified that traits and situations intersected in the sense that some traits were more important in some situations if an individual was to be an effective leader (Yukl, 2006). Stogdill's (1974) second study reported on 10 traits associated with leadership in a positive way. These were (1) drive for responsibility and task completion, (2) vigor and persistence in pursuit of goals, (3) venturesomeness and originality in problem solving, (4) drive to exercise initiative in social situations, (5) self-confidence and sense of personal identity, (6) willingness to accept consequences of decisions and actions, (7) readiness to absorb personal stress, (8) willingness to tolerate frustration and delay, (9) ability to influence other people's behavior, and (10) the capacity to structure social interaction systems to the goal to be achieved (Northouse, 2010).

Mann (1959) determined that leaders were strong in traits such as (1) intelligence, (2) masculinity, (3) adjustment, (4) dominance, (5) extroversion, and (6) conservatism. He agreed that traits could help differentiate leaders from nonleaders. Lord, DeVader, and Alliger (1986) reviewed Mann's work and concluded that (1) intelligence, (2) masculinity, and (3) dominance are very important traits that people use to distinguish leaders. Kirkpatrick and Locke (1991) argued that leaders and nonleaders differ on six traits: (1) drive, (2) desire to lead, (3) honesty and integrity, (4) self-confidence, (5) cognitive ability, and (6) knowledge of the business. These writers argued for a nurture and nature perspective in that they believed that people can learn these traits, be born with them, or both. Summarizing the traits identified above suggests five that are mentioned most frequently: These are (1) intelligence, (2) self-confidence, (3) determination, (4) integrity, and (5) sociability. It is these five that we will focus on (Northouse, 2010).

Intelligence

Zaccaro, Kemp, and Bader (2004) found that leaders and nonleaders differ in their intellectual ability in that leaders have higher levels of intelligence than nonleaders. Their research suggests that having certain abilities helps one be a better leader—these are strong verbal, perceptual, and reasoning abilities. Conversely, their research also indicates that it may be counterproductive if a leader's intelligence is a lot higher than his or her followers' intelligence (Dubrin, 2007). This situation could lead to an inability to effectively communicate with followers as leaders may be too advanced in their thinking to be accepted and understood by their followers. Intelligence does allow leaders to more effectively develop social judgment and complex problem-solving skills. It also appears to be positively associated with effective leadership (Dubrin, 2007; Northouse, 2010).

Self-Confidence

Self-confidence means that you have a positive perspective on your ability to make judgments, to make decisions, and to develop ideas (Daft, 2005). Self-confidence aids people to develop as leaders (Yukl, 2006). It helps individuals to be assured of their skills, knowledge, abilities, and competencies. It encourages leaders to consider that influencing others is right and appropriate. It allows individuals to believe that their decisions will make a difference. In addition to being self-confident, it is important for a leader to be able to express that confidence to followers; one example of exhibiting self-confidence is being calm, cool, and collected in a crisis situation (Dubrin, 2007).

Determination

Determination is a trait that we like to call "stick-to-it-ive-ness." Others would describe it as having a task orientation—a desire to get the job done. Dubrin (2007) calls it tenacity. Daft (2005) calls it drive and says that it is related to having high energy. Many leaders have this sense of "stick-to-it-ive-ness"—this desire to finish the job and to do it well. Initiative, persistence, dominance, and drive go along with determination. Leaders with determination are willing to be assertive, to be proactive, and to persevere when the going gets tough. Determined leaders will demonstrate a sense of dominance, especially when followers need explicit direction and when there is little or no time to explain the reason for the direction being given.

Integrity

We like to think of integrity as consistency between what you believe, what you think, what you say, and what you do. Integrity is being trustworthy and honest. It is taking responsibility for one's actions and holding fast to strong principles. Followers trust and have confidence in leaders with integrity because these leaders do what they say they will do (Daft, 2005; Yukl, 2006). In the 1990s and 2000s, many political and business leaders abused the trust of their followers; consequently, trust of followers toward their leaders is absent in many organizations (Daft, 2005). This led to cynicism on the part of followers toward leaders in these arenas because many were disappointed in what was believed to be hypocritical behavior on the part of leaders. As those of you reading this casebook become leaders, you can be sure that your followers will demand that you demonstrate integrity in your beliefs, thoughts, words, and actions.

Sociability

Sociability is an important trait for leaders. Leaders who are sociable are more inclined to pursue enjoyable social relationships. They are empathetic to the concerns and needs of others and want the best for them. They exhibit friendliness, courtesy, tactfulness, diplomacy, and an outgoing personality. Their interpersonal skills are above average, and they develop a higher level of cooperation with, and among, their followers (Northouse, 2010).

These five traits are substantive contributors to effective leadership. However, the other traits listed earlier also contribute to effective leadership. Collins (2004) argues that two traits exemplify those with the highest level of leadership—a sense of humility and a steely resolve to get the job done. Their sense of humility means that they accept and take the blame when things go wrong but give others the credit when things go right. Their steely resolve means that they will find a way to go through, over, under, or around obstacles.

The Five-Factor Personality Model

Since the early 1980s, researchers have come to generally agree on five factors that determine an individual's personality. These factors are known as the Big Five and include neuroticism, extraversion, openness or intellect, agreeableness, and conscientiousness or dependability (Judge, Bono, Ilies, & Gerhardt, 2002; Yukl, 2006). Judge et al. (2002) found empirical support for personality traits being associated with effective leadership. In particular, extroversion, conscientiousness, and openness are positively associated with effective leadership, in that order of importance. Neuroticism is ranked third with openness but is negatively associated with effective leadership—in other words, less is better. Finally, agreeableness was only weakly, albeit positively, associated with effective leadership (Northouse, 2010).

Emotional Intelligence

Emotional intelligence combines our affective domain (emotions) with our cognitive domain (thinking) (Yukl, 2006). It is concerned with our understanding of emotions and applying this understanding to the tasks we engage in throughout our lives. Mayer, Salovey, and Caruso (2000) used four components to define emotional intelligence: being aware of one's ability to perceive and express emotions, having the ability to control our own emotions while behaving with integrity and honesty, being empathetic toward others and sensing organizational concerns, and effectively managing our own emotions and those involved in our relationships with other people (Dubrin, 2007). Another researcher (Goleman, 1995, 1998) suggests that emotional intelligence encompasses social and personal competencies, with social competence consisting of empathy, communication, and conflict management, while personal competence involves motivation, conscientiousness, self-regulation, confidence, and self-awareness (Northouse, 2010).

Emotional intelligence is a relatively new concept in leadership trait research. There is debate on how important it is in people's lives, with some arguing that it is very important in success at home, school, and work and others saying that it is somewhat important. It is reasonable to suggest that emotional intelligence is important to effective leadership as leaders with more sensitivity to their own emotions and the effect of their emotions on other individuals should be more effective (Yukl, 2006). Dubrin (2007) says that emotional intelligence is a supplement to cognitive ability and that leader effectiveness needs more than only emotional intelligence. More research is needed to give us a better understanding of the relationship between emotional intelligence and effective leadership.

How Does the Trait Approach Work?

The trait approach to leadership is not relational. It concentrates on leaders with no focus on followers or situations. The trait approach emphasizes that effective leadership is about having leaders with specific traits. Inherent in the trait approach is the suggestion that organizations will have better performance if they put people with specific leadership traits into particular leadership positions. In other words, selecting the right people will improve organizational performance (Northouse, 2010).

◪ References

Bass, B. M. (1990). *Bass and Stogdill's handbook of leadership: A survey of theory and research.* New York: Free Press.

Collins, J. (2004). Level 5 leadership: The triumph of humility and fierce resolve. In *Collection of articles—Best of HBR on leadership: Stealth leadership* (pp. 15–30). Boston: Harvard Business School Press.

Daft, R. L. (2005). *The leadership experience* (3rd ed.). Mason, OH: Thomson, South-Western.

Dubrin, A. (2007). *Leadership: Research findings, practice, and skills.* New York: Houghton Mifflin.

Goleman, D. (1995). *Emotional intelligence.* New York: Bantam.

Goleman, D. (1998). *Working with emotional intelligence.* New York: Bantam.

Jago, A. G. (1982). Leadership: Perspectives in theory and research. *Management Science, 28*(3), 315–336.

Judge, T. A., Bono, J. E., Ilies, R., & Gerhardt, M. V. (2002). Personality and leadership: A qualitative and quantitative review. *Journal of Applied Psychology, 87,* 765–780.

Kirkpatrick, S. A., & Locke, E. A. (1991). Leadership: Do traits matter? *The Executive, 5,* 48–60.

Lord, R. G., DeVader, C. L., & Alliger, G. M. (1986). A meta-analysis of the relation between personality traits and leadership perceptions: An application of validity generalization procedures. *Journal of Applied Psychology, 71,* 402–420.

Mann, R. D. (1959). A review of the relationship between personality and performance in small groups. *Psychological Bulletin, 56,* 241–270.

Mayer, J. D., Salovey, P., & Caruso, D. R. (2000). Models of emotional intelligence. In R. J. Sternberg (Ed.), *Handbook of intelligence* (pp. 396–420). Cambridge, UK: Cambridge University Press.

McCormick, J. & Stone, N. (1992). From national champion to global competitor: An interview with Thomson's Alain Gomez. In W. Bennis (Ed.) *Leaders on leadership: Interviews with top executives* (pp. 119–136). Boston, MA: Harvard Business Review.

Northouse, P. G. (2010). *Leadership: Theory and practice* (5th ed.). Thousand Oaks, CA: Sage.

Stogdill, R. M. (1948). Personal factors associated with leadership: A survey of the literature. *Journal of Psychology, 25,* 35–71.

Stogdill, R. M. (1974). *Handbook of leadership: A survey of theory and research.* New York: Free Press.

Yukl, G. (2006). *Leadership in organizations* (6th ed.). Upper Saddle River, NJ: Pearson-Prentice Hall.

Zaccaro, S. J., Kemp, C., & Bader, P. (2004). Leader traits and attributes. In J. Antonakis, A. T. Cianciolo, & R. J. Sternberg (Eds.), *The nature of leadership* (pp. 101–124). Thousand Oaks, CA: Sage.

⊠ The Cases

LG Group: Developing Tomorrow's Global Leaders

The firm's chairman has announced a corporate goal of increasing revenues from $38 billion to $380 billion between 1995 and 2005. Most of this increase is expected to come from new international sales. As a consequence, the firm must add an estimated 1,400 new global leaders to its management ranks. The chairman and his team must determine what these new global leaders should look like and how to develop them.

Vista-Sci Health Care, Inc.

The new senior vice president of marketing at Vista-Sci Health Care, Inc. must decide which of two very good candidates he should promote to the position from which he has just been promoted. Both of the candidates have demonstrated strengths and weaknesses in their current jobs; the question is whether these competencies and other personal characteristics will make them a good fit for their new roles.

⊠ The Reading

The Character of Leadership

Scratch the surface of a true leader, or look beneath his or her personality, and you'll find character. The traits and values that make up the character of a good business leader are, for the most part, similar to those that make up the character of an outstanding citizen. These authors describe the traits and values that make up the character of leadership.

--- LG Group ---

Developing Tomorrow's Global Leaders

Prepared by J. Stewart Black and Allen J. Morrison
in collaboration with Young Chul Chang

On February 22, 1995, Bon Moo Koo, 51, took over the helm of the LG Group, one of the three largest Korean *chaebols*. Like a newly recommissioned ship, LG had recently undergone significant renovation and appeared to be in great sailing shape. The renovation and refurbishing had been directed by the former chairman, Mr. Cha-Kyung Koo, Mr. Bon Moo Koo's father. After steering through some stormy seas from 1985 to 1991, the clouds had cleared and LG's future looked sunny and bright. Group revenues had increased each year from 1991 through 1994, when they stood at a record US$38 billion.

Firmly established as the new captain, Chairman Koo was determined to build upon the legacy of his father and set a brave new course by transforming LG Group from a great Korean company into a world-class enterprise. To do this, he would need to lead the group into the uncharted waters of global competition. In 1995, Chairman Koo announced "LEAP 2005," his vision of the future. Of all the different elements of this vision, the goal of increasing revenue to US$380 billion by 2005 with fifty per cent coming from international sales was the most challenging. The emotion behind LEAP 2005 is conveyed in the following statement by Chairman Koo:

> If we do not compete on the world stage, we will have difficulty surviving. I announced this lofty target to prevent us from becoming complacent with our past successes.

In late 1997, nearly three years after Chairman Koo took office and just over seven years away from the magical date of 2005, Mr. Y. K. Kim faced a significant challenge in translating the Chairman's vision into reality. Mr. Kim was the head of the LG Human Resource (HR) team that was charged with the task of identifying and developing "HIPOs" (high potential individuals) and the global leaders that LG would need in the future. Mr. Kim, representing the Office of the Chairman, worked closely with Dr. Michael Lee, Managing Director of LG Academy (LGA). LGA was the central training center for the entire LG Group with an annual budget of US$28 million and a professional staff of nearly 70 people.

Together Mr. Kim and Dr. Lee recognized that if LG achieved its revenue targets, it would likely be the largest private enterprise on earth. As such, the HR team estimated that LG would need approximately 1,400 new global leaders by 2005. About half would be Korean and half would be non-Korean. The central challenge for the HR team was to identify, hire, retain, and develop these needed global leaders.

Background

To understand what a quantum leap Chairman Koo's aspirations represented, it is necessary to understand some background on the country and businesses of Korea.

                    Version: (A) 1999-01-22

Korea's Economic Development

Korea's economic development over the last 50 years was nothing short of phenomenal. Prior to World War II, Korea's economy was primarily that of a third world, agrarian country. In the mid-1930s, about two-thirds of the working population were engaged in agriculture. Like many agrarian societies, the literacy rate in 1935 was only about 20 per cent.

Although the country began to make some progress after the end of World War II, the Korean civil war reversed those gains and took a heavy toll on the country. Economically, the civil war devastated the country's industrial base. After the end of the war in 1953, virtually the entire industrial base of what is now South Korea had to be rebuilt. This base was rebuilt and thereafter developed with amazing success.

A few key statistics could provide a clear picture of the dramatic transformation of this country and its economy. In 1953, per capita GNP was just US$67. By 1963, it had risen to US$91. By 1973, it stood at US$302. In 1983, per capita GNP had skyrocketed to US$2,014. By 1993, it had more than tripled to US$7,513. Nominal per capita GNP was projected to exceed US$30,000 by 2005, and by 2020 was expected to top US$77,000.

The transformation of the people was in many respects just as dramatic. From 1945 to 1995, the percentage of the working population in agriculture dropped from 67 per cent to just under seven per cent. As people moved from farms to factories, from villages to cities, literacy rates increased to 72 per cent by 1962, and to 98 per cent by 1996.

Korea's economic transformation took it from a third world country to a position on a par with many developed countries such as Italy and Spain in terms of per capita GNP. Many observers gave a significant portion of the credit to the various government officials and bureaucrats who guided Korea's industrial policy and to Korean business leaders who, during this period, built up some of the largest companies in the world.

Korean Chaebols

The primary economic engines for Korea's economic growth were the *chaebols*. Although Korean *chaebols* were often referred to as conglomerates, the term captured only part of the nature of *chaebols*. Like conglomerates, most Korean *chaebols* had a variety of companies operating in various industries. However, Korean *chaebols* were not legal entities because holding companies were not legally allowed in Korea. Consequently, the companies affiliated with each *chaebol* were a confederation held together by controlling families. Typically, the founding family controlled a majority of the stock in the related companies. The center of this web of companies was usually the "Office of the Chairman." In most cases, the chairman was a senior member of the controlling family. Nearly all of the large Korean *chaebols* started as small companies established by entrepreneurs.

Chaebols received their real boost in the 1960s. Devastated by the ravages of war, the government of South Korea was determined to rebuild the country. To ensure that the country's limited resources were used effectively and efficiently, the government targeted specific companies as engines of economic growth. The government used financial incentives in terms of taxes and protection from foreign competition to nurture and support these selected companies. *Chaebols* were given preferential access to loans and foreign exchange as well as subsidized interest rates. Government officials also used indirect influence to guide *chaebols* into new industries such as shipbuilding, automobiles, and steel.

Chaebols were the main drivers behind Korea's economic growth between 1960 and 1990. In 1996, the top 30 *chaebols* accounted for over 50 per cent of Korea's GDP. The top four *chaebols* employed only three per cent of the population, yet accounted for 60 per cent of all exports and nearly a third of all company revenues within Korea.

Ironically, the phenomenal success of the country and the *chaebols* created new challenges and problems. As the country's wealth increased and the society became more democratized, organized labor movements proliferated. During the late 1980s, workers staged a number of strikes to demonstrate the sincerity of their demands for higher wages and better working conditions. Subsequently, wage rates increased dramatically. From 1985 to 1990, wages jumped 143 per cent, not including the cost of new benefits that were also part of these new wage packages. By contrast, wages in Japan during this same period rose only 18 per cent overall. People also began to worry about so much economic power in the hands of so few individuals and families. While *chaebols* contributed to the rapid industrialization and economic growth of the country, many Koreans became increasingly concerned about their economic power and resource misallocation.

In response to mounting public concerns and growing international pressure, the government began a series of reforms. The reforms were designed to "level the playing field" and provide medium and small-sized companies with greater opportunities to grow. The *chaebols* did not openly embrace every reform, and consequently, these reforms often moved slowly. Still the government was determined, and in some cases unilaterally changed a number of policies, such as removing the subsidized loans and restricted access to foreign exchange that the *chaebols* enjoyed.

LG Group History

LG began in 1947 as a small chemical company, called the Rakhee Chemical Works. The company was established by Mr. Bon Moo Koo's grandfather, Mr. In-Hwoi Koo, and initially manufactured household items such as hair combs, toothpaste, and soaps. From this base, the company expanded into more complex plastic products. As it expanded, LG created a tradition of pushing into new technological frontiers. For example, LG produced the first radio in Korea in 1958, as well as the country's first refrigerator. LG also led South Korea's push into greater energy self-sufficiency with the building of the Homan Oil Refinery in 1967.

Low Cost Strategy (1947–1987)

From its foundation and through most of its early history, LG focused on competing through low cost manufacturing. LG competed with other multinational corporations by leveraging Korea's low cost labor and government-subsidized cost of capital. LG also strongly emphasized high production volumes. As LG expanded into a variety of plastic products and consumer electronics, it continued its strategy of under-pricing competitors with products of acceptable, although not superior, quality. In the context of this strategy, it established the Lucky-GoldStar brand as a low-cost and acceptable quality products manufacturer.

As LG moved forward on its low cost strategy, it developed significant manufacturing capabilities. Some managers were concerned that this was achieved at the cost of under-emphasizing marketing competencies. Managers focused on producing high volumes and getting per unit costs as low as possible rather than on finding out what customers wanted, developing high quality products, or expanding marketing capabilities.

This general strategic orientation held for most of the businesses and industries into which LG expanded. By 1987, LG had businesses in chemicals, communications, energy, electronics, finance, insurance, machinery, metals, sports, and trade. While LG was strong in Korea, it was not an international technology or quality leader in any of its business segments, especially relative to world class foreign competitors.

Value Strategy (1987–1995)

By the mid-1980s, it was clear that the strategic thrust of LG needed to change. Several factors contributed to this recognition.

First, by the mid-1980s Korean consumers were more sophisticated than they had been during the 1960s and 1970s, and were increasingly aware of and demanding higher quality products. Also, the rising standard of living increased the ability of Koreans to afford higher quality products and services. Most Korean consumers were no longer happy with low quality, even if it did come at a low price.

Second, under international pressure, the Korean government began to relax trade barriers that made it easier for foreign companies to compete with LG in Korea. In many cases, these foreign companies had significantly higher product quality and features and, because of lower trade barriers, were increasingly price competitive with domestic Korean companies. This was extremely important given that a vast majority of LG revenues came from domestic sales (approximately 70 per cent in 1980).

Third, the cost competitiveness of Korean companies began to slip. As wage rates increased in Korea, low cost labor began to erode as a source of comparative advantage. In addition, other countries, such as China, had significantly lower labor costs and were also coming up the technology curve. Consequently, competitors in developing Asian countries were quickly pushing LG out of its traditional low cost position. For example, Chinese companies were increasingly able to produce consumer electronics (such as fans) that, while not technically sophisticated, were reasonably reliable and significantly cheaper, allowing them to under-price and out-position Korean competitors.

By the mid-to-late 1980s, these external changes started showing up in LG's financial performance. Between 1986 and 1987, sales dropped by US$1 billion (about a seven per cent decline) and profits fell by 18 per cent.

Refurbishing the Ship

Although the ship was not in any real danger of sinking, LG was listing badly and taking on water. It needed some serious refurbishing and

restructuring. It was unthinkable for the aging Chairman, Cha-Kyung Koo, to hand over the helm until the ship was righted. To assist in turning LG around, Chairman Koo retained McKinsey & Co. as an advisor and undertook an extensive internal audit.

Given the environmental shifts, it was clear that LG had to become a value rather than a low cost player. This meant that customers, rather than low cost, had to become the dominant force in company decisions. But, what did customers really want? How did they use LG's products? What did they expect in terms of product reliability or service? These types of questions began to dominate LG and put customers at the center of its new strategic philosophy.

It was also clear that LG had to change its decision-making style. Like many Korean organizations, LG had a history of relatively centralized decision making and a top-down management process. This worked fine as long as the organization was small enough for top management to know everything that was going on and as long as the marketplace was fairly homogeneous. However, by the late-1980s LG had become a huge organization with revenues approaching US$20 billion and over 80,000 employees. Furthermore, whereas early in its history LG had been primarily focused on the domestic Korean market, increasingly it focused more on international markets. These markets and their customers often differed, not only from Korean markets and customers, but from each other as well. Consequently, it was impossible for top managers to know everything that was going on in such a large organization and across such diverse markets and customers. LG's management approach had to become more decentralized and more participative in nature. Decisions needed to be pushed down to where the action was.

The new management approach was implemented and was typically referred to in LG as "management by self-control." It allowed for much greater autonomy than had ever existed in the Group. Although most managers welcomed the opportunity for greater decision-making autonomy, many lacked experience with it. These managers had to change their mind set from flawlessly executing orders to determining strategic direction.

To facilitate and reinforce this new approach, LG was restructured. In 1987, LG's various affiliated companies were divided into 21 "Cultural Units." The cultural units consisted of multiple Strategic Business Units (SBUs) grouped together by common 'cultural' characteristics. SBU heads were given full profit and loss responsibility for their units, were expected to formulate specific competitive strategies, and were held accountable for results. Cultural Unit presidents focused on integration and coordination across SBUs.

Within SBUs, middle managers were charged with reviewing and reengineering business processes to ensure that they were efficient and effective. This reengineering was guided by the central strategic theme of providing value to the customer. This required managers to have a clear idea of customer needs, values, and preferences. In general, LG's top management wanted businesses structured and operated so that for a given amount of money spent, customers would get more of what they wanted in a product or service, and more than what they would get from a competitor's product or service.

Although managers kept a vigilant eye on costs, greater attention was also paid to quality than ever before. New and intense initiatives around 'zero-defects' were undertaken and supported from the highest levels. Customer satisfaction became a key measure and important input into quality improvement programs.

By 1994, the results of all these efforts were beginning to show. Sales had increased each year from 1991 through 1994. The rate of return for the entire Group rose from a low in 1991 of just under one per cent to nearly four per cent in 1994. Net income was up nearly 800 per cent, rising from US$128 million in 1991 to US$965 million in 1994.

New Face and Image

With the ship righted and ready to sail on a brighter course, it was time for a public recommissioning. This recommissioning occurred on January 1, 1995. On that date, Lucky-GoldStar Group officially changed its name to the LG Group. A new corporate identity program was launched, the center of which was a new Group logo—'The Face of the Future.' The logo was designed to symbolize five key concepts which (translated directly from Korean) were:

> The World
> The Future
> Youth
> Humans
> Technology

These concepts were believed to be the keys to LG's future growth and prosperity.

Leap 2005

When Mr. Bon Moo Koo took over as Chairman in 1995 (about one month after the public recommissioning), growth was the center of his new vision for the Group. He charted a course in his Leap 2005 initiative that would take LG on a journey from being a leading company in Korea to being a leading company in the world. In the process, LG would become one of the largest and most admired enterprises in the world.

Basic Philosophy

To achieve the general objectives of Leap 2005, Chairman Koo articulated a basic philosophy. This philosophy was set forth with four key points:

1. Compete from a global perspective
   - Compete with world-class companies in the global market

- Secure global management systems to be competitive on a world and regional basis
- Secure and utilize people, finance, and technology from a global perspective to create world class business systems

2. Create maximum value for customers, employees, and shareholders

3. Conduct business with integrity

4. Contribute to social development as a corporate citizen

This basic philosophy reaffirmed elements that had a long tradition in LG as well as adding new emphasis to other elements. The focus on valuing employees had been in LG from the beginning, as had the philosophy of contributing to social development through good corporate citizenship. The focus on creating customer value was relatively new, having been introduced with the restructuring efforts that started in 1987. However, the emphases on the global market and world class competitors were totally new, as was the greater emphasis on creating value for shareholders. Executives hoped that combining traditional philosophies with compatible new ones would provide employees with needed anchors so that they did not feel completely adrift while at the same time directing their attention toward new horizons.

Transitioning From the Old LG Culture

The new global orientation of LG required a new culture to support it. Although parts of the old culture did not fit the new environment, it did have valuable components. Consequently, the objective was to reaffirm what was still valid and add new cultural elements that were necessary for future success. The old culture was most often described by three words: stability, harmony, and respect.

Stability

In general, LG had a history of being a relatively stable company and culture. The company did not make radical shifts in strategy or practice. If LG entered a country, it tended to stay there. If it entered a new product or business segment, it tended to stick with it. Neither poor performing businesses nor managers were easily dropped from the Group.

Harmony

From its beginning, LG placed considerable emphasis on harmony. Some of that emphasis may have stemmed from its history. Mr. In-Hwoi Koo, the founding Chairman, believed strongly that harmony rather than conflict should dominate the atmosphere at work.

Respect

The emphasis on respect was reinforced both at the company and national level. Respect for authority and hierarchy have had a long cultural tradition in Korea. Much of this tradition tied back to Confusion philosophy that held: "Let the king be king. Let the subject be subject. Let the father be father. Let the son be son. In this there is order." As a consequence, respect for management authority and the roles of individual workers were strong values in LG.

The Chairman wanted the new culture to keep the tradition of harmony as well as respect for the individual. Stability, in contrast, could not be sustained. Technological innovations, mergers, acquisitions, divestitures, alliances, and so on, happened at such a rapid pace in the global environment that to accomplish the ambitions of Leap 2005, LG had no choice but to become more agile. Furthermore, unlike the past, Korea would no longer be a protected market, but instead would become increasingly open to foreign competitors. Consequently, even stability at home could not be sustained. For LG to be a world leader, it would need to be as quick and nimble as the best global competitors.

The cultural value of respect would also need to play out differently in the future than it had in the past. In the past, respect had translated into a top down management style. However, beginning with the reorganization in 1987, it had become increasingly clear that while respect for others would always be important, top down management and strong emphasis on hierarchy would not allow LG to respond to the market as quickly as needed to stay competitive.

Establishing the New LG Culture

While retaining certain elements of the past culture, LG's top management tried to establish and reinforce four new cultural elements: challenge, speed, simplicity, boundarylessness.

Challenge

In many ways this new element was in direct contrast to the old value of stability. Going forward, LG needed to develop a culture that thrived on challenge rather than one that relied on stability. According to Chairman Koo, a business objective was challenging if the way to accomplish it was unknown. In other words, if you knew exactly how to accomplish an objective, then it was not challenging. On the other hand, an objective that you did not know how to reach would challenge you to think differently and to come up with "break-through" innovations.

Speed

The second new cultural element—speed— was critical to success in the fast-changing global environment. Managers had to develop a new perspective on time-based competition. Most managers were used to thinking about a year in terms of 365 days. But in fast-paced industries such as the Internet, "web years" lasted perhaps 90 days. In other words, as much changed on "the web" in 90 days as changed in

traditional industries in a year. Consequently, as LG pushed into new markets and higher technology industries, speed had to be a central value that permeated the Group's culture.

Simplicity

In a world as complex as the one LG was entering, keeping things as simple as possible was absolutely essential. For greater product reliability, fewer parts and simpler designs were necessary. Greater product simplicity would also help keep costs down. Quicker service time would require simpler products and business processes. Each additional step in a business process represented both increased costs and time delays, neither of which added value for the customer. If LG did not instill a cultural value around simplicity, the natural complexity of the global environment could cause the Group to respond with complex products and business processes that could turn into a tangled mess.

Boundarylessness

The rapid pace and sophisticated nature of the global environment made the past structure and practice of separated departments and sequentially "handing off" projects—from product research to product design to engineering to manufacturing to marketing to sales—unworkable. Functional, geographic, and even business boundaries of the past needed to become less like fortress walls and more like fuzzy lines. People from different disciplines and geographies increasingly needed to work together to analyze problems and figure out solutions.

⊠ Strategic Orientation of LG

The growth objectives articulated by the Chairman in Leap 2005 were highly ambitious. LG was to grow from around US$38 billion in 1994 to US$380 billion by 2005. This objective represented a true challenge because no one knew exactly how to get there, even though by year-end 1996 Group revenues had increased to US$73 billion. But growing revenues at any cost, such as profitability, was not acceptable. The Chairman made it clear that to be considered one of the best companies in the world, LG's financial performance also had to be among the best in the world.

Focus

New financial objectives meant that LG could no longer carry marginal businesses with poor performance. Either the managers heading those businesses had to fix them so that they were growing and making money or they would need to prepare them for divestiture. Although divestiture would need to happen in a way that honored LG's commitment to employees and retained remaining employees' loyalty to the Group, if a business could not be fixed to be a leader in its industry, it would be sold or shut down.

Focus would also be essential in terms of LG's geographic strategy. Although LG would compete across the globe, it would focus on *strategic markets*. Strategic markets were selected according to two primary criteria. The first was the expected economic growth and size of the market. The second was the extent of business opportunity in that market. Business opportunity was a function of how open the market would be to foreign firms, how intense the competition would be in that market, and what LG's capabilities were for competing there.

Based on expected economic growth and business opportunities, China and Southeast Asia were identified as strategic markets. These markets were expected to grow by eight to ten per cent a year in real terms through 2005. In addition, these markets were increasingly open to foreign trade and investment, and LG had good capabilities for competing there.

Eastern Europe, Central and South America, the Middle East and Africa were all regions with potential economic growth, but were expected to grow more slowly than China

and Southeast Asia. Furthermore, government restrictions and LG's relatively weak competitive positions made them less attractive. Still, LG did not intend to ignore these regions. In fact, LG had plans to establish regional headquarters in Europe, South America, Africa and the Middle East in the near future because of the market potential in these regions.

The developed markets of the United States, Japan, and Western Europe were expected to grow at much slower rates (one to three per cent). Although these markets were relatively open, competition was quite intense, and LG generally had no particular competitive advantage in these markets. Thus, LG would continue to compete there because of the size of these markets, but would focus on China and Southeast Asia as areas of strategic growth.

Avenues of Growth

Simplified, LG could grow through existing and new products, and through existing and new geographies. The specific avenues of growth in each quadrant of this matrix are captured in Exhibit 1. Of the four cells in the matrix, managers anticipated that growth in the "existing products, existing markets" would be the most difficult. Significant revenue growth in this cell would require a product revolution in terms of new technologies or business models.

Technological revolution typically comes in two forms. The first is product technology innovation. This type of innovation provides products that do things that they never did before. As a consequence, customers of the previous product generation replace their old products with the new ones, and new customers are so enticed by the features and capabilities that they enter the market in significant numbers for the first time. The second technology revolution happens through process innovation. This type of innovation allows the product to be produced faster or more cost efficiently.

Exhibit I Avenues of Growth for LG

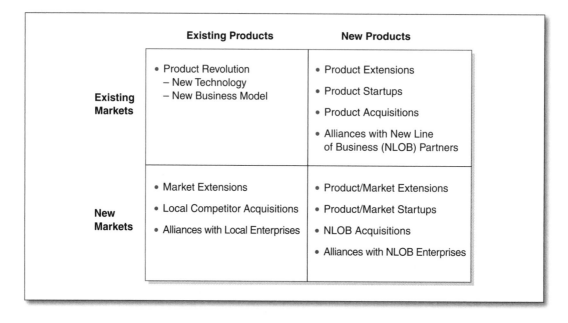

	Existing Products	New Products

Existing Markets	• Product Revolution
	  – New Technology
	  – New Business Model
		• Product Extensions
		
		• Product Startups
		
		• Product Acquisitions
		
		• Alliances with New Line of Business (NLOB) Partners

New Markets	• Market Extensions • Local Competitor Acquisitions • Alliances with Local Enterprises	• Product/Market Extensions • Product/Market Startups • NLOB Acquisitions • Alliances with NLOB Enterprises

A business model revolution produces significant growth with existing products in existing markets because business process innovations provide significantly better value to customers. The significantly better value causes customers to purchase from the new "system" in significant numbers. Wal-Mart did this in discount retailing and Microsoft did this with pre-installed operating system software.

Growth in the other three quadrants comes from extensions, start ups, acquisitions, and various forms of alliances. While each of these activities shares some common managerial capabilities, each requires its own unique set of managerial capabilities for success. Each avenue of growth is difficult to manage successfully. Even if specific managers focused on just one of these avenues of growth, in order to grow ten-fold in ten years, LG would need hundreds of world-class managers in each of these cells and for each of these growth strategies.

Investment Decisions and Cash Flow

To reach growth objectives, top LG managers recognized that financial resources would need to be invested wisely for the greatest possible return. No longer would simple pay-back assessments be adequate. In the future, approved investments would not only need to pay back the original investment but would need to provide an attractive return on that investment based on a future cash flow analysis. With these heightened investment requirements, LG would need a cadre of managers with more sophisticated knowledge of finance.

Customer Satisfaction

Chairman Koo believed that sustained revenue growth would only come through satisfying customers' needs. This orientation had already begun to be instilled throughout the Group by the restructuring his father had directed.

Chairman Koo wanted to build on that. Customer satisfaction was established as a key measure of success in going forward. However, the Chairman did not want the organization to simply react to customer satisfaction and "fix things when customers were dissatisfied," but he wanted proactive management that would anticipate customer needs and satisfy them before the customer ever had a chance to voice dissatisfaction.

Quality

Increasingly sophisticated customers in Korea and around the world wanted products that were reliable and of high quality. To have the most satisfied customers, LG would need world class quality in their products and services. Consequently, Leap 2005 continued the emphasis on high quality and zero defect initiatives.

Product Technology

Customers also wanted products with "the latest and greatest" features. Consequently, Leap 2005 stressed the role of technology and its acquisition. To have the most satisfied customers, LG would need leading-edge product technology and innovations to ensure that, compared to competitors, LG products had superior features and capabilities. In particular, Chairman Koo stressed the importance of acquiring differentiating technology.

Process Technology

Customers also wanted the greatest possible value, which meant that they wanted the best possible features in products and services for the lowest price. Therefore, acquisition of process technology was also important. Key managers believed that innovations enabling products to be made more cheaply, more reliably, or more quickly would enhance not only the value proposition made to customers, but LG's internal profit margins. Therefore, acquisition of process technology also became an important part of Leap 2005.

◾ Leader Development Challenge

Top management and the HR team were convinced that LG could not achieve the objectives of Leap 2005 without substantially more global leaders. Because LG had a domestic orientation in the past and because of the speed with which Leap 2005 required LG to change course to a global setting, leadership development emerged as one of the biggest challenges within the Group.

Working Environment

To be a leading global company, senior executives felt that LG would need to create a global working environment that included both Korean and non-Korean leaders. The Chairman articulated several aspirations that would demonstrate that LG was well on its way to creating a global working environment:

- Fill three to four business president positions with non-Koreans out of the nearly 50 positions (see Exhibits 2 and 3 for an overall review of LG's current size and structure).
- Fill 20 per cent of executive positions at the office of the Chairman in Seoul with non-Koreans.
- Fill most top executive positions of foreign affiliates (approximately 129) with local national managers.

These were ambitious goals, but some executives were worried that if LG did not achieve these aspirations, it would encounter the same problem that Japanese multinational corporations had experienced. Several studies found that Japanese companies had significant difficulty attracting and then hanging on to top local executive talent in countries such as the U.S. This was primarily because local managers got frustrated by the "Bamboo Ceiling." The bamboo ceiling was the barrier non-Japanese

Exhibit 2 LG Group Overall Status, 1996

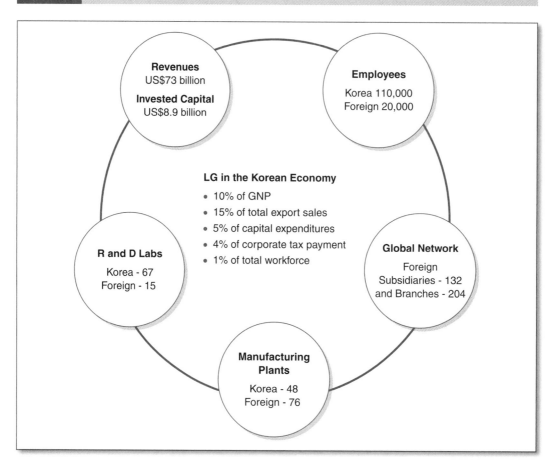

Exhibit 3 LG Businesses, 1996

**Trade and Services and Others
(31.3% of Total Revenue)**

- LG International Corp
- LG Construction Co. Ltd.
- LG Engineering Co. Ltd.
- LG Energy Co. Ltd.
- LG Mart Co. Ltd.
- LG Department Store Co. Ltd.
- LG Ad Inc.
- LG EDS System
- LG Investment Inc.

- Han Moo Development Co. Ltd.
- LG Homeshopping Inc.
- LG Sports Ltd.
- LG Leisure Co. Ltd.
- LG Economic Research Institute

**Chemicals and Energy
(25% of Total Revenue)**

- LG Chemical Co. Ltd.
- LG Petrochemical Co. Ltd.
- LG MMA Corp.

- LG Owens Corning Corp.
- LG Siltron, Inc.
- LG AlliedSignal Corp
- LG Caltex Oil Corp.
- LG Caltex Gas Corp
- LG Oil Products Sales Co. Ltd.
- Hoyu Tanker Co. Ltd.
- Wonjeon Energy Co. Ltd.

Electric and Electronics (23.7% of Total Revenue)

- LG Electronics Inc.
- LG Electro-Components Ltd.
- LG Semicon Co. Ltd.
- LG Honeywell Co. Ltd.
- LG Industrial System Co. Ltd.

- LG Soft Ltd.
- LG Information & Communication Ltd.
- LG Telecom Ltd.

Finance (15% of Total Revenue)

- LG Securities Co. Ltd.
- LG Investment Trust Management Co.
- LG Insurance Co. Ltd.
- LG Credit Card Co. Ltd.
- LG Finance Co. Ltd.
- LG Futures Co. Ltd.
- LG Merchant Banking Corp.

Machinery and Metals (5% of Total Revenue)

- LG Cable & Machinery Ltd.
- LG Metal Corp.

executives ran into at a certain point in the hierarchy of the Japanese subsidiary. In the U.S., many American executives felt that they could rise only to a certain level within the Japanese foreign affiliates and no higher. American executives often felt that above that level only "Japanese expatriate managers need apply." Consequently, smart and capable managers would simply use their experience in a Japanese company as a springboard to better positions in other companies. This turnover of top local talent hurt the financial performance of Japanese companies throughout the world.

Some managers thought Korean companies, if they were not careful, would run into the same problem. Many felt that if LG could not attract and retain the best management and executive talent wherever in the world that talent existed, it would not be competitive with more culturally open-minded companies. But how could the Chairman's aspirations be achieved? What would need to take place for this to be accomplished? How could numerous non-Koreans be effectively integrated into the head offices in Seoul? Where would they find three or four non-Koreans capable of being company presidents and effectively interacting

with other Korean company presidents within the Group? These and other questions plagued the HR team.

Needed Competencies

Beyond these specific aspirations, LG had a much broader set of leadership needs. Mr. Kim estimated that LG needed 1,400 new capable global leaders to achieve the growth objectives of Leap 2005. What competencies would these individuals need? Mr. Kim could generate a list of 20 or 30 needed competencies off the top of his head, but which ones were the truly important ones? With limited time and resources, LG could not afford to take a "shot gun" approach to global leader development. The HR team needed to identify a limited set of competencies on which they could focus assessment and development activities.

Development of Non-Korean Global Leaders

Since it was expected that 50 per cent of revenues in 2005 would come from international sales, Mr. Kim expected that 50 per cent of the 1,400 new global leaders would need to be non-Korean. This meant that 700 non-Korean managers would need to be identified and brought up to world-class standards in short order (see Exhibit 4). Most senior LG executives believed that all company CEOs in LG would need to have a global orientation and global leadership capabilities. In general, the feeling was that as one went down the ranks of managers, the percentage of managers needing to be global leaders declined. This view was more or less true for both Korean and non-Korean future leaders.

But the 700 non-Korean global leaders only scratched the surface of the non-Korean leadership development challenge. Given that half of the targeted US$380 billion in revenues by 2005 was expected to come from international sales, it was estimated that LG

Exhibit 4 The Composition and Orientation of Future Global Leaders at LG

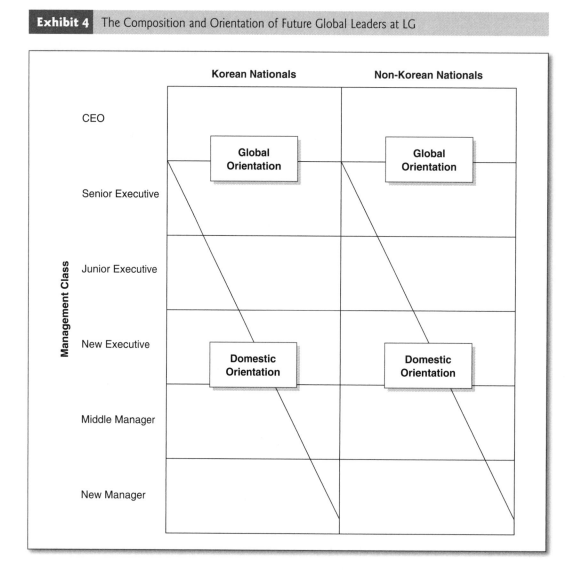

would need approximately 340,000 foreign employees. (In 1996, LG had 110,000 Korean employees, 20,000 non-Korean employees). With a typical manager-to-employee ratio of 1-to-100, LG would need approximately 3,400 non-Korean managers, compared to the 200 it had in 1996.

LG's non-Korean leadership development needs were further complicated by the fact that LG's regional focus for growth was China and Southeast Asia. These were areas in which world-class managerial talent was in relatively short supply. Furthermore, LG was not the only company that had targeted this region. Companies like General Motors, Coca-Cola, Exxon, Philips, Ericsson, Sony and other multinationals were equally committed to the region and had been aggressively acquiring and retaining the best local managerial talent.

How should LG identify high potential managerial talent in the region? What comparative advantage did LG have in acquiring and retaining this talent compared to global competitors such as General Motors or Philips? Furthermore, how should LG develop these high potential individuals once they were hired? Also, was it even possible for a Korea-based team to effectively create and effectively implement a development plan for non-Korean managers? In other words, given that 700 future top LG leaders would be non-Korean, could a group composed of Koreans effectively hire, train, and retain this group? Would culture or other filters cause the HR team to look at information, interpret behavior, structure problems and solutions in ways that would be culturally bound and perhaps not be effective in meeting management development objectives?

Programs

Although Mr. Kim and Dr. Lee did not have the answers to all these questions, several programs were in place at the LG Academy to try to address these leadership development challenges. (See Exhibit 5 for a brief description of each program.) These programs spanned the entire range of employees, from non-managerial employees through company presidents.

The HR team recognized that younger employees and managers needed to be cultivated and developed early if LG were to have strong global leaders 20 years in the future, but these young managers would not be ready to assume significant global responsibilities by 2005. Even if they could be ready, would LG's culture allow a 35-year-old to run a significant business with international operations? Mr. Kim and Dr. Lee wondered if they should concentrate their energy on developing managers who were currently in their 40s.

Prioritization and Decision Time

In September 1997, the HR team met to decide how to proceed. Some members thought the issues needed more study. For example, clearly identifying the critical capabilities of future global leaders was a major challenge. Some argued that to make sure that the right capabilities were identified, more thought and data were needed. Other members of the team felt they knew enough to proceed without more research.

In addition to identifying leadership competencies, the HR team needed to determine how an agreed-upon set of leadership competencies should be developed. The team had identified a variety of approaches to assess the competencies of current LG managers—pencil and paper tests, supervisor evaluations, assessment centers, job performance, expert assessments, and so on. Would each of these be relevant for every career stage? While new managers would basically do whatever they were asked, Mr. Kim and Dr. Lee, in particular, wondered if senior managers would ever agree to participate in a pencil and paper test. They also wondered if current job performance

Exhibit 5 Global Leadership Programs

Non-Manager	Manager	General Manager	Director	VP	President

Global Business Communication

Host Manager

Global Mindset

Global MBA

Global Business Leader

Global Business Consortium

Global CEO Conference

Global Business Communication:	Short seminar designed to teach fundamental principles of cross-cultural communication.
Host Manager:	Program designed to help host country managers understand the strategy and structure of LG.
Global Mind-set:	Program intended to raise understanding of business globalization and the forces behind it.
Global MBA:	Two-Year MBA program. First half completed in Korea and the second half completed in the U.S.
Global Business Leader:	Six-Week program with modules in Korea, the U.S., and countries in Southeast Asia.
Global Business Consortium:	Focuses on strategic benchmarking among six member countries (ABB, BT, Lufthansa, SKF, SCB, and LG).
Global CEO Conference:	Designed to help senior executives address critical issues relative to LG competitive position.

would be a good indicator of potential in young managers. Also, would supervisor evaluations be valid for young managers who might very well have bosses that were not very high potential global leaders themselves?

Once high potential managers were identified and the gaps between existing versus desired leadership competencies were determined, the approach to develop these competencies had yet to be worked out. What role should job rotation and experience play in developing future leaders? What about international assignments? Should the nature of the assignment differ for young managers versus older managers? What about formal training and education programs? What sorts of programs would really be effective?

As members of the HR team grappled with these issues, the task ahead seemed daunting. In an effort to better structure the discussion, Mr. Kim and Dr. Lee agreed to focus the team on three key questions: (1) What were the key needed capabilities of future global leaders? (2) How should these capabilities be developed? (3) Could the team take the same approach to both these issues with Korean and non-Korean managers? With just over seven years remaining under Leap 2005, the HR team was under increasing pressure to not only find answers to these questions, but to put in place the infrastructure required to quickly develop the next generation of leaders at LG.

Vista-Sci Health Care Inc.

Prepared by Jeffrey Gandz

For Allun Jones, this had been a good day. Senior vice-president, marketing and sales of Vista-Sci Health Care Inc.'s (Vista-Sci's) pharmaceutical division at 35—not bad for a university general arts graduate who had started at Vista-Sci as a medical representative, detailing its products to doctors and pharmacists, some 13 years ago. Now he would be responsible for the domestic marketing and sales functions of the pharmaceutical division of a multinational company that had some leading prescription and non-prescription brands ranging from antibiotics to skin creams.

Reporting to him, was a vice-president, product management who supervised a staff of eight product managers and assistant product managers, a vice-president, marketing research and her staff, a vice-president, marketing services and his staff, and a sales force of some 155 medical representatives, district managers and internal sales and sales training staff who reported to the vice-president, sales.

This promotion was a big one that would place him firmly on the next step in his career path, one that he believed could lead to the chief executive officer's (CEO's) job in seven to 10 years. But he knew that it was an opportunity that required continued and indeed accelerated performance on his part; nothing came easily at Vista-Sci and performance was everything!

One rather urgent issue was his replacement as vice-president, product management. The role was a challenging one—he had been doing it for almost seven years, and those years had been difficult but exciting times. He had two candidates, both of whom had stellar records of performance as product managers but, as

Version: (A) 2006-03-31

personalities and in their previous career paths, they were as different as any two people could be. Which one should he recommend? Or should he do the unexpected and look outside the domestic operation or even outside the company? This latter option would be an unusual one to take; Vista-Sci had an outstanding reputation as a developer of talent in the industry and tended to promote from within its own ranks.

⬛ The Vice-President-Product Management Role

Vista-Sci was a company that had embraced the marketing philosophy earlier and more completely than most pharmaceutical firms. Everything was focused on the customer, defined as the user of the company's products rather than the channels through which they were sold, prescribed or recommended. The firm spent millions of dollars on market research, believed that it was knowledgeable about customers' wants, needs and buying behaviors, and its research and development, marketing and sales efforts were driven by an intense commitment to customer satisfaction.

This marketing orientation pervaded the company. Packaging engineers were focused on making the products appealing and accessible to customers, researchers were searching for more appealing dosage regimens, leading to many products being reformulated into one-a-day, time-released formats; even accounts receivable staff were seeking ways in which the trades could spread their payments for seasonal products over a full year so that they would not run out of stock during "slow" periods, thereby inconveniencing customers.

But while this marketing orientation was intensely customer-focused, it also had a strong bottom-line orientation. Shareholders were to be delighted because the company was successful in satisfying customer needs. So every initiative, every new product, package, flavor, distribution drive was expected to pay off in bottom-line results.

Product managers were key players in executing this marketing orientation. Each of these men and women was expected to be a marketing professional. Many had formal business education—most had MBAs from well-recognized schools; some had started with the company as medical representatives (prescription products) or sales representatives (non-prescription products); many had science undergraduate degrees in disciplines such as pharmacy, pharmacology or biochemistry. Each was responsible for the performance of one or more products; its marketing, advertising, packaging, forecasting, line-extension development and the many other activities that went into product management.

These product managers shared many resources. When they wanted some market research, they would make the request of the vice-president, market research; their request might be competing with 10, 20 or more requests from other product managers. Sales force time was allocated to products, and product managers had to make their cases why their product, as opposed to some other product, should be allocated time by the sales force in, for example, the first quarter of next year.

There were formal mechanisms for planning priorities; for example, there was a "sales calendar" established annually, and product managers pitched for their allocation of sales time. There were systems development schedules and priorities, market research efforts were allocated to various products in a planned and budgeted way. But it was well known that the most "effective" product managers got the favored treatment from all those staffs that supported the marketing programs. It was one thing for product managers to get their products allocated for sales force attention . . . and quite another to get the sales force motivated and excited about actually detailing or selling that product to doctors and pharmacists.

Product managers who made effective presentations, who related well to the sales force and who listened to the sales representatives' ideas about how to sell the products seemed to get more attention than others. Market researchers, packaging engineers, even credit analysts had their favorites among the company's eight product managers—usually the ones who took time to give them the "big picture," thanked them for their work, gave credit where credit was due and emphasized the team's efforts. There were other product managers who seemed to have more trouble getting the kind of involvement, participation and commitment from the marketing services, sales and other support functions. They were either too demanding or not demanding enough; too academic in their approach to marketing or not thoughtful enough, constantly promoting hare-brained schemes to support their products.

The product managers also maintained a number of external relationships. The company used three different advertising agencies among which it distributed its brands. Here, again, it was clear that some product managers seemed to get much better performance from agency personnel than others. Top copywriters and creative directors could make a huge difference in marketing a product and some of the product managers seemed to attract the very best agency personnel to work on their assignments. Others attracted lesser talent.

The vice-president product management was really the director of this marketing thrust, even though many of the key players did not report to this position. Packaging reported through production, accounting personnel through the controller, sales staff through the vice-president, sales. It was the responsibility of the vice-president product management to recruit, train and develop the product management staff and to ensure that while each was driving and promoting the interests of the assigned products, the whole unit worked as a team. It was the closest thing to corporate lion-taming that Allun Jones had ever experienced! Now he was moving onwards and upwards, and he needed to find a replacement. Two candidates were apparent—both had strengths, and both had weaknesses.

✄ Jamie Hernandez

When she joined Vista-Sci six years previously, Hernandez had just been terminated from her job with Ashridge Pharmaceuticals in England. She explained why to anyone who asked:

> One day the president was musing aloud about why sales were below plan. I told him: I'd just spent three days out with different members of the field sales force and we'd spent more time in coffee shops than in doctors' offices. I just thought that we weren't pushing hard enough. Ten minutes later, my boss, the vice-president marketing, was in my office telling me that I was being let go. No matter that I was absolutely right—he agreed with me . . . it was lack of sales effort. But I had managed to embarrass the vice-president of sales and he had insisted that my boss fire me, virtually as a condition for continued support by the sales department. So, despite being right, I was sacked—fired! Just shows, you can be right and wrong at the same time!

When he had interviewed Hernandez in the United Kingdom, Jones had been immediately attracted to her openness, her apparent willingness to learn from this incident, and her obvious enthusiasm for the industry and for the marketing role. Hernandez had been a pre-med student at a prestigious medical school in the United Kingdom but had not completed her program. "I was probably too young, had a great time at university, but my grades weren't that great! I just felt that being a doctor wasn't what I really wanted." So, without a degree but with some knowledge of pharmacology, physiology and anatomy, she had applied to a pharmaceutical company as a medical representative, calling on doctors in her assigned territory in London. She'd done that for three years:

But there's just so many *Readers Digests* you can read while waiting for doctors to see you. After a while, I was just bored stiff. The problem was, you couldn't get ahead in that company unless you have a university degree . . . I was stuck! It didn't matter how good I was at my job. In fact, I was working only three days a week—I could get all my assigned calls done in that time, my area manager didn't want me to do any more because it would show up other representatives and make it hard for him to explain why they weren't doing more. So I took up golf!

One day, coming back on a train from a meeting at head office, she'd started talking to a man who was the president of an engineering firm selling to the petro-chemical industry in Europe. He was drinking pretty heavily on the train and, by the time they reached London, he was semi-conscious. She helped him into a taxi and sent him on his way, not, however, before he'd given her a business card and said, "If you're ever looking for a job, give me a call."

The next day, she did. He couldn't remember the event at all! But, despite that—or maybe because of it—she ended up as the Redders Instrumentation and Valve sales manager for Europe.

Great title, reasonable salary, a Jaguar as a company car, and lots of incentive pay for building the business. It was a great two years . . . but it came to an end when Redders was acquired by a larger company and my job was reduced in scope and opportunity. They wanted to keep me, but I just didn't see my future selling safety relief valves and instruments to petrochemical plants in Northeastern England.

While working as a medical representative at the pharmaceutical firm, Hernandez had enrolled in a continuing education program at a local polytechnic (community college) leading to a diploma in marketing. Armed with this accreditation, she applied for a job as a product manager at a very large U.S.-based multi-national pharmaceutical firm. She was successful in a series of full-day interviews, parted on good terms from Redders and joined Ashridge Pharmaceutical where she'd been completely happy until the day she was fired. This entire story had come out during her interview with Allun Jones:

It was one of the most refreshing and candid job interviews I think that I've ever conducted. That's the great thing with Jamie . . . what you see is what you get! She speaks her mind, tells it the way it is. Totally transparent. Passionate about what she wants to do, totally committed. And she's that way with everyone, from the CEO of the company to an accounts receivable clerk. And they all seem to respond well to her. They like working with her or for her; she never has any difficulty getting the best talent to work on her projects, new assistant product supervisors (freshly minted graduates, straight out of business school who are assigned to work for product managers) seem to want to work with her, despite the fact that she does not have the MBA-type education that others have.

True, her outspokenness does cause some ripples. Jamie does not suffer fools wisely and she sometimes is fast to judge people as fools. Her excitability is both an asset and a liability. There are few weeks that go by when I don't have someone in my office raising questions or complaints about how she's handled something. What I notice, however, is that they are not people who are directly involved in her projects. Rather, they are "observers" and they usually point out that Jamie is different from others, maybe just doesn't fit the usual Vista-Sci model. As far as I've been concerned, at least in the past, that's been a good thing. We need some more diversity around here . . . and Jamie's different. The outspokenness? Well she usually says "What do you expect, with a Scottish mother and a Mexican father . . . bland?"

There was one incident that showed what a driving personality Hernandez was. One of her products was a specialized, bactericidal mouthwash that was positioned at dentists and dental hygienists to be recommended to their patients. It was very successful in this niche, with very high gross margins, limited advertising expenditures, but only seven per cent share of the total mouthwash market. Hernandez wanted to reposition this brand into the broader consumer market. She felt that with the professional endorsements, the highly appealing characteristics of the product and with the right kind of approach she could drive market share up to the 20 per cent to 25 per cent range.

The issue was that Vista-Sci already had a mouthwash brand with 35 per cent share of market, positioned against this broader market. "No problem," said Hernandez; "Sure we'll cannibalize some of that market share but, overall, we'll boost our corporate market share by 10 or so share points." And she'd commissioned the research to support her point. In comparison tests and conjoint analysis studies, she had built the case for doing it. It convinced pretty well everyone . . . except the product manager of the other, consumer-oriented mouthwash brand. He was not, and never would be, convinced. Discussions had gotten pretty heated before Hernandez had been told to back off. Still, every chance she got, she

made the point that they could be doing better in the mouthwash category if the company had accepted her approach.

There were other sources of friction. The company used a "full-costing" approach to making product "go/no-go" launch decisions; Hernandez—who, at that time had been studying for her MBA at a local university in the evenings[2]—had become convinced that they were making bad decisions by following this approach, that what they should really do was use a marginal-contribution approach. So, when making her proposal, that's how she did it. Routinely, the finance department sent back her analysis and told her to do it "the right way." She did . . . and it was "her" way! Of course, in the end, she did it their way because she wanted to get her projects approved. But she also wanted to make her point. "Eventually," she said, "they'll change. Sure I make a few waves, but if you don't, then people will keep on doing the same old things in the same old ways. I think I know how hard I can push and when to back off."

Unlike some of the product managers, Hernandez seemed to be liked and respected by all her peers. When there was hard work to be done and they needed help, she pitched in. When it was time to relax and party . . . Hernandez usually got the party organized, was the first to arrive and the last to leave. When others had ideas, she gave credit to them and she was reluctant to claim credit for her own initiatives. Had there been a vote for the "most popular product manager in the company" among both the product managers and sales force, she'd have won hands-down. To some extent, there was such a vote. Each year, all the product and assistant product managers in the company (not just the pharmaceutical division) held a "copy competition" where they presented their advertising strategies and creative work. Hernandez had won this competition in three of the last four years, partly due

[2]She completed her MBA in three years of evening and weekend study.

to the quality of the advertising she and her advertising agencies developed and partly because of the overall respect with which she was held by her peers.

Her official performance record was outstanding. Vista-Sci had a disciplined multi-factor scorecard approach to assessing performance and, on every measure, Hernandez had received top scores and maximum bonus. Sales of her products were booming, profit margins were on or above stretch targets, she got great scores from sales force reports on her effectiveness in working with them, her advertising agencies put their best creative people on her product assignments and the corporate marketing research manager reported that she framed her research issues better than anyone else in the company. It was, overall, a very positive picture.

Managers at Hernandez's level received a lot of unofficial feedback but also underwent an annual performance appraisal. Based on the competencies associated with the role, each product manager was given an overall rating that ranged from Unsatisfactory (1) through Needs Improvement (2), Satisfactory (3), Good (4), to Outstanding (5). These ratings determined the personal component of the annual bonus with Unsatisfactory receiving zero bonus and Outstanding receiving a bonus that was 50 per cent of base salary. The difference between Good and Outstanding was 15 per cent, a significant amount. More important, getting an Outstanding rating was really considered the key to being considered for promotion at the next available opportunity.

Allun Jones could only remember one time during Hernandez's career at Vista-Sci when her performance had been an issue. About three years ago, Hernandez had come to see him one day, visibly distressed. Her mother had been diagnosed with Alzheimer's disease about a year ago—she had not mentioned this to Jones—and now appeared to be deteriorating fairly quickly.

Allun—I'm going to have to spend more time with her, especially until we can figure out what to do. You know, some of the weekend work and late nights will just have to be spent with my family—the other one, not the Vista-Sci one! And I think that I'll definitely use up my accumulated vacation this year and, maybe, even apply for a leave of absence for a couple of months.

They had discussed her workload and agreed that she could assign a couple of her minor brands to others and also put more responsibility on her product supervisors—she had two people whom she had trained really well and Jones felt that they could pick up any slack caused by Jamie backing off a little and even coping with a leave of absence for a couple of months.

There was one additional assignment that Jones needed completed during that year. For some time, he had been thinking of re-shuffling the brand allocations among the various product managers since he felt that some were relatively lightly loaded while others seemed overloaded. He also thought that they might be able to reduce the product management staff by at least one or two product managers (of the total of seven) and, perhaps, four or five of assistant product managers. There was some considerable pressure for him to do so; corporate was asking for a steady five per cent annual increase in "people productivity" and the marketing department had been lagging this for several years.

Following several meetings, Jones had suggested to Hernandez that she interview the current product managers and their assistants, as well as others inside and outside the company with whom they worked, and then make her recommendations. After a month, he had met with her to review progress; she had not yet started the interviews but promised to do so "within the next few weeks." After another couple of months had gone by, Jones raised it in a regular monthly meeting. Hernandez reported that she had started interviews but had not yet formed any opinions about reorganization. Soon afterwards, Hernandez' mother's condition had deteriorated further and she took six weeks accumulated vacation time followed by a three-month leave of absence. At least that's what she was supposed to do. Actually, she called in fairly frequently and stayed in touch with her product supervisors on a pretty regular basis. Toward the end of this period she had made the difficult decision to place her mother in a nursing home.

On her return to work, full-time, Jones had spoken to her about the reorganization project:

> Jamie, the reorganization project is way, way behind schedule. And it forms 30 per cent of your official goals for this year. . . . It could affect your bonus calculation this year. What's the problem?

Hernandez responded

> Well, I've spoken to several of the people—just informal discussions really—but I can't honestly say that I can see any areas where people seemed underworked or there seems to be any slack. We're doing real well in sales and I think that our advertising and research are better than ever. But I'll get some more focus on it and get back to you next month.

She didn't and, what's more, her annual performance rating had been due within the next couple of weeks. "What rating should I give her?" Jones had wondered. "If I downgrade her from Outstanding to Good, it would cost her quite a lot in bonus and might affect her prospects for promotion." Jones also knew that it would be hard to justify the downgrade to his boss, the CEO, who thought very highly of Hernandez. He had talked it over with the

vice-president, human resources. "Be careful," he'd said. "Jamie is pretty valuable to us and we'd hate to get her upset over this—after all, it was a different type of assignment . . . not her usual work. And there was her family problems . . . you'd expect some things to be done less than perfectly."

In the end, Jones had decided to ignore the unfinished project and had given Hernandez an "Outstanding" rating. He also decided, based in his own analysis, to downsize the product management department by five people. It was not a popular choice and certainly disrupted the "team" environment for a while but he felt that it needed to be done.

With Hernandez' mother settled into a good nursing home, things returned to normal in the Vista-Sci product management group. Hernandez was back to her normal self, doing her usual, outstanding job.

Michael Upshaw

"When it comes to personality," Jones observed, "You couldn't have a greater difference than between Jamie Hernandez and Michael Upshaw. Nor, for that matter, could you have people with more different backgrounds."

Michael Upshaw had been brought up in the Midwestern United States, the son of a small-town college professor and a homemaker. He had been educated at a local high school where he'd been active in military cadets through the Reserve Officers Training Corps (ROTC), in both high school and college and, with the support of his local congressman, had won a place at West Point, the U.S. Army College. He'd ranked in the top third of his class, graduated as an army engineer, and then served three years in the army, two of them in Vietnam attached to a front-line infantry regiment where he had been slightly wounded and had eventually been honorably discharged.

Upshaw spoke little about his military service. In fact, he spoke little about himself at all. After the military, he had won a scholarship to a prestigious business school, graduating—again in the top third of his class—with an MBA and not a great deal of sense about what he wanted to do with the rest of his life.

He had been recruited by Vista-Sci while he was at business school and moved into the company in an assistant product manager role. Over the next three years Upshaw had worked for three different product managers as well as serving on a couple of special task forces, one working on a department-wide forecasting system and the other on a project for the chairman of Vista-Sci International, scoping out possibilities for site location of the international division's world headquarters. He had received good or outstanding appraisals after all of these assignments. Invariably these reviews singled out his thoughtful, disciplined approach to all the tasks he undertook. He took direction extremely well but, when he was left on his own, demonstrated reasonable initiative and resourcefulness. He blended in well with any team on which he was placed, pulled his weight on the team and was thought of as a good colleague by those who worked with him.

Promoted to product manager about five years ago, Upshaw had managed his products with disciplined thoroughness. Never an "ideas man" himself, he nevertheless was open to ideas from others, listened carefully to them and usually made good choices. His documentation of everything—from marketing plans to minutes of packaging meetings—was extensive and accurate.

Allun Jones made a point of discussing the performance and development needs of all of his staff with people with whom they frequently interacted. In reviewing his product managers' performance with John Middlestadt, the account supervisor at one of his advertising agencies, John had said:

I'm always impressed with how well-prepared Mike (Upshaw) is. His creative briefs are first rate and, largely because of that, his projects run very smoothly. Come to think of it, I don't think that I can recall a single case where the budget ran over the forecasted amount or even when a project was delayed. No—Michael operates with military precision!

The other thing that helps him is his choice of people to work with. Some of your people attract the more way-out, unorthodox members of our creative staff. Jamie, for instance—now she's always pushing for unusual, breakthrough creative ideas for print and television advertising and even some creative media buy packages ... she was one of the first into cable bundles ... turned out to be a great buy. Michael, on the other hand ... well, he assembles a good team and then gets really good performance from them. It's a more "controlled" creative product ... but it's good.

Allun had pushed the account supervisor: "I hear you. But tell me, honestly, if you had to assemble an absolutely first class creative team headed by a strong marketing person, would you go for Mike?" There was a long pause before John answered:

I'm not sure. I know that I'd sleep well at night if I had Mike running the team. There would be no surprises and a pretty good product in the end. But I suspect that someone like Jamie would walk away with the awards for the best advertising campaign more often than Mike. Of course, you'd put a lot more work into the project as well. ... I mean, she'd need more supervision than Michael.

Jones had met several times with Michael Upshaw over the last two years to discuss his career aspirations. Unlike most other members of his Marketing staff, Michael had seldom asked about promotion or what it took to get ahead. He'd asked him about this once, suggesting almost that maybe Michael lacked some ambition. His response had been, characteristically cool:

> I suppose that I get that from having been in the military. You get used to having to put time in working on lower level jobs, some of which aren't all that exciting. I guess that you get used to just doing a good job and hoping and expecting that someone will notice and give you an opportunity to take on bigger challenges and responsibilities. I think that the same thing happens in business—not much point in putting myself forward if the job performance is not there. . . . I just let the performance speak for itself.

Allun Jones had also noticed that Michael did not seem to attract high potential junior staff the same way that others, including Jamie, did. While the people that he managed always spoke well of him, and believed that they had benefited from his teaching and coaching, he didn't seem to have the same magnetism as Jamie. When she went on campus recruiting trips and made presentations, there were crowds of students who came up to her asking questions and trying to impress her; when Michael did recruiting trips the responses were less enthusiastic—people listened politely but did not seem as eager to engage him in discussion.

People who worked for Michael found him to be a good boss—considerate, caring, willing to spend time with them. Sometimes Allun wondered if they had it a little too good—he remembered always feeling stretched and on the edge of having too much to do in too short a time when he had been a junior product manager or supervisor. Maybe Michael's superior organizing skills meant that his people had an easier time of it or maybe he just didn't stretch his people far enough.

Jones summarized:

> He's good. Sometimes he's very good. But he's not, you know, exciting! He would be a good, safe appointment as vice-president, product management. He'd make the routine decisions himself and probably come to me to talk through the tough ones. But I'm not convinced that we'd get any breakthroughs with Michael. At best, he'd do as good a job as I've been doing after he got some more experience.

The Decision

There were many thoughts on Allun Jones's mind as he drove home that night, not all of them making him feel comfortable.

> Michael or Jamie? Which one would be best for the job; how would each react if the other got it . . . and did that really matter? How would the decision be viewed by the other product managers and assistant product managers at Vista-Sci, both in the pharmaceutical and other divisions?

He was also conscious of the fact that this was the first major "people" decision that he would be making in his new role. How this worked out may well determine his own future with Vista-Sci.

The Character of Leadership

James C. Sarros, Brian K. Cooper, and Joseph C. Santora

> *I have a dream today . . . I have a dream that my four little children will one day live in a nation where they will not be judged by the color of their skin but by the content of their character. I have a dream today.*

> Martin Luther King, Jr.
> Speech on steps of Lincoln Memorial,
> Civil Rights March, 28 August 1963

Scratch the surface of a true leader, or look beneath his or her personality, and you'll find character. The traits and values that make up the character of a good business leader are, for the most part, similar to those that make up the character of an outstanding citizen. These authors describe the traits and values that make up the character of leadership.

Character has come in from the cold. Once the poor cousin of clinical psychology and behavioural studies, character is once again recognized as a critically important component of personality and therefore, of what makes people tick. Its importance to leadership is considerable.

⊠ Character in Leadership

Not surprisingly, the importance of the character of leadership is making inroads in the business world. Johnson & Johnson (J&J), the major manufacturer of health care products in the United States, views character as a leadership essential. Former Chairman Ralph Larsen believes that people with character can give a company a significant competitive advantage.

The company actively seeks to recruit and be represented by people of exceptional character. Johnson & Johnson's stance is supported by research which suggests that in leadership, good character counts. According to Frances Hesselbein, the author and chairman of the Drucker Foundation, leadership that achieves results goes beyond *how to be*, and becomes *how to do*; this type of leadership is all about character. So in other words, in order to get things done personally and organizationally, one first needs to get in touch with his or her character.

Leaders with character achieve results that transcend everyday organizational imperatives and outcomes. A study of world leaders over the past 150 years asserts that managers who possess strong character will create a better world for everyone, while leadership generally is vital to the social, moral, economic, and political fabrics of society.

For example, Theresa Gattung is the CEO of Telecom NZ, a New Zealand telecommunications company. Her candour about her vulnerabilities, as well as her philosophy on leadership, has won her the admiration of her male colleagues. She recognizes that good leadership consists more of character than personality:

AUTHORS' NOTE: The study on which this article is based was made possible through the generous support of the Australian Institute of Management (Queensland division). We appreciate the contributions of Dr. Anne Hartican, research assistant, Monash University, to this study.

When I went to management school 20 years ago, I thought it was about personality, desire, determination, and a little bit of technique. I didn't actually realise it was about character, and that struck me more as I have gone along. . . . The leaders whom people respect and will follow have the characteristics of being themselves, of being passionate about what they are doing, communicating that in a heartfelt way that touches hearts.

However, we often take the character of leadership for granted. We expect good leaders to be strong in character, that is, to have a moral imperative underwrite their actions. These leaders with character have been identified as *authentic* leaders: They are what they believe in; show consistency between their values, ethical reasoning and actions; develop positive psychological states such as confidence, optimism, hope, and resilience in themselves and their associates; and are widely known and respected for their integrity.

Nonetheless, the key attributes of authentic leaders, or leaders with character, remain problematic. To identify these attributes and better understand them, we undertook a study. This paper is based on that study and in it we identify the three underlying dimensions of leadership character—universalism, transformation, and benevolence.

We also suggest ways of further enhancing these dimensions and their constituent attributes.

Universalism represents an understanding, appreciation, and tolerance for the welfare of people generally, and is a macro perspective approach to work and life. The character attributes of respectfulness, fairness, cooperativeness, and compassion in particular fit best with this definition of universalism.

Transformation is consistent with the concept of transformational leadership as an activity that inspires others in the achievement of long-term, visionary goals. The character

attributes of courage and passion best represent this factor. Transformation is a situation-specific process that relies on the competence and self-reliance of the incumbent in their delivery of inspired and values-driven strategic direction for the enterprise.

Benevolence is a micro approach to work, and focuses on concern for the welfare of others through one's daily interactions. Selflessness, integrity, and organization loyalty best represent the characteristics of benevolence.

I. Universalism

Universalism is the outward expression of leadership character and is made manifest by respectfulness for others, fairness, cooperativeness, compassion, spiritual respect, and humility.

Respectfulness

Juliana Chugg, the former Managing Director of General Mills Australasia, illustrated respect for her workers by dramatically altering the time employees needed to spend at the workplace by closing the doors at 1pm every Friday. Against the board's advice, this decision allowed the company's executives and factory workers to start their weekends earlier. More importantly, this action resulted in no job losses or salary reductions, no drop in productivity, and no increase in working hours on other days during the week. Chugg, who now heads up General Mills' head office in Minneapolis, Minnesota, is the new face of home baking giant Betty Crocker, a $1 billion business in the US alone. As a relatively young mother in charge of a diverse international company, Chugg understands the need to balance her personal and work demands: "The role of a managing director is not to make all the decisions. It is to get the people who have access to the right information together so that, collectively, they are able to make better decisions than they would on their own." Chugg received the Victorian Businesswoman of the Year award in 2000 for her visionary and caring approach to business.

Fairness

Fairness is treating people equitably and in a just manner. Max De Pree, the former CEO of furniture maker Herman Miller, is guided by a deep concern for others. His approach to life manifests itself in his approach to work and the way in which Herman Miller conducts its business affairs. De Pree believes a corporation is a community of people, all of whom are valued. His main contention is that when you look after your people with care and consideration, they in turn look after you.

Former Chrysler CEO Lee Iacocca was known to say that if you talk to people in their own language and you do it well, they'll say, "God, he said exactly what I was thinking." And when your people begin to respect you, Iacocca claimed "they'll follow you to the death," metaphorically speaking.

Cooperation

The ability to work as a team has been praised as a strategic advantage. Unfortunately, many corporations prevent good teamwork through antiquated organizational structures and protocols. However, creating new office towers with transparent offices, mezzanine floors, and atrium-style meeting places may not necessarily promote a more cooperative workplace. Attitudes need to change also. One way of influencing attitudinal change is by linking individuals' sense of identity with the organization's destiny. The more a leader assists workers in defining their work identities, the greater the chance of encouraging worker commitment and building a cooperative workplace.

Merck, a leading pharmaceutical products and services company in the U.S., lists its recognition of its employees' diversity and teamwork capacities as one its core values. It promotes teamwork by providing employees with work that is meaningful in a safe and dynamic workplace. Therefore, building cooperation as an attribute of character requires commitment, possible corporate redesign, and consciousness of client needs, both internal and external.

Compassion

Compassion has deep religious connotations, for it refers to showing concern for the suffering or welfare of others, and shows mercy to others. In a company sense, compassion manifests itself when leaders make an effort to understand the needs of their employees and take steps to address those needs and concerns. A compassionate leader takes the Atticus Finch approach (the attorney in Harper Lee's 1962 novel *To Kill a Mockingbird*), which means walking around in another person's shoes, and climbing around under their skin, to understand what it looks like from their side of the ledger: "You never understand a person until you consider things from his point of view . . . until you climb into his skin and walk around in it."

Linda Nicholls, chairperson of Australia Post, argues that recent terrorist activities and the spate of corporate collapses around the globe have given rise to widespread social concerns for safety, security, and certainty. Nicholls argues that leaders need to show compassion because of the fears such events have generated, and to balance the drive for innovation, risk and growth with the human need for safety and security.

Peter Sommers, managing director of Merck's Australian division, provides an anecdote that exhibits how compassion for employees takes precedence to work demands:

> We've got stock-take this Thursday. The mother of one of the women who works in our factory died a few days ago, and the funeral is going to be on stock-take day. We only do stock-take once a year; it's a very, very big day. The employee's manager and I have both said, "Well, if the funeral is on stock-take day, then stock-take will have to stop for an hour." It's a very

important day, it's a full day, I work a 12-hour day and I'm usually exhausted. But we will go to our employee's mother's funeral to give support, because we care for our people. They're not just numbers here. Each person is treated as an individual, we know their needs, and we try to cater to some of their wants.

Spiritual Respect

Today's organizations are multidimensional; they provide services and products at an ever-increasing rate and superior quality, and achieve these outcomes through a multicultural and diverse workforce. Leaders who respect these differences in workers' backgrounds, cultures, and beliefs help build vibrant and relevant workplaces.

Respect for individual beliefs and customs has a long history. In Athenian society, Plato viewed leadership as "an activity with utility for the polis, the activity of giving direction to the community of citizens in the management of their common affairs, especially with a view to the training and improvement of their souls." The reference to soul suggests that leaders engage the full person and help make him or her a productive and morally strong member of society through their contributions in the workplace.

In recent years, the Track-Type Tractors Division of Caterpillar Inc. has experienced unprecedented improvement across the board by establishing workplace values and making employees feel important in the organization. Jim Despain, vice president of this division, acknowledges that leadership is "about others and not about self. It is about trust and not about power. It is about producing results by creating cultures where people know it's okay to be unique and different, so they willingly take off their masks, express themselves, and do great things." This approach confirms the view that workers can achieve great things with the right type of encouragement and respect.

Humility

Fifth Century BC Chinese Taoist philosopher Lao-Tzu described humility as the capacity to keep yourself from putting the self before others and argued that in doing so, one can become a leader among men.

Despite broad acknowledgement of its importance, being humble does not sit comfortably with the healthy egos of many executives. Some CEOs operate under the mistaken beliefs that they are infallible, and that to admit error or concede a superior point of argument is a weakness. Sometimes a leader becomes a boss to get the job done, and there's not much room for humility when the job demands action.

A recent study of over 2,000 Australian executives revealed that often executives were democratic and collegial at the beginning of the working week, but often resorted to authoritarian direction giving at week's end in order to meet deadlines. There was no room for humility in those situations. Humility may be an anachronism in a world recognized by the combat of commerce rather than by cooperative and collegial workplaces. For instance, when managers are asked to apply Benjamin Franklin's (1784) "Moral Virtues" to contemporary society, there is a predictable resistance to Franklin's virtue of humility, which is to "imitate Jesus and Socrates." Today's executives see themselves as more worldly and upbeat than that, regardless of the valuable lessons implicit in the statement.

When we examine humility across cultures, there are compelling differences. For example, Japanese CEOs have been known to resign when their projected company profits fell short of the mark. These businessmen blamed themselves for their company's poor performance. When the world's largest bank, Mizuho Holdings, experienced severe computer breakdowns that delayed business transactions, CEO Terunobu Maeda took swift action. He cut the pay of the employees directly involved in the computer system integration, as well as taking a personal pay cut of

50% for six months. Leaders who shift responsibility back to themselves in good times as well as bad have strength of character that goes beyond standard leadership constructs. These leaders possess the attributes commonly referred to as servant leadership. One of the key elements of this leadership philosophy is humility, or the capacity to commit to your workers as much as you do to the bottom line. The guiding principle of servant leadership is to serve rather than to lead. Serving your workers, being a steward of their efforts, takes a considerable dose of humility and rests on a strong sense of self-identity.

Many western business leaders may reject humility as a desirable or useful attribute in today's fast moving, competitive world. Nonetheless, the common characteristics of company leaders who have achieved outstanding and sustainable financial performance in this dynamic environment include modesty, humility, quietness, and self-effacing behavior. These attributes are indicators of leaders quietly aware of their roles in the overall scheme of things. Humility therefore appears to be about a realistic sense of perspective, an acceptance of one's strengths and weaknesses.

2. Transformation

Transformation is how leaders achieve universal and benevolent outcomes, and is the second main factor of leadership character. Transformational leaders with character have courage, passion, wisdom, competency, and self-discipline in their leadership repertoire.

Courage

From a business perspective, courage is having strong convictions about the strategic objectives of the company and being prepared to harness the minds of workers and company resources to achieve those objectives. There are no second-place getters in this approach to business. Courage is not constrained by fear of the unknown and thrives in the problems and promises of dynamic environments.

Managerial courage includes the willingness to do what is right in the face of risk. With "risk" there is a possibility of failure or loss and no guarantee that everything will turn out fine. Acting with courage may result in unpleasant experiences, yet it is a fundamental ingredient of leadership.

Corporate courage manifests itself in many ways. G eneral Electric (GE) requires law firms on its panels to compete for projects through online, eBay-style auctions which force competing bids to a financial bottom line that allows for comparability across all contenders who are promoting their wares. This innovative and courageous approach coaxes the best out of competitors. From this perspective, courage is immediate and localized.

Michelle Peluso, the chief executive of Travelocity, a US travel company, exemplifies courage. She knows that being innovative requires risk and facing the possibility of failure. Peluso proposed an innovative business model which she believed would assist Travelocity regain ground lost to the company's key competitors. Peluso's business model, "seamless connectivity", focuses on customer and supplier satisfaction. Implementing the model required an investment in technology and training. Investors expressed concern about the time it would take to implement Peluso's strategy and questioned whether it was the right approach. Peluso was unwavering in the face of mounting ambivalence. She believed that her business model was compatible with the company's philosophy of doing things differently and having a long-term view.

Peluso did not yield to these pressures. Instead, she worked hard to influence investors by developing a strong rapport with employees and encouraging them to be innovative and passionate about their work. She introduced a weekly prize for outstanding and innovative work by staff. She also mentors twenty-five "exceptional" Travelocity employees.

Peluso's courage and conviction appear to have paid off handsomely. Travelocity has recently been certified as an official third-party distributor for the Intercontinental Hotels Group because of its supplier-friendly policies.

Passion

Passion is about energy and deeply committed enthusiasm to producing the best one can. In business, passion is an indicator of a company's guiding principles, its *raison d'etre*, and helps others identify the underlying culture of the organization. Unilever is a top ranking Fortune Global 500 company, with over US$46 billion in revenues, US$7 billion in operating profit, and over 240,000 employees globally. The company is a world leader in ice cream, frozen foods, teas, and the second-largest manufacturer of laundry, skin cleansing and hair-care products. Its corporate slogan, "Your passion. Our strength," represents "total commitment to exceptional standards of performance and productivity, to working together effectively and to a willingness to embrace new ideas and to learn continuously" (Unilever, 2004).

John McFarlane (2003), the CEO of the ANZ bank in Australia, believes that leadership is about choosing to make a difference and that when you reflect on making a difference it must be in areas about which one is passionate. A leader's passion can make a significant difference in the degree to which she inspires others or provides focus and motivation for the organisation.

Leadership guru Warren Bennis thinks passion is inherent in effective leadership: "We are productive when we do what we love to do". For example, toward the end of his seventh year as president of the University of Cincinnati, Bennis was giving a talk at the Harvard School of Education. During question time the dean asked Bennis not if he "enjoyed", but whether if he "loved" being president of the University of Cincinnati. Bennis acknowledged that he didn't know, but on reflection realized that he did not love the job of president. For Bennis, this realization was a major turning point in his life, as it made him realize that his passion lay in teaching and writing. If passion or love of your work or vocation is missing, then choose another vocation.

Wisdom

Wisdom is the ability to draw on one's knowledge and experience to make well-formed judgments. It also involves the use of one's power and personal authority to implement an effective course of action.

Wisdom underpins major decisions. Former BP CEO John Browne was the first CEO in the oil industry to openly acknowledge the impact the industry was having on the environment, and to highlight the ways of reducing greenhouse gas emissions. Browne advocated a responsible approach to limiting the energy industry's impact on the environment through BP's "Beyond Petroleum" campaign. This approach could have impacted on the company's bottom line, but the wisdom of the decision was that it tapped into the moral conscience of society at the time.

Compare Browne to Lee Raymond, his counterpart at Exxon Mobil. Raymond initially was skeptical about global warming. Consequently, Raymond is said to have become the "energy executive everyone loves to blame for the industry's PR problems". Exxon became the target of a boycott in Europe, which encouraged Raymond to change his stance. Recognizing the positive impact Browne's approach had on BP's corporate image, Exxon Mobil subsequently launched its own green ad campaign.

Competence

Those actively pursuing a career as a leader need to be competent in order to maintain the confidence of others. They need to be expert in something to the extent that their expertise commands the respect of peers and followers. According to the former Australian Governor-General, Sir Ninian Stephens (1997):

The first and most important ingredient of leadership seems to me to be to possess a rounded and comprehensive knowledge of the subject matter with which you are dealing and about which you want others to act in a particular way.

FedEx's founder and CEO, Fred Smith, exemplifies the power of competence. Awarded *Chief Executive* Magazine's 2004 CEO of the Year prize, Smith was recognised for his ability to take FedEx from being "just an idea to being a great company".

Smith says that his vision for creating FedEx was the result of studying a mathematical discipline called topology. Through this study he realized that if you connected all points on a network through a central hub, the resulting efficiencies could be huge.

For Smith, competence does matter. When asked what it takes to be a leader who creates a company and then builds it up to a $25 billion-a-year business, employing 240,000 employees and contractors, Smith advocates "continual learning and education and the discipline to apply those lessons to your operation." He also advises others to make the time and effort to benchmark and learn the lessons of history.

Self-Discipline

Leaders with self-discipline exercise appropriate personal control over their thoughts and actions and are able to manage and express emotions in constructive ways. They are well organised and able to persist in the face of difficulties. Through self-discipline, leaders engender confidence in their followers that they can be relied upon to make rational and logical decisions. As a consequence, their capacity to influence others often increases. Lao Tzu proposed that through mastering ourselves we find true power.

Author and former CEO of international medical technology company, Medtronics, Bill George (2004) argues that self-discipline is the attribute that converts values into consistent action. George describes his successor at Medtronics, CEO Art Collins, as a highly self-disciplined leader as his ego and emotions don't get in the way of taking appropriate action. Collin's consistency in his disposition, behaviours and decisions lets employees know where he stands on important issues.

Self-discipline requires the maturity to do what is needed, not always what is desired in the present moment. Amy Brinkley, Chief Risk Officer, Bank of America, exhibits such maturity. Brinkley (2003) includes self-discipline as a key component of her personal equation for success and in order to maintain the right balance between her roles as bank executive, wife, mother and as a member of her church and community: "I try very hard to be fully in the zone I am in at the moment. I give everything I have at that moment to what I am focusing on. I also abide by my own operating principles like staying away from voice mails and e-mails when I am with my kids and my husband."

As a means of maintaining a balance between professional and personal roles, self-discipline is an important component of effective leadership.

▧ 3. Benevolence

The third major dimension of leadership character is benevolence, and is associated with loyalty, selflessness, integrity, and honesty.

Loyalty

Leaders who demonstrate organisational loyalty show a deep commitment to building organisational sustainability. Such leaders have been described as having the resolve to do whatever it takes to make a company great irrespective how hard the decisions or how difficult the task.

Take Anne Mulcahy, the CEO of Xerox, as a case in point. Mulcahy has exhibited a deep loyalty to her organisation. When she was asked by the board to take on the role of CEO,

Xerox was in financial crises, with a $17.1 billion debt and $154 million in cash. In 2000 the stock fell from $63.69 a share to $4.43.

While Mulcahy had an excellent reputation within Xerox, she had no prior CEO experience. Despite the dire financial position of the company, the board recognized Mulcahy was straightforward, hard-working, disciplined, and fiercely loyal to the company. Mulcahy accepted the CEO role based on a sense of duty and loyalty.

When Xerox's external financial advisors suggested Mulcahy consider filing for bankruptcy, the easier way out, she refused to do so. According to Joe Mancini, Xerox's Director of Corporate Financial Analysis, the company's financial advisors didn't think Mulcahy had the courage to make the painful but necessary changes to save Xerox. But Mulcahy indeed did have what it takes.

In her efforts to achieve what can only be described as an extraordinary corporate turnaround, it is claimed that Mulcahy did not take a single weekend off in two years. Timothy R. Coleman, a senior managing director at the private equity firm, Blackstone, said of Mulcahy at the time: "She was leading by example. Everybody at Xerox knew she was working hard, and that she was working hard for them."

Organizational loyalty, as a component of character, means commitment to the idea and ideals of the company as much as it does to the nature of its business.

Selflessness

The character attribute of selflessness requires leaders to put others' interests ahead of their own.

Ping Fu, a founding member of Raindrop Geomagic, a North Carolina-based innovative software company, is a leader who demonstrates a capacity for selflessness. Fu took on the role of CEO in 2001 when the company's viability was threatened. The company was running out of money and the venture capital markets were drying up.

Under Fu's leadership, several cost-cutting initiatives were implemented, which included laying off almost half the company's employees. Those who remained took pay cuts. In her efforts to save the business, Fu loaned the company money in order to pay its workers. She also declined to take a pay check until the company straightened out its financial situation.

Raindrop Geomagic board member Peter Fuss acknowledges Fu's personal sacrifices. He says she invested considerable time and was tenacious in her efforts to rebuild the company.

Integrity

The word *integrity* comes from the Latin word 'integritas', meaning wholeness, coherence, rightness, or purity. Integrity has been defined as consistency between word and deed or "the perceived degree of congruence between the values expressed by words and those expressed through action."

Integrity is the most often cited element of corporate mission statements. In most cases, integrity refers to honest representation of a company's values and operating protocols. Texas Instruments (TI) refers to "representing ourselves and our intentions truthfully" as evidence of their integrity. General Electric (GE) identifies integrity as a "worldwide reputation for honest and reliable business conduct." The Gillette Company highlights "mutual respect and ethical behavior" as hallmarks of integrity.

Roger Corbett (2004), the CEO and Managing Director of Woolworths, Australia's largest supermarket chain, consisting of more than 150,000 employees and 1,500 stores, believes integrity is the glue that holds his values and the organization's success together: "The closer you can get the business towards integrity and the further away from cynicism, then that really is a good measure of the effectiveness of your business . . . integrity of purpose and example, of lifestyle and attitude, are probably the most important cultural contributions a leader can make to the business."

Honesty

Honesty is absolutely essential to leadership and character. People value working for leaders they can trust. Lindsay Cane is the Chief Executive Officer of an Australian national sporting body, Netball Australia. Her views on honesty and integrity testify to their important role in building leadership character.

Netball Australia receives public funds and is involved with over a million people nationally. Cane (2004) believes her ability to win the confidence of others is critical to the success of the organization, and relies on her capacity to be honest and direct:

> I think it's really important I be seen as a very sound, honest person with high integrity and I need people to want to do business with me. The capacity to build relationships which relates to trust and listening and respect and empathy, those are very important things because they absolutely affect sponsorship outcomes, business financial outcomes, what money we get from the government, from corporate Australia, what money we might get in the future from our members.

Successful leaders are open and honest with others, but they also understand that maintaining trust requires them to exercise discretion in how they use and disclose information. They take care to avoid violating confidences and do not carelessly divulge potentially harmful information.

Greg Dooley, the Australian General Manager of international financial services and technology company Computershare, rates honesty as the most important character attribute of leadership: "If you're dishonest as a leader then you've got no chance. As soon as you lose trust you may as well give up the ghost." Dooley differentiates between withholding information and deceiving someone. He acknowledges that being open and honest with people may at times be difficult when you have commercially sensitive information that you can't disclose. However, Dooley argues that appropriately withholding information is critical to Computershare's business: "Clients need to know that they can trust us, that we'll be able to handle that information and deal with it on a needs-to-know basis."

A leader's capacity for honesty can help followers work constructively on solving issues and problems. American leadership development consultant Joan Lloyd (2001) says: "I think most employees today are hungry for some good old-fashioned honesty." Employees prefer to work for leaders who they trust can be honest with them about the reality of their circumstances. Lloyd argues that the best leaders are respected, in part, because they level with people and tell it like it is.

Future of Leadership With Character

Our study identified three underlying dimensions or factors of leadership character. Universalism represents an understanding, appreciation, and tolerance for the welfare of people generally, and is a macro perspective approach to work. Transformation is consistent with the concept of transformational leadership as an activity that inspires others in the achievement of long-term, visionary goals. Transformation is a situation-specific process that relies on the competence and self-reliance of the incumbent in their delivery of inspired and values-driven strategic direction for the enterprise. The third dimension, Benevolence, is a micro approach to work, and focuses on concern for the welfare of others through one's daily interactions. As a process, Transformation can be seen as the link between Universalism as the externally-focused manifestation of leadership character and internally-focused Benevolent intentions. We propose that leaders who manifest courage (setting a long-term direction and taking people along without fear) with passion (energy and enthusiasm) are more often associated with outcomes that have external as well as internal benefits, and are typical of character-led organizations.

CHAPTER

3

Leadership Skills Approach

I am amazed to see people running companies who do not have the creativity to respond in a dynamic environment. In an unforgiving, fast-paced business climate, you are infinitely better prepared if you are a creative person. Good communicators have an enormous advantage over poor communicators because so much of running a company is inspirational, external and internal, that is, inspiring your employees, shareholders, industry analysts, and customers.

—Craig Conway[1]

In a manner similar to the trait approach, the skills approach to leadership is a leader-centered perspective. But the two approaches are different in that in the trait approach, we focused on personality traits that are considered inherent and relatively stable from birth, whereas in this chapter, we focus on a person's "skills and abilities that can be learned and developed" (Northouse, 2010). Skills suggest what leaders can achieve, whereas traits suggest who they are based on their intrinsic characteristics. The skills approach implies that skills, knowledge, and abilities are required for a leader to be effective. In this chapter, we focus on two studies that defined the skills approach: Katz (1974) and Mumford, Zaccaro, Harding, Jacobs, and Fleishman (2000).

---

[1]Craig Conway is the former President and Chief Executive Officer of PeopleSoft.

Katz's Three-Skills Approach

Katz's (1974) seminal article on the skills approach to leadership suggested that leadership (i.e., effective administration) is based on three skills: technical, human, and conceptual.

Technical Skills

Technical skill is proficiency, based on specific knowledge, in a particular area of work. To have technical skills means that a person is competent and knowledgeable with respect to the activities specific to an organization, the organization's rules and standard operating procedures, and the organization's products and services (Katz, 1974; Yukl, 2006). Technical skill is most important at supervisory levels of management, less important for middle managers, and least important for top managers such as CEOs and senior managers. Finally, technical skill is proficiency in working with *things*.

Human Skills

In contrast to technical skills, human (or interpersonal) skills are proficiency in working with *people* based on a person's knowledge about *people* and how they behave, how they operate in groups, how to communicate effectively with them, and their motives, attitudes, and feelings. They are the skills required to effectively influence superiors, peers, and subordinates in the achievement of organizational goals. These skills enable a leader to influence team or group members to work together to accomplish organizational goals and objectives. Human skill proficiency means that leaders know their thoughts on different issues and, simultaneously, become cognizant of the thoughts of others. Consequently, leaders with higher levels of interpersonal skills are better able to adapt their own ideas to other people's ideas, especially when this will aid in achieving organizational goals more quickly and efficiently. These leaders are more sensitive and empathetic to what motivates others, create an atmosphere of trust for their followers, and take others' needs and motivations into account when deciding what to do to achieve organizational goals. Interpersonal skills are required at all three levels of management: supervisory, middle management, and senior management (Katz, 1974; Yukl, 2006).

Conceptual Skills

Conceptual skills allow you to think through and work with ideas. Leaders with higher levels of conceptual skills are good at thinking through the ideas that form an organization and its vision for the future, expressing these ideas in verbal and written forms, and understanding and expressing the economic principles underlying their organization's effectiveness. These leaders are comfortable asking "what if" or hypothetical questions and working with abstract ideas. Conceptual skills allow leaders to give abstract ideas meaning and to make sense of abstract ideas for their superiors, peers, and subordinates. This skill is most important for top managers, less important for middle managers, and least important for supervisory managers (Northouse, 2010). We would offer one caveat. While conceptual skills are less important at lower levels of management, to be promoted to higher levels of management, it is important to develop and demonstrate this skill at all levels of management (Yukl, 2006). It is a skill that can be learned; consequently, I encourage you to take advantage of every opportunity to develop and the ability to learn conceptually.

Recent research used a four-skill model similar to Katz', which includes interpersonal, cognitive, business, and strategic skills. Results show that although interpersonal and cognitive skills were required more than business and strategic skills for those on the lower levels of management, as leaders climbed the career ladder, higher levels of all four of these leadership skills became necessary (Mumford, Campion & Morgeson, 2007).

Leadership Skills Model

This approach suggests that leadership is not just the purview of a few people born with traits that make them effective leaders. The skills approach implies that many people have leadership potential, and if they can learn from their experiences, they can become more effective leaders. This means involvement with activities and/or exposure to people and events leading to an increase in skills, knowledge, and abilities. This model is different from a "what leaders do" approach and focuses on capabilities that make leaders effective (Mumford, Zaccaro, Harding, et al., 2000; Northouse, 2010). The leadership skills approach by Mumford, Zaccaro, Harding, et al. (2000) has five elements: individual attributes, competencies, leadership outcomes, career experiences, and environmental influences.

Competencies are the most important element—the "kingpin"—in this model. Competencies lead to leadership outcomes but themselves are affected by a leader's individual attributes. In addition, the impact of leaders' attributes on leaders' competencies and leaders' competencies on outcomes is dependent on career experiences and environmental influences. In the next few paragraphs, we describe competencies, how attributes affect competencies, and how competencies affect leadership outcomes, and we briefly discuss the impact of career experiences on attributes and competencies and the impact of environmental influences on attributes, competencies, and outcomes.

Leader Competencies

Mumford, Zaccaro, Harding, et al. (2000) identified three competencies that result in effective leadership: problem solving, social judgment, and knowledge. These three work together and separately to affect outcomes.

Problem-Solving Skills. These are creative abilities that leaders bring to unique, vague, "hard to get a handle on" organizational problems. These skills include the following: defining problems and issues that are important, accumulating information related to the problem/issue, developing new ways to comprehend each problem/issue, and developing unique, first-of-its-kind alternatives for solving the problems/issues. Problem-solving skills operate in the context of an organization and its environment and require that leaders be aware of their own capacities and challenges relative to the problem/issue and the organizational context (Mumford, Zaccaro, Connelly, & Marks, 2000). The solutions or alternatives developed to solve problems and issues require that leaders be conscious of the time required to develop and execute solutions—whether the solutions are achieving short-term and/or long-term objectives, whether these objectives are organizational or personal, and the external context such as the industry, national, and international environments (Mumford, Zaccaro, Harding, et al., 2000).

Social Judgment Skills. These are skills that enable leaders to comprehend people and the social systems within which they work, play, and have a social life (e.g., friends and family) (Zaccaro, Mumford, Connelly, Marks, & Gilbert, 2000). Social judgment skills facilitate working with others to lead change, solve problems, and make sense of issues. Mumford and colleagues (Mumford, Zaccaro, Harding, et al., 2000) outlined four elements important to social judgment skills: perspective taking, social perceptiveness, behavioral flexibility, and social performance.

Perspective taking is sensitivity to others' objectives and perspective; it is an empathic perspective to solving problems, and it means that leaders actively seek out knowledge regarding people, their organization's social fabric, and how these two very important areas of knowledge intersect with each other.

Whereas perspective taking is associated with others' attitudes, *social perceptiveness* is about leaders knowing what people will do when confronted with proposed changes. *Behavioral flexibility* means being able to change what one does when confronted with others' attitudes and intended actions based on knowledge gained through perspective taking and social perceptiveness, respectively. Leaders with behavioral flexibility understand that there are many different paths to achieving change and the goals and objectives associated with change.

Social performance means being skilled in several leadership competencies. Some of these are abilities in persuading and communicating in order to convey one's own vision to others in the organization, abilities in mediation that enable the leader to mediate interpersonal conflict related to change and to lessen resistance to change, and abilities in coaching and mentoring by giving subordinates support and direction as they work to achieve organizational objectives and goals.

To summarize, Northouse (2010) stated that

> social judgment skills are about being sensitive to how your ideas fit in with others. Can you understand others and their unique needs and motivations? Are you flexible and can you adapt your own ideas to others? Last, can you work with others even when there are resistance and change? Social judgment skills are the people skills required to advance change in an organization.

Knowledge. Knowledge is the gathering of information and the development of mental structures to organize that information in a meaningful way. These mental structures are called schema, which means a diagrammatic representation or depiction. Knowledgeable leaders have more highly developed and complex schemata that they use to collect and organize data. Knowledge is linked to a leader's problem-solving skills. More knowledgeable leaders are able to consider complex organizational issues and to develop alternative and appropriate strategies for change. Knowledge allows leaders to use prior incidents to constructively plan for and change the future.

Individual Attributes

Mumford and his colleagues (e.g., Mumford, Zaccaro, Harding, et al., 2000) identified four attributes that affect the three leader competencies (problem-solving skills, social judgment skills, and knowledge) and, through these competencies, leader performance.

General Cognitive Ability. Think "perceptual processing, information processing, general reasoning skills, creative and divergent thinking capacities, and memory skills" (Northouse, 2010). This is a brief description of general cognitive ability. This type of intelligence grows as we age to early adulthood but declines as we grow older. General cognitive ability positively affects a leader's ability to acquire knowledge and complex problem-solving skills (Northouse, 2010).

Crystallized Cognitive Ability. Think "intelligence that develops because of experience." As we age and gain more experience, we acquire intelligence—this is crystallized cognitive ability. This type of intelligence remains relatively consistent and generally does not diminish as we age. As our crystallized cognitive ability increases, it positively affects our leadership potential by increasing our social judgment skills, conceptual ability, and problem-solving skills.

Motivation. Motivation affects leadership competencies in several ways. We discuss three ways in which motivation helps in the development of leadership competencies. First, a person must want to lead—there must be a willingness to engage in solving complex organizational issues and problems. Second, leaders must be willing to exert influence—to be willing to be dominant within a group of people. Finally, the leader must be willing to advance the "social good" of the organization (Northouse, 2010; Yukl, 2006).

Personality. This is the fourth attribute positively linked to leadership competencies. Northouse (2010) gives three examples of personality that affect how motivated leaders are able to resolve organizational issues and problems. They are tolerance for ambiguity, openness, and curiosity. Leaders with confidence and adaptability may be helpful in situations of conflict. The skills model suggests that personality traits that aid in developing leader competencies lead to better leader performance (Mumford, Zaccaro, Harding, et al., 2000).

Leadership Outcomes

Individual attributes lead to leader competencies, which lead to leadership outcomes. It is noteworthy that without the development of leader competencies, individual attributes may have little effect on leadership outcomes. This reminds us that the leadership competencies element is the "kingpin" component of the leadership skills model. We discuss two leadership outcomes: effective problem solving and leader performance.

Effective Problem Solving. Mumford and his colleagues (e.g., Mumford, Zaccaro, Harding, et al., 2000) developed the skills model to explain variation in the ability of leaders to solve problems—this makes it a capability model. An effective problem solver develops unique, original, and high-quality solutions to issues and problems. Leaders with higher levels of competencies will be more effective problem solvers.

Performance. This outcome refers to the individual leader's job performance—how well he or she has performed. This is usually evaluated by objective external measures. Better performance leads to better evaluations. Leaders whose performance is better will receive better annual evaluations, larger merit pay increases, and recognition as better leaders. Effective problem solving and leader performance are linked, even though they are separate ways of measuring leadership outcomes.

Career Experiences

Career experiences affect both individual attributes and leadership competencies. We believe that some career assignments may develop a leader's motivation to be a better problem solver or be better at interacting with people. These career assignments may also help increase a leader's crystallized cognitive ability. Of course, this depends on being in assignments that have been progressively more difficult, with long-term problems and issues, and at increasingly higher levels in the organization's hierarchy. Arguing that leaders develop as a result of their career experiences suggests that leaders can learn leadership abilities and are not necessarily born with leadership abilities (Mumford, Zaccaro, Harding, et al., 2000; Northouse, 2010).

Environmental Influences

These are factors that are external to individual attributes, leader competencies, and career experiences and that affect leadership outcomes along with the effect of individual attributes through leadership competencies. We will not discuss particular external influences. However, we acknowledge that they exist and that they may affect a leader's ability to be an effective problem solver. They are factors that are considered beyond the control of the leader. Of course, leaders who use the environment as an excuse for their poor performance may not be allowed to continue in their leadership role/position if external factors are not the real cause of poor performance. Top-tier leaders use the environment with great caution and only when they are sure it is the real reason.

How Does the Leadership Skills Approach Work?

The leadership skills approach is mainly a descriptive model. This approach allows students of leadership to comprehend what it takes to be an effective leader rather than offering prescriptive ways to be an effective leader.

Katz's (1974) three-skills approach implies that where one is in an organization determines how important each skill is to a leader's effectiveness. The leadership skills approach (Mumford, Zaccaro, Harding, et al., 2000) is a much more complex model of leadership effectiveness that is based on rigorous research conducted on U.S. Army officers who ranged in rank from second lieutenant to colonel. This model suggests that leadership effectiveness as measured by outcomes is a direct result of leader competencies and the indirect result of individual attributes working through leader competencies. Finally, the model contends that career experiences work indirectly to affect leadership outcomes, while environmental influences work indirectly and directly to influence leadership outcomes.

◪ References

Ashby, M. D., & Miles, S. A. (2002). Leaders talk leadership: Top executives speak their minds. Oxford: Oxford University Press.

Katz, R. L. (1974, September/October). Skills of an effective administrator, *Harvard Business Review,* *52*(5), 90–102.

Mumford, M. D., Zaccaro, S. J., Connelly, M. S., & Marks, M. A. (2000). Leadership skills: Conclusions and future directions. *The Leadership Quarterly, 11*(1), 155–170.

Mumford, M. D., Zaccaro, S. J., Harding, F. D., Jacobs, T., & Fleishman, E. A. (2000). Leadership skills for a changing world: Solving complex problems. *The Leadership Quarterly, 11*(1), 11–35.

Mumford, T.V., Campion, M.A., & Morgeson, F.P. (2007). The leadership skills strataplex: Leadership skill requirements across organizational levels. *Leadership Quarterly*, 18, (pp. 154–166).

Northouse, P. G. (2010). *Leadership: Theory and practice* (5th ed.). Thousand Oaks, CA: Sage.

Yukl, G. (2006). *Leadership in organizations* (6th ed.). Upper Saddle River, NJ: Pearson-Prentice Hall.

Zaccaro, S. J., Mumford, M. D., Connelly, M. S., Marks, M. A., & Gilbert, J. A. (2000). Assessment of leader problem-solving capabilities. *The Leadership Quarterly, 11*(1), 37–64.

The Cases

Coaching for Exceptional Performance Workshop

Informal coaching opportunities occur in the course of daily activities. In this workshop, students are provided with ways to improve their responsiveness to these opportunities. The format is a series of sessions in which students and each member of their teams, in turn, play the role of the director of operations for a software products business. Two staff members drop in to see the director, on their initiative, to ask for ideas, help, guidance or a decision on an issue. The director knows key details about each staff member's background and development needs, but does not know in advance what the specific issues or concerns are. It is necessary to explore these issues or concerns before any decision can be made. The students' performances are videotaped and critiqued in terms of identifying each staff member's problem(s); the effectiveness of responses to the immediate problems; and contribution to that staff members' longer-term growth or awareness through coaching.

Consulting for George Lancia

A young recent graduate has just been hired as a consultant by the tired owner of a small syndicate. His task is to solve the many problems existing within the various businesses, including restaurants, real estate, and a retirement home. The financial situation is severe, and there are several personnel conflicts. He must resolve these problems while effectively managing the owner.

The Reading

Train Dogs Not Leaders

Leaders can be trained, but highly successful leaders, this author writes, can be developed. The burden is on the organization to develop leaders—to actively involve leaders in recruitment and selection, development, career-move decisions and other leadership activities. These executives also recruit the best prospects, challenge them constantly and manage them. Leadership, the author notes, may be the only sustainable advantage today, which is why it should never be left to chance.

Coaching for Exceptional Performance Workshop

Prepared by Jane Howell

◪ Overview

The objective of the Coaching for Exceptional Performance Workshop is to improve your responsiveness to informal coaching opportunities that occur in the course of daily activities.

The format of the workshop is a series of sessions in which you (and each member of your team in turn) will play the role of Terry Hepburn, the director of operations for the software products business of the Multi-Product Manufacturing (MPM) Company. Two of your staff members will drop in to see you, on their initiative, to ask for your ideas, help, guidance or a decision on an issue. You have only six minutes to see each staff member in this informal coaching session since you have to leave for another important meeting at head office.

Terry Hepburn knows key details about each staff member's background and development needs but does *not* know in advance what the specific issues or concerns are. It will be necessary to explore these issues or concerns before any decision can be made. Depending on the situation, the staff member may be looking for your ideas, guidance or emotional support rather than for an actual decision.

The *quality* of your coaching performance as Terry Hepburn will be critiqued in terms of: your identification of each staff member's problem(s); the effectiveness of your responses to the immediate problems; and your contribution to that staff member's longer-term growth or awareness through coaching.

◪ How the Role Play Works

Every member of your team will play the role of Terry Hepburn in turn. When each person

does so, the other team members will play staff roles.

Each of the staff roles is typical of those you might meet in any organization:

- an over-conscientious manager who is very critical of staff and who can't delegate;
- an insecure supervisor who is very reluctant to make decisions and take responsibility;
- a frustrated supervisor whose ambitions have not been taken seriously and who has been passed over for promotion;
- an ambitious and talented analyst who pushes hard for recognition;
- a very competent manager who is eager for promotion;
- a brilliant engineer who lacks interpersonal and conflict resolution skills;
- a dedicated production supervisor who believes manufacturing should be the company's number one priority.

You will also take a turn playing the role of one of these staff members for the purposes of visits to other team members when they are acting as Terry Hepburn. You should play your staff role with conviction and sincerity.

Your facilitator will set up the sequence of coaching interviews, and give you further details of the staff character you are to play.

◪ Summary

There will be as many 12-minute rounds as there are members on your team.

AUTHOR'S NOTE: This workshop is a revision and extension of the Coaching Workshop prepared by Citicorp.

Version: (A) 2000-05-29

In one round, you will be Terry Hepburn, director of operations; you will meet with two of your staff members and deal with the issues they bring to you.

In two other rounds, you will be a staff member visiting Terry Hepburn to discuss an issue you have.

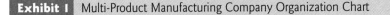 **Multi-Product Manufacturing (MPM) Company**

An organization chart of the MPM Company can be found in Exhibit 1. A brief description of the job responsibilities and functions follows.

Exhibit 1	Multi-Product Manufacturing Company Organization Chart

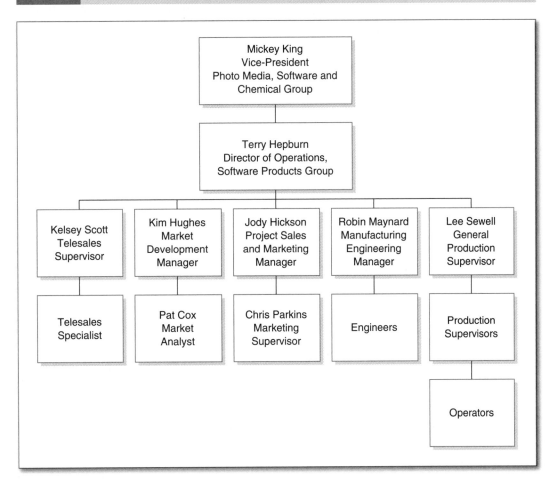

Mickey King — Vice-President, Photo Media, Software and Chemical Group

Terry Hepburn — Director of Operations, Software Products Business

Terry's Staff

Kelsey Scott — Telesales Supervisor: supports all group products (four telesales coordinators and one specialist)

Kim Hughes — Market Development Manager: supports all group products under Mickey King's sector (three analysts, including Pat Cox)

Jody Hickson — Project Sales and Marketing Manager, Software Products Business: two regional sales managers, one marketing supervisor (Chris Parkins), one secretary/assistant

Robin Maynard — Manufacturing Engineering Manager, Software Discs: responsible for technical aspects of manufacturing the product, i.e., quality improvements, cost improvements (five engineers)

Lee Sewell — General Production Supervisor: responsible for all aspects of manufacturing software discs (three shift supervisors and 10 process workers)

Functions

Telesales

- expand sales revenue through selling to C and B accounts in Mickey's group;
- implement special project assignments that expand sales for various businesses

Market Development

- develop new markets and track competitive activity

- liaise with MPM Company's key distributors

Project Management

- responsible for all aspects of marketing and sales of current business and developing new business opportunities

Engineering

- support manufacturing in both day-to-day and long-term troubleshooting with respect to the technical aspects of manufacturing the product, i.e. quality improvements, cost improvements;
- to investigate, recommend and implement modifications to processing equipment

Manufacturing

- manufacture the product, meeting cost, quality and service goals

✉ What You Already Know About Your Staff Members

Kim Hughes—Market Development Manager, Photo Media, Software and Chemical Group

Kim, age 35, has been employed by MPM Company for 14 years, seven years in the current position. Kim leads a group of three analysts, including Pat.

Kim is meticulous and accurate at administrative tasks, completes assignments on time, and avoids risks at all costs. Kim tends to over-supervise staff members in order to guarantee that their work is perfect. Due to poor delegation skills, lack of rapport with staff members, and drive for perfection, Kim works overtime practically every evening. In your opinion, Kim has peaked as far as promotion potential is concerned.

You assigned Kim to assist your boss, Mickey, on a feasibility study for a new information system to track sales leads.

Pat Cox—Market Analyst for Kim in Market Development

Pat, age 27, joined MPM Company as a market analyst 18 months ago. Pat shows intelligence and initiative, and tries to broaden his/her knowledge of departmental activities. Pat has made several creative procedural recommendations, which have been successfully implemented.

Pat is ambitious and easily bored with routine work. Kim has complained about Pat's careless attention to detail.

Terry believes Pat will be ready for promotion or transfer within six months.

Kelsey Scott—Telesales Supervisor, Photo Media, Software and Chemical Group

Kelsey Scott, age 31, has worked in the manufacturing industry for 10 years, the last six with MPM Company. Kelsey's tenure in the telesales supervisor role is three months. Kelsey's performance as an analyst was adequate and Kelsey was promoted to the current role as the best of a weak group of candidates.

Kelsey lacks self-confidence, is reluctant to make decisions, and avoids confronting staff with mistakes. Kelsey constantly brings simple problems to Terry to solve.

Jody Hickson—Project Sales and Marketing Manager, Software Products Business

Jody Hickson, age 31, joined MPM Company four years ago, and has been in his/her current role for two years. Jody has been designated as a high potential employee. Previously, Jody was an executive account manager at Xerox The Document Company, and has developed a rich network of contacts in the local business community over time. Recently, Jody has been hinting to you at every opportunity that the timing is right for a promotion to a higher-level sales management position.

Chris Parkins—Marketing Supervisor, Software Products Business

Chris Parkins, age 41, has 18 years of marketing experience, 12 years with MPM Company, eight years in the present position. Chris lacks a university education, but is totally familiar with marketing practices. Chris's current performance is satisfactory.

Your major concern about Chris is lack of ambition and creativity. Chris could be marginally effective as a manager although you have serious doubts about Chris's ability and motivation to advance.

Robin Maynard—Manufacturing Engineering Manager, All Products in Mickey's Group

Robin Maynard, age 42, has been with MPM Company for four years, working for Terry in Mickey's businesses. Robin is a brilliant engineer but needs to work on interpersonal skills. Robin has a tendency to be short with people and unable to empathize. Robin views engineering as the most important function in the company and therefore undervalues other colleagues' contributions.

Lee and Robin have difficulty resolving their own disputes and tend to look to higher management for solutions.

Lee Sewell—General Production Supervisor, Software Products Business

Lee, age 38, joined MPM Company 10 years ago and has been in his/her current position for three years. Lee has broad exposure to manufacturing across the company and takes great pride in achieving monthly production and revenue targets. Lee is fastidious about safety and ensures all precautions are taken in the manufacturing process. At times Lee can have too narrow a focus on "process" at the risk of losing sight of costs.

Lee has difficulty with the way engineering prioritizes its projects and feels manufacturing process issues must be first and foremost at all times.

Consulting for George Lancia

Prepared by Michelle Linton under the supervision of Elizabeth M.A. Grasby

Cam Matthews shook his head as he looked over the financial statements in front of him. It was June 1993, and he had been hired as a consultant to bring George Lancia's organization under control. George, who wanted a break from the management of his various businesses, was concerned about the successes of his investments. Cam, a 24-year-old recent business graduate, knew upon reading the statements that the financial position was worse than George realized. Cam's foremost concern was how to manage and to relate to George. Cam believed significant changes would have to be made. He wondered what problems he should anticipate.

George Lancia

George Lancia was the 45-year-old owner of the organization. He had worked on his own in order to support himself through high school. Upon graduation, he worked as a surveyor's assistant for two years, after which he sold securities for five years. At various times during these years he had owned a movie theatre, a drive-in theatre, and a restaurant. He had also begun to buy and sell real estate, including rental properties, and had created a substantial amount of wealth through these dealings.

In 1985, George was approached by Kevin Gibson with the idea of leading a syndicate to invest in several fast food restaurants in Eastern Ontario. George agreed to invest in this venture. By 1988, the restaurants' performances had failed to improve and George was forced to buy out the other investors.

Three years later, George was approached with another investment opportunity, a nursing home and retirement lodge in the small town of Sterling, Ontario. George responded with an offer that was accepted in principle; however, the actual agreement was still being completed by the lawyers.

George built a new house in 1991. By this time, all of his cash was tied up in six restaurants, the retirement home, the rental properties, and the new house.

Management Structure

George's investments were set up as individual, numbered corporations. In theory, this structure

Version: (A) 2001-08-01

was intended to protect him from personal liability and to save the structure from problems in a single unit. However, two sources of exposure could not be avoided. Both George's reputation and his borrowing ability within this very small town would be hindered if any of the individual corporations were to go bankrupt. The banks and creditors had recently begun to ask for personal guarantees on any new debt requested by George.

In general, George made all decisions and approved all spending. His primary source of control was monthly financial statements, which he often viewed several months late and did not trust the accuracy of. He seldom had direct contact with his front-line employees.

George's secretary, Sharon, was 23 years old and had received a college diploma in bookkeeping. Sharon had been named the controller of the company. She prepared financial statements, managed the payroll, and handled supplier relationships. Her assistant, Caroline, who was 24 years old with a commerce degree from Brock University, helped Sharon prepare the financial statements. Both women had a difficult time remaining productive during the day; statements were occasionally late or inaccurate. George was aware of this situation but wondered how the office computers would be run and the filing and banking handled without Sharon and Caroline. Because George wished to avoid any conflict, Sharon had an effective veto on the decisions in her area.

Restaurants

Kevin Gibson was the general manager of the restaurant operations. He was 22 years old when he started working for George. Kevin had no formal management education but had managed fast-food restaurants since the age of 18. George had given him full control over decisions at first, claiming that he "would totally step aside and let Kevin do his thing." When commenting on his own management approach, George said he "preferred to sell an idea rather than tell people what to do." George would review the monthly financial statements and then hold "grilling sessions" during which he would ask Kevin for explanations of any apparent poor results. Kevin would then be asked to project the next month's results. George would write down these projections and file them to be pulled out and pointed to during next month's "grilling session." George received other information informally from time to time, in the form of phone calls from banks, suppliers, employees, or the franchiser, whenever there were problems.

For various reasons, Kevin was unable to provide positive results over time, causing George to lose patience and to take back the formal authority. Currently, Kevin had no authority to make any decisions without George's approval; however, he did anyway. Most of the restaurant staff and suppliers had never heard of George and assumed Kevin was the owner. George wondered who would manage the restaurants if Kevin left and therefore did not want to create any friction between himself and Kevin. Additionally, George hoped Kevin would repay the money he had loaned him on a handshake to finance Kevin's house.

Jeff Cranney, a 35-year-old with no management education or former management experience, managed the restaurant in Cobourg. He had invested a substantial amount of cash to build the store in 1991 and currently held 49 per cent of the shares. However, this restaurant was not managed effectively and had significant operating problems. George was worried that he would be forced to buy Jeff out if these concerns were addressed.

John and Lucy Wilson approached George in September 1992 and asked him to sell them the restaurant in Peterborough. They provided two houses as a down payment and intended to pay the rest over time. From the perspectives of the bank, the employees, and the landlord, George remained responsible for the asset. John and Lucy were middle-aged with no management education or supervisory experience.

John worked as a linesman for a power company; Lucy was a health care aide. George wanted to avoid any conflict here as well to prevent "being left with a real mess."

The Sterling Manor

The Sterling Manor was a nursing home and retirement lodge that housed 62 residents and employed close to 50 employees. The negotiations between George and the retirement home's initial owners, the Vaughans, were intense. The Vaughans, the Ministry of Health, and the bank had expressed considerable doubt about George's ability to run the home successfully. It was exp ected that any additional conflicts or problems would further hinder their perception of him.

At the same time, major changes in the industry were pending. The government had developed stricter regulations to increase the level of quality and service in the industry. These regulations stipulated how the funding should be allocated among nursing, food services, and housekeeping. These changes would reduce net profit considerably, and management would face a much greater challenge than before, when financing was plentiful and regulations minimal.

Linda Baxter was the administrator of the Sterling Manor. She had been a nursing assistant for 25 years and had a diploma in long-term care management. Linda was very personable and concerned about doing a good job. However, she lacked several important technical skills regarding computers, time management, and supervising. She had been hired by the Vaughans and continued to report to them on a regular basis. Whenever she and George disagreed, Linda stated that she still worked for the Vaughans and threatened to seek their decisions. The administration of the home was very disorganized. Phones went unanswered, and Linda's desk was piled with paperwork and mail dating back to 1989. Linda lacked focus or direction and felt that

she was accomplishing very little. With the pending regulations, Linda was worried that others would question her competence; therefore, she reacted defensively when anyone attempted to get involved in her work.

Heather Irvin was the director of nursing at the Manor. She was a registered nurse with 30 years' experience. Heather found it difficult to organize and run a staff while dealing with all the conflict and confusion among George, Linda, and the Vaughans. She recognized the importance of management control in a nursing organization, where health and lives are at stake. It was her opinion that Linda did not understand how to operate a health business. So, in order to protect her own position, Heather refused to listen to Linda. Instead, she complained constantly to George about Linda. Because George knew very little about nursing, he could not effectively evaluate Heather's work. He worried about what would happen if she quit. He had not heard any negative comments from anyone else about her work, so he basically gave her complete freedom.

Real Estate

Margaret Dennett managed the apartment building in Belleville. She had been given authority to make decisions about the tenants and daily operations but continually called George about problems she encountered. George did not have the time to find a replacement for her and therefore, to prevent upsetting Margaret, did not attempt to change the situation.

Performance

Restaurants

The restaurant operation had performed poorly for the past three years. The stores had reached their overdraft limit several times, and George had been forced to inject $70,000 from his personal line of credit. Labor productivity was low, quality and service were substandard, current marketing activities were expensive and ineffective, and relations with banks, suppliers, and the franchisers were very poor. In the spring of 1993, Kevin had diverted $70,000 cash from the restaurants to secure equipment and working capital for an ice cream store, a venture that had lost $3,000 per month since its inception.

The Sterling Manor

The Sterling Manor had been barely breaking even for the past several months and was near its overdraft limit. The new union was in the midst of contract arbitration that, when completed in late 1993, would likely expose the home to a retroactive wage settlement of between $200,000 and $500,000. Whenever George accumulated money in the business, the Vaughans withdrew it as advance payment on the Manor's purchase price. George did not want to jeopardize the sale and was therefore reluctant to approach the Vaughans about this.

George did not understand the Ministry of Health's new funding model and did not know whether the home would be a good purchase, or even if it would survive, under the new system. George did not seem aware of the severity of the Manor's financial position.

George had almost reached the limit of his personal credit line and could not count on significant cash flows from his businesses in the short term. He had pledged to limit his withdrawals from the Manor; there were minimal funds coming from the restaurant operations; and recent vacancies had eliminated any positive cash flow from his rental properties.

◤ George and Cam

George and Cam had met several times during the spring of 1993. By this time, George

was tired and wanted nothing more than to hand over the reins of his business to someone else and step back for a while. He wanted to remove himself from day-to-day management of all assets and to remain merely as a hands-off investor. In June, George hired Cam as a consultant, asking him to prepare a plan to bring the organization under control, specifically, to "find a way to clean up all the junk on my plate."

Cam had graduated in 1992 with a degree in business administration from Wilfrid Laurier University and had started working as a consultant to medium-sized businesses. His experience consisted of co-op positions[2] with large companies, part-time restaurant management during school, and research and consulting since his final year of school.

During their initial meetings together, George repeatedly said to Cam:

> I've promoted myself to the level of my own incompetence. I know that now, and so from here on, I'm going to be like Henry Ford—I'm going to hire the expertise that I lack myself. That's where you come in—you have the education that I missed out on. I'll give you the benefit of my 25 years' experience in business, and you give me the benefit of your education.

Cam knew from the start that it would be a grave mistake to underestimate the value of George's "school of hard knocks" education, but felt that he, too, had several significant contributions to make. Cam wondered where to start. He wanted to make sure he had a good understanding of the organization and its problems before he made recommendations or attempted any changes. Cam also wondered if he should expect any problems in dealing with George.

---

[2] The university offered a business program that combined regular course work with work terms at various companies.

Train Dogs, Develop Leaders

By Jeffrey Gandz

There is an old Chinese proverb: "Give a man a fish and he will eat for a day. Teach a man to fish and he will eat for the rest of his life." But what happens when there are no more fish to catch?

That is the limitation with training. Successful training ensures that a person will act predictably in response to a given stimulus. Pavlov trained dogs to respond to bells and the provision of food . . . so well, indeed, that they even salivated when the food was not presented. And B.F. Skinner was able to train chickens to behave predictably with a wide variety of different reward ratios.

I am not arguing against training. People need knowledge and skills to develop the competencies required to do their jobs. But what does this have to do with leadership? Organizations need leaders to be able to assess situations that are frequently complex and seldom identical to past situations. Leaders must recognize patterns without assuming that a situation is identical to one they have encountered before. They must be able to use analogies to make inferences, and figure out what to do when they encounter new situations. In short, they must use and develop their judgment to the point where it becomes wisdom.

In the pursuit of leadership talent, organizations tend to hire for knowledge, train for skills, develop for judgment—and hope for wisdom. When wisdom does not materialize, they are forced to hire it. Certainly, there is nothing wrong with selective hiring, but organizations should hire to enrich their gene pool, not because their internal reproductive system has failed.

When organizations look at their leadership pipelines, the demographic facts of life stare them in the face. Through the last two decades, the severe, short-lived recession and painful downsizings of the 1980s taught them how to stay lean. Out went multiple layers, "assistants-to" and the narrow spans of control that allowed leaders to spend time developing people. Senior executives could boast of personally "managing" 20-30 people by e-mail. But "lean" turned into anorexic as organizations starved their people of developmental experiences and the counselling of those who had gone before.

Now organizations have 50-somethings with judgment and wisdom, but their 30-somethings have only skills and knowledge. The question is, can organizations accelerate the development of this leadership talent?

◿ Leadership Can Be Developed

In the unending nature-versus-nurture debate about leadership, I stand firmly in the middle Leaders are 'born', innate leadership talent can be accelerated But not everyone with skills and knowledge will develop judgment The challenge of human resource development is to accelerate the development of high-quality leadership in organizations, increase the yield of mature leaders from the pool of high potentials, and create a *pipeline* of management talent that delivers leaders where and when they are needed (While the term 'leadership pipeline' has been used by many authors over many years, it is described in greatest detail in *The Leadership Pipeline*, by Ram Charan, Stephen J. Drotter and Jim Noel, Jossey-Bass Publishers, 2001; also see article, The Leadership Pipeline, by Charan and Drotter, *Ivey Business Journal*, May/June 2001).

Research in the field of leadership development is not conclusive, but my 25 years of teaching experience leads me to several conclusions:

- It pays to start with excellent talent. This requires the commitment of senior executives because recruiting the very best prospects is both expensive and challenging Top performers are the best recruiters of top talent.

- It pays to channel high potentials into the "right" experiences. Challenging job assignments and well-designed learning programs encourage individual development.

- Learning does not simply "happen." "Doing" without reflecting does not lead to learning. When learning is combined with "doing"—the concept of action-learning—the loop is effectively closed. This also happens when individuals receive excellent coaching from caring mentors. It does not happen when high potentials are assigned to supervisors who have no interest or skill in leadership development.

- Development must be integrated with personal career management and organizational development. It is pointless and expensive to pour money into developing people who have no leadership challenges.

Figure 1	Hierarchy of Leadership Development

- There must be "on-" and "off-ramps." Some high potentials are late bloomers. Others fail to live up to their original promise or decline to commit to their own development.
- High potentials must be managed differently. They are high-maintenance and their development must be accelerated. They require frequent, in-depth, project-based performance reviews and consistent reassurance that they are high-potentials.

⬛ The Role of HRD in Leadership Development

Human resource departments play an important role in leadership development, especially in multidimensional businesses or conglomerates. The best organizations view leadership development as a treasury function. They centralize ownership of high-potential leaders and their value to the organization, rather than downloading responsibility to the departments where the high potentials happen to be working.

The onus is on the HR Development function to:

Make the connection between corporate and business-unit strategies. When leadership development is disconnected from strategy, the leadership pipeline becomes clogged or sucks air. High potentials leave the organization for lack of opportunities, or the organization struggles to implement strategies without leadership resources.

Integrate critical HR systems around the leadership development challenge, as shown in Figure 2. Common flaws in HR

Figure 2 Integrated Leadership Development Systems

development are: development without succession planning, information systems that are inadequate for inventorying talent and experiences, and assessment and evaluation systems that make no allowance for talent spotting and deployment.

Manage the development and deployment of the infrastructure of leadership development activities, including assessments, evaluations, programs, courses and career tracking.

Advise and consult on individual career plans and developmental moves, working with candidates, supervisors, mentors and top management.

Brief management on developments in leadership thinking.

Seek and evaluate "outside" leadership development resources (e.g., consultants, academics, organizations).

Benchmark development leadership practices against high-performing organizations.

⬚ A Commitment to Leadership Development

Some 30 or 40 years ago, everyone assumed that great grapes grew only in selected regions of certain countries, and that great wines developed from those grapes as a matter of chance. Vintages that showed promise were left to mature for many years. No longer. As a result of the careful selection, feeding and pruning of vines, yields have increased and maturation periods have decreased. Excellent wines are produced in shorter time frames and in regions of the world previously known only for their "plonk."

It is no accident that some companies have great leadership bench strength and others do not. That is because some companies work at developing leadership. Their senior executives are actively involved in recruitment and selection, development, career-move decisions, and other leadership activities. They recruit the best prospects, challenge them constantly, manage them centrally and locally, and utilize the "off ramp" when the candidate wants to abandon the fast track or his or her potential does not match the needs of the organization.

In an increasingly competitive and boundaryless world, leadership may be the only sustainable competitive advantage. That is why leadership should never be left to chance.

4

Leader Style Approach

It's often the best leaders that are most resistant to change. And about 20 percent of my leaders didn't make the transition. They were command-and-control, wonderful leaders but wanted to stay command and control and couldn't transition over. And I had nothing against that. It's like a basketball player who can score 30 points a game. But if you're going to go into a real, unique style of team offense and team defense, if a person can't adjust, it's probably better that they get traded to another team. And so, all of us have to change.

—John Chambers[1]

The leadership style approach is different from the trait approach and the skills approach. The trait approach emphasized the personality characteristics of leaders. The skills approach focused on the leader's competencies. The leadership style approach accentuates leader behaviors—in other words, what leaders do and how they act, particularly toward subordinates, in a multitude of situations to change subordinate performance and influence subordinate behavior (Yukl, 2006).

These behaviors can be distilled into two broad types: initiating structure (task behavior) and consideration (relationship behavior). Task behavior makes it easier for group members (subordinates) to accomplish goals and objectives. Relationship behavior makes it easier for group members (subordinates) to feel at ease with the context in which they are operating, with other members of the group, and with who they are themselves. The ultimate objective of the leadership style approach is to help in our understanding of how leaders integrate these two broad conceptualizations of behaviors to positively influence group members in efforts to achieve personal and organizational goals and objectives (Northouse, 2010).

---

[1]John Chambers is CEO and Chairman of Cisco Systems.

Consequently, we describe three streams of research that focus on task and relationship behaviors and their intersection. The first stream was conducted at the Ohio State University (e.g., Stogdill, 1948) and pursued style research to demonstrate the need to account for more than leaders' traits (Dubrin, 2007). The second stream was conducted at the University of Michigan (e.g., Likert, 1961, 1967) and examined how leadership happened in small groups. The third stream (Blake & Mouton, 1964, 1978, 1985) researched how leaders used relationship and task behaviors in an organizational context (Yukl, 2006).

The Ohio State Studies

As we see from Table 4.1, the Ohio State University studies found that leader behaviors clustered under two broad categories: initiating structure and consideration (Stogdill, 1974). Characteristics of both are included in Table 4.1.

Table 4.1   Task Behavior and Relationship Behavior

	Task Behavior	Relationship Behavior
Ohio State studies	*Initiating structure* Organizing work Giving work structure Defining role responsibilities Scheduling work activities	*Consideration* Building respect, trust, liking, and camaraderie between followers and leaders
University of Michigan studies	*Production orientation* Stress technical aspects Stress production aspects Workers viewed as way to get work done	*Employee orientation* Workers viewed with a strong human relations aspect Leaders treat workers as human beings, value workers individuality, give attention to workers' needs
Blake and Mouton's grid	*Concern for production* Achieving tasks Making policy decisions Developing new products Optimizing processes Maximizing workload Increasing sales volume	*Concern for people* Attending to people Building commitment and trust Promoting worker personal worth Providing good work conditions Maintaining fair salary/benefits Promoting good social relations

SOURCE: Adapted from Northouse (2010). Copyright © 2010, Sage Publications, Inc.

These two behaviors were viewed as two separate and different continua. This means that an individual can be high on both, low on both, or high on one and low on the other (Daft, 2005). In addition, these behaviors need to be considered in context as in some situations, high consideration and low initiating structure may be appropriate, whereas in others, the opposite may be appropriate. Being high on both is the best form of leadership, but this is very difficult for many individuals (Daft, 2005; Northouse, 2010).

The University of Michigan Studies

As reported in Table 4.1, this body of research found results similar to the Ohio State studies. Their two broad categories were production orientation and employee orientation. Characteristics of both are included in Table 4.1.

Contrary to the Ohio State studies, initially, these two types of leader behaviors were argued to be on opposite ends of one continuum (Daft, 2005), thus suggesting that leaders high on production orientation had to be low on employee orientation and vice versa. Later, the Michigan researchers came to agree with the Ohio State studies and view the two types of leader behavior as two separate continua. This meant that leaders could be viewed as being able to have high production and employee orientations. Some research viewed this as being valuable for employee satisfaction and employee performance, but most research was inconclusive (Northouse, 2010; Yukl, 2006).

The Blake and Mouton Grid

Blake and Mouton (1964, 1978, 1985) developed their leadership grid to demonstrate that leaders helped organizations achieve their goals through two leader orientations: concern for production and concern for people. These two orientations resemble task behavior and relationship behavior, as shown in Table 4.1. Using the grid, the researchers developed five leadership styles.

The *authority–compliance* style describes leaders who are results driven with little or no concern for people except to organize them in a way that keeps them from interfering with getting the job done. Communication with followers is limited and used only to give instructions regarding the task. These leaders are controlling, hard driving, overpowering, and demanding—not nice people to work for. Some research suggests a higher turnover rate under this style of leadership (Yukl, 2006).

The *country club* style describes leaders with a high concern for people and a low concern for results or production. These leaders focus on meeting people's needs and creating a positive environment in which to work. Turnover rates seem to decrease under these leaders (Yukl, 2006).

Impoverished management describes leaders who have little or no concern for people or for production (Daft, 2005). They do enough to not get fired, but mentally, they have probably already defected from the organization.

The *middle-of-the-road* style describes leaders who have a moderate concern for people and for production (Daft, 2005). These leaders are compromisers who do not push production hard or push to meet the needs of their followers to the maximum limit.

Team management-style leaders emphasize interpersonal relationships and getting results. These leaders help employees focus on and commit to their work and promote teamwork and a high level of participation in work-related decisions by employees. Northouse (2010) suggests that the following phrases describe these leaders: "stimulates participation, acts determined, gets issues into the open, makes priorities clear, follows through, behaves open-mindedly, and enjoys working."

The team management style integrates high concerns for people and for production. It is possible to use a high concern for people and a high concern for production but not in an integrative manner. These leaders switch from the authority–compliance style to the country club style depending on the situation. An example would be the benevolent dictator who acts graciously to get the job done. This style is called *paternalistic/maternalistic,* and leaders who use this style do so because they consider that people are not associated with what it takes to achieve the organization's goals and purposes.

The final style based on the leadership grid is *opportunism.* This refers to a leader who opportunistically uses any combination of the five styles to advance his or her career.

Blake and Mouton (1985) argue that leaders usually have a style that is most dominant and one that is their backup style. Leaders revert to their backup style when the dominant style is not working and they are under a great deal of pressure (Northouse, 2010).

How Does the Leadership Style Work?

This style helps students, practitioners, and academics to assess leadership based on two broad dimensions: task behavior and relationship behavior. It does not tell leaders what to do but describes the major dimensions of what they do in their relationships with their job and their followers. This style suggests to leaders that how they affect followers "occurs through the tasks they perform as well as in the relationships they create" (Northouse, 2010). There may be a situation perspective to the leadership style approach in that some followers may need to be directed more, while others may need to be nurtured and supported more (Yukl, 2006).

References

Blake, R. R., & Mouton, J. S. (1964). *The managerial grid.* Houston, TX: Gulf.

Blake, R. R., & Mouton, J. S. (1978). *The new managerial grid.* Houston, TX: Gulf.

Blake, R. R., & Mouton, J. S. (1985). *The managerial grid III.* Houston, TX: Gulf.

Chambers, J. (2009). McKinsey conversations with global leaders: John Chambers of Cisco. *McKinsey Quarterly.* Retrieved August 6, 2009, from http://www.mckinseyquaterly.com/Strategy/Strategic_Thinking/McKinsey_conversations_with_global_leaders_John_Chambers_of_Cisco_2400

Daft, R. L. (2005). *The leadership experience* (3rd ed.). Mason, OH: Thomson, South-Western.

Dubrin, A. (2007). *Leadership: Research findings, practice, and skills.* New York: Houghton Mifflin.

Likert, R. (1961). *New patterns of management.* New York: McGraw-Hill.

Likert, R. (1967). *The human organization: Its management and value.* New York: McGraw-Hill.

Northouse, P. G. (2010). *Leadership: Theory and practice* (5th ed.). Thousand Oaks, CA: Sage.

Stogdill, R. M. (1948). Personal factors associated with leadership: A survey of the literature. *Journal of Psychology, 25,* 35–71.

Stogdill, R. M. (1974). *Handbook of leadership: A survey of theory and research.* New York: Free Press.

Yukl, G. (2006). *Leadership in organizations* (6th ed.). Upper Saddle River, NJ: Pearson/Prentice Hall.

⬚ The Cases

Technosoft Russia

A supervisor at a telesales office has received very low ratings on an employee survey, and the marketing manager is concerned that this team leader is not performing well. The marketing manager must decide what actions are needed to improve the leadership skills of this supervisor.

Consultancy Development Organization

The director of Consultancy Development Organization (CDO), a not-for-profit organization that helps develop the consultancy profession in India, needs to respond to CDO's poor morale and specifically to the recent incident with the deputy director of projects. The director's encounter with the deputy director was the latest in a series of frustrating experiences that he has faced since joining CDO the previous year. The director needs to decide whether to resign from CDO or to continue trying to improve the situation.

⬚ The Reading

Navigating Through Leadership Transitions: Making It Past the Twists and Turns

Adaptability is a must-have for a leader. At different points and for different reasons, he or she must change behavior to succeed. This author shares the advice she's given to business leaders.

Technosoft Russia

Prepared by Fyodor Suzdalev under the supervision of James A. Erskine

On February 13, 2002, Ivan Chaikovsky, sales and marketing manager, finally received all responses from the Technosoft telesales team in Saint Petersburg regarding the performance of team leader Olga Peterson. Staff members had given Peterson a very low rating and Chaikovsky was not sure how best to proceed.

⬚ Technosoft

Technosoft, a global high-tech company with a corporate headquarters in the United States, opened a representative office in Saint Petersburg, Russia, in 1993. At the time, Russia was only three years into the post communist era, and the business

Version: (A) 2004-06-30

environment was not totally stable. Nevertheless, the Technosoft business had a very dynamic start and, by 2002, the representative office in Saint Petersburg had over 80 people on staff.

The Technosoft Saint Petersburg office was responsible for business development in Russia and ex-USSR countries like Ukraine, Byelorussia and Kazakhstan but excluding the Baltic countries (Latvia, Estonia, and Lithuania). Technosoft Saint Petersburg reported to the Eastern European H eadquarters (EEHQ) located in Vienna. EEHQ was responsible for business development in Eastern European countries like Poland, Czech Republic and Hungary and, in turn, EEHQ reported to the European Headquarters (EHQ) located in Amsterdam. EHQ was responsible for Europe, the Middle East and Africa (EMEA). The last link in the chain was the link between EHQ and corporate headquarters in the United States. Each representative office and regional headquarters had a general manager (GM) who was responsible for territory revenues and all business development spending (see Exhibit 1).

Technosoft produced a wide range of software and hardware products for business and consumer markets. All products were developed in the United States, but operations like hardware production, compact disc recording, printing, packaging and shipping were performed in several production sites or operation centres. Physical units or stock keeping units (SKUs) like hardware items, software

Exhibit 1 Technosoft Corporate Structure

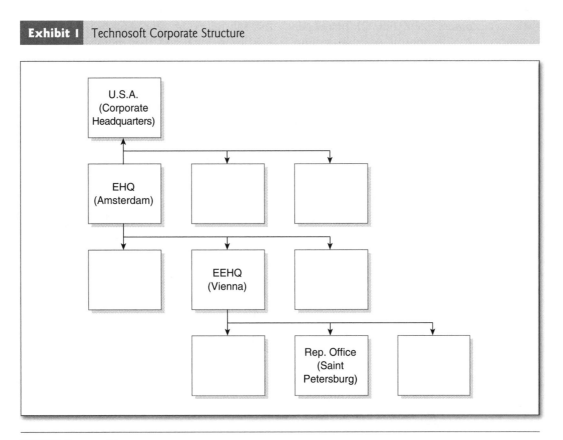

SOURCE: Company files.

Exhibit 2 Value Chain

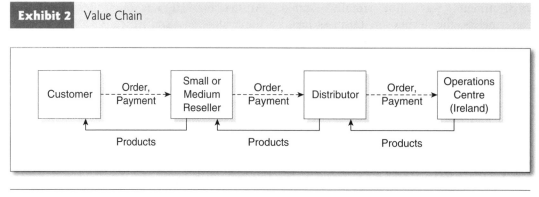

SOURCE: Company files.

packages and licence agreements for corporate clients were shipped to distributors. Distributors then shipped SKUs to small and medium resellers, and resellers transferred them to customers (see Exhibit 2). In any particular country, Technosoft could have hundreds of small and medium resellers but relatively few distributors.

Technosoft small and medium resellers were the key part of the value chain. Most resellers added value to Technosoft products by working closely with a customer, understanding problems and providing a turn-key solution, often using third-party software and hardware. Some resellers specialized in training and support for Technosoft products, and some were developing their own products using Technosoft products for a component of their own solutions.

Budgeting

A country budget consisted of revenues collected through the channel and expenses like payroll, premises and marketing expenses. Production and operating costs were excluded except for the costs incurred by creating localized versions of the products. This job was usually done by OC but the cost was transferred to the country budget. Marketing expenses included outsourcing and third-party orders.

Each GM was responsible for the budget of its own territory. The budget was formed on the subsidiary or representative office level, usually in June, and then revised in January every year. The budget procedure always included several day-long discussions with regional headquarter management concerning product forecasts, marketing plans and headcounts. Approved budgets were aggregated on regional levels and then passed to the next level (e.g., from EEHQ to EHQ) and the procedure repeated. During the year, business performance was closely monitored by headquarter management, and quarterly business review sessions were held in each Technosoft subsidiary or representative office.

Even though each Technosoft subsidiary or representative office had relative freedom in deciding what to do at the country level, each country management was supposed to apply corporate guidelines and regional marketing programs. Otherwise, the subsidiary had to explain why it had not applied them. Usually the price of explaining "why not" was much higher than that of simply implementing corporate guidelines and programs.

Each country allocated funds in the country budget for special programs/projects. At a country level, a program champion was typically assigned. In many cases, this program champion had other responsibilities within their department and had to form a "virtual" team across other departments to move projects along. This "horizontal" co-operation was an extremely important form of organizational design in Technosoft. For a program to be successful, its champion had to know key people in other units, their motives, relative power and their bosses. Usually this knowledge came after employees had spent six to 12 months in the organization.

Each special program was measured independently on the country level. If the program performed the best in comparison to other countries, its GM got additional bargaining power during budget approval process. Poor results in such a program could lessen the GM's credibility and, eventually, the country's reputation.

Performance Review

During the performance review process, managers assessed past performance of their subordinates and held discussions about future goals and actions. Performance review results affected employees' bonuses and potential promotion. The GM's performance was measured not only by budget and programs performance but also by his direct subordinates and the organizational health index (OHI). OHI was calculated annually based on results of performance review process, an integral part of which was the Technosoft poll.

There were two types of staff in Technosoft: full-time employees (FTEs) and temporary employees (TEs). FTEs had perpetual employment agreements and were on the Technosoft payroll. TEs had a limited period of employment in their contracts, usually three months, and in most cases were on some outsourcing company's payroll, though they had Technosoft e-mail addresses, access

to Technosoft information resources and sat in a Technosoft office. Each month, Technosoft informed the payroll company about the TEs' monthly compensation and quarterly about renewing their contracts. TEs did not have many benefits, which FTEs had, such as stock option plans and health insurance. FTE headcount was kept small worldwide and increased very conservatively. On the other hand, the TE headcount varied widely.

The corporate performance review process involved the FTEs only. All collected data was stored in a corporate database, and every FTE's performance history was available from the start of their employment. Nevertheless, on the country level, some managers used some elements of the performance review program on their own initiative to manage and evaluate TEs. At the start of 2002, approximately 35 per cent of the headcount in the Saint Petersburg representative office were TEs.

An important part of the performance review process, the Technosoft poll, was generated by only the FTEs. The poll was a long, Web-based questionnaire that was designed to measure the company's "internal climate." The questionnaire took more than 20 minutes to answer and included various sections about understanding company priorities and goals, customer satisfaction, job satisfaction, compensation, work environment and an evaluation of the manager's performance.

The poll was always conducted by an external, independent company. Every year, usually in May, all the FTEs received a link to the personal Web-page where the questionnaire was located. Each FTE had to follow their personal link and fill out the questionnaire. FTEs were supposed to complete this task within a 15-day timeframe. All data collected by the external company were passed to the corporate level, processed (OHI was calculated at this stage) and then distributed back to the country level. Apart from the aggregated results of a particular country, these data contained the regional average and the last year's results for comparison. The data were then discussed on the country level to identify areas for improvement and to create an action plan.

Each country assigned a "champ" to supervise the poll. This person was responsible for the response rate and the post discussion of results. The poll was a high priority program in Technosoft, and response rates of all countries were closely monitored by regional headquarters. Every GM wanted to keep the response rate at least as high as other countries (in many cases, greater than 90 per cent). Program champs tried to stimulate colleagues to participate in the poll using incentives like a free computer mouse or other such gadgets.

The poll section in which each FTE evaluated their immediate manager was one of the most important parts of the poll. Managers who were responsible for lower-level supervisory staff used a specific section of the poll to evaluate the performance of these leaders. The results of this poll had a direct impact on each individual's performance review. Company standards required at least 75 per cent positive answers ("strongly agree" and "agree" answers on the five-point scale for each question.) A low mark meant poor performance, a low bonus and, potentially, a demotion or dismissal.

◪ Technosoft Saint Petersburg

On the country level, each representative office comprised several business units. One of the business units in Technosoft Saint Petersburg was the small and medium business unit (SMB). The SMB director, Dubrovsky, had worked for Technosoft since 1995. The SMB unit brought in approximately 60 per cent of Technosoft Saint Petersburg's revenue and was responsible for all channel activities,

value chain monitoring and small and medium enterprise business development. Dubrovsky was a talented manager who had a great respect for Sergei Zolotov, the GM, since 1996, in Technosoft Saint Petersburg (see Exhibit 3).

Technosoft did not sell directly to customers and, before 1999, had almost no contact with small and medium enterprises. However, in 1999, Technosoft headquarters' corporate decided to push the idea of working with small and medium customers directly. Although the value chain was left unchanged, the Technosoft sales forces in the various SMB units were challenged to understand the market and organize direct marketing activities targeted on SMB customers. The marketing efforts produced leads which, in turn, had to be passed on to resellers. Technosoft Saint Petersburg had neither the expertise nor the tools to use direct marketing methods or to handle generated leads. Dubrovsky hired Chaikovsky in August of 1999 as the SMB sales representative.

One of Chaikovsky's primary tasks was to decide which database to use for the sales and marketing activities to SMBs. He could either collect and maintain an inhouse database or use an agency list. The latter was usually less expensive than the former. Chaikovsky decided to build an inhouse database based on a key outsource agency that provided support services for Technosoft customers and already maintained a purchases database. By the summer of 2000, a new customer database was created, and regular data updating routines were set up and controlled by Technosoft Saint Petersburg.

By this time, Chaikovsky had won the support and admiration of Dubrovsky. Chaikovsky kept all promises, was conservatively proactive and never let Dubrovsky down. Chaikovsky always asked for Dubrovsky's advice in order to test the water before going forward with some idea. Chaikovsky felt that Dubrovsky had an exceptional gift in determining the feasibility of

Exhibit 3   Technosoft Saint Petersburg Organization Chart

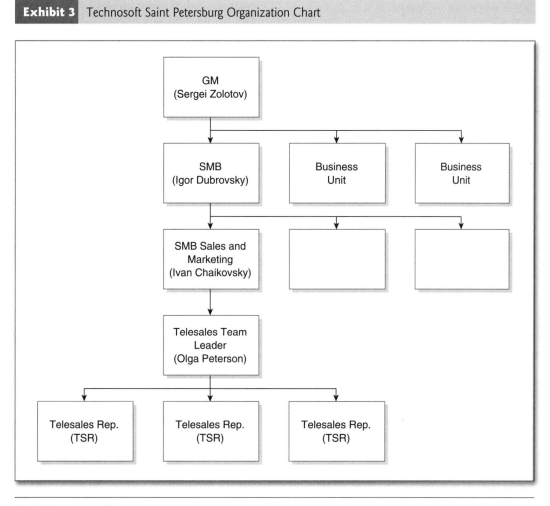

SOURCE: Company files.

new ideas. Usually this preliminary assessment helped everyone to understand the gaps in the business concept and to decide whether to collect additional data or drop the concept. However, in some situations Dubrovsky's position was imposed on Chaikovsky, despite his lack of agreement with it.

Even though Chaikovsky's SMB unit had a good database and was doing direct marketing work, he was worried about potential clients (leads) generated by his activities who were not being passed on to resellers and were eventually being lost. In response, Chaikovsky created a lead referral system where all generated leads could be captured and then distributed to resellers. The cost of developing the software was small, and Chaikovsky easily persuaded Dubrovsky to launch the project. Chaikovsky's system was developed and became one of the best practices in Eastern Europe. Eventually this system was replaced by a centralized corporate-wide sales and marketing support system (SMSS) and was implemented in every country.

Telesales Project

The lead referral system was a step in the right direction, but the system itself could not resolve the task of actively monitoring and following up on the leads. Moreover, Technosoft wanted to be sure that resellers did their best in order to maximize Technosoft's part in any deal to satisfy its customers. Chaikovsky knew that, in some countries, telesales representatives were hired to follow-up on leads. These salespeople also made proactive calls to customers and hence became another source of leads.

Chaikovsky wanted to use telesales to generate and follow up leads in order to have a full cycle of working with SMBs. Chaikovsky knew that direct sales, even by phone, was an extremely powerful instrument. Other countries, like the United Kingdom, had successfully used a telesales force for generating leads. Most were using an outsourced telesales force with non-Technosoft management and the "many-to-many" telesales model where telesales representatives (TSRs) did not have an assigned sales territory and worked through assigned call lists. Hence, one customer could be assigned to different TSRs during different sales campaigns.

From the very beginning Chaikovsky knew that he wanted to fully utilize the relationship between the TSR and the customer when they got to know each other over a long period of time. Therefore he wanted to use the "one-to-many" telesales model where each TSR had an assigned sales territory and the opportunity to create a long-term relationship with customers. The one-to-many sales model was more complex and expensive, required well-trained TSRs and low staff turnover. It meant a long-term commitment but promised much higher returns than the many-to-many model. In the one-to-many model, TSRs used all marketing activities such as direct mailings, marketing programs and customer events as an additional lever or sometimes to occasionally call customers.

Customers who were interested in buying Technosoft products or who had some issue that could be resolved only by a reseller, were transferred by the TSR to the reseller by SMSS (see Exhibit 4). TSRs were responsible for regularly monitoring the sales pipeline and contacting resellers when necessary.

Chaikovsky first approached Dubrovsky with his telesales idea in September 2000. Dubrovsky's first reaction was not encouraging. He had real concerns about the idea. He said: "Technosoft already has a channel and it is the resellers' job to sell. We don't want to confuse the customers. In addition, the telesales project is a long-term commitment, and I'm not sure that Russian customers are ready to buy over the phone." Chaikovsky tried to persuade Dubrovsky to test the concept. The factor that helped to change Dubrovsky's mind was that the U.S. subsidiary was also building a telesales force, and they were doing it using the "one-to-many" model. In addition, EHQ had started to develop its own telesales concept. After two months, Dubrovsky finally agreed to support Chaikovsky's request to the GM for additional budget allocation.

Inspired by this small victory, Chaikovsky created a comprehensive description of future telesales business processes. He discussed these with colleagues in the SMB unit and with key people in other units (see Exhibit 5). Finally, Chaikovsky and Dubrovsky made a presentation to the GM in December and got his support. Additional budget would be allocated from January 2001 for one TSR to test the concept. Even though he had approved the telesales project, Dubrovsky remained reserved about its success.

Ironically, in December, EHQ launched an "SMB Telesales" program which was to be rolled out all over the EMEA. Suddenly telesales became a priority and appeared in many GM scorecards. Subsidiaries were encouraged to allocate funds for this project. The commitment for this project was so high that the EHQ program manager received additional funds to be distributed among countries that were

Exhibit 4 Telesale Process

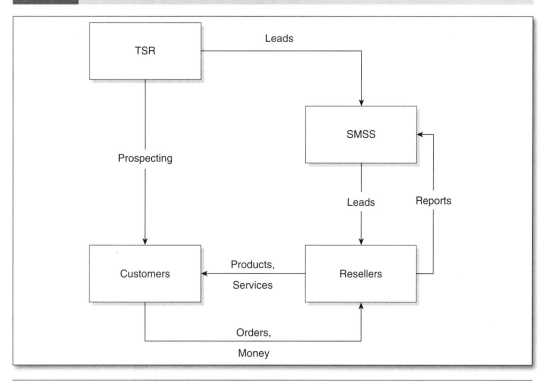

Exhibit 5 Telesales Project Timeline

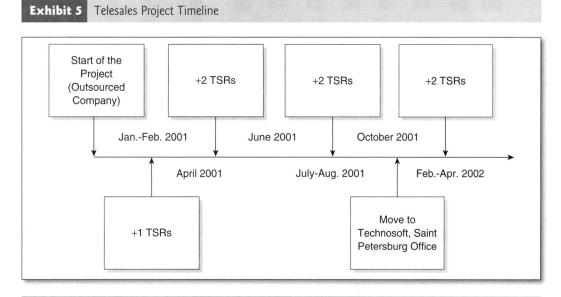

implementing telesales projects. Technosoft Saint Petersburg was in a good position. Chaikovsky's budget was extended to include up to four TSRs over the next six months. Nevertheless, he followed Dubrovsky's strong advice and moved ahead with caution.

The project was started at an outsourcing vendor's location to provide customer support. The vendor was responsible for administration, service and all the necessary equipment like telephones, Internet connection and personal computers. Technosoft Saint Petersburg organized all the training activities and managed the work. The first TSR hired was a former vendor employee who had been working in customer support service and had a good knowledge of Technosoft products. January 2001 was spent polishing up all the procedures, signing agreements with resellers and training them, preparing the working environment and training the TSR. In February 2001, the first TSR started work and the project was launched.

February and March sales results showed that the concept was very well-accepted by customers and resellers. Surprisingly, customers were not put off by the TSR making "cold" calls. In April, Chaikovsky hired two more TSRs who had been recommended to him even though they did not have telesales experience. Chaikovsky had difficulty in finding adequate candidates and hired a recruitment agency. Unfortunately, the agency did not change the trend: good candidates were rare. Usually, successful people with telesales experience did not want to stay in telesales, and it was difficult to find a person who was smart, mobile and committed to spending at least one year in the telesales position. Chaikovsky did the primary selection of candidates, and then all selected candidates had to be approved by Dubrovsky.

Telesales Team Leader

Chaikovsky understood that he would not be able to manage a telesales team forever and still be responsible for his other projects as well, so he and Dubrovsky decided that the telesales project should eventually have its own team leader. In June 2001, Chaikovsky was about to hire a young woman, Olga Peterson, who had substantial sales experience. He felt other TSRs could obviously benefit from her experience, but she would require a higher salary than the current TSRs. Chaikovsky was unsure what to offer her when Dubrovsky suggested making her a team leader at the same salary as the TSRs. Chaikovsky preferred to wait at least three months before making such a decision since Peterson did not have any managerial experience. He finally agreed, especially as he could offer a lower salary to Peterson in return for the opportunity for her to become a manager. In addition, Chaikovsky thought it would be a good idea to make Peterson's compensation dependent on the performance of the group. Chaikovsky did not feel totally comfortable with this decision, but he reassured himself that everything would be fine. Peterson seemed to be a good person, and the other TSRs accepted her well at the beginning, admitting her superiority in sales skills.

By summer 2001, Chaikovsky, in co-operation with the Technosoft human resource manager, had developed formal job descriptions for the TSRs and the team leader. During July and August of 2001, two more TSRs were hired, making six members in the telesales team, including the team leader, Olga Peterson. At the same time, Chaikovsky and Dubrovsky made a decision to move the telesales team from the outsourcing vendor's site into the Technosoft office in Saint Petersburg in order to make the team more visible and manageable and to exploit the current facilities of Technosoft's office, including Internet connections and phone lines. From the very beginning, the idea was to build the telesales project inhouse so there was no point in delaying relocation of the telesales force from the vendor site. All TSRs and the team leader stayed on as TEs and continued their employment contracts with the outsource vendor.

In February 2002, the telesales project at Technosoft Saint Petersburg added two more TSRs. With eight members on board, it was becoming highly visible, both on a country and a regional level. Following Dubrovsky's advice, Chaikovsky held several meetings with other business units to present the project and introduce the team and to explain how things worked and discuss possible synergies and ideas. Sergei Zolotov, Technosoft's GM, attended one of telesales team staff meetings held by Chaikovsky. Chaikovsky presented the team and all procedures and then asked each TSR to speak about their territory, customers, findings and sales results. Zolotov was delighted by the team performance, made several valuable comments and came up with even more ideas for future development.

A Technosoft EMEA internal conference was scheduled for April, and Chaikovsky had been asked to report on the successes in the telesales project. The budgeting process for the next year was going to start soon, and Chaikovsky saw this as a good opportunity to request additional TSR positions. By summer 2002, he wanted the telesales group to have 14 members.

Telesales Poll

Chaikovsky used the same procedures and processes to manage the telesales group as Technosoft managers used for the FTE group: staff meetings and personal reviews. Staff meetings were used to share information, discuss common issues, compliment and punish publicly. Personal reviews were used to assess individual performance, monitor goals, identify weak points and advise on courses of action. At the beginning, Chaikovsky held staff meetings and personal reviews every week, but when TSRs got used to their responsibilities and procedures, this habit converted into bi-weekly staff meetings and monthly personal reviews. Besides, Chaikovsky was a very approachable person, and the TSRs could

ask him a question or have a chat anytime. Once a quarter Chaikovsky did "team building" activities devoted to the celebration of good quarter results.

Despite the fact that a comprehensive training program was developed for new TSRs, Chaikovsky spent a lot of time doing personal review sessions, trying to coach people to help them perform. He tried to understand personal problems and find unique strengths in each person. By December 2001, staff meetings were held once a month, and Chaikovsky stopped doing personal reviews, delegating the job to Peterson. He attended her first meeting with each TSR and gave her some feedback.

Before that, Chaikovsky and Peterson discussed how the staff meetings should be conducted, what the agenda could be, points to review in detail and how to behave. At the first meeting, Chaikovsky allowed Peterson to lead the discussion but steered the direction where necessary. After this meeting, Chaikovsky was basically satisfied with the way that Peterson controlled the discussion. His feedback was concerned with a specific part of the discussion. Peterson seemed to ask the right questions, but they sounded too formal and did not invite conversation; the goal of each performance review. Peterson promised to take this input into account.

In January, some rumors about conflicts between TSRs and Peterson came to Chaikovsky's attention. Chaikovsky spoke with some of the TSRs who complained about "stupid" call plans, unrealistic targets and constant push. Chaikovsky shared these concerns with Peterson, but she reassured him that the situation was under her control.

By February 2002, the one year anniversary of the project, Chaikovsky thought it would be a good idea to conduct a Technosoft poll among the telesales group even though the group were all TEs. He informed the Technosoft human resource manager about his idea and received full support. Chaikovsky created his own questionnaire, incorporating some questions and ideas from the corporate poll. Using a company internal tool, he put the Web-based questionnaire on the Technosoft intranet and asked the TSR team to fill it out. The questionnaire did not contain any personal information. The telesales poll contained sections about Chaikovsky's and Peterson's performances as managers. The part concerning Peterson was filled out only by the five TSRs who had been working with Peterson at least six months. The two newest TSRs hired in February did not participate in the poll.

▧ Telesales Poll Results

Poll results revealed some interesting information (see Exhibits 6, 7, and 8), but the part concerning Olga Peterson was discouraging. Peterson was not performing very well as a team leader. Chaikovsky was concerned and not sure what he should do.

Exhibit 6 Olga Peterson's Telesales Poll Results

Question	Strongly Disagree	Disagree	Neutral	Agree	Strongly Agree
1. I clearly understand Olga Peterson's mission.	1	1	2	1	
2. Olga Peterson's contribution to the group success is tangible.	1	2	2		
3. Olga Peterson's suggestions for SMB Telesales business improvement are relevant.		1	3	1	
4. Olga Peterson knows how to exploit various tools (SBL, Sprut, Technosoft Office, Technosoft Sales) for Telesales Business.		1	2	2	
5. Olga Peterson helps me to achieve my quota.	1	1	1	1	1
6. I ask Olga Peterson when I have a problem.	1	1	2	1	
7. Olga Peterson helps me to solve my problems.	1		3	1	
8. Olga Peterson helps me to determine priorities in my work.	2	2	1		
9. Olga Peterson is candid and honest when giving me feedback on my performance.			4	1	

Question	Strongly Disagree	Disagree	Neutral	Agree	Strongly Agree
10. Olga Peterson helps me to work with SBL smartly.		1	2	2	
11. Olga Peterson builds co-operation and teamwork within my work group.	1	1	2	1	

SOURCE: Company files.

Exhibit 7   Ivan Chaikovsky Telesales Poll Results

Question	Strongly Disagree	Disagree	Neutral	Agree	Strongly Agree
I have confidence in the effectiveness of Ivan Chaikovsky.					5
Ivan Chaikovsky helps me determine priorities for my work.			1	4	
Ivan Chaikovsky sets high but achievable standards of performance.			1	4	
Ivan Chaikovsky is candid and honest when giving me feedback on my performance.			2	2	1
Ivan Chaikovsky builds co-operation and teamwork within my work group.			2	2	1

SOURCE: Company files.

Exhibit 8	Telesales Project's Poll Results

Question	Strongly Disagree	Disagree	Neutral	Agree	Strongly Agree
I work toward clear goals.					5
I have the authority to carry out the responsibilities assigned to me.			2	2	1
My work gives me a feeling of personal accomplishment.			1	1	3
When I do an excellent job, my accomplishments are recognized.		1	3	1	
I feel supported when I take risks in getting my work done.		1	2	1	1
I have received the training I need to do my job effectively.			2	2	1
I can see a clear link between my work and my work group's objectives.			1	1	3
My work group works toward clear goals.			3	1	1
The people in my work group co-operate to get the job done.		1	1	2	1
I would recommend my work group as a good place to work.			1	4	
I am encouraged to work co-operatively with people in other groups.			3	1	1
My total compensation package (base pay, bonus, benefits) is fair.		1	4		
I believe Technosoft delivers best-in-class products.				1	4
I clearly understand Technosoft's vision.				2	3

Question	Strongly Disagree	Disagree	Neutral	Agree	Strongly Agree
I have confidence in the leadership of the GM of my subsidiary/region.					5
Even if I were offered a comparable position with similar pay and benefits at another company, I would stay at Technosoft.				3	2
I expect to work for Technosoft for _____. (Neutral = Don't know, Agree = 2–4 years, Strongly agree = 4–10 years)			3	1	1
In my organization, senior management demonstrates through their actions that customer and partner satisfaction is a top priority.					5
How would you rate the satisfaction of your organization's customers? (Agree = Satisfied)			2	3	
I have the authority to make decisions in the best interest of customers.			3	2	
I have a clear understanding of customer needs and expectations.					5
The information I need to do my job is accessible and applicable.			3	1	1
People at Technosoft have a passion for the work they do.					5

SOURCE: Company files.

Consultancy Development Organization

Unnat Kohli wrote this case under the supervision of W. Glenn Rowe

It was just after 3 p.m. on Friday, January 4, 2008. Rohit Sharma, director of Consultancy Development Organization, stormed into the office of the deputy director of projects, Mukesh Kumar:

> One of our organization's prestigious members, Krish Industrial Consulting Limited, has complained that it received the information on the Mahanadi Electrical Company proposal from us after the last date for submission. As a result, it has lost the opportunity to participate. Why was it delayed?

Kumar replied:

> It takes time to gather information. We engaged New Infotech Limited to collect the information. They took their time to send the information. We have to follow government rules to get it printed in our newsletter, *Business Opportunities*, and then it is mailed to all members. There are procedures. What can I do if there is a delay? I have to follow these procedures.

"Do we have any plan to reduce the time lag so we can get the information to our members in time for them to use it?" asked Sharma.

"No. We work as the government tells us from time to time," replied Kumar.

Sharma could not believe what he had just heard. This was not the first time that he had felt let down by his employees. He left the room feeling embarrassed and vowing to himself that this latest incident would be the last.

✉ Consultancy Development Organization

In January 1990, Consultancy Development Organization (CDO) was set up by the Indian government in conjunction with the Indian consultancy industry as a not-for-profit body to help develop the Indian consultancy profession. CDO acted as a facilitator by providing information on consulting opportunities, a database on consultants and a platform for policy suggestions and networking. Among its main activities, CDO organized annual conferences and training programs and published a fortnightly publication on business opportunities, which listed CDO's expected consulting assignments.

CDO was based in Chennai (see Exhibit 1) and its membership included 200 individual consultants and 40 consultancy companies. It was headed by a full-time director, Rohit Sharma, who was supported by eight professionals and 20 support staff (see Exhibit 2). The Governing Council (the board) of CDO comprised 20 members, of which two-thirds (14 members) were elected by the general membership and the remaining members were nominated by the government. CDO's chairman was appointed directly by the government for a fixed two-year term. Approximately three-quarters of CDO's annual expenses were met through government grants.

✉ Rohit Sharma

Rohit Sharma joined CDO in October 2007, as a full-time director. He had an MBA from the Indian Institute of Management (IIM) in Ahmedabad, India's premier business school.

Version: (A) 2008-04-18

Exhibit I   Map of India

SOURCE: Office of the Registrar General and Census Commissioner, India, "India 2001: State Map." Retrieved from http://www.censusindia.gov.in/maps/State_Maps/maps.htm, accessed April 12, 2008.

Prior to joining CDO, Sharma had worked for 20 years in various positions in the industry, consulting both in India and abroad. Sharma had a reputation for being a hard task master and a dynamic, hard-working person with a vision.

Sharma had been appointed to the post of director by the Ministry of Industrial Promotion, which was the nodal government ministry in charge of CDO. Prior to Sharma's appointment, the Ministry of Industrial Promotion had used the CDO director position as a parking place for unwanted government officials, a practice that had led to three directors joining and leaving CDO in the last three years. Nevertheless, Sharma accepted the challenge of leading CDO and turning it into a leading player.

Exhibit 2 Organization Chart of Consultancy Development Organization

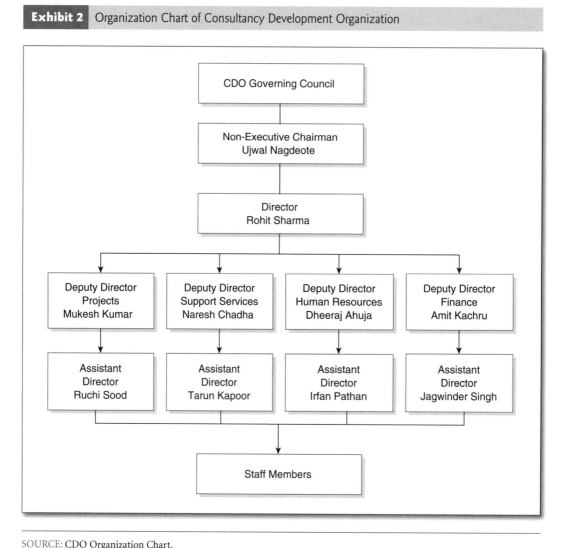

SOURCE: CDO Organization Chart.

 Mukesh Kumar

Mukesh Kumar received an engineering degree from Delhi University. After graduation, he worked as a junior engineer in a government organization. He joined CDO in 1992 as an assistant manager and had progressed through the ranks to become one of four deputy directors who reported to the director. Kumar was hard working and knowledgeable but lacked ambition and drive. He was currently the deputy director of projects at CDO, the second-most prestigious profile in CDO after the director.

Naresh Chadha

Naresh Chadha, a commerce graduate, had been employed at CDO since its inception in 1990. He was politically well connected and regarded as a hands-on employee. He had worked in various positions in CDO, ranging from administration to marketing, and was currently deputy director of support services. His work included organizing annual conferences and conventions. He reported to the director.

Dheeraj Ahuja and Amit Kachru

Dheeraj Ahuja and Amit Kachru were the other two deputy directors at CDO who reported to Rohit Sharma. They were responsible for human resources and finance, respectively. Prior to joining CDO the previous year, both Ahuja and Kachru had spent their entire careers serving the Indian government in various roles.

Ujwal Nagdeote

Ujwal Nagdeote was the non-executive chairman of CDO, appointed by the government. He was a politically well-connected, knowledgeable and respected figure in the industry. Nagdeote served on the board of a dozen leading Indian companies and played a dormant role in the affairs of CDO.

Organization Culture

CDO had four deputy directors and four assistant directors. The deputy directors reported to the director, and the assistant directors reported to the deputy directors (see Exhibit 2). The director, deputy directors and assistant directors comprised the officer category, and the 20 support staff (personal assistants, secretaries, clerks and peons[2]) comprised the Class II category. Each officer had at least one personal assistant or secretary and one peon. All clerks worked in the administration wing of CDO, where all files were located.

In 1990, when CDO was established, the staff was recruited according to the structure prevalent in government organizations. In the early 1990s, clerks were needed for typing and administrative tasks, and the peons were required to run office errands, such as delivering files, dispatching letters, serving water, and preparing tea and coffee for the officers. However, by 2008, computers were available to all the officers, and coffee and tea machines were common in the office. The clerks and peons did not have enough work; however, they were very difficult to fire, because they had job security, in accordance with the government system.

At all levels of the organization, the salaries were fixed and equal with no variable pay or rewards system. As a result, employees had no incentive to perform. Until Sharma's appointment, no outside appointments had been made for the past 10 years. The culture was not very professional, and government organizations constantly interfered, wanting to use the CDO facilities (such as CDO's office car) and staff for their own purposes. As a result, morale within CDO was poor.

Rohit Sharma's First Week In Office

When Sharma joined CDO in October 2007, he was greeted by Naresh Chadha and Mukesh Kumar, two of his four direct reports. That week, the attendance was abysmally low. Sharma learned that most of the staff were absent because it was Diwali[3] season. Even though Diwali was five weeks away, some of the employees had taken time off to be with their families and friends. They had scant regard for Sharma, which was reinforced through their absence. Sharma was aghast to see that no one on the administration staff had bothered to fill the water coolers with fresh water or to clear the cupboards in his office.

National Convention

CDO was organizing the National Convention scheduled for January 15, 2008. For this annual

[2]Peons were persons of menial position, such as messengers and servants.

[3]Diwali, the festival of lights, is an important festival celebrated throughout India.

conference, eminent speakers had been invited to address consulting issues and discuss their experiences with the participants, generally the member organizations and individuals and executives from the corporate sector.

On January 4, 2008, Sharma went to the office of Naresh Chadha, the deputy director in charge of the National Convention to inquire about the conference's progress, particularly the number of speakers that had confirmed and the number of participants that had registered.

"We sent letters to the members. Their responses continue until the last date. We have not set any targets. Do not worry. We will have good numbers," replied Chadha, casually sipping his tea and eating pakoras.[4]

Sharma returned to his own office an unhappy person. He was feeling uneasy: there was not much response to show and most activities had been delayed. The annual conference was not expected to be successful. The attitude of most employees was callous and inept. The fiscal year-end was on March 31, and he was concerned that CDO's performance would be seen as much below average.

International Consultancy Congress

The International Consultancy Congress was scheduled to be held in London, England, from February 3 to 6, 2008. Sharma thought it would be a good opportunity to interact and network with consultancy organizations in other countries. He considered taking one of his officers with him to boost morale.

According to government rules, any foreign visit had to be approved by the Ministry of Industrial Promotion. Thus, Sharma had sent the proposal for his own participation and that of Naresh Chadha on December 1, 2007. After several follow-up attempts, he was informed on January 3, 2008 that the proposal had not been accepted. This rejection had a further demoralizing effect on employees who now thought that Sharma, despite all his talk, was not able to do much.

Sharma's First Three Months

Sharma realized quickly that employee morale at CDO was very low and was compounded by the absence of career development and low remuneration. The company had no clear strategy or direction. The government grants took care of the salaries of staff and the administrative expenses. Consequently, employees had no motivation to perform or to increase the business.

"How are we expected to facilitate our members?" asked Sharma.

"It is not our concern. In any case, the members pay very little and our salaries are paid by the government. You should not worry so much. Whether you undertake the same or more activities, you will be paid the same salary," advised Kumar.

Sharma faced the choice of continuing on the path of his predecessors (i.e., doing nothing new and having an easy time) or working towards a turnaround strategy for the organization and setting it on a growth path.

The December 28, 2007 Meeting

Sharma had called a meeting of all officers and staff on Friday, December 28, at 9 a.m. He asked them for ideas for the growth of CDO. Divergent views were expressed:

> CDO has been in existence for 18 years and has been doing well. It can continue to function as such.

> The government grant received annually is sufficient to pay for the salaries and some activities only.

---

[4]Pakoras are a deep-fried South Asian fritter made by dipping pieces of vegetable in a chickpea flour batter. They are generally eaten as a snack.

We are a government controlled organization. We undertake activities as directed by the controlling Ministry of Industrial Promotion.

There is no incentive for extra effort or growth. Following the government pay scales, we get the same salary whether we do the same activities or take up more.

Members of CDO pay very small subscription [membership fee]. They are not interested in any major initiatives, which may lead to their paying more subscription.

Sharma disagreed. He observed that he had joined the organization because he believed it had great potential. Consultancy was fast growing, and India had an edge in the global consultancy field because of a large professionally skilled pool of workers and the relatively low cost of consultants. CDO could greatly help in developing the consultancy profession in the country. He outlined his five-year vision:

- CDO should be fully self-supporting and not dependent on government grants. For this purpose, CDO must increase its income from its own activities by at least five times.
- CDO should function on a non-government pattern and the employees need to be accountable for results.
- CDO should strive for a 10-fold increase in memberships, both individual and corporate. The members must benefit from CDO's activities. They must receive information about a larger number of business opportunities within the country and abroad, online, without delay.
- CDO should help consultants in consultancy exports, through studies, data collection and providing opportunities for networking.
- CDO should function as facilitator by using its government links for policy intervention to promote the profession.

- CDO should also take up consultancy assignments that can be outsourced to its members, to generate income and to help employ its members.
- Support staff need to be given work responsibility after being trained in new skills that can be useful for the organization.
- Employee morale needs to improve, performance needs to be linked to incentives and promotions need to be introduced.

Some of the executives were enthusiastic but only if these changes could lead to better prospects for themselves. Others expressed apprehension, particularly regarding the operational freedom they would have from the controlling ministry. The Governing Council also had to be consulted for endorsement.

Mahanadi Electrical Proposal Incident

Mahanadi Electrical Company (MEC) was an electricity distribution utility in the eastern state of Orissa (see Exhibit 1), which supplied electricity to about one-fourth of the state. The distribution system was very old, and breakdowns were frequent, as were the failure of transformers and interruptions to the electrical supply. Consumers were unhappy, and the State Electricity Regulation Commission had asked MEC to revamp the distribution system. Accordingly, the company had invited bids for consultancy work, which involved the preparation of a feasibility report for the revamping of the distribution system. This major assignment was worth about US$2.5 million, and few consultancy companies had the necessary competency in this field.

Krish Industrial Consulting Limited (KICL), a founding member of CDO and one of the competing companies bidding on the MEC project, was confident of being awarded the assignment and was waiting to receive the information needed to bid for the job. On behalf of CDO, New Infotech Limited (to whom this work was outsourced) was collecting information regarding potential consultancy assignments from tender notices published in newspapers, websites and other sources. This information was then passed to CDO, which published it in a fortnightly newsletter that was mailed to all of its members. The last date for receipt of bids by MEC was December 15, 2007, but KICL received the CDO newsletter with the information on this assignment on January 1, 2008. The CEO of KICL had expressed his disappointment to Sharma regarding the delay.

January 4, 2008 Incident

On January 4, Sharma stormed into the office of Kumar to inquire about the MEC proposal and why it had been delayed. Kumar had been non-apologetic and unfazed that KICL lost the opportunity to participate. He had justified the situation by suggesting he had been following government guidelines.

Sharma could not believe Kumar's lackadaisical attitude. KICL was an important member of CDO, yet Kumar seemed unperturbed by KICL's loss of business because of CDO's delay and ineptness. Kumar's attitude was a clear reflection of the state of affairs in the organization. Sharma left the room very frustrated. Things needed to improve or CDO would lose its elite status as the nodal agency for consultancy in India, and his career would be at stake.

Sharma wondered whether he had made a mistake by accepting the director's position and whether he could do anything to improve the situation at CDO.

Navigating Through Leadership Transitions

Making It Past the Twists and Turns

By Christine M. Riordan

All things change; nothing abides. Into the same river, one cannot step twice.

—Heraclitus

Agility and adaptability are mandatory these days, as leaders prepare, manage, and sometimes reinvent themselves in order to navigate the twists, turns, and transitions they must make. Otherwise, making the wrong move could eventually scuttle a once-promising leadership career.

Many points in our jobs and careers require, even demand, changes in our leadership behaviors, competencies, attitudes, and thinking. How well we navigate these potentially treacherous junctures often determines our ultimate success—or failure—as leaders.

Whether change involves the strategic direction of the corporation, a merger, acquisition or reorganization, the development of a new product line or a shift in the competitive market place, or new bosses or co-workers, leaders must constantly monitor their environment and adjust their leadership skills to match the new demands. This requirement for constant personal modification can be daunting for anyone not agile enough to adapt.

It is imperative that leaders determine how they need to adjust their leadership behaviors and style to navigate the changes surrounding them. This task sounds easy, but it is often very difficult. This article describes tactics leaders can use to reach this goal.

What Happens When Times Change

Sometimes, leaders do not recognize environmental changes or, perhaps more importantly, the need for them to behave differently because of these changes. Leaders will often cling to the past or continue "business as usual." They think that past behaviors that have proven successful will again carry them into the future. While they are correct in many respects, one set and style of behaviors rarely moves a person seamlessly throughout his or her leadership career. At each transition, a leader must be prepared to adopt new and different behaviors to succeed. This ability (or failure) to recognize, navigate, and make personal changes influences the effectiveness of leaders over time.

For example, a woman I will call Barbara, a vice president of operations for a major insurance company, found herself in unfamiliar waters when the business went through a major review process. One result was a restructuring that established a new strategy and accompanying performance goals. Barbara retained her position but had a new boss, new strategic objectives, new performance demands, and new teammates. Her boss no w expected Barbara to focus most of her time and energy on being accountable and delivering results.

Over time, however, she had difficulty changing her behavior, attitudes, and thinking to match the new strategy and goals. She was unaccustomed to being personally accountable and the high demands from her new boss. Her supervisor provided feedback during the transition, but after a year of trying to help Barbara, he decided she was not delivering. Further, Barbara did not seem able or willing to make the personal leadership transformations needed to support the new strategic direction and environment, nor was she able to help her subordinates make the transition. While the company rarely fired

anyone, Barbara's supervisor eventually let her go. She had worked for the company for 27 years.

Transitions: Potentially Turbulent Waters

If they are to demonstrate and retain their value, leaders must steer their organizations through various transitions. Failure to handle such transitions adequately can result in career disaster. Successful navigation, on the other hand, results in vital lessons learned, greater flexibility and adaptability, and stronger leadership skills. With each transition, leaders must adapt their skills to face the new set of challenges.

Ron Parker, executive vice president of Human Resources at PepsiCo, notes that successful leaders must be "learning agile". "You have to be agile in your approach to complex issues," he says. Parker indicates that corporations need people who can change with the times. "You cannot stay in a steady state in a competitive global environment. That which is not broken today should be broken tomorrow. We look at the entire value chain and are constantly asking ourselves what needs to change." Leaders need to be asking themselves the same questions: How and what do I need to change to keep up with the future and to be of value to this organization?

Leaders commonly face several major types of transitions in their careers. Each of these requires an adjustment in behaviors, capabilities, attitudes, and thinking. Some of these major transitional challenges are described below.

Change in Job/Role

The most common transition for which a leader will need to change is taking on a new role or job. Charan, Drotter, and Noel (May/June 2001, *Ivey Business Journal*) note six passages an individual makes while progressing in leadership roles through an enterprise: from managing self to managing others; to managing other managers; to functional management; to business leadership; to group leadership; and to enterprise leadership.

At each passage, the person must acquire new skills and competencies to make major transitions. The skills that made a leader successful in a previous role are typically not sufficient for the new role.

This need to adapt also comes about in lateral moves, changes in jobs that may occur due to restructuring, reorganizations, or mergers and acquisitions. Additionally, as the leader grows and develops in his/her job, he or she must look for new ways to improve performance and value within that role.

For example, Jason worked in state government as the manager of a department. He was a high achiever and extremely successful in the technical aspects of his job. He developed quite a reputation for his expertise and was proud of it. Jason received a promotion to a management position, in part because of this expertise.

After becoming a manager, Jason networked only with people at his level of seniority and skill. He had a hierarchical mentality but proved ineffective at networking with those above him and neglected to network with those below him. He was also into strictly maintaining the status quo in his unit, even though the entire division was undergoing dramatic changes. He was quick to dismiss new and innovative ideas.

This attitude frustrated many of his subordinates, who saw other work units making dramatic improvements in processes and outcomes. As part of the performance appraisal process, Jason's subordinates completed feedback evaluations on his performance. Each year they became more devastating. It was clear his leadership style was weighing down both him and his work unit. Yet, rather than following the feedback and trying to change, he attributed the negative results to external factors. He blamed his failure on things other than his own behavior. For example, he thought, since the evaluations were given to subordinates right after they had received their raise information, they were angry about their wages and not at Jason.

As the feedback became increasingly worse, Jason stopped socializing and talking casually with his subordinates. He never went to lunch or stopped by subordinates' offices to chat. He became negative and abrasive, and seemed to embody and intensify bad management practices. He became the butt of jokes and gossip among his peers and subordinates. No one took him seriously anymore. Finally, after receiving yet another crushing evaluation from his subordinates, he simply resigned. While Jason had been an excellent individual performer, he had never been able to become a manager of others.

Change in People

Sometimes the people we work with change jobs. Working with different bosses, peers, and subordinates is an important transition and one in which leaders must ride the waves. Learning to interact productively with new people who have diverse ideas, styles, and preferences is a difficult challenge. While learning such lessons seems basic, many leaders fail to navigate people changes—particularly when they get a new boss.

For example, Bob was leading a new product development group in a professional services firm. In one year, his direct boss changed along with the leader one level above. Bob's old boss was very hands off in his leadership style, not asking for much information about the performance of the unit. He also did not spend any time helping Bob succeed.

When the new leadership arrived, it recognized that Bob had been successful in implementing new product lines. However, it also believed that there was room for improvement in both the number of products developed and the way in which he introduced these inside the firm.

To start the unit down the path of improvement, Bob's new boss began asking him for strategic and execution plans for the development department. Rather than taking this request as an opportunity to demonstrate his understanding of how to reshape the development department, Bob felt threatened by these requests and thus resisted any requests for information. His behaviour became adversarial when dealing with any suggestions for change. He longed for the days when his old boss simply left him alone and he was not accountable.

Bob talked negatively about the changes occurring within the firm and about his bosses to others inside and outside of the firm. Bob's bosses and co-workers, of course, became aware of this unconstructive behavior. Bob consequently gained a reputation for being uncooperative, for not being a team player, and as being a person that others did not trust. Bob's new bosses started questioning whether he could run the development department effectively. Eventually, the bosses brought in someone new to run the department; the individual reduced Bob's job scope.

In another example, Tom was a senior vice president at a financial services firm that recently transferred him to a new region within the same corporation. He had two vice presidents reporting to him. Though Tom had been in this role in another region, this was the first time he worked with these particular vice presidents.

After a few months, Tom realized that he was having difficulty connecting and working with one of his vice presidents. Therefore, Tom elicited the advice of an executive coach who helped him understand that there were simple differences of style between Tom and his vice president. They also determined that the other vice president had a style very similar to Tom's, which made that relationship easier to navigate. Rather than trying to change the vice president to suit his own style, Tom made some simple adjustments in his interactions. Today, his relationships with his two vice presidents are strong. Moreover, he continues to adjust his style slightly to relate to them each more effectively.

Change in the Marketplace

Markets change in many ways and leaders who are effective in transitions pay attention to these market changes. They understand the need to keep abreast of the business, industry, and marketplace trends. They do not take things for granted.

As the director of a major business line for a consumer products firm, Sara had seen her line grow for many years. However, the competitive environment changed, not only in her region but all over the country. She started to see a significant reduction in interest and sales. Rather than look at how the organization had designed or positioned the product relative to the competitive market and changing consumer interests, she poured more money into advertising and marketing.

Yet, sales continued to erode. She blamed the reduction in sales on national trends. Eventually, other leaders in the organization began to take control of the situation. Sarah lost significant amounts of autonomy, as senior leaders began telling her what to do and reduced her responsibilities. Other leaders in the firm restructured and repositioned the business line to respond to the changing consumer interests. Over time, sales began to increase again.

Change in Strategy/Products

Often in response to the competitive environment, firms will look at changing their strategy and/or their product mix. Leaders must adjust their organizational thinking and way of doing business when the enterprise shifts direction. Yet, many leaders have difficulty making this transition.

Leaders who successfully embrace this type of change become the enablers, or the people who help promote, accept, and make the change happen. The organization values these types of leaders because they ensure strategic growth.

On the other hand, it is difficult for the organization when leaders become "open resistors" to the change or actively work against the changes. They may engage in activities such as sabotaging change efforts, promoting to keep things the same, arguing openly against the changes in meetings, or creating coalitions to fight the change effort. They may also become "nay-sayers" or openly criticize the changes and those involved in it. Leaders who are not successfully transitioning may also become "passive resistors" or privately refuse to support the change, though they do no overtly resist the change. However, they also do not do anything to enable the change. Finally, some individuals may be unwary resistors or not be aware that they are resisting the change effort. They simply revert to what they know, which could be old processes, old priorities, and old strategies.

For example, Bill was a vice president of sales for a consumer services and products firm for an entire state. He had hundreds of sales people as well as 35 sales managers. The company decided to roll out a completely new product line as a way to grow business and buffer predicted declines in its traditional lines of business. While the new product line complemented the existing lines, it did represent a major strategic shift that required sales people to acquire a new knowledge base for the products and to learn how to cross sell the products. Additionally, it meant that Bill needed to keep up with sales results, the competition, and the marketplace in three different, but related, lines of business.

Bill had strong relationships with his sales people and managers. He just figured that he could keep doing things the same without making any major adjustments. Over time, sales in the old product lines started to drop while sales in the new product lines became limited. Bill could not figure out a way to turn things around. In short, he could not get out of the mindset of doing business in the same way. He rarely sought out information about the local marketplace, nor did he read industry or company literature that discussed market and strategy changes. Over time and after much coaching, the senior leaders of the firm moved Bill into a less demanding position. He just could not transition into being a strategic leader who focused on new ways of operating.

◣ How Transitions Impact a Leader's Performance

As these and other transition points come up during a leader's tenure, he or she needs to be prepared to advance through them. Perhaps the most common mistake is that the leader does not recognize the critical juncture in the leadership river and, therefore, fails to respond or make the correct turns. Over time, this failure to transition affects the performance of the leader. In a similar situation, the leader may recognize the juncture, but does not know how to respond and change. Performance also suffers. As depicted in the figure below, we can generally categorize a leader's ability to navigate transition points on three levels:

1. Staying ahead—these leaders have the ability to recognize transition points; this type of leader generally navigates all changes and transition points with ease while maintaining high levels of performance

2. Keeping up—these leaders have the ability to recognize the transition points; performance may dip for a slight period as the leader adjusts to the new situation, but the leader is able to respond and bring performance back to peak levels—until the next transition point; over time however, the leader's overall performance is high, leading to success in the role

3. Falling behind—these leaders may or may not recognize the transition points; they generally do not know how to respond or choose to not respond; over time, their leadership performance suffers; these leaders are the ones who commonly lose their leadership roles or have their leadership roles reduced.

One should recognize that sometimes there is a fourth level of response. A leader may choose not to navigate a transition point. That is, the leader may decide that he or she does not want to make the transition. This situation could occur for a variety of reasons, including the leader's philosophical disagreement with the changes or her belief that the change will fail with the given resources. Ultimately, this type of leader often decides to move proactively into another situation within the firm or sometimes outside of the firm. As an example, we commonly see very successful founders of entrepreneurial ventures leave the organization they started because they do not want to become the type of leader needed to take the firm to the next level.

For example, Dan was a very successful senior executive with a major indemnity company in the northeast. Brought into the organization to help turn around the performance of the eastern region, Dan thrived in this role for several years. The company, however, decided to change strategy. Dan did not philosophically agree with the changes. Rather than staying with the organization, Dan decided to leave. He knew that he was not the right person to make the next set of changes and felt that he and the firm would be better off with someone else in the role.

✉ Company Responses to Leadership Transitions

It is extremely expensive and disruptive for an organization to see leaders fail or to have leaders who are ill equipped for their positions. As a result, companies are beginning to recognize how critical it is to help their leaders make a transition through the more difficult situations. For example, Burlington Northern Santa Fe Railway offers an executive education class for new leaders. This class focuses exclusively on what changes the new leaders need to make in their new roles, how to handle these changes, and what challenges they may face.

In 2003, *The Economist* estimated that organizations were already spending more than

Exhibit 1

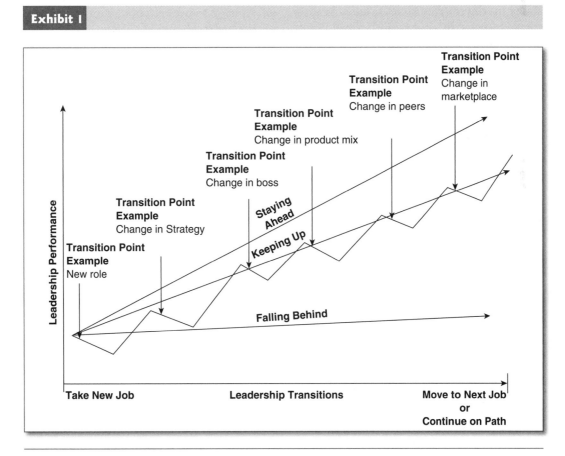

$1 billion providing coaches for their employees; it projected that this expenditure would double in two years. This growth in the executive coaching industry is in part due to the increase in companies' recognition that leaders commonly need assistance in managing the transitions, and that an external party may help the leaders gain the needed skills, abilities, and fresh perspective.

Individual Transition Skills Needed

While organizations may try to facilitate transitions, navigating transitions is a skill that leaders need to acquire if they do not already possess it.

Successful leaders focus on their ability to navigate changes in the environment and their ability to reinvent themselves to adapt to those changes. Generally, successful navigation and personal reinvention require three things: 1) a change in attitude and thinking; 2) a change in competencies and skills; and 3) a change in behaviors.

Changing one area is not usually sufficient to navigate transitions successfully. For example, Sandra was a successful corporate relations manager for a consumer products company. She had a successful performance results record, worked well with others, and prided herself on being open to developmental feedback. As Sandra moved up and the organization changed, it became obvious that she needed advanced leadership skills and competencies in strategic thinking and positioning, managing change, and project management. Sandra knew she needed to change, and was open to feedback. While her attitude was positive, she had a difficult time acquiring the advanced skills she needed. It took many different types of development activities and continuous feedback for Sandra to develop these skills. Eventually she succeeded, though her performance suffered a bit while she learned to change her behaviors.

You can ask yourself several questions to determine if you will navigate transitions easily (see box at end of article). If you answer "No" to any of these questions, you can take several developmental actions to help reinvent yourself and navigate difficult transitions.

Specific Steps

Navigating transitions is not something you do only for the organization. It is something you do for yourself. As such, you need to take charge of developing the skills you need to periodically reinvent and realign yourself with environmental changes.

One key is to dedicate yourself to becoming a student of leadership throughout your career. Study effective leadership practices. Knowledge of what constitutes effective leadership at each stage of your career is fundamental. At each transition point, your perspective on leadership should change as you work to acquire advanced leadership skills and competencies. Acquiring such knowledge can save many errors, reduce learning time, and improve your leadership success.

A second key is to look in the mirror. Your leadership effectiveness begins with you. You need to answer important questions such as how does your leadership style need to change, what roles and responsibilities do others expect you to give them, what type of leader do you want to be, and what type of leader do you need to be at each transition point? Are you a steward for the organization or do you collude with the status quo? Do you need to change your attitude and thinking, your competencies, and/or your behaviors to navigate the transition?

A third key is being open to feedback and coaching—*really* open to feedback and coaching. You should understand that sometimes this feedback is unpleasant, challenges our egos, and simply stings a bit. However, getting one-on-one feedback and advice from a boss, executive coach, or mentor is invaluable. It is important to seek feedback and suggestions for leadership development throughout your career.

As you hit transition points, being open to feedback and coaching may help you adjust faster. Additionally, other people can serve as a sounding board for ideas for leadership development activities targeted towards your specific needs; help identify different types of activities, which will help you practice the skills; and provide valuable coaching or feedback based on observation and interaction with you. Finally, having someone who provides honest feedback can affirm the things that you do well and potentially prevent you from adopting attitudes, thinking and behaviors that may derail your career.

A fourth key is recognizing that effective leadership takes lots of practice and reflection. As part of the transition, try doing things differently, but be reflective. If something goes well, reflect on why it went well. If something does not go well, ask why it did not and what can you do differently.

The fifth key is observing and learning from other successful leaders. Observe people who seem to flourish in their leadership roles. It is equally important, though, to learn from people who are not succeeding in their leadership roles. Some of the most powerful learning occurs by observing "what not to do" in a situation.

Finally, make sure that you understand the business, industry, and community in which you operate. Stay current about industry and company trends. Attend conferences and classes, listen to and participate in business conversations, or go back to school for an advanced degree if appropriate. You will only be able to identify transition points if you know what the competitive environment looks like and understand the challenges that the company may be facing.

Outstanding leaders recognize the need to modify their skills, attitudes, and behaviors frequently to smoothly maneuver through their careers and leadership challenges. They also recognize that while they may need assistance along the way, no one else can make the changes for them. They are the only ones who can successfully navigate their own leadership river.

Assessing Your Capability to Navigate Transitions

Evaluate your skill in each of the competencies listed below to assess your agility to adapt and navigate leadership transitions.

Adaptability and Openness to Change—the ability to respond to new demands and challenges and to maintain a constructive, positive outlook about change.

- Do new challenges excite you and are you willing to tackle them?
- When presented with a change in the organization, do you view it as an opportunity rather than a threat?
- Do you challenge status quo within the organization?

Self-awareness—the ability to recognize when you do not possess the skills/competencies needed to navigate the transition and the ability to recognize that you need to change competencies, behaviors, and/or attitude.

- Do you recognize when you need to gain some new capabilities or change behaviors and/or attitude?
- Are you willing to learn or seek help when needed?

(Continued)

(Continued)

- Are you willing to admit that you have to change to succeed?
- Do you proactively work on expanding your capabilities/competencies?
- Do you commonly ask yourself, if I were to start this job all over again, what would I need to do differently?

Leadership Maturity—the felt responsibility to make the changes in competencies, behaviors, and attitude needed to support the direction of the organization and to be successful in the role.

- Do you feel that it is important to improve as a leader to help the organization succeed?
- Do you look for ways in which you can be better to help the organization achieve its goals?
- Do you recognize that a change in attitude can result in a change of behavior?
- Do you seek to understand why changes are needed?
- Are you an active steward of the organization and its goals?

Leadership Resilience—the ability to rebound from setbacks and/or changes.

- When things do not go well, do you work to make them better?
- When there is a setback, do you reflect on what happened and look for ways to improve?

Strategic Thinking—the ability to look ahead and behind to determine the best plan for improvement.

- Do you proactively look for ways to improve?
- Do you periodically question your own assumptions, ideas, and thinking?
- Are you able to define the issues or problems clearly to determine appropriate actions?
- Do you focus on the big picture *and* the details in planning how to change?
- Do you periodically conduct a reality test of yourself to see if you are on track?

Business Acumen—developing a deeper understanding of the business so that you understand how the business is changing and why and how you might need to change as a leader

- Do you proactively seek to know more about the business so that you can help move it in the direction it needs to go?
- Do you pay attention to industry trends, market trends, and strategic shifts that are taking place?
- Do you apply these trends to how you might need to change as a leader?

5

The Situational Approach to Leadership

My management philosophy starts with the basics: thoroughly understand the environment in which you're managing. That means knowing the strengths and weaknesses of the company, its competitive position, its competitors, and where the markets for the products you're offering are heading. With that thorough understanding, you have to decide on the strategy that you intend to pursue.

—Gary Wendt[1]

Contrary to other theories of leadership that are descriptive, the situational approach to leadership is prescriptive. This leadership approach tells leaders what to do in different situations and what not to do in other situations. This approach is widely used in leadership development and training and has been refined and revised several times (Blanchard, Zigami, & Nelson, 1993).

The situational leadership theory has two underlying assumptions. First, as situations vary, so must a person's leadership. This means that leaders are able to adapt their styles to different situations. Second, leadership is made up of a directive component and a supportive component, and these two components have to be exercised appropriately based on the context. To assess the appropriate level of each component, it is critical that leaders evaluate their subordinates and determine their level of competence and commitment to a given task or job. Inherent in this latter assumption is that subordinates' levels of competence and commitment may change over time, requiring that leaders change their level of direction and

---

[1]Gary Wendt is the former chairman and CEO of Conseco.

personal support to match these changing needs in their employees. The situational leadership approach suggests that leaders who are more capable of assessing what their subordinates need and changing their own style will be more effective as leaders (Dubrin, 2007).

This approach to leadership suggests that understanding situational leadership is best accomplished by discussing the two underlying principles: leadership style and subordinates' level of development (Northouse, 2010).

Leadership Styles and Subordinate Developmental Level

As in Chapter 4, leadership style describes a leader's behavior when he or she tries to influence others. Thus, it includes directive or task behaviors and supportive or relationship behaviors.

These two groups of behaviors help subordinates to accomplish goals and to be positively encouraged in how they feel about their job, their coworkers, and themselves. Four styles based on being directive and supportive are suggested by the situational leadership approach: directing, coaching, supporting, and delegating. These styles are described, accompanied by brief descriptions of when and why they should be used based on the developmental level exhibited by subordinates with respect to their competencies for and their commitment to getting the job done.

Directing Leadership Style

This style is directive and nonsupportive. Leader communications are focused on getting the job done with little or no communication effort focused on supportive behaviors. The

Table 5.1 Directive and Supportive Behaviors for Situational Leadership

Directive behaviors aid in goal achievement	Some supportive behaviors are
by giving directions	asking for input
by establishing goals	problem solving
by establishing methods of evaluation	praising
by setting time lines	sharing information regarding self
by defining roles	listening
by showing how to achieve goals	job related
In addition, directive behaviors	Supportive behaviors help subordinates to
clarify what is to be accomplished	feel comfortable with the situation
clarify how it is to be accomplished	feel comfortable with their coworkers
clarify who will accomplish it	feel comfortable with themselves
Often through one-way communication	Often through two-way communication

SOURCE: Adapted from Northouse (2010). Copyright © 2010, Sage Publications, Inc.

communication effort is one-way and emphasizes instructions that give subordinates direction about what to do and how to do it. This style is associated with close and careful supervision (Northouse, 2010).

This style is most appropriate when subordinates are most committed but least competent in what to do and how to do it—when they have a low development level (D1); see the Situational Leadership II model in Northouse (2010). Because they are most committed, the level of leader support can be minimal, while the level of direction has to be high because subordinates are least competent. The reason for the lower level of competence is generally because subordinates are new to the job or task to be accomplished (Dubrin, 2007).

Coaching Leadership Style

This style is highly directive and highly supportive. Communications from the leader to followers focus on getting the job done and on employees' emotional and social needs. Communication is two-way in that leaders communicate to subordinates and encourage input from subordinates. Leaders still decide on what needs to be accomplished and how it will be accomplished (Northouse, 2010).

This style is most appropriate when subordinates have some competence but a lower level of commitment. They are learning their job but losing some of their commitment to and motivation for the job—when they have a moderate development level (D2); see the Situational Leadership II model in Northouse (2010). In this situation, the leader still needs to be directive but also needs to be supportive (Dubrin, 2007).

Supporting Leadership Style

This style is highly supportive but relatively low on direction. The leader focuses on supportive behaviors in his or her communications to subordinates to bring out the skills required to accomplish the task. Subordinates have control over day-to-day operations, but the leader is still available for problem solving if needed. These leaders give deserved recognition to subordinates in a timely manner and support subordinates socially when needed (Northouse, 2010).

This style is most appropriate when subordinates have the required job skills but lack the necessary commitment because they are uncertain whether they have the necessary skills—when they have a moderate developmental level (D3); see the Situational Leadership II model in Northouse (2010). Direction is not required in this situation, but a lot of encouragement is needed to support subordinates in using their well-developed skill sets (Dubrin, 2007).

Delegating Leadership Style

The delegating style is best described as low direction and low support. In this approach, employees have more confidence and motivation when leaders are less directive and less supportive. Leaders agree with subordinates on the result but then back off and allow subordinates to be responsible for accomplishing the desired result. In essence, the leader gives the employees control and avoids any unnecessary social support (Northouse, 2010).

This approach is appropriate when subordinates are very skilled and highly committed—when they have a high developmental level (D4); see the Situational Leadership II model in

Northouse (2010). In this situation, giving subordinates more control and less social support is best because of their seasoned skills and motivation to do their best for the organization. Being even a little directive or supportive may cause subordinates to work less skillfully and with less commitment as they sense a lack of trust on the part of their leaders (Dubrin, 2007).

How Does the Situational Approach to Leadership Work?

The key to this approach is to understand that subordinates individually and as a group move along the developmental continuum. This movement could occur from day to day, week to week, or even over longer periods depending on the subordinates and the task to be accomplished. Effective leaders discern where subordinates are and adapt their style appropriately.

Questions that help leaders discern where subordinates are on the developmental continuum are as follows: What job needs to be accomplished? How difficult is the job? Do subordinates have the necessary skills to accomplish the job? Are subordinates sufficiently motivated to start and complete the job? In addition, understanding the directive and supportive behaviors available to leaders will enable them to use the appropriate behaviors depending on the answers to these questions (Northouse, 2010). The trait approach (Chapter 2) and the contingency approach (Chapter 6) suggest that leader style is fixed; the situational approach to leadership suggests that leaders need to behave in a manner that is adaptive and flexible (Yukl, 2006).

References

Ashby, M. D., & Miles, S. A. (2002). *Leaders talk leadership: Top executives speak their minds.* Oxford: Oxford University Press.

Blanchard, K., Zigami, D., & Nelson, R. (1993). Situational leadership after 25 years: A retrospective. *Journal of Leadership Studies, 1*(1), 22–36.

Dubrin, A. (2007). *Leadership: Research findings, practice, and skills.* New York: Houghton Mifflin.

Northouse, P. G. (2010). *Leadership: Theory and practice* (5th ed.). Thousand Oaks, CA: Sage.

Yukl, G. (2006). *Leadership in organizations* (6th ed.). Upper Saddle River, NJ: Pearson/Prentice Hall.

The Cases

Brookfield Properties: Crisis Leadership Following September 11, 2001

Brookfield Properties is a publicly held North American commercial real estate company focused on the ownership, management, and development of premier office properties located in the downtown core of selected North American markets. Most of Brookfield's assets are in the United States, with headquarters in New York and an executive office in Toronto. Four of the properties that Brookfield owns are adjacent to the World Trade Center site, and on September 11, 2001, the terrorist attacks had an immediate impact on Brookfield employees, tenants, and physical property. With little reliable information and in the face of chaos and human tragedy, the president and chief executive officer must develop an action plan that will ensure the safety of all employees and tenants, deal with grief and suffering, assess the damage, enable the company to return to business as usual, and reassure investors and the media of the company's commitment to restoring Brookfield's position of market strength.

Elite, Inc. (A)

Elite, Inc. is a highly successful public relations firm. Elite's chief financial officer has been spending 18-hour days in an effort to get his work done. The newly appointed chief executive officer must determine the cause of the excessive workload and develop a strategy to deal with the chief financial officer's performance.

▧ The Reading

Making Difficult Decisions in Turbulent Times

In turbulent times, some leaders make tough choices with courage and conviction. Others, however, remain indecisive. But most executives find ways to cope with uncertainty, ways that enable them to make sense of a confusing situation. In this article, the author describes seven strategies that leaders can use to cope with ambiguity and complexity when making decisions. He also points out their drawbacks, underlining the need to take great care when deploying these strategies.

Brookfield Properties

Crisis Leadership Following September 11, 2001

*Elizabeth O'Neil prepared this case under
the supervision of Kathleen Slaughter*

It was 4 p.m. on September 11, 2001, and Bruce Flatt, president and chief executive officer (CEO) of Brookfield Properties Corporation, had just approved the press release that would be issued shortly from the Toronto, Canada, office. The World Trade Center (WTC) in New York City had been the target of terrorist bombings that morning and the city was in chaos. Brookfield's four properties adjacent to the WTC appeared to have sustained considerable damage, but no concrete information was available. It seemed that employees and tenants had been safely evacuated. Flatt had to quickly formulate an action plan to manage this crisis and then get some input from Ric Clark and John Zuccotti, who ran Brookfield's U.S. operations.

▧ Brookfield Properties Corporation

Brookfield Properties Corporation was a publicly held North American commercial real estate company whose origins were in sports facility management.

In 1924, Canadian Arena Corporation, the predecessor to Brookfield, built the Montreal Forum to provide facilities for hockey and other sporting and cultural events. Until 1972, Brookfield's earnings were derived principally from the ownership of the Montreal Forum and the Montreal Canadiens of the National Hockey League.

During the 1960s, Brookfield expanded into various facets of the real estate business

Version: (A) 2003-01-13

and, in 1976, the company began to shift its focus to commercial real estate interests.

In 1990, a strategic decision was made to focus Brookfield's investments in premier office properties in select, high-growth, supply-constrained North American markets, including New York, Toronto, Boston, Calgary, Denver and Minneapolis. Over the next few years, the accumulation of these assets was completed through various purchases, including that of the former real estate assets of BCE Inc., Olympia & York, and Gentra Inc. (see Exhibit 1).

| **Exhibit 1** | Portfolio Listing—Commercial Properties by Region |

JUNE 30, 2002	Number of Properties	Leased	Office	Retail/ Other	Leasable Area	Effective Ownership Interest	Brookfield's Effective Interest
		%	000's Sq.Ft.	000's Sq.Ft.	000's Sq.Ft.	%	000's Sq.Ft.
NEW YORK							
World Financial Center							
Tower One	1	99.4%	1,520	108	1,628	100%	1,628
Tower Two	1	100.0%	2,455	36	2,491	100%	2,491
Tower Four	1	100.0%	1,711	89	1,800	51%	917
Retail		72.3%	—	287	287	100%	287
One Liberty Plaza	1	93.0%	2,194	20	2,214	100%	2,214
245 Park Avenue	1	99.9%	1,631	62	1,693	100%	1,693
Development sites							
CIBC World Markets Tower	1	—	1,200	—	1,200	100%	1,200
Penn Station	1	—	2,500	—	2,500	100%	2,500
	7	97.9%	13,211	602	13,813		12,930
TORONTO							
BCE Place							
Canada Trust Tower	1	99.6%	1,127	18	1,145	50%	573
Bay Wellington Tower	1	97.6%	1,295	42	1,337	100%	1,337
Retail, parking and office	2	98.3%	137	809	946	75%	705
Exchange Tower Block	2	98.4%	1,137	256	1,393	51%	708
HSBC Building	1	94.2%	188	37	225	100%	225
Queen's Quay Terminal	1	97.6%	428	74	502	100%	502
Other	3	92.4%	1,198	137	1,335	28%	380

JUNE 30, 2002	Number of Properties	Leased	Office	Retail/ Other	Leasable Area	Effective Ownership Interest	Brookfield's Effective Interest
Development sites							
Bay-Adelaide Centre	1	—	1,000	800	1,800	50%	900
Hudson's Bay Centre	1	—	535	557	1,092	25%	273
BCE Place III	1	—	800	—	800	65%	520
	14	96.9%	7,845	2,730	10,575		6,123
BOSTON							
53 State Street	1	99.9%	1,091	70	1,161	51%	592
75 State Street	1	93.8%	742	260	1,002	51%	511
	2	97.4%	1,833	330	2,163		1,103
DENVER							
Republic Plaza Office	1	95.1%	1,247	—	1,247	100%	1,247
Development and other	1	—	400	548	948	100%	948
Trade Center	2	90.1%	767	43	810	100%	810
Colorado State Bank Building	1	97.5%	412	—	412	50%	206
	5	93.9%	2,826	591	3,417		3,211
CALGARY							
Bankers Hall	3	91.4%	1,955	750	2,705	100%	2,705
Fifth Avenue Place	2	99.6%	1,427	254	1,681	50%	841
Petro-Canada Centre	2	98.0%	1,707	245	1,952	50%	976
Other	1	81.2%	—	108	108	100%	108
	8	95.5%	5,089	1,357	6,446		4,630
MINNEAPOLIS							
33 South Sixth Street (formerly City Center)	2	88.0%	1,082	695	1,777	100%	1,777
Dam Plaza	2	93.8%	593	638	1,231	100%	1,231
	4	90.4%	1,675	1,333	3,008		3,008
OTHER							
Royal Centre, Vancouver	1	92.4%	493	362	855	100%	855
Other	9	96.6%	2,920	884	3,804	100%	3,804
	10	95.3%	3,413	1,246	4,659		4,659

(Continued)

Exhibit 1 (Continued)							
JUNE 30, 2002	**Number of Properties**	**Leased**	**Office**	**Retail/ Other**	**Leasable Area**	**Effective Ownership Interest**	**Brookfield's Effective Interest**
Total portfolio	50	96.1%	35,892	8,189	44,081		35,664
Less other shareholders' interests							1,212
Brookfield's net effective ownership interest							34,452

SOURCE: Company files.

In September of 2001, Brookfield's market capitalization was approximately US$9 billion, with 80 per cent of the assets held in the United States. Of the company's nearly 2,000 employees throughout North America, two-thirds were operating employees located in Brookfield's properties.

In addition to commercial property management, Brookfield operated an office management services business, which managed over 120 million square feet of real estate, and owned a master-planned residential development business, which accounted for approximately eight per cent of Brookfield's asset value and constructed 3,000 single family homes annually (see Exhibit 2).

Brookfield was an inter-listed company whose shares traded on both the New York and Toronto stock exchanges under the symbol BPO.

▧ Competitive Strengths

Success at Brookfield was attributed to the strong teamwork demonstrated by employees, the customer service excellence that was a part of the corporate culture, and the company's strategic portfolio management.

In addition, senior management believed the company was well positioned for continued growth based on the following factors.

Unique, High-Quality Portfolio

Brookfield's portfolio of landmark office properties, including the World Financial Center complex in Manhattan and BCE Place in Toronto, was recognized as unique in North America. The office properties were modern, averaged 1.4 million square feet in size and were focused in the central business districts of select, major North American cities. Eighty-five per cent of Brookfield's portfolio was located in cities known for their ongoing high demand, such as New York, Boston and Toronto, ensuring stable, long-term growth.

Superior Quality Tenants

The quality and location of Brookfield's office properties, combined with a high commitment to service excellence, attracted highly successful organizations as tenants. Brookfield counted Merrill Lynch, JP Morgan Chase, Goldman Sachs, CIBC World Markets, RBC Financial Group,

| Exhibit 2 | Brookfield at a Glance |

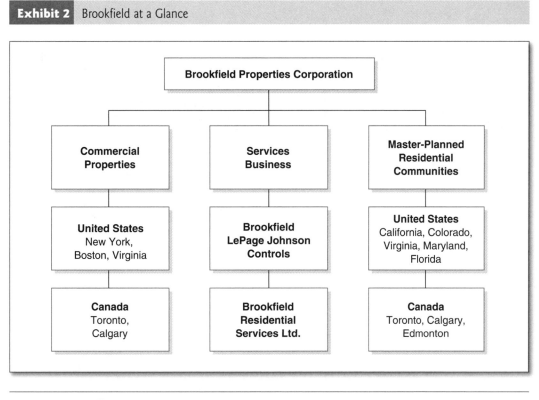

SOURCE: Company files.

Petro-Canada, Lehman Brothers and TD Canada Trust among its clients. These clients possessed high credit quality and therefore ensured the long-term sustainability of rental revenues.

Financial Strength

A conservative debt structure, quality streams of cash flow and the ability to retain cash flow provided financial strength and flexibility to fuel strategic growth. Brookfield's financial performance was captured in its Fact Sheet (see Exhibit 3).

Market Leadership

The second largest office property company in North America by total market capitalization—over US$9 billion—Brookfield had established a

leadership position in the key North American office markets with premier properties in prime downtown locations. In addition,

- Brookfield's master-planned community business was the largest Canadian-based residential development operation and among the largest home builders and land developers in the United States; and
- The services business was the largest provider of property management services in Canada.

Commitment to Customer Service Excellence

Brookfield was a leader in the real estate industry in providing innovative and timely customer

Exhibit 3 Fact Sheet

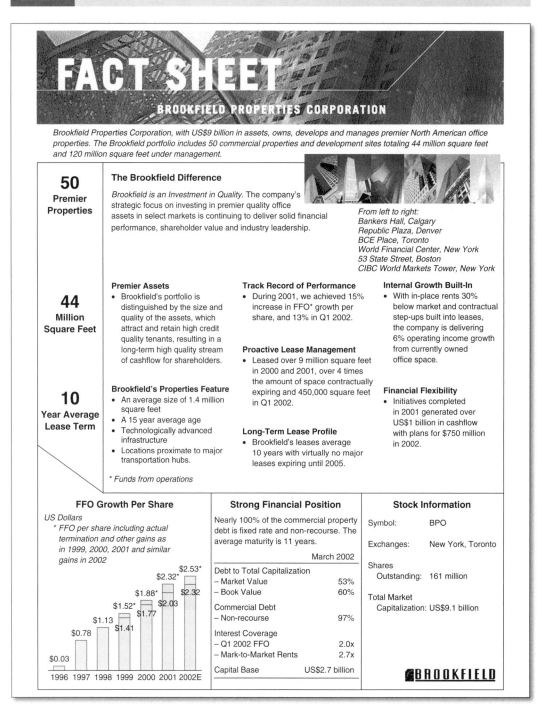

FACT SHEET
BROOKFIELD PROPERTIES CORPORATION

Brookfield Properties Corporation, with US$9 billion in assets, owns, develops and manages premier North American office properties. The Brookfield portfolio includes 50 commercial properties and development sites totaling 44 million square feet and 120 million square feet under management.

50
Premier Properties

The Brookfield Difference

Brookfield is an Investment in Quality. The company's strategic focus on investing in premier quality office assets in select markets is continuing to deliver solid financial performance, shareholder value and industry leadership.

From left to right:
Bankers Hall, Calgary
Republic Plaza, Denver
BCE Place, Toronto
World Financial Center, New York
53 State Street, Boston
CIBC World Markets Tower, New York

44
Million Square Feet

Premier Assets
- Brookfield's portfolio is distinguished by the size and quality of the assets, which attract and retain high credit quality tenants, resulting in a long-term high quality stream of cashflow for shareholders.

Brookfield's Properties Feature
- An average size of 1.4 million square feet
- A 15 year average age
- Technologically advanced infrastructure
- Locations proximate to major transportation hubs.

* Funds from operations

10
Year Average Lease Term

Track Record of Performance
- During 2001, we achieved 15% increase in FFO* growth per share, and 13% in Q1 2002.

Proactive Lease Management
- Leased over 9 million square feet in 2000 and 2001, over 4 times the amount of space contractually expiring and 450,000 square feet in Q1 2002.

Long-Term Lease Profile
- Brookfield's leases average 10 years with virtually no major leases expiring until 2005.

Internal Growth Built-In
- With in-place rents 30% below market and contractual step-ups built into leases, the company is delivering 6% operating income growth from currently owned office space.

Financial Flexibility
- Initiatives completed in 2001 generated over US$1 billion in cashflow with plans for $750 million in 2002.

FFO Growth Per Share

US Dollars
* FFO per share including actual termination and other gains as in 1999, 2000, 2001 and similar gains in 2002

1996	$0.03
1997	$0.78
1998	$1.13
1999	$1.52* / $1.41
2000	$1.88* / $1.77
2001	$2.32* / $2.03
2002E	$2.53* / $2.32

Strong Financial Position

Nearly 100% of the commercial property debt is fixed rate and non-recourse. The average maturity is 11 years.

	March 2002
Debt to Total Capitalization	
– Market Value	53%
– Book Value	60%
Commercial Debt	
– Non-recourse	97%
Interest Coverage	
– Q1 2002 FFO	2.0x
– Mark-to-Market Rents	2.7x
Capital Base	US$2.7 billion

Stock Information

Symbol:	BPO
Exchanges:	New York, Toronto
Shares Outstanding:	161 million
Total Market Capitalization:	US$9.1 billion

BROOKFIELD

BROOKFIELD

From left to right:
Petro-Canada Centre, Calgary
One Liberty Plaza, New York
Exchange Tower, Toronto

Strategic Priorities

- Maintain record of growth in FFO per share of greater than 15% and total cash return on equity of 20%
- Low-risk, high-return development of office properties on existing sites.
- Sale of partnership interests with institutional investors to surface value in mature assets.
- Acquisition of premier office assets in existing or new markets, consistent with current portfolio.

25
Major Properties Represent

80%
Of the Portfolio

Portfolio Distribution by Square Feet

New York 36%
Toronto 24%
Boston 5%
Denver 7%
Calgary 14%
Minneapolis 7%
Other 7%

Geographic Distribution
(By net operating income)

80% New York Toronto Boston
20% Denver Calgary Minneapolis

Value Per Share Comparison

Fully diluted shares outstanding:
165.5 million
(US Dollars)

Book Value	Market Value	NAV Analyst Consensus	NAV Brookfield
$12.32	$20.00	$22.50	$23.50

Average Lease Term (Years)

Brookfield's leasing profile is one of the strongest in the industry with one of the lowest rollover rates of any major North American office company.

Midtown New York	Downtown New York	Calgary	Toronto	Boston	Minneapolis	Denver	Average
14	11	9	5	6	5	5	10

Brookfield's average lease term across the portfolio is 10 years.

In New York and Boston, virtually no leases expire until 2005.

Five Year Common Share Dividend History

(US dollars)	1998	1999	2000	2001	2002
Mar. 31	–	–	–	–	0.10
Jun. 30	0.07	0.10	0.12	0.13	–
Sept. 30	–	–	–	0.10	
Dec. 31	0.09	0.12	0.13	0.10	–

*Effective September 2001, Brookfield initiated quarterly dividend payments replacing the semi-annual payment schedule. Record dates are set on the first business day of March, June, September and December.

Expected Earnings Release Dates

Quarter	Period Ending	Expected Release Dates
First	Mar. 31, 2002	Apr 22, 2002
Second	Jun. 30, 2002	July 31, 2002
Third	Sept. 30, 2002	Oct. 30, 2002
Fourth	Dec. 31, 2002	Feb. 2003

Investor Relations Contacts

Katherine C. Vyse,
Senior Vice President,
Investor Relations & Communications
Tel: (416) 369-8246
Fax : (416) 865-1288
E-mail: kvyse@brookfieldproperties.com

Melissa J. Coley, Vice President,
Investor Relations
Tel: (212) 417–7000
Fax : (212) 417–7194
Email: mcoley@brookfieldproperties.com

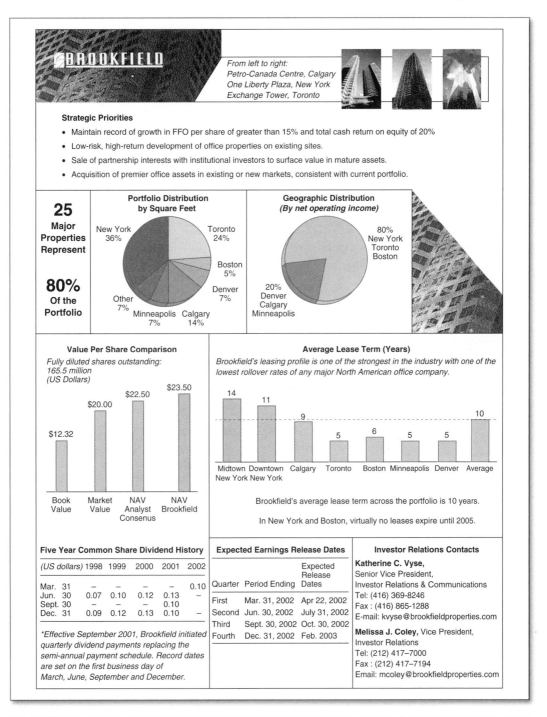

SOURCE: Company files.

service programs at the property level and for each individual tenant. This commitment was backed by extensive training and proactive recruitment practices that were embraced by the Brookfield team.

Brookfield's Management Team and Corporate Culture

Brookfield was a lean, fairly flat organization managed by a team of senior employees who worked hard to maintain the company's reputation for excellence (see Exhibits 3, 4 and 5).

Roles tended to be fluid, with employees often taking on projects and responsibilities that were not formally a part of their job description. The pace was fast but disciplined, and after a long day it was not uncommon for the group to socialize together.

Within the tight-knit group, communication was not a problem. In describing the effectiveness of communications at Brookfield, Melissa Coley, director of arts and events marketing in New York, said, "It's easy to know what's going on around here. Our offices are close to each other, we eat lunch together, we just *know* what's going on. In fact, if Ric didn't stop by my office once a day to ask how things were going, I'd wonder what was up."

Exhibit 4 Management Team Bios

Gordon Arnell

Chairman, Brookfield Properties Corporation

Gordon Arnell brings with him more than 25 years of real estate industry experience. Gordon joined Brookfield's predecessor company, Carena Developments Limited, in 1989 as President and CEO and was subsequently appointed Chairman and CEO of Brookfield. In April 2000, he assumed the role of Chairman.

Prior to joining Brookfield, Gordon was a senior executive at several major real estate companies, including: Oxford Development Group Ltd. of Edmonton; Trizec Corporation Ltd. of Calgary; and Trilea Centres Inc. A lawyer by training, he also practiced litigation and commercial law in Calgary.

Gordon holds Bachelor of Arts and Bachelor of Law degrees from the University of Alberta and was called to the Bar of Alberta in 1958. He is a Director of Brookfield Properties Corporation, Brookfield Financial Properties Ltd. and BPO Properties Ltd.

Ric Cark

President and CEO, US Commercial Operations

Ric is the President and Chief Executive of Brookfield's US commercial operations. Ric has been with Brookfield and its New York based affiliate, Brookfield Financial Properties (and its predecessor company, Olympia and York) since 1984 in various senior roles including Chief Operating Officer, Executive Vice President, and Director of Leasing.

Ric is a Certified Public Accountant and holds a business degree from the Indiana University of Pennsylvania. He is a member of the Brookfield Financial Properties' Board of Directors, a member of The Real Estate Board of New York's Board of Governors and a member of the Lincoln Centre Real Estate and Construction Council.

Steven Douglas
EVP and CFO, Brookfield
Properties Corporation

Steve Douglas was appointed Executive Vice President and Chief Financial Officer in July 2001, following four years as Senior Vice President and Chief Financial Officer and three years in various senior management positions at Brookfield. In his current role, he is responsible for corporate finance, reporting, tax and treasury for Brookfield and its subsidiaries. Prior to joining the company, Steve was affiliated with Ernst and Young in Toronto.

Steve is a Chartered Accountant and holds a Bachelor of Commerce degree from Laurentian University in Sudbury, Ontario.

Katherine Vyse
Sr. VP, Investor Relations
and Communications

Katherine Vyse joined Brookfield in early 2000. Her 14 year business career includes a similar role at a major North American real estate company and 10 years in the Financial Services industry. Katherine is currently responsible for expanding Brookfield's investor relations program and developing new investor relations and corporate communications vehicles and programs.

Katherine holds an MBA degree from the Ivey School of Business, a Bachelor of Arts degree from the University of Western Ontario in London, Ontario and a Retail Management Diploma from Sheridan College in Oakville. Katherine is a member of the Board of Directors of Canadian Investor Relations Institute (CIRI), Ontario Chapter.

Mark Brown
SVP, Finance

Mark Brown was appointed Senior Vice President, Finance in July 2001. Mark joined Brookfield in 2000 and has primary responsibility for managing the finance function for the U.S. commercial operations and contributing to the company's corporate financial strategies.

Prior to joining Brookfield, Mark spent 9 years with Salomon Smith Barney and Citicorp Real Estate, Inc. He holds a Masters of Business Administration from York University and a Bachelor of Commerce degree from Laurentian University.

John Zuccotti
Deputy Chairman,
Brookfield Properties

John E. Zuccotti, Deputy Chairman of Brookfield Properties Corporation, has specialized throughout his career in planning, housing, real estate and municipal law. He has played a leading role in the development process of major residential and commercial projects in the New York metropolitan area, served as director or trustee of many planning and development boards and has lectured at numerous institutions including Harvard, Columbia and Yale. John also served as the first Deputy Mayor of the city of New York from 1975 through 1977.

Prior to joining Brookfield, John served as President and Chief Executive Officer of Olympia and York Companies (U.S.A) and as a Partner in the law firms of Brown & Wood and Tufo & Zuccotti.

(Continued)

Exhibit 4 (Continued)

John graduated from Princeton University in 1959 and received his law degree from Yale University Law School in 1963. He was an officer in the United States Army.

Bruce Flatt
President and CEO,
Brookfield Properties

Bruce has been President and Chief Executive Officer since April 2000. Before joining Brookfield, he held a number of senior management positions at Hees International Bancorp Inc. from 1989 to 1992, and also worked for Arthur Young International, which is now part of Ernst & Young.

Bruce is a Chartered Accountant and holds a business degree from the University of Manitoba. Bruce is a director of Brookfield Properties Corporation, EdperPartners Limited, Noranda Inc. and Brascan Corporation.

Dennis Friedrich
EVP and COO,
Brookfield Properties

Dennis Friedrich was appointed Chief Operating Officer of Brookfield's US commercial operations in July 2001 following his role as head of Strategic Initiatives for the US property portfolio. In his current position, Dennis oversees Brookfield's commercial property operations comprising 18 million square feet of premier office space in New York, Boston, Denver and Minneapolis.

Prior to joining Brookfield, Dennis was co-head of Jones Lang LaSalle's Tenant Advisory practice in New York. He holds a business degree in finance from Baruch College and is a member of the Real Estate Board of New York.

David Arthur
President and CEO,
Canadian Operations

President and CEO of Brookfield's Canadian operations since February 1998, David is also Chairman of Brookfield LePage Johnson Controls. Through his 15 year career at Brookfield, David held the positions of President and Chief Executive Officer of Brookfield Commercial Properties Ltd., President and Chief Executive Officer of Brookfield Management Services Ltd. and a number of other management positions at related real estate companies. While at Brookfield, David has been involved in several major property acquisitions and new contracts, including the acquisition of the landmark Bankers Hall and Fifth Ave. Place complexes in Calgary.

David started his career with Cadillac Fairview and Cambridge Leaseholds. He holds a Master of Science in Urban Land Economics from the University of British Columbia and Bachelor of Urban and Regional Planning from the University of Waterloo. David is President of the Canadian Institute of Public and Private Real Estate Companies (CIPPREC) and is a member of the Young Presidents' Organization (YPO).

SOURCE: Company files.

Exhibit 5 Commercial Property Operations Organizational Chart

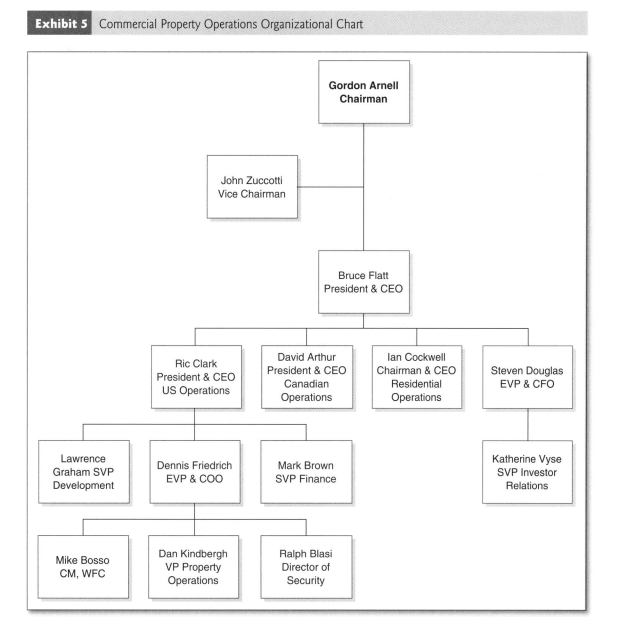

In Ric Clark's words:

This company was built around smart, dedicated, energetic, decent hardworking people. Since 90 per cent of our New York employees have been with Brookfield for over 10 years, it makes sense that our corporate culture in New York is collegial. Our philosophy is 'lead by example, share the credit, be a team player,' and that's what we try to do around here. As part of that team, I try to make myself available to anyone who has an idea or an opinion to share—actually, more people than I'd care to admit have my personal cell phone number.

Outside hiring did happen when necessary, but whenever possible, employees were grown in-house. Clark's own career path was an excellent example of this progression. He began his career as a financial analyst, then became an analyst in the leasing department, and eventually worked his way up to become the director of leasing. He was then made chief operating officer (COO) for Brookfield's U.S. operations and eventually became president of the same.

Having been involved with new hires at all levels, Clark cared "more about what a person is all about than what his or her background is." This philosophy was well respected by his colleagues, one of whom remarked: "Ric's got a *great* gut. He sure knows how to pick 'em!"

Bruce Flatt's colleagues also exhibited a great deal of trust in and respect for his leadership. One of his senior vice-presidents (SVPs) said about his style:

> Bruce is very, very good at recognizing the efforts of others in a genuine way. He always remembers to stop to say a simple "thank you" and lavishes praise publicly when things go well. And he is always calm and even-tempered, even when something goes wrong, which is a valuable talent when you are trying to encourage others to assume greater responsibilities, take risks and be creative. He is a true leader whom others gladly follow.

It was generally agreed that this culture of hard work, camaraderie, respect and trust was consistent across all Brookfield's North American offices.

September 11th—World Trade Center Attacks

On September 11, 2001, the world watched in horror as the twin towers of New York City's World Trade Center (WTC) were destroyed by what appeared to be acts of terrorism.

At 8:48 a.m. on that fateful Tuesday, a hijacked passenger jet (American Airlines Flight 11 out of Boston) crashed into the North Tower of the World Trade Center, causing a massive fire through several storeys of the building. Eighteen minutes later, at 9:03 a.m., a second hijacked jet (United Airlines Flight 175 out of Boston) crashed into the South Tower of the WTC and exploded, dispelling any thoughts that New Yorkers may have had about the crashes being accidental.

By 9:17 a.m., New York City airports were shut down by the Federal Aviation Association (FAA), and the Port Authority closed all bridges and tunnels in the New York area.

For the first time in U.S. history, at 9:40 that morning, the FAA halted all American flight operations across the country, and air traffic was diverted to the closest Canadian airports.

At 9:43 a.m., a third hijacked jet (American Airlines Flight 77) crashed into the Pentagon, which was then evacuated along with the White House. At 9:59 a.m. the South Tower of the World Trade Center collapsed. At 10:00 a.m., a fourth hijacked jet (United Airlines Flight 93) crashed just south of Pittsburgh in Somerset County, Pennsylvania. And at 10:28 a.m., the North Tower of the WTC fell.

In New York, Mayor Giuliani urged all New Yorkers to stay home if they had not yet come into the city. U.S. President George W. Bush reported that all security measures possible were being taken and asked for prayers from the public. Senior FBI sources reported that they assumed the four hijacked planes were part of a terrorist attack and that they suspected that Saudi militant Osama bin Laden was involved, based on "new and specific" information.

Media information coming out of Lower Manhattan was unreliable as the area had been declared a no-fly zone and the press could not access the WTC area, which had been cordoned off for several blocks. This led to much speculation as to the extent of the damage. Still, reports of death and critical injury made it to the forefront and, by mid-afternoon, 2,100 total injuries in New York were reported, with many more expected as rescue efforts progressed.

 ## Adjacent Buildings

With the general state of chaos and confusion in Lower Manhattan, it was impossible to say with any certainty what the extent of the damage was to the buildings surrounding the World Trade Center. Building 7 of the WTC was reported to be on fire due to its proximity to the WTC attacks. With phone lines down and access to the immediate area blocked off, accurate information was unavailable, but it was assumed that buildings in the surrounding area had suffered severely. Speculation also arose regarding damage done to the World Trade Center slurry (or "bathtub") wall—the structure that protected the WTC from water leakage from the nearby Hudson River.

Four of Brookfield's properties, comprising approximately 30 per cent of the company's total portfolio, were immediately adjacent to the WTC towers (see Exhibit 6) and had clearly sustained damage, but it was not known how much. In fact, three of these properties stood between the WTC and the Hudson River, and it was clear that other properties in the area were on fire or were severely damaged. The major tenants of these properties included:

Exhibit 6 Lower Manhattan Properties

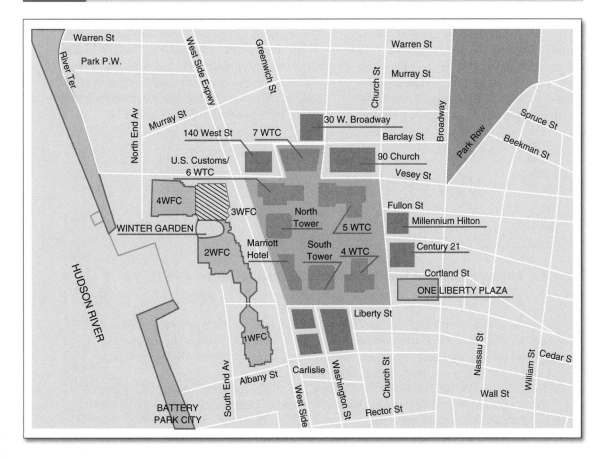

- One World Financial Center (Lehman Brothers, Dow Jones, National Financial Services, and RBC Dain Rauscher);
- Two and Four World Financial Center (Merrill Lynch); and
- One Liberty Plaza (Goldman Sachs, Cleary Gottlieb, NASD, Bank of Nova Scotia, Zurich, and Royal Bank of Canada).

Lastly, it was reported in the media that One Liberty Plaza (a 2.2 million square foot property that was 100 per cent owned by Brookfield) was on fire and in the process of collapsing.

⬚ Brookfield Responds

About that morning in New York, Clark said:

> I came into the office early that morning, around 7:00 a.m. I was working quietly in my office when I heard an explosion and felt the building shake. I ran to the other side of the floor [facing the World Trade Center] and

saw a hole in about six floors of the building. It was a giant fireball.

After calling home, I called Bruce and told him what had happened. He wanted to come to New York, but I told him not to come. I said "Bruce, don't do it. Don't come." It just wasn't safe. After the first plane hit, we evacuated all our employees and tenants— it was better to send them home than risk any potential harm.

Fortunately, Brookfield's corporate director of security, Ralph Blasi, had upgraded security procedures three years earlier when he assumed his position. He had hired a firm to develop emergency and disaster plans and manuals for all tenants, beginning with the New York properties, and all tenant evacuation plans had been revised. Prior to these changes, all 30,000 tenants had planned to evacuate into the Winter Garden area (a glassed-in atrium between the World Financial Center buildings) which had a capacity of approximately 2,500 people. Plans were changed to ensure the safe and timely passage of all tenants in the event that an evacuation would be necessary (see Exhibit 7).

| Exhibit 7 | Disaster Planner Has Lessons From 9/11 |

New York Times, July 10, 2002
Commercial Real Estate

Disaster Planner Has Lessons From 9/11 to Offer, and Boston Listens

By Michael Brick

As Ralph A. Blasi remembers it, the man who was trying to enter the World Financial Center on Sept. 11 as buildings burned nearby claimed to be a Verizon employee. The man would not take no for an answer, says Mr. Blasi, the director of security for Brookfield Financial Properties, manager of the World Financial Center.

"Punch this guy in the face, as hard as you can," Mr. Blasi says he remembers telling one of his security guards, delivering an order that was effective in changing the man's mind before the punch itself needed to be delivered.

That is Mr. Blasi's favorite part of the story. He includes it every time he talks about the evacuation. It is funny, in a dark way, and it gets his audience's attention. But of far more importance to the property managers here in Boston who have asked Mr. Blasi to repeat his story is what he did in the years before the terrorist attacks in drawing up an evacuation plan.

"I was totally fascinated with the way he delivered it, the no-nonsense story," said Michael Quinn, a senior vice president of Meredith & Grew who manages the 24-story building at 160 Federal Street in Boston and who is president of the local Building Owners and Managers Association. "You could see him choking up. It was like he was reliving the whole thing."

Mr. Quinn heard the story with officials of the local fire, police and emergency management departments, and they have asked all the managers of this city's skyscrapers to come hear Mr. Blasi tell it again in July. The point of Mr. Blasi's story is that landlords must join together to make disaster and security plans. Such coordination is a hard sell, because these landlords are direct competitors who closely guard every aspect of their operations and services from one another, using the information to attract and retain the same tenants.

But now, in these times of rattled nerves, Mr. Quinn said, the landlords are changing their minds.

"It's not really going to cost any money to coordinate our evacuation plans with the city, but I think it's an effective marketing tool, something you can take back to your tenants," Mr. Quinn said. "The idea right now is to renew your tenants."

Mr. Blasi's story is particularly harrowing when he tells it in his own office at the World Financial Center in New York, where he sits before a picture window overlooking ground zero and, at its edge, the damaged shell of the Winter Garden. He did that for a visitor late last spring, before all the property managers in Boston became interested. The story begins with his background.

He was a 22-year veteran of the New York Police Department, including stints on patrol in Queens and Brooklyn and a job as a homicide detective. He retired in 1995, did a little bartending and private investigation and eventually took the job with Brookfield. In 1997, he started asking World Financial Center tenants, including Merrill Lynch, Lehman Brothers, Dow Jones and Fidelity Investments, about their evacuation plans. He checked with the Mercantile Exchange, too.

All told, by his count, about 30,000 people planned to gather in the Winter Garden, a 10-story atrium with glass ceiling panels that served as a public entryway to the World Financial Center and connection to the World Trade Center through the North Bridge. It was built to hold 2,500 people—a fact that greatly affected his disaster planning.

When the first airplane hit the World Trade Center on Sept. 11, Mr. Blasi's staff cordoned off access to the North Bridge with ropes and posted a guard there, sending workers from the World Financial Center out into the streets. And turning away the man who claimed to be from Verizon.

That left room for people from the twin towers to evacuate across the North Bridge, which was eventually destroyed, and through the Winter Garden. Debris and bodies fell through the ceiling into the atrium, but many workers who might have been underneath were already trudging up the West Side Highway.

"The biggest thing now is showing there's a clear need to know what your neighbors are doing," Mr. Blasi said. "Everybody has their own plan, but nobody's talking." He has not taken this story on the road as a public speaker espousing some new management trend. In fact, Mr. Blasi has traveled to tell his story only in Boston and Minneapolis, the two cities outside New York where Brookfield owns substantial amounts of office space in crowded downtown towers.

(Continued)

Exhibit 7 (Continued)

For Brookfield, the business purpose is not to promote Mr. Blasi but to enhance security for the company's tenants, said Richard B. Clark, the chief executive of the Brookfield Properties Corporation, which owns 95 percent of the company that employs Mr. Blasi.

"Security is only as good as the weakest link in the area," Mr. Clark said.

Here in Boston, the story has resonated.

"If you had all of these tenants evacuate out into this," Lt. James Hasson of the Boston Police Department said as he drove a cruiser down Congress Street, "it would clog the street up, and this is a major artery. This is the extent of the high rises in Boston, but it's a lot of workers, if you can imagine them pouring out."

Property managers have extensively discussed security since Sept. 11, obviously, but only now are they beginning to coordinate their efforts. Mr. Quinn said he was just now beginning to ask his competitors about their plans, but he fears that "most buildings are likely to go to Post Office Square," a 1.54-acre park in the Financial District.

Until these recent discussions, Mr. Quinn said, managers had focused on their own individual buildings, making decisions about what to spend on guards and cameras and electronic identification cards.

But now, as rents decline, they are pressed to find less expensive tactics without compromising safety. Rents in the best high-rises downtown here have fallen to around $45 a square foot, from $70 in 2000 and $59 a year ago. Various brokers and building managers here estimate that security costs have risen 10 to 20 percent since September, adding 50 cents to $1 a square foot to average annual asking rents, excluding any effects of the cost of terrorism insurance.

"You don't want to be too secure," said James E. Fox, an asset manager for CB Richard Ellis who handles 1 Beacon Street, a one-million-square-foot office tower downtown with 50 tenants who employ a total of 3,500 people. "You want to show your tenants that you're being cost-effective, but also safe."

That, in part, is why managers like Mr. Fox plan to go hear Mr. Blasi talk, as soon as Mr. Quinn can bring him back to Boston.

As property managers set budgets for 2003, said Stephen P. Lynch, executive managing director of the Boston office of the real estate services firm Cushman & Wakefield, they are looking for ways to market the notion of enhanced safety without spending a lot on added security. Coordinating their plans and communicating their intentions may be unusual, he said, but it is inexpensive.

"This is one topic area where landlords are in open dialogue," Mr. Lynch said.

SOURCE: Reprinted with permission from The New York Times.

Flatt remembered his last conversation with Clark around 10:30 that morning, just before cellular phone connections went down. Clark told him:

Bruce—Ralph, Dan, and Mike are staying at the site. They're helping other buildings in the area evacuate. There are already cops on every street corner and they're trying to get everyone out of the area. I needed a security escort just to walk to the WFC buildings. I'm heading out of here now—I'll call you when I reach the Madison Avenue offices.

Flatt had seen the second WTC tower collapse on television shortly thereafter and had not had any contact with Clark since.

✕ Brookfield's Relationship With Local Officials

Many official government agencies had arrived at the scene of the attacks to assist with rescue efforts and to maintain order. Flatt knew the main agencies that Brookfield would have to work with:

- At the federal level: FEMA—Federal Emergency Management Agency;
- At the state level: The National Guard; and
- At the local level: The New York City Department of Design & Construction (DDC), The New York City Office of Emergency Management (OEM), the Office of the Mayor of New York, and the New York City police and fire departments.

Brookfield had always maintained good relations with government authorities, which Flatt felt would ease their interactions over the coming days and weeks. He also knew that having John Zuccotti, former deputy mayor of New York, as Brookfield's co-chairman would be an advantage. Zuccotti was always well prepared to act as the statesman in government dealings.

✕ Conclusion

It was 4 p.m. on September 11th, and Flatt sat at his desk, overwhelmed by the day's events and trying to decide what to do next. Brookfield had issued a press release (see Exhibit 8), but how would he make sure all employees and tenants were safe? How would they assess the damage and get beyond government barriers to start repairs, if that was even feasible? How would he deal with the grief and suffering being experienced by employees and tenants? Would offering reassurances of a plan to return to business as usual be insensitive with the degree of personal trauma being experienced? How could he reassure Brookfield's investors and the media of this commitment to restoring Brookfield's position of market strength? What was the best way to deploy his staff and structure communications to most effectively accomplish all this?

It was a critical time, filled with shock, horror, pain, suffering and potentially severe business losses. In the midst of chaos and uncertainty, Brookfield needed an action plan, quickly.

Exhibit 8	September 11th Press Release

Brookfield Responds to New York City Tragedy

New York, New York, September 11, 2001—(4:00 PM ETN) (BPO: NYSE/TSE)

Brookfield Properties Corporation, in response to the tragic events in the U.S., reported that its emergency plans were implemented, including the evacuation of tenants and employees from One Liberty Plaza and the World Financial Center, adjacent to the World Trade Center in downtown New York.

Bruce Flatt, President and CEO of Brookfield said: "We feel great empathy for the individuals and families involved in this tragedy and our hearts go out to them."

(Continued)

Exhibit 8 (Continued)

Brookfield has no ownership interest in the World Trade Center. Brookfield owns 100% of One Liberty Plaza, and 100% of Towers One and Two and 50% of Tower Four of the World Financial Center. From all accounts to date, Brookfield's properties sustained no structural damage. Glass replacement and clean-up programs will commence at the earliest opportunity.

Brookfield is co-operating with government and security authorities.

Mr. Flatt concluded "Our prayers go out to all of the victims of this great tragedy and their families."

* * * * * * * * * * * * *

Brookfield Properties Corporation, with over US$8 billion in assets, owns, develops and manages premier North American office properties. Brookfield also operates real estate service businesses and develops residential master-planned communities. The Brookfield portfolio spans 60 commercial properties and development sites totaling 46 million square feet. Brookfield is inter-listed on the New York and Toronto Stock Exchanges under the symbol BPO. For more information, visit the Brookfield Properties website at www.brookfieldproperties.com.

Contact Information

Katherine C. Vyse
Senior Vice President, Investor Relations and Communications
Brookfield Properties Corporation
Tel: (416) 369-8246
Fax: (416) 865-1288
Email: kvyse@brookfieldproperties.com

Elite Inc. (A)

Jessica Frisch prepared this case under the supervision
of Ann Frost and Lyn Purdy

It was April 1, 2000, and Fran Benson, chief executive officer (CEO) of Elite Inc., had just entered her office for the day. As usual, Benson went directly to her computer to check her e-mail. To her dismay, she had received another late-night message from Greg Jakes, the company's chief financial officer (CFO). Recently, Jakes had been spending 18-hour days at the office trying to get his work done. Jakes spent inordinate amounts of time checking over his daily tasks and projects and, even with the long hours at work, he could not meet his deadlines. With increasing pressure from the board of directors, Benson knew something had to be done about Jakes.

Company Background

Elite Incorporated, a highly successful public relations firm, was founded in Toronto,

Version: (A) 2003-10-06

Ontario, in 1960. The company's founders, Carl and Frank MacNeil, studied business at the University of Toronto, and the brothers had always had a keen business sense. Upon Frank's graduation in 1958, he took a job as a financial analyst with a large Canadian bank in order to gain business experience and learn more about the Canadian marketplace. When Carl graduated two years later, the brothers started up their own public relations firm using capital from their family and a substantial loan. Frank assumed the role of president and CEO while Carl assumed the role of vice-president, operations.

Elite became an incorporated business in 1972. For the next two decades, the company experienced great success with growing profits and healthy financial stability. The early 1990s, however, were troublesome for Elite. In 1991, Frank and Carl decided to purchase a new head office building in downtown Toronto. The combination of the large financial investment and the overall recession put the company into extreme financial difficulties. Nonetheless, with strong commitment from the management team, the company was profitable again by the first quarter of 1993. In 2000, Elite had 400 employees, offices in Toronto, Montreal and Winnipeg, and the brothers had received numerous awards for entrepreneurial excellence.

Company Culture

From its beginnings in the early 1960s, a distinct corporate culture could be observed at Elite. The small work force of 50 employees was flexible and co-operative, creating a relaxed and enjoyable atmosphere. Management and employees had a close relationship with open lines of communication. Daily meetings between executives and middle management and weekly meetings between middle management and employees helped keep information flowing throughout the organization. Employees reported a high level of job satisfaction. Frank and Carl, excited about their new business, would often take employees out for drinks on Fridays after work.

As the company continued to grow in the 1970s, the culture began to change. The co-operative nature of Elite had turned far more competitive; employees competed against one another for bonuses and pay increases. Also, Frank and Carl were less involved in the business than they had been in the company's formative years. As the work force grew to over 200 people, a gap formed between management and employees; there seemed to be no goal congruence between employee goals and corporate objectives. New employees did not take the same pride in the company's success as those who helped start the business from scratch.

One noticeable aspect of the company culture in the late 1970s concerned the employee demographics. With the exception of the clerical and administrative staff, 95 per cent of Elite's managers were male. This trend continued into the 1990s. Frank and Carl became concerned with the corporate culture at Elite, and their concerns were validated when employees chose to unionize in 1980.

Many factors led Elite employees to form a union. First, the flow of communication within the company had broken down. Although daily and weekly meetings were once a core part of Elite's culture, by the late 1970s, meetings were often skipped or cancelled altogether. Senior executives worked on the top floor of head office; management completely isolated themselves from the teams they were responsible for leading. Employees felt that management did not have respect for them, their needs or their ideas. Second, an 'us' versus 'them' culture had evolved in the company. All the power and decision making was in the hands of a few senior managers. Elite employees were not empowered to make decisions regarding their work; employees always had to ask for senior management approval, even when making minor changes to their projects. The third major factor that contributed to unionization was the punitive method of leadership at the company. Employees reported incidents of being screamed at for doing something 'wrong.'

The Service Employees International Union (SEIU) local formed in 1980, and it took years for Elite's management to adapt to its presence. Although management's relationship with the union had been somewhat amicable throughout the 1980s and 1990s, tension could be felt between management and the union. Frank and Carl often reminisced about the way things used to be at Elite.

A Change in Leadership

During the financial troubles of the early 1990s, employees and management worked together to revive the company. However, the 1990s presented many corporate challenges that required long hours at the office; Frank and Carl were working very hard and were becoming tired.

Frank MacNeil, CEO of Elite, decided to retire in 1999. Carl, VP Operations, also decided that he wanted to leave the company to pursue another business opportunity. Elite would need a new CEO. Frank was a perceptive individual and a realistic manager; he realized Elite's culture had deteriorated. Before leaving the company, he thought it was essential to obtain some guidance. Frank wanted suggestions about improving internal relations, and most importantly, he wanted recommendations regarding what he should look for in a new CEO.

Frank sought the advice of Rob Packard, a well-respected management consultant in the Toronto area. Packard agreed that many areas of the company needed improvement. Regarding the search for a new CEO, Packard looked Frank in the eye and said, "You need something fresh in here to shake things up."

A New CEO in 1999

Frank and Carl received several applications for the CEO position. They spent weeks going through resumes and interviewing candidates until they found Fran Benson. Benson was the vice-president of operations at a rival public relations firm in the Toronto area. She was admired by her employees and praised by the executive team. Benson had an undergraduate degree in mathematics and an MBA degree from a renowned Canadian business school. Frank felt that she was exactly what the company needed. Benson accepted the position on November 8, 1999, and she knew that she had a big job ahead of her. She spent hours in meetings with Frank and Carl, and she obtained advice, suggestions and records from Packard.

Benson started the transition by introducing herself to the employees. She met with each department individually; she set up coffee and doughnuts and spent time exchanging ideas and objectives regarding the company's direction. Benson knew it would be critical to create a strong bond with both her employees and, in particular, with her senior management team.

One senior manager remaining with Elite was Greg Jakes, the company's CFO. Jakes was an essential member of Benson's team, but unfortunately, Benson had already received some mixed reviews regarding his performance.

Greg Jakes

Jakes, a 50-year-old husband and father of five, was a loyal member of the Elite team. He had a business degree from McMaster University and was a certified management accountant (CMA). Prior to joining Elite, Jakes had held a management position at a multinational accounting firm for eight years. His recommendations from his former employer were positive; however, Elite was warned that as the organization grew, "Jakes would only be able to take the company so far."

Jakes was hired in the early 1980s as the CFO. He led the finance team at head office, consisting originally of five employees and growing to 13 employees by 2000. Jakes was responsible for compiling Elite's financial statements, conducting risk management analysis and investing the organization's funds. Jakes also worked with the information technology (IT) department on occasional projects. During the early 1990s, Jakes helped Elite overcome its financial troubles. He showed a high level of commitment and had in-depth knowledge of Elite's financial systems and general ledger.

Jakes had been the CFO of Elite for his entire career with the company, and when the CEO position became available, he eagerly applied. However, unknown to Jakes, there was no chance of his getting the promotion. The board of directors felt that he lacked the necessary leadership skills to advance and, furthermore, they did not consider him to be highly effective as the chief financial officer.

Jakes certainly had some positive attributes. He was known in Elite as a very nice man with a great sense of humor. He was liked by his co-workers, was known as a pleasant boss, and he was respected for being a good husband and father. Unfortunately, Jakes also presented some serious problems.

Throughout the years, Jakes had not been able to keep pace with the increasing level of complexity in the organization and within his role. In fact, it had become evident that Jakes had difficulty getting his work done and, for whatever reason, this situation was allowed to persist. Jakes spent far too much time paying attention to the details of his work. He was afraid of making a mistake and therefore spent inordinate amounts of time checking over his daily tasks and projects. It was not uncommon for Jakes to spend 18-hour days at the office to get things done. Even then, he could not meet the deadlines; the company's monthly financial statements often came out four weeks late. Jakes's behavior rubbed off on his team as well; the finance department repeatedly handed in late assignments or did not get assignments done at all. Jakes had so many projects going at once that he could rarely meet people's requests; he would start a task and would forget about it as he moved on to the next one. He did not know how to delegate, and it sometimes seemed as though he did not have a firm understanding of his work. Often, Jakes would be unable to answer questions about the material he was working on.

Furthermore, Jakes was not proactively managing the cash of the company. Frank and Carl had continuously asked him to research the diversification of Elite's investments, but Jakes never followed up on the requests. Every day that Jakes waited was costing the company significantly.

Benson's Task

Benson had been warned about Jakes when she took the position of CEO. There were so many challenges for Benson that, five months into the job, she had not yet addressed the situation. Despite the fact that Jakes had been turned down for the position of CEO, he had been very receptive to Benson. He helped her adapt to the company by sharing information and knowledge.

In the first few months of Benson's time with Elite, she had recognized many of Jakes's traits about which she had been forewarned. She had given him three new projects, and two were already past deadline. Also, she had received many late-night e-mails from Jakes regarding work that should have easily been completed during regular office hours.

Benson wanted to make a good impression with the board of directors at Elite, and she realized that she needed her entire executive to be motivated, competent and reliable. Furthermore, the company's board of directors, consisting of 12 major shareholders, had noticed Jakes's inefficiencies, and they were demanding that the situation be resolved. The board members were empathetic to his historical importance to the company; however, they were demanding changes in his behavior.

Benson needed Jakes to improve in three key areas: she needed him to re-engineer the company's financial systems, to be proactive about the company's financial issues and, at the very least, she needed him get his work done on time. Jakes was a pivotal figure in Elite, and Benson wondered how she could help him improve his performance.

Making Difficult Decisions in Turbulent Times

By Michael A. Roberto

In their own way, complexity and ambiguity tyrannize decision making. What managers need are strategies for making clear, accurate judgments under stressful conditions.

Napoleon Bonaparte once said that, "Nothing is more difficult, and therefore more precious, than to be able to decide." He recognized that a few critical decisions put leaders to the test. In turbulent times, some leaders make tough choices with courage and conviction. Others cannot cope with the complexity and uncertainty. They remain indecisive, and their rivals gain the upper hand.

Like Napoleon, today's business leaders must cope with a great deal of ambiguity as they make important choices about the future. They face uncertainty with regard to world politics, macroeconomic growth and stability, technology and changing consumer tastes. Many worry that an unknown event will transform their entire industry in a matter of a few weeks or months.

Most executives find ways to cope with this uncertainty. They adopt strategies for simplifying complex situations so that they can make decisions quickly and effectively. These strategies enable managers to make sense of a confusing situation. In this article, I describe seven strategies that leaders can employ to cope with ambiguity and complexity as they make critical decisions. The strategies are reasoning by analogy, imitation, rules of thumb, reformulation, deference to experts, rigorous debate, and experimentation. These strategies often prove very effective because they enable leaders to make accurate judgments under stressful conditions. Unfortunately, each of these strategies has serious drawbacks as well. When employing these techniques, many leaders draw the wrong conclusions, make biased estimates, pursue flawed policies, or impede the development of commitment within their management teams. Thus, leaders must use these strategies with great care.

⊠ I. Reasoning by Analogy

Business leaders often draw analogies with past experiences when faced with a complex problem. They draw comparisons to similar situations or circumstances from their past or the history of other organizations, and deduce certain lessons from those experiences. John Rau, a former CEO and business school dean, argues that analogies provide a wealth of information: "The fundamental laws of economics, production, financial processes and human behaviour and interaction do not change from company to company or industry to industry. Reading about other companies makes me a better decision maker because it provides a store of analogies." (J. Rau, "Two Stages of Decision Making," *Management Review,* December 1999). Indeed, researchers have shown that people in a variety of fields, from foreign policy to firefighting, reason by analogy as a means of coping with complexity and ambiguity. They enable people to diagnose a complex situation very quickly and to identify a manageable set of options for serious consideration.

Analogies prove especially useful when decision makers do not have access to complete information and do not have the time or ability to conduct a comprehensive analysis of alternatives.

Unfortunately, most analogies are imperfect. No two situations are identical. Many decision makers spot the similarities between situations very quickly, but they often ignore critical differences. In foreign policy, officials often refer to the "Munich analogy" when making decisions. When confronted with international aggression, many world leaders argue against appeasement by drawing comparisons to Hitler's belligerence during the 1930s. They argue that British Prime Minister Chamberlain's decision to appease Hitler in 1938 actually encouraged him to pursue further expansion. Political scientists Richard Neustadt and Ernest May point out, however, that not every situation parallels the circumstances in Europe in the late 1930s. For example, they argue that President Truman would have been well served to identify the differences, as well as the similarities, between Korea in 1950 and Czechoslovakia in 1938. Ignoring these distinctions may have impaired the United States' strategy during the Korean conflict.

Business leaders often draw imperfect analogies as well. Take the recent dot-com boom, for example. Several market research firms projected the growth of on-line advertising by drawing analogies between the internet and other forms of media. They examined the historical growth in advertising in other media industries and projected Internet growth by selecting the analogy that they deemed most appropriate. In doing so, they failed to recognize the critical differences between the Web and other media such as television and radio. Similarly, many research firms project the demand for new technologies by drawing analogies to the adoption rates for VCRs, personal computers and cell phones. Again, the differences among these technologies are often rather striking, yet they receive scant attention.

Analogies prove especially useful when decision makers do not have access to complete information and do not have the time or ability to conduct a comprehensive analysis of alternatives.

⊠ 2. Imitation

When faced with uncertainty and environmental turbulence, some business leaders emulate the strategies and practices of other highly successful firms. After all, why reinvent the wheel; one way to simplify a complex problem is to find someone who has already solved it. Learning from others can pay huge dividends. At General Electric, former CEO Jack Welch launched a major best practice initiative in 1988. He credits this initiative with fundamentally changing the way that GE does business and produces substantial productivity gains. Welch and his management team identified approximately 20 organizations that had long track records of more rapid productivity growth than GE. For more than a year, GE managers studied a few of these firms very closely. They borrowed ideas liberally from these organizations and adapted others' strategies and processes to fit GE's businesses. For instance, they learned "Quick Market Intelligence" from Wal-Mart and new product development methods from Hewlett-Packard and Chrysler. Over time, imitating others became a way of life at GE, and it produced amazing results.

All of this learning sounds wonderful, but imitation has its drawbacks. In many industries, firms engage in "herd behaviour." They begin to adopt similar business strategies, rather than develop and preserve unique sources of competitive advantage. Take, for example, the credit card industry. Many firms have tried to emulate the highly successful business model developed by Capital One. Over time, company marketing and distribution policies have begun to look alike, rivalry has intensified, and industry profitability has eroded. Consider too the many instances in which a leading firm decides to merge with a rival, touching off a wave of copycat acquisitions throughout an industry.

In times of great turbulence and ambiguity, executives may feel safe imitating their rivals rather than going out on a limb with a novel business strategy. However, the essence of good strategy is to develop a unique system of activities that enables the organization to differentiate itself from the competition or to deliver products and services at a lower cost than its rivals. Simply copying the strategies and practices of rival firms will not produce a unique and defensible strategic position. It takes great courage to stand alone when rivals engage in herd behaviour, but it can pay huge dividends. Being different does not mean that a firm refuses to learn from others. For instance, General Dynamics studied its rivals very closely during the turmoil in the defence industry in the early 1990s, and observed that many firms had decided to pursue commercial diversification to compensate for diminishing military spending. The company's historical analysis indicated that aerospace firms had not fared well during past diversification efforts. Therefore, it chose to focus on defence despite the precipitous decline in industry demand. Many rivals ridiculed this strategy at the time. Yet for the past decade, General Dynamics has generated shareholder returns well in excess of that of most large competitors.

3. Rules of Thumb

In many situations, managers cope with ambiguity and complexity by adopting a rule of thumb, or heuristic, to simplify a complicated decision. These shortcuts reduce the amount of information that decision makers need to process, and shorten the time required to analyze a complex problem. Often, an entire industry or profession adopts a common rule of thumb. For example, mortgage lenders assume that consumers should spend no more than 28 percent of their gross monthly income on mortgage payments and other home-related expenses. This provides a simple method for weeding out consumers with high default risk. Computer hardware engineers and software programmers have adopted many rules of thumb to simplify their work. Many of us are familiar with one such rule, Moore's Law, which predicts that the processing power of computer chips will double approximately every

18 months. Finally, the conventional wisdom in the venture capital industry used to suggest that firms should demonstrate four consecutive quarters of profits before launching an initial public offering. Alas, many venture capitalists regret abandoning this rule during the dot-com frenzy of the late 1990s.

Many executives also develop heuristics for their own firms. For instance, Dennis Kozlowski, CEO of Tyco International, uses a few rules of thumb to simplify his firm's acquisition screening and evaluation process. Tyco considers hundreds of potential acquisition targets per year. Conducting an in-depth analysis of each firm would take enormous time and effort. To streamline the decision process, Kozlowski and his management team only consider deals that are friendly and immediately accretive to earnings. These two rules of thumb enable managers to weed out unattractive deals very quickly and to conserve precious organizational resources.

In most cases, heuristics enable managers to cope with ambiguity and to make sound judgments in an efficient manner. Rules of thumb can be dangerous, though. They do not apply equally well to all situations—there are always exceptions to the rule. While industries and firms employ many idiosyncratic rules of thumb, researchers also have identified several, more general heuristics that can lead to systematic biases in judgment. Let's consider two prominent shortcuts: availability and anchoring. Individuals typically do not conduct a thorough statistical analysis to assess the likelihood that a particular event will take place in order to estimate probabilities. Vivid experiences and recent events usually come to mind very quickly and have undue influence on people's decision making. This availability heuristic usually serves people well. However, in some cases, easily recalled information does not always prove relevant to the current situation and may distort our predictions.

When making estimates, many people also begin with an initial number drawn from some information accessible to them at the time, and they adjust their estimate up or down from that starting point. Unfortunately, the initial number often serves as an overly powerful anchor, and restrains individuals from making a sufficient adjustment. Researchers have shown that this "anchoring bias" affects decision making even if people know that the initial starting point is a random number drawn from the spin of a roulette wheel! In sum, many different rules of thumb provide a powerful means of coping with uncertainty and complexity. But they also impair managerial judgment when people fail to recognize their drawbacks and limitations.

⊠ 4. Reformulation

Social psychologist Karl Weick has noted that decision makers can gain traction on complex problems by reframing them as "mere problems." Complicated issues can overwhelm people because they cannot cope cognitively and emotionally with the uncertainty, complexity and stress associated with trying to solve the problem. Redefining a serious challenge as a series of smaller problems enables people to make decisions more manageable. They can adopt a strategy of "small wins" in order to build momentum and make steady progress toward achieving the overall objective.

Business leaders employ this strategy all the time. For example, when Bill Anders took over General Dynamics in 1991, the company stood at the brink of bankruptcy. He framed the immediate problem as the need to generate the cash required to pay down the enormous amount of debt carried on the company's balance sheet. To address this issue, the firm divested several businesses and sold a number of assets. Then, Anders and his team set out to tackle a series of other problems that had contributed to the firm's poor performance. Another example occurred when Julie Morath became the Chief Operating Officer at Minnesota Children's Hospital and set out to tackle the complicated and highly sensitive

problem of medical errors. To make early progress, she broke down the challenge into a series of smaller initiatives, and gradually shifted the organization's entire approach to patient safety.

The risk associated with a "small wins" strategy is that leaders might choose to make incremental adjustments in a firm's strategy, while missing the opportunity and the necessity for more radical changes. My colleague, Clayton Christensen, has written extensively about how firms can become fixated on making incremental improvements while failing to recognize disruptive changes in technology. Effective managers utilize a "small wins" approach but recognize its limitations. For instance, when Kevin Dougherty and his team crafted an e-commerce strategy for Sun Life's group insurance business, they focused first on the opportunity to create value by transferring existing business processes to the Web. After experiencing some success, they recognized the incremental nature of many of the changes that they had made. Dougherty and his team worried that a competitor might use the Internet to create a completely different business model. They did not want to be "Amazoned" by such a rival. Therefore, the team began intense discussions about the possibility of more radical changes in the business unit's strategy. Dougherty's team coped effectively with uncertainty by keeping their eye on the big picture while pursuing a series of small wins.

⊠ 5. Deference To Experts

Most executives rely heavily on experts in a pertinent domain to inform their decision-making in complicated situations. Occasionally, top teams bring in outsiders who can offer knowledge and experience that is unavailable within the firm. On many senior teams, managers defer to other members who have relevant expertise on a particular issue. These experts have credibility, and command respect from others inside as well as outside the organization. For example, I have observed a top team in which one member exerted a great deal of influence on acquisition decisions because he had negotiated many merger deals throughout his career.

When making complex, unstructured decisions, experts can play an important role because they bring to bear a rich accumulation of experiences from which they can draw inferences, develop hypotheses and pose challenging questions. Their experience enables them to recognize patterns over time and across situations. They can use this pattern recognition ability to simplify complex situations very quickly and effectively.

Some teams, however, do not make good decisions when they defer to experts. Experienced members of a group can dominate a discussion and discourage constructive dissent. As a result, teams may converge prematurely on a suboptimal alternative. The Kennedy administration's infamous decision to support an invasion of the Bay of Pigs provides a vivid example of this phenomenon. In that decision process, experts from the Central Intelligence Agency exerted undue influence during the decision-making process. During those early days of the Kennedy administration, less experienced advisers deferred to the CIA officials, and even engaged in self-censorship when they held opposing views. Consequently, the Kennedy team failed to test critical assumptions embedded in the CIA plans and considered a very narrow range of options. By all accounts, the input and advocacy of a few highly credible experts proved to be a burden rather than a blessing.

Deference to experts may also diminish a team's commitment to a decision, and thereby impede implementation. Consider the case of a division president who typically assigned a small subgroup of his management team to analyze decisions in detail. For each situation, the division president selected individuals with relevant expertise. The subgroup developed and evaluated alternatives, and then shared their recommendation with the entire team. Naturally, others viewed these recommendations as a fait accompli and did not feel comfortable expressing dissent during the team meetings. If they had objections, they waited to raise them at some future date, often derailing the implementation process. In short, deference to experts may diminish commitment if other team members feel that they have not had an adequate opportunity to express their views and to influence the final decision.

✎ 6. Rigorous Debate

Rather than relying on expert judgments, some management teams may wish to grapple with ill-structured decisions by stimulating a rigorous debate among all members. In situations of great uncertainty, a lively debate can clarify and refine people's ideas, and enhance shared understanding of complex problems. In his book, *Only the Paranoid Survive* (Currency/Doubleday, 1996), Intel chairman Andy Grove explained that "debates are like the process through which a photographer sharpens the contrast when developing a print. The clearer images that result permit management to make a more informed—and more likely correct—call." Indeed, constructive conflict encourages the generation of multiple alternatives and ensures that teams will critically evaluate each option. Healthy debate also enables managers to separate facts from assumptions, and to surface and evaluate the latter very carefully.

> *Many successful business leaders employ constructive conflict as a means of clarifying and sharpening their ideas during uncertain times.*

For instance, Chuck Knight, the former CEO of Emerson Electric, always sparked heated debates during his firm's strategic planning meetings. He asked tough questions and forced his managers to examine all sides of an issue. Knight believed that debate provided a clearer assessment of the threats and uncertainties in the competitive landscape. Similarly, Jack Welch often explained that constructive conflict was an essential feature of strategic planning at General Electric. As one of his colleagues once said, "Jack will chase you around the room, throwing arguments and objections at you. Then you fight back . . . if you win, you never know if you've convinced him or if he agreed with you all along and was just making you strut your stuff." (J.L. Bower, "Jack Welch: General Electric's Revolutionary," Harvard Business School Case Study 0-394-065).

Conflict and dissent can prove to be very productive if managed appropriately. However, many debates result in a stalemate between opposing camps within management teams. Subgroups retrench into rigid opposing positions and cannot resolve their differences. Often, these stalemates lead to interpersonal conflict, ranging from personality clashes to emotional outbursts and personal attacks. This dysfunctional form of conflict makes it difficult to build commitment, and diminishes the likelihood that team members will want to cooperate with one another during implementation. For these reasons, leaders must adopt a variety of techniques for managing conflict effectively. These include discouraging the use of inflammatory language, asking people to argue several different sides of an issue, shifting people out of their traditional roles, and requiring teams to revisit key facts and assumptions when an impasse is reached.

7. Experimentation

The final technique that executives employ to cope with ambiguity in strategic decision-making is experimentation. In this mode, managers avoid making a big bet under murky conditions. Instead, they stage a small test, gather feedback and adjust their strategy based upon what they have learned. They may run a second experiment at that point, or managers could decide to make a much bolder move. Alternatively, they could decide to abandon the project. This type of learning process enables managers to gradually reduce uncertainty and gather new information about customers and markets. For instance, throughout Home Depot's history, managers have tested new retailing concepts that they were not certain would become popular with customers. During the test, they gathered customer feedback and evaluated various measures of performance. Then, they made a decision regarding how to proceed. Many of these concepts evolved over time based upon the learning from these experiments.

When managers engage in experimentation, they need to be aware of the sunk-cost effect—the tendency for people to escalate commitment to a course of action in which they have made substantial prior investments of time, money or other resources. If people behaved rationally, they would make choices based on the marginal costs and benefits of their actions. The amount of any previous unrecoverable investment in that activity should not affect the current decision. Unrecoverable investments represent sunk costs that should not be relevant to current choices. However, research demonstrates that people often do consider past investment decisions when choosing future courses of action. In particular, individuals tend to pursue activities in which they have made prior investments. Often, they become overly committed to certain activities despite consistently poor results. As a result, individuals often escalate their commitment to failing courses of action. The sunk-cost effect can make it particularly difficult for decision makers to abandon unsuccessful experiments. Because managers do not want to "waste" their prior investment of time, energy and money, they may persist with future tests or scale up projects despite signs of poor performance during the initial experiment.

Process Evaluation

There is no magic bullet when it comes to making complex decisions in a turbulent environment. Managers must develop a repertoire of strategies that they can employ under these conditions. Moreover, they need to develop their management team's capability to utilize these practices and techniques. At the same time, leaders must be keenly aware of the risks associated with each strategy, and they need to raise the awareness of those around them. Leaders should not stop there. They also must audit their decision-making processes, preferably in real time. As their management teams discuss complicated problems, leaders need to step back and assess the quality of the decision-making process. They must identify the strategies that managers are using to cope with uncertainty and complexity, and try to spot any dysfunctional behaviour. To audit their decision process, leaders can ask some simple questions: What shortcuts are we employing? Is the team converging prematurely on a single alternative? Are experts exerting undue influence? Have we drawn the appropriate analogy? Are we engaging in herd behaviour? Have we discouraged dissent? Leaders ought to encourage their entire management team to ask these kinds of questions. They should strive to raise everyone's awareness about process issues. By doing so, leaders will enhance their team's ability to make tough choices under stressful and uncertain conditions, and hopefully, avoid the dismal fate of the Emperor Napoleon.

The Contingency Theory of Leadership

Those parameters are going to be different for different individuals. And for the same individual, they're going to be different for different tasks. Some people are going to be very inexperienced in certain things, so you need to be careful about setting the parameters of where they have authority and where they need to stop to seek clarification. Other people have experience, skills, and a track record, and within certain areas you want to give them a lot of latitude.

—Robert Howard[1]

In Chapter 5, we described the situational approach to leadership as an approach that suggested to the leader what to do in different situations. This requires a great deal of flexibility on the part of the leader (Yukl, 2006). In the contingency theory of leadership, it is assumed that the leader's style is relatively stable and needs to be matched with the most appropriate situation for the leader's style (Daft, 2005). Fiedler and Chemers (1974) call contingency theory a leader–match theory. The closer the match between leader style and a particular situation, the more effective the leader will be.

Leadership Styles

As with the theories in Chapters 4 and 5, in contingency theory leadership, styles are broadly described as falling into two categories: task motivated and relationship motivated (Dubrin, 2007). Fiedler (1967) placed these two styles on opposite ends of a continuum and developed a

---

[1]Robert Howard is the chairman and CEO of Levi Strauss & Co.

scale he called the Least Preferred Coworker (LPC) scale. When a leader scores high on the LPC, it means that the leader is relationship oriented, whereas being low on the LPC means that the leader is task oriented (Daft, 2005). Task-oriented leaders want to achieve goals. Relationship-oriented leaders want to develop close relationships with their followers (Yukl, 2006).

Situational Variables

The contingency model helps leaders evaluate three variables using a dichotomous measure. In essence, leaders ask three questions: Are the leader–member relations good or poor? Is the task structure high or low? Is the leader's position power strong or weak? Answering these three questions allows leaders to determine what situation they are in and whether their style is a good match for that situation (see Figure 6.1).

Criteria for assessing these three variables are shown in Table 6.1. The variables need to be assessed in the order they are presented in Figure 6.1 and Table 6.1. As these are fairly self-explanatory, we will discuss the intersection of leadership styles with the situations defined by these three variables.

As mentioned, the order of these three variables is important. Leaders should examine leader–member relations, then task structure, and, finally, position power (Yukl, 2006). Good leader–member relations combined with high task structure and strong leader position power (Position 1 in Figure 6.1) is a very favorable situation for leaders. Poor leader–member relations combined with low task structure and weak leader position power (Position 8 in Figure 6.1) is the most unfavorable situation for leaders.

Contingency theory suggests that leaders with a low LPC score (those who are very task motivated) will be most effective in these two situations. In addition, leaders with middle LPC scores will be effective in Position 1 as well as being effective when the situation is assessed as being somewhat less favorable (Positions 2 to 3 in Figure 6.1). Furthermore, leaders with low LPC scores are effective in Positions 2 to 3. Finally, in situations that are moderately favorable to somewhat less favorable (Positions 4 to 7 in Figure 6.1), leaders with a high LPC score (very relationship oriented) will be most effective (Dubrin, 2007).

Figure 6.1   Contingency Model

Leader–Member Relations	GOOD				POOR			
Task Structure	High Structure		Low Structure		High Structure		Low Structure	
Position Power	Strong Power	Weak Power	Strong Power	Weak Power	Strong Power	Weak Power	Strong Power	Weak Power
	1	2	3	4	5	6	7	8
Preferred Leadership Style	Low LPCs Middle LPCs				High LPCs			Low LPCs

SOURCE: Adapted from Fielder (1967). Used by permission.

Table 6.1	Three Variables in the Contingency Model	
Leader-member relations	**Good**	**Poor**
	Subordinates like leader trust leader get along with leader	Atmosphere unfriendly friction between leader/followers Followers no confidence in leader no loyalty to leader not attracted to leader
Task structure	**High**	**Low**
	Task accomplishment requirements clear few paths to achieving task end to task clear solutions limited	Task accomplishment requirements vague and unclear many paths to achieving task end to task vague many correct solutions
Leader's position power	**Strong**	**Weak**
	Leader has authority to hire subordinates fire subordinates promote give pay raises	Leader has no authority to hire subordinates fire subordinates promote give pay raises

SOURCE: Adapted from Northouse (2010). Copyright © 2010, Sage Publications, Inc.

How Does the Contingency Theory of Leadership Work?

The answer to this question is not entirely clear. Why are leaders with low LPC scores best in very favorable and most unfavorable situations? And why are leaders with high LPC scores most effective in situations that are moderately favorable? These are two questions that are still unanswered. Fiedler (1995) has suggested why a mismatch between situation and style may not work. A mismatch leads to anxiety and stress, more stress leads to coping mechanisms developed earlier in a leader's career, and these less developed coping mechanisms lead to bad leader decisions and, consequently, negative task outcomes (Northouse, 2010).

However, while we may not be able to explain why a mismatch between style and situation does not work and a match does work, we can predict whether a leader will be effective in certain situations and not in others. Consequently, assess several work-related situations based on the three variables in the contingency model, assess your own leadership style (are you mostly task oriented, relationship oriented, or somewhere in the middle?), and choose the best situation for your leadership style (Daft, 2005).

References

Daft, R. L. (2005). *The leadership experience* (3rd ed.). Mason, OH: Thomson, South-Western.

Dubrin, A. (2007). *Leadership: Research findings, practice, and skills.* New York: Houghton Mifflin.

Fiedler, F. E. (1967). *A theory of leadership effectiveness.* New York: McGraw-Hill.

Fiedler, F. E. (1995). Reflections by an accidental theorist. *Leadership Quarterly, 6*(4), 453–461.

Fiedler, F. E., & Chemers, M. M. (1974). *Leadership and effective management.* Glenview, IL: Scott, Foresman.

Howard, R. (1992). Values make the company: An interview with Robert Haas. In W. Bennis (Ed.), *Leaders on leadership: Interviews with top executives* (pp. 33–53). Boston, MA: Harvard Business Review.

Northouse, P. G. (2010). *Leadership: Theory and practice* (5th ed.). Thousand Oaks, CA: Sage.

Yukl, G. (2006). *Leadership in organizations* (6th ed.). Upper Saddle River, NJ: Pearson/Prentice Hall.

The Cases

A Difficult Hiring Decision at Central Bank

The case is designed to encourage readers to select among three highly qualified candidates for an important managerial position. In doing so, readers are required to establish the set of criteria that they believe should be taken into account when making an important hiring decision for the bank. Through the process of considering and prioritizing potential criteria with respect to the three candidates, readers are led to evaluate and reflect on the vision, mission, and core value of the bank.

Christina Gold Leading Change at Western Union

The chief executive officer of Western Union had just begun implementing a new organization structure. Changing the structure sent out a clear message of Gold's desire to change the company's mind-set to a new, more global culture. Already the CEO was finding that leaders in the United States were reluctant to give up control of product lines. At the regional level, she had keen leaders in place who wanted to push out the responsibility within their own regions and move toward a decentralized plan. While the CEO supported this notion in principle, she wanted to ensure that the right leaders could be placed in decentralized offices in order to execute on the six strategic pillars that she had laid out for the organization. One thing was certain—the CEO had made it clear that no revenue decreases would be forgiven amid the change. Many considerations had arisen: What pace of change should she take? How would she deal with resistance to change? How could she ensure that the new structure would support Western Union's global expansion?

The Reading

What Engages Employees the Most, or the Ten Cs of Employee Engagement

In selecting this reading, we looked for one that suggested leaders need to be high on relationship behaviors. We believe that most businesses will be in that middle portion (Positions 4 to 7) on the contingency model, and this is where the model suggests that we need relationship-oriented leaders.

Practitioners and academics have argued that an engaged workforce can create competitive advantage. These authors say that it is imperative for leaders to identify the level of engagement in their organization and implement behavioral strategies that will facilitate full engagement. In clear terms, they describe how leaders can do that.

A Difficult Hiring Decision at Central Bank

Prepared by Mark S. Schwartz and Hazel Copp

The Challenge

Martin Smith, vice-president (VP), Regional Sales at Central Bank, had recently been let go, and the search for his replacement was taking place. As part of the recruitment process, several candidates for the position needed to be ranked, while taking into account Central Bank's recently established vision, mission, and values (see Exhibit 1).

Exhibit 1	Central Bank's Vision, Mission, and Values

Vision
- To be the leader in client relationships.

Mission (Employees)
- To create an environment where all employees can excel.

Mission (Clients)
- To help them achieve what matters to them.

Mission (Community)
- To make a real difference in our communities.

Mission (Shareholders)
- To build the highest total return for shareholders.

Core Values: Trust
- Act with integrity, honesty, and transparency, open and candid, treat others with dignity and fairness, behave according to ethical principles, operate with integrity and support our colleagues.

Core Values: Teamwork
- Work collaboratively with others; share info; respect opinions of others, listen attentively, ask for input and feedback.

Core Values: Accountability
- Live up to commitments, accept overall responsibility for behavior, admit mistakes and learn from them, seek clarity on roles.

Version: (A) 2009-09-15

⊠ Background

The position would require managing a number of employees in a region just outside of Toronto (see Exhibit 2).

Through conversations with Smith's former supervisor, Central Bank's Executive Resources established the background that led to Smith's dismissal:

- "Values driven" and well liked by his staff
- Strong community ties/profile
- Lowest turnover rate in segment
- Employee satisfaction scores in middle of pack
- Region in last place; results poor/growth stalled
- Integration of new segment incomplete
- Critical new processes/procedures not bought into or implemented
- Dismissed the previous week, decision unpopular in Region
- Three years away from early retirement, 30 years with Central Bank

---

Exhibit 2   Job Posting: Vice President, Sales

Business Unit Description

With over 1,200 locations in the Canadian marketplace, our premiere Retail Banking segment represents the soul of the Central Bank brand and is the key to our long-term success. Our in-branch retail professionals provide a range of financial services to clients, from savings and chequing accounts, mortgages and loans, small business credit solutions and investment products, to complete financial planning.

Purpose of Position

To lead effective and profitable sales execution of multiple customer offers in the Region and to maximize the contribution generated by its retail customers. Lead the advancement of the Region's market share and profitability through delivery of an excellent customer and employee experience.

Work closely and cooperatively with internal service and operations providers and other regional colleagues to better position Central Bank as the pre-eminent financial services provider in Canada. To improve Central Bank's reputation with customers, regulators and government and create an environment where employees can excel.

Provide leadership to the design and execution of segment-wide and cross-segment initiatives.

Accountabilities of Positions (Key Outcomes and Activities)

Establish a vision and clear purpose for the region; inspire commitment to the vision in employees and colleagues in a manner that puts the best interests of Central Bank and its customers first.

Develop, communicate and manage an aggressive regional sales plan aligned to national strategies and based on a deep understanding of regional market conditions, customer segments and resource requirements; drive the sales, business development and sales management processes for the region.

(Continued)

Exhibit 2 (Continued)

Build a customer-focused, high-performing sales team in the region that focuses on maximizing profitability, growth and customer loyalty; employ rigorous hiring practices/policies to ensure newly hired and current sales staff subscribe to all of Central Bank's values and professional standards.

Ensure all delegated roles, responsibilities and accountabilities are well defined and understood; apply metrics to measure and manage performance and foster continuous improvement.

Lead employees through periods of organizational change and maintain high levels of motivation during transition period; coach and mentor staff; actively support staff in their professional growth and personal development.

Deliver customer offers in accordance with core Central Bank business strategies, risk management requirements and Brand standards; build keen awareness of governance and regulatory requirements and closely manage process to monitor adherence.

Develop close partnerships with local leaders of all customer segments; build integrated sales plans where possible to maximize customer coverage.

Model the values of the organization internally and in the community; encourage staff to actively participate in their communities and publicly acknowledge their efforts.

Competencies (Skills and Knowledge)

Highly developed leadership skills; experience turning around a business or managing significant business change is highly desirable.

Proven ability to develop and manage a world-class sales force in a highly competitive business environment. Candidates must have:

- a track record for delivering aggressive financial and business growth targets;
- a staffing model and experience recruiting high performing sales staff;
- a well-honed and highly successful coaching methodology;
- demonstrated sales prospecting and sales tracking capabilities.

Expert knowledge of business and financial planning processes is required; demonstrated financial discipline and cost management capabilities.

Ability to manage relationships between various customer offers, delivery channels and support/supplier groups; demonstrated ability to work collaboratively across Central Bank to achieve collective business goals and satisfy customer needs.

Ability to instill respect for risk management and compliance requirements and deliver effective processes/systems to manage all aspects of operational, regulatory, market, credit and reputational risk.

Ability to translate strategic intent into action, communicate action/direction openly and effectively up, down and across the region.

Able to represent Central Bank in various external communities of interest.

Attributes Required

Trustworthy (e.g., Integrity); Relationship builder; Team Player/Builder; Accountability (i.e., Results orientation); Customer focus; Adaptability

Smith's former supervisor also provided a summary of "what went wrong":

- Need to be liked got in the way of critical changes
- Thought there was a trade-off between performance and values
- Couldn't make the tough people calls
- Said he bought into sales process/disciplines but didn't enforce the process
- Hadn't built appropriate relationships with colleagues in other strategic business units; no previous goodwill to help smooth integration of new segment
- Business continually left on table due to poor teamwork between segments
- Would blame others (often Head Office) for lack of success
- Should have moved on Smith earlier, *but* he'd been around for so long

Smith's former supervisor provided an indication of what he believed was needed:

- Major turnaround
- Build new team; exit players who can't deliver
- Hire well; recruit people who can deliver and have required values
- Get buy-in into new sales processes/value of a more disciplined approach
- Employ a person who can build trust/relationships with other segments to grow business
- Hire a candidate who could ultimately prove to be a good "succession" candidate.

The Candidates

Following an initial screening and interview process (see Exhibit 3) conducted by Central Bank's Executive Resources, the number of final candidates had been reduced to three. The following provides a summary of each of the final candidate's profiles.

Exhibit 3	Interview Questions/Responses of the Three Candidates

1. Describe the culture in which you do your best work.

Charlotte Webb:

I'm the sort of person who likes a work environment that provides some challenges professionally. So far, Central Bank has provided that for me. What's most important to me now is the ability to grow career-wise. I like working with bright people, in an organization that is willing to take some risks. I'm not talking about recklessness, but I like working for an organization that wants to operate at the "cutting edge" with respect to conducting business, one that is attuned to the market, uses technology and analytics to the fullest, and knows where it wants to play. It's also important to me how organizations treat their people, that people are rewarded not only for achieving goals, but for how they are achieved as well.

Scott Warren:

I guess I can speak best about the Royal, which puts a heavy focus on being number one. That's the sort of place where I do my best work. I like everything to be fast paced, with clear deadlines to meet. As well, when the firm allows its managers and employees to take reasonable risks, and be rewarded for results, that's best for me, that's when I'm most motivated. I also like "hands-off" managers, I really don't like being micromanaged.

(Continued)

Exhibit 3	(Continued)

James Skinner:

The First Northern bank culture works for me, it's critical to me that employees and customers are treated with respect and dignity, where people can work as a team. I don't subscribe to the "star" system, where only the top performers receive all of the rewards. I like to think through the short- and long-term implications of what we do, and I appreciate a culture that supports that. I really dislike the "churn" that results from poor planning and last minute changes. Those sorts of twists and turns are really tough on people.

2. What's the toughest call you have had to make?

Charlotte Webb:

While working at a Central Bank branch as a summer student, a friend of my dad's came in, and asked me for some personal information on his ex-wife's bank accounts. They were going through an ugly divorce, and it was very awkward for me given my family's connection to say no, and my desire to please an important customer. I knew that I shouldn't give him the information, and I politely refused, but he became very vocal and threatened to pull out his accounts. I knew I was doing the right thing but it was pretty tough, I was so junior at the time.

Scott Warren:

I can't say anything I've ever had to do was really that "tough" or "difficult." I guess I'm just the sort of person who does what has to be done, and tries not to think too much about it afterwards. But if I had to pick something, it would be when I was working as an executive director in corporate finance in Australia, and there was pressure coming from Head Office to close off our loan book, since we were beginning to close down Australia. One of our clients was in trouble could easily have been put on the watch list. He had a seasonal business and was desperate to buy more time. It was still within my discretion in terms of what to do, but it was somewhat of a tough call to let his account ride since I could have had some difficulties with Toronto, but I did think the guy deserved a chance, and in the end everything worked out and we got our money back.

James Skinner:

Well, it probably was last year when my wife got sick, and I had to give up an opportunity to become a senior VP in the Calgary office. It was an opportunity that I had been waiting for, for years. In the end you make the right decision for your family, but it wasn't easy, letting the opportunity that I had worked for slip through my fingers.

3. What would you be afraid to find if you got this job?

Charlotte Webb:

I wouldn't exactly say "afraid" is the right word, but if you're asking me what I think the biggest challenges would be, I would say winning over the staff, who will know I don't have a lot of line experience, and introducing sales discipline to the group, but it's a challenge I'm happy to accept. It's not the first time I've gone in without all the required skills, but I think my record shows I've not only met the desired targets, but exceeded them as well.

Scott Warren:

I'm concerned that it would take forever for me to get ahead, and that people don't really get rewarded for producing results. I'm willing to do whatever it takes, to deliver, but my expectation would be that I would be rewarded accordingly.

James Skinner:

This is a very important question for me, so I'm very glad you asked it. I am concerned whether Central Bank is more focused on the "numbers" than on people. I know this is perhaps the wrong perception, but I'm also concerned about teamwork issues at Central Bank; too many "silos" and "revolving doors." It's certainly perceived to be a very different culture here, but despite my concerns, I believe I'm up for the challenge.

4. How do you feel about the recent emphasis being placed on corporate governance?

Charlotte Webb:

It certainly has been a lot of work for managers throughout the organization. I used to spend 5 per cent of my time on what I would loosely call governance, but in the last year that has shot up to 45 per cent. No one could argue that this isn't critical, or necessary, but I certainly would hope that once we have installed the governance engine, that the time requirements will be reduced. It's not just about enforcing rules and regulations and policies, it's also about making sure you've hired the right people.

Scott Warren:

I guess you're referring to Sarbanes-Oxley and the Basel Accord stuff. I'm really not sure whether it will make a difference at the end of the day in terms of discouraging the "bad apples"—I think all of those CEOs and CFOs involved in the recent scandals knew what they were doing was wrong, but did it anyways. People always seem to find a way around laws and regulations. But at the end of the day, it's important for the banks to comply with what the regulators want, because none of us can afford to lose the trust of our customers. But hopefully as the checks and balances are built into the system, it won't continue to be as cumbersome as it has been at the front end.

James Skinner:

I'm very happy to see the renewed emphasis being placed on corporate governance. It's been needed for a while to remind everyone of the importance of having rules and regulations. I think that people have forgotten that firms have responsibilities to their shareholders and the public. I believe that unfortunately sometimes very ethical people can be placed into an organization with certain pressures to perform that can make them do some very bad things. We need to renew the public's faith in the corporate world, and this seems to be the best way of doing it.

5. Describe an ethical dilemma you have faced in the workplace and how it was resolved.

Charlotte Webb:

I was in an awkward situation a few years ago. The department was required to dramatically reduce its expenditures. What this meant was that we could no longer sponsor things like department lunches, or have prizes for reaching certain goals. At first the managers accepted it, but then a number of people started to become upset when they saw how the VP, who enforced

Exhibit 3	(Continued)

the rules with all of us, was continuing to spend on lavish dinners, staying at upscale hotels, and continuing to use limos. None of these expenses seemed to lead to a return on business, everyone could see the VP taking people out, he wasn't even discreet about it. When people started complaining to me, I decided to see the VP. I suggested to him that he might be setting a poor example for everyone, and that he might want to cut down on the expenses before someone decided to raise the issue with his supervisor. He became very annoyed, said he wasn't really prepared to discuss it with me further, that there was an agenda that I wasn't fully aware of. Although it appeared afterwards that he did in fact cut down on some of the excesses, unfortunately our working relationship was strained from then on, in fact sometimes he was quite verbally abusive to me, and on one occasion he even pushed me to tears in front of a group of colleagues. After that, I just took the first opportunity I could to move out of that division.

Scott Warren:

I'm not sure if I've ever really faced a true ethical dilemma, but I did have an issue once that related to Royal's Code of Conduct. In about half my branches, I have responsibility for wealth management, we were courting some high net worth individuals, and I wanted to plan a day that they would really enjoy and differentiate us from the other banks. But that meant taking me over my approved entertainment budget. I knew Royal's code spoke about "moderate" business entertainment, but these were some pretty important potential clients. I wanted to take them golfing and for dinner at Glen Abbey, since I certainly couldn't take them to the local municipal course. I debated whether I needed to get my supervisor's approval since I suspected my supervisor would probably stick to the code, and wouldn't be able to see the bigger picture. As it happened, my supervisor was away on vacation, and I was able to get it approved by Head Office. When my supervisor returned he was very upset at first that I had gone over his head to get approval, until he found out that I managed to bring in about $30 million dollars in new assets, which he agreed justified the few thousand spent.

James Skinner:

I think I've probably faced many ethical dilemmas over my career. It's hard to pick just one, but if I had to it would probably be the story of how I met my wife at First Northern bank. She was my administrative assistant at the time, and I struggled with whether to disclose the relationship, particularly when it became more serious, knowing that it was "taboo," that it was frowned upon. The way we resolved it though was to hide the relationship, to the point where no one had any idea we were together. In the end the dilemma resolved itself, we ended up getting married, my wife ended up leaving the bank, and no one knew any differently.

Candidate: Charlotte Webb (Internal Candidate)

Current Position: Senior Director, Customer Experience, Marketing Division (Toronto)

Status: First round interview with VP, Executive Resources completed

Background

Webb was the only internal candidate to be short-listed. She worked at Central Bank during summers while in university, initially as a teller, and then in the marketing division and for one year between her undergraduate and postgraduate degrees. Webb was recruited to the World Bank from the London School of Economics, and assigned to the World Bank offices in Geneva and Washington, DC, for a total of four years.

A desire to return to Canada prompted her to reconnect with Central Bank. Initially hired as a senior analyst in January of 1998 by the Corporate Strategy unit, she had exposure to many of Central Bank's businesses and, while in that role, led a number of strategically critical and enterprise-wide projects. In 2001, Webb was seconded into Central Bank's Small Business Division to help implement a new go-to-market strategy she had crafted. The role was made permanent, and she was appointed general manager (GM), Small Business Sales and Operations in early 2002. In January of 2004, Webb applied for and secured her current role in the Marketing Division (see attached resume, Exhibit 4, for greater detail).

Exhibit 4	Résumé: Charlotte M. Webb

Charlotte M. Webb
177 Roxborough Drive, Toronto, Ontario M8T 2C7
Phone: 416-376-8827
E-mail: charlotte.webb@cibc.ca

Career Summary

Seasoned author and executor of far reaching corporate strategies that deliver tangible business results. Demonstrated thought, people and values leadership capabilities. Award winning corporate and community citizen.

Education

1994 Masters in Economics, London School of Economics, London, England
1991 Bachelor of Science, Applied Mathematics & Statistics, University of Waterloo (Ontario Scholar—full scholarship to university)

Professional Experience

Central Bank: 1998–Present
February 2003–Present
Senior Director, Customer Experience & Communication, Marketing Division

- Led initiative to transform customer experience at Central Bank in all delivery channels. Worked across SBU lines to engage all relevant participants in cultural and operational changes required to position Central Bank as the premiere Canadian Bank.
- Diagnosed root causes of customer dissatisfaction and defection; segmented issues into employee and operations related challenges and recommended solutions. Received approval for 80% of suggestions, achieving buy-in from all business units and infrastructure groups. (Cost reduction delaying implementation of remaining 20%).
- Developed innovative training programs for front line staff that minimized time away from customers, provided a standard Central Bank customer interface across Central Bank, improving both customer and employee satisfaction ratings.

(Continued)

Exhibit 4 (Continued)

- Worked with product groups and front line management to reduce product "fatigue"; reduced number and complexity of products available, producing just-in-time interactive training modules that significantly increased sales volumes.
- With process re-engineering specialists, explored solutions to common customer irritants related to lengthy or unreliable processes/procedures; liaised with Technology & Operations Division to resolve existing challenges and gain support for new initiatives.

August 2000–January 2003
General Manager, Small Business Sales & Operations

- Led Small Business executives through design of new go-to-market strategy for segment; assessed lifetime value of small business client by conducting statistical and segmentation analysis; analysed competitive environment and best practices.
- Provided strategic options and led deliberations to validate and choose optimal direction; worked with VP, Strategic Initiatives to translate strategy into operational plan for deployment across Canada.
- Implemented new sales and resourcing model for segment which included new client team configuration, revised roles and accountabilities and new sales discipline. Provided tools to assess sales versus service capabilities and introduced new compensation plan to incent sales force.
- Worked with central operations group to achieve better efficiencies and improve client service; liaised with Branch Banking group to facilitate improved in-branch service of Small Business clients and to increase cross selling opportunities.
- Achieved: 24% revenue growth, versus corporate target of 12%; ten point increase in client satisfaction ratings, grew market share by 5%.

May 1998–August 2000
Senior Analyst, Corporate Strategy, Office of the Chairman
Responsibilities included leading projects, analyzing/developing new business opportunities; providing analytical support for key business decisions.
Projects included:

- Customer Strategy Project for Business Segment: Led customer preference/conjoint statistical analysis, resulting in the divesture of unprofitable unit and increased investment in profitable business.
- Growth Strategy for E-Business venture: Worked with McKinsey to explore feasibility of moving successful banking venture into US and European markets. Helped develop detailed go forward plan, emphasizing regulatory challenges and recommending alliance partners.

August 1994–November 1997
The World Bank, Washington, D.C.; Geneva

- Supporting teams comprised of World Bank, Eastern European Development Commission and the United Nations in the financial restructuring of the Balkan States.
- Conducted preliminary needs assessment for economic reconstruction of the Ukraine. Supported commission examining banking needs/functions in various developing countries.

Scholarships and Awards

1999	Present: Rated "exceeds expectation" on all performance evaluations
2004, 2002, 2001	Quarterly Achiever Award Recipient
1991	Big Sister of the Year Award
1992	Young Woman of Distinction, Toronto YWCA
1987	Ontario Scholar
1987	University of Waterloo Entrance Scholarship

Affiliations:

- United Way Coordinator and Spokesperson
- Run for the Cure Campaign Manager for GTA
- Board of Directors, Centre for Family Literacy
- Chair of Fund Raising, Bayview Centre for Abused Women

People were eager to work for Webb because of the emphasis she put on personal development. Many of her "graduates" had gone on to bigger and better roles because of the challenges/exposure she provided and her willingness to hire on potential and coach/mentor for missing skills.

Webb was currently viewed as one of Central Bank's highest potential level 10s. She sustained high performance ratings over the last six years and had been the recipient of numerous internal awards based on her superior contributions to the organization. While this new position would constitute Webb's first front-line role, this experience would fill an important development gap for her.

At her most recent performance review, Webb requested just such an opportunity to round out her experience and wondered aloud how many more years she was destined to spend at the same level. She also voiced disappointment that Central Bank had gone outside the organization repeatedly for VP hires, overlooking talented insiders. Retaining Webb was a priority for Central Bank.

Education

Havergal alumnus. Has undergraduate degree in Mathematics and Statistics from the University of Waterloo. Graduate of the London School of Economics.

Strengths Relative to This Role

- Highly intelligent, superior analytic and strategic skills
- Very eager to learn, had taken every opportunity to acquire new skills/perspectives
- Big-picture thinker, had long-term perspective
- Very high energy level, expected a lot of herself and others
- Positive, can-do attitude, engaging, gots things done
- Quick study, had grasped complex and diverse business equations with relative ease
- Superior knowledge of financial needs and delivery preferences of this segment's customers (currently leading initiative to enhance the quality of customer experience in all delivery channels)
- Had successfully developed strategies, objectives and sales programs for several business segments, key contributor to the sales measurement and tracking systems currently in use
- Had operationalized and executed a sales program for Small Business that resulted in aggressive growth, successfully led a roll-out of sales process across Canada

- Respected and well liked by her team, Employee Commitment Index (ECI) scores among highest in Bank
- Very principled, good examples of doing the right, rather than the expedient, thing
- Good influencing skills, successfully delivered initiatives across SBU lines despite competing agendas

For Consideration

- Minimal front-line interaction, had "knowing" rather than "doing" perspective of sales
- Had hired several professional staff, but never exited anyone
- While her roles had clearly influenced the direction of the business, most of her interactions had been with Head Office types
- Had led "thought" turnaround, rather than "people/business" turnaround
- Could personalize issues, on occasion, cared too much and got emotional
- Thinks very quickly, question whether she could bring others (slower staff) along
- Suspect she will always do "the right thing" but occasionally came across a bit pedantic/righteous
- Once raised concerns over supervisor's seemingly improper use of his expense account, matter later resolved as a "misunderstanding"

Of Interest

- This candidate had been very active in both Central Bank's Run for the Cure and United Way efforts. Several years ago, Webb was named "Young Woman of Distinction" by the Toronto YWCA for her work with the Big Sisters' group. Albeit junior, she was a popular member of Central Bank's informal women's network

- Webb is the niece of a Central Bank Board member. The Director commented on "Webb's great interest in this role" when he bumped into the hiring manager at a recent social gathering

Webb was five months pregnant, and it was not clear how long a maternity leave she would require.

Candidate: Scott Warren

Current Position: VP, Retail Bank, Toronto West & Hamilton, Regional Bank

Status: Interviewed by executive search firm and VP, Executive Resources, Central Bank

Background

Warren originally planned to pursue a career in the foreign service or international law but a stint with Nesbitt Burns (between his undergraduate and law degrees) sharpened his interest in financial services. Recruited to McKinsey's Montreal office after articling with a prominent Ottawa law firm. Recruited by Regional Bank (former client) two years later to work on a high-profile new venture in Australia; Warren returned to Toronto after the venture was terminated and was put on an accelerated management program. Served 12-month stints in both Audit and Risk and was then selected from bank's high-potential pool to work as executive assistant to Regional Bank's chairman. Warren moved out of the chairman's office into his first executive posting and his first line role. He had been in this post, the smallest territory nationally, since December 2001 (see Exhibit 5).

Warren was chafing against Regional Bank's long-term and disciplined approach to development and felt that he should have been moved to a bigger, more complex mandate or promoted to senior vice-president (SVP). He believed that he could move up the ladder

| **Exhibit 5** | Résumé: T. Scott Warren |

T. Scott Warren
28 Bayview Crescent, Oakville, ON M3P 1B9
Telephone: 905-846-3321 (Home); 416-307-2215 (Business); 416-537-9856 (Cell)
Confidential e-mail address: melissaandscott@rogers.com

Profile

A seasoned financial services professional with broad managerial experience. Motivated by challenging environment, aggressive goals, teamwork and the opportunity to make a tangible contribution to an organization's performance.

Professional Experience

Royal Bank of Canada
December 2002–Present
Regional Vice President, Toronto West & Hamilton

- Led all aspects of Regional Bank's retail business in Toronto West & Hamilton area; executed dramatic turnaround of region (last to first place) within first 18 months. Sales volumes increased by 60%; significantly exceeding profitability and cost management targets. Steps to achievements:
- Assessed existing branch location and resource deployment; closed branches in four unprofitable locations, piloted two new state of the art branches with enhanced physical design and front-end technology.
- Significantly upgraded Regional talent pool, exiting 35% and redeploying 15% of workforce; designed and implemented comprehensive assessment process (now adopted by Regional Bank overall) for sales ability; seeded region with top talent identified in recruitment blitz.
- Used available Customer Relationship Management (CRM) tools and Risk Management expertise to mine more affluent pockets in region, greatly increasing the number in profitable customers and reducing credit losses.
- Helped design and pilot training program for front line staff; content included advanced use of CRM tools, prospecting techniques and selling "the Regional Bank way".
- Re-segmented customer population along "share of wallet" and potential to cross-sell lines; focused efforts on high yield sales activities resulting in increased sales volume of most profitable products.
- Negotiated successful referral program with Regional Bank colleagues to grow customer base.
- Led measure and manage project for Regional Bank Branch Banking, redesigning sales metrics and rewards.

(Continued)

Exhibit 5 (Continued)

October 2001–October 2002
Acting Vice President, Office of the President & CEO

- Chosen from the high potential pool for assignment. Responsible for ensuring the smooth operation of the President & CEO's business day by anticipating needs, organizing events, undertaking strategic analysis and preparing presentations. Work with departments throughout the organization to deliver pertinent and timely information to the President and CEO's office.
- Operate as a conduit for information from the bank's various divisions to the President & CEO's office.

June 2000–October 2001
Accelerated Management Program, Toronto, Canada

- *Audit Division:* Participated in audits of Wealth Management and Retail Banking units in Canada, West Indies and Guernsey. Co-led project to define new Audit philosophy for Regional Bank and to enhance the effectiveness of the function.
- *Risk Management:* Assigned to Credit Adjudication for Commercial Bank Group; participated in initiative to re-engineer end-to-end credit processes relating to Commercial and Corporate Banking.

February 1998–March 2000
Executive Director, Regional Bank, Australia

- Crafted strategy, provided legal expertise for Regional Bank entry into Australian corporate finance market; led integration efforts with newly acquired firm.
- Originated, negotiated and executed senior debt, mezzanine and equity financings for acquisitions, leveraged buy-outs, and other structured corporate finance transactions.
- Developed valuation models and negotiated to sell Regional Bank's corporate finance business in Australia.

January 1996–February 1998
Management Consultant, McKinsey & Co., Montreal, Canada

- Created customer profitability strategy for Travel and Hospitality client. Helped reposition brand, did service profit chain analysis and recommended product and service innovations which resulted in brand turnaround.
- Helped Canadian Oil & Gas company launch new venture for European exploration and production, significantly broadening their operating base and increasing profitability.
- Performed business unit, product/channel and customer profitability studies for retail wealth management business unit, resulting in product bundling and pricing policy changes.
- Developed acquisition and integration strategy for Corporate banking arm of leading Canadian bank. Developed detailed integration plan and managed "first 100 days" project teams, including contractual negotiations, regulatory requirements and infrastructure build.

May 1994–May 1995
Articling Student, Wise, Strong & Kessler, Barristers and Solicitors, Ottawa, Ontario

- Provided corporate, commercial, securities, tax, insolvency, and litigation legal services.

Education

1994 LLB (Bachelor of Laws), Osgoode Hall Law School, York University
1991 BA (with Honors), Government, Harvard University

Achievements and Interests

Fluent in French
Currently working on MBA (Richard Ivey School of Business, The University of Western Ontario)
Qualified for and completed the Boston and NYC marathons in 2003 and 2004
Competitive skier—competed with Team Canada in 1994 Winter Games
Member of the National Club (nominated to run in Presidential election 2005)

more quickly here, given (in his view) Central Bank's penchant for hiring externally and promoting on perceived potential rather than experience. Warren was told by Regional Bank in March that a move was imminent but this promise seemed to have been lost in the noise around the massive restructuring of Regional Bank's senior ranks. Most troubling was the fact that Warren's sponsor had been exited.

Education

Toronto French School Alumnus; BA, Government, Harvard; LLB, Osgoode Hall Law School, York University

Strengths Relative to This Role

- Extremely bright, versatile player; voracious learner
- Driven, results oriented, huge capacity for work
- Executed turnaround of small, but lucrative territory, moved area from last to first place in 18 months
- Exited 35 per cent of sales staff and redeployed additional 15 per cent more
- Designed hiring profile/recruitment process for sales staff now adopted by the rest of the bank

- Increased sales volumes by 60 per cent for the last two years, significantly exceeding profitability and cost management targets
- Worked closely with customer relationship management (CRM) area and Risk Management to hone prospecting skills and reduce losses
- Contributed to and piloted new sales training program for Regional Bank, led national initiative to "measure and manage" more effectively
- Key contributor to bank initiatives within his division and across the bank
- Moved to west end of the city to better participate in community activities

For Consideration

- Hinted of intellectual arrogance, a bit condescending around Regional Bank's "superiority"
- Difficult to get handle on what Warren personally accomplished in Australia; became vague when pressed for details, alluded to Regional Bank strategic gaffe
- Believe Warren cares about people but suspect he doesn't always show it
- Intense, could be overpowering for more reticent team members

- May not always give credit to others; seemed to be a one-man show on occasion
- Activity level on the job and elsewhere was awesome, but how much is too much?
- Enthusiasm engaging but candidate interrupted, wanted to speak rather than listen

Warren's tenure in any position had not exceeded two years—not sure how much success candidate can claim for projects initiated before his arrival or executed after his departure.

Of Interest

- Warren was working on his MBA (Richard Ivey School of Business, University of Western Ontario) and was actively campaigning to be the next and youngest president of the National Club, which he hoped to revitalize. He was also an avid runner (finishing both the Boston and New York marathons in the middle of the pack) and longtime skier (visited his family's chalet at Mount Tremblant in Quebec as often as possible).

A preliminary and very discreet reference was obtained from a former peer (now a SVP at Central Bank) of Warren's at Regional Bank. The individual confirmed Warren's long-term potential, superior results and high-potential status at Regional Bank but described him as "overly ambitious" and "political."

Candidate: James (Jim) Skinner

Current Position: District Vice-President, First Northern Bank

Status: Interviewed by executive search firm and VP, Executive Resources, Central Bank

Background

Skinner grew up in Toronto's East End, where his father owned a printing business. He ran the office for his father for two years after his graduation from Ryerson University. At the suggestion of the manager, Skinner joined the local First Northern Bank branch where his family banked. He progressed through the ranks to Bank Manager (including a two-year stint in the West Indies) and was moved through increasingly senior roles in Human Resources, Commercial Bank and Risk Management, returning to retail banking as a District Vice-President in 2000 (see attached resume, Exhibit 6, for more detail).

Exhibit 6   Résumé: James (Jim) Skinner

James (Jim) Skinner
11 Moorecroft Road, Ajax, Ont, M4N 2S5
Home: 905-777-0456; Business: 416-437-8813
E-mail: jamess@rogers.ca

Professional Experience

Bank of First Northern
1979 to present
February 2004—Present
On interim assignment with EVP, Retail Branch Banking.

Projects include:

- Initiative examining correlation between employee and customer satisfaction.
- Macro planning for replacement of segment's aging executive population.
- Roll out of new technology/CRM tools to branch network.

March 2000–December 2003
District Vice President, Toronto East

- Assumed responsibility for troubled Toronto East Region during restructuring of GTA regional territories. Merged two smaller districts into largest mandate in Ontario, reduced FTE and rolled out new sales process concurrently.
- Formed Employee Association to ensure employee voice heard during major transition, to augment communication strategy and garner input/insight into regional dynamics and build marketing strategies.
- Assessed staff for sales versus servicing skills, finding jobs for all employees displaced in process; introduced disciplined sales process to Region, traveling to all branches at least bi-monthly to personally coach branch managers and communicate expectations to all levels.
- Initiated annual "Customer First Award" for District employee who best exemplifies customer service and monthly award (extra vacation days or gift certificates) for "Best Assist" given for teamwork resulting in new or expanded business.
- Built strong alliances with segment peers to increase business flow and provide broader market and community coverage.
- Recognized as most improved district in 2001. Received Best District Award (Ontario) 2003 and 2004 for highest sales volumes, top quartile Employee Commitment and lowest NIX ratio.

October 1998–March 2000
General Manager, Credit, Ontario Region

- Co-led initiative to re-engineer credit approving/adjudication and compliance reporting process for Small Business and Agriculture portfolios.
- Engaged line staff in streamlining front end credit approval processes, using behavioural scoring and technology assisted decisioning tools.
- Introduced base line accreditation requirements for Risk Managers and credit training for all front line originators.
- Dramatically reduced credit losses and significantly improved credit approval time.

August 1996–October 1998
General Manager, Small Business Banking, Central Toronto

- Implemented Small Business strategy in Central Toronto, the largest market in Canada; led the change management effort to reposition the Small Business offer, adding wealth management products to traditional credit focus.
- Chaired the GTA Risk Committee, significantly improving the region's risk profile through the development and implementation of sound risk and governance practices and policies.

(Continued)

Exhibit 6 (Continued)

- Achieved highest improvement award in Employee Index in 1997.
- Publicly recognized for strong contribution to operations and infrastructure groups.
- Partnered with external groups to develop added value programs for Small Business clients.
- Delivered on cost containment and client retention targets, exceeding sales targets by 31%.

June 1995–August 1996
General Manager, Service Effectiveness, Western Canada, Calgary
Seconded to Regional Head Office to deploy successful sales & services strategies developed for Main Branch, Calgary across the Western Division.

- Developed and implemented a business retention and development plan for the Division;
- Expanded the Regional Call Centre's mandate to augment customer support;
- Aligned service response to segments, providing differentiated service to high value customers;
- Developed and implemented Local Market Management in the Division;
- Met retention objectives and exceeded sales targets by 120MM by year end.

August 1992–May 1995
Director, Retail and Private Banking Services, Main Branch, Calgary
Responsible for managing Retail and Private Banking, Main Branch, Calgary

- Designed and launched a customer-centric sales and service model; differentiated high net worth customer experience from standard service
- Restructured Main Branch to better implement new customer strategy, make productivity gains and increase profitability.
- Increased individual sales capacity by 95%, increased branch customer satisfaction ratings (in top 10 branches nationally). Won national Customer Service Excellence Award.

June 1990–July 1992
Human Resources Officer, Head Office, Toronto
Seconded to Human Resources to help implement a major restructuring of Retail Banking; provided field perspective for organization design, training and recruitment specialists:

- Conducted span of control and capacity planning for realigned districts;
- Helped design and facilitate new training and orientation programs;
- Revamped roles and responsibilities for newly crafted line positions;
- Established selection criteria for senior District leaders and conducted first line interviews.

1985–1990
Branch Manager

- Managed increasingly larger and more complex branches in Ontario, Western Canada and Atlantic Canada. Key achievements: (1) The effective leadership and development of staff; (2) Continually exceeding sales and profitability goals.

1979–1985

- Progressed through a number of line roles to Branch Manager

Education

1996   EMBA, University of Toronto
1991   Fellow, Institute of Canadian Bankers
1981   Canadian Securities Course
1975   Business Administration Diploma, Ryerson

Affiliations

Director, Canadian Parkinson Society
Treasurer, Pickering Lions Club
Trustee, Separate School Board, Durham Region
Coach, Boys Intermediate Soccer

Beginning in 1996, First No rthern Bank agreed to sponsor Skinner's executive MBA (EMBA) program in recognition of his strong leadership capabilities and to supplement his rather weak academic background.

Skinner was in the process of moving to Calgary to a larger and more senior District VP role (with a promise to re-evaluate the role for possible upgrading to SVP) when his wife became seriously ill. Skinner elected to remain in Toronto where family support and better treat- ment is available to his wife. His old role was backfilled quickly with a rising star, and Skinner has spent the last 10 months without portfolio, working on special assignments and getting pro- gressively frustrated. He was open to talking to headhunters for the first time in his career.

Education

High School; Business Administration Diploma, Ryerson University; Fellow, Institute of Canadian Bankers; Canadian Securities Course; EMBA, University of Toronto.

Strengths Relative to This Role

- People management/motivation was a key strength

- Able to build trust, trusted advisor to senior management and staff alike
- Clearly saw the correlation between employee satisfaction and customer satisfaction
- Track record for turning around under-performing units
- Grounded in First Northern Bank way: doing more with less, employees for life, if humanly possible
- Didn't shoot from the hip, down to earth, honest and open
- Achieved results through people and teamwork
- Results focused, takes time to under- stand the variables
- Strong on process, cutting time and money where possible
- Mature, strong communicator

For Consideration

- While capable of meeting immedi- ate business and "values" needs, Skinner may be a less viable succes- sion candidate
- Not clear if Skinner could take necessary tough stand without usual First Northern Bank safety net for employees

- Whether Skinner was committed to leaving Firs t Northern Bank was unclear; Skinner's ability to adjust to/change Central Bank's culture was also questionable
- Significant front-line experience, but candidate lacked analytical/strategic depth

Of Interest

- Skinner, a First Northern Bank lifer, was reluctant to leave but felt he needed to find a "real job" soon. He was concerned about the adverse publicity Central Bank had generated over the last few years and his perception that it "chews up and spits out executives," "eating its young," to quote Skinner
- During the interview (his first, in 26 years) Skinner confessed he was very nervous about starting over again at 50 and was worried about adjusting to a new corporate culture
- His wife required periodic visits to the Mayo Clinic and First Northern Bank had been very supportive with time off and professional support for him and his three teenagers. He wondered if Central Bank would be as helpful and compassionate

Christina Gold Leading Change at Western Union

Prepared by Jordan Mitchell under the supervision of Professor Alison Konrad

◊ Introduction

In early 2003, Christina Gold, chief executive officer (CEO) of Western Union, had just begun implementing a new organization structure. Gold had joined Western Union in May 2002 with a key focus of unifying the company's U.S. operations with its international division. In guiding the company to act as one entity, Gold proposed a change from a U.S. centric product line focus to a regional structure with three main divisions: the Americas; Europe, Africa, the Middle East and South Asia; and Asia-Pacific.

Changing the structure sent out a clear message of Gold's desired change in mindset to a new type of global culture. Already,

Gold was finding that leaders in the United States were reluctant to give up control of product lines. At the regional level, she had keen leaders who wanted to push out the responsibility within their own regions and move towards a decentralized plan. While Gold supported this notion in principle, she wanted to ensure that the right leaders could be placed in decentralized offices in order to execute on the six strategic pillars that she had laid out for the organization. As well, she wanted to match responsibility with authority by giving the regional heads profit and loss responsibility. With this responsibility at the regional level, she wondered how new products would develop under a regional structure. Gold was also

Version: (A) 2009-09-17

aware of the need to consider recruiting, training and development of new leaders as the company was growing most rapidly in emerging markets, such as India, China, Eastern Europe and Africa.

One thing was certain—Gold had made it clear that no revenue decreases would be forgiven amidst the change. Many considerations had arisen: What pace of change should she take? How would she deal with the resistance to change? How could she ensure that the new structure would support Western Union's global expansion?

◼ Christina Gold

Born in 1947 in the Netherlands, Gold moved to Canada at age five. She attended Carleton University in Ottawa where she earned a degree in geography in 1969, and upon graduating, secured a job at a coupon-centre clearinghouse. A year later in 1970, she joined Avon Canada as an entry-level inventory control clerk. Gold worked her way up through more than 20 positions before being promoted to president of the entire Canadian Avon division in 1989. Gold became well known for training sales representatives on selling techniques and time management. Dedicating time to joining representatives on sales calls, Gold explained her rationale, "I'd go out with the sales reps who were doing well and with the ones who were doing badly, and I'd pass what the successful ones were doing on to the others."[2]

In November 1993, Gold was selected from a number of candidates to run the entire North American Avon organization in New York.

For several months, she and her husband maintained a commuting marriage between New York and Montreal before he was able to relocate to New York. Within six months at Avon, she was credited with rejuvenating the energy level among sales representatives, with one sales representative sending her flowers with a note saying, "Thanks for bringing springtime back to Avon."[3] In a show of appreciation to the sales force, Gold asked that all salaried Avon employees hand-write 100 thank-you notes to representatives. But Gold clarified an important aspect of communication, "Motivation isn't all prizes and things. It's listening."[4]

In 1996, Gold was promoted to lead the development of global direct-selling in an executive vice-president role, and in the same year was named one of the top 25 U.S. managers. During the same time, Gold was one of the three women insiders predicted to be promoted to the CEO post of Avon; however, all three of the internal candidates were passed over for Charles Perrin, former CEO of Duracell International Inc.[5] Gold left Avon in early 1998 after a 28-year career and established The Beaconsfield Group, a consultancy focused on global direct-selling and marketing/distribution strategies.[6] In September 1999, Gold was selected as the CEO of Excel Communications, a $1.3 billion Dallas-based firm, to lead the company's rollout of direct telecommunications selling. With the changing infrastructure in the telecommunications landscape within the next three years, Gold successfully launched a direct-selling strategy. In May 2002, Gold transitioned after Bell Canada Enterprises (BCE) sold the company. Gold became president

---

[2]Claudia Deutsch, "Avon's Montreal recruit has Gold touch with reps," *New York Times*, April 5, 1994, p. B10.

[3]Ibid.

[4]Ibid.

[5]"Avon chooses outsider as heir apparent," *The Record*, December 12, 1997, p. B03.

[6]"New CEO at Excel Communications. . . ," *PR Newswire*, September 15, 1999.

of First Data Corporation's largest division— Western Union.

◣ First Data Corporation in Brief

First Data Corporation was established in 1992, when American Express spun off the division through an initial public offering.[7] Three years later in 1995, First Data merged with First Financial Management Corporation, which owned Western Union.

First Data's focus was facilitating the purchase of goods and services through almost any form of payment. In carrying out its business aim, First Data provided electronic commerce and payment services solutions to three million merchants, 1,400 card issuers and millions of individuals by the end of 2002. As First Data stated on its website, "You may not realize it, but First Data touches your life every day. Whether writing a check at the supermarket, buying dinner with your credit card or ordering a book online, we're connecting with you to make those transactions happen—safely and securely."[8] It had four central business segments: payment services, merchant services, card issuing services and emerging payments.

First Data had realized steady growth and had experienced a compound annual growth rate of 7.5 per cent in revenues and 21.6 per cent in net income from 1998 to 2002.[9] As of the end of 2002, First Data had revenues of $7.6 billion and net income of $1.2 billion.[10] First Data's strategy to grow hinged on expanding the reach of its core businesses, developing long-term

contractual agreements with customers for steady and predictable revenue flows and responding to new e-commerce initiatives.

◣ Western Union in Brief

Western Union was founded in Rochester, New York, as The New York and Mississippi Valley Printing Telegraph Company in 1851. When the name changed to Western Union, the intent was to integrate acquired companies and unite the United States from east to west. Western Union had a number of firsts, such as the invention of the stock ticker in 1866, the electronic money transfer in 1871, the credit card in 1914, the singing telegram in 1933 and intercity facsimile service in 1935.[11]

Western Union posted sales of $3.2 billion in 2002, an 18 per cent increase from the prior year.[12] Eighty per cent of Western Union's revenues came from consumer-to-consumer (C2C) money transfers.[13] The number of consumer money transfers grew from 55.8 million in 2001 to 67.8 in 2002 with predictions that the number of these transfers would rise to more than 80 million in 2003. The remaining 20 per cent of revenues was derived from consumer-to-business (C2B) transactions.

By early 2003, Western Union had approximately 4,500 employees of which 40 per cent were based in the United States. Most of the workforce was non-unionized except for 1,200 call centre employees located in the Missouri, U.S. branch office. Western Union operated in 182,000 locations in 195 countries. More than 59,000 of the locations were located in North America (United States, Canada and Mexico),

---

[7]First Data Fact Sheet, Company Documents.

[8]First Data Corporate Website, www.firstdatacorp.com, accessed December 23, 2004.

[9]First Data Annual Report, www.sec.gov, accessed December 31, 2002, p.17.

[10]Ibid.

[11]Western Union Fact Sheet, Company Documents.

[12]First Data Annual Report, www.sec.gov, December 31, 2002, p.33.

[13]Ibid.

while the remaining 123,000 were made up of international agent locations. Agreements with international agents were typically made with banks and national post offices.

⌧ Agent Network

All of Western Union's international agents entered information into a common data processing system, where the payment was processed and made available to the receiving location. A consumer sending money paid a transfer fee on the amount sent to the receiver. Both the "sending" and "receiving" agents received a commission as did Western Union's corporate operation. Western Union also benefited from the differences in exchange rate spreads, which it recorded as additional revenue.

Robin Heller, Western Union's soon-to-be vice-president, operations talked about how the company maintained consistency across its expansive agent network:

> We have to ensure the same brand promise whether someone is at a retail brick-and-mortar location, online or by telephone. We do that by asking for the same pieces of information in the same order and we make it very easy to execute. From that, we look at what we need to do to add to our training, the forms we use or the screens that agents use. We use the same system across the entire world.

Christina Gold shared her view of what it took to lead a geographically separated operation:

> You have to be sensitive to other cultures and other people, and that's true in New York City as well as in Bangkok. Each person's needs are different, and the leader has to be aware and flexible enough to work with each person effectively. One thing that does get in the way

is language and communication issues. Using abbreviations and acronyms in Japan, for example, can make people feel ostracized. It's not inclusive. People feel left out or misunderstood. Another thing that can happen is that people do not understand what you are asking of them—they don't see it as a directive, but rather as a general comment. So to be effective in a global team requires more patience, more focus, you need to repeat things and get feedback to ensure people understand each other. Everything takes more thought and more patience. It's important not to jump to conclusions and to really listen.

⌧ Western Union's Consumer

Western Union's major consumer segment was the migrant worker who earned money in one country and used money transfer services to send funds to family and loved ones in another country. This target consumer typically did not have a bank account. Hikmet Ersek, senior vice-president, EMEA (Europe/Middle East/Africa and South Asia), Western Union stated, "We're dealing with a lot of immigrants who may experience problems in their host countries and where they work. The idea is that they will be served well and with a smile."

Heller spoke about the importance of customizing the Western Union experience to significantly different audiences:

> Our agents will try to localize the look and feel and the location of the office. They do the marketing at a local level. Take Africa for instance: in Africa there's a big festival culture so, we do skits or little plays at the festival to advertise our services.

See Exhibit 1 for an example of Western Union's advertising from around the world.

Exhibit 1   Examples of Global Western Union Advertising

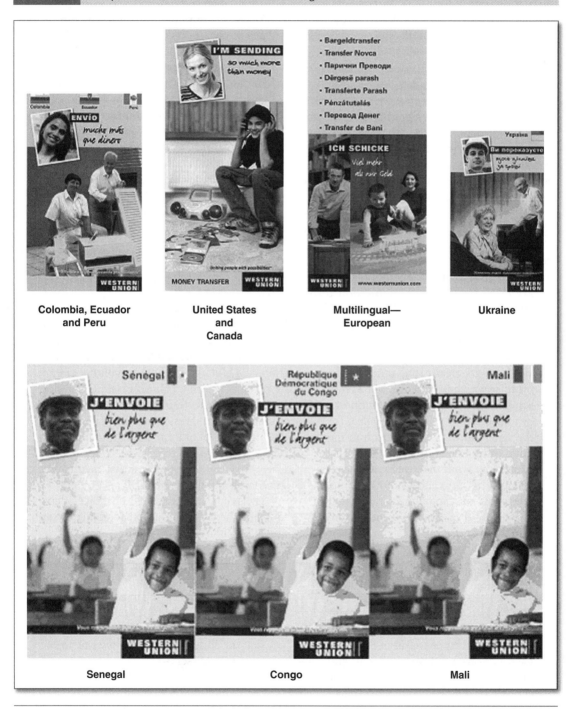

≋ Western Union's Strategy

By late 2002, Gold and her executive team had developed six core strategies for Western Union:

1. Develop a global brand

2. Enhance global network distribution

3. Expand adjacent markets such as WesternUnion.com and Prepaid services

4. Develop future business leaders within the organization

5. Increase productivity

6. Execute on service excellence

Gold talked about the driver of Western Union's growth and the challenges going forward:

> [The driver is] obviously the core business, which is the money transfer business. The consumer-to-consumer business is the growth engine. We're looking to grow our commercial business, our bill-payment business in the United States. And we're now extending that globally. We are starting to develop (our prepaid business) around the globe. Our challenge and our opportunity is to keep that growth in the double digits. I think part of it's really looking at building the right brand for Western Union. The fact we're growing so quickly and growing around the globe are key things as we develop our business and our brand in India and China.

≋ Reorganization

In order to align the company's organizational structure to the six core strategic focuses, Gold began a reorganizing program in early 2003. Prior to the reorganization effort, the structure mirrored Western Union's parent company, First Data, in that it had a U.S. business and an international business.

The executive team was made up of Christina Gold as president and six other senior executives. Four senior vice-presidents were in charge of the following product lines: Consumer Money Transfer, Mexican Money Transfer, Bill Payments and Corporate Services. One executive commented on the individuals responsible for the worldwide development of products: "The four executives run those products for the entire world, but they are very U.S.-centric."

The other two executive positions were Western Union's chief financial officer (CFO) and the senior vice-president of Western Union International. Annmarie Neal, senior vice-president, Talent, First Data and co-acting senior vice-president of human resources for Western Union, was one of the first to draw out a rough version of the new structure on a white board. She talked about the goals in making a change to the structure:

> The main impetus is to allow Western Union to bring their services to market more effectively. The second major reason is to manage redundancy. We have a head of marketing for both the U.S. and international businesses. So one of the biggest thrusts is to have brand consistency across the globe. We also want to build the financial infrastructure and really place the financial decisioning in the right areas. With information technology, the aim is to have common platforms. For human resources, the idea is to have the ability to move talent around the globe. Whether that be from South East Asia or to the Americas. Western Union is very domestic in resources, but we see all the growth coming from other areas.

Alternatives Considered

In developing the new proposed structure, Gold and her executive team first established the core strategic focuses and looked at each region and considered structures that would be effective. Alternatives included making minor changes to the product line-focused structure, rolling out a structure organized by functional area such as sales, marketing, operations, finance and IT or considering a structure based on geography. The team chose to reorganize the company into a decentralized structure covering three main regions: the Americas; Europe, the Middle East and Africa; and Asia/Pacific. Annmarie Neal described the process for choosing a regional structure:

> We really wanted to reflect the global business and cut down on the idea of a domestic and international business. So, it became pretty obvious that we would choose a regional structure, but our organizational structure is constantly evolving. When we looked at a product organization structure, we realized pretty quickly that it wasn't going to work, simply because we had a number of products in the domestic business. But we really had only one business in the international market, which was money transfers. So we discarded that option pretty quickly. One of the big debates was the corporate role of marketing and what should be done at the regional level. We decided that strategy for loyalty and brand would reside at the corporate level whereas the execution of such strategies would be done in the regions.

Gold gave her view:

> Currently, we have a domestic business and an international division. It doesn't make sense for a global business the way it is now; whatever country you're in is 'domestic.' So, [the idea is to] have a regional structure. [My hope is that] we will have common goals and share a lot more ideas. There will be a lot more communication and sharing of resources. For example, the plan is to have a global marketing plan whereas currently we have separate marketing for domestic and each international area. It'll be much better from a customer perspective because the global services allows each region to spend their time focusing on specific customer needs.

Challenges With Reorganizing

In making the change, Gold had to first convince the Fir st Data management team and then the First Data board of directors. The total cost of the restructuring was estimated at US$4 million and included provisions for relocation and recruitment in a few key positions. Gold's one central mandate for the organization was that revenues could not be negatively affected. In facilitating the change, Gold used her executive team, as well as the services of human resources, to define the key processes, design the structure of the new organization and define responsibility within the structure.

Defining Responsibility

In defining responsibility, two main issues had arisen: Who would lead the development of new products? and Who would have profit and loss accountability in the organization?

Development of New Products

The company had been promoting four new business areas: commercial services, the website, WesternUnion.com and the prepaid card.

Prepaid cards included a gamut of products ranging from prepaid wireless and telephone cards to prepaid debit cards.

Company executives needed to decide whether there should be a product leader or whether regional leaders could take on the responsibility. Some executives argued that sufficient time could not be devoted to developing them at a regional level. Ersek stated:

> Something like the prepaid card is led by a product manager. I think that until it becomes big enough, it should stay under the product manager and then it is handed over to the regional heads. See, prepaid cards for me makes up about $200,000 in revenues, out of over $1.5 billion in revenues. My priority will be the larger numbers. But a product manager can put the marketing effort into this, build the product and then hand it off.

⌖ Profit and Loss (P&L) Responsibility

Another central challenge was deciding on whether profit and loss responsibility should rest with the regional heads or whether it should be based on corridors. Western Union defined corridors as, "country-to-country money-transfer pairs"[14] such as the U.S.-Mexico, UAE-India and Spain-Morocco. The company's worldwide operations had approximately 15,000 corridors[15] with approximately 500 of the top corridors making up 80 per cent of money transfer activity. Changes in the corridors were heavily influenced by immigration patterns, country regulations and geo-economic conditions.[16]

While it was common that many corridors would be based within one region, such as the United States to Mexico under the Americas canopy, it was also common that corridors crossed international frontiers. Ersek explained:

> We have the unique challenge of sending and receiving. If I send money from Spain to Brazil, I need someone in Brazil. One of the big discussions is whether to have region or corridor heads. Some people feel that we needed to give the P&L responsibility to corridor heads. I am against this. Part of the reason is that there have been big dynamic changes in corridor traffic.

Some managers felt that changes to corridor traffic were heavily linked to external factors outside of the control of Western Union making it too difficult to hold leaders responsible for top-line revenue results. Other executives believed that responsibility would be clearer if it mirrored the transaction flow between countries.

⌖ Decentralization at the Regional Level

While decentralization was not a prerequisite in the new regional design, some executives felt that decentralization would enable the regions to get closer to the company's customers.

In the Europe, Middle East, Africa and South Asia division, the recently appointed Vice-President, Hikmet Ersek, wanted to decentralize the region by opening up a number of smaller offices in each country. Ersek believed the plan would put Western Union closer to its customers and agents allowing faster response times and enhanced service. Ersek stated, "I want to move from having five offices to having 35 or more different

---

[14]First Data Annual Report, www.sec.gov, December 31, 2002, p. 34.

[15]Ibid.

[16]Ibid.

offices—like small agile teams. Obviously, there are some things that need to be central, like creating the brand and network development."

However, moving to the decentralized plan had its challenges. Ersek indicated:

> In order to decentralize, there are lots of questions from the legal and finance departments at the headquarters in Denver. Eventually, I want to put an office in Tashkent. However for many people Tashkent is an unknown quantity and they have some concerns. Finding the right people is a challenge. In a place like Tashkent, in Uzbekistan, we would have to find people who understood the code of conduct. We have to have people that we can trust. They need to accept and understand what it means to be part of a U.S. and a global company. Also, many of the local agents think that we are opening up branches. So, we have to assure them that we are opening up offices to support the agents.

Other executives felt that decentralization had its limits due to cost and human resource constraints. Neal balanced Ersek's view:

> I want to listen to all of the ideas around the globe. But, decentralizing regions could add to a significant increase in infrastructure cost. There's colonization in spirit and I think with some adaptation it could work. Where it gets tricky, is making a change without thinking through implications for the rest of the organization. We need to think about leveraging opportunities around the globe.

Recruiting for New Positions

Proposed changes in leadership included moving the head of Western Union International in Paris, France, to the company's headquarters in Colorado to assume the position of president of Western Union Americas, including all countries on both continents.

Formerly the senior Vice-President for Eastern Europe, Hikmet Ersek, had taken the role as the senior vice president responsible for Europe, the Middle East, Africa and South Asia. A role was still required to be filled for the Asia-Pacific division as the former president of the Asian division had left the company. Two new corporate roles were set to be created: senior vice-president of business development to be filled by Mike Yerington, a 30-year Western Union veteran, and senior vice-president, operations to be filled by Robin Heller. Scott Schierman would continue as chief financial officer with greater day-to-day operational duties.

Overall, Western Union recruited approximately 500 individuals a year—some of the roles were to fill the four per cent attrition rate, while others were to fill positions created by internal growth. One of the major challenges was recruiting individuals who possessed an understanding of operating in China and India. While growth was through adding agents in both countries, Western Union did not have to recruit staff in each location. However, the company needed to place people at the corporate level to manage the marketing, operations and information technological consistency. As Neal explained: "A lot of folks confuse being global with being from a different country. It doesn't mean that you're global if you have a different colored passport. We're looking for people that have a global mindset."

Executive Development Programs

As of early 2003, First Data was making changes to the company's development program. Previously, the program was called First Leaders, which contained 12 modules whereby participants could learn about aspects of leadership such as enhancing communication, risk-taking, conflict resolution and motivating employees. Jana Johnson, vice-president, executive development, First Data commented on the old program:

> What you had was a director sitting in a room with administrative assistants and attendance was not mandatory. So, a lot of times people wouldn't come or people would attend a call on their cell phone and the types of issues that were coming up weren't necessarily helpful for everyone.

With the effectiveness of the old program dwindling, First Data executives planned a new leadership series, "First Executives," that was more in line with developing a pipeline of leaders for top management positions. Johnson explained the burning need at the First Data level, "At the First Data level, one of the critical things was succession planning and we identified 134 top critical positions. Specifically the goal was to have three high-confidence candidates per critical role by 2007."

The new program—First Executives—had 30 participants at an original cost of $7,500 per person in First Data of which 15 were Western Union executives. The plan was to add another 30 participants by the end of 2003. Each participant was given an executive coach that helped develop managerial and leadership abilities. In addition, they were all given mentors and given the opportunity to shadow a senior executive.

◪ The Culture Change

The words "culture change" were frequently talked about within both First Data and Western Union. First Data had the reputation of being a conservative culture steeped in the financial industry. Some observers felt that the Western Union had a stronger identity due to its history and product focus. Ersek talked about the difference in the culture between Western Union and its parent:

> A company like First Data is driven by statistics, this has to be the case if

you are listed on America's "Most Admired" list and if you are a major employer. With Western Union outside of America we still have the pioneering spirit that made Western Union famous in America. For Western Union International, the sky is the limit. We are still growing in double-digits.

Johnson talked about change in both organizations:

> It's a culture of change and we need leadership change. We're big and we know we're big. We know we need to change but we're just not sure what we need to change into. You can't control change, but you have to learn how to manage it and how to lead it. It's the messiness of change. And, it is messy.

Heller offered her view of changing Western Union:

> The biggest issue is probably the fear of the unknown and the fear of change. It's very important that we have the talent in place first and then we can look at the restructuring. You can always do any amount of restructuring or managing change that you need to do if you have the right people.

◪ Gold as the Leader of the Change

"She was masterful at reading the organization's readiness," commented Neal on Gold's leadership in initiating the organizational design change. Executives credited Gold with instilling a deep understanding of branding and marketing at Western Union while managing disparate personalities and cultures. Heller explained how Gold fostered leadership among Western Union executives and how she was leading the change:

> She doesn't bring rank into the situation. She always has time for us—she has a high level of accessibility and with her grinding schedule it's amazing. She's very much about inquiring and asking instead of telling. She gives feedback and ideas and listens openly to other ideas. Everyone has a voice. But don't take that the wrong way. She can make decisions. She can definitely make decisions! She takes it all in and then makes the call.

Ersek talked about his relationship with Gold:

> She gives autonomy, but she also keeps a hand on things. She is tough and has high standards and expects all her managers to adhere to these standards. This is something I admire very much about her, because she doesn't expect anything of anybody she cannot deliver herself. And, sometimes, I say, "Christina, that's not doable," and she says, "I'll help you do it." After she understood my region, her leadership has basically been, "What's your decision Hikmet?" And through that, she is sending signs to others that the responsibility is being pushed into the regions.

Neal observed Gold:

> Christina's a very tough executive. And by tough, I mean that she sets very high objectives. She is constantly stretching her executives. Christina is masterful in managing the globe and I don't mean just the employees. I'm talking about developing strong relationships with our agents and with government officials. I think a major thing about her leadership is how she empowers her revenue-generator executives. It's hard to keep track with some being several hours away and in a different time zones. But, she seems to manage this exceptionally well.

▧ Considerations Moving Forward

Gold was eager to lead Western Union through a major structural change from a company organized by product line to a geographically aligned organization. Gold wanted to ensure that the structure would support the company's strategic aims and give strength to Western Union's global expansion. She had a number of considerations: the pace of change, how to assuage resistance to the change and how to ensure that the new structure would help to follow the new strategic direction.

What Engages Employees the Most, or The Ten C's of Employee Engagement

By Gerard H. Seijts and Dan Crim

Practitioners and academics have argued that an engaged workforce can create competitive advantage. These authors say that it is imperative for leaders to identify the level of engagement in their organization and implement behavioural strategies that will facilitate full engagement. In clear terms, they describe how leaders can do that.

A professor in a recent executive education program on leadership elicited a lot of laughs by telling the following joke: "A CEO was asked how many people work in his company: 'About half of them,' he responded." After the session, several participants put a more serious face on the problem when, while chatting, they bemoaned the fact that, in their organization, a significant number of people had mentally "checked out."

Quite clearly, CEOs and managers should be very concerned about a waste of time, effort and resources in their organizations. The reason is simple: If people are not engaged, how can these same leaders attain those business objectives that are critical to improving organizational performance?

What do we mean by employee engagement? How much does a lack of employee engagement cost an organization? What steps can leaders take to make employees want to give it their best? These and other questions are the focus of this article.

What Is Employee Engagement?

An engaged employee is a person who is fully involved in, and enthusiastic about, his or her work. In his book, *Getting Engaged: The New Workplace Loyalty* , author Tim Rutledge explains that truly engaged employees are attracted to, and inspired by, their work ("I want to do this"), committed ("I am dedicated to the success of what I am doing"), and fascinated ("I love what I am doing"). Engaged employees care about the future of the company and are willing to invest the discretionary effort—exceeding duty's call—to see that the organization succeeds. In his book, Rutledge urged managers to implement retention plans so that they could keep their top talent. The need to do so is supported by a 1998 McKinsey & Co. study entitled *The War for Talent* that reported that a shortage of skilled employees was an emerging trend. Today, there is widespread

agreement among academics and practitioners that engaged employees are those who are emotionally connected to the organization and cognitively vigilant.

Is There a Crisis in Employee Engagement?

We believe that executives must be concerned about the level of engagement in the workplace. For example, the Gallup Management Journal publishes a semi-annual Employment Engagement Index. The most recent U.S. results indicate that:

- Only 29 percent of employees are actively engaged in their jobs. These employees work with passion and feel a profound connection to their company. People that are actively engaged help move the organization forward.
- Fifty-four percent of employees are not engaged. These employees have essentially "checked out," sleepwalking through their workday and putting time—but not passion—into their work. These people embody what Jack Welch said several years ago. To paraphrase him: "Never mistake activity for accomplishment."
- Seventeen percent of employees are actively disengaged. These employees are busy acting out their unhappiness, undermining what their engaged co-workers are trying to accomplish.

A Towers Perrin 2005 Global Workforce Survey involving about 85,000 people working full-time for large and midsized firms found similarly disturbing findings. Only 14 percent of all employees worldwide were highly engaged in their job. The number of Canadians that reported being highly engaged was 17 percent. Sixty-two percent of the employees surveyed indicated they were moderately engaged at best; 66 percent of employees in Canada were moderately engaged. And 24 percent reported that they are actively disengaged; the corresponding number in Canada was 17 percent. (See article by Towers Perrin authors elsewhere in this issue.)

The survey also indicated that on a country-by-country basis, the percentages of highly engaged, moderately engaged, and actively disengaged employees varied considerably. And the results showed some interesting, perhaps counter-intuitive, results. For example, Mexico and Brazil have the highest percentages of engaged employees, while Japan and Italy have the largest percentages of disengaged employees. In their report, the authors interpreted these and other findings as an indication that employee engagement has relatively little to do with macro-economic conditions. Instead, it is the unique elements of the work experience that are most likely to influence engagement.

Does Engagement Really Make A Difference?

Should executives be concerned about these findings? Perhaps a more interesting question to executives is: "Is there a strong relationship between, say, high scores on employee engagement indices and organizational performance?" It seems obvious that engaged employees are more productive than their disengaged counterparts. For example, a recent meta-analysis published in the *Journal of Applied Psychology* concluded that, "employee satisfaction and engagement are related to meaningful business outcomes at a magnitude that is important to many organizations." A compelling question is this: How much more productive is an engaged workforce compared to a non-engaged workforce?

Several case studies shine some light on the practical significance of an engaged workforce. For example, New Century Financial Corporation, a U.S. specialty mortgage banking company, found that account executives in the wholesale division who were actively disengaged produced 28 percent less revenue than their colleagues who were engaged. Furthermore, those not engaged generated 23 percent less revenue than their engaged counterparts. Engaged employees also outperformed the not engaged and actively disengaged employees in other divisions. New Century Financial Corporation statistics also showed that employee engagement does not merely correlate with bottom line results—it *drives* results.

Employee engagement also affects the mindset of people. Engaged employees believe that they can make a difference in the organizations they work for. Confidence in the knowledge, skills, and abilities that people possess – in both themselves and others—is a powerful predictor of behavior and subsequent performance. Thus, consider some of the results of the Towers Perrin survey cited earlier:

- Eighty-four percent of highly engaged employees believe they can positively impact the quality of their organization's products, compared with only 31 percent of the disengaged.
- Seventy-two percent of highly engaged employees believe they can positively affect customer service, versus 27 percent of the disengaged.
- Sixty-eight percent of highly engaged employees believe they can positively impact costs in their job or unit, compared with just 19 percent of the disengaged.

Given these data, it is not difficult to understand that companies that do a better job of engaging their employees do outperform their competition. Employee engagement can not only make a real difference, it can set the great organizations apart from the merely good ones.

Leading the Turnaround

Consider the words of Ralph Stayer, CEO of Johnsonville Sausage. In the book, *Flight of the*

Buffalo: Soaring to Excellence, Learning to Let Employees Lead, he writes:

> I learned what I had to in order to succeed, but I never thought that learning was all that important. My willingness to do whatever it takes to succeed is what fueled Johnsonville's growth. In 1980 I hit the wall. I realized that if I kept doing what I had always done, I was going to keep getting what I was getting. And I didn't like what I was getting. I would never achieve my dream. I could see the rest of my business life being a never-ending stream of crises, problems, and dropped balls. We could keep growing and have decent profits, but it wasn't the success I was looking for.

The CEO observed that his employees were disinterested in their work. They were careless—dropping equipment, wasting materials, and often not accepting any responsibility for their work. They showed up for work, did what they were told to do, and, at the end of their shift, went home; the same routine would be repeated the next day. An employee-attitude survey showed average results. To Stayer, it appeared that the only person who was excited about Johnsonville was himself. He began to feel like a baby-sitter for his executives and staff. Stayer also realized that he could not inspire Johnsonville to greatness and as a result, the business he was running was becoming vulnerable.

Stayer found solutions to these problems in a meeting with Lee Thayer, a communications professor. Thayer explained to Stayer that a critical task for a leader is to create a climate that enables employees to unleash their potential. It is not the job of a CEO to make employees listen to what you have to say; it is about setting up the system so that people want to listen. The combination of the right environment and a culture that creates wants instead of requirements places few limits on what employees can achieve. Thayer's message

resonated with Stayer, as it should among business executives.

Stayer began to recognize the difference between compliance and commitment, and that an engaged workforce was what he needed to help improve organizational performance. He also learned that he needed to change his own leadership behaviour first. Leaders cannot "demand" more engagement and stronger performance; they can't stand on the sideline and speak only "when the play goes wrong" if an engaged workforce and great performance are what they desire. But what should leaders do, or consider doing, to increase the level of engagement among employees?

✄ The Ten C's of Employee Engagement

How can leaders engage employees' heads, hearts, and hands? The literature offers several avenues for action; we summarize these as the Ten C's of employee engagement.

1. Connect: Leaders must show that they value employees. In *First, Break All the Rules*, Marcus Buckingham and Curt Coffman argue that managers trump companies. Employee-focused initiatives such as profit sharing and implementing work–life balance initiatives are important. However, if employees' relationship with their managers is fractured, then no amount of perks will persuade employees to perform at top levels. Employee engagement is a direct reflection of how employees feel about their relationship with the boss. Employees look at whether organizations and their leader walk the talk when they proclaim that, "Our employees are our most valuable asset."

One anecdote illustrates the Connect dimension well. In November 2003, the CEO of WestJet Airlines, Clive Beddoe, was invited to give a presentation to the Canadian Club of London. Beddoe showed up late, a few minutes before he was to deliver his speech. He had met with WestJet employees at the London Airport and had taken a few minutes to explain the corporate strategy and some new initiatives to them. He also answered employees' questions. To paraphrase Beddoe, "We had a great discussion that took a bit longer than I had anticipated." Beddoe's actions showed that he cares about the employees. The employees, sensing that he is sincere, care about Beddoe and the organization; they "reward" his behavior with engagement.

2. Career: Leaders should provide challenging and meaningful work with opportunities for career advancement. Most people want to do new things in their job. For example, do organizations provide job rotation for their top talent? Are people assigned stretch goals? Do leaders hold people accountable for progress? Are jobs enriched in duties and responsibilities? Good leaders challenge employees; but at the same time, they must instill the confidence that the challenges can be met. Not giving people the knowledge and tools to be successful is unethical and de-motivating; it is also likely to lead to stress, frustration, and, ultimately, lack of engagement. In her book *Confidence: How Winning Streaks and Losing Streaks Begin and End*, Rosabeth Moss Kanter explains that confidence is based on three cornerstones: accountability, collaboration, and initiative.

3. Clarity: Leaders must communicate a clear vision. People want to understand the vision that senior leadership has for the organization, and the goals that leaders or departmental heads have for the division, unit, or team. Success in life and organizations is, to a great extent, determined by how clear individuals are about their goals and what they really want to achieve. In sum, employees need to understand what the organization's goals are, why they are important, and how the goals can best be attained. Clarity about what the organization stands for, what it wants to achieve, and how people can contribute to the organization's success is not always evident. Consider, for example, what Jack Stack, CEO of SRC

Holdings Corp., wrote about the importance of teaching the basics of business:

> The most crippling problem in American business is sheer ignorance about how business works. What we see is a whole mess of people going to a baseball game and nobody is telling them what the rules are. That baseball game is business. People try to steal from first base to second base, but they don't even know how that fits into the big picture. What we try to do is break down business in such a way that employees realize that in order to win the World Series, you've got to steal x number of bases, hit y number of RBIs and have the pitchers pitch z number of innings. And if you put all these variables together, you can really attain your hopes and dreams . . . don't use information to intimidate, control or manipulate people. Use it to teach people how to work together to achieve common goals and thereby gain control over their lives.

4. Convey: Leaders clarify their expectations about employees and provide feedback on their functioning in the organization. Good leaders establish processes and procedures that help people master important tasks and facilitate goal achievement. There is a great anecdote about the legendary UCLA basketball coach, John Wooden. He showed how important feedback—positive and constructive—is in the pursuit of greatness. Among the secrets of his phenomenal success was that he kept detailed diaries on each of his players. He kept track of small improvements he felt the players could make and did make. At the end of each practice, he would share his thoughts with the players. The lesson here is that good leaders work daily to improve the skills of their people and create small wins that help the team, unit, or organization perform at its best.

5. Congratulate: Business leaders can learn a great deal from Wooden's approach. Surveys show that, over and over, employees feel that they receive immediate feedback when their performance is poor, or below expectations. These same employees also report that praise and recognition for strong performance is much less common. Exceptional leaders give recognition, and they do so a lot; they coach and convey.

6. Contribute: People want to know that their input matters and that they are contributing to the organization's success in a meaningful way. This might be easy to articulate in settings such as hospitals and educational institutions. But what about, say, the retail industry? Sears Roebuck & Co. started a turnaround in 1992. Part of the turnaround plan was the development of a set of measures—known as Total Performance Indicators—which gauged how well Sears was doing with its employees, customers, and investors. The implementation of the measurement system led to three startling conclusions. First, an employee's understanding of the connection between her work—as operationalized by specific job-relevant behaviors—and the strategic objectives of the company had a positive impact on job performance. Second, an employee's attitude towards the job and the company had the greatest impact on loyalty and customer service than all the other employee factors combined. Third, improvements in employee attitude led to improvements in job-relevant behavior; this, in turn, increased customer satisfaction and an improvement in revenue growth. In sum, good leaders help people see and feel how they are contributing to the organization's success and future.

7. Control: Employees value control over the flow and pace of their jobs and leaders can create opportunities for employees to exercise this control. Do leaders consult with their employees with regard to their needs? For example, is it possible to accommodate the needs of a mother or an employee infected with HIV so that they can attend to childcare concerns or a medical appointment? Are leaders flexible and attuned to the needs of the employees as well as the organization? Do leaders involve employees in decision making, particularly when employees will be directly affected by the decision? Do employees have a say in setting goals or milestones that are deemed important? Are employees able to voice their ideas, and does leadership show that contributions are valued? H. Norman Schwartzkopf, retired U.S. Army General, once remarked:

> I have seen competent leaders who stood in front of a platoon and all they saw was a platoon. But great leaders stand in front of a platoon and see it as 44 individuals, each of whom has aspirations, each of whom wants to live, each of whom wants to do good.

A feeling of "being in on things," and of being given opportunities to participate in decision making often reduces stress; it also creates trust and a culture where people want to take ownership of problems and their solutions. There are numerous examples of organizations whose implementation of an open-book management style and creating room for employees to contribute to making decisions had a positive effect on engagement and organizational performance. The success of Microsoft, for example, stems in part from Bill Gates' belief that smart people anywhere in the company should have the power to drive an initiative. Initiatives such as Six Sigma are dependent, in part, on the active participation of employees on the shop floor.

8. Collaborate: Studies show that, when employees work in teams and have the trust and cooperation of their team members, they outperform individuals and teams which lack good relationships. Great leaders are team builders; they create an environment that fosters trust and collaboration. Surveys indicate that being cared about by colleagues is a strong

predictor of employee engagement. Thus, a continuous challenge for leaders is to rally individuals to collaborate on organizational, departmental, and group goals, while excluding individuals pursuing their self-interest.

9. Credibility: Leaders should strive to maintain a company's reputation and demonstrate high ethical standards. People want to be proud of their jobs, their performance, and their organization. WestJet Airlines is among the most admired organizations in Canada. The company has achieved numerous awards. For example, in 2005, it earned the number one spot for best corporate culture in Canada. On September 26, 2005, WestJet launched the "Because We're Owners!" campaign. Why do WestJet employees care so much about their organization? Why do over 85 percent of them own shares in the company? Employees believe so strongly in what WestJet is trying to do and are so excited about its strong performance record that they commit their own money into shares.

10. Confidence: Good leaders help create confidence in a company by being exemplars of high ethical and performance standards. To illustrate, consider what happened to Harry Stonecipher, the former CEO of Boeing. He made the restoration of corporate ethics in the organization a top priority but was soon after embarrassed by the disclosure of an extramarital affair with a female employee. His poor judgment impaired his ability to lead and he lost a key ingredient for success—credibility. Thus the board asked him to resign. Employees working at Qwest and Continental Airlines were so embarrassed about working for their organizations that they would not wear their company's uniform on their way to and from work. At WorldCom, most employees were shocked, horrified, and embarrassed when the accounting scandal broke at the company. New leadership was faced with the major challenges of regaining public trust and fostering employee engagement.

Practitioners and academics have argued that competitive advantage can be gained by creating an engaged workforce. The data and argument that that we present above are a compelling case why leaders need to make employee engagement one of their priorities. Leaders should actively try to identify the level of engagement in their organization, find the reasons behind the lack of full engagement, strive to eliminate those reasons, and implement behavioral strategies that will facilitate full engagement. These efforts should be ongoing. Employee engagement is hard to achieve and if not sustained by leaders it can wither with relative ease.

CHAPTER 7

The Path–Goal Theory of Leadership

You have to be able to be very tough and very supportive, if supportive is needed. And you have to give others room. But that doesn't mean you abdicate authority, because you have been entrusted with authority if you lead something and then you have to exert it.

—Dan Vasella[1]

The path–goal theory of leadership is similar to the situational and contingency theories of leadership in that it prescribes appropriate leadership styles for interacting with subordinates. It is different from the situational and contingency theories in that path–goal theory adds more variables to what leaders need to consider in their relationships with employees. In essence, the path–goal theory of leadership "is about how leaders motivate subordinates to accomplish designated goals" (Northouse, 2010).

Based on expectancy theory, path–goal theory suggests that employees will be motivated if three conditions are met. These are the following: Employees believe in their ability to perform their assigned work-related tasks, they believe that their work-related efforts will lead to appropriate outcomes, and they believe that these work-related outcomes will be meaningful.

The key to understanding the path–goal theory of leadership is to think about the path that subordinates must follow to achieve goals assigned. Subordinates are motivated by their leader to achieve these goals when leaders clearly define the goals, clarify the path to completing the goals, remove obstacles to completing the goals, and provide support to help achieve the assigned goals (Northouse, 2010). This is illustrated in Figure 7.1.

---

[1]Dan Vasella is the CEO and chairman of Novartis AG.

| **Figure 7.1** | The Basic Idea Behind Path–Goal Theory |

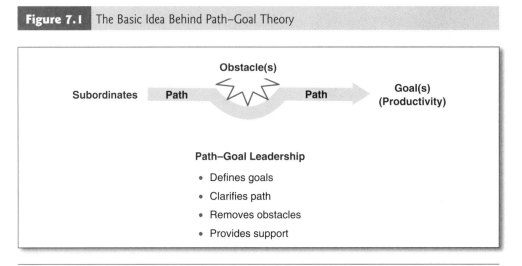

SOURCE: From Northouse (2010). Copyright © 2010, Sage Publications, Inc. Reprinted with permission.

Path–goal theory has several components that leaders need to assess if they are to create a positive association between subordinate motivation and goal achievement. Different leadership behaviors will differentially affect subordinate motivation, and this impact will depend on subordinate and task characteristics (Northouse, 2010). These four components of path–goal theory are shown in Figure 7.2.

| **Figure 7.2** | Major Components of Path–Goal Theory |

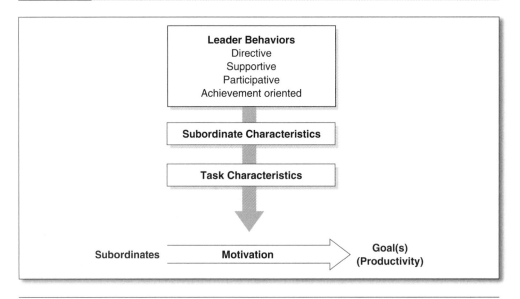

SOURCE: From Northouse (2010). Copyright © 2010, Sage Publications, Inc. Reprinted with permission.

Leader Behaviors

Initially, four leader behaviors were assessed but with the understanding that others would be examined as research continued. These were directive, supportive, participative, and achievement oriented (House & Mitchell, 1974; Yukl, 2006).

Directive Leadership

This leadership style emphasizes giving direction to subordinates regarding their tasks (Daft, 2005). These directions include the result expected, how the task will be accomplished, and the schedule for task completion. In addition, the leader clarifies performance expectations and explicitly outlines the required standard operating procedures, rules, and regulations (Yukl, 2006). This style increases subordinate morale when there is task ambiguity (Dubrin, 2007) and is similar to the task-oriented or initiating structure style (Daft, 2005).

Supportive Leadership

These leaders are approachable (i.e., maintain an open-door policy), friendly, and empathetic to their subordinates' needs and well-being (Yukl, 2006). They expend extra effort to ensure the workplace has an enjoyable environment, and they create an atmosphere of honor, respect, and equality for their subordinates in the workplace. This style is most appropriate for improving morale when tasks are boring, frustrating, repetitive, stressful, and dissatisfying. Subordinates who are uncertain of their capabilities, situation, and future appreciate this style more (Dubrin, 2007). In addition, this style is similar to the people-oriented or consideration style (Daft, 2005).

Participative Leadership

These leaders encourage employees to actively participate in the decision-making process that determines how the group will achieve its goals. They do this through consultation, solicitation of employee suggestions, and using employee ideas in the decision-making process (Daft, 2005). This style is most likely to enhance the morale of subordinates who are well motivated and engaged in tasks that are nonrepetitive (Dubrin, 2007).

Achievement-Oriented Leadership

This leadership style challenges employees to work at a performance level that is the best possible. The leader sets a very high standard and continuously seeks to improve performance above that initial standard (Daft, 2005). Achievement-oriented leaders also express a great deal of confidence in the abilities of employees to set and achieve very demanding goals (Yukl, 2006). This style is most appropriate for improving morale when subordinates have a high need to achieve and are working on tasks that are characterized by variety and ambiguity (Dubrin, 2007).

The path–goal theory is different from trait theory in that leaders are not constrained to a leadership style that depends on their personality. It is also different from contingency theory in that leaders do not have to be matched to particular situations or the situation changed to match leader style. House and Mitchell (1974) argue that leaders may be flexible (similar to situational leadership in Chapter 5) and exercise all or any of the four styles described above. They suggest that it will depend on the subordinate and task characteristics. In addition, leaders may integrate styles should the situation require a blending of two or more styles (Dubrin, 2007). In the next two sections, we describe the subordinate and task characteristics on which the impact of leader behavior on subordinate motivation depends.

Subordinate Characteristics

Several characteristics determine how much satisfaction (present or future) subordinates will obtain from a leader's behavior. Four have been studied intensely. These are "subordinates' needs for affiliation, preferences for structure, desires for control, and self-perceived level of task ability" (Northouse, 2010).

Subordinates with a higher need for affiliation should prefer supportive leadership because friendly, concerned leadership will give these subordinates greater satisfaction. On the other hand, subordinates who work in uncertain situations and have a tendency to be dogmatic and authoritarian should prefer directive leadership because this type of leadership gives "psychological structure and task clarity" (Northouse, 2010).

Whether subordinates have an internal or external locus of control determines which leader behaviors give more satisfaction. Internal locus of control suggests that subordinates believe that the decisions they make affect what happens in their lives, while external locus of control suggests that subordinates believe that what happens in their lives is beyond their control. Subordinates with an internal locus of control should find participative leadership more satisfying because it gives a greater feeling of being in charge and of being an important part of the decision-making process. On the other hand, subordinates with an external locus of control should prefer directive leadership because it parallels their belief that external forces control what happens to them (Northouse, 2010).

Finally, self-perceived level of task ability is important in determining how leader behaviors affect subordinates' satisfaction and motivation. Subordinates with a higher perception of their own competence at performing specific tasks should prefer less directive leaders. As subordinates assess that they are becoming more competent, directive leadership may become superfluous and seem more controlling than necessary (Northouse, 2010).

Task Characteristics

Task characteristics also have a major effect on how leader behaviors affect subordinates' satisfaction and motivation. These characteristics include the subordinates' task design, the organization's formal authority system, and subordinates' primary work group (Northouse, 2010). For example, when there is task clarity and structure, well-established norms and customs, and a clear formal authority system, subordinates will not need leaders to provide goal clarity or coaching in how to achieve these goals. Subordinates will consider that their work is of value and that they can accomplish their tasks. Leaders in this situation may be viewed as more controlling than necessary, having little or no empathy and, therefore, unnecessary.

Other situations may need leaders to be more involved. In a context where there is goal ambiguity, leaders can provide structure. Repetitive tasks may require supportive leadership given the mechanical nature of these tasks. When there is a weak authority system, leadership may be required to provide clarity regarding rules and what is needed to accomplish assigned work. Finally, leaders may be required to encourage teamwork and acceptance of role responsibility when group norms and customs are weak.

Path–goal theory has a special focus on assisting subordinates to get around, over, under, or through obstacles that are keeping them from achieving their tasks. Obstacles may be responsible for subordinates having feelings of frustration, uncertainty, and being threatened. Path–goal theory implies that leaders should assist subordinates in getting around these obstacles or in removing the obstacles from the path to task completion. Helping subordinates in this way will increase their perceived level of task ability and their level of satisfaction and motivation.

House (1996) has reformulated path–goal theory by adding four new leader behaviors. These are facilitating subordinates' work, decision-making processes that are more group oriented, allowing work groups to network and represent themselves, and providing leader behavior that is based on values that are not focused solely on the bottom line. The essence of the reformulated theory is no different from the original—subordinates need leaders who will provide what is needed in the subordinates' environment and what is needed to make up for deficient skills, knowledge, and abilities (Northouse, 2010).

How Does Path–Goal Leadership Theory Work?

Table 7.1 suggests several possible ways the path–goal theory of leadership can integrate leader behavior with subordinate and task characteristics. While the theory is conceptually complex, it is also very pragmatic and gives direction to leaders with respect to assisting subordinates in accomplishing their work in a manner that provides them with satisfaction and motivation. The theory assumes flexibility on the part of leaders and suggests that leaders should choose leader behaviors that best suit subordinate needs and work situations. We provide some examples in the next paragraph.

Table 7.1 Path–Goal Theory: How It Works

Leader Behavior	Group Members	Task Characteristics
Directive leadership "Provides guidance and psychological structure"	Dogmatic Authoritarian	Ambiguous Unclear rules Complex
Supportive leadership "Provides nurturance"	Unsatisfied Need affiliation Need human touch	Repetitive Unchallenging Mundane and mechanical
Participative "Provides involvement"	Autonomous Need for control Need for clarity	Ambiguous Unclear Unstructured
Achievement oriented "Provides challenges"	High expectations Need to excel	Ambiguous Challenging Complex

SOURCE: From Northouse (2010). Copyright © 2010, Sage Publications, Inc. Reprinted with permission.

First, if you as a leader see that the path is ambiguous, rules are unclear, and there is complexity and that subordinates are authoritarian and dogmatic, you should be a directive leader to provide guidance and psychological structure. Second, if the work is repetitive, not very challenging, mundane, and mechanical and if subordinates are unsatisfied, need a human touch, and have a higher need for affiliation, you should be a supportive leader to develop and provide a nurturing atmosphere. Third, when you see that the path is ambiguous, the way is unclear, the task is unstructured, and subordinates have a need for autonomy, control, and clarity, you need to be a participative leader who invites subordinates into the decision-making process. Finally, if the path is ambiguous, the task is challenging and complex, and subordinates have high expectations for what they can achieve and a higher need to excel, you need to be an achievement-oriented leader who challenges subordinates.

Of course, as we mentioned earlier, leaders may find it appropriate to exercise two leader behaviors simultaneously. It may be that the situation and subordinate characteristics call for you as a leader to be achievement oriented and supportive (Dubrin, 2007). We find that in our teaching, we set a high standard for students to challenge them to achieve, and we offer as much support as possible (without doing the work for them) to help and encourage them to achieve to the best of their abilities. There is an ethical component to this leader behavior. You have to know your students well enough to have expectations for achievement on their part that are achievable.

Leaders who are effective meet subordinates' needs. They help subordinates set goals and determine the path to take in achieving these goals. Effective leaders assist subordinates in getting around, getting through, or removing obstacles. Finally, leaders are effective when they assist subordinates in the achievement of their goals by guiding, directing, and coaching them along the right path.

References

Daft, R. L. (2005). *The leadership experience* (3rd ed.). Mason, OH: Thomson, South-Western.

Dubrin, A. (2007). *Leadership: Research findings, practice, and skills.* New York: Houghton Mifflin.

House, R. J. (1996). Path–goal theory of leadership: Lessons, legacy, and a reformulated theory. *Leadership Quarterly, 7*(3), 323–352.

House, R. J., & Mitchell, R. R. (1974). Path–goal theory of leadership. *Journal of Contemporary Business, 3,* 81–97.

McKinsey conversations with global leaders: Dan Vasella of Novartis. *McKinsey Quarterly.* Accessed on August 6, 2006, from http://www.mckinseyquarterly.com/Strategy/Strategic_Thinking/McKinsey_con versations_with_global_leaders_Dan_Vasella_of_Novartis_2401

Northouse, P. G. (2010). *Leadership: Theory and practice* (5th ed.). Thousand Oaks, CA: Sage.

Yukl, G. (2006). *Leadership in organizations* (6th ed.). Upper Saddle River, NJ: Pearson/Prentice Hall.

The Cases

General Electric: From Jack Welch to Jeffrey Immelt

This case describes the leadership initiatives of two of General Electric's (GE) chief executive officers: Jack Welch and Jeffrey Immelt. Under Jack Welch's leadership, GE, one of the most admired firms in the world, began its transformation from a manufacturing conglomerate to one that focused on services. Welch's stature as a management leader grew as GE's stock price increased. Many of Welch's management practices were adopted by

American and global organizations. While his changes resulted in excellent financial performance sustained over a long period of time, not all within GE agreed with his methods. Welch's departure in 2001 triggered a steep decline in GE's stock price. His successor, Jeffrey Immelt, took over the company days before the terrorist attacks in September 2001 and has spent the last few years preparing the firm for its next stage of growth.

Blinds to Go: Staffing a Retail Expansion

Blinds to Go is a manufacturer and retailer of customized window coverings. The company has been steadily expanding the number of its stores across North America. The vice chairman is concerned with the lack of staff in some of these newly expanded stores. With plans for an initial public offering within the next 2 years, senior management must determine what changes need to be made to the recruitment strategy and how to develop staff that will help them achieve the company's growth objectives.

◤ The Reading

Learning Goals or Performance Goals: Is It the Journey or the Destination?

Every manager has his or her eye on the finish line, but sometimes what you do or don't do during the race is more important than winning it.

General Electric

From Jack Welch to Jeffrey Immelt

Prepared by Ken Mark under the supervision of Stewart Thornhill

◤ Introduction

General Electric (GE) is a U.S. conglomerate with businesses in a wide range of industries, including aerospace, power systems, health care, commercial finance and consumer finance. In 2007, GE earned US$22.5 billion in net profit from US$170 billion in sales. In 2008, GE expected to generate US$30 billion in cash from operations. Driving GE's growth was what many commentators considered to be the "deepest bench of executive talent in U.S. business,"[2] the result of two decades of investment in its management training programs by its former chief executive officer (CEO), John F. (Jack) Welch, Jr. The current CEO, Jeffrey Immelt, took over from Jack Welch four days before September 11, 2001, and had spent the last few years preparing the firm for its next stage of growth.

Version: (A) 2008-04-18

⊠ General Electric

GE's roots could be traced back to a Menlo Park, New Jersey laboratory where Thomas Alva Edison invented the incandescent electric lamp. GE was founded when Thomson-Houston Electric and Edison General Electric merged in 1892. Its first few products included light bulbs, motors, elevators, and toasters. Growing organically and through acquisitions, GE's revenues reached $27 billion in 1981. By 2007, its businesses sold a wide variety of products such as lighting, industrial equipment and vehicles, materials, and services such as the generation and transmission of electricity, and asset finance. Its divisions included GE Industrial, GE Infrastructure, GE Healthcare, GE Commercial Finance, GE Consumer Finance, and NBC Universal.[3]

For more than 125 years, GE was a leader in management practices, "establishing its strength with the disciplined oversight of some of the world's most effective business people."[4]

When he became chairman and CEO in 1972, Reginald Jones was the seventh man to lead General Electric since Edison. Jones focused on shifting the company's attention to growth areas such as services, transportation, materials and natural resources, and away from electrical equipment and appliances. He implemented the concept of strategic planning at GE, creating 43 strategic business units to oversee strategic planning for its groups, divisions and departments. By 1977, in order to manage the information generated by 43 strategic plans, Jones added another management layer, sectors, on top of the strategic business units. Sectors represented high level groupings of businesses: consumer products, power systems, and technical products.[5]

In the 1970s, Jones was voted CEO of the Year three times by his peers, with one leading business journal dubbing him CEO of the Decade in 1979. When he retired in 1981, the Wall Street Journal proclaimed Jones a "management legend." Under Jones's administration, the company's sales more than doubled ($10 billion to $27 billion) and earnings grew even faster ($572 million to $1.7 billion).[6]

Jack Welch Becomes CEO

In terms of his early working life, Welch had:

> Worked for GE not much more than a year when in 1961 he abruptly quit his $10,500 job as a junior engineer in Pittsfield, Mass. He felt stifled by the company's bureaucracy, underappreciated by his boss, and offended by the civil service-style $1,000 raise he was given. Welch wanted out, and to get out he had accepted a job offer from International Minerals & Chemicals in Skokie, Ill.
>
> But Reuben Gutoff, then a young executive a layer up from Welch, had other ideas. He had been impressed by the young upstart and was shocked to hear of his impending departure and farewell party just two days away. Desperate to keep him, Gutoff coaxed Welch and his wife, Carolyn, out to

---

[2]Diane Brady, "Jack Welch: Management Evangelist," *BusinessWeek*, October 25, 2004. Available at http://www.businessweek .com/magazine/content/04_43/b3905032_mz072.htm, accessed November 12, 2007.

[3]http://en.wikipedia.org/wiki/General_Electric, accessed November 12, 2007.

[4]General Electric, "Our History: Our Company." Available at http://www.ge.com/company/history/index.html, accessed June 4, 2007.

[5]Christopher A. Bartlett and Meg Wozny, "GE's Two-Decade Transformation: Jack Welch's Leadership," Harvard Business School Case, May 3, 2005, pp. 1–2.

[6]Christopher A. Bartlett and Meg Wozny, "GE's Two-Decade Transformation: Jack Welch's Leadership," Harvard Business School Case, May 3, 2005, p. 2.

dinner that night. For four straight hours at the Yellow Aster in Pittsfield, he made his pitch: Gutoff swore he would prevent Welch from being entangled in GE red tape and vowed to create for him a small-company environment with big-company resources. These were themes that would later dominate Welch's own thinking as CEO.[7]

In his memoirs, Welch noted that the CEO's job was "close to 75 per cent about people and 25 per cent about other stuff."[8]

But Welch knew that his path to become CEO of GE was anything but smooth. As he recalled:

The odds were against me. Many of my peers regarded me as the round peg in a square hole, too different for GE. I was brutally honest and outspoken. I was impatient and, to many, abrasive. My behavior wasn't the norm, especially the frequent parties at local bars to celebrate business victories, large or small.[9]

For Welch, there was a seven-person "horse race" to become CEO that was, in his words, "brutal, complicated by heavy politics and big egos, my own included. It was awful."[10] In the end, however, Welch prevailed, becoming CEO in April 1981. Later, he learned that he had been left off the short list of candidates until late into the process. Welch recalled:

I didn't know that when the list was narrowed to ten names by 1975, I still wasn't on it.... One official HR [human resources] view of me stated at the time: "Not on best candidate list despite past operating success. Emerging issue is overwhelming results focus. Intimidating subordinate relationships. Seeds of company stewardship concerns. Present business adversity will severely test. Watching closely."[11]

1981 to 1987: Number One or Number Two and Delayering

Welch wanted the company to do away with its formal reporting structure and unnecessary bureaucracy. He wanted to recreate the firm along the lines of the nimble plastics organization he had come from. He stated:

I knew the benefits of staying small, even as GE was getting bigger. The good businesses had to be sorted out from the bad ones.... We had to act faster and get the damn bureaucracy out of the way.[12]

Welch developed this strategy based on work by Peter Drucker, a management thinker, who asked: "If you weren't already in the business, would you enter it today? And if the answer is no, what are you going to do about it?"[13] Welch communicated his restructuring efforts by insisting that any GE business be the number one or number two business in its industry, or be fixed, sold or closed. He illustrated this concept with the use of a three-circle tool. The

[7]John A. Byrne, "How Jack Welch Runs GE," *BusinessWeek*, June 8, 1998. Available at http://www.businessweek.com/1998/23/b3581001.htm, accessed June 4, 2007.

[8]Jack Welch, *Straight from the Gut*, Warner Books, New York, 2001, p. xii.

[9]Jack Welch, *Straight from the Gut*, Warner Books, New York, 2001, p. xii.

[10]Ibid, p. xiii.

[11]Ibid, p. 77.

[12]Ibid, p. 92.

[13]Ibid, p. 108.

businesses inside the three circles—services, high technology, and core—could attain (or had attained) top positions in their industries. The selected few included many service businesses, such as financial and information systems. Outside of the three circles were organizations in manufacturing-heavy sectors facing a high degree of competition from lower cost rivals, such as central air conditioning, housewares, small appliances and semiconductors.

Employment at GE fell from 404,000 in 1980 to 330,000 by 1984 and 292,000 by 1989. The changes prompted strong reactions from former employees and community leaders. Welch was the target of further criticism when he invested nearly $75 million into a major upgrade of Crotonville, GE's management development center.[14] Welch saw leadership training as key to GE's growth.

In addition, Welch undertook a streamlining exercise. By his estimate, GE in 1980 had too many layers of management, in some cases as many as 12 levels between the factory floor and the CEO's office. The sector level was removed, and a massive downsizing effort put into place.

Compared with the traditional norm of five to eight direct reports per manager, GE senior managers had 15 or more direct reports. Successful senior managers shrugged off their workload, indicating that Welch liberated them to behave like entrepreneurs. They argued that the extra pressure forced them to set strict priorities on how they spent their time, and to abandon many past procedures. Observers believed GE was running two main risks: having inadequate internal communication between senior managers and people who now reported to each of them; and the overwork, stress, demotivation and inefficiency on the part of managers down the line who had extra work assigned by their hard-pressed superiors. In

1989, an article in the *Harvard Business Review* reported "much bitter internal frustration and ill-feeling among the troops at GE."[15]

During this period, Welch earned his "Neutron Jack" moniker, a reference to a type of bomb that would kill people while leaving buildings intact. On the other hand, Welch could see that changes had to be made to make GE more competitive. He recalled:

> Truth was, we were the first big healthy and profitable company in the mainstream that took actions to get more competitive. . . . There was no stage set for us. We looked too good, too strong, too profitable, to be restructuring. . . . However, we were facing our own reality. In 1980, the U.S. economy was in a recession. Inflation was rampant. Oil sold for $30 a barrel, and some predicted it would go to $100 if we could even get it. And the Japanese, benefiting from a weak yen and good technology, were increasing their exports into many of our mainstream businesses from cars to consumer electronics.[16]

But Welch's strategy was not simply a cost-reduction effort: from 1981 to 1987, while 200 businesses were sold, 370 were acquired, for a net spend of $10 billion.

The turmoil that these changes caused earned Welch the title of "toughest boss in America," in a *Fortune* magazine survey of the 10 most hard-nosed senior executives. In tallying the votes, Welch received twice as many nominations as the runners-up. "Managers at GE used to hide out-of-favor employees from Welch's gun sights so they could keep their jobs," *Fortune* said. "According to former

---

[14]Ibid, p. 121.

[15]"General Electric Learns the Corporate and Human Costs of Delayering," *Financial Times*, September 25, 1989, p. 44.

[16]Jack Welch, *Straight from the Gut*, Warner Books, New York, 2001, pp. 125–126.

employees, Welch conducts meetings so aggressively that people tremble."[17] But Welch's credibility was bolstered by GE's stock performance:

> After years of being stuck, GE stock and the market began to take off, reinforcing the idea that we were on the right track. For many years, stock options weren't worth all that much. In 1981, when I became chairman, options gains for everyone at GE totaled only $6 million. The next year, they jumped to $38 million, and then $52 million in 1985. For the first time, people at GE were starting to feel good times in their pocketbooks. The buy-in had begun.[18]

Late 1980s: Work-Out, Boundaryless and Best Practices

Welch used GE's Crotonville facility to upgrade the level of management skills and to instill a common corporate culture. After reading comments from participants, Welch realized that many of them were frustrated when they returned to their offices because many of their superiors had discounted the Crotonville experience and worked actively to maintain the status quo. Welch wondered:

> Why can't we get the Crotonville openness everywhere? . . . We have to re-create the Crotonville Pit [a circular, tiered lecture hall at Crotonville] all over the company. . . . The Crotonville Pit was working because people felt free to speak. While I was technically their "boss," I had little or no impact on their personal careers—especially in the lower-level classes. . . . Work-Out was patterned after the traditional New

England town meetings. Groups of 40 to 100 employees were invested to share their views on the business and the bureaucracy that got in their way, particularly approvals, reports, meetings and measurements. Work-Out meant just what the words implied: taking unnecessary work out of the system.[19]

Work-Out sessions were held over two to three days. The team's manager would start the session with a presentation, after which the manager would leave the facility. Without their superior present, the remaining employees, with the help of a neutral facilitator, would list problems and develop solutions for many of the challenges in the business. Then the manager returned, listening to employees present their many ideas for change. Managers were expected to make an immediate yes-or-no decision on 75 per cent of the ideas presented. Welch was pleased with Work-Out:

> Work-Out had become a huge success. . . . Ideas were flowing faster all over the company. I was groping for a way to describe this, something that might capture the whole organization—and take idea sharing to the next level. . . . I kept talking about all the boundaries that Work-Out was breaking down. Suddenly, the word *boundaryless* popped into my head. . . . The boundaryless company . . . would remove all the barriers among the functions: engineering, manufacturing, marketing and the rest. It would recognize no distinction between "domestic" and "foreign" operations. . . . Boundaryless would also open us up to the best ideas and practices from other companies.[20]

[17]"Fortune Survey Lists Nation's Toughest Bosses," *The Washington Post*, July 19, 1984, p. B3.

[18]Jack Welch, *Straight from the Gut*, Warner Books, New York, 2001, p. 173.

[19]Jack Welch, *Straight from the Gut*, Warner Books, New York, 2001, p. 182.

[20]Ibid, pp. 185–187.

Welch's relentless pursuit of ideas to increase productivity—from both inside and outside of the company—resulted in the birth of a related movement called Best Practices. In the summer of 1988, Welch gave Michael Frazier of GE's Business Development department a simple challenge: How can we learn from other companies that are achieving higher productivity growth than GE? Frazier selected for study nine companies with different best practices, including Ford, Hewlett-Packard, Xerox and Toshiba. In addition to specific tools and practices, Frazier's team also identified several characteristics common to the successful companies: they focused more on developing effective processes than on controlling individual activities; they used customer satisfaction as their main gauge of performance; they treated their suppliers as partners and they emphasized the need for a constant stream of high-quality new products designed for efficient manufacturing. On reviewing Frazier's report, Welch became an instant convert and committed to a major new training program to introduce Best Practices thinking throughout the organization, integrating it into the ongoing agenda of Work-Out teams.[21]

To encourage employees to put extra effort into reaching their goals, Welch instituted the idea of "stretch." He was frustrated with the compromise that was occurring as work teams tried to lower targets and top management tried to raise targets. With stretch, teams were asked to develop two plans: the first reflecting what they expected to do; and the second that reflected the toughest targets they thought they had a chance of reaching. Welch explained:

The team knows they're going to be measured against the prior year and relative performance against competitors—not against a highly negotiated internal number. Their stretch target keeps them reaching. . . . Sometimes we found cases where managers at lower levels took stretch numbers and called them budgets, punishing those who missed. I don't think it happens much anymore, but I wouldn't bet on it.[22]

1990s: Six Sigma and the Vitality Curve

One well-known program popularized by GE was process improvement, or Six Sigma. As a result of GE's Best Practices program, Welch learned from Lawrence Bossidy, a former GE executive, how AlliedSignal's Six Sigma quality program was improving quality, lowering costs and increasing productivity. Welch asked Gary Reiner, a vice-president, to lead a quality initiative for GE. On the basis of Reiner's findings, Welch announced a goal of reaching Six Sigma quality levels company-wide by the year 2000, describing the program as "the biggest opportunity for growth, increased profitability, and individual employee satisfaction in the history of our company."[23] Subsequently, every GE employee underwent at least minimal training in Six Sigma, whose terms and tools became part of the global language of GE. For example, expressions like "CTQ" were used to refer to customer requirements that were "critical to quality" in new products or services.[24]

---

[21]Christopher A. Bartlett and Meg Wozny, "GE's Two-Decade Transformation: Jack Welch's Leadership," Harvard Business School Case, May 3, 2005, p. 5.

[22]Jack Welch, *Straight from the Gut*, Warner Books, New York, 2001, p. 386.

[23]Christopher A. Bartlett and Meg Wozny, "GE's Two-Decade Transformation: Jack Welch's Leadership," Harvard Business School Case, May 3, 2005, p. 12.

[24]Matt Murray, "Can GE Find Another Conductor Like Jack Welch?" *The Wall Street Journal* Europe, April 13, 2000.

Whereas Six Sigma was focused on process improvement, to develop GE's talent pool, Welch looked to differentiate his people. He remarked: "In manufacturing, we try to stamp out variance. With people, variance is everything." Welch knew that identifying and ranking people in a large organization was not a simple task. GE began using what became known as 360-degree evaluations, in which managers and supervisors were evaluated by their subordinates and their peers as well as by their bosses. One exception was Welch. He did not get evaluated by his subordinates. "I've peaked out," he said. Nor did he evaluate the top executives immediately below him.[25]

Next, Welch put in place an assessment based on a "vitality curve," roughly shaped like a bell curve. He asked his managers to rank all their staff into the "top 20," "the Vital 70" and the "bottom 10," with the intent to force executives to differentiate their employees. The "top 20" were groomed for larger assignments, and the "bottom 10" were coached out of the organization. In addition, Welch advocated categorizing employees as "A, B or C" players. He explained that how both assessment tools worked together:

> The vitality curve is the dynamic way we sort out As, Bs, and Cs. . . . Ranking employees on a 20-70-10 grid forces managers to make tough decisions. The vitality curve doesn't perfectly translate to my A-B-C evaluation of talent. It's possible—even likely—for A players to be in the vital 70. That's because not every A player has the ambition to go further in the organization. Yet, they still want to be the

best at what they do. Managers who can't differentiate soon find themselves in the C category.[26]

Welch reinforced the importance of the ranking system by matching it with an appropriate compensation structure. The A players received raises that were two to three times the increases given to Bs, and the As also received a significant portion of the stock option grants. C players received no raises or options. Welch admitted:

> Dealing with the bottom 10 is tougher. . . . Some think it's cruel or brutal to remove the bottom 10 per cent of our people. It isn't. It's just the opposite. What I think is brutal and "false kindness" is keeping people around who aren't going to grow and prosper. There's no cruelty like waiting and telling people late in their careers that they don't belong.[27]

In GE's people review process, known as "Session C," managers were expected to discuss and defend their choices and rankings. During these sessions, Welch was known to challenge his managers' talent decisions aggressively, expecting them to defend their choices with passion. Welch was prone to making quick judgment calls on talent, and these snap decisions could be perceived both positively and negatively. An observer commented:

> Welch is impetuous, inclined to make lightning strikes and wage blitzkrieg. His decisions on people, assets, and strategies can be made in a heartbeat; one bad review with Jack may be the

---

[25]Frank Swoboda, "Up Against the Walls," *The Washington Post*, February 27, 1994, p. H01.

[26]Jack Welch, *Straight from the Gut*, Warner Books, New York, 2001, p. 160.

[27]Ibid, 2001, pp. 160–162.

end of a long career. And the record shows that many of Welch's snap decisions have turned out to be stupendous blunders.[28]

One example was Welch's purchase of Kidder Peabody, then one of Wall Street's most prominent investment banks. Although his board of directors was opposed to the idea, Welch's persuasive arguments carried the day. But merging the two cultures proved more difficult than he imagined. Welch stated that at Kidder Peabody, "the concept of idea sharing and team play was completely foreign. If you were in investment banking or trading and your group had a good year, it didn't matter what happened to the firm overall."[29] In addition, Kidder Peabody was hit by two public scandals: insider trading and fictitious trades that led to a $350 million writedown. Another example was NBC's partnership with Vince McMahon in January 2001 to launch the XFL, an alternative football league to the NFL. After losing $35 million on the venture in four months, and accompanied by falling viewership, the league shut down in May 2001.[30]

Some managers were worn down by the constantly evolving programs. A chemist who once worked for GE Power Systems stated:

It's management by buzzword. People chant Jack's slogans without thinking intelligently about what they're doing. I've been stretched so much I feel like Gumby. All Welch understands is increasing profits. That, and getting rid of people, is what he considers a vision. Good people, tremendous people, have been let go, and it is hurting our business. I'm trying to meet the competition, but his policies aren't helping me. It's crazy, and the craziness has got to stop.[31]

Welch believed otherwise: "No one at GE loses a job because of a missed quarter, a missed year, or a mistake. That's nonsense and everyone knows it. . . . People get second chances."[32]

Over his tenure as CEO, Welch had grown GE's market capitalization by 27 times, from $18 billion to $500 billion. The company was trading 28 times forward earnings versus about 24 for the Standard & Poor's 500.[33] See Exhibit 1 for selected GE information over 25 years.

After two decades as GE's CEO, Welch retired, nominating Jeffrey Immelt as his successor. Immelt was one of three candidates short-listed for the job. Observers noted that Immelt was "starting his tenure at the end of an unprecedented bull market and in the midst of a global economic slowdown."[34] Despite GE's consistent earnings growth even during the economic downturn, GE's stock had fallen 33 per cent from its high of about $60 per share in August 2000. Many attributed this steady drop to the anticipation surrounding Welch's departure.[35]

Immelt's first day on the job was September 7, 2001, four days before the terrorist attacks in the United States.

---

[28]Thomas F. Boyle, *At Any Cost*, Vintage Books, New York, 1998, pp. 11–12.

[29]Jack Welch, *Straight from the Gut*, Warner Books, New York, 2001, p. 222.

[30]Eric Boehlert, "Why the XFL Tanked." Available at http://archive.salon.com/ent/feature/2001/05/11/xfl_demise/index.html, accessed January 11, 2008.

[31]Thomas F. Boyle, *At Any Cost: Jack Welch, General Electric, and the Pursuit of Profit*, Vintage Books, New York, 1998, p. 223.

[32]Ibid, p. 274.

[33]William Hanley, "An Eye on GE as Jack Bows Out," *National Post*, August 23, 2001, p. D01.

[34]Daniel Eisenberg and Julie Rawe, "Jack Who?" *Time*, September 10, 2001, p. 42.

[35]Ibid.

| Exhibit I | GE: Selected Information From 1981 to 2008 |

($ billions)	1981	1986	1991	1996	2001	2006
Revenues	27.2	36.7	52.3	79.2	125.9	163.4
Net Profit	1.7	2.5	2.6	7.3	14.1	20.7

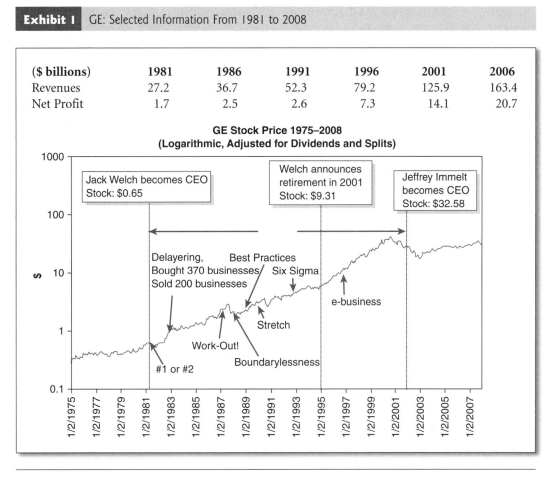

GE Stock Price 1975–2008
(Logarithmic, Adjusted for Dividends and Splits)

SOURCE: Case writers. Stock information from finance.yahoo.com, accessed January 5, 2008.

The Transition From Welch to Jeffrey Immelt

Immelt joined GE in 1982 and held several global leadership positions in GE's Plastics, Appliance and Medical businesses.[36] At GE Medical, his last assignment before becoming CEO, Immelt became a star by:

persuading a growing number of cash-strapped hospitals to trade in their old-fashioned equipment for digital machines that were capable of generating more dynamic images much faster. He inked lucrative, long-term deals with such hospital giants as HCA and Premier, and bought a number of smaller companies to round out his product line, all the while growing GE's market share from 25 per cent to 34 per cent and moving the company into services such as data mining.[37]

[36]"Jeff Immelt, CEO." Available at http://www.ge.com/company/leadership/ceo.html, accessed January 6, 2008.

[37]Daniel Eisenberg and Julie Rawe, "Jack Who?" *Time*, September 10, 2001, p. 42.

Only the ninth man to lead GE since 1896, Immelt followed in the footsteps of his predecessors by abandoning the leadership approach favored by Welch. In contrast with Welch's need to control and cajole his management, Immelt was "less a commander than a commanding presence."[38] "If you, say, missed your numbers, you wouldn't leave a meeting with him feeling beat up but more like you let your dad down," said Peter Foss, a longtime friend and colleague of Immelt's and president of GE Polymerland, part of GE's plastics business.[39] Immelt believed that leaders exhibited three traits:

> It's curiosity. It's being good with people. And it's having perseverance, hard work, thick skin. Those are the three traits that every successful person I've ever known has in common.[40]

Immelt aimed to continue GE's transition "from a low-margin manufacturer to a more lucrative services company."[41] During Welch's tenure, although revenues from services had grown from 15 per cent of revenues to 70 per cent, the majority of the revenues came from GE Capital (renamed GE Consumer Finance and GE Commercial Finance). In 2001, Immelt believed there was still room to grow services in many of its divisions, such as aircraft maintenance and monitoring contracts, and medical software and billing services.[42] There were differences in strategic approach as well. Whereas Welch had courted Wall Street by setting—and hitting—pinpoint earnings targets, Immelt gave the Street's short-term demands a back seat to long-term strategy.

Whereas Welch rapidly rotated managers through different divisions to develop generalists, Immelt wanted to keep them in place longer to develop specialists. Immelt explained:

> I absolutely loathe the notion of professional management. Which is not an endorsement of unprofessional management but a statement that, for instance, the best jet engines are built by jet-engine people, not by appliance people. Rotate managers too fast, moreover, and they won't experience the fallout from their mistakes—nor will they invest in innovations that don't have an immediate payoff.[43]

By 2007, Immelt had divested GE units representing 40 per cent of revenues. To grow $20 billion a year and more, new investments were made in areas where sizeable players had an advantage. Infrastructure and infrastructure technology, according to Immelt, was "a $70 billion business that will grow 15 per cent a year for the next five years. That's a business where small people need not apply."[44] In addition, Immelt was focused on growing revenues in emerging markets such as China, India, Turkey, Eastern Europe, Russia, and Latin America. Immelt believed that the international arena was where GE's future growth would come:

> In 2007, for the first time in the history of GE, we'll have more revenue outside the United States that we'll have inside the United States. Our

---

[38]Jerry Useem, "Another Boss Another Revolution," *Fortune*, April 5, 2004, p. 112.

[39]Daniel Eisenberg and Julie Rawe, "Jack Who?" *Time*, September 10, 2001, p. 42.

[40]David Lieberman, "GE Chief Sees Growth Opportunities in 2008," *USA Today*, December 14, 2007, p. B1.

[41]Daniel Eisenberg and Julie Rawe, "Jack Who?" *Time*, September 10, 2001, p. 42.

[42]Ibid.

[43]Jerry Useem, "Another Boss Another Revolution," *Fortune*, April 5, 2004, p. 112.

[44]David Lieberman, "GE Chief Sees Growth Opportunities in 2008," *USA Today*, December 14, 2007, p. B1.

business outside the United States will grow between 15 per cent and 20 per cent next year. We're a $172 billion company. In 2008, with the U.S. economy growing at 1.5 per cent, we'll grow revenue by 15 per cent because we're in the right places with the right products at the right time.[45]

Blinds To Go

Staffing a Retail Expansion

Prepared by Ken Mark under the supervision of Fernando Olivera and Ann Frost

◪ Introduction

"Staffing stores is our most challenging issue as we plan our expansion across North America," exclaimed Nkere Udofia, vice-chairman of Montreal-based Blinds To Go (BTG). "There are locations now where we've got physical store buildings built that are sitting unstaffed. How are we going to recruit and develop enough people to meet our growth objectives? What changes should our company make?" It was August 2, 2000 and Udofia knew that if Blinds To Go was to continue to grow 50 per cent in sales and add 50 stores per year, the issue of staffing would be front and centre.

◪ The Development of the Blinds To Go Retail Concept

This retail fabricator of window dressings began as a one-man operation. Growing up in the Côte-des-Neiges district in Montreal, Canada, David Shiller, the patriarch of the Shiller family, started in business in 1954. Stephen Shiller, his son, joined the business in the mid-1970s, convincing his father to focus on selling blinds. Called "Au Bon Marché," as it was known in Quebec, the Shillers began to create the production system that allowed them to cut the normal six- to eight-week delivery time frame for custom blinds to 48 hours. The customer response was overwhelming and the business took off.

Stephen Shiller exclaimed:

We gave them food, kept them busy while they waited for their blinds to be ready. The factory was literally next to the store and we offered our one-hour delivery guarantee, which kept our customers happy. Our St. Leonard store, the prototype for the current Blinds To Go stores, opened in 1991. Prior to that, people used to drive for up to 100 miles to come to our stores.

At that point, in early 1994, we realized what a hot concept we had on our hands—our sales were higher for each consecutive store opened, and none of our competitors could replicate our model. They were either manufacturers or retailers: none were both. None could hope to deliver the 48-hour turnaround we promised, had our unique sales model, which is 100 per cent commission-based, or had our attention to customer needs.

Version: (A) 2001-10-09

[45]Ibid.

By June 2000, Blinds To Go operated 120 corporate-owned stores across North America (80 U.S. stores, 40 Canadian stores), generating in excess of US$1.0 million in sales per store (having a staff of between six to 20 people per store). Blinds To Go expected to add an average of 50 new stores per year for the next five years, 80 per cent of which was targeted to be U.S. expansion stores.

Retail Operations

It was senior management's belief that quality of staff was even more important than store location, the surrounding customer demographics or advertising. Stephen Shiller, president, tested this belief with the East Mississauga, Ontario store.

In 1999, the East Mississauga store had experienced declining sales and high employee turnover. Analysing the demographic data surrounding the store left management with the impression that the store was a victim of poor location and cannibalization from another BTG store 10 miles away. However, Stephen Shiller suspected that the real problem was in the quality of the store's staff. Stephen Shiller commented:

> We let the store continue on its downward sales trend as we trained a management team for this store. Although I was quite sure that the quality of people was at fault, I was determined to use this as a lesson to show the rest of the company how important it was to have first-class talent. After six months of waiting, we put in an 'A' management team and trained staff. In one week, we doubled our sales and we tripled our sales in one month. That was a lesson we must never forget.

There were four staff roles in the stores— the sales associate, the selling supervisor, the assistant store manager and the store manager. The sales associates were the most junior employees and their job was to follow a set plan to help walk-in customers purchase a set of blinds. If they proved to be consistent sales performers, they would be promoted to selling supervisors or assistant store managers. Selling supervisors were assistant managers in training and usually had been one of the best sales associates. Assistant managers were in charge of the store when the store manager was not scheduled to work. The store manager was directly responsible for overall store operations, including closing sales, motivating and developing staff, and handling customer service issues such as repairs and returns.

Generally, a very good sales associate was promoted to selling supervisor six to nine months after hiring date. To become a store manager generally took another six to 18 months. However, because of the enormous variation in personal potential, these progression targets were by no means fixed.

The BTG selling process involved a very high level of interaction with the customer, which set a very high level of service expectation. At the retail stores, the emphasis on customer satisfaction and sale closure led to a higher volume of orders relative to their retail competition. Outlined in the Blinds To Go University Manual (training program for new sales staff) were the following four operating guidelines:

- Service and Satisfy Every Customer
- Never Lose a Sale
- Make the Customer Feel Special
- Bring the Manager Into Every Sale to Give the Customer "Old Fashion Service"

Salespeople were expected to bond with a customer through a personal greeting, then ask open-ended questions about their product needs. The purpose of the next few minutes of interchange between associate and customer was to understand the customer's primary concerns and work towards a sale by resolving those issues. Next, associates emphasized to the customer the quality of the product, large selection and warranties. At this point, the associate would listen to any customer objections, and try to address them. The associate would price the product(s), then introduce the customer to the store manager. After walking the store manager through the order, the associate would deduct any relevant coupons, then attempt to close the sale.

All employees of BTG, even up to the president, prided themselves on being able to sell blinds to customers. During store visits, it was not uncommon to see senior management helping out the staff in dealing with an overflow of customers.

⊠ Compensation of Retail Staff

The commission-based structure fostered a high-energy, sales hungry culture at Blinds To Go. Todd Martin, the director of retail planning and operations explained:

> We know people come to us because they need blinds. An example of our culture in action is a manager who is unhappy with closing eight of 10 sales, because with the tools at his disposal, he should be able to close all 10. Even if the customer is just looking because they want to buy a house in six months, we can take their worries away from them. He should be able to sell to 10 out of 10 customers.

Todd Martin also believed there was a healthy competitive environment among sales associates. He offered:

> In the store, there are no rules on grabbing customers—in my two years

here, I've never seen a problem with staff fighting for customers.

As BTG grew from a one-store operation, the Shillers kept a commission pay structure for its salesforce, believing that it best motivated performance. From experience, they knew that a suitable salesperson could, with the commission structure, make more money at BTG than at a comparable retail outlet. The focus had been on hiring energetic, personable people who loved the thrill of a sale.

⊠ A Change in Compensation Results in Sales Decline

In 1996, the Shillers decided to change the compensation system from full commission to salary. This change was the result of a recommendation from a newly hired vice-president of store operation who had been the vice-president of a major U.S. clothing retailer. Her intention was to attract more recruits for Blinds To Go's expansion phase by standardizing store operations and compensation. At that time, there were already 15 stores and expansion was underway. Based on her prior experience at the U.S. retailer, she led the change from full commission to paying sales associates a wage of Cdn$8 per hour. This was intended to make sales associates less entrepreneurial and more customer-service focused. Store manager compensation was also revised to reflect a higher base salary component relative to commissions. A more casual uniform was mandated in place of the business casual attire that was being worn at stores. In an attempt to differentiate the roles of sales associates and store management, it was decided that the store manager would no longer be involved in the sale. Though skeptical of this recommendation, the Shillers reluctantly agreed to proceed as suggested, rolling out these changes in 1996.

Sales declined between 10 per cent to 30 per cent in both new and existing stores from

1996 to 1997. Overall staff turnover increased to more than 40 per cent from a pre-1995 figure of 15 per cent. This problem was further exacerbated by the fact that rapid store expansion into Toronto, Philadelphia and Detroit had required the deployment of skilled store staff, thinning the ranks of existing stores. The Shillers attributed this decline in performance primarily to the change in the compensation structure.

⊠ BTG Reverts to Commission-Based Compensation

Unsatisfied with this turn of events, a change was made in the leadership of the stores' team. A variation of the commission-based compensation plan was brought back in May 1998 (see Exhibit 1). Udofia explained why he

Exhibit I	BTG Pay Structure History		
Corporate Formula	**Original**	**1995 to 1996**	**Current**
Sales Associate	$3 to $5/hr + 3% sales	$8/hr	$6 to $8/hr minimum, *or* 6% sales (whichever was higher)
Managers/Assistants	$10,000 to $20,000/yr + 1.5% – 3% of overall store sales	$25,000 to $40,000/yr + 0.25% – 0.5% of overall store sales	$10,000 to $20,000/yr + 1.5% – 2.5% of overall store sales
Actual Results	**Original**	**1995 to 1996**	**Current**
Sales Associate Top 20% of class ($14,000/sales/week)	$620/wk	$320/wk	$840/wk
Sales Associate Average Success ($10,000/sales/week)	$500/wk	$320/wk	$600/wk
Sales Associate Marginal Performer ($6,000/sales/week)	$380/wk	$320/wk	$360/wk
Sales Associate Poor Performer ($3,000/sales/week)	$290/wk	$320/wk	$240/wk
Manager Top 20% (2.5% of store sales)	$75,000/yr	$52,500/yr	$67,500/yr
Manager Average Success (1.2% of stores sales)	$50,000/yr	$40,000/yr	$50,000/yr
Manager Poor Performer	$35,000/yr	$35,000/yr	$40,000/yr

believed that commission was key to the sales culture of Blinds To Go:

> When we made the 1996 change, the base salary of $8/hour made it much easier to staff the store, but we were attracting a lower caliber of people— our best commission-based people did not like it and left. Having learned our lesson, we went back to our roots, brought back the old culture and experienced a sales turnaround. But, we've never 100 per cent recovered from it and are still playing catch-up today.

Since the return to commission-based compensation in 1998, store sales improved across the board, and within a few months, stores were posting between 10 per cent to 30 per cent increases in sales from the previous year (see Exhibit 2).

Exhibit 2 Sales Turnaround			
	Pre-1994	1995 to 1996	1997 to 2000
New stores/year	N/A	25	20
New store average sales	$1 million	$0.7 million	$1.2 million
Versus comparable store sales year ago	3%	−20%	+15%

This dramatic turnaround was accomplished with the aid of several other initiatives. First, all U.S. district sales managers (DSMs) were brought to Toronto to see top-performing stores, thus establishing a performance benchmark. Next, a BTG employee stock option plan for store employees (all full-time sales associates were made partners and given shares in the company) was implemented along with a sales award and recognition program. Also, weekly development conference calls between senior management and the district sales managers and training managers were set up for the purpose of constant updates and to facilitate group learning. Finally, a manager/assistant training program was tested in the U.S. in early 1998.[46]

The 1998 shift back to commission caused another huge turnover in BTG stores. This was unfortunate, because, from a staffing perspective, BTG had still not fully recovered from the previous compensation change. The need for additional staff was further aggravated due to BTG's continued push for growth and the tight U.S and Canadian labor markets (four per cent unemployment) in which it operated.

Another concern was that a commission-based compensation structure would not work in the U.S. Martin explained:

> The U.S. folks seemed uncomfortable with 100 per cent commission. They seem to prefer a straight wage or salary. Thus, we have not figured out our compensation system, but for now, it's largely commission based. We know that for the people who are good, they will figure out what they need and go get it. Commission for us is like an insurance

---

[46] This program eventually evolved into the Legends Training Program, where the best training managers at BTG were relocated to new regions to motivate, train and coach new store employees.

policy on our hires—the better you are the more you make. If you don't like servicing the customers, you leave.

Along with the reversion to the proven BTG compensation structure, Blinds To Go emphasized the practice of promoting their managers from within. Senior management believed that sales managers had to be properly motivated and provided them with a combination of store sales commission and opportunities for rapid advancement in the growing organization. However, being a top salesperson did not necessarily guarantee promotion, as Blinds To Go also looked at a matrix of sales, drive, presence, and people skills. Martin explained: "So even with the top salespeople, they have to be solid in their other attributes to be chosen for management. If the person is driven, he or she will ask for what it takes to be promoted."

✎ Attracting Quality Retail Sales Candidates

BTG was looking for people who possessed certain sales-driven qualities. Martin explained:

> We look for people who have the 'gift of the gab,' no ego, are honest, like sales, are driven and hungry for an opportunity, and have good leadership and good people skills. People have to possess these core values. We're partners—we want other people who want to be our partners. We pay for performance. You bet on yourself. You get rewarded because you're performing. Entry-level sales associates get 1,000 stock options after 90-days. At another successful retailer start-up that has since gone public, their people only received 500 options each.

Having recognized that quality of staff was paramount, BTG devoted resources to ensure

that it hired the right people as it was estimated that 80 per cent of their expansion needs would be for new U.S. stores. BTG store staff was very diverse. In terms of gender, it was a 50/50 split between men and women. Among associates, high school was the most common education level, followed by college students, then college graduates. In Ontario, Canada, 20 per cent of the associates were recent immigrants who had college or professional qualifications. The average age of associates was distributed over a typical bell curve between the ages of 18 to 50.

Over the last few years, BTG had tried several recruiting methods to varying degrees of success. There were several formal and informal programs that worked to entice qualified personnel to apply to BTG.

Employee Referral

Having current staff refer friends and family to BTG seemed to be the most effective way to attract a candidate already briefed on the BTG concept. A recent addition to create an incentive to refer was the "BMW" contest where staff could win the use of a BMW car for a year if they referred 10 eventual hires that stayed for at least three months. Employee referrals alone did not currently satisfy BTG's hiring needs.

Internet Sourcing

BTG used the Internet in two ways: BTG solicited résumés at its blindstogo.com site; DSMs and recruiters actively searched online job sites like Monster.com and other job sites to contact potential candidates.

DSM Compensation Readjustment

To put more emphasis on staffing in early 2000, DSMs' incentive bonus was changed from a sales target to new staff quota target. Historically, district sales managers had received an incentive bonus based on sales. Thus, a large part of the DSM's role had evolved to include recruiting responsibilities—the DSM now had to hire 10 new sales associates a month.

BTG Retail Recruiters

Professional recruiters were hired in early February 1998 and had been paid annual salaries ranging from $30,000 to $60,000. Recruiters generate leads through cold calls (in-person and via telephone), networking referrals, colleges, job fairs, the Internet, and employment centres. Even though they were given some training and recruiting objectives, the initial recruiters had averaged around four hires per month (against the company objective of four hires a week). "Overall, the performance was sub-optimal," lamented Martin. "By paying them a base salary, we divorced performance from pay and they became administrators." For recruiters, a switch was made in early 2000 to a mix of salary and commission. "They will still need to average four hires a week—but we've increased our training and the 'per hire' commission will focus them on results," Martin concluded.

Newspaper Advertising

BTG used weekly newspaper advertising for nine months starting in mid-1998. Although this method generated a sufficient number of candidate leads, senior management believed that this medium did not generate the quality of candidates that it needed—newspaper advertising attracted people who did not possess the skills and core values that BTG was looking for.

Store Generated Leads

Each BTG had a "help wanted" sign on its window, and walk-in traffic, along with customer referrals, resulted in some sales associates becoming hired. Overall, this was very successful only in stores located in densely populated areas with foot traffic.

The Hiring Process at Blinds To Go

Once potential candidates were persuaded to apply, a store visit was arranged. The purpose of this visit was to acquaint the potential candidates with the BTG environment and for them to get an overview of the job of a sales associate. Subsequently, the DSM administered a telephone interview. If the candidates were selected to proceed beyond this screen, two additional face-to-face interviews awaited them—one with the DSM and another with the store manager. BTG hired associates against these six criteria:

1. "Gift for Gab"

2. Outgoing personality

3. Energetic and motivated

4. Honest

5. Likes sales or dealing with people

6. Positive

If the candidate was selected to be a sales associate, then references were checked and offers extended.

✎ The Results of Hiring Procedures

Before collecting data, it was the impression of senior management at BTG that the most effective method of attracting quality candidates was employee referral, followed by Internet sourcing, and then DSM recruitment. To confirm their suspicions, BTG tracked the yield of different hiring methods for June and July 2000 and as of the end of July, had the results shown in Table 1.

Martin explained that the highest ratio of leads to hire was in the employee referrals. This was partially attributed to the fact that referrals generally pursued employment with BTG,

Table 1	Yield of Different Hiring Methods		
Recruiting Method	**June**	**July**	**Total (2 mth)**
Cold Call (Recruiters)	9	0	9
Walk-ins	31	16	47
Internet	9	3	12
Employee Referral	39	20	59
DSM hires (Direct/Rehires/College)	8	8	16
Total	96	47	143

excited by the opportunity that a friend or family member who was a BTG employee had recounted. Cold calling was thought to have the lowest close rate because the recruiter had to first educate, then convince potential recruits. But cold calling was thought to be time-efficient if the recruiter was good. Recruiters were focused on non-store sources (cold calling, Internet, schools, etc.), store sources (store walk-ins and employee referrals) were handled by the DSM. Recruiters were now paid $20,000 a year with a bonus of $150 to $500 for each successful hire, defined as a hire who stayed at least three months.

Staff Turnover

BTG also began tracking staff turnover and had created a turnover list from existing data (see Table 2). A large percentage of staff voluntary turnover occurred in their first four months. The higher turnover after eight months was partly due to termination because of sales underperformance. Also, sales associates who were not progressing as fast as their peers would inevitably be dissatisfied, leaving for other jobs.

Blinds To Go Future Needs

BTG needed additional staff to proceed with its expansion plan of 50 stores per year and to fill current store requirements (see Table 3).

Udofia had one more pressing concern on his mind:

> We're planning an initial public offering in the next one to two years. The key to our success is our ability to recruit and develop enough people to meet our growth objectives.

He wondered what strategy he should follow to meet the staffing challenge ahead.

Table 2	Number of Staff Leaving and Length of Stay (Numbers from June and July 2000)		
Length of Stay	**1 to 4 Months**	**5 to 8 Months**	**8+ Months**
Total	29	12	13

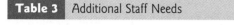 **Table 3** Additional Staff Needs		
Position	Current Complement	Extra Personnel Needed for Expansion (per year)
Sales Associate	1,000	500
Selling Supervisor	150	50
Asst. Store Manager	150	50
Store Manager	150	50

Learning Goals or Performance Goals

Is It the Journey or the Destination?

By Gerard H. Seijts and Gary P. Latham

While setting goals is important, setting an outcome goal—rather than a learning goal—can have a negative impact on an individual's performance. This is especially true when acquiring skills and knowledge is more important than being persistent and working harder. Instead of focusing on the end result, a learning goal focuses attention on the discovery of effective strategies to attain and sustain desired results. These authors build a compelling case for learning goals' superiority and describe the positive impact they can have on leadership, performance appraisal, and professional development.

⬚ The Good and the Bad of Setting Goals

Nearly all executives understand the importance of goal setting. And yet, most organizations have no idea how to manage specific, challenging goals, or what are sometimes labelled "stretch goals." For example, some organizations may ask employees to double sales or reduce product-development time but fail to provide those employees with the knowledge they need to meet these goals. It is foolish and even immoral for organizations to assign employees stretch goals without equipping them with the resources to succeed—and still punish them when they fail to reach those goals. This lack of guidance often leads to stress, burnout, and in some instances, unethical behaviour.

The Lucent scandal is a compelling example of what can happen when people feel undue pressure to make the numbers. Richard McGinn, the former CEO of Lucent, prided himself for imposing "audacious" goals on his managers, believing that such a push would produce dream results. In 2000, McGinn pushed his managers to produce results they could not deliver—not, apparently, without

AUTHORS' NOTE: The authors acknowledge the suggestions of Paul Beamish and Ed Locke in preparing this paper.

crossing the line. The pressures that McGinn applied were described in a complaint that a former Lucent employee filed, charging that McGinn and the company had set unreachable goals that caused them to mislead the public. Empirical research supports this claim, namely that setting unrealistic performance-outcome goals sometimes causes people to engage in unacceptable or illegal behaviour.

These findings point to a fault with the type of goal that was set, namely the performance-outcome goal. Setting a learning goal, on the other hand, is likely to be far more effective in helping individuals discover radical, out-of-the-box ideas or action plans that will enable organizations to regain and sustain a competitive edge. This paper discusses both types of goals and explains why learning goals can be more effective and when it is more appropriate to use them.

Goal Mechanisms

Generally speaking, there are at least four benefits of setting goals.

1. Specific performance goals affect an employee's choice about what to focus on, or which actions are goal relevant and which are not.

2. Goals help employees adjust their effort and persistence according to the goal's level of difficulty.

3. Goals help employees persist until they have reached them.

However, these three motivational mechanisms alone are not always sufficient for attaining a goal.

4. A fourth benefit of goal setting has to do more with cognition than motivation. Specifically, it has to do with the fact that a certain type of goal, the learning goal, helps employees acquire the knowledge

to understand and apply what they are doing. For complex tasks, setting goals based on one's knowledge stimulates the development of task strategies to complete those tasks. For example, the Weyerhaeuser Company discovered that unionized truck drivers who had been assigned a specific high-performance goal in terms of the number of trips per day from the logging site to the mill started to work "smarter rather than harder." After being assigned goals, truck drivers developed tactics to attain them. These included the use of radios to coordinate their efforts so that a truck would always be at the site when logs were available for loading. Performance increased because drivers drew on their existing knowledge to attain their goal. While they already knew how to use a radio, they chose to apply this knowledge in such a way that productivity increased.

Motivation or Knowledge Acquisition?

Goal setting is viewed by most executives and behavioral scientists as a motivational technique. The fact is, however, that most of the tasks that scientists have studied have been straightforward, so that the effect of a goal on an employee's choice, effort, and persistence could be easily assessed. But what happens when the task is not straightforward? Anecdotal evidence and empirical research provide a thought-provoking answer.

The ordeal of Wagner Dodge and the 15 firefighters under his command illustrates the difference between working hard (motivation) and working smart (knowledge acquisition). The ordeal is described by leadership expert Michael Useem in The Leadership Moment. A hellish, fast-moving forest-and-grass fire caused the group to run for their lives. With less than a minute remaining until the fire would swallow the group, Dodge discovered a way for the group to survive. He started an "escape fire" that cleared a small area of flammable prairie grass and bushes. As Useem states, Dodge survived because "he had literally burned a hole in the raging fire." However, Dodge's crew ignored his order to jump inside the expanding ring of fire and all of them died while trying to outrun the blaze. For Dodge, working smart, that is, knowledge acquisition, led to a far better result than "working hard."

In the context of running a successful business, Dell Computer Corporation CEO Michael Dell emphasizes the importance of information and knowledge acquisition:

> It's all about knowledge and execution. Traditionally, it was thought that lack of capital was the barrier to entry into a new competitive market. Take a look around, and you'll see that's just not true anymore. Information will increasingly become both a tool to help businesses hone their competitive edge and a weapon to protect them against the competition. Besides Dell, there are countless successful companies that are thriving now despite the fact that they started with little more than passion and a good idea. There are also many that failed, for the very same reason. The difference is that the thriving companies gathered the knowledge that gave them a substantial edge over their competition, which they then used to improve their execution, whatever their product or service. Those that didn't simply didn't make it.

In sum, a person's quest to be effective is influenced by ability and motivation, so that in the end, performance is a function of creative imagination or learning, AND sheer effort and persistence. This is particularly true for tasks where an individual lacks the requisite knowledge or skill to master those tasks. Thus, we see that setting a performance goal can have a downside.

Performance-Outcome Goals and Their Downside

Acquiring knowledge before setting a performance-outcome goal can be critically important. On the other hand, setting a specific performance goal can damage a person's effectiveness in the early stages of learning. This is because in the early stage of learning a person's attention needs to be focused on discovering and mastering the processes required to perform well, rather than on reaching a certain level of performance.

This reality highlights the fact that the attentional demands that can be imposed on people are limited. Trying to attain a specific performance goal places additional demands on people, so much so that they are unable to devote the necessary cognitive resources to mastering the task. A performance-outcome goal often distracts attention from the discovery of task-relevant strategies. For example, focusing on a score of 95 may prevent a novice golfer from focusing on mastering the swing and weight transfer, and using the proper clubs to shoot 95. Unwittingly, the golfer has diverted the cognitive resources necessary for understanding the task to a self-regulatory activity, namely shooting 95. The golfer has focused on scoring at the expense of acquiring the skills to become a better golfer. In the process, the golfer has exposed the downside of setting a performance goal.

Learning Goals or Performance-Outcome Goals

That setting specific performance goals can sometimes actually worsen performance is at first glance astonishing in that this conclusion is at odds with the accumulated findings of over a quarter of a century of research in the behavioral sciences.

For at least three decades, this research has shown that goal setting is a powerful and effective motivational technique. Specifically, the research shows again and again that a performance goal influences choice, effort, and the persistence needed to attain it. However, it is often forgotten that performance at a high level is a function of ability as well as motivation. Consequently, we wondered what would happen if the goal of certain tasks, say those for which minimal prior learning or performance routines existed, was switched to knowledge acquisition instead of motivation. (In situations where learning rather than an increase in motivation is required, setting a specific performance goal is not likely to be prudent. Perhaps a specific high-learning goal should be set instead. For example, a novice golfer should consider setting a high learning goal such as learning how to hold a club or when to use a specific iron. In short, the novice golfer must learn how to play the game before becoming concerned with attaining a challenging performance outcome [e.g., a score of 95].)

To test our idea, we examined the effects of learning versus performance-outcome goals by using a complex business simulation, namely, the Cellular Industry Business Game (CIBG). The CIBG is an interactive, computer-based simulation that is based on the events that occurred in the U.S. cellular telephone industry. It uses a complex set of formulas to link the various strategic choices to performance outcomes. The CIBG consists of 13 rounds of decision making, each corresponding to one year of activity. Participants were asked to make decisions concerning ten areas of activity during each round. Examples of the strategic options are pricing, advertising, sales-force, cost containment, finance, geographic scope, and alliances with other companies. Each area of activity allowed numerous choices. For example, in the finance area, participants could raise funds by issuing bonds, public shares or dividends, or by borrowing from the bank.

The evolution of the cellular telephone industry was predetermined in the simulation. For example, during the first eight decision periods (simulating the industry's first eight years) competition was restricted by region.

Following year eight, however, the telecommunications industry experienced a radical environmental change in the form of deregulation. Hence, participants in the simulation were given several warnings that deregulation was likely to occur. The strategic options that were viable before deregulation were no longer effective. Thus, to maintain or increase market share, participants now needed to discover a new set of strategies. This aspect of the CIBG simulation reflects a business environment where past success strategies are by no means a guarantee for future success.

The participants assigned a specific high-learning goal were told to identify and implement six or more strategies for increasing market share. The results revealed that:

1. Performance was highest for individuals who had a specific high learning goal. Their market share was almost twice as high as those with a performance outcome goal. There was no significant difference in performance among individuals with a performance goal, or those who were simply urged to do their best.

2. Individuals who had a learning goal took the time necessary to acquire the knowledge to perform the task effectively and to analyze the task-relevant information that was available to them.

3. Those with a learning goal were convinced that they were capable of mastering the task. This suggests that the increase in self-efficacy resulting from a learning goal occurs as a result of the discovery of appropriate strategies for task mastery. A performance goal, on the other hand, can lead to a highly unsystematic "mad scramble" for solutions.

4. Those with a learning goal had a higher commitment to their goal than did those with a performance goal. The correlation between goal commitment and performance was also significant.

These research findings are consistent with the observations of the CEOs cited throughout the paper.

Why Learning Goals?

How does a learning goal differ from a performance-outcome goal? What explains the superiority of a learning goal over a performance goal for a complex task? How can specific challenging learning goals be applied in business settings?

Learning Goals, Performance Goals and the Efficacy of the Former

The primary distinction between performance and learning goals lies in the framing of the instructions given to employees. Hence, the difference between these two types of goals is first and foremost a "mindset." The respective instructions focus attention on two different domains-motivation versus ability. A performance goal, as the name implies, frames the instructions so that an employee's focus is on task performance (e.g., attain 20 percent market share by the end of the next fiscal year). The search for information to attain the goal is neither mentioned nor implied because knowledge and skills are considered a given for tasks that require primarily choice, effort, or persistence. Similarly, a learning goal frames the instructions in terms of knowledge or skill acquisition (e.g., discover three effective strategies to increase market share). A learning goal draws attention away from the end result to the discovery of effective task processes. Once an employee has the knowledge and skills necessary to perform the task, a specific performance goal should be set to direct attention to the exertion of effort and persistence required to achieve it. The performance goal cues individuals to use strategies or performance routines that the person knows are effective. Setting a learning goal for a task that is relatively straightforward wastes time. It is also ineffective in that the person has already mastered the requisite performance routines and is aware of the requisite job behaviors.

In short, learning goals help people progress to the point where performance-outcome goals increase one's effectiveness. The focus of a learning goal is to increase one's knowledge (ability); the focus of a performance goal is to increase one's motivation to implement that knowledge. Therefore, both learning and performance goals are needed to be successful. But, as noted earlier, our research shows that a performance goal should not be set until an employee has the knowledge to attain it.

Practical Applications of Learning Goals

Based on our findings, as well as the experiences of the CEOs we have cited, there are at least 3 areas where the application of learning goals should prove particularly helpful in improving performance—leadership, performance management and professional development.

1. Leadership

Jack Welch once stated that, "An organization's ability to learn and translate that learning into action is the ultimate competitive advantage. . . . I wish we'd understood all along how much leverage you can get from the flow of ideas among all business units . . . the enormous advantage we have today is that we can run GE as a laboratory for ideas."

Three examples suggest the benefits of having a leader focus employee attention on the attainment of learning goals. First, when Andy Grove was the CEO at Intel Corporation, he was obsessed with learning as much as possible about the changing environment.

In Grove's own words, "I attribute Intel's ability to sustain success to being constantly on the alert for threats, either technological or competitive in nature." Second, Sam Walton continued to refine his business strategies and discover ways for improving his stores. He never stopped learning from competitors, customers, and his own employees. He believed that there was at least one good idea he could learn, even from his worst competitor. Walton passed on this philosophy to his employees. As Kurt Bernard, a retailing consultant, noted:

> When he meets you . . . he proceeds to extract every piece of information in your possession. He always makes little notes. And he pushes on and on. After two and a half hours, he left, and I was totally drained. I wasn't sure what I had just met, but I was sure we would hear more from him.

Leaders such as Welch, Grove and Walton would increase the effectiveness of their workforce if they set specific high learning goals for sharing ideas among divisions, identifying potential threats in the environment, or extracting ideas from competitors, customers and employees.

Third, the primary use of learning goals at Goldman Sachs, as described by Steve Kerr, is to develop present and future leaders. For example, a sales manager might be asked to join or even lead a taskforce whose goal is to discover a new process for product development. People's leadership skills are developed by assigning specific learning goals that require these people to go outside their comfort zone.

2. Performance Management

Coca-Cola Foods and PricewaterhouseCoopers (PWC) are among the many companies that have incorporated goal setting into their coaching and mentoring practices. The goals are typically performance outcomes or behavioral goals that are within employees' repertory of knowledge and abilities to increase in frequency (e.g., communicate the objectives of the program to coworkers).

PWC, which recognizes that this approach is not effective for every employee, also sets learning goals. For example, like other organizations, they hire job applicants for their aptitude rather than their existing skills. New employees,

therefore, benefit from mentors who actively help them discover ways to develop their competencies within the firm, and who assign them specific, high learning, rather than performance, goals. Employees assigned challenging learning goals in the early stages of their job typically outperform those who are initially given specific high performance targets.

Learning goals are also appropriate for seasoned managers. For example, those who operate in global organizations find it fruitful to focus on ways to effectively manage a myriad of social identity groups so as to minimize rigidity, insensitivity, and intolerance. Newly formed work teams, especially culturally diverse teams, need time to gel. Ilya Adler observed that managers view, "the cultural issue as an additional burden to the already difficult task of making a team function effectively." Focusing on the end result before team dynamics have been ironed out can hurt the team's performance. Thus, a team leader may be well advised to focus on the discovery of 3–5 strategies, processes, or procedures for accelerating effective interaction and teamwork, particularly ways of fostering understanding of local customs and values and developing mutual understanding and trust. In contrast, assigning a culturally diverse work team a specific performance goal before the team's rules of conduct have become accepted is likely to lead to prolonged "storming" and "norming." Indeed, it is not uncommon to see culturally diverse teams spend more time working out their differences than doing the actual work.

3. Professional Development

Jack Welch often moved his top executives from one functional area to another. Similar to the mentoring practice at PWC, he did this to broaden their knowledge base. When this is done in any organization today, employees should be asked to come up with a specific number of ideas that would help them improve the performance of their respective businesses. Welch also introduced the Work-Out, a forum that was intended to enable management and employees to share knowledge. Facilitators of these types of sessions should be asked to set a goal of discovering a specific number of ideas or strategies that will improve organizational effectiveness.

Other executives also ensure the ongoing professional development of their senior executives through job rotation. The purpose of the rotation is to "shake the executives up," provide them with opportunities to learn new perspectives, get them out of their comfort zones, and develop greater creativity. To ensure that this occurs, specific learning goals should be set to ensure that the broad perspective to which the executives are exposed actually helps the company make decisions in a cohesive fashion.

⚲ In the End, Goals Can Be Different

Today's workforce is under intense pressure to produce tangible results. Workers are perpetually in a "performance mode." This is a plus when known performance routines continue to be effective, and when the issue is fostering the conditions for a highly motivated workforce. In such instances, countless studies in the behavioral sciences support the significant motivational benefits of setting specific, challenging performance goals.

However, a high-performing workforce is a function of both high ability and motivation. This is particularly true in today's business environment in which organizations face rapidly changing technologies, information overload, escalating competitive pressures, and a host of other challenges. Hence the importance of knowing that learning goals and performance goals are different. They differ in the behavior/actions required to attain them and in their appropriateness for increasing an organization's effectiveness.

The purpose of a learning goal is to stimulate one's imagination, to engage in discovery, and to "think outside the box." The purpose of a performance goal is to choose to exert effort and to persist in the attainment of a desired objective or outcome using the knowledge one already possesses. Thus, the behavior of a person with a learning goal is to systematically search for new ideas, actively seek feedback, be reflective, and execute a specific number of ideas in order to test newly formed hypotheses. The behavior of a person with a performance goal is to focus on known ways to use the knowledge and skills that have already been mastered. When the strategy for an organization is already known and the ways to implement it have been deciphered, setting performance goals for an individual or team is appropriate. When an effective strategy requires innovation that has yet to emerge, specific high learning goals should be set.

CHAPTER

8

The Leader–Member Exchange Theory of Leadership

As leadership and other functions change and combine within organizations at all levels, role management and career/life management grow in importance. Through periodic developmental feedback, the global leader can help individuals actively manage their careers and their personal lives.

—Goldsmith, Greenberg, Roberston, &
Hu-Chan (2003, p. 139)

A s the quote above suggests, the leader–member exchange (LMX) theory of leadership is concerned with the interactions between leaders and followers (Daft, 2005). The trait, skills, and style approaches to leadership emphasized leadership from the leader's perspective. Situational, contingency, and path–goal theories of leadership are centered on the follower and the context in which the leader and follower interact with each other. In essence, these theories are about what leaders do to each of their followers (Northouse, 2010). The focal point in LMX theory is the dyadic relationship between a leader and each of his or her followers. In other words, LMX theory is concerned with the differential nature of the relationships between leaders and each of their followers (Daft, 2005; Dubrin, 2007; Yukl, 2006). We will describe two waves of studies that have examined the LMX theory of leadership.

The Early Studies

Graen and his colleagues (Dansereau, Graen, & Haga, 1975; Graen, 1976; Graen & Cashman, 1975) were the forerunners in the early studies related to LMX theory. They emphasized the vertical dyadic linkages that leaders developed with each subordinate. The relationship that a leader developed with his or her workgroup was the combination of all of these vertically dyadic relationships. This led to two broad types of relationships: those considered in-group relationships and those considered out-group relationships.

Relationships within the in-group are marked by mutual trust, respect, liking, and reciprocal influence. In-group relationships develop when leaders and followers negotiate that followers do more than required by their job description, and leaders provide more than that required by the formal hierarchy. In-group members are given more responsibility, more participation in decision making, more interesting job assignments, more tangible rewards, and more support for career advancement. In contrast, relationships within the out-group are marked by formal communication based on job descriptions. (Daft, 2005; Dubrin, 2007; Yukl, 2006). In addition, in-group members communicate more, are more involved, and are more dependable than out-group members (Dansereau et al., 1975). Out-group members do what is required and no more (Yukl, 2006). They may be physically present but will only do what is necessary to retain their jobs. Mentally, they may have defected from their jobs, even though they still come to work, do enough to keep their jobs, and then go home. They will not go the extra mile that is often required to achieve higher levels of effectiveness.

The Later Studies

Whereas early studies focused on the differential nature of in-groups and out-groups, the later studies focused on enhancing organizational effectiveness. Essentially, empirically based studies have found that where there are higher-quality leader–member exchanges, there are lower employee turnover, better employee evaluations, more frequent promotions, better work assignments, more participation by employees in decision making, enhanced commitment to the organization, more favorable attitudes toward the job, and greater support and interest from the leader (Graen & Uhl-Bien, 1995; Liden, Wayne, & Stilwell, 1993; Northouse, 2010).

In essence, these studies demonstrated that leader–member exchange quality was positively related to results for leaders, their followers, the groups in which leaders and followers interacted with each other, and the organization as a whole (Graen & Uhl-Bien, 1995). This suggests that organizations where leaders develop good working relationships with each individual subordinate will outperform those organizations where the leader–member exchange reflects mostly out-group member relationships (Yukl, 2006).

Leadership Making

The later studies led to a prescriptive approach to leadership that has come to be called *leadership making*. Leadership making suggests that leaders need to form high-quality, or in-group, exchanges with nearly all of their subordinates, not just a small minority. Leadership making is also about the development of partnership networks beyond the workgroup throughout the rest of the organization. Developing these networks should lead to better organizational performance and greater career progress for those leaders who engage in this practice (Graen & Uhl-Bien, 1995; Northouse, 2010).

There are three phases to leadership making (Graen & Uhl-Bien, 1991). They are the stranger phase, the acquaintance phase, and the partnership phase (Daft, 2005). In the stranger phase, the leader–member exchanges resemble those described earlier as out-group exchanges. In this phase, members are more concerned with their own self-interest than with what is best for the group.

In the acquaintance phase, the leader or member makes an offer to do more for the other. This is a testing period during which the leader and the subordinate are checking each other out to see if they trust each other enough to shift to in-group status or the partnership phase. During this phase, member self-interest lessens, and there is more of a focus on the group's goals and objectives.

In the mature partnership phase, leader–member exchanges are similar in quality to in-group exchanges described earlier. Leader–members who are in this stage with each other have developed a high level of "mutual trust, respect and obligation toward each other" (Northouse, 2010). Each leader–member relationship has been tested, and there is a confidence that the leader and member can count on each other. In this stage, leaders positively affect each member and are positively affected by each member. These leader–member exchanges go much farther than those previously defined as out-group exchanges in that there is a transformational nature to these exchanges that allows leaders and followers to pursue what is better for the team and the organization rather than their own self-interests (Northouse, 2010).

First Impressions

Some research (Liden et al., 1993) suggests that the leaders and members need to be aware that first impressions matter. Their results suggest that the initial expectations of leaders toward members and initial member expectations of leaders were positively associated with the leader–member exchanges 2 and 6 weeks later. In addition, initial expectations of the members toward their leader were good predictors of leader–member exchange quality 6 months into the relationship. This means that the leader–member exchange may be formed in the first days and that the old adage—You have only one chance to make a good impression—may be true (Dubrin, 2007).

How Does the LMX Theory of Leadership Work?

The LMX theory of leadership is both descriptive and prescriptive. In both cases, the heart of the LMX theory is the vertical dyadic relationship developed between a leader and each of her or his subordinates.

From a descriptive sense, LMX theory implies that we need to understand that in-groups and out-groups exist in groups and organizations and that as leaders, we participate in their development. Goal accomplishment with in-groups is substantively different than with out-groups. In-group members willingly work harder than required and are more innovative in accomplishing goals. Consequently, leaders give in-group members more opportunities, more responsibilities, more support, and more time.

Out-group members work differently than in-group members with their leaders. They work strictly within the guidelines governing organizational roles and only do the minimum necessary. Leaders are fair to these group members in that they respond to them by strictly adhering to any contractual obligations. However, they are not given any special treatment by their leaders. These out-group members receive the benefits that they are due and required based on their contract but nothing more.

From a prescriptive sense, Graen and Uhl-Bien's (1991) leadership-making model allows us to comprehend LMX theory the most. Their prescription is to develop relationships with all subordinates who are similar to those described earlier for in-group members. In other words, give all subordinates the chance to accept new responsibilities, nurture better-quality relationships with each subordinate, develop relationships based on trust and respect with all subordinates, and make the whole workgroup an in-group (Daft, 2005). Finally, leaders should form high-quality partnerships with people throughout the organization (Daft, 2005; Northouse, 2010).

Whether we view the LMX theory of leadership as descriptive or prescriptive, it works by emphasizing the dyadic relationship that both leaders and followers see as special and unique. Northouse (2010) suggests that "when these relationships are of high quality, the goals of the leader, the followers, and the organization are all advanced." Implied in this statement is that these goals are clearly defined and understood, as well as shared among all leaders and followers—this may be one of the prime responsibilities of leaders: to ensure the development of high-quality relationships between leaders and each follower. We encourage each of you to be willing to lead others but to also understand the responsibility you take on for developing special, unique relationships with each of your subordinates.

◤ References

Dansereau, F., Graen, G. B., & Haga, W. (1975). A vertical dyad linkage to leadership in formal organizations. *Organizational Behavior and Human Performance, 13*, 46–78.

Daft, R. L. (2005). *The leadership experience* (3rd ed.). Mason, OH: Thomson, South-Western.

Dubrin, A. (2007). *Leadership: Research findings, practice, and skills.* New York: Houghton Mifflin.

Graen, G. B. (1976). Role-making processes within complex organizations. In M. D. Dunnette (Ed.), *Handbook of industrial and organizational psychology* (pp. 1202–1245). Chicago: Rand McNally.

Graen, G. B., & Cashman, J. (1975). A role-making model of leadership in formal organizations: A developmental approach. In J. G. Hunt & L. L. Larson (Eds.), *Leadership frontiers* (pp. 143–166). Kent, OH: Kent State University Press.

Graen, G. B., & Uhl-Bien, M. (1991). The transformation of professionals into self-managing and partially self-designing contributions: Toward a theory of leadership-making. *Journal of Management Systems, 3*(3), 25–39.

Graen, G. B., & Uhl-Bien, M. (1995). Relationship-based approach to leadership: Development of leader–member exchange (LMX) theory of leadership over 25 years: Applying a multi-level, multi-domain perspective. *Leadership Quarterly, 6*(2), 219–247.

Goldsmith, M., Greenberg, C. L., Robertson, A., & Hu-Chan, M. (2003). *Global leadership: The next generation.* Upper Saddle River, NJ: Financial Times Prentice Hall.

Liden, R. C., Wayne, S. J., & Stilwell, D. (1993). A longitudinal study on the early development of leader–member exchange. *Journal of Applied Psychology, 78*, 662–674.

Northouse, P. G. (2010). *Leadership: Theory and practice* (5th ed.). Thousand Oaks, CA: Sage.

Yukl, G. (2006). *Leadership in organizations* (6th ed.). Upper Saddle River, NJ: Pearson/Prentice Hall.

◼ The Cases

Carnegie Industrial: The Leadership Development Centre

A director within the leadership development program of a large multinational organization must decide how to manage a very difficult conversation she must have with her assistant director. The assistant director, who is older and more experienced (although less educated), interviewed for the director's position and didn't get it. The assistant director has never been happy reporting to her much younger boss and has felt consistently left out of major decisions. The assistant director had confronted the director about her feelings and threatened to resign. How should the director handle this difficult conversation?

Moez Kassam: Consulting Intern

A summer assignment is turning into a nightmare for an intern at a large consulting firm. He has just received his third reprimand from his boss and is concerned how this relationship is distracting him from the project he needs to complete and how it could hurt his chances of obtaining full-time employment. He must decide how he can salvage the relationship with his boss and whether this organization is the best fit for him.

◼ The Reading

On Leadership: Leadership and Loyalty

Leaders expect their followers to be loyal and to be able to depend on their loyalty. Good leaders understand that there is a difference between real loyalty and a related but different concept—fealty. Smart leaders understand that fealty is demanded, whereas loyalty is earned. In this article, the author notes some things that leaders can do to earn loyalty.

Carnegie Industrial

The Leadership Development Centre

Prepared by Ken Mark under the supervision of Michael Sider

◼ Introduction

Even though she knew it was coming, Shannon Copley, a director at Carnegie Industrial's Leadership Development Centre, was taken aback by her co-worker's outburst of emotion.

Eleanor Galvin, the assistant director, had just issued what sounded like an ultimatum, her voice trembling with anger. Galvin was livid that she was not being considered for a full-time position in Copley's communications program.

   Version: (A) 2008-01-03

It was May 12, 2007, and both women were standing outside Copley's office in Somerville, Massachusetts. With colleagues watching her, Copley wondered how best to respond.

◪ Carnegie Industrial

Carnegie Industrial (Carnegie), headquartered in Stamford, Connecticut, was one of the biggest corporations in the United States with $125 billion in annual sales and 45,000 employees. Part of the S&P 500 since 1985, Carnegie was both a manufacturer of products for the engineering and construction industry and an industrial consulting firm, with clients primarily from the U.S. northeast. Carnegie had grown rapidly in the past decade as a result of a series of acquisitions. As a result, its workforce comprised at least four distinct cultures. In an effort to amalgamate the group, a leadership centre, patterned after General Electric's Crotonville facility, was built in Somerville, Massachusetts, in April 2001. Somerville was chosen for its location, which was central to the various Carnegie offices.

The Leadership Development Centre, or LDC, was housed in a refurbished factory, completely renovated to modern standards. A staff of 25 was led by Executive Director Elizabeth Silver and three directors. The LDC offered a menu of courses and leadership development modules. All new hires at Carnegie spent a week at the LDC as part of their orientation at the firm. The curriculum for these new hires focused on team work, financial analysis skills and the basics of project management. The leadership modules were reserved for grooming talent at the mid- and senior-level management ranks. In addition to the specialized programs in team-building, finance and project management, courses in two general areas were available: technical competency (specialized courses in engineering or science) and communications (courses in conflict resolution, negotiation, and written and oral communication).

◪ Shannon Copley and Eleanor Galvin

Shannon Copley had been hired as director of the LDC communications program in April 2006, with a mandate to revive the program, which had foundered in the past three years as evidenced by its poor reviews. Attendees complained that the materials were either outdated or bland, and the instruction uninspiring. Although the former director had been relieved of his duties, Silver had retained the four staff members. Through an executive search firm, the LDC had interviewed several candidates for the director's position and had narrowed its search to two candidates, Copley and Galvin.

Copley, in her early 30s, had recently completed her PhD in English and Communications from a well-respected Eastern U.S. school and for the past three years had been working in the investor relations practice of a prominent Boston-based consulting firm. She was both articulate and approachable, and was known for her innovative thinking and her project management skills. Copley had an informal business approach that valued results over decorum and hierarchy. Copley would arrive at work in casual clothing, wearing Birkenstocks. She encouraged her staff, all of whom were in their late 20s and early 30s, to dress in a similar manner. She disliked meetings, preferring to communicate through email or personal contact. When she did gather staff for meetings, she was informal but efficient. She ran her meetings quickly, with lots of casual banter and humor, and her staff seemed to appreciate both the brevity of the meetings and Copley's enthusiasm. When clients addressed her as "Miss Copley," she would correct them with a wave of her hand. "Call me Shannon," she would say. On the other hand, Copley could be business-like when the situation called for it: when the consulting firm faced an accelerated deadline for the completion of a client project, Copley was able to work efficiently within her team setting to complete the job ahead of time. Her collabora tive style was appreciated by her co-workers and superiors, and she had been recently promoted to manager level. Most recently, Copley had created an effective communications program for one of the firm's clients, and the program was winning plaudits from users. When Copley was interviewed for the position, she impressed Silver with her candor, innovative thinking and confidence:

> I've seen effective and ineffective programs. And effective programs are typically more than remedial in nature and accessible to employees throughout the business. Your previous communications program was both inaccessible and remedial. It sent the message that, if you used it, you were in need of help. When your managers sent staff to the program, the staff felt they were being criticized— that their communications skills weren't adequate. Furthermore, there were some important areas that the previous program wasn't equipped to handle, like working with the business's growing number of overseas managers whose English language skills put them at a disadvantage here in the U.S. Programs like this should be open to all associates, whether they're native English speakers or not. Everyone can benefit from improved communications. I know there's some apprehension about the costs of such a program—if we make it less remedial and open it up to lots of people as

a viable part of their leadership training in the company, there would be many candidates being coached—but we shouldn't limit it to the ones who need remedial help. We should use dedicated personnel for the coaching, and have learning teams from the different ranks. Junior team members can learn from seniors and vice versa. If you hire me, some of the program elements may seem avant-garde but they'd represent current thinking in the field. Don't hire me if you don't want change.

Eleanor Galvin, the other candidate for the director's position, held a master's degree in English from Oxford University and had spent 20 years in the human resources department of an international technical services firm, where she had specialized, among other things, in the leadership development of managers for whom English was a second language. Galvin was 50 years old. A conservative person by nature, Galvin preferred formal business attire at all times and dressed immaculately in expensive business suits. She was known for her attention to detail and her love of protocol and process. Galvin was reserved, cool and analytical in her business approach, but beneath the reserve was a professional respect for co-workers and clients. Galvin had been instrumental in working with her team to develop a well-regarded coaching program. Although her team of subordinates had initially envisaged a broad-reaching, high-impact (but costly) program, Galvin was able to work with them to create a more focused and thriftier version. The team never seemed to disagree with Galvin's suggestions because she was the most senior person on the team. Since joining the firm, Galvin had been promoted through four ranks from assistant manager to senior director. Her superiors praised Galvin for her no-nonsense business style. "Miss Galvin's tough but fair," quipped a junior employee. Two months earlier, Galvin left the job to be closer to her family in Somerville, and was actively seeking another position.

When Galvin was interviewed for the director's job, Silver was pleased with her grasp of the objectives and her precise answers:

> We should aim to help employees who can improve the most and we should do this in a cost-effective way. There should be clear deliverables, and regular progress updates. Although we would welcome suggestions from our team members—after all, the best ideas can come from anywhere—we need to keep this program focused. The last program was very good but the material could be refreshed. Let's not throw out the baby with the bathwater, so to speak. Too much change can be confusing to everyone, especially before we do the required analysis of existing processes.

◪ The "Communicate!" Program Is Created

Although Silver was impressed by both Copley and Galvin, she decided to offer Copley the director's job on the basis of her superior academic credentials and her previous experience creating a communications program, which Silver believed would bolster both Copley's credibility in the training sessions and the LDC's credibility throughout the organization. An assistant director's position was created and offered to Galvin. Silver was delighted when Galvin accepted despite the assistant director's position being only half-time. Silver strongly believed that the skills sets of the two hires were complementary and that both could work together to build an excellent program. Certainly, the two women had different approaches, but Silver believed that increased diversity of thought and personality in the workplace could lead to better results.

"I trust you to turn this program around," Silver said to Copley on her first day of work. "Here is your budget, here are your people, and you have free rein to shape this program. The only caveat is that I would like you to work closely with Eleanor Galvin."

"No problem," replied Copley, confidently. It was April 2006, and Carnegie's recruiting season was just under way. Copley knew that she had at least a month before the new hires were ready for training. In addition, mid-level and senior staff were busy completing mid-year reports and interviewing candidates. Copley called a meeting of her five team members (four from the previous director's team and Galvin) for a brainstorming session. They developed a list of priorities, then identified key action items. The sign-up web page on the intranet was updated, presentations were scheduled for each of the business units and a curriculum outline was developed.

In the first few weeks, Copley sensed that Galvin was having trouble adjusting to her new role as the second-in-charge. On the first day, for example, Galvin had approached Copley and, shaking her hand, congratulated her on her appointment. Galvin had thanked her, assured her that she was looking forward to working with her and then said: "I'm a little confused, though, as to which office should be mine." Silver had previously asked Copley whether it was "okay with her" to share an office with Galvin for a few weeks until better offices became available for both. Copley had agreed with the arrangement and had assumed that Galvin would also have no problems with the arrangement. However, for Galvin, the lack of an office was a bigger deal than Copley had anticipated. "I just feel," said Galvin, "that it looks bad to the staff and to the whole organization to have two directors sharing an office. Can you try to find me an office of my own as soon as possible?"

Although she was a little surprised at the exchange, Copley talked to Silver, made a few telephone calls, spoke to one of her managers and found an office for Galvin. Galvin seemed delighted with the larger office, which had a window facing the park. Indeed, she spent a day at the company storage building looking for new office furniture.

Within six months, the communications program was generating positive reviews. The program's four managers—who were all in their late 20s—seemed to be excited about the new direction of the program, and they could often be seen spending time on program work after normal business hours. Copley and Galvin led training sessions for the managers once a week. Copley soon felt quite close to her managers, kindred spirits in many ways. Two of them had PhDs, and the other two had MBAs. They were young, bright, enthusiastic and incredibly quick learners. Copley often told Silver that working with them was one of the best things about her new job. These managers were the people who would help popularize the new program throughout the organization and train new program instructors—they were the core of the program—and Copley felt lucky to be able to mentor them.

Galvin, however, had some trouble with the managers. At the first training session, she seemed defensive, as if disconcerted by working with people who had the same if not more education. She spent a lot of time lecturing, used PowerPoint presentations and didn't entertain many questions. Copley, in contrast, passed out readings ahead of time and ran her sessions as small-group discussions. The managers seemed to respond with greater interest to Copley's training, but Copley felt that the difference in style between Galvin and herself was perhaps a good thing—the kind of balance that Silver was looking for in the program. Still, she noticed that the managers spent a lot of time with her and almost invariably brought any problems they encountered to her, not to Galvin. Silver was worried that she was unintentionally disempowering Galvin in front of the other staff, a move that would make more work for Copley and cause Galvin obvious concern.

As time went on, Galvin, in Copley's opinion, continued to have trouble adjusting to the more collaborative, informal environment Copley wanted to create. In training sessions or when meeting with others in the organization in an attempt to sell the new program, Galvin continued to be almost rigidly methodical: she was more comfortable with one person after another speaking in turn, preferably starting with junior employees and ending with the most senior employee in the room. Her body language suggested that she had difficulty tolerating "push back" or "constructive criticism," although she had less of an issue when she was addressing the junior staff. Some managers within the company responded well to Galvin's style, however, and Copley continued to feel that Galvin, although quite different from her, was an asset to the program. Furthermore, Copley had by now found several portfolios in which Galvin's training and her aptitude for analysis and process were benefits (the development of communications courses targeted specifically at international leaders, for example), and Copley had made sure that these portfolios kept Galvin away from the more central decision-making process in the program, and, often, away from Copley's office.

⊠ Rumors and Reports

In March, 2007, one month before the new program had completed its first year of operation, a friend from her old firm called Copley to tell her that he had met Galvin at a conference the week before. According to Copley's friend, Galvin had been actively soliciting offers from other employers at the conference. He had overheard her say that she was quite unhappy with the situation at Carnegie—that she felt "secondary" and "unappreciated" and would welcome a chance to run a program of her own. Her friend had also heard her say that she did not like being subordinate to someone nearly 20 years her junior. Copley recalled that at a dinner that both she and Galvin attended, she had overheard Galvin introducing herself as "one of the two directors" of the communications program. Copley had let it go without saying anything, although her husband, who had also overheard the comment, was angry.

In April 2007, with the program's first annual review of employee performance looming, Copley tried not to let what she had heard affect her judgment. She thought she would give Galvin a "very good," one notch short of "outstanding," because Galvin had indeed attained the goals Copley had set for her, and in the demanding environment of a new initiative. However, Cop ley felt that Galvin was still trying too hard to lecture to the managers, and that although her guidance was sound, her tone was condescending. One manager confided to Copley that, on more than one occasion, participants had noted on their feedback forms that they found Galvin "arrogant" and "aloof." And yet program enrollment was up 100 per cent, and positive reviews had tripled during the year. Silver was clearly happy at this rapid turnaround. In addition, Copley, Galvin and their team were accomplishing this feat with a smaller budget than before. The communications team was lauded for its success in improving skills across the organization, and Copley received a steady stream of congratulatory emails, which she shared with her staff. Talk at the management ranks suggested promoting Copley into an operating role within a few years. Galvin wasn't a great "fit," to be sure, but Copley had to admit she was part of the program's success.

Before actually writing Galvin's review, Copley met with her to discuss the process that would be used for the review. Galvin expressed concern with the use of "360-degree" feedback that incorporated managers' reviews of their superiors. Copley argued that she felt the managers' feedback was vital, given their centrality to the program and their very strong qualifications and performance. By this time, Copley was growing weary of Galvin's constant conservatism. She seemed to be trying to protect the status quo. Galvin, however, continued to argue vociferously that only her superior

should provide feedback. Finally, Copley said, "Okay, if you only want my feedback, then I'm happy to limit the appraisal to my response alone." Galvin looked shocked. "I wasn't talking about your feedback, Shannon," she said. "I was talking about direct feedback from Elizabeth." Copley, confused, told her that Galvin reported directly to her, not to Silver. Galvin insisted that, as one of the two program directors, she reported to Silver, and angrily left the office. A few minutes later, Silver phoned Copley to say that she had just met with Galvin, who was unclear about the chain of command, and that Silver had informed Galvin "in the clearest possible terms" that Galvin reported to Copley.

Two weeks after the reviews were completed, Silver approached Copley:

We're very pleased with your performance, Shannon, and we hope that you're happy with your role. We certainly want to keep you here. I want to tell you this in person because, as you know, the firm is facing difficult times and we have cutbacks across the organization. Fortunately, I made it clear that your program has my full support and, as a result, we shielded it from the cuts. The unfortunate thing is that we won't be able to expand the program as we discussed a year ago. In fact, I don't know if we'll be able to put in a budget increase in the next two years or so. I hope you understand.

Copley replied, "I can work quite well with the budget you've given us, Elizabeth. We'll make do." As she walked out of Copley's small office, Silver said, "I should also tell you that we're looking for your enrollment numbers to increase and your ratings to increase next year. This was the condition the management team asked of us, in exchange for protecting the current level of funding." Copley looked back and smiled.

⊠ A Difficult Conversation

Although Copley was happy to accept the challenge of increasing program enrollment and ratings on the current budget, she knew that the decision to freeze funding would not be taken well by Galvin, who wanted a full-time position. Indeed, Copley had just met with Galvin to talk about Galvin's completed performance review. Deciding that she did not want what might be simply differences in leadership style to affect the objectivity of her review, Copley had, at the last minute, decided to give Galvin an "outstanding" rating, despite her own reservations about Galvin's performance and the equivocal feedback from the managers. However, during the meeting, Galvin had used Copley's review to suggest that she be given a full-time position. Copley had told her that funds were frozen. Galvin had suggested letting one or two of the managers go, thereby freeing funds for a full-time position. Copley had responded that her

suggestion wasn't an option. Galvin had left the meeting angrily and had called in sick the next day.

On May 12, 2007, Galvin approached Copley's office, and, standing in the doorway, burst out in tears:

> It's not fair to me not to provide me with a full-time position. I've worked really hard—as hard as you—over the past year, and my contributions have been central to this program's success. But you, Shannon, have basically alienated me from the managers, and you've deliberately kept me out of the loop during some of the most important program decisions this year. You don't trust me, and this is the first place I've ever worked where I wasn't trusted. It really hurts, and I can't go on like this. You either tell me right now how you feel about me and whether you'll ever support a full-time position, or I quit.

Moez Kassam

Consulting Intern

Prepared by Ebrahim El Kalza under the supervision of James A. Erskine

> That's not at the Matthews standard! You're going to have to perform at a higher level if you want to work here!

Summer Associate Moez Kassam slowly rubbed his temples as his senior manager, Sherif Mahfouz, at Matthews Management Consulting stormed out of the client office they shared. It was early August 2003, and Kassam had been in Abu Dhabi for only two weeks. Already his dream assignment was

becoming a nightmare. He felt he could do no right, and was beginning to lose confidence in his abilities. This was the third time he had been scolded, and he felt his chance of leveraging the internship into a full-time offer with Matthews was in serious jeopardy.

⊠ The Consulting Industry

Since the burst of the dot-com bubble in 2000, many articles, in business magazines, had

Version: (A) 2006-06-07

characterized the industry's decline and even forecasted its demise. With the consulting industry's role in scandals such as Enron, the glut of MBA graduates available and their lack of accountability, some of the shine had certainly rubbed off the industry.

Strategy consultants offered wisdom in exchange for money; they helped a client's top executives navigate the strategic challenges in leading companies. The fortunes of consultants depended on the future prospects of large corporations. Although, in theory, poor economic conditions could create work for consultants, the reality was that a corporation's budget for consultants was typically the first to go in tough times.

During the dot-com boom, strategy consulting companies had been faced with two serious threats: their "general" approach was being outflanked by smaller, more specialized e-commerce experts, and the Internet start-up frenzy created a serious war for talent. Many consulting companies had been forced to offer ludicrous pay packages and hire a large number of employees to handle the high volume of business. When the dot-com bubble burst, losses mounted, clients disappeared and growth came to a halt. Heavy lay-offs were necessary to recoup the lost investment in e-commerce, and many international offices were closed. This left many firms with an uncertain future, and those who remained suffered from low employee morale.

In the wake of these hard times, consulting companies began to restructure to deal with the changing business environment. The migration of former consultants into the industry allowed large corporations to build in-house consulting units, decreasing the demand for professional strategic advice. The increased competition for clients resulted in increased hours and shrinking case lengths for consultants, as well as a bias towards "over-selling" cases by partners in order to attract business.

Matthews Management Consulting

The Firm

Matthews was a top-tier global strategy consulting firm, with a reputation for producing implementable, data-driven solutions for its clients. In exchange for large fees, Fortune 500 clients were supplied a high-powered team of bright and capable consultants to tackle their most difficult business problems.

The firm consistently ranked among the top-three consulting firms in the world, and employed more than 2,000 people in 20 countries. Consulting at this level was considered a prestigious business, and the lucrative compensation packages, early exposure to senior executives and key decision makers, and the numerous opportunities available upon leaving the firm attracted the best and brightest from top-ranked business, engineering and liberal arts programs. The average stint at a consulting firm ranged from two to four years, and alumni were typically lured by their clients into high-paying executive positions in large multinationals or used the network and skills they accumulated to launch a new company.

As coveted as they were, internships and full-time placements at Matthews were not easy to come by. Since the firm's competitive advantage was based on providing clients with "the best and the brightest," hiring procedures were strenuous and highly competitive. A want-to-be consultant was required to pass two or three rounds of case and fit interviews, meeting with several senior consultants at each stage. Even so, only half of summer interns were offered full-time positions.

The rewards of a career in consulting came at a price. Consultants typically worked between 60 and 90 hours per week, maintained an unpredictable and onerous travel schedule and often spent up to four days a week at the client site. If a client happened to be overseas, a consultant could be asked to relocate for the duration of the engagement, which could last up to six months or more. The intense commitment and uncertainty resulted in family and social pressure, stress and often burnout.

Structure

Matthews employed a "one firm" or global model: all professionals were paid out of a consolidated bonus pool. Although each office had its own identity and core clients, this system made it in everyone's interest to share resources, such as people and expertise, across all offices to best meet client needs. Occasionally, consultants were staffed on two cases at once in order to maximize their utility and expedite their

development. This was widely known as the "50/50" staffing model, but consultants often joked about how it was really "80/80" due to competing demands and heavy workloads.

Teams were composed of the best available mixture of industry experience and expertise. A partner with knowledge of a particular industry would sell the firm's services in what was referred to as a "bake-off"; a company looking for advice invited a number of consulting firms to propose a preliminary solution, approach, plan and fee structure. The company would then select from among the proposals. Once a case was sold, the partner would bring in a manager, who subsequently staffed the team with the appropriate mix of consultants and associates (see Exhibit 1).

Exhibit 1   Typical Team Structure and Roles

Partner

A partner, or principal, extensive industry has expertise and 10 years of consulting experience. A partner's duties include selling the engagement, appointing a manager to head the tactical team, providing guidance, working closely with the client's CEO (or equivalent) and delivering the final presentation.

Manager

The manager is the tactical leader of the team and is responsible for assembling the team, working with the partner to prepare a hypothesis (or "answer first"), defining the analysis required to verify the hypothesis, identifying the different work streams and assembling the right team to complete them. Managers typically work the most hours and are under the greatest strain.

Case Team Leader

A senior consultant with two to three years of experience is referred to as a Case Team Leader, or CTL. CTLs support the manager by taking on one or two work streams, and are expected to help develop some of the more junior members of the team.

Consultant

The consultant position is either a promotion for star associates, or an entry level positive for MBA hires. Consultants are expected to take ownership of a work stream and are given direct client interaction.

> **Associate Consultant**
>
> Associate consultants are undergraduate hires. They typically have little previous work experience, and are given intensive training in their early months. Associate work is usually quite analytical, and there is very limited, if any, client exposure. Parts of work streams are carved out for and owned by an associate. Ideally, responsibility is increased as the associates demonstrate their ability. After two years, successful associates will be promoted to senior associates and have their MBA sponsored by the firm, contingent on a promise to return for at least two years upon its completion.

Culture

Matthews Worldwide

Matthews's employees often said how astounded they were by the high similarity of different offices, no doubt due to a very strong and discriminating culture. Many related it to an old law firm, where you had to earn your stripes and the right to speak, and more importantly, the right to be heard.

The firm prided itself on offering clients data-driven, profit-focused results, and offering employees world-class training and access to the best clients. It also provided several unique opportunities to employees, including stints in foreign offices, postings to a not-for-profit subsidiary and invitations to world-wide social events.

Matthews Toronto

The Toronto office staffed about 40 consultants at various levels and had been hit especially hard by layoffs due to the tough economic climate. Despite being merged with a nearby U.S. office, Matthews Toronto worked hard to maintain a distinct Canadian identity, becoming known for expertise in pulp and paper, mining, forestry and financial services, as well as its reputation for hard work and a sociable climate. Matthews Toronto hired its associates from the top business and engineering programs in Canada.

Moez Kassam

Moez Kassam knew from a young age that he wanted to be in business, and from his first job at 14 washing dishes, he knew he wanted to be the boss. Graduating at the top of his high school class with acceptance letters from Canada's top business schools in hand and an offer to work for a top consumer packaged goods company, he knew he was off to the right start. By the summer of 2002, Kassam had worked for three top-tier corporations, had started two businesses and had launched the first youth-initiated international trade mission in Canadian history. Still, he felt like he was not getting the most out of his business education. Upon reviewing his options and consulting with many mentors and friends, Kassam applied and was accepted into the honors program at The University of Western Ontario with the hopes of becoming a strategy consultant.

With four years of business schooling, including the first year of his HBA and three years at another institution, some corporate experience under his belt and a knack for speaking his mind, Kassam felt confident that he was well positioned for success and a career in consulting.

> My value proposition is different from most want-to-be consultants. I've had some great and unique experiences for someone my age and learned a lot of useful skills along the way. I also love thinking up creative ideas to tough business problems. Consulting is the best way for me to solidify and test out these skills and ideas. It'll be great training for when I'm ready to run my own business.

By working extremely hard, Kassam focused and achieved an A average during the first semester of his sophomore year. He spent the winter break learning about the various firms and preparing for the strenuous interviews. In early March, he received a phone call from Matthews Consulting offering him the summer internship he desired most. He accepted on the spot.

⊠ The Abu Dhabi Engagement

Kassam started his internship at Matthews on May 26, 2003, and spent the first week training and meeting the Toronto staff. He was well rested from his month-long trip to Egypt and was eager to get to work. Two other fellow students from a different section were also hired as interns, as well as an MBA graduate. Matthew's human resources staff had hinted during training that the Toronto office did not have enough analysts to meet demand, and that they would hope to extend offers for full-time positions to all the interns, provided they met performance standards.

After completing his first assignment—a diagnostic on the operations of a large U.S. paper mill—with a satisfactory performance review, Kassam waited to be staffed on his next project. When word went around the office of an opportunity in Abu Dhabi, Kassam sent an e-mail to the manager on the project, Sunjay Singh, detailing his desire to participate. Kassam cited how his ability to speak Arabic would be helpful in communicating with the client, as well as his past international work experience in Malaysia and Mexico. He took a measured risk by copying the partner heading the project on the e-mail, since associates, let alone interns, rarely communicated directly with partners. Singh seemed to be impressed by Kassam's keenness and commended him on his initiative.

Kassam was disappointed to learn that he would not be staffed on the case, but continued to send the manager research papers that he deemed relevant to the Abu Dhabi

project. On a Thursday afternoon in mid-July, already one week into the case, he received a call from the partner asking if he could be ready to leave for Abu Dhabi the next day. They would need his help, the partner said, to complete some customer interviews in Arabic. Kassam was ecstatic about the opportunity and went home to pack his suitcase.

The Client

The client was one of the largest private equity firms in the Middle East and the largest consumer user of consultants in the region. Many of the client's top managers were former consultants themselves and, as such, were shrewd project managers and quite business-savvy. This was the first time Matthews had worked with this client, and the project was viewed as a vital foothold in establishing a Middle Eastern presence.

The client was looking to invest hundreds of millions of dollars in a novel and risky manufacturing technology that utilized some of the country's natural resources. Matthews had been asked to determine the economic feasibility of such an investment, and to render a "go" or "no-go" decision in one month's time. The client selected Matthews based on demonstrated experience in the industry and the promise of a data-driven solution.

The Matthews Team

Matthews staffed a five-person team on the project: an experienced manager, two case team leaders who were mere months away from promotion to manager and two very junior associates. The senior staff all had experience in the client's industry, and one of the junior associates had only worked on private equity cases. The team was drawn from four Matthews's offices: Toronto, London, Paris and the fledgling Middle Eastern practice based in Beirut, Lebanon (see Exhibit 2).

Exhibit 2	Team Member Profiles

Chris McKibbin, Partner

Education:	MBA (Insead)
Expertise:	Pulp & Paper, Financial Services, Insurance
Experience:	Investment banking (2 years), Matthews Consulting (9 years)
Languages:	English, French, Spanish
Home office:	Toronto, Canada

Sunjay Singh, Manager

Education:	B. Eng., MBA (MIT)
Expertise:	Airline, Insurance, M&A, Private Equity
Experience:	Manufacturing (2 years), Matthews Consulting (7 years)
Language:	English, Urdu
Home office:	Toronto, Canada

Sherif Mahfouz, CTL/Manager

Education:	B. Eng., Masters in Government & Policy (Harvard)
Expertise:	Middle East, Private Equity
Experience:	Civil engineer (3 years), Consulting (7 years), Matthews Consulting (2 years)
Languages:	English, French, Arabic
Home office:	Paris, France (Middle East practice reports to Paris under the current structure)

Shenny Morstern, Senior Consultant

Education:	MBA (Insead)
Expertise:	Retail, Airline, Insurance, Financial Services
Experience:	Matthews Consulting (6 years)
Languages:	English, French
Home office:	London, UK

Jean Brisebois, Associate Consultant

Education:	B. Com. (HEC Paris)
Expertise:	Private Equity
Experience:	Matthews Consulting (2 years)
Languages:	English, French
Home office:	Paris, France

Mike Brown, Associate Consultant

Education:	B. Com. (Queens)
Expertise:	Retail
Experience:	Matthews Consulting (1 year)
Languages:	English
Home office:	Toronto, Canada

(Continued)

Exhibit 2	(Continued)

Moez Kassam, Associate Consultant Intern[a]

Education:	HBA Candidate (Ivey)
Expertise:	Pulp & Paper
Experience:	Venture Capital (internship), Marketing (internship), various international assignments
Languages:	English, French, Arabic
Home office:	Toronto, Canada

a. A late appointment to the team.

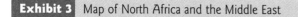 Working in Abu Dhabi

Abu Dhabi, an island off the coast of Saudi Arabia in the Arabian Sea, was the conservative capital of the United Arab Emirates (UAE) (see Exhibit 3). The UAE was an oil-rich country of 2.5 million people, one-quarter of which were descendents of the nation's founding tribes. These "Nationals," as they were called, enjoyed special privileges, including access to

Exhibit 3	Map of North Africa and the Middle East

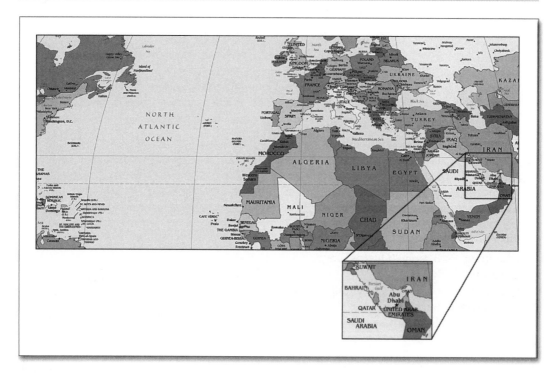

the benefits of designated petrol trusts that provided them with subsidized housing, health care, education, full employment and many other incentives. The rest of the population was largely composed of Arab, Indian and South-East Asian immigrants and Western expatriates working for large multinational subsidiaries. The intense heat, which often surpassed 50°C, made summer a time for vacations to more palatable climates. This left the city desolate and hot, with not much to do.

As soon as he arrived, Kassam was quickly introduced to the team and the client managers, and put to work. Since the engagement was already in progress, he was handed a series of binders and reports to review in order to ramp up and was given several assignments and deadlines. He was to source, book and complete 50 customer interviews across five Middle Eastern countries in his first two weeks. No further direction was given, and Kassam began to think of ways to tackle the problem. He drafted a list of questions for his direct supervisor, Mahfouz, who was to monitor his performance and provide guidance when necessary.

When provided with the questions, Mahfouz made it clear that he was quite busy and that Kassam would have to learn to be a source of solutions rather than questions. Mahfouz took Kassam through his first three interviews, and then left him to complete the rest. Kassam was instructed to thoroughly complete a pre-written questionnaire for each interview, enter it into a word processor and e-mail it to Mahfouz for review.

Although he knew that consulting was a demanding profession, Kassam was not prepared for the intensity of this project. He found himself working 16 hours a day, seven days a week, without pause for the four weeks he was there. He had worked overseas before, but never for this long under such strenuous circumstances or without access to friends or family. The number of complex political challenges he faced within the team and with the

client only added to the pressure and made it difficult to dedicate himself to his work.

Sherif Mahfouz

Mahfouz was in his early 40s and had been with Matthews for just over one year but had more than seven years of consulting experience in the Middle East with a competing firm, an engineering degree, a Harvard graduate degree in public policy, experience in the industry and spoke three languages including Arabic. He had been hired in order to help build Matthews's Middle Eastern business. Through informal conversation, Mahfouz's goals became clear to Kassam: to establish Matthews's presence in the Middle East and leverage that into a partnership in the firm. Mahfouz even mentioned that there may be opportunities in the new office, assuming Kassam performed well. Mahfouz worked especially hard, juggling several engagements at once, and often appeared tired and stressed. He had just built a new house in Beirut and would often speak of it fondly and wonder out loud when he would finally have time to enjoy it.

The First Incident

In the first week, Kassam worked hard to complete 15 interviews and scheduled 10 more for the following week. He spent every spare minute reading up on the company and industry and discussing the progress of the other work streams. While on the phone with a customer, Mahfouz walked into the client office, customer surveys in hand, and cast Kassam a sideways glance. Kassam finished the interview, updated Mahfouz on his progress so far and asked him what he thought of the work he had already completed.

I'm glad you're getting the hang of it, but we're behind schedule here. The client needs 50 interviews done, and done well. I'm under a lot of pressure to get this done, and I can't do that while you're submitting this kind of trash to me. There are spelling mistakes and errors in the documents. Some questions are incomplete. I can't put my name on this. I want them fixed, and I want to have a schedule for the interviews in my hand ASAP. This is not some school project. This is serious business.

Mahfouz went on to correct him on an Arabic word he had heard Kassam mispronounce in his last interview, handed him a stack of completed interviews covered in red ink and walked out of the room. Kassam began to browse through the stack and noticed that although there were a few typos, he thought that many of the edits were subjective and frivolous. He was angry at himself for making so many careless errors, and felt that he was off to a rocky start with his new boss.

At nearly 10 p.m., Mahfouz walked back into the room, silently packed his laptop computer, folded away the schedule Kassam had left for him on his desk and, without looking directly at him, told Kassam he would require an update at breakfast the next morning, 7:30 a.m. sharp. Frustrated because his first interview was at 9 a.m. and he knew he would once again get very little sleep, and embarrassed by the way he was being treated, Kassam finished the edits and quickly summarized the week's findings. As he made back for the hotel, he checked his watch. It was 12:30 a.m.

☒ The Second Incident

Kassam showed up at breakfast 10 minutes late, and found that Mahfouz had finished his breakfast and was impatiently reading the paper. As he sat down, Mahfouz said nothing.

Feeling awkward, Kassam got up to get his breakfast from the buffet. As he came back to the table, Mahfouz was checking his watch, and glanced up at Kassam, who started to apologize for being late. It was 7:45. Kassam pulled out his notes for the update and began reading. Mahfouz raised his hand and told him to finish his breakfast. There was no longer time to go through the update. Ten minutes later, Mahfouz asked for the bill, put on his suit jacket and walked to the door. Kassam left his half-finished breakfast and followed him out. Mahfouz walked three paces ahead of Kassam the entire way to the client office.

As soon as they settled in, Mahfouz mentioned that he would be in a senior meeting all morning, and that he would leave for the city of Doha, in nearby Qatar, that evening. He would debrief with Kassam before leaving. Kassam spent the hour before his interview improving his weekly update and e-mailing it to Mahfouz. Five minutes before his first scheduled interview, a senior member of the client's team, Laurent, knocked and entered the office. After asking where Mahfouz was, he began to question Kassam first on his progress and then on his background and experience. Kassam gave very general answers and assured Laurent that everything was going well. As soon as Laurent left, Kassam let out a sigh of relief.

At lunch, Kassam mentioned what had happened to one of the other associates. The associate explained that this was not surprising, since the client's management team, comprising former consultants, was disgruntled because it did not receive the team of people that it was promised. The management team claimed that Matthews had "pulled a bait-and-switch" and had replaced the industry experts they promised at the point of sale with a team of younger, less experienced (and consequently less expensive) consultants. Kassam felt that his youth and lack of experience were likely to exacerbate the issue.

During their debrief meeting, Mahfouz asked Kassam how the morning had gone. He thanked him for the update and commended him on a job well done. Soon after, he asked if Kassam had spoken to Laurent. Kassam reiterated the conversation and mentioned that he had felt uncomfortable during Laurent's probing. Mahfouz grimaced and said that he would speak to Laurent and Singh on the issue.

The next morning, Singh called Kassam into an empty office, and began to chastise him on speaking with the client.

> Sherif told me about your conversation with Laurent. The client is already wary about the age of the team. The last thing we need right now is more problems. I don't want you speaking to him again. Any questions on the progress of your work should be directed to Sherif or me. Is that clear?

Before Kassam could respond, Singh checked his watch, told him he was late for a client update and walked out of the room.

⊠ The Third Incident

The team continued to work throughout another weekend in one room, while Kassam worked through his interviews in another. He had developed the habit of e-mailing an update to Mahfouz at the end of each day and was receiving positive feedback on his progress. Halfway through the following week, Mahfouz appeared at the office for the first time in five days. Kassam asked him about his trip and was told that he would hear all about it at lunch. Mahfouz seemed in high spirits, and Kassam felt that perhaps their relationship was improving. Mahfouz asked Kassam for a written update on the status and findings of the interviews for the morning's client meeting. With two scheduled interviews, Kassam knew he would be pressed to complete the report on time.

Scared of jeopardizing Mahfouz's good mood, he promised it would be completed by the required time.

With only 45 minutes to complete the necessary document, Kassam amalgamated the daily updates he had sent Mahfouz over the past two weeks and formatted them for clarity and coherence. Since Mahfouz had commended him on his updates, Kassam felt confident that it would be satisfactory.

Mahfouz rushed in minutes before his meeting, picked up the document, thanked Kassam and rushed out.

Just before their scheduled lunch, Mahfouz came back into the office, with a foul look on his face. He proceeded to yell at Kassam for the lack of care he took in putting together the document.

> That's not at the Matthews standard! You're going to have to perform at a higher level if you want to work here! I trust you to help me prepare for a client meeting, and you give me this? You had better get your act together. I want a proper summary and updated plan by the time I get back from lunch with Sunjay!

Tired, frustrated, and angry, with no family, friends, or mentor to turn to, Kassam sat alone at his desk and contemplated his options. He knew how critical teamwork was to the position, and he did not want to appear incapable in front of the team's manager. Kassam wondered if consulting was the right career for him. More importantly, he felt that not receiving an offer would be detrimental to finding an alternative full-time position in the fall. All of his hard work seemed to be going to waste over what he felt were small and avoidable errors. He counted the days until his return to Canada and marked the date on his calendar. He wondered what he could do to salvage something positive during his remaining days in Abu Dhabi.

On Leadership

Leadership and Loyalty

By Jeffrey Gandz

Leaders expect their followers to be loyal and to be able to depend on their loyalty. This is why we have such a visceral reaction when a David Radler turns on a Conrad Black or an Andrew Fastow cooperates with the prosecution to give evidence against his superiors at Enron. Emotive phrases like "ratting" or "biting the hand that has fed you" find their way into otherwise sober commentary. They conjure up childhood prohibitions on snitching and sneaking.

Leaders themselves have been known to go into paroxysms of rage followed by periods of deep hurt and even depression when they find that support on which they had counted is no longer there. And individuals have paid a steep price when their leaders conclude that they are no longer loyal and cannot be trusted to do their bidding, and so find themselves marginalized in decision making and personally shunned.

Good leaders understand that there is a difference between real *loyalty* and a related but different concept—*fealty*.

⬚ Give Me Loyalty, Not Fealty

Both loyalty and fealty share some things in common; they call for allegiance, faithfulness, and fidelity. But they differ in one remarkable respect. Loyalty embraces the concept of allegiance to an authority to whom such faithfulness is lawfully and morally due. Fealty, on the other hand, describes the fidelity of a vassal, slave or feudal tenant to his lord and master or, in modern parlance, the unqualified fidelity of a person to his or her boss.

Fealty is dangerous in corporations as well as in other social organizations. It leads to unethical, corrupt and often illegal actions spreading to the many rather than the few, to covering up those actions sometimes to the point of obstructing justice. Loyalty, on the other hand, is a positive dimension of business since it provides a force of energy that binds people together in the pursuit of worthwhile goals.

Fealty can be coerced or bought. Consequently, when the power relationship no longer exists or a better "deal" is available elsewhere—from another employer, or a prosecutor offering a more lenient sentence—the bond of fidelity is snapped. This is not an act of disloyalty but, rather, a belated recognition that the bond was composed only of self interest. The more enlightened that self-interest, the more individuals will act in ways that are beneficial to them.

Loyalty is made of sterner stuff. It is built on sound moral foundations, of which lawfulness is one but is not the only one. People who are bound by common values and moral beliefs are not easily deterred from supporting each other. They are neither discouraged by adversity nor deflected by better offers.

It explains why many people do work for which there is little extrinsic reward, why they serve their countries or churches or other social movements as volunteers or in poorly paid positions; why they choose to work for companies that pursue socially responsible and responsive policies; why they are attracted to companies that have reputations for treating individuals and groups with dignity and respect, who are committed to their development, who provide employees with the opportunity to speak up and speak out about things with which they disagree, who have good whistle-blowing policies and who do not tolerate leaders who do not support these value-driven actions.

Such moral beliefs are not necessarily inconsistent with the capitalist system or the obligations of private sector managers to maximize shareholder value. Creation of economic activity leads to better lives for people, generation of profits results in investment in growth and contribution of taxes, and so on. Business can be and often is a force for good. But, sometimes, business activity does create conflict between personal morality and financially attractive activities. Ask me to be involved in a company selling tobacco products and I will say "No!" Ask me to endorse advertising approaches that deliberately mislead potential customers and, again, you cannot expect my loyalty to the company, my boss, my colleagues on the executive team to guarantee my assent to the advertising campaign. Generate profits for shareholders at the expense of environmental depredation, and you violate my sense of corporate social responsibility. Do this often, and any bonds of loyalty that might have been generated in the past, erode.

Moral beliefs are not unchangeable. Not that long ago, many people had deeply held beliefs about separation of races, the evil of religions other than their own, or relationships between same-gender couples. These values were supported by the laws of those times. There are still people who hold to these beliefs, who are prepared to go to extraordinary, sometimes illegal lengths to preserve them and who willingly give their loyalty to leaders who espouse them. These time-warps are troubling to many people yet they form part of today's operating environments for business.

Individuals' moral development is also dynamic. Some have strong foundations through family or early institutional influences while others grow up in more free-thinking environments. Some views change over time, others remain stable.

Some people are quick to realize that what they are being asked to do by their bosses is wrong, others either don't question, accepting that their boss must be doing the right thing because he or she *is* their boss, or going along with the request because they accept that "that's the way it's done in this business." Such moral naivety is not evil, but it can lead to bad things.

Smart leaders understand that fealty is demanded whereas loyalty is earned. And they earn this loyalty by doing a number of things:

- They understand the values of the people they lead and try to build their business strategies, plans, processes and practices in ways that are congruent with those values. This is the acid test of the "respect for the individual" that we see in so many organizations' value statements.
- They are sensitive to and respect changes in moral values within the societies in which they operate. Occasionally this will put them at odds with prevailing societal values and they must make difficult personal decisions either to conform or quit.
- When they see other leaders in their organizations acting in ways that are morally offensive, they speak up . . . sometimes at personal risk. They channel their dissent constructively . . . chaining oneself to railings is not usually an effective way to challenge corporate decisions! But they seldom just go along with the decision as an act of fealty.
- They promote debate about contentious issues to ensure that there is openness and transparency and that people do not feel that expressions of doubt are interpreted as "disloyalty."

Above all else, smart leaders understand: Never, never expect or depend on fealty—earn loyalty!

Transformational Leadership

Leaders who can spark our imaginations with a compelling vision of a worth-while end that stretches us beyond what is known today and who can show us a clear path to our objectives are the ones we follow. In the future, the leadership role will focus more on the development of an effective strategy, the creation of the vision, and an understanding of their impact, and will empower others to carry out the implementation of the plan.

—Goldsmith, Greenberg, Robertson, & Hu-Chan (2003, p. 118)

Transformational leadership is an involved, complex process that binds leaders and followers together in the transformation or changing of followers, organizations, or even whole nations. It involves leaders interacting with followers with respect to their "emotions, values, ethics, standards, and long-term goals, and includes assessing followers' motives, satisfying their needs, and treating them as full human beings" (Northouse, 2010). While all theories of leadership involve influence, transformational leadership is about an extraordinary ability to influence that encourages followers to achieve something well above what was expected by themselves or their leaders.

Early researchers in the area of transformational leadership coined the term (Downton, 1973) and tried to integrate the responsibilities of leaders and followers (Burns, 1978). In particular, Burns (1978) described leaders as people who could understand the motives of followers and, therefore, be able to achieve the goals of followers and leaders. As we discussed in Chapter 1, he considered leadership different from power because leadership is a concept that cannot be separated from the needs of followers.

Burns (1978) differentiated between transactional and transformational leadership. He described transactional leadership as that which emphasizes exchanges between followers and leaders. This idea of exchange is easily seen at most levels in many different types of organizations.

He described transformational leadership as that process through which leaders engage with followers and develop a connection (one that did not previously exist) that increases the morals and motivation of the follower and the leader. Because of this process, leaders assist followers in achieving their potential to the fullest (Yukl, 2006).

Bass and colleagues (Bass, 1998; Bass & Riggio, 2006; Bass & Steidlmeier, 1999) differentiated between leadership that raised the morals of followers and that which transformed people, organizations, and nations in a negative manner. They called this *pseudotransformational* leadership, to describe leaders who are power hungry, have perverted moral values, and are exploitative. In particular, this form of leadership emphasizes the leader's self-interest in a manner that is self-aggrandizing and contrary to the interests of his or her followers (Northouse, 2010). Kenneth Lay and Jeff Skilling might be examples of this form of leadership in their roles as chair and CEO of Enron, respectively. Authentic transformational leaders put the interests of followers above their own interests and, in so doing, emphasize the collective good for leaders and followers (Howell & Avolio, 1992).

Charismatic Leadership

"Charisma is a special quality of leaders whose purposes, powers, and extraordinary determination differentiate them from others" (Dubrin, 2007, p. 68). Weber (1947) emphasized the extraordinary nature of this personality trait but also argued that followers were important in that they confirmed that their leaders had charisma (Bryman, 1992; House, 1976). The influence exercised by charismatic leaders comes from their personal power, not their position power. Their personal qualities help their personal power to transcend the influence they have from position power (Daft, 2005).

House (1976) provided a theory of charismatic leadership that linked personality characteristics to leader behaviors and, through leader behaviors, effects on followers. Weber (1947) and House (1976) both argued that these effects would be more likely to happen when followers were in stressful situations because this is when followers want deliverance from their problems. A major revision to House's conceptualization has been offered by Shamir, House, and Arthur (1993). They argue that charismatic leadership transforms how followers view themselves and strives to tie each follower's identity to the organization's collective identity (Northouse, 2010). In other words, charismatic leadership is effective because each follower's sense of identity is linked to the identity of his or her organization.

A Transformational Leadership Model

Bass and his colleagues (Avolio, 1999; Bass, 1985, 1990; Bass & Avolio, 1993, 1994) refined and expanded the models suggested by Burns (1978) and House (1976). Bass (1985) added to Burns's model by focusing more on the needs of followers than on the needs of leaders, by focusing on situations where the outcomes could be negative, and by placing transformational and transactional leadership on a single continuum as opposed to considering them independent continua. He extended House's model by emphasizing the emotional components of charisma and by arguing that while charisma may be a necessary condition for transformational leadership, it is not a sufficient condition—more than charisma is needed.

Transformational leadership inspires subordinates to achieve more than expected because (a) it increases individuals' awareness regarding the significance of task outcomes, (b) it encourages subordinates to go beyond their own self-interest to the interests of others in their team and organization, and (c) it motivates subordinates to take care of needs that operate at a higher level (Bass, 1985; Yukl, 2006).

There are eight factors in the transformational and transactional leadership model. These are separated into three types of factors: (1) transformational factors consisting of idealized influence, individualized consideration, inspirational motivation, and intellectual stimulation; (2) transactional factors consisting of contingent reward, management by exception (active), and management by exception (passive); and (3) one nontransformational/nontransactional factor, that being laissez-faire (Yukl, 2006).

Transformational Leadership Factors

This form of leadership is about improving each follower's performance and helping followers develop to their highest potential (Avolio, 1999; Bass & Avolio, 1990). In addition, transformational leaders move subordinates to work for the interests of others over and above their own interests and, in so doing, cause significant, positive changes to happen for the good of the team and organization (Dubrin, 2007; Kuhnert, 1994).

Idealized Influence or Charisma. Leaders with this factor are strong role models followers want to emulate and with whom they want to identify. They generally exhibit very high moral and ethical standards of conduct and usually do the right thing when confronted with ethical and moral choices. Followers develop a deep respect for these leaders and generally have a high level of trust in them. These leaders give followers a shared vision and a strong sense of mission with which followers identify (Northouse, 2010).

Inspirational Motivation. Leaders with this factor share high expectations with followers and motivate them to share in the organization's vision with a high degree of commitment. These leaders encourage followers to achieve more in the interests of the group than they would if they tried to achieve their own self-interests. These leaders increase team spirit through coaching, encouraging, and supporting followers (Yukl, 2006).

Intellectual Stimulation. Leaders with this factor encourage subordinates to be innovative and creative. These leaders support followers as they challenge the deeply held beliefs and values of their leaders, their organizations, and themselves. This encourages followers to innovatively handle organizational problems (Yukl, 2006).

Individualized Consideration. Leaders with this factor are very supportive and take great care to listen to and understand their followers' needs. They appropriately coach and give advice to their followers and help them to achieve self-actualization. These leaders delegate to assist followers in developing through work-related challenges and care for employees in a way appropriate for each employee. If employees need nurturance, the leader will nurture; if employees need task structure, the leader will provide structure (Northouse, 2010).

   Transformational leadership achieves different and more positive outcomes than transactional leadership. The latter achieves expected results while the former achieves much more than expected. The reason is that under transformational leaders, followers are inspired to work for the good of the organization and subordinate their own self-interests to those of the organization.

Transactional Leadership Factors

As suggested above, transactional leadership is different from transformational leadership in expected outcomes. The reason is that under transactional leaders, there is no individualization of followers' needs and no emphasis on followers' personal development—these leaders treat their followers as members of a homogeneous group. These leaders develop a relationship with their followers based on the exchange of something valuable to followers for the achievement of the leader's goals and the goals of the followers. These leaders are influential because their subordinates' interests are connected to the interests of each leader (Kuhnert, 1994; Kuhnert & Lewis, 1987).

Contingent Reward. This factor describes a process whereby leaders and followers exchange effort by followers for specific rewards from leaders. This process implies agreement between leaders and followers on what needs to be accomplished and what each person in the process will receive. This agreement is usually done prior to the exchange of effort and reward.

Management by Exception (MBE). This factor has two forms—active and passive. The former involves corrective criticism, while the latter involves negative feedback and negative reinforcement. Leaders who use MBE (active) closely monitor their subordinates to see if they are violating the rules or making mistakes. When rules are violated and/or mistakes made, these leaders take corrective action by discussing with their subordinates what they did wrong and how to do things right. Contrary to the MBE (active) way of leading, leaders who use MBE (passive) *do not closely monitor subordinates* but wait until problems occur and/or standards are violated. Based on their poor performance, these leaders give subordinates low evaluations without discussing their performance and how to improve. Both forms of MBE use a reinforcement pattern that is more negative than the more positive pattern used by leaders using contingent reward.

The Nonleadership Factor

As leaders move further from transformational leadership through transactional leadership, they come to laissez-faire leadership. Individuals in leadership positions who exercise this type of leadership actually abdicate their leadership responsibilities. This is absentee leadership (Northouse, 2010). These leaders try to not make decisions or to delay making decisions longer than they should, provide subordinates with little or no performance feedback, and ignore the needs of subordinates. These leaders have a "what will be will be" or "hands-off, let-things-ride" approach with no effort to even exchange rewards for effort by subordinates. Leaders who do not communicate with their subordinates or have any plans for their organization exemplify this type of leadership.

Other Perspectives of Transformational Leadership

Two other streams of research contribute to our comprehension of transformational leadership: These streams are research conducted by Bennis and Nanus (1985) and Kouzes and Posner (1987, 2002). Bennis and Nanus interviewed 90 leaders and, from these leaders' answers to several questions, developed strategies that enable organizations to be transformed. Kouzes and Posner interviewed 1,300 middle- to senior-level leaders in private and public organizations. They asked each leader to tell about his or her "personal best" leader experiences. From the answers these leaders provided, Kouzes and Posner developed their version of a transformational leadership model.

The Bennis and Nanus (1985) Transformational Leadership Model

Bennis and Nanus (1985) asked questions such as the following: "What are your strengths and weaknesses? What past events most influenced your leadership approach? What were the critical points in your career?" (Northouse, 2010). The answers to these questions provided four strategies that transcend leaders or organizations in their usefulness for transforming organizations.

First, leaders need to have a clear, compelling, believable, and attractive *vision* of their organization's future. Second, they need to be *social architects* who shape the shared meanings maintained by individuals in organizations. These leaders set a direction that allows subordinates to follow new organizational values and share a new organizational identity. Third, leaders need to develop within followers a *trust* based on setting and consistently implementing a direction, even though there may be a high degree of uncertainty surrounding the vision. Fourth, leaders need to use *creative deployment of self through positive self-regard.* This means that leaders know their strengths and weaknesses and focus on their strengths, not their weaknesses. This creates feelings of confidence and positive expectations in their followers and builds a learning philosophy throughout their organizations.

The Kouzes and Posner (1987, 2002) Transformational Leadership Model

On the basis of their interviews with middle- to senior-level managers, Kouzes and Posner (1987, 2002) found five strategies through content analyzing the answers to their "personal best" leadership experiences questions.

First, leaders need to *model the way* by knowing their own voice and expressing it to their followers, peers, and superiors through verbal communication and their own behaviors. Second, leaders need to develop and *inspire a shared vision* that compels individuals to act or behave in accordance with the vision. These inspired and shared visions challenge followers, peers, and others to achieve something that goes beyond the status quo. Third, leaders need to *challenge the process.* This means having a willingness to step out into unfamiliar areas, to experiment, to innovate, and to take risks to improve their organizations. These leaders take risks one step at a time and learn as they make mistakes.

Fourth, leaders need to *enable others to act.* They collaborate and develop trust with others; they treat others with respect and dignity; they willingly listen to others' viewpoints, even if they are different from the norm; they support others in their decisions; they emphasize teamwork and cooperation; and, finally, they enable others to give to their organizations because these others feel good about their leaders, their job, their organizations, and themselves.

Fifth, leaders need to *encourage the heart.* This suggests that leaders should recognize the need inherent in people for support and recognition. This means praising people for work done well and celebrating to demonstrate appreciation when others do good work.

This model focuses on leader behaviors and is prescriptive. It describes what needs to be done to effectively lead others to embrace and willingly support organizational transformations. The model is not about people with special abilities. Kouzes and Posner (1987, 2002) argue that these five principles are available to all who willingly practice them as they lead others.

How Does the Transformational Leadership Approach Work?

This approach to leadership is a broad-based perspective that describes what leaders need to do to formulate and implement major organizational change (Daft, 2005). These transformational leaders pursue some or most of the following steps.

First, they develop an organizational culture open to change by empowering subordinates to change, encouraging transparency in conversations related to change, and supporting them in trying innovative and different ways of achieving organizational goals. Second, they provide a strong example of moral values and ethical behavior that followers want to imitate because they have developed a trust and belief in these leaders and what they stand for.

Third, they help a vision to emerge that sets a direction for the organization. This vision transcends the various interests of individuals and different groups within the organization while clearly determining the organization's identity. Fourth, they become social architects who clarify the beliefs, values, and norms that are required to accomplish organizational change. Finally, they encourage people to work together, to build trust in their leaders and each other, and to rejoice when others accomplish goals related to the vision for change (Northouse, 2010).

References

Avolio, B. J. (1999). *Leadership in organizations* (6th ed.). Upper Saddle River, NJ: Pearson/Prentice Hall.

Bass, B. M. (1985). *Leadership and performance beyond expectations.* New York: Free Press.

Bass, B. M. (1990). From transactional to transformational leadership: Learning to share the vision, *Organizational Dynamics, 18,* 19–31.

Bass, B. M. (1998). The ethics of transformational leadership. In J. Ciulla (Ed.), *Ethics: The heart of leadership* (pp. 169–192). Westport, CT: Praeger.

Bass, B. M., & Avolio, B. J. (1990). The implications of transactional and transformational leadership for individual, team, and organizational development. *Research in Organizational Change and Development, 4,* 231–272.

Bass, B. M., & Avolio, B. J. (1993). Transformational leadership: A response to critiques. In M. M. Chemers & R. Ayman (Eds.), *Leadership theory and research: Perspectives and directions* (pp. 49–80). San Diego: Academic Press.

Bass, B. M., & Avolio, B. J. (1994). *Improving organizational effectiveness through transformational leadership.* Thousand Oaks, CA: Sage.

Bass, B. M., & Riggio, R. E. (2006). *Transformational leadership* (2nd ed.). Mahwah, NJ: Lawrence Erlbaum.

Bass, B. M., & Steidlmeier, P. (1999). Ethics, character, and authentic transformational leadership. *Leadership Quarterly, 10,* 81–227.

Bennis, W. G., & Nanus, B. (1985). *Leaders: The strategies for taking charge.* New York: Harper & Row.

Burns, J. M. (1978). *Leadership.* New York: Harper & Row.

Bryman, A. (1992). *Charisma and leadership in organizations.* London: Sage.

Daft, R. L. (2005). *The leadership experience* (3rd ed.). Mason, OH: Thomson, South-Western.

Downton, J. V. (1973). *Rebel leadership: Commitment and charisma in a revolutionary process.* New York: Free Press.

Dubrin, A. (2007). *Leadership: Research findings, practice, and skills.* New York: Houghton Mifflin.

Goldsmith, M., Greenberg, C. L., Robertson, A., & Hu-Chan, M. (2003). *Global leadership: The next generation.* Upper Saddle River, NJ: Financial Times Prentice Hall.

House, R. J. (1976). A 1976 theory of charismatic leadership. In J. G. Hunt & L. L. Larson (Eds.), *Leadership: The cutting edge* (pp. 189–207). Carbondale: Southern Illinois University Press.

Howell, J. M., & Avolio, B. J. (1992). The ethics of charismatic leadership: Submission or liberation? *Academy of Management Executive, 6*(2), 43–54.

Kouzes, J. M., & Posner, B. Z. (1987). *The leadership challenge: How to get extraordinary things done in organizations.* San Francisco: Jossey-Bass.

Kouzes, J. M., & Posner, B. Z. (2002). *The leadership challenge* (3rd ed.). San Francisco: Jossey-Bass.

Kuhnert, K. W. (1994). Transforming leadership: Developing people through delegation. In B. M. Bass & B. J. Avolio (Eds.), *Improving organizational effectiveness through transformational leadership* (pp. 10–25). Thousand Oaks, CA: Sage.

Kuhnert, K. W., & Lewis, P. (1987). Transactional and transformational leadership: A constructive/developmental analysis. *Academy of Management Review, 12*(4), 648–657.

Northouse, P. G. (2010). *Leadership: Theory and practice* (5th ed.). Thousand Oaks, CA: Sage.

Shamir, B., House, R. J., & Arthur, M. B. (1993). The motivational effects of charismatic leadership: A self-concept-based theory. *Organization Science, 4*(4), 577–594.

Weber, M. (1947). *The theory of social and economic organizations* (T. Parsons, Trans.). New York: Free Press.

Yukl, G. (2006). *Leadership in organizations* (6th ed.). Upper Saddle River, NJ: Pearson/Prentice Hall.

▨ The Cases

Mayor Rudolph Giuliani, Knight of the British Empire

Rudolph Giuliani was the mayor of New York City during the events of September 11, 2001, and became world renowned for his leadership. Outlined is a description of his background, his first few years in office, the troubles he faced in his last year in office, and the sudden shift in his popularity post–September 11, 2001.

Spar Applied Systems: Anna's Challenge

The director of human resources must contend with internal and external pressures to make changes quickly and smoothly for the new year. She has been with the company for 6 months. In her capacity as director of human resources, she has spent her time establishing a baseline for the division so that she can then create a departmental vision and strategy for 2000. It will be one of the most interesting challenges of her career. Since joining, she has gained an understanding of the division's future direction from its leadership team. The team is under the direction of the division's new general manager.

▨ The Reading

Drucker's Challenge: Communication and the Emotional Glass Ceiling

The supreme challenge for a leader is to change human behavior, a formidable, if not impossible, task. But the leader who is emotionally intelligent (who is aware of and comfortable with his or her own self) will have a far greater chance of changing the behavior of others than a leader who is not aware of himself or herself. Using theories from esteemed management thinker Peter Drucker, the author points out that leaders who inspire are those who have resolved their own identity crisis. But that is much easier said than done, and the daunting nature of the task is encapsulated in Drucker's Challenge, which states that every human being has an emotional glass ceiling, a natural "resistance to changing" identity. This ceiling is broken only when communication is so compelling that it overcomes that resistance. How leaders can accomplish this goal is the subject of this article.

Mayor Rudolph Giuliani, Knight of the British Empire

Prepared by Ken Mark under the supervision of Christina A. Cavanagh

Introduction

Rudolph Giuliani, the mayor of New York City, was going to receive a honorary knighthood from Britain, announced the *National Post* on October 15, 2001. The award, reported in the British press on Saturday and confirmed by official sources on October 14, 2001, followed Giuliani's widely praised leadership in the wake of the September 11 terrorist attacks on New York that killed thousands of people and destroyed the twin towers of the World Trade Center. The award, "Knight of the British Empire," was the highest honor the Queen could bestow on a foreign citizen.

Britain's *Sunday Telegraph* newspaper quoted a Buckingham Palace official saying:

> The Queen believes that Rudolph Giuliani was an inspiration to political leaders around the world, as well as to his city. She was grateful for his support for Britons bereaved by the tragedy and feels

that this will also be a gesture of solidarity between America and Britain. Her regard for Mayor Giuliani is reflected in her desire to present the honour in person at Buckingham Palace.

Rudy Giuliani, Mayor of New York City

Giuliani had spent his adult life searching for missions impossible enough to suit his extravagant sense of self. A child of Brooklyn who was raised in a family of fire fighters, cops and criminals, he chose the path of righteousness and turned his life into a war against evil as he defined it. As a U.S. attorney in New York during the 1980s, Giuliani was perhaps the most effective prosecutor in the country, locking up Mafia bosses, crooked politicians and Wall Street inside traders.

When Giuliani was elected mayor of New York City in 1993, more than a million

---

AUTHOR'S NOTE: This case has been written on the basis of published sources only. Consequently, the interpretation and perspectives presented in this case are not necessarily those of Rudolph Giuliani or any of his employees.

Version: (A) 2003-02-12

New Yorkers were on welfare, violent crime and crack cocaine had ravaged whole neighborhoods, and taxes and unemployment were sky-high. It was fashionable to dismiss the place as ungovernable. Mayor Giuliani made good on his promise, doing away with New York's traditional politics of soft and ineffectual symbolism. The public was shocked and delighted to find that the streets were safer and cleaner. And the public did not care how he did it. If Giuliani picked fights big and small, if he purged government of those he deemed insufficiently loyal, so be it, "People didn't elect me to be a conciliator," Giuliani said.

He governed by hammering everyone else into submission, but in areas where that strategy was ineffective, such as the reform of the city schools, he failed to make improvements. Although by 1997 he had cut crime by two-thirds, his job-approval rating had declined to 32 per cent. New York City was getting better, but the mayor seemed to be getting worse. Black minority leaders complained that his aggressive cops were practising racial profiling, stopping and frisking people because of their race. Giuliani launched campaigns against jaywalkers, street vendors, noisy car alarms, and a crusade against publicly funded art that offended his moral sensibilities. But the pose seemed hypocritical at best when Giuliani, whose wife had not been seen at City Hall in years, began courting another woman, Judi Nathan.

In typical New York fashion, he was a dichotomous mix of public sentiment and disdain. *Time* magazine reported, on May 28, 2001, that Giuliani was poised to leave his office on a wave of goodwill, with opportunities for future office. Despite announcing the end of his marriage to the press corps before he told his wife, he had garnered a level of public sympathy not usually available to adulterers, thought to be due to his unfortunate bout of prostate cancer overriding the simultaneous appearance of his new girlfriend.

As a public figure, his life was more than just an open book. It was a constant and daily analysis of every aspect of his colorful life. Perhaps not since the Princess of Wales had a public figure become so newsworthy even if only on a local scale. There were hundreds of stories written about him and just as many colorful headlines announcing the firing of his estranged wife's staff and rumors of him leaving the New York City mayor's mansion due to the ongoing divorce drama.

◼ The Transformation Begins

Through circumstances both inexplicable and extraordinary, a controversial mayor who was set to leave office in 2002 took the reigns of a crisis on what became known as the twenty-first century's "Day of Infamy"—September 11, 2001. Countless newspapers published stories of Giuliani mobilizing the city's emergency services, running through smoke-filled basements wearing a gas mask and urging survivors to head north. As *Newsweek* reported, September 24, 2001:

> Giuliani, wearing a gas mask, was led running through a smoke-filled basement maze and out the other side of the Merrill Lynch building on Barclay Street, where the soot they're now calling "gray snow" was a foot deep. Stripping off the gas mask, Giuliani and a small group set off on foot for a mile hike up Church Street, urging the ghostly, ash-caked survivors to "Go north! Go north!" A distraught African American woman approached, and the mayor touched her face, telling her "It's going to be OK." Farther up, a young rowdy got the mayoral "Shhhhhh!" he deserved. That set the tone. He was sensitive and tough and totally on top of everything. Even his press criticism was, for once, on target.

And even his harshest critics offered nothing but sincere praise.

In recent years, Rudy Giuliani has been a cranky and not terribly effective mayor, too distracted by marital and health problems to work on the city's surging murder rate. But in this cataclysm, which he rightly called "the most difficult week in the history of New York," the city and the country have found that the most elusive of all democratic treasures—real leadership.[1]

A *Barron's* report, on September 24, 2001, was even more on point:

It is no secret that disaster has yielded a remarkable change in the public persona of Rudy Giuliani. Vanished is the mean mayor who badgered hot-dog vendors, threatened museums, sought to bludgeon dissent and indulged in an open and nasty row with his estranged wife. And in his place is, well, the essential Rudy: generous, sympathetic, indefatigable, levelheaded, unfailingly reassuring, a man for all crises.

The real Rudy, in other words. We say that because we've known Rudy for something close to a quarter of a century; indeed, for a spell between government jobs he represented Dow Jones, the parent company of Barron's, and, we can personally attest, was one hell of a lawyer. More to the point, he was also that rare combination of tough when he had to be and tender when he should have been, funny, bright and argumentative (natch), a great guy to knock off a bottle or two of vino with. Rudy has done a lot of silly things as mayor, but it doesn't

surprise us one whit that when the unimaginable happened, he did everything right and with incomparable style.[2]

As his popularity soared, Giuliani played with thoughts of returning to serve a third term. *Time* magazine reported on October 8, 2001 that Giuliani had received 15 per cent of the primary vote, all from write-in ballots. This result underlined Giuliani's undiminished popularity in the eyes of the public:

On a typical day last week, he found simple words to console the two children of Inspector Anthony Infante at St. Theresa's in the morning, then managed the ego of the Rev. Jesse Jackson as he took advantage of Giuliani's media entourage to nominate himself negotiator-in-chief. In the evening, Giuliani called on a stricken crowd at Temple Emanu-El to stand and applaud Neil Levin, the head of the Port Authority, who died helping his employees escape. Reverting to tireless cheerleader, he ended his day at Yankee Stadium watching Roger Clemens pitch against Tampa Bay.[3]

Bolstered by this show of support from the public, Giuliani summoned the three leading mayoral candidates to his office at Pier 92 and demanded to be allowed to stay in office for another three months—or else he would enter the mayoral race against them and win. Al Sharpton, a supporter for Fernando Ferrer in the 2002 New York mayoral election was unimpressed with this move. Unmoved by Giuliani's achievements, he referred to reports of Giuliani's heroics on September 11, 2001, arguing that on that day, "We would have come together (as a city) if Bozo was the mayor."

---

[1]Jonathan Alter, "Grit, Guts and Rudy Giuliani", *Newsweek*, September 24, 2001.

[2]Alan Abelson, "Up & Down Wall Street: Weighing Consequences", *Barron's*, September 24, 2001.

[3]Margaret Carlson, "Patriotic Splurging", *Time*, October 15, 2001.

Spar Applied Systems

Anna's Challenge

Prepared by Laura Erksine under the supervision of Jane M. Howell

It was September 1993 and Anna Solari had been with Spar Applied Systems for six months. In her capacity as director of human resources, she had spent her time establishing a baseline for the division so that she could then create a departmental vision and strategy for 2000. It would be one of the most interesting challenges of her career. Since joining, Anna had gained an understanding of the division's future direction from its leadership team. The team was under the direction of Stephen Miller, the division's new general manager. Since there was internal and external pressure to make the changes quickly and smoothly, Anna knew the vision for human resources had to be in place well before the new year.

⊠ Spar Aerospace Limited

Spar Aerospace Limited was Canada's premier space company and was a recognized leader in the space-based communications, robotics, informatics, aviation and defense industries. The company began in 1968 as a spin-off from de Havil land Aircraft, and was re-organized into four decentralized business segments over a period of two decades: space, communications, aviation and defense and informatics (see Exhibit 1).

The company employed approximately 2,500 people worldwide and approximately 60 per cent of Spar's sales originated outside Canada. Spar's expertise enabled Canada to become the third country in outer space and the company continued to innovate with achievements such as communications satellites, the Canadarm, and the compression of digital communication signals.

⊠ Spar Applied Systems

Spar's Aviation and Defense area featured two distinct businesses, one of which was Applied Systems Group (ASG). ASG was born through a merger between Spar Defense Systems and the newly acquired, but bankrupt, Leigh Instruments Limited in 1990. ASG designed and supplied communication, flight safety, surveillance and navigation equipment to space, military, and aerospace organizations around the world. It also offered advanced manufacturing services for complex electronic assemblies and systems. These government contracts represented close to 100 per cent of ASG's business.

The flight safety systems products included deployable emergency locator beacons, and flight data and cockpit voice recorders that collected, monitored, and analyzed aircraft flight information to assess equipment condition and improve flight safety procedures. Communications and intelligence products included integrated shipboard naval communications systems, ground-based aircraft navigation beacons, and infrared surveillance systems. Advanced manufacturing incorporated the assembly of high quality, low volume, highly complex electronic assemblies and systems to meet stringent military and space specifications.

ASG operated out of two facilities in the Ottawa Valley (Kanata and Carleton Place),

Version: (A) 2001-08-10

Exhibit 1 Organizational Chart

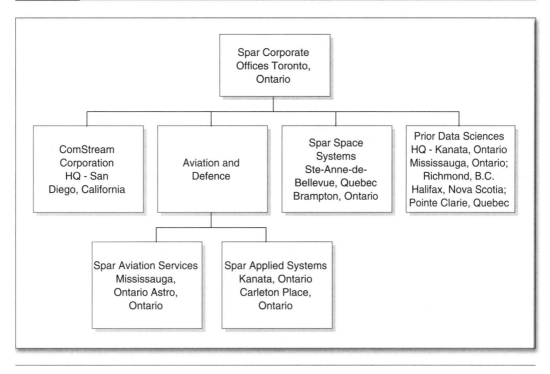

SOURCE: Company files.

employed 340 people (43 per cent manufacturing, 20 per cent engineering and technical, 17 per cent sales and professional, and 20 per cent other), and was the only non-unionized area of Spar. Historically, ASG's customers were primarily government-based and included Canada's Department of National Defense, the U.S. Navy and Coast Guard, as well as organizations in other international governments. For government customers, ASG had cost-plus contracts which guaranteed a minimum profit for the company, even if there were delays or occasions when the project went over budget. Customers were often told by ASG what they needed rather than delivering requirements or specifications to ASG.

Due to shrinking defense budgets, the aviation and defense industry was becoming increasingly competitive. As government contracts diminished, ASG sought more commercially oriented aviation customers who required fixed-price contracts. This meant ASG would have to finish on time and on, or under, budget in order to guarantee a profit. Time to market was becoming a critical factor in winning bids. Competition was coming from larger-scale, highly flexible, and vertically integrated companies such as Hughes Aircraft and McDonnell Douglas who were global in both strength and influence. Their capabilities, competencies, and capacities, especially related to technology and products, overshadowed those at ASG.

Applied Systems had other reasons to be concerned. More than 70 per cent of its revenues came from heritage programs that were nearing completion; it operated in too many fragmented lines of business; and a significant portion of the lines of business in their portfolio were nearing an 'end-of-life' status. The Applied Systems division of Spar had just started to become profitable two years after the acquisition of the Leigh Instruments assets. In the fall of 1993, ASG made up 9.1 per cent of the revenues and 33.3 per cent of the profits of Spar Aerospace. Members of ASG's leadership were wondering how to sustain this newfound profitability.

Although the employees at ASG were among the most skilled in their fields, the company did not know how to best direct their energy. They were very comfortable working in their current environment. In the era of cost-plus contracts, they had lots of time to work on a project because deadlines were often extended. Engineers possessed the ability to dedicate themselves to designing and creating superior (sometimes over-engineered) technology, even at the expense of manufacturability. Most importantly, employees could focus on their design and manufacturing tasks because they were being directed and led by a program manager. The program manager had the responsibility of customer contact, maintaining a schedule, and looking after the "business" details. The work was very independent and narrow as specific people were asked to contribute to different phases based on their skill sets and their experience. Overall, company strategy was unimportant to ASG's engineers. Phases moved sequentially through design and manufacturing with little interaction.

Following the formation of ASG in 1990, the executive management group of Spar Aerospace Limited wanted to see the company become more firmly established in the commercial aerospace and defense industry. They felt that by adapting their military products to suit commercial aviation customers, ASG could be successful. Stephen Miller, vice-president of marketing and government relations in Spar's corporate office, was selected as general manager and joined ASG in September 1992.

Stephen Miller

Stephen Miller, in his early 40s, had more than 20 years of experience in government and the aerospace industry. He quickly determined from his initial size-up that ASG was ill-prepared to compete in an increasingly commercial marketplace. ASG had products designed for military and government clients, had a technology rather than a customer focus, and lacked the internal attitude to move as quickly and efficiently as these new customers would require. Stephen saw an urgent need to change and established three personal objectives. First, he wanted to change the culture at ASG so dramatically that any of his successors would be unable to revert to the way things were in the fall of 1992. Stephen wanted to change the culture from being technology-driven, reactive, internally focused, and controlling to one that would be market-driven, strategic, externally focused, and liberating. Second, he wanted the division to make money for more than six months in a row. Finally, he wanted to develop a long-term strategy that would make sense in a global context and eliminate the short-term planning with which the company was familiar. If successful, these objectives would increase both the flexibility and resiliency of the organization.

Stephen also wanted to create a culture that fostered teamwork, open communication, accountability, and recognition of performance in a skilled, challenged workforce. He strongly believed that the organization was capable of greater achievements if properly managed and motivated. He knew that the functions had to be more integrated to eliminate the functional silos currently in place. He also realized that too many changes too quickly might upset the current workforce and, although committed to his goals, Stephen was worried. ASG attracted very highly skilled employees who would be valued by competitors. Stephen was well aware that he needed the intellectual capital of ASG's employees in order to move into the commercial marketplace.

One of Stephen's first moves was to take his management team (see Exhibit 2) off-site to hammer out a mission statement and

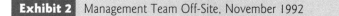

Exhibit 2 Management Team Off-Site, November 1992

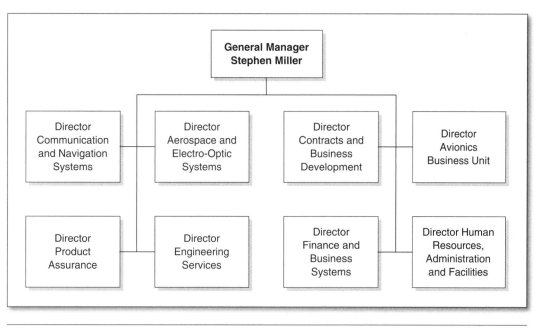

SOURCE: Company files.

develop a strategic plan. The group achieved consensus on the following:

> Building on our heritage, we will become the market leader in informatics-based integrated digital communications and flight safety systems and services, with a particular focus on satisfying the changing needs of the global defense market. We will grow to be a fast-paced, high performance, $250 million a year enterprise, with returns in the top 25 per cent of our industry by the year 2000.

The management team also reached consensus about a vision, later introduced and discussed with ASG employees in a series of meetings (see Exhibit 3). They also developed a three-part strategy that was intended to link organizational activities to the strategic plan. First, through business development, ASG had

to capture significantly higher dollar volumes of profitable business. Second, programs had to be executed effectively (on budget, on schedule, and satisfying the customer). Third, ASG's employees needed to provide value to customers by being responsive and by delivering top quality products.

By the first quarter of 1993, Stephen was feeling confident about ASG's future ability to make progress with the initiatives, except for human resources. Unlike the present ASG and many other organizations, he wanted human resources to play a crucial role in Applied Systems' strategic plan by implementing the vision at a structural and organizational level. In order to find a leader for the new human resources role, Stephen went outside the organization to recruit Anna Solari from a high technology firm that did not compete with ASG. Anna was selected because of her strengths in integrated human resources systems, organizational development and change leadership.

Exhibit 3 Applied Systems Group

Vision

- We will grow to be a $250 million/year enterprise by the year 2000.
- We will attain a prominent and respected position in the new world order, climbing the systems chain, entering new markets that build on our heritage and growing those products and services that are relevant to our future.
- We will be recognized as being the best at what we do, on a global scale, winning consistently in excess of 70 per cent of the markets and opportunities we pursue.
- We will achieve total customer satisfaction by understanding their needs and through 100 per cent performance of our industry.
- We are mastering the concepts of teamwork and organizational growth; we will exploit its strengths to create an exciting and vibrant entity, attractive to both our customers and employees.

Anna Solari

After receiving a Bachelor of Social Sciences in Psychology from the University of Ottawa in 1986, Anna Solari became a consultant with a large firm specializing in Human Resources consulting. From there, her 10-year career took her to two different commercial high technology firms, where she had a wide range of human resources responsibilities. Anna moved to Applied Systems in March 1993, six months after Stephen Miller had taken the role of general manager. Having recently managed the rapid growth and merger of a smaller company, she was interested in the challenges presented by a mature, relatively successful company that had to change in order to survive. When she met with Stephen, his energy and enthusiasm for radical change helped to finalize her decision to take the new job.

Just as Anna joined Applied Systems, there were a number of labor relations issues that needed to be addressed. All of Spar's divisions, with the exception of ASG, were unionized. There was regular pressure to change that situation and ASG had always maintained a labor relations component within its human resources staff to attempt to prevent a union from taking hold. The last attempt ended just as Anna arrived and was the most successful yet,

where the union came close to getting the necessary 50 per cent plus one vote for certification. Reasons behind the drive were thought to be the ASG employees comparing their representation to the other Spar divisions and the difficulty that arose from attempting to mix the Leigh and Defense cultures following the acquisition. Due to closed communication paths and a lack of employee involvement, there was a feeling of "us versus them". Although the company was still not represented, the drive was so close to being successful that it was enough to give Spar management a wake-up call. Unsure of the reasons behind the drive, management breathed a sigh of relief and hoped something, anything, would end the union threat. Since then, Anna had tried to gather an understanding of the current state of affairs, a baseline, in order to create a human resources vision that would be compatible with the company's strategic direction and proactive in preventing a union drive from recurring.

The Baseline Audit

By September 1993, Anna felt she had gathered and digested a wide range of data and opinions regarding the current state of the human resources function at ASG. Given the continuing internal and external pressures to make changes, Anna reviewed the information she had amassed in order to develop a plan for implementing needed changes quickly that could be smoothly aligned with a vision for human resources and consistent with ASG's mission.

Anna gathered the following observations during the "baseline audit" that she later shared with the case writer:

Organizational Structure

The company's leadership team had already discussed possible structures to eliminate the top-heavy pyramid in place when Anna joined. Instead of an organization revolving around program management with functional departments operating in isolation, upper management wanted a structure organized by process (winning new business, supporting the company, and delivering product) that functioned in integrated teams created for specific contracts. Their idea was that people would have a "home" based on the skills they possessed but would join one or more project teams for the length of the business contracts. Although this was a radical departure from the current structure, Stephen, Anna, and the others felt it was an important way to decrease their time to market and become more responsive to their increasing commercial customer base.

Spans of Control/ Management Responsibility

Anna recalled: "What I walked into was a very traditional, hierarchical organization with four or five layers of management. It started with the general manager/VP. Under him were director levels and those director levels may or may not have fallen within the senior management categories. If not, directors might have had senior management who then had middle level management. Middle level management might have also had entry level management or supervisors below it." (See Exhibit 4 for a departmental organization chart.) The organization was very

top-heavy which forced large spans of control at the lower levels in the company. For example, people at the very top may have only had four or five people reporting to them while entry-level supervisors were responsible for 25 or 30 people. In addition, the accountability rested with those who possessed the 'manager' title whereas the real profit and loss impact resided with the general workforce.

Culture

Despite Stephen's initiatives and relationships with his management team, Anna found the culture at ASG was quite formal, hierarchical, and traditional. To a certain degree it was bureaucratic and also lived under the threat of third-party intervention. The descriptors used were: technology-driven; resource-led; tactical; reactive; 'thing' (rather than people) sensitive; closed; controlling; introspective; divided; and marginal performer. Anna had conducted many focus groups of 20 to 25 employees during her baselining and these employees identified issues such as the color of the paint on the walls, poor ventilation, and questions about health and safety standards, among others. Anna started to worry:

> Because [I] wanted to make real changes in areas that impacted the bottom line and had a return on investment such as equity, behavior shifts, overtime policies and sick leave. If [the employees] were upset about paint, what would happen when we introduced things that affected their pocketbooks?

She wondered how to cope with another possible attempt at unionization without allowing that threat to overshadow any decisions that needed to be made.

Communication

There was very little face-to-face communication in ASG and the basis for information flow

Exhibit 4 Engineering Department Organization Chart, February 1992

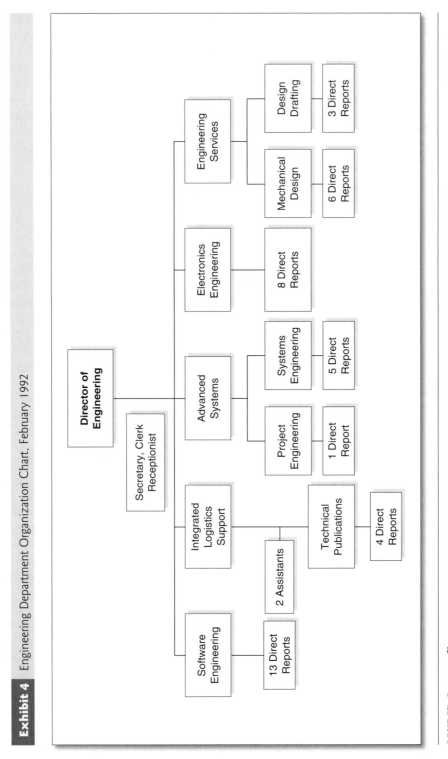

SOURCE: Company files.

was formal, one-way, top-down, and written. Approval processes went up through the levels of the company, across the top, and back down again. As a result, decision making was delayed. Occasionally, the general manager would give a formal "state of the union" address to all employees that might allow for questions at the

end. If you wanted to speak to someone, an appointment was made through managers' secretaries in advance. Communication seemed to Anna to be too formal and too inefficient. She vividly recalled an exchange with a member of the management team that occurred in her first weeks at ASG (see Exhibit 5).

Exhibit 5 An Early Communications Example—Setting Up a Meeting

Anna's Secretary:	Anna, Mr. Smith would like to set up a meeting with you. Why don't you give me your calendar so I can organize the meeting with Mr. Smith's secretary? I can also set up any other meetings you need to have without bothering you for your availability.
Anna:	Thanks for the offer but I like to keep my own schedule. Do you know where Mr. Smith's office is? I'll just walk over and talk to him right now.
Anna's Secretary:	Oh, I don't think that is a very good idea. We don't really do things like that around here.
Anna:	That's OK. If Mr. Smith needs to see me, I am free right now and I'll just walk over to see him.
Anna's Secretary:	[Gives directions to a secretary's office with a closed outer door that leads into Mr. Smith's inner office (also with a closed door).]
Anna:	Good morning, I am here to see Mr. Smith. He wanted to speak with me.
Mr. Smith's Secretary:	Do you have an appointment?
Anna:	No, but is Mr. Smith in his office?
Mr. Smith's Secretary:	Yes, but. . . .
Anna:	Is he with somebody or on the phone?
Mr. Smith's Secretary:	No, but. . . [as Anna knocked on Mr. Smith's door]. You really shouldn't be doing that.
Anna:	Mr. Smith, I understand you wanted to see me.
Mr. Smith:	Yes, but I am not really prepared for a meeting right now.
Anna:	How long will it take? I can meet you in the cafeteria in 15 minutes.
Mr. Smith:	Well, 15 minutes should be enough time but I would prefer to have the meeting here in my office.
Anna:	That's fine. I'll be back in 15 minutes.

When Anna returned 15 minutes later, Mr. Smith's secretary was very surprised when Anna greeted her but didn't ask permission to see Mr. Smith. Anna knocked on Mr. Smith's door, entered, and the meeting began.

Recruiting and Training

Recruitment was a reactive process designed to fill gaps. People leaving the organization were replaced using a position description developed many years ago and faithfully adhered to over time. The human resources department solicited resumes based on the information from a given department that an employee would be leaving or that growth required additional personnel. The target audience for filling gaps was industry.

> The organization had always targeted [the high technology defense] industry and, in fact, they broke out of the mold a little bit when they hired me. We did not focus a lot on the new [college and university] grads because experience was very important to us.

> Traditional roles were defined: "a technician is a technician, a technologist is a technologist and at no point in time do those two roles meet."

The human resources department had limited involvement in the new employee orientation. New employees filled out tax and registration paperwork and received a policy manual that explained the company "rules" (absenteeism, benefits, company hours, bathroom and cigarette breaks, etc.). One striking example that stood out to Anna was the rule that employees were not permitted to sleep at their workstations during working hours. New employees then reported directly to their manager who immediately integrated them into their roles. Information about ASG and their role in the organization was picked up from their manager and their peers.

Training was also an informal process. Members of the human resources department arranged for a given employee to receive certain courses in response to a request from that employee's manager. ASG employees already possessing the necessary skills provided the specific technical courses (usually lasting a few hours) and managers could request specific "trainers". If the necessary courses were not available on site, Applied Systems reimbursed employees' tuition at a local community college. This procedure was unusual because ASG provided most courses. Training was conducted on company time and increased technical skills led to jumps in job grades and corresponding pay

increases. There were 54 pay grades within ASG. Managers and employees did not need to show an immediate business need or an opportunity to use the new technical knowledge to participate in training, just a desire to learn the new skills.

Performance Appraisal and Review

Employee performance appraisals, which were conducted annually, determined merit increases for each employee. Each person's appraisal was conducted by his or her immediate manager and was based on a rating system that ranged from excellent to poor. Technical elements like quality and quantity of work were evaluated, as were factors like adherence to health and safety standards, and punctuality. Some employees indicated to Anna that they did not interact with their managers enough to be evaluated by them, while some managers complained of the time it took to complete the reviews. Merit increases were at the discretion of each manager and came from a pool of funds distributed from higher levels of the organization. As a result, Anna learned that pay equity and equality were not being maintained throughout ASG because a connection was not directly made between the performance appraisal and the amount of the merit pay.

Compensation and Benefits

Anna felt that the benefits program at Spar was one of the best that she had seen, "not only in the industry but extending into the high tech area, including software." The benefit package included everything from dental coverage to disability programs. In addition, employees at ASG were very well paid. Based on information collected by ASG from its industry hires and marketplace research, Anna found the company's compensation policy was 30 per cent above market rate. Although employee satisfaction was not a problem, Anna realized that excessively high salary levels reflected poor business practices and were inconsistent with actual divisional financial performance.

Salary administration was based on 54 job grades (secretary: 1 to 6, technician: 1 to 6, etc.) and each grade had very specific tasks that those people within it could complete. Anna described the mentality by saying:

> People knew their box and they did not want anybody stepping into their box, and, by the same token, did not want to step out of their box.

This is where the inequity was manifested. Some people with the same roles could be making salaries that differed by up to $10,000 annually because of seniority and performance appraisals.

◪ Vision 2000

Anna, with the assistance of members of the management group and employees of ASG, wanted to design an organization that would be more competitive, more flexible, and ready to grow through mergers and acquisitions. The employees were highly skilled and very innovative in nature; however, they were demographically diverse and tended to operate within the silos fostered by the hierarchical organization. Given that ASG had created a strategy and a vision for 2000, Anna's task was to develop a vision for human resources that was compatible with Stephen Miller's strategy of capturing higher volumes of profitable business, executing effectively, and providing value to the customers. How could employee development, succession planning, and the new organizational structure be introduced and what were the best recruiting and training practices, performance evaluation process, and compensation plan? She also wondered if the labor relations component needed to change in order to prevent a successful union drive. After establishing the vision, how would the transition occur to get them there?

Drucker's Challenge

Communication and the Emotional Glass Ceiling

By Paul Wieand

Building social capital is imperative for a leader today. But to meet that challenge, a leader must do nothing less than change human behaviour, a formidable, if not impossible, task.

During the past two decades, no psychological concept has had a greater influence on leadership development than emotional intelligence. On the other hand, no other concept in the past 20 years is so tied to ancient wisdom: 2,000 years ago

Socrates declared that the attainment of self-knowledge is humanity's greatest challenge; Aristotle added that this challenge was about managing our emotional life with intelligence. This is at the heart of leadership development in today's complex, dynamic business environment.

This article will describe the relationship between psychological complexity, human potential and communications, and how they relate to emotional intelligence and, ultimately, build social capital.

The Importance of Peter Drucker

The current popularity of emotional intelligence can be seen as a discontinuous extension of the psychological revolution during the '60s and early '70s, when the human potential movement, popularized by Abraham Maslow, dominated business literature.

In the history of business, Peter Drucker stands alone as a bridge between that earlier era and today. Drucker is both an intellectual and a pragmatist, and at 92, he has observed the major changes in both epochs and been a force of change himself. In his work he consistently points out that while the context of organizations and leadership has changed, human nature has not.

Drucker also understands the need for complexity. He says, "We can't learn anything by simplifying difficult issues. We have got to complexify them." Ultimately, Drucker values simplicity, but he realizes that "getting there" means making connections to the past and to related fields. His work is a tool for making these connections. Before discussing Drucker further, it is necessary to identify what is, and what is not, truly new about the concept of emotional intelligence.

Emotional Intelligence

By themselves, the discoveries in emotional intelligence are not new. What is new is that for the first time we can scientifically validate, through brain scanning technology, the fact that our emotions play a central role in moulding thinking and logic. New discoveries in neurophysiology have also advanced our understanding of the critical relationship between emotions and values.

With respect to human development, two significant issues have emerged which have an immediate impact on, and practical application for, leadership development. One is that the emotional component of the brain, the limbic system, is capable of hijacking both our intellect and our values. What is not new is that this hijacking occurs without our awareness. This is simply not good, for when the thinking and the processing of values are controlled by emotions outside of awareness, humans have a strong tendency to develop attitudes and behaviours that destroy trust and relationships. Values can be determined on an ad hoc basis, leading to inconsistency in relationships and decision making.

A second significant fact is that the emotional system is changed neither easily nor quickly. Making significant changes to the limbic system usually requires approximately one year; making those changes enduring ones is highly dependent on social interaction. This scientific discovery sounded the death knell for the idea that significant, enduring change can take place quickly, by insight alone, or in isolation, outside of a relationship. Reading about or studying emotional intelligence is as likely to have an impact on its development as reading a book on playing golf. Emotional intelligence is acquired through experience, in relationships.

Identity and the Emotional Glass Ceiling

Thirty years before the discovery of emotional intelligence, Drucker noted that deep and fundamental human change takes place at the level of identity. He observed that such change is most likely to occur as a result of communication in the form of social interaction around shared values. To paraphrase Drucker, the most effective communication requires altering the emotions of others. The most powerful communication may be nothing more, but nothing less than, shared experience, without any logic whatever.

If Drucker is right, emotional intelligence becomes a powerful tool for moving an individual toward realizing his or her potential only when the change is grounded in his or her identity. In other words, increasing emotional intelligence requires altering identity. At the same time, science has shown us that identity's emotional component is the most difficult and complex to alter. Drucker observed that altering emotions is, for the most part, a communications challenge that succeeds only when it breaks through a person's "emotional glass ceiling." Psychologists often refer to this event as a boundary experience.

Drucker's Challenge

In 1969, Drucker wrote one of his few theoretical and psychological papers and presented it to the Fellows of the International Academy of Management, in Tokyo. One of the most insightful statements in this paper brings together psychological complexity, human potential and communication in a way that can shed light on the practical application of emotional intelligence. We call this statement "Drucker's Challenge," and it states: "At its most powerful, communication brings about conversion, that is, a change of personality, values, beliefs, aspirations. But this is a rare existential event, and one against which the basic psychological forces of every human being are strongly organized."

Drucker's Challenge recognizes that every human being has an emotional glass ceiling, a natural resistance to changing identity. Moreover, this ceiling is broken only when communication is so compelling that it overcomes that resistance.

While this is not a revelation for a psychologist, it presents a unique and profound challenge for most executive coaches, the individuals who are usually responsible for significantly increasing another person's emotional intelligence. It is a challenge because the basic psychological forces of "every" human being are strongly organized against achieving higher emotional intelligence.

There is a myth about the difficulty and complexity of human development, and to understand it we must first understand the relationship between identity and emotional intelligence.

The Identity System: Reconceptualizing Emotional Intelligence

Emotional intelligence is an evolving concept, one that lacks even a standard definition. More important, it is not grounded in an integrated existential context. Understanding the existential component of Drucker's Challenge is a necessary first step in effectively using emotional intelligence as a vehicle for human development. An appreciation of the identity system can greatly facilitate that understanding.

The foundation of identity rests on three major, interrelated psychological and existential factors.

1. The relationship between emotional intelligence and identity: Much of the current literature would lead you to believe that emotional intelligence is an independent system that subsumes identity. In fact, it is the other way around. Identity is the whole system and emotional intelligence is just one component of that identity. When Drucker refers to a "rare existential event," he refers to what is required to alter the identity system. Any perceived change in emotional intelligence will be short lived if it is not accompanied by a change in identity. Moreover, this is not only a rare event. It is an existential one that alters personality, values, beliefs and aspirations.

2. The core components of the identity system: Here, again, psychology and neuroscience have come together and, in a way, reached a consensus. Identity is composed of three primary components that can be viewed as the brain's core subsystems—emotions, values and intellect.

Neuroscience has revealed that all three subsystems are processed in different parts of the brain. What makes emotional intelligence such a powerful concept is that the emotions play a unique and powerful role in altering identity. Leaders function at their best—when they are consistent in their values, actions and words, and therefore, trust is high—when they are aware of their emotions and maintain a balance between emotions, values and the intellect, and when values are the leading subsystem in identity. When emotions remain outside of awareness, they—along with intellect—tend to drive the identity system. Behaviours that are inconsistent because they are emotionally driven are often rationalized, and it becomes difficult to have values that remain consistent. The result is that words and action tend to be inconsistent and serve only the individual, who has little empathy or regard for others. The primary by-product is a decrease in open, honest communication, which over time, tends to lead to distrust.

When values are the driver—overriding both emotional reactivity and intellectual rationalization—words and actions become consistent, creating attitudes and behaviours that foster open, honest communication. This consistent communication in turn creates trusting relationships.

3. The dynamics of identity. If it is to adapt and survive, every system, including human identity, needs an "organizing principle." The task of the organizing principle is to help the system reach its potential. One way to isolate the most powerful organizing principle in human identity is to examine the characteristics of people who survive and adapt at the extreme boundaries of human existence. In other words, what are the personality traits that actually grow under the most adverse circumstances? The question is all the more interesting since Drucker's Challenge states that the basic psychological forces of every human being are strongly organized against change.

The Survivor Personality

Extensive research has been done on two groups of people who meet these criteria, wartime paratrooper survivors and concentration camp survivors. The research reveals that these "survivor personalities" have two characteristics in common, both of which involve very adaptive emotional capabilities.

First, values are the driver of the survivor personality. While the intellect can change at the speed of thought and emotions can change at the speed of impulse, values are relatively constant and tend to change at the speed of trust. Values, because they transcend the individual, can infuse an individual with the need for continuity and stability, both of which are necessary to survive under extreme conditions. Victor Frankl, the Viennese psychiatrist and concentration camp survivor, and author of *Man's Search for Meaning*, observed that extreme, tortuous conditions actually strengthened certain identities because the conditions forced people to clarify their values.

A second characteristic these survivors have in common is that they are able to use a broader range of emotions than other personality types. This makes them better able to adapt to complex social situations and enables them to develop social support systems. Al Seibert, a psychologist, former paratrooper and the originator of the "survivor personality," found that the survivor personality is predominantly paradoxical; it is made up of combinations of opposites. Survivor personalities have an ability to be humble and fierce, strong and vulnerable, logical and intuitive, self-confident and self-critical, serious and playful. They use their emotions in a way that makes them both strong and flexible, and they use them to get the best out of others. But to have core values that are consistent yet flexible requires that an individual have an extremely adaptive emotional capacity. Researchers often describe individuals with these capabilities as genuine and authentic.

Authenticity and Exceptional Leadership

The connection between authenticity and exceptional leadership is very significant. Authenticity can be viewed as the most advanced form of identity and the ideal condition for increasing the effectiveness of emotional intelligence. It is characterized by an emotional capacity that continuously strives to reach its potential in a way that maximizes trusting relationships. Increasing emotional intelligence is a complex challenge, one that involves breaking through one's own emotional glass ceiling as a necessary first step, and then using this capacity to help others do the same in a way that transcends individual differences.

The authentic person communicates trust by being genuine and non-defensive, and by allowing consistent access to his or her value system. Values, particularly empathy, are clearly developed and communicated, so that authentic people are true to both themselves and others. Being true to humanity gives authenticity a transcendent quality by elevating dignity and respecting differences in people and cultures.

Increasing authenticity requires courage—the courage to be oneself—without sacrificing the values that bond leaders with others. When authenticity is viewed in this way, empathy becomes an act of courage and trust becomes the foundation of communication. Words are the least powerful form of communication, an artifact of the failed theory that logic and rational thought alone are the supreme elements of effective communication. Drucker is correct when he says that, "the whole person comes with the words." Identity, who you are, speaks louder than words.

Human potential, especially for leaders, cannot be a derivative of IQ alone. In an age in which IQ, in the form of intellectual capital, has become a commodity, EQ has become the driver of competitive advantage. Most organizations will continue to fail to build high-performance cultures if they do not require leaders at every level of the organization to have a high degree of emotional intelligence.

Authenticity and the Post-Modern Leader

Estimates suggest that 70-80 per cent of major reorganizations and re-engineering efforts fail over the long term. The primary reason for failure is the destruction of social capital. From the beginning of the Industrial Revolution until the last few decades, physical capital was the most valued form of capital. As the technological revolution evolved and then exploded during the '80s and '90s, a premium was placed on intellectual capital. We did not realize that this shift occurred, to a great extent, at the expense of social capital, and until its demise came to be seen as a crisis.

Very few companies have historically factored in, in any meaningful way, the social and relational consequence of major organizational change. Most reorganizations, even today, emphasize changes in strategy, structure and cost reductions; they do not give equal weight to the human issues and the reorganization's negative impact on social capital. When most organizations make major changes, they fail to manage the emotional component intelligently, something that requires "authentic" leadership. In our experience, however, senior management in general, and CEOs in particular, too often resist breaking through their own emotional glass ceiling. They are not authentic leaders.

Many executives that were trained as leaders, especially during the '60s, have failed to realize that the demands of building social capital, the "people" component in the business world, have changed. Maximizing human potential has become one of the most important and enduring competitive advantages, primarily in its ability to retain and attract talent. Without doubt, today's post-technological revolution has changed the requirements for leadership.

Margaret Mead was perhaps the first anthropologist to see the new challenges facing organizations in the industrialized world. In her 1970 book *Culture and Commitment*, she writes, "We are the first generation to develop our identity during a time when the forces of change are greater than the forces of non-change." Winston Churchill, a contemporary of Mead, wrote, "We are shaping the world faster than we can change ourselves, and we are applying to the present the habits of the past." The existential psychologist E. Van Deurzen-Smith states that, "The cultural component of identity has never before been so unstable, and this instability is anxiety-producing."

In today's world, leaders must not only be able to help people in the organization realize their human potential. They must also be able to lead during a time of instability, uncertainty and continuous change. To do so, leaders must be emotionally flexible, paradoxical, non-defensive, empathic and values-driven. In short, leaders must model authenticity.

Executive coach Peter Koestenbaum claims that leaders today must address "existential quandaries" similar to those found in Drucker's Challenge. He writes, "Nothing is more practical [today] than for people to deepen themselves. The more you understand the human condition, the more effective you are as a businessperson. Human depth makes business sense." His primary solution is to help executives become more authentic and to deepen their understanding of human nature.

Technical competence is still a necessity today, but leaders who can role model authenticity at every level of the organization are equally important. This new reality is reflected in the current emphasis by some of the world's most admired companies on developing the emotional intelligence of leaders. Leaders who are both technically competent and authentic have the greatest ability to attract and retain talent and build social capital. Building social capital begins

with deepening the capacity of leaders to model authenticity. This requires changes at the level of identity. An authentic leader then has the emotional flexibility and strength to deal with the discontinuity of change, and to create a reasonable sense of stability during tremendous upheaval.

Once an organization understands that who a leader is as a person speaks more powerfully than what he or she says, the connection between identity and communications becomes clear. Authenticity and effective communications are mutually inclusive, and no organization in today's world runs well in the long run without effective communications.

Authentic leaders are able to manage their own emotional lives with intelligence and leverage, by evoking higher levels of emotional intelligence in others in the organization. Howard Gardner, a Harvard psychologist and author of Leading Minds: An Anatomy of Leadership, offers valuable insight into the human and emotional process that takes place when leaders can leverage their own development to help others develop those same qualities. At the risk of oversimplifying his work, Gardner views authentic leaders as those who have the ability to create a sense of group identity. They serve as role models with whom the group identifies and which it can emulate. With a sense of trust at the core of these relationships, open, honest, candid and empathic communication leads to strong relationships that create stability amidst uncertainty and change. The leader's stability is experienced as a part of the group's stability. Gardner adds a powerful insight into the emotional process that enables this to take place: "It is the particular burden of the leader to help other individuals determine their personal, social and moral identities; more often than not, leaders inspire, in part, because of how they have resolved their own identity issues."

Breaking Through

When leaders find the courage and humility to identify and break through their own emotional glass ceiling, they can begin to do the same for others. As leaders develop a better understanding of the nature of human change and its connection to effective communication, they become more realistic about the time frame and the knowledge required for successful leadership development and cultural change. They recognize that the short-term cost of building social capital far outweighs its long-term benefits, both financial and human.

Drucker's Challenge reflects the magnitude of the effort required to increase emotional intelligence in leaders. There are no quick or easy ways to accomplish these changes in identity. Change begins with a realistic appraisal of the self, a process of reflection that increases self-knowledge and leads to a humble acceptance of one's real limitations and recognition of one's strengths. When leaders develop a more accurate self-concept,

they can utilize those around them to compensate for their natural limitations and leverage their strengths. Clarification of values is paramount so that leadership, work life, and values are more closely aligned, over time, creating stability and a passion and commitment to work. Howe ver, one must realize that a deeper awareness of the complexity of emotions and how they influence decision making and reacting to others is critical.

These are the difficult and rewarding challenges of leadership development in today's complex and rapidly changing world. Leadership development, at its best, is human development. You simply cannot be a world-class leader if you are first of all, not a world-class person, and you cannot be a world-class person if you are not authentic. This is why authenticity is the most advanced form of emotional intelligence.

Authentic Leadership

Daina Mazutis

The University of Western Ontario

"Why is it so hard to lead yourself?" The answer, in my experience, lies in the differences between your idealized self and your real self. The key to being able to develop yourself as a leader is to narrow that gap by developing a deep self-awareness.

—Bill George[1]

As a response to the seemingly pervasive ethical scandals that dominated the business headlines at the beginning of this century, the public demand for more honest, more trustworthy, and more genuine leadership has become increasingly animated. Both practitioners and social scientists have heeded this call and attempted to define a new approach to leadership that is based on the positive characteristics, behaviours, and capabilities of authentic leaders. Although still in its early developmental stages, the theoretical and practical approaches to understanding authentic leadership are presented in this chapter.

Authentic Leadership Defined

Authentic leadership was first defined by Luthans and Avolio (2003) as a process described as being a style:

> which results in both greater self-awareness and self-regulated positive behaviors on the part of leaders and associates, fostering positive self-development. The authentic

---

[1]Bill George is a former CEO of Medtronics Inc.

leader is confident, hopeful, optimistic, resilient, transparent, moral/ethical, future-oriented, and gives priority to developing associates to be leaders. (p. 243)

Since then, multiple definitions of authentic leadership have been explored, each conceived from a unique standpoint and emphasizing different components of the theory. Intrapersonal, interpersonal, and developmental definitions are considered below (Northouse, 2010).

Intrapersonal definitions, such as the one developed by Shamir and Eilam (2005), focus on the leader himself or herself. In this view, authentic leaders have highly developed systems of self-knowledge and self-regulation. They have realistic concepts of self that are rooted in strong values and base their actions on these core values, exhibiting genuine leadership and leading from conviction (Shamir & Eilam, 2005). These values include loyalty, responsibility, trustworthiness, integrity, accountability, respect, and fairness, in addition to attributes such as self-awareness, emotional intelligence, and self-certainty (Michie & Gooty, 2005). This approach also stresses the importance of the intrapersonal experiences of authentic leaders, both in the role that their personal life stories have had in their development as well as in the role that followers play in affirming the legitimacy of the leader and his or her behaviour (Gardner, Avolio, Luthans, May, & Walumbwa, 2005; Shamir & Eilam, 2005).

Interpersonal definitions, on the other hand, emphasize the relational aspect of authentic leadership, which is dependent on the reciprocal interactions of leaders and followers (Eagly, 2005). Here, authentic leaders are seen not only as hopeful and optimistic, but also as builders of confidence, hope, and trust (Avolio, Gardner, Walumbwa, Luthans, & May, 2004). Through positive modeling, personal and social identification, emotional contagion, and positive social exchanges, authentic leaders foster positive follower attitudes and outcomes (Avolio & Gardner, 2005; Gardner et al., 2005). However, only if followers identify with the values of the leader will positive outcomes arise; there must therefore be a high degree of buy-in from followers for authentic leadership to be effective (Northouse, 2010).

Developmental definitions assert that both intrapersonal characteristics and interpersonal behaviours are qualities that can be developed into authentic leadership. Several researchers, for example, have suggested that positive psychological capabilities such as self-awareness, internalized moral perspective, balanced processing, and relational transparency are skills that can be taught. These capabilities are thus not conceived of as static personality traits but rather as behaviours that can be nurtured and developed over time or can even be triggered by major life events. Many explorations of authentic leadership take this explicitly developmental approach (Avolio & Gardner, 2005).

From a theoretical perspective, however, the most recent definition of authentic leadership that best captures the intrapersonal, interpersonal, and developmental approaches is

a pattern of leader behavior that draws upon and promotes both positive psychological capacities and a positive ethical climate, to foster greater self-awareness, an internalized moral perspective, balanced processing of information, and relational transparency on the part of leaders working with followers, fostering positive self-development. (Walumbwa, Avolio, Gardner, Wernsing, & Peterson, 2008, p. 94)

Although complex, this definition includes many of the components of authentic leadership that are currently being developed in the social science literature. This theoretical approach to authentic leadership is discussed in the next section, followed by a brief discussion of the more practical approach that has evolved simultaneously in the popular business press.

Theoretical Approaches

Research on authentic leadership was originally spearheaded out of the University of Nebraska, where Luthans and Avolio (2003) first wrote about authentic leadership development as a model of leadership that was more ethical and more humane than what was being portrayed in the popular business press after the ethical scandals at WorldCom, Tyco, and Enron, to name a few. Although other models of leadership, such as transformational leadership, also include positive components, the meaning of authentic transformational leadership had yet to be fully explored. The related fields of ethics, positive psychology, and positive organizational scholarship were drawn upon in this foundational period (Northouse, 2010).

In addition to Luthans and Avolio's (2003) developmental perspective, different models of authentic leadership have also been proposed. As discussed above, some of these models focused on leader values and attributes (e.g., Michie & Gooty, 2005), while others have focused on the interpersonal effects of authentic leadership. For example, Ilies, Morgeson, and Nahrgang's (2005) model focused on the outcomes of authentic leadership and the positive effects on follower well-being. Similarly, both Avolio and colleagues (2004) and Gardner and colleagues (2005) argued that authentic leadership has positive effects on follower trust, hope, and positive emotions, resulting in increased meaningfulness, commitment, engagement, and workplace well-being. Empirically, authentic leadership has been shown to be a strong predictor of group-level leadership outcomes such as employee job satisfaction and performance (Walumbwa et al., 2008). Theoretically, authentic leadership has also been applied to firm-level outcomes such as organizational learning (Mazutis & Slawinski, 2008).

Recent theoretical and empirical work, however, has converged around four primary components that form the core of authentic leadership theory: self-awareness, relational transparency, internalized moral perspective, and balanced processing (Avolio & Gardner, 2005; Gardner et al., 2005; Ilies et al., 2005; Kernis, 2003; Mazutis & Slawinski, 2008; Northouse, 2010; Walumbwa et al., 2008). These four essential elements of authentic leadership are discussed in detail below.

Self-Awareness

Ilies and colleagues (2005) define a leader's self-awareness as "awareness of, and trust in, one's own personal characteristics, values, motives, feelings, and cognitions. Self-awareness includes knowledge of one's inherent contradictory self-aspects and the role of these contradictions in influencing one's thoughts, feelings, actions and behaviors" (p. 377). Because self-aware leaders understand their strengths and weaknesses, are tuned in to how their behavior affects others, and know who they are and what they stand for, other people perceive these leaders as more authentic (Gardner et al., 2005; Kernis, 2003).

Internalized Moral Perspective

The internalized moral perspective component of authentic leadership describes a process of self-regulation whereby "leaders align their values with their intentions and actions" (Avolio & Gardner, 2005, p. 325). Authentic leaders will resist external pressures that are contrary to their moral standards through an internal regulation process that ensures that their values are congruent with the anticipated outcomes of a behavior (Gardner et al., 2005). By aligning their values and actions and acting according to their own "true selves," leaders demonstrate consistency in what they say and what they do that translates into more authentic leadership.

Balanced Processing

Balanced processing is also referred to as *unbiased processing*. Authentic leaders are able to hear, interpret, and process both negative and positive information in an objective manner before making decisions or taking any action. This includes objectively evaluating their own words and deeds without ignoring or distorting anything that has been presented (Kernis, 2003), including interpretations of their own leadership style (Gardner et al., 2005). Balanced processing is linked to a leader's integrity and character (Ilies et al., 2005) as other perspectives are considered along with the leader's own, thus increasing attributions of authenticity.

Relational Transparency

It is not enough to be self-aware, congruent in values and actions, and objective in one's interpretations; an authentic leader must also be willing to communicate this information in an open and honest manner with others through truthful self-disclosure (Ilies et al., 2005). If it is difficult to be aware and unbiased about one's own weaknesses, it is even more difficult to expose these weaknesses to others in the organization. However, being transparent with one's feelings, motives, and inclinations builds trust and feelings of stability, fostering teamwork and cooperation (Gardner et al., 2005; Kernis, 2003). Leaders who demonstrate relational transparency will therefore be perceived as more real and more authentic.

Other Factors That Influence Authentic Leadership

Researchers have also identified several other elements that influence authentic leadership development, including (1) positive psychological capacities, (2) moral reasoning, and (3) critical life events (Northouse, 2010). First, it has been argued that authentic leaders possess the positive psychological attributes of confidence, hope, optimism, and resilience (Luthans & Avolio, 2003). These traitlike characteristics could be seen as fixed aspects of personality; however, they can also be developed through training or coaching. Confident, hopeful, optimistic, and resilient leaders welcome challenges, inspire followers, and expect favorable outcomes, yet they also adapt positively to unfavorable ones (Avolio & Gardner, 2005).

Second, moral reasoning might be an important antecedent to authentic leadership. Moral reasoning refers to the capacity to make ethical decisions. Although this develops over a lifetime, this capacity allows authentic leaders to make more balanced decisions that serve the greater good over time (Northouse, 2010).

Last, several researchers have also pointed out the role of critical life events, both positive and negative, that can act as catalysts for change, promoting individual growth, learning, and understanding and helping individuals become stronger, more authentic leaders (Luthans & Avolio, 2003; Shamir & Eilam, 2005).

Practical Approaches

At the same time as a theory of authentic leadership was being developed in academia, business practitioners were also discussing the need for more honest, ethical, and accountable models of leadership. This gave rise to several practical how-to books about authentic leadership such as *Authentic Leadership: Courage in Action* by Robert Terry (1993) and *Authentic Leadership: Rediscovering the Secrets to Creating Lasting Value* by Bill George (2003). Most recently, Goffee and Jones (2006), professors and consultants at the London Business School, also published *Why Should Anyone Be Lead by You? What It Takes to Be an Authentic Leader*. These more popular practical approaches to authentic leadership are briefly described in this section.

Robert Terry's (1993) approach to authentic leadership revolves around his Authentic Action Wheel, a diagnostic tool designed to help leaders answer fundamental questions such as "What is really, *really* going on and what are we going to do about it?" Problems in the organization are categorized into six areas: meaning, mission, power, structure, resources, and existence. By locating a problem in one of these areas, leaders can then select an appropriate response that most faithfully addresses the root cause of the issue. This alignment allows leaders to base their actions on what is really happening in the organization, resulting in more authentic leadership (Northouse, 2010).

Bill George (2003), the former CEO of Medtronic and now a professor at Harvard Business School, popularized the term *authentic leadership* again a decade later by reflecting on his 30 years of business success. His approach can be seen as encompassing intrapersonal, interpersonal, and developmental aspects of authentic leaders. Specifically, authentic leadership has five core dimensions (purpose, values, relationships, self-discipline, and heart) that authentic leaders can access (or learn to access) through their behavior, passion, consistency, connectedness, and compassion. In general, authentic leaders display the following characteristics: (1) They are passionate about their purpose; (2) they have strong values and act on those values; (3) they establish trusting relationships with others; (4) they embody focus, determination, consistency, and self-discipline; and (5) they are genuinely compassionate, leading with heart.

Last, the authentic leadership approach proposed by Goffee and Jones (2006) is mostly intrapersonal, focusing on the relationship between the leader and the led. In this view, leadership is always situational, nonhierarchical, and relational and has little to do with fixed personal character traits. Here, authentic leaders are seen as particularly skilled at navigating the many tensions that are inherent in leading others, such as communicating (but not too much) and remaining true to oneself (but also conforming). The book presents some interesting insights into managing these paradoxes, providing many examples of how authentic leaders are better able to adapt their own strengths and weaknesses to the situation at hand.

How Does Authentic Leadership Work?

An empirically tested model of authentic leadership is still being developed, so important questions about its effectiveness have yet to be entirely substantiated. However, both theoretical and practical perspectives suggest that authentic leadership goes beyond a trait-based or a merely relational approach to leadership. Rather, authentic leaders may possess some key characteristics (such as confidence, hope, optimism, and resiliency) or core capabilities (such as self-awareness, relational transparency, internalized moral perspective, and balanced processing), but these abilities can also be developed over time and are enacted in relation to others. At the heart of most interpretations of authentic leadership is the notion that it is the opposite of the selfish and self-serving portrayals of corporate greed that dominated the headlines at the beginning of this century. Rather, authentic leaders have strong values upon which they act, trying to be honest with themselves and others; authentic leaders are transparent and trustworthy, striving to do what is right or good for their followers, their organizations and society as a whole. As such, authentic leadership theory provides, at minimum, some insightful questions for those seeking a more positive and more ethical approach to leadership and leadership development.

◰ References

Avolio, B. J., Gardner, W. L., Walumbwa, F. O., Luthans, F., & May, D. R. (2004). Unlocking the mask: A look at the process by which authentic leaders impact follower attitudes and behavior. *Leadership Quarterly, 15*, 801–823.

Avolio, B. J., & Gardner, W. L. (2005). Authentic leadership development: Getting to the root of positive forms of leadership. *Leadership Quarterly, 16*, 315–338.

Eagly, A. H. (2005). Achieving relational authenticity in leadership: Does gender matter? *Leadership Quarterly, 16*, 459–474.

Gardner, W. L., Avolio, B. J., Luthans, F., May, D. R., & Walumbwa, F. O. (2005). Can you see the real me? A self-based model of authentic leader and follower development. *Leadership Quarterly, 16*, 343–372.

George, B. (2003). *Authentic leadership: Rediscovering the secrets to creating lasting value.* San Francisco: Jossey-Bass.

Goffee, R., & Jones, G. (2006). *Why should anyone be led by you? What it takes to be an authentic leader.* Boston: Harvard Business School Press.

Ilies, R., Morgeson, F. P., & Nahrgang, J. D. (2005). Authentic leadership and eudaemonic well-being: Understanding leader–follower outcomes. *Leadership Quarterly, 16*, 373–394.

Kernis, M. H. (2003). Toward a conceptualization of optimal self-esteem. *Psychological Inquiry, 14*, 1–26.

Luthans, F., & Avolio, B. J. (2003). Authentic leadership development. In K. S. Cameron, J. E. Dutton, & R. E. Quinn (Eds.), *Positive organizational scholarship* (pp. 241–258). San Francisco: Berrett-Koehler.

Mazutis, D., & Slawinski, N. (2008). Leading organizational learning through authentic dialogue. *Management Learning, 39*(4), 437–456.

Michie, S., & Gooty, J. (2005). Values, emotions, and authenticity: Will the real leader please stand up? *Leadership Quarterly, 16*(3), 441–457.

Northouse, P. G. (2010). *Leadership: Theory and practice* (5th ed.). Thousand Oaks, CA: Sage.

Shamir, B., & Eilam, G. (2005). What's your story? A life-stories approach to authentic leadership development. *Leadership Quarterly, 16*, 395–417.

Terry, R. W. (1993). *Authentic leadership: Courage in action.* San Francisco: Jossey-Bass.

Walumbwa, F. O., Avolio, B. J., Gardner, W. L., Wernsing, T. S., & Peterson, S. J. (2008). Authentic leadership: Development and validation of a theory-based measure. *Journal of Management, 34*(1), 89–126.

◰ The Case

Goedehoop: When Social Issues Become Strategic

This case chronicles a change process to counteract the epidemic of HIV/AIDS in a coal mine in South Africa that impacts the sustainability of the organization. The case illustrates the type of leadership activities needed to deal with a compelling environmental force affecting business. It shows how a wide range of stakeholders needs to be involved and systems and practices instituted for sustainable change to be implemented. It raises the question of the role of business in society.

⊠ The Reading

Compelling Visions: Content, Context, Credibility, and Collaboration

The "vision thing" is still with us, but while leaders insist on having a compelling vision, the fact is that many—both the leaders and the visions—leave people standing still, unmoved. A leader who engages stakeholders when developing a vision will, in the end, articulate one that resonates strongly and impels people to act.

Goedehoop

When Social Issues Become Strategic

Prepared by Verity Hawarden under the supervision of Margie Sutherland

Dr. Brian Brink, senior vice-president of health at Anglo American South Africa, looked across his office in Johannesburg and reflected on the success of the HIV/AIDS programme at Goedehoop Colliery. By mid-2007, the programme had been recognised and applauded internationally; HIV infections and AIDS were "under control" at the mine and Goedehoop was considered to be a role model for the corporate response to AIDS in South Africa. His predicament now was what he should do in the next three months to ensure that all the other Anglo business units were as proactive as Goedehoop (pronounced "Ghood-uh-hoorp").

Brink had been actively involved in HIV/AIDS issues since the mid-1980s and was the driving force behind Anglo American's highly admired response to the epidemic. He

acknowledged that the management of HIV and AIDS was an ongoing challenge for the Anglo companies operating in countries with a high burden of HIV disease. He was all too aware that the greatest risk was in eastern and southern Africa, where it was estimated that the HIV prevalence among Anglo employees was 18 per cent at the end of June 2007.[1] While he was extremely satisfied by Goedehoop Colliery's management of the syndrome, the high prevalence statistic of the Anglo group in sub-Saharan Africa worried him.

The reality was alarming. "The global epidemic of HIV/AIDS was rapidly becoming the worst infectious-disease catastrophe in recorded history."[2] South Africa was one of the most severely affected countries worldwide and the potential economic consequences were disturbing due to the fact that over five million

---

AUTHOR'S NOTE: For ease of use and due to other academic references doing the same, the term "disease" is used throughout this case.

Version: (A) 2009-01-28

[1]http://www.angloamerican.co.uk/static/reports/2006/rts/hc-hiv-aids.htm, accessed April 11, 2007, and meeting with Dr. Brian Brink on Oct. 8, 2007.

[2]S. Rosen, J. Simon, J.R. Vincent, W. MacLeod, M. Fox and D.M. Thea, "AIDS is your business." *Harvard Business Review*, Feb. 2003, p. 81.

South Africans were infected by the HI virus.[3] It was reported that the overall HIV prevalence statistic in South Africa by mid-2006 was 11.2 per cent (19.2 per cent of adults between the ages of 20 to 64 were infected).[4] South African companies faced high risks to both direct and indirect costs as AIDS killed mainly young and middle-aged adults in their most productive years. By the end of 2007, approximately 2,170,000 people had died of AIDS-related deaths in South Africa, of whom approximately 355,000 died in 2006.[5] In mid-2007, the South African population was estimated to be 47.9 million;[6] therefore, deaths from AIDS to mid-2007 equated to approximately 4.5 per cent of the total population.

Brink knew that mining companies that responded positively to the HIV/AIDS epidemic also showed the greatest productivity and profitability. Goedehoo p Colliery was a case in point. While most coal mines within Anglo Coal South Africa were following suit with increasingly successful HIV/AIDS programmes, it was the Anglo companies mining other minerals in South Africa that were not responding to the syndrome at the same level as Goedehoop. Brink understood the importance of effective management leadership to ensure a successful response. He knew that, ultimately, the productivity and profitability of Anglo American South Africa would be adversely affected if all companies within the group did not take real ownership of the HIV/AIDS problem.

Anglo and AIDS

Anglo American plc was formed in May 1999 through the combination of Anglo American Corporation of South Africa (AACSA) and Minorco. It had its primary listing on the London Stock Exchange and was majority-owned by U.K. institutions. AACSA was founded in 1917 by Sir Ernest Oppenheimer to exploit the gold mining potential of the East Rand.[7] Employing approximately 160,000 people worldwide,[8] the Anglo American Group was a global leader in mining activities, owning a diversified range of businesses covering platinum, gold, diamonds, coal, base and ferrous metals, industrial minerals, paper and packaging.[9] Anglo American plc's coal interests were held through its wholly-owned Anglo Coal business, one of the world's largest private sector coal producers and exporters. Anglo Coal had mining operations in South Africa, Australia, Colombia, China and Venezuela.[10]

Anglo Coal had a 100 per cent shareholding in Goedehoop Colliery, one of its nine South African coal mines. Goedehoop Colliery was located 40 kilometres southeast of Witbank in the province of Mpumalanga, 180 kilometres east of Johannesburg. Employing

---

[3]Bureau for Economic Research, "The impact of HIV/AIDS on selected business sectors in South Africa, 2005," Survey conducted by the Bureau for Economic Research and funded by the South African Business Coalition on HIV and AIDS, 2005.

[4]R.E. Dorrington, D. Bradshaw, L. Johnson and T. Daniel, "The Demographic Impact of HIV/AIDS in South Africa," *National and Provincial Indicators 2006*, Centre for Actuarial Research, South African Medical Research Council, Actuarial Society of South Africa, Cape Town, 2006, http://www.mrc.ac.za/bod/DemographicImpactHIVIndicators.pdf, accessed Oct. 15, 2007.

[5]Ibid.

[6]Statistics South Africa, "Mid-year population estimates, 2007 (P0302)," 2007, http://www.statssa.gov.za/publications/P0302/P03022007.pdf, accessed Oct. 4, 2007.

[7]http://www.angloamerican.co.uk/article/?afw_source_key=19ED07F3-C5AB-427C-BACE-6DABAC9037A7, accessed April 11, 2007.

[8]Anglo American plc Annual Report 2006.

[9]http://www.angloamerican.co.uk/ourbusiness, accessed April 11, 2007.

[10]http://www.angloamerican.co.uk/ourbusiness/thebusinesses/coal/geographiclocations, accessed April 11, 2007.

almost 2,000 permanent staff and just under 1,000 contractors, Goedehoop (Afrikaans for the term "good hope") produced both domestic coal and high-grade thermal coal for export customers. While a small quantity of low-grade coal was produced for the domestic market, Goedehoop Colliery was one of Anglo Coal's South African export mines. In 2005, Goedehoop won an award for being the safest colliery in Anglo Coal worldwide. Goedehoop's objective for 2006 was to be "the safest and lowest cost producer of green coal in Anglo Coal."[11] All employees were constantly driven by the mantra "SHE first . . . always!" which meant a strong focus on safety, health and the environment. Employees understood that adherence to these three factors contributed towards greater production and productivity, resulting in lower costs and higher profitability.

Anglo American plc's Group HIV/AIDS policy, first introduced in 1990, stated that Anglo "recognised the human tragedy caused by the HIV/AIDS epidemic . . . we are concerned about the gravity and implications of the epidemic for our operating companies."[12] In addition, Anglo American plc became increasingly concerned over the last decade about the health and well-being of its employees, their families and the communities in which the employees lived.[13]

Dr. Jan Pienaar, chief medical officer for Anglo Coal South Africa, asserted that "Anglo Coal holds the view that holistically healthy employees are key to the long term success of Anglo Coal."[14] Brink supported the latter assertion:

> Those organisations responding to HIV/AIDS with strong leadership at the CEO level, impact assessments based on real data, negotiated HIV/AIDS policies, up-to-date strategic HIV/AIDS responses, specific HIV/AIDS performance indicators and targets, and ongoing monitoring and evaluation also happen to show the greatest productivity, the most effective cost containment and the greatest profitability. A good response to HIV/AIDS is synonymous with good management, good business and a good investment.[15]

The Business of AIDS

The impact of HIV/AIDS on life expectancy and the South African economy was profound. In 2001, South African life expectancy was 51 years.[16] Estimates from 2007 suggested that by 2010, South African life expectancy would drop to only 42 years and the epidemic would have had a marked impact on firms' costs, productivity and demand for products.[17] It had been established that the scale and speed of the epidemic was much worse than was initially expected and the demographic, social and economic consequences would have a dramatic

---

[11]Anglo Coal, "Raising the AIDS bar at Goedehoop Colliery" brochure, Exhibit C.

[12]Anglo Coal, "Raising the AIDS bar at Goedehoop Colliery" brochure, Exhibit A.

[13]GBC (Global Business Coalition) Awards for Business Excellence 2007—submission by Anglo Coal South Africa.

[14]Ibid.

[15]Bureau for Economic Research, "The impact of HIV/AIDS on selected business sectors in South Africa, 2005," Survey conducted by the Bureau for Economic Research and funded by the South African Business Coalition on HIV and AIDS, 2005, p. 37.

[16]Statistics South Africa, "Mid-year population estimates, 2005 (P0302)," 2005, http://www.statssa.gov.za/publications/P0302/P03022005.pdf, accessed Oct. 3, 2007.

[17]J. D. Lewis, "Assessing the demographic and economic impact of HIV/AIDS" in *AIDS and South Africa: the social expression of a pandemic*, Palgrave Macmillan, New York, 2005, Chapter 5.

macro economic impact.[18] Gross domestic product (GDP) is one economic indicator that enables a measurement of economic output. Research had determined that the South African GDP level in 2010 would be 17 per cent lower in an AIDS scenario than it would have been if AIDS did not exist.[19]

The macro economic impact of HIV/AIDS on business was felt as a result of several factors, specifically, a lower supply of labour, lower labour productivity through absenteeism and illness, cost pressures for companies through higher benefit payments and replacement costs, and a lower customer base as the purchasing population decreased.[20] Private sector involvement in responding to the HIV/AIDS epidemic was thus crucial due to the economic impact being experienced.[21]

The impact of the above factors on business presented a growing challenge for management to create shareholder value if, in addition, it did not take certain social issues into account. Companies were held accountable by public opinion; they wanted to be viewed as responsible corporate citizens making a positive impact in the community.[22] Business could no longer distance itself from society; the extent to which a company was socially responsible was crucial for a positive public evaluation.[23] Bearing in mind the growing demand by shareholders for companies to manage their business with a triple bottom-line focus, it became apparent that companies could not simply have a rational response to the AIDS crisis, meaning that their response was based only on a cost-benefit ratio. A reasonable response was also required; this being when the company acknowledged it had a moral duty to respond to its employees regardless of whether there was an implied cost or benefit in doing so.[24] A further challenge experienced by companies when considering a response to HIV/AIDS was the profound denial regarding the epidemic accompanied by stigma and discrimination towards infected individuals. The cultural taboo surrounding the disease had ensured that AIDS remained a silent killer.

In South Africa, the mining sector was one of the worst HIV/AIDS-affected industries, particularly as this sector employed predominantly semi-skilled and unskilled workers. Fifty-five per cent of surveyed mines reported that profitability had been adversely affected by HIV/AIDS. Harmony, a significant gold mine in South Africa, estimated in 2005 that HIV/AIDS-related costs could amount to 7.5 per cent of its total labour cost for the following 15 years. The high HIV prevalence rate, especially among migrant mineworkers, was thought to be related to their long separations from regular partners/spouses, compounded by easy access to commercial sex workers.[25]

---

[18]United Nations, "General Assembly special session on HIV/AIDS," 2001, http://www.un.org/ga/aids/coverage, accessed April 18, 2006.

[19]C. Arndt and J. Lewis, "The macro-implications of HIV/AIDS in South Africa: a preliminary assessment," *South African Journal of Economics*, 68:5, Dec. 2000, pp. 856–887.

[20]K. Quattek, "The economic impact of AIDS in South Africa: a dark cloud on the horizon," Konrad Adenauer Stiftung Occasional Paper, June 2000, p. 49.

[21]C. Arndt and J. Lewis, "The macro-implications of HIV/AIDS in South Africa: a preliminary assessment," *South African Journal of Economics*, 68:5, Dec. 2000, pp. 856–887.

[22]D. Dickinson, "Corporate South Africa's response to HIV/AIDS: why so slow?" *Journal of Southern African Studies*, 30:3, Sept. 2004, pp. 627–649.

[23]A. Whiteside and C. Sunter, *AIDS: the challenge for South Africa*, Human & Rousseau (Pty) Ltd., Cape Town, 2004.

[24]N. Nattrass, *The moral economy of AIDS in South Africa*, Cambridge University Press, Cambridge, 2004.

[25]Bureau for Economic Research, "The impact of HIV/AIDS on selected business sectors in South Africa, 2005," Survey conducted by the Bureau for Economic Research and funded by the South African Business Coalition on HIV and AIDS, 2005.

⚑ Leading the Way

John Standish-White had a mining engineering degree from the University of the Witwatersrand, a blasting certificate and, prior to joining Goede hoop, was the general manager at Greenside Colliery from 1999 to 2003. In his early 40s, with a relaxed and easy demeanour, Standish-White realised during these years that it was time he became involved in responding to HIV/AIDS. In 1999, a mine worker at Greenside, Sello Malefane,[26] applied to take voluntary ill-health retirement from the mine. Standish-White knew Malefane by sight and name as he consciously involved himself with his employees. He always visited staff in hospital who had been admitted either due to illness or mine accidents. Malefane was a semi-skilled mine worker and it was fairly clear to Standish-White that he was terminally ill with AIDS. Malefane opted to take early ill-health retirement and return home to Lesotho, a neighbouring country to South Africa. Standish-White offered that his personal driver take Malefane home to the rural hills of Lesotho. After a long and tiring journey, which eventually ended in painfully slow progress on tracks more suited to transport on horseback, Malefane and the driver arrived at Malefane's home. Standish-White's driver reported back to Standish-White about how shaken he had been by the despair and wailing of Malefane's family members when they first set eyes on him. Malefane was a shadow of his former self; he was unrecognisable; he was very, very ill. Not many weeks later, Malefane was dead.

Standish-White realised it was time for him to take action. In the late 1990s, HIV/AIDS was relatively unknown. People were scared to learn more about it and, as Standish-White stated, "All AIDS talks were a doom and gloom show."[27] It was time for him to show some compassion and to do something that would be proudly South African. He realised he could save lives. There was fresh ground to be explored! Anglo's head office had not yet issued specific HIV/AIDS guidelines to follow, so Standish-White simply persevered through trial and error to put in place some effective action and response programme.

Standish-White recounted how, late one afternoon, he picked up a sex worker at the crossroads outside the mine and, in his wife's car, took her to the "usual place under the gum trees," where she explained the local sex industry to him.[28] In addition to including the sex workers, he radically restructured the Goedehoop AIDS committee on his arrival there, firing at least half of the members including all of those who did not know their own HIV status. "You need to be very tough when you start out," acknowledged Standish-White. "You need to have the courage to do the difficult and the uncomfortable."

⚑ Goedehoop Goes "Green"

Standish-White had been appointed regional general manager of Goed ehoop in 2003. In August 2003, the voluntary counselling and testing (VCT) uptake was at five per cent. Standish-White and his team realised that an HIV/AIDS programme would not be successful without a structured campaign and buy-in from employees. "My main vision and drive was that with great communication you can do all sorts of things. We got the people going, got everybody aligned and raised the trust levels. We had to get our hands dirty and go and look at what AIDS was really doing to our country."[29] Goedehoop management understood that initiatives in the boardroom would have little impact at an operational level if they were not

---

[26]Name has been changed to protect his identity.

[27]Interview with John Standish-White at Anglo Coal Head Office, Johannesburg, on May 4, 2007.

[28]Ibid.

[29]HIV and AIDS Initiatives at Anglo Coal Goedehoop Colliery DVD, Shadowy Meadows Productions.

communicated and implemented in a simple, practical, user-friendly manner. By encouraging both vertical and horizontal communication at all levels, Standish-White believed he managed to change employees' sexual behaviour.[30] He asserted that the disease should be approached as a form of business risk and, whether employees were in a threatening situation deep underground in a mine shaft or whether they were in a questionable sexual situation, they should know the key questions to ask themselves when doing a risk assessment.

The 5GH approach was implemented at the Colliery and was endorsed by the Goedehoop Lekgotla team ("lekgotla" is a Tswana term for meeting place; pronounced "leh-ghort-la"). The team was made up of management and labour union leadership. The Goedehoop AIDS committee was founded and named the SIDA Shipani Committee ("SIDA" is Portuguese for AIDS and "Shipani" is an Nguni term for team).[31] It consisted of senior management, medical staff, union representatives, traditional healers and informal settlement leaders. In addition, it was assisted by a full-time AIDS coordinator and 30 workplace peer educators.

5GH was based on the following five elements:

- Status
- Education (and "qaphela!" or awareness)
- Care for our people
- Partnerships
- 100 per cent personal protective equipment (PPE)

In order for the programme to succeed, the approach had to be relevant, innovative, positive and easily understood, as South African mines were characterised by employees with very diverse home languages and varied education levels. A Confidentiality Pledge was signed on an annual basis by SIDA Shipani members, peer educators, medical personnel and Anglo Coal Highveld Hospital, which reinforced commitment to the 5GH campaign (see Exhibit 1). The above five elements and the Confidentiality Pledge encouraged great interest and allegiance to taking action against AIDS throughout the operation. In addition, they effectively communicated the benefits and importance of learning more about the HIV/AIDS pandemic. Standish-White realised it was important that the HIV/AIDS message be taken back to peoples' families.[32]

Status

Of the five elements, knowing one's status formed the foundation and main focus of the campaign. VCT was actively encouraged on an ongoing basis. Measurement of VCT uptake was evaluated annually, with the clock being set back to zero in January of each year. In 2005, the VCT uptake had increased to 96 per cent and by the end of 2006, Goedehoop had managed to achieve an uptake of 98.3 per cent. The promotion of Visible Felt Leadership at Goedehoop was constantly in place, with Sir Mark Moody-Stuart, U.K.-based Anglo American plc chairman, himself having been orally tested for HIV at Goedehoop in March 2005. Testers took the oral tests to work areas, including going underground or to night shifts, which removed excuses for non-testing.

VCT uptake had been incorporated into all bonus incentive schemes for the full workforce and a weekly departmental VCT progress report was communicated to all employees (see Exhibit 2). Goedehoop worked hard to ensure that its VCT campaign remained people-focused and did not become mechanistic and numbers-driven.[33] Simon Ndlangamandla, an

---

[30]Interview with John Standish-White at Anglo Coal Head Office, Johannesburg, on May 4, 2007.

[31]Anglo Coal, "Raising the AIDS bar at Goedehoop Colliery" brochure, point 3.1,

[32]HIV and AIDS Initiatives at Anglo Coal Goedehoop Colliery DVD, Shadowy Meadows Productions.

[33]Anglo Coal, "Raising the AIDS bar at Goedehoop Colliery" brochure, point 3.3.1.

| **Exhibit 1** | Latent Confidentiality Pledge |

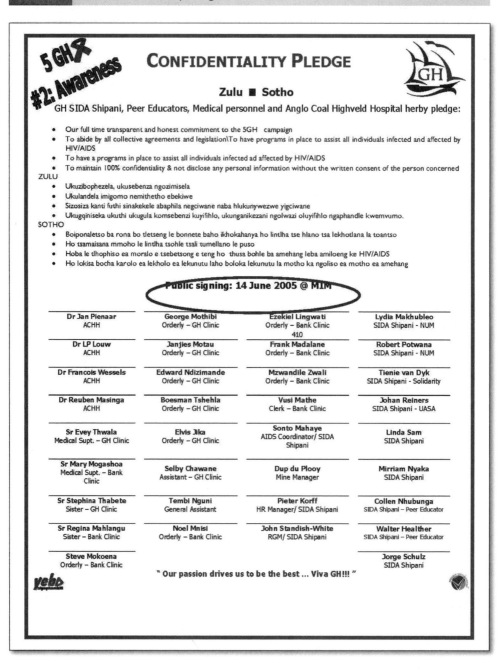

orderly at Anglo Coal Highveld Hospital, was an HIV-positive man in his early 40s who stressed the importance of VCT, acknowledging that if he had not been tested, he "wouldn't be here today." His message to others was, "If you are negative, stay negative—if you are positive,

Exhibit 2 Departmental VCT Statistics

Goedehoop Colliery
SIDA SHIPANI Campaign: Element 1 = Status

VCT STATISTICS : Mine Employees per Area tested in 2006 — 01December 06

	Human Resources			Finance & Admin*			Technical Services**			GH Plant Processing***		
	Act	VCT	%	Act	VCT	%	Act	VCT	%	Act	VCT	%
Officials	57	55	96%	70	65	93%	44	38	86%	11	11	100%
Snr Skilled	1	0	0%	0	0		0	0		9	9	100%
Skilled	38	37	97%	2	2	100%	25	25	100%	59	59	100%
Total	96	92	93%	72	67	93%	69	63	91%	79	79	100%

* includes: Security   ** includes: Survey, VOHE, Geology,   *** includes: Environment

	Plant 2 Processing			Plant 5 Processing			GH Plant Engineering			Plant 2 Engineering		
	Act	VCT	%	Act	VCT	%	Act	VCT	%	Act	VCT	%
Officials	9	9	100%	2	2	100%	12	12	100%	7	7	100%
Snr Skilled	9	9	100%	3	3	100%	40	40	100%	26	26	100%
Skilled	47	47	100%	26	26	100%	29	29	100%	21	21	100%
Total	65	65	100%	31	31	100%	81	81	100%	54	54	100%

	Plant 5 Engineering			Simunye # Engineering			South # Engineering			Block 5 Engineering		
	Act	VCT	%	Act	VCT	%	Act	VCT	%	Act	VCT	%
Officials	2	2	100%	10	9	90%	8	8	100%	3	3	100%
Snr Skilled	8	8	100%	33	25	76%	31	29	94%	20	20	100%
Skilled	7	7	100%	20	20	100%	19	19	100%	16	16	100%
Total	17	17	100%	63	54	86%	58	56	93%	39	39	100%

	Hope # Engineering			VL Engineering			Surface Engineering			Simunye # Mining		
	Act	VCT	%	Act	VCT	%	Act	VCT	%	Act	VCT	%
Officials	13	13	100%	10	9	90%	32	32	100%	18	18	100%
Snr Skilled	70	63	90%	57	53	93%	20	20	100%	3	2	67%
Skilled	41	39	95%	42	41	98%	77	75	97%	137	125	91%
Total	124	115	93%	109	103	94%	129	127	98%	158	145	92%

	South # Mining			Block 5 Mining			Hope # Mining			VL Mining		
	Act	VCT	%	Act	VCT	%	Act	VCT	%	Act	VCT	%
Officials	11	11	100%	13	13	100%	37	33	89%	26	24	92%
Snr Skilled	2	2	100%	1	1	100%	7	6	86%	6	6	100%
Skilled	101	100	99%	68	68	100%	238	226	95%	184	171	93%
Total	114	113	99%	82	82	100%	282	265	94%	216	201	93%

	Trainees			Men			Women			care stats		
	Act	VCT	%	Act	VCT	%	Act	VCT	%	HIV+		%
Officials	10	7	67%	361	343	95%	60	54	90%	HIV+	356	18%
Snr Skilled	11	11	100%	342	343	100%	13	13	100%	New inf	26	0.42%
Skilled				1104	1105	100%	57	50	88%	ART	131	
Total	21	18	86%	1807	1735	96%	130	117	90%			

	Other VCT
Paid by Others	46
Contractors	318
Ex Employees	24
Dependants	56
Visitors	15
Total	459

Total Employees 2006			
	Act	VCT	%
Officials	423	405	96%
Snr Skilled	355	344	97%
Skilled	1161	1146	99%
Total	1937	1895	98%

Total VCT to date	
Mine	1895
Other	459
Total	2354

it is not the end of the world."[34] Nursing Sister Evey Thwala asserted that "It gives one great relief if you talk about your status, especially to the people you live with and those you work with."[35]

Awareness

"To get management and everybody together to talk about one thing is not an easy job to do. So you have to convince them that actually we're talking one language," noted Sonto Mahaye, HIV/AIDS coordinator at Goede hoop.[36] The SIDA Shipani members used various tools to help raise awareness about AIDS at the mine and in the community, some examples being the Daily Safety Bulletin (see Exhibit 3), which included a weekly AIDS message and which reached everybody verbally at the beginning of each shift; a two-day Imphilo/Wellness drive, which was held at the weekly induction programme for new and ex-leave employees; weekly AIDS days every Tuesday; rural and urban AIDS tours as well as area AIDS "blitzes" by community and work place peer educators; and road shows and SAMs (shock awareness meetings). World AIDS Day on the 1st of December was celebrated with great festivity each year and placed itself on the annual calendar as the target date on which 100 per cent of the mine's employees would have received VCT for that year.

Joe Marais, a middle-aged white man and Solidarity Union Representative, admitted that "Previously we all just knew about AIDS from what we read in the papers and we all thought it was a black person's disease or a poor person's disease. As soon as the programme at Goedehoop started, I think we all were quite shocked, especially my constituency. We were quite shocked to find out that it can happen to anybody."[37]

"Khuluma" (pronounced "koo-loo-muh") means talk in isiZulu, and chat shows (khulumisanas) were regularly held to which all employees and their dependants were invited to attend. "People should be educated about this problem, even the Unions. They like the idea because it teaches people about this problem we see everyday. We at Goedehoop are happy that we are learning," stated Sixanananaxa Nizi of the National Union of Mineworkers (NUM).[38] Educational handouts were often distributed either by means of posters or attached to payslips (in English, Sotho and Zulu), one of these being the "Slippery Slope and the way back" (see Exhibit 4), an AIDS-on-one-page handout, which concisely summarised AIDS in an easily understood way.

Care, Support, and Treatment

Once employees had been encouraged to know their status, it was imperative that a support system was in place to respond to those individuals who needed further treatment. Two fully equipped clinics serviced by four professional nurses, as well as easy access to the nearby local hospital, were readily available. Free antiretroviral therapy (ART) and free nutritional supplements were provided to all HIV-positive permanent employees. The success of ART was noted by the decrease in absenteeism at work. "Our employees should die of old age and not of AIDS," noted Dr. Pienaar. Viral loads and CD4 counts were monitored regularly and counselling sessions were held frequently. Support was extended to

---

[34]GBC (Global Business Coalition) Awards for Business Excellence 2007—submission by Anglo Coal South Africa, p. 14.

[35]HIV and AIDS Initiatives at Anglo Coal Goedehoop Colliery DVD, Shadowy Meadows Productions.

[36]Ibid.

[37]Ibid.

[38]Ibid.

the community by peer educators who provided home-based care.

Jorge Schulz was a burly, middle-aged white man who had been working at Goedehoop for eight years as a fitter. He was HIV-positive and was the only employee who had disclosed his status to the mine management and all his colleagues. He talked emotionally about the spirit of acceptance, the lack of discrimination and about how buoyed up he was by the response from his community. He received his medication free of charge and stated that he was 90 per cent healthy and fully productive at work. Schulz acknowledged that the treatment he received from Goedehoop was "like walking into paradise; I feel at home, I feel loved."[39]

Partnerships

An important contributor to the success of the programme was the successful partnership between mine management and the three recognised unions: NUM, Solidarity and United Association of South Africa. "One of the big things is our managers information meeting—without that, you don't get your message across," noted Nick Bull of the United Association of South Africa.[40]

In addition, trust and supportive partnerships existed with Anglo Coal Highveld Hospital, Anglo American Corporate Office, schools, churches, non-governmental organisations, traditional healers and the surrounding communities. Fifty per cent of the community peer educators were sex workers themselves. "Relationship with the people is most important," stressed Sonto Mahaye. This statement was reinforced by Standish-White: "The emotional side is important; you need to start feeling it . . . you start to get to know some of your people on the mines; all the time celebrating the programme and making it an enjoyable journey. An energy-add is what cracked the ice on our property."[41]

Protection

Open talk about sex was encouraged. Standish-White believed that AIDS was everyone's problem. He even kept a wooden penis on his desk so that HIV/AIDS was "always in your face." In 2006, Goedehoop distributed about 23,000 free condoms per month to the surrounding community near the colliery (see Exhibit 5). Femidoms were freely available from both clinics. Use of protection ensured that the HIV-negative people stayed negative and the positive people protected their partners.

Achievements and Challenges

Goedehoop kept a very detailed database on all the HIV statistics, which was updated weekly. At the end of 2006, there were 362 HIV-positive employees out of the total of 2,000, of whom 129 were taking antiretrovirals. In 2005, 51 new infections were recorded. This dropped to 27 new infections in 2006, a decrease of 47 per cent. What was alarming, though, was that by the end of April 2007 (when more than half the VCT had already been completed for the year), 17 new infections had been recorded, revealing that there was still work to be done. Brink's ultimate goal was to have zero new HIV infections, zero employees and family members becoming sick or dying from AIDS, and zero babies born HIV-positive in employees' families.[42]

---

[39]Ibid.

[40]Ibid.

[41]Ibid.

[42]http://www.angloamerican.co.uk/article/?afw_source_key=14052965-CC7F-43EEADCA7ED39F33ECA1&xsl_menu_parent=/cr/hivaids/ourresponse, accessed June 4, 2007.

Exhibit 3 Daily Safety Bulletin (DSB)

Daily Safety Bulletin DSB

Daily Safety, Health & Environmental Bulletin : Goedehoop Colliery

"SHE first … always!"

14-Mar-06

S	LTI
H	MTC
E	

The last 48 hours

LTI = Lost time injury
MTC = Medical treatment case

OTTO

OHSAS 18001
ISO 14001

ANGLO COAL

1. Today's SHE tips from the people / Likeletso tlhokomeliso ka basebetsi / Iziluleko zabasebenzi (GH)

* Do not learn safety by accident!!!! - John Kewana - HR Assistant - Boarding House
* Wash hands before handling food!!!! - Oupa Nkosi - Assistant Training Officer - Training Centre
* Educate your children about the importance of caring for the environment!!!! - Ananiase Mohaebe - Block 5

GoedeBingo No's

12,34,53,28,83,50,60,84,13,63,59,5,21,16,44,43,69,64,19,82
78,23,33,62,65,58,40,26,37,85,80,8,73,31,86,1,39,42,25,66,10

Today's Bingo No **10**

60 4 RA

STOP! Think before you ACT and TUNE into 60 4 RA.
60 seconds to think, 4 steps to safety and assess the RISK

yebo siyaphambili!

Proudly GH and proudly SA

4. SHE statistics

Progressive Fatality Free Production Shifts	315
Date of last lost time injury 19 - Feb -06	159
Working days to go to 1 000 FFPS	314
Date of last fatal accident	31-Oct-05
Prog. Actual LTI Target 0.00 (C2005 LTIFR = 0.4)	0.12
Prog. Anglo Coal (SA) LTI (Target 2006 = 0.00)	0.27
Chairman's Shield competition	1st
LTISR (Target 0.00) ACTUAL YTD	6.79

Weekly AIDS News

2006 VCT ytd   68%
VCT Induction   96%
Condoms distributed mtd   1600

Impilo support for this week - John Blaundish-White and Robeth Potwana
Come on guys lets make a commitment to our VCT.

2a: Previous Day: Injuries / Incidents / Izingozi

No	Date	Name	Dept.	Time	Place Inj./ Inc.occurred.	Severity	HOD	Nature of injury	Cause of Injury / Description	Hazard ID	Acc. Report	Alc.& drug test

2b: Month to date: Injuries /Incidents /Izingozi

					Days accident free : 2							
9	10-Mar	Jack Mkosi	Mining	02h00	Section 3 - Imvubu	MTC	Archew Fulton	Hairline Fracture on tip of right middle finger	Caught between temporary jack & handle	Lack of hazard identification	Yes	Not tested

3: Hospitalisation: Injuries or illness / Likolane

Name	Section	Reason	HOD	Hospital
Tandile Ndloyani	HR	Multiple injuries MVA	Dave Miller	MidmedH
Petros Mngometulu	Eng Serv	Multiple injuries MVA	Tony Lowe	Cosmos
Isaac Motoana	Eng Serv	Medical	Tony Lowe	ACHH
Medhat Mdrwilla	South #	Chest Problem	Archew Fulton	ACHH

Daily DSB BU reality check

SIYANQOBA RECOVERY PLAN = No. 5 Seam

Section	21-Jan	06-Mar	Today
Fezela	8 030	10 697	9 273
Dzansansa	-5 593	-28 516	-28 804
Total UG	2 437	-17 819	-19 531
Block 10 pit	- 3 257	-3 419	-4 352
Total No. 5 Seam	- 820	-21 238	-23 883

Best siyanqoba performance: Fezela
Worst Siyanqoba performance: Dzansansa

Comment:
Dzansansa
Well done Felela. Keep the ball rolling guys, that's great!
Dzansansa water control improved, now for the tons!!!
Minipit - rain causing production delays
Performance excellence through our people

Yebo # 1

5: Production yesterday / Umkhiqizo

GOEDEHOOP PRODUCTION

ROM Mining Feed

Area	Daily target	Daily actual
2 Seam		
Hope 2 Seam	17 575	22 321
Vlak 4 Seam u/g	15 929	15 626
Vlak 4 Seam o/c	828	600
Sterkop 2 Seam	8 600	6 921
South 2 Seam	6 500	4 153
Total 2 & 4 Seam	48 759	48 623
5 Seam u/g	2 100	559
Block 10 o/c	900	1 001
Total 5 Seam	3 000	1 560
Total Goedehoop	52 759	50 381

Block 27 Development:	Total 894m	
Daily (target 5.4m)		5.4m
Monthly prog (target 105m)		23.4m
CONCOR overall progress		(-85.6m)

GOEDEHOOP PLANT

FTP	Daily Target	Daily Actual
2S Double stage (A)	8 900	14 290
2S Single stage (C)	6 400	8 085
4S Single stage (B)	6 400	6 065
Total	29 100	34 569
Discard retreat	4 800	5 528
Trains railed	3	3

Weekly Qualities

GH - MJ/kg	28.15	28.00
AAC - MJ/kg	27.45	27.82
LAC - Ash %	7.5	7.0

Plant 2	13 400	13 800
Plant 5	3 200	3 496
Total	16 600	17 296
Trains railed	1	1

Weekly Qualities

LAC - Ash %	7.7	7.0
PRE - Ash%	10.5	10.2
AAC - MJ/kg	27.2	27.36

Annual 2006 tons

ROM	Target GH	8.7Mt
	Trend GH	8.1Mt
	Target BANK	4.9Mt
	Trend BANK	4.1Mt
FTP	Target GH	8.7Mt
	Trend GH	8.1Mt
	Target BANK	4.9Mt
	Trend BANK	4.1Mt
Saleable	Target GH	8.2Mt
	Trend GH	5.3Mt
	Target GH	3.3Mt
	Trend BANK	1.6Mt
Total Saleable tons	Target	9.4Mt
	Trend	7.1Mt

(Continued)

Exhibit 3 (Continued)

6. Dust & Noise / Lerata & Lerole

Average dust: **1.82**   % < 8 mg/m³ **91%**

mg/m³			
HOPE 5/6	3.24	Simunye	1.49
HOPE 7/8	0.61	Mangwegwe	0.06
HOPE 9/10	1.32	Siyeza	0.11
HOPE 11/12	0.11	Ngwenya	0.12
STOOPING	0.43	FIZELA	2.30
GH Plant	0.16	DZANGARA	1.31
Plant 2	0.47	SAVUBU	1.49
Plant 5	0.85	USHEJANE	0.74
		KHOMANANI	5.78
		ISIKHONYANE	3.58
		SIZIMISELE	2.81

8. Human Resources Info / Tlhakiso ya tsa baseshedi

Labour Statistics

	Officials	Snr Staffed	Staffed	Total
GH	430	354	1211	1995

9. Birthday corner - Happy birthday to you!!

Somtsheni Sithandile - Mining Operator - Hope #
Mahlangu Moyeni - Engineering Operator - Surface Services
Rendani Podile Podile - Snr Personnel Asst - Surface Services
Khosi Martin - Mining Operator - Wakisagta 4 #
De Jongh Danniel - Boilermaker - Plant Surface
Keli Boniswa - Mining Asst - Simunye #

10. HR Message

11. HOD Message   Dave Miller

Denial & Die

HIV/AIDS is no longer a death sentence, is something that can be managed.

2 Saving Tips Residential users
* Use compact fluorescent lights lampa (CFL) instead of ordinary bulbs
* Switch Off lights
* Use low-energy lamps for exterior lighting and
* Do not install multiple lights on single switch

Respect

If you want to be respected by your fellow workers, you must respect them.

Remember respect is earned !!!

7. Environment

SPILL SORB BINS

As part of emergency response, demarcate your spill sorb bin used for fuel/chemical spills.

It is often found that these bins are used for domestic waste and is not acceptable.

Theme of the week

Clean up your fuel spills.
Area of focus: Connor Block8

12. Bank team Yebo corner

THANK YOU "YEBO" TEAM FOR YOUR HARD WORK OVER THE PAST MONTHS.

GH2000

Diversity Update: 2006 1st Quarter

= **1.33**   17% decline

* disappointing decline BUT still a positive score coming in at above 1.0
* makala thank you to all for participating & please remain committed to GH Diversity journey
* 5 x Legotla working teams to revisit action plans and address areas of concern
* Diversity scoring to continue on a quarterly basis ... GH North to be included in due course
* Diversity @ GH North = huge success thanks to all ... awaiting Report # 2 and Legotla caucus

13. Financial Indicators / Tsa lichelete / Ezozimali

Anglo share price
S.A Rand/US $ Exchange rate

		Budget	Actual
		R213.64 Prog.	
		R6.30 Stores	6,139,395
		5,911,574	

F.O.B. Cash cost (Cost of production + selling cost)

	Year to Feb-2006		Outlook 2006	
	Budget	Actual	Budget	Actual
GH 2 & 4 Seam	R 169.11	R 179.34	R 165.00	R 166.12
Bank 5	R 226.11	R 304.56	R 266.74	R 262.29

14. Diary for today / Liketsahalo tsa kajeno   March 13, 2006

TIME	GH	VENUE	RESPONSIBLE
06:00	5-5 Meeting Khomanani	South Shaft	All Concerned
06:00	5-5 Meeting	BK Plants	All Concerned
06:00	Block 5 Imbizo Session	Block 5	All Concerned
06:40	Simunye # 5-5 Meeting	Simunye Shaft	All Concerned
07:00	Block 5 Focus Meeting	Block 5	All Concerned
07:00	GH Snr Manager Performance Appraisals	Guest House	As per JS-W Prog
07:15	HR Focus Meeting	Training Centre	All Concerned
	Bank Focus Meeting & Underground		All Concerned
08:00	MM Innovation Meeting	BK Plants	All Concerned
08:00	Geological Indaba	Luiperdskloof	All Concerned
08:30	ATD Review	ACTDS Lapa	Tony L.
13:30	MIM	Kopanang Hall	All Concerned
14:40	Simunye # 5-5 Meeting	Simunye Shaft	All Concerned
22:40	Simunye # 5-5 Meeting	Simunye Shaft	All Concerned

15. General / Dwonko wonke

GOEDEHOOP

1

Exhibit 4 AIDS-on-One-Page Handout

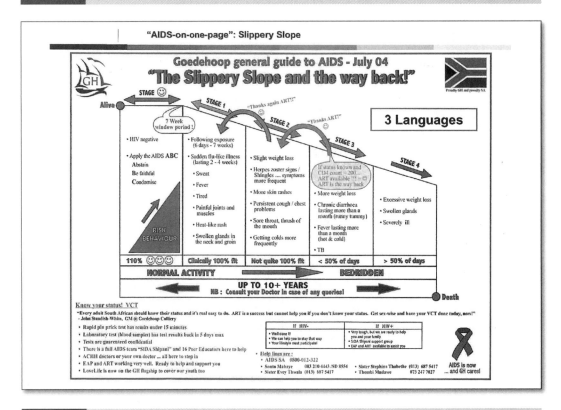

Exhibit 5 Condom Distribution Points

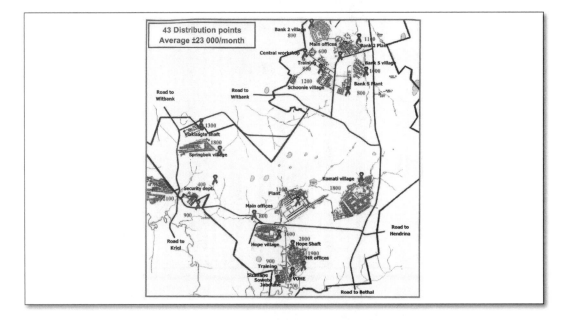

But the programme was not without its challenges. The colliery had to soundproof the medical sister's room to ensure that discussions within remained private. Mistakes were made. In one instance, a medical vehicle arrived to collect HIV-positive employees to take them to the hospital for their monthly prescription of antiretroviral therapy. While the reason for the trip should have remained confidential, the driver announced to the crowd in a loud voice the purpose of his transfer. Needless to say, no passengers came forward for the ride. Standish-White said that they overcame the mistakes by talking about them.

Goedehoop Colliery's efforts did not go unnoticed. It won the South African weekly newspaper *Mail & Guardian*'s "Investing in Life" Award in August 2005 for the Best Corporate Response to AIDS in South Africa. In May 2006, the Colliery was awarded a "Highly Commended" certificate at the Global Business Coalition Gala Awards banquet held in London, a function that was attended by more than 1,600 guests. Goedehoop was identified as the centre of best practice for HIV/AIDS initiatives in the Anglo American group and yet the mine was conscious of trying to continuously improve its programme.

Return on Investment

"I've been so enriched by the way Goedehoop has risen to this challenge. The support that I've had from head office has been superb and the whole mine is united in its pride. We're the number one mine on HIV/AIDS," noted Standish-White. "I know that at least I have saved one life, hopefully many more."[43]

The majority of funding for the components of the 5GH campaign was borne by Goedehoop. The annual budget allocation to the campaign was approximately R1.5m (US $220 000[44]) which excluded:

- The provision of ART, which was sponsored by Anglo American plc
- The provision of condoms, which were subsidised by the government
- The management of the two loveLife[45] centres, which were covered by a R30 million donation from Anglo American plc to loveLife
- Costs incurred for peer educators, which were sponsored by Project South Africa (PSA)[46]

Many South African industry-specific charters had been designed to assist the sectors in meeting black economic empowerment (BEE[47])

---

[43]HIV and AIDS Initiatives at Anglo Coal Goedehoop Colliery DVD, Shadowy Meadows Productions, and interview with John Standish-White at Anglo Coal Head Office, Johannesburg, May 4, 2007.

[44]South African Rand/U.S. Dollar exchange rate in Oct. 2007: approximately R6.75/$1.00 (Standard Bank).

[45]loveLife is an NGO that incorporates the lessons of more than 15 years of international HIV prevention, and a two-year process of consultation and planning—including a thorough assessment of international HIV prevention efforts and extensive focus group research with young South Africans. http://www.lovelife.org.za/corporate/research/research.html.

[46]Anglo Coal, "Raising the AIDS bar at Goedehoop Colliery" brochure, point 3.2.

[47]Black economic empowerment (BEE) is a strategy aimed at increasing black participation at all levels in South Africa's economy. It aims to redress imbalances of the past by seeking substantially and equitably to transfer ownership, management, industry and operational expertise, as well as proportionate control of South Africa's financial and economic resources, to the majority of its citizens. It also aims to ensure sustainable, broader and meaningful participation in the economy by black South Africans. http://www.southafrica.info/public_services/citizens/travelkit-bee.htm.

guidelines. A key component of the mining charter was the scorecard, which provided a framework for measuring the BEE process in the sector.[48] One of the recommendations in the mining scorecard was that approximately 1.5 per cent per annum of post-tax operating profit be directed towards corporate social investment. In the case of Anglo American plc, this figure easily covered all ART costs.

Goedehoop Colliery was a high-profile mine for Anglo Coal. As a flagship colliery, it made over an approximate billion Rand profit in each of the three years up to 2006. This allowed it easily to cover the cost of treatment, which in 2006 amounted to less than R400 per person per month. Standish-White agreed that the business case for responding to AIDS was a "no brainer." Ninety eight per cent of the employees who were taking ART were at work every day and they only needed a day off every six months for a CD4 cell count check-up. Labour turnover and absenteeism had noticeably decreased.[49]

The financial commitment may appear high but Brink advised that the cost of not putting a worker through the AIDS programme was $32,000 per worker.[50] Goedehoop's success was an inspiration to all Anglo American operations, more so because far fewer employees were contracting tuberculosis (TB), which is an infectious disease commonly affecting the lungs. This was a welcome side-effect of the company's efforts to tackle HIV. The number of new cases of TB had dropped by almost 75 per cent since 2001. "TB has recently taken a lower profile" said Dr. Pienaar. "It was a social problem at one time—now it has devolved into being just a medical matter."[51]

Next Steps for Brink and the Team

Sitting in his Anglo head office, Brink contemplated his main challenges. He realised that the group had not yet managed to successfully stop new HIV infections. In addition, he understood how crucial it was for infected employees to gain early access to care, support and treatment. Brink knew that these two areas could be addressed by increasing the uptake of testing. South Africa labour legislation stated that it was illegal to enforce compulsory HIV/AIDS testing in an organisation. How could Brink push the importance of testing? How could he persuade all the Anglo business units to respond optimally in the next three months to the HIV/AIDS challenge?

Furthermore, at the end of 2006 Standish-White was promoted to Anglo head office in Johannesburg to take up a position as head of underground operations. Brink wondered if the change in leadership at Goedehoop would impact the mine's 5GH programme and if Goedehoop, with new leadership in place, could attain the goal for the whole group—zero new HIV infections.

Glossary

Acquired: The virus is not spread through casual or inadvertent contact; a person has to do something which exposes him/her to the virus.

AIDS: This is the second stage of the H.I. virus and is fully referred to as the acquired immunodeficiency syndrome or acquired immune deficiency syndrome.

[48]http://www.southafrica.info/doing_business/trends/empowerment/charters.htm, accessed June 5, 2007.

[49]Interview with John Standish-White at Anglo Coal Head Office, Johannesburg, on May 4, 2007.

[50]Interviews with Dr. Brian Brink at Anglo American Head Office, Johannesburg, on April 2 and 8 October 8, 2007. The figure refers to the projected lifetime cost to the company for an infected employee who does not obtain treatment (costs arriving from absenteeism, health care, early retirement, death benefits, replacement costs, etc.).

[51]http://www.angloamerican.co.uk/static/reports/2006/rts/hc-hiv-aids.htm, accessed April 11, 2007.

Antiretrovirals: The name given to any class of medication which suppresses HIV and thereby slows the destruction of a person's immune system (AIDS Law Project, 2005).

CD4+T cells: CD4 cells are vital components of the human immune system. One type of CD4 cell (which is attacked by HIV) is the CD4 positive T cell. This cell organises the body's overall immune response to foreign bodies and infections. This T helper cell is the prime target of the HI virus, the particles of which attach themselves to the CD4 cell. Once the virus has penetrated the wall of the CD4 cell it is safe from the immune system because it copies the cell's DNA so that it cannot be identified and destroyed by the body's defence mechanisms. In a healthy person there are on average 1,200 CD4 cells per microlitre of blood. As infection progresses, the number will fall. When the CD4 cell count falls below 200, opportunistic infections begin to occur and a person is said to have AIDS (Barnett and Whiteside, 2002).

Epidemic: A rate of disease that reaches unexpectedly high levels, affecting a large number of people in a relatively short time (Barnett & Whiteside, 2002).

HIV: Refers to an epidemic know as the human immunodeficiency virus and is a cause of the syndrome known as AIDS. HIV attacks a particular set of cells in the human immune system known as CD4 cells. HIV can only be transmitted through contaminated body fluids in sufficient quantities. The main modes of contamination are unsafe sex; transmission from infected mother to child; use of infected blood or blood products; intravenous drug use with contaminated needles; and other blood transmission modes (bleeding wounds) (Barnett and Whiteside, 2002).

Immunodeficiency: The virus attacks a person's immune system and makes it less capable of fighting infections.

Non-governmental organisation (NGO): A community-based organisation with its own management structure; it is not part of the structure of government.

Pandemic: Epidemic of world-wide proportion (Barnett and Whiteside, 2002).

Syndrome: AIDS is not a disease. It presents itself as a number of diseases that come about as the immune system fails; hence, a syndrome (Barnett and Whiteside, 2002).

Traditional healer: A practitioner of herbal medicine and counselling in traditional African societies. The philosophy is based on a belief in ancestral spirits. Also known as a "Sangoma" in local African dialect (traditional healers were known as "witch doctors" by colonialists).

Triple bottom-line: The idea that companies can simultaneously service social and environmental goals and earn profits (Davis, 2005).

Compelling Visions

Content, Context, Credibility and Collaboration

By Jeffrey Gandz

One of my favorite Peanuts cartoons shows Lucy, once again, lecturing Charlie Brown on the meaning of life:

> 'Charlie Brown, life is like a deck chair on a cruise ship. Passengers open up these canvas deck chairs so they can sit in the sun. Some people place their chairs facing the rear of the ship so they can see where they've been. Other people face their chairs forward—they want to see

where they're going. On the cruise ship of life, which way is your deck chair facing?'

Replies Charlie, 'I've never been able to get one unfolded.'

Unlike Charlie Brown, leaders today must have a vision. There are many stakeholders—employees, shareholders, governments, special interest groups, and the media—who simply demand to know, "Where is this organization going and what is going to get it there?" Everyone who is a leader or wants to be a leader—of an organization, division, department or team—must be able to formulate, articulate and communicate a compelling vision if they are to engage and inspire people to follow them. They must also ensure that their followers find meaning in this vision, the context in which they operate. If followers can find this meaning, if they can grab on to it, hold it in their hands and make it a mental bookmark, their actions are likely to reflect and support their leader's vision.

Some visions compel people to act whereas others leave people cold or even alienate them from their leaders. This causes some leaders to give up on the visioning challenge, to let their actions rather than their words convey a sense of direction. Other leaders are simply reticent when it comes to establishing clear, directional targets for their organizations. Perhaps they don't want to be held to account for reaching or not reaching these targets; perhaps they don't want to publically commit to some strategic direction; perhaps they think that a clear vision may appeal to one group and turn off another.

There may be many reasons for rejecting visioning as a useful exercise. Yet, as we emerge from another U.S. electoral season with a president who appears to have triumphed because his vision for America and the power with which he projected it prevailed over others, it is time to re-examine

"the V word" and ask what makes one vision particularly compelling and capable of engaging people, and what makes yet another vision unsalable and essentially leaves people feeling cold.

Compelling Visions

Compelling visions that move people to action, change their behaviors, focus on key priorities, and follow the pathway that the leader lays out, have three attributes that can be summarized under the broad headings of content, context and credibility. Beyond that, they are developed as part of a collaborative process that engages key stakeholders.

The Content of Visions

Compelling visions are not just slogans. For example, consider General Electric's "We bring good things to life" or "Imagination at Work", Nikon's "Our Aspirations—Meeting needs. Exceeding expectations", "Honda's "How we see things" or Coca-Cola's "It's the real thing." These may all have worked well as advertising slogans or signature lines, but they didn't lay out with any degree of clarity what the leadership of these organizations wishes them to become in the future. Toronto-Dominion Bank's vision, "To be the Better Bank," is more goal-oriented, while Manulife Financial's is more specific, stating boldly that its vision " . . . is to be the most professional life insurance company in the world: providing the very best financial protection and investment management services tailored to customers in every market where we do business." These vision statements give a better sense of where those companies are heading. But, since they are targeted to multiple stakeholders, they also lack the specificity that some of those stakeholders would like to see.

The content or substance of a leader's vision must appeal to would-be followers as well as the leader. This appeal generally rests on the belief of followers-to-be that the leader can deliver something that they want and need—the feeling that their leader serves their needs and that they can achieve through their leader. They might assume this servant-leader role for altruistic reasons, without care for her or his own needs, or on the other hand, to satisfy their own needs through satisfying the desires of their followers.

Effective leaders are good at understanding the wide variety of physical, economic, psychosocial, and emotional needs that people have, and in their ability to tailor a "vision" so that it promises to satisfy unmet needs. The person who doesn't have a job, can't pay the rent, has a family to support and has other basic needs may be attracted to any vision that seems to promise material rewards and security. Someone who has savings, a secure pension or is near retirement age may not care too much about getting paid more, but may put a high value on the social satisfaction that they get from doing their job—the quality of interaction that they have with clients, suppliers, co-workers, and so on. Someone who has a high need for achievement may be attracted to an audacious vision; someone who has a high need for security may reject that same vision in favor of one that promises security and stability. Charismatic or transformational leaders can get followers to transcend their narrow, personal "economic" interests and embrace the leader's mission, whereas transactional leaders operate on a more material plane. Both types have to develop a content-rich vision to motivate people to follow them.

For any leader, the challenge is to figure out what will "turn people on," at least those people who will be essential for achieving the vision. The problems arise when very different, sometimes totally contradictory, things turn on the people who need to be motivated to follow. A CEO or executive team may be turned on by profit growth, especially when they have substantial stock options that vest when certain profitability targets are met. The union leader may see these profitability targets being achieved only through plant closures, loss of jobs and consequent reduction in union membership. Little surprise, then, that the union leader does not enthusiastically embrace the leadership vision. For the vision of profitable growth to be embraced by both union leaders and management, each has to see a payoff somewhere in the content of that vision. It is not essential that everyone agrees with every aspect of a vision, only that they find something in that vision which resonates with them.

Even within management teams, there may be a lack of buy-in to certain corporate visions. A risk-averse CEO who has a substantial portion of his personal wealth tied up in in-the-money options may embrace a vision that emphasizes slow and steady domestic growth. On the other hand, the head of the international division may be focused on the higher-risk strategy of entering emerging markets.

The problem with many enterprise-level visions is that they have to be crafted to appeal to multiple stakeholders or, at a minimum, so as not to create conflict among any interests that have some countervailing power. This is a high hurdle for visionaries to overcome. One vision has to appeal to shareholders, managerial and non-managerial employees, partners, customers, governments, supply-chain participants, and community activists. Such "enterprise" visions, as they are referred to, often lack the focus or an edge. Indeed, many corporations are vague about their visions, at least in public, preferring instead to focus on their broader "missions," often stated in socially progressive, non-threatening ways. Who can argue with British Petroleum's "Beyond Petroleum" in an environmentally-conscious world or Archer-Daniel-Midland's "To unlock the potential of nature to improve the quality of life"?

Vision and the Necessity for Context

If visions are to motivate, especially employees, it's essential that employees find the vision meaningful in the context of their work. A vision for an HR department may well be "to create the best employment brand of any company in our industry," or for a risk management department of a bank to embrace "the highest risk-adjusted return in our industry," or for the marketing department of a food processing company to "have 50 percent of sales in products that are less than five years old that match the lifestyles of busy people today." This means that there may be several visions within a company. All need to be aligned with the company's overall mission, though each would have a particular meaning for a selected constituency in the enterprise. Each person should have a line of sight to the firm's higher-level organizational mission and vision, and be able to see how they can contribute to its fulfillment by realizing their own visions. This means that everyone with a leadership role in an enterprise, from a team leader to department manager to business unit manager, to functional leader and CEO, must be involved in "the visioning thing." It's not just one, over-arching vision from on high that does it.

Individuals' salient wants and needs are dynamic, and vary by circumstances, time and place. Desperate people, experiencing material or psychological threats to their immediate wellbeing, are primed to respond to a leader who promises the hope of delivering them from their current situations.

We see this most evidently in the sociopolitical context. Martin Luther King, Jr. drew on a deep vein of anger and frustration in the civil rights community and mobilized Afro-Americans to action. Barack Obama called for an era of change for an American population frustrated and angry with the Bush administration. Margaret Thatcher roused the British from their welfare-state torpor in the 1970s and got that country moving again, although there are still many people who would say it was in the wrong direction.

But we also see the ability of a vision to mobilize in a corporate context. Jack Welch used the powerful vision of "being number one or number two in each market we are in" to focus a number of the small, powerful business units in the conglomerate-like General Electric. He subsequently used powerful visions such as "the largest small company on earth, smart, agile, nimble" to bust the silo mentality and excessive bureaucracy that characterized the GE that he had inherited from his predecessors. The contexts for these visions were situations in which employees felt constrained, restricted and dissatisfied with the way the company operated. As well, shareholders were unhappy with results that were negatively influenced by the slow, resource-wasteful practices of the "old" GE, suppliers who found the company hard to deal with, customers who were unhappy with product and service reliability and quality, and even unions and employees that saw the only real security in the face of free trade and Japanese competition was in superior performance.

A business leader in a turnaround situation may be able to articulate a vision that compels people to act, whereas that same vision, articulated a year earlier or later, before the enterprise has run into trouble or after it has started a recovery, may well fall on deaf ears. One who seeks to build a long-lasting institution by making long-term investments may attract few people to that vision when the stock price is low; however, such a course of action may stimulate interest when the organization is performing well. One whose vision focuses on innovation and creativity may stimulate followers to action when the basics are working well, though he or she may fail to do so when the fundamentals of the business need fixing. There are times when there are several competing visions and a leader must consider the relative power of his or her vision to move people who may be torn between competing, attractive alternatives.

Time and circumstances may compel a shift of a particular vision. As the economic slowdown of early 2008 merged with the global banking meltdown of the second half of the year, most companies had to re-think their goals in light of what was achievable over a specific time frame. As competitors succeed in reducing a market leader's advantage,, that leader may have to adjust the vision. Michael Dell discovered this when Hewlett-Packard, under the leadership of Mark Hurd, achieved supply-chain economics comparable to Dell's. Dell found that the shift to notebook computers required potential buyers to have a tactile experience. This persuaded Dell to re-embrace the retail distribution channel that it had abandoned many years previously, when it switched to the Dell Direct business model.

While flexibility is required to deal with dramatically changed circumstances, constant vision changing inevitably creates confusion and consternation, a lack of faith that the leadership knows where they are heading. Vision drift is a constant danger and the "vision-du-jour" phenomenon is to be avoided at all costs. The President and CEO of TD Bank Financial Group, Ed Clark, continues to focus on creating a truly North American powerhouse in the face of an economic slowdown, a continued focus that has some critics calling for a time-out from the pursuit of this goal. But Clark is determined and very conscious of the fact that any perceived weakening of resolve could derail the achievement of a worthwhile, long-term aspiration for the Bank. This is not some innate stubbornness, but rather the resolve of a leader for whom the creation of an enduring institution is a higher-order imperative.

▧ Credibility: Of Vision and Visionary

There are those who just have dreams and those whose dreams will inspire others to follow them. The difference may have more to do with the credibility of the visionary rather than with the content of the vision.

The leader with a good track record, who is known for having achieved what they set out to do in the past, who "knows the business" and is recognized as an expert by those they are seeking to influence, is more likely to inspire a following than one who lacks such credentials, other things being equal. Such a leader has personal credibility which, when allied with the right content and context may provide powerful transformational leadership. Such was the case with Lou Gerstner, a former, highly successful

CEO of RJR Nabisco, who was hired to turn a moribund IBM around and transform it from a product-focused company into one that had a blend of products and services. He had an impressive track record at American Express and, importantly, was not steeped in the culture of IBM, a culture that had spawned a great company in the period 1950—1990, but was in danger of strangling it in the much faster-moving, high-technology environment of the 1990s.

But such personal credibility may not outweigh a vision that lacks substantive appeal and is credible in its own right. Has this been done before? When and where? By whom? With what resources? A vision may be appealing and the visionary may have some degree of personal credibility, but if the vision seems too fantastic, too implausible, it will not be seen as compelling, an absolute must for any successful leadership vision. When Mike Zafirovski came to Nortel Networks from Motorola, he came with high personal credibility. However, the company was in so much trouble, faced such serious financial problems, and had an innovation deficit compounded by the need to limit R&D expenditures that personal credibility could not carry the day. Individuals that might have made it possible for Nortel to succeed had defected to competitors, where they saw the resources required to be a leader in the telecommunications field. Those that remained at Nortel discovered that they did not have the resource base to compete effectively against the Cisco's and Alcatel-Lucent's of this world.

Then sometimes, we see a newcomer who, armed with words but without a history of deeds, and who may lack a degree of evidence-based credibility, can nevertheless still be persuasive. In Barack Obama's presidential campaign, we saw a leader whose oratory, command of language and personal presence in a context where people were desperate for new leadership—but one who carried a very thin resume—elected to the most powerful office on earth. This charismatic leader may inspire a following based on little except their "magnetic" force, a force that is magnified and distributed through the mass media. This charisma may exist independently of their other leadership attributes or may substantially add to them. One thinks of a Steve Jobs at Apple, Warren Buffet of Berkshire Hathaway, or Herb Kelleher of Southwest Airlines, as examples of charismatic leaders who have founded or resurrected businesses.

◪ Collaboration: Whose Vision Is It, Anyway?

Throughout history there have been individuals who have seen something that others did not see, who were able to articulate that "something" and build followers, and manage those followers through the many changes called for by the vision. Bill Gates and Bill Allen did this with Microsoft, Steve Jobs and Steve Wozniak did it at Apple; in earlier generations there were Thomas Edison, David Sarnoff, and Timothy Eaton to name just a few. But there have been many failures as well; prophets who could not change the minds of others, false messiahs, CEO's who promised the world and failed to deliver, team leaders who could not get the support of their teams and eventually were either deposed or who left under their own steam.

Several acolytes of Jack Welch failed to deliver for their organizations when they sought to "import" elements of the GE culture to their new organizations. Bob Nardelli failed to deliver at Home Depot, and Jim McNerney did not lead 3M to greater performance. Both of the organizations they joined had strong cultures and, while neither of them had sterling performance records in the years immediately before their arrival, they were not organizations that recognized that they were in trouble and in need of a savior. The visions that Nardelli and McNerney tried to impose on their new organizations were rejected by employees and failed to deliver business results that were satisfactory to shareholders.

For any new leader, the challenge is to create a vision that reflects the wants, needs and aspirations of those who will be tasked with achieving it. Such visions are borne from the dissatisfaction that people have with the current situation and

their perception that there could be something better. The leader may have an important role in generating this dissatisfaction and in postulating a better way, but he or she will do so with great sensitivity to the way that people view the past and present. The challenge is to *envision* rather than to have a vision, and this is best done by engaging people in the process of developing that vision and giving them a meaningful opportunity to shape the product of this engagement. Commitment to it will develop only from this empowerment; mere involvement in a process will not result in commitment. The truly compelling vision has content, context and credibility; the process of developing it is collaborative. When people can say "That's my vision" or at least lay claim to having influenced it, it's an indication that the task of execution has started well.

This need for collaboration when framing a vision requires what Jack Welch called "aggressive-patience" on the part of a leader. While challenging the status quo, leaders must respect those who have contributed to success in the past and seek their involvement and engagement in developing the way forward. This takes time and some process skills. Leaders must approach the visioning process with an open mind, not an empty mind, one that is receptive to the concerns and inputs of those who will have a stake in the emerging vision and on whom the achievement of that vision depends. If this takes some time, if people find it necessary to develop a new vision in a gradual, iterative way, then this must be viewed as an investment in developing commitment.

◪ Does Your Vision Compel Action?

These four characteristics of a compelling vision—content, context, credibility and collaboration—are summarized in the figure, below. They suggest a set of screening questions that should be asked when any vision is being conceived, developed and articulated.

Exhibit 1

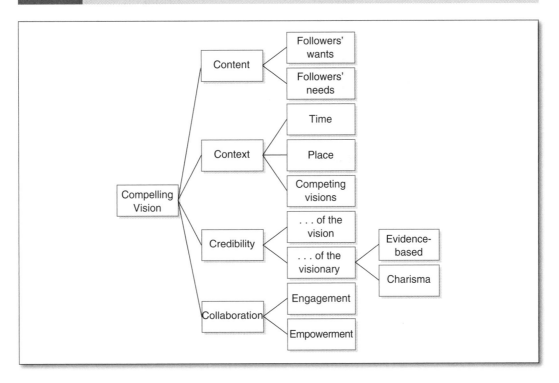

Characteristics of Compelling Visions

- Has this vision been developed in a collaborative way with those that will be responsible for its enactment?
- Does the content or substance of the vision appeal to the salient wants and needs of those you seek to inspire?
- Even if all elements of the vision do not appeal to all followers, will all those essential to making it happen see something of value for them in it?
- Is the vision articulated clearly so that followers will clearly see what's in it for them?
- Is the timing for launching the vision right or should it be delayed to the point at which potential followers will receive it better?
- Is the proposition in the vision credible to those who must embrace it?
- Are you personally credible in the role of visionary?

If the answers to all of these are "Yes" then your vision may compel action; less than that, and there is a chance that it will fall short of achieving this goal and may need rethinking or reformulating.

One of Barbra Streisand's popular songs says, "The vision ain't the solution, it's all in the execution." The emphasis on execution is important, but it must not exclude developing a compelling vision that will stimulate minds, engage passions, and move feet. The cost of launching a vision that fails to inspire is the loss of the visionary's credibility. . . . Get it right the first time!

CHAPTER

11

Team Leadership

You can best lead a complicated organization through a team approach, in part to obtain more information, in part to obtain different points of view and, maybe equally important, to get the buy-in and support that is necessary to execute. The strongest part of the culture of our organization is teamwork, and we've found that the more diverse our teams, the more productive they can be.

—Hank McKinnell[1]

Being an effective leader means understanding the nature of leadership as it applies to leading teams. Some researchers (Zaccaro, Rittman, & Marks, 2001) suggest that leadership may be the most important element in whether teams succeed or fail. Contrary to previous leadership theories, where we focused on a leader and followers, in this chapter, the leadership function can be exercised by the leader in charge of the team, shared by members of the team, or both (Daft, 2005). Some researchers refer to this shared leadership model as team leadership capacity (Day, Gronn, & Salas, 2004).

The Team Leadership Model

The team leadership model described in this chapter gives central importance to team leadership capacity in achieving team effectiveness. When the word *leadership* is used, it refers to team leadership capacity. The model itself offers a way of thinking for leaders sharing the team leadership role and should be used to determine team issues and problems as well as several alternatives to resolve these issues and problems while being cognizant of the team's resources and capabilities and the external challenges and opportunities.

---

[1]Hank McKinnell is the former chairman and chief executive officer of Pfizer.

Figure 11.1	Hill's Model for Team Leadership

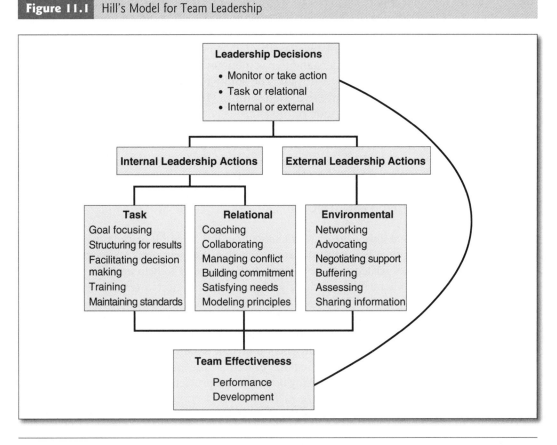

SOURCE: From Northouse (2010). Copyright © 2010, Sage Publications, Inc. Reprinted with permission.

The word *external* could mean the organization external to the team and/or the environment external to the organization of which the team is a part. Figure 11.1 summarizes the team leadership model used in this chapter.

Effective leadership in teams assumes behavioral flexibility, problem-solving skills applicable to teams, and using discretion when determining if leader intervention is necessary. In the model in Figure 11.1, the first box suggests that leadership decisions affect team effectiveness directly and through internal and external actions that leaders can decide to take or not take.

Leadership Decisions

These decisions are as follows: (1) Should I continue to monitor, or do I need to take action? (2) If I need to take action, is it task or relationship focused or both? (3) If I need to take action, do I need to intervene inside the team or in the team's external environment (the organization or the environment external to the organization)?

Should I Continue Monitoring or Take Action Now? Knowing when to take action is a very important leadership skill to develop. Intervening too soon could be more damaging to team effectiveness than waiting. However, waiting could sometimes cause more damage than intervening now. This skill develops through experience (similar to most leadership skills), and leaders need to understand that sometimes they will intervene too soon or too late, but sometimes they will get it right. The ability to get it right generally increases as leaders develop more experience in a team setting. The important thing to remember is to learn from intervening too soon or too late.

To determine when to intervene, leaders need information. This requires the ability to scan and monitor the internal team dynamics and the external environment in which the team operates. In addition, formal leaders need to let informal team leaders share this task and be open to informal team leaders coming to them with internal team problems and external environmental issues that could help or hinder the team (Barge, 1996; Fleishman et al., 1991; Kogler-Hill, 2007).

Should I Intervene to Take Care of Relational and/or Task Needs? If team leaders decide they need to intervene, then they must determine whether intervention is necessary to improve problems and issues related to task/structure and/or whether to help improve interpersonal relations among team members, including the team leaders. Effective team leadership focuses on both task and relational issues/problems as a high level of task productivity, combined with superior intrateam relationships, leads to best team performance and development. For virtual teams, it may be necessary to focus on intrateam relationships and then work on fixing issues/problems related to getting the job or task done (Kinlaw, 1998; Pauleen, 2004). Trying to fix task-related problems first may exacerbate the intrateam relationship problems to such a degree that it may make fixing both types of problems much more difficult.

Should I Intervene Within the Team or External to the Team? This decision is also very important. In the previous paragraph, we suggested that team leaders need to focus on task and intrateam relations. It is also important for team leaders to know when and if they need to intervene between the team and its external environment—be it within the larger organization or even external to the organization. Effective team leaders are able to balance the internal and external demands placed on their teams and to know if and when to intervene in one or in both.

Leadership Actions

The leadership decisions described above affect team performance and development through the actions team leaders take internally and externally. These actions are listed in Figure 11.1 and are based on research that discusses team performance. It is important for team leaders to assess the problem and select the right action or set of actions. The model in Figure 11.1 is a good guide for inexperienced team leaders and will become more useful as leaders gain experience that allows them to internalize the model to the point where it becomes almost tacit—that is, leaders respond to situations without even thinking about the model.

The actions listed in the model are not all inclusive, and astute team leaders will add others and maybe delete some as they gain leadership experience in a team environment. What is most important is developing the ability to discern when an intervention is needed and the appropriate action to take during the intervention.

Internal task leadership actions are used to improve a team's ability to get the job done. They include the following:

- Being focused on appropriate goals
- Having the right structure to achieve the team's goals
- Having a process that makes decision making easier
- Training team members through developmental/educational seminars
- Setting and maintaining appropriate standards for individual and team performance

Internal relational actions are those required to improve team members' interpersonal skills and intrateam relationships. They include the following:

- Coaching to improve interpersonal skills
- Encouraging collaboration among team members
- Managing conflict to allow intellectual conflict but not personal conflict
- Enhancing team commitment
- Satisfying the trust and support needs of team members
- Being fair and consistent in exercising principled behavior

External leadership actions are those required to keep the team protected from the external environment but, at the same time, to keep the team connected to the external environment. These include the following:

- Networking to form alliances and gain access to information
- Advocating for the team with those who affect its environment
- Negotiating with senior management for recognition, support, and resources
- Protecting team members from environmental diversions
- Examining external indicants of effectiveness (e.g., customer satisfaction surveys)
- Providing team members with appropriate external information

One practice that worked for me was having my boss's boss speak to my team at the start of a difficult project. This was much appreciated by the team members and showed the team members that senior management supported the project.

The critical point is that team member needs, in support of the goals agreed upon, are met either by the team leader or other team members. Of course, the better this is done, no matter by whom, the better will be team effectiveness (Kogler-Hill, 2007).

Team Effectiveness

Team effectiveness consists of two overarching dimensions: team performance and team development. Team performance refers to whether and how well team tasks were accomplished, and team development refers to how well the team was maintained in accomplishing the team's tasks. Several researchers have suggested criteria for assessing team effectiveness. In this casebook, we will use the Larson and LaFasto's (1989) criteria.

We will present these criteria in the form of questions to help in assessing team effectiveness. The better a team is assessed to be on these criteria, the better the team is performing:

- Does the team have specific, realizable, clearly articulated goals?
- Does the team have a results-oriented structure?
- Are team members capable?
- Is there unity with respect to commitment to the team's goals?

- Is there a collaborative climate among team members?
- Are there standards of excellence to guide the team?
- Is there external support and recognition for the team?
- Is team leadership effective?

These criteria are important in assessing team effectiveness. Effective team leaders will find formal and informal ways of examining themselves and their team against these criteria. Finally, team leaders must be willing to take action to correct weaknesses on any of these criteria (Kogler-Hill, 2007).

How Does the Team Leadership Model Work?

The model in this chapter is a mental map for helping team leaders constantly assess their team's effectiveness, as well as when and where the team's leaders need to intervene. If an intervention is needed, is it internal task, internal relational, or external? This constant analysis is necessary for continuous team improvement. Just as hockey general managers need to continuously assess their team coaches and players, whether winning or losing, team leaders in nonsports organizations need to continuously push for improvement and, for example, must know when it is appropriate to change the coach and/or team members. The team leadership model assists in this push for continuous improvement and helps determine weaknesses that might need an intervention on the part of a member of the team's shared leadership structure.

To continue with the sports analogy, it may be necessary for the team captain to hold a players-only meeting, it may be appropriate for the coach to change team strategy when playing different teams, and/or it might be appropriate for the general manager to change the coach and/or team players. Lou Lamoriello, the general manager of the New Jersey Devils National Hockey League team, changed his team's coach with eight games to play at the end of the 2000 season and ended up winning the Stanley Cup. Since he became the general manager in 1987, the Devils have won three Stanley Cups (he is tied with Ken Holland of the Detroit Red Wings for the most by any general manager since 1987), and Lamoriello has done this with a different coach each time whereas Ken Holland has done it with only two different coaches.

References

Ashby, M. D., & Miles, S. A. (2002). *Leaders talk leadership: Top executives speak their minds.* Oxford: Oxford University Press.

Barge, J. K. (1996). Leadership skills and the dialectic of leadership in group decision making. In R. Y. Hirokawa & M. S. Poole (Eds.), *Communication and group decision making* (2nd ed., pp. 301–342). Thousand Oaks, CA: Sage.

Daft, R. L. (2005). *The leadership experience* (3rd ed.). Mason, OH: Thomson, South-Western.

Day, D. V., Gronn, P., & Salas, E. (2004). Leadership capacity in teams. *Leadership Quarterly, 15,* 857–880.

Fleishman, E. A., Mumford, M. D., Zaccaro, S. J., Levin, K. Y., Korotkin, A. L., & Hein, M. B. (1991). Taxonomic efforts in the description of leader behavior: A synthesis and functional interpretation. *Leadership Quarterly, 2*(4), 245–287.

Kinlaw, D. C. (1998). *Superior teams: What they are and how to develop them.* Hampshire, UK: Grove.

Kogler Hill, S. E. (2007). Team leadership. In P. G. Northouse (Ed.), *Leadership: Theory and practice* (4th ed., pp. 207–236). Thousand Oaks, CA: Sage.

Larson, C. E., & LaFasto, F. M. J. (1989). *Teamwork: What must go right/what can go wrong.* Newbury Park, CA: Sage.

Northouse, P. G. (2010). *Leadership: Theory and practice* (5th ed.). Thousand Oaks, CA: Sage.

Pauleen, D. J. (2004). An inductively derived model of leader-initiated relationship building with virtual team members. *Journal of Management Information Systems, 20*(3), 227–256.

Zaccaro, S. J., Rittman, A. L., & Marks, M. A. (2001). Team leadership. *Leadership Quarterly, 12,* 451–483.

The Cases

The 1996 Everest Tragedy

In May 1996, two world-renowned climbers, along with some of their clients and guides, perished on Mount Everest in the mountain's deadliest tragedy to date. The accounts of survivors imply that biased decision making contributed to the tragedy. Did a decision lead to this tragedy, or was it an unfortunate mountaineering accident? The case provides the opportunity to explore decision biases such as framing, escalation of commitment, anchoring, and overconfidence and the issues of leadership style, group behavior, team management, and communication.

Chuck MacKinnon

A bank supervisor must contend with various personnel problems, specifically highlighting individuals—both subordinates and superiors. His immediate supervisor said that the new group was supposed to be great, his new position fun. In the view of his boss' boss, the group had major problems. He soon discovered that he had more problems than he had anticipated. How was he to deal with a dysfunctional group when his superiors disagreed about whether or not there were problems and were also personally antagonistic?

The Reading

X-Teams: New Ways of Leading in a New World

Like a country, an organization can't be too inward looking. Over there, on the outside, lies much of the intelligence and many of the resources that it must have to innovate and lead.

The 1996 Everest Tragedy

Prepared by Khushwant Pittenger

Introduction

According to Jon Krakauer, "attempting to climb Everest is an intrinsically irrational act—a triumph of desire over sensibility. Any person who would seriously consider it is almost by definition beyond the sway of reasoned argument."[2] Yet, Krakauer was one of 150 climbers and

Version: (A) 2004-03-30

[2]Jon Krakauer, *Into Thin Air: A Personal Account of the Mt. Everest Disaster*, Anchor Books, New York, 1997, p. xvii.

their 300 Sherpa guides and porters who were in the process of climbing Mount Everest on the weekend of May 10, 1996, the deadliest in the mountain's history.[3] That season, a record number of 98 climbers had reached the summit, yet 15 climbers had died on the mountain, 11 during the weekend of May 10.[4] The deaths might have been written off as a natural element of the sport and the increasing commercialization of the mountain, had it not involved two of the most experienced and famous climbers in the world and some of their clients of questionable abilities, who had paid approximately $70,000 each to set foot on top of the world. Krakauer was one of the fortunate clients who lived to tell the story. Other survivors have published their accounts as well.[5]

☒ International Competition and the Mountain Without Mercy

Rob Hall's expedition group, Adventure Consultants Gui ded Expedition (Adventure Consultants), had boasted in an American mountaineering journal 100 per cent success in reaching the Mount Everest summit.[6] Hall perhaps had reason to be boastful: he had climbed Mount Everest four times. In six years, he had guided 39 clients to the summit, more than the total number of people who had reached the summit in the 20 years following Sir Edmund Hillary's first climb in May 1953.[7]

On this particular weekend, the accomplished New Zealander, Rob Hall, was guiding a party of eight—his largest client team ever. He was, however, not the only famous climber with clients on the mountain. Scott Fischer of Seattle was the leader of Mountain Madness Guided Expedition (Mountain Madness). He also had eight clients, and his company was a direct competitor of Adventure Consultants Guided Expedition, Rob Hall's company. Actually, Hall had "stolen" Jon Krakauer from Fischer's expedition by offering *Outside* magazine, which sponsored Krakauer, a sweeter deal in exchange for publicity. In addition, 14 other expeditions from around the world, including a team sponsored by IMAX, were on the mountain in spring 1996 with lofty ambition.[8] No doubt, this was a remarkable story in the making.

Everest's summit is the highest in the world, with a height of 29,028 feet. It is a place where the difference between life and death may be only one small step. One wrong step can plunge a climber to death either in Nepal or China. More than 150 climbers have died on their way up to the summit or on their way down from the summit.[9] "Going to the summit is entirely optional but returning is mandatory."[10] A significant number of climbers die on their return from the summit when they run out of energy, oxygen, thinking ability and daylight. It is a place where the most minor ailments turn deadly, people lose their desire to eat and the thinking level becomes that of a child. Minor wounds do not heal, a dry cough cracks ribs, exposure of

---

[3]J. Adler and R. Nordland, "High Risk," *Newsweek*, Society Section, May 27, 1996, p. 50.

[4]B. Coburn, *Everest: Mountain Without Mercy*, National Geographic Society, New York, 1997.

[5]A. Boukreev, and G.W. DeWalt, *The Climb*, St. Martin's Press, New York, 1997; D. Breashears, *High Exposure: An Enduring Passion for Everest and Unforgiving Places*, Simon & Schuster, New York, 1999; B. Weathers, *Left for Dead: My Journey Home from Everest*, Villard Books, New York, 2000.

[6]J. Adler and R. Nordland, "High Risk," *Newsweek*, Society Section, May 27, 1996, p. 50.

[7]B. Coburn, *Everest: Mountain Without Mercy*, National Geographic Society, New York, 1997.

[8]Jon Krakauer, *Into Thin Air: A Personal Account of the Mt. Everest Disaster*, Anchor Books, New York, 1997.

[9]B. Coburn, *Everest: Mountain Without Mercy*, National Geographic Society, New York, 1997.

[10]B. Weathers, *Left for Dead: My Journey Home from Everest*, Villard Books, New York, 2000.

limbs to the elements can instantly make them as fragile as glass and the body starts to eat into its own muscle to stay alive. It is a place where severe storms develop quickly and unpredictably and often rob climbers of their most precious resource—sight. On the average, only one in seven climbers actually reaches the summit, and yet approximately 700 people have reached the summit.[11] One can only wonder why anyone would want to climb Mount Everest. The answer can be found in the British mountaineer George Mallory's classic 1928 response, "Because it's there." George Mallory is speculated to have died on his way down from the summit.

Obviously, death on Mount Everest is neither unexpected nor unusual. Yet, the world was in shock when 11 climbers perished on the mountain during the weekend of May 10, 1996. Particularly newsworthy were the deaths of Rob Hall and Scott Fischer, two of the most experienced climbers in the world. Fischer had gained world-wide notoriety in 1994 for climbing Everest without supplemental oxygen and removing 5,000 pounds of trash from the mountain as part of the Sagarmatha Environmental Expedition.[12] The experience and the fame seemed to have made Fischer confident— perhaps overconfident. When asked about the risks, he was noted to tell a reporter shortly before the 1996 climb, "I believe 100 per cent I am coming back. . . . My wife believes 100 per cent I'm coming back."[13] Fischer cajoled Krakauer into joining his expedition to write an article for *Outside* magazine with statements like, "Hey, experience is overrated. It's not the altitude that is important, it's your attitude. You'll do fine. . . . These days, I'm telling you, we've built a yellow brick road to the summit."[14]

Fischer made these claims even though he had never guided a commercial expedition to the summit, he suffered from a chronic clinical illness related to gastrointestinal parasites and he had reached the summit only after three previous unsuccessful attempts. Fischer died on his return from the summit only 1,000 feet from the safety of Camp Four.

Fischer's attitude seemed to match that of his rival commercial operator, Rob Hall, of Adventure Consultants. Hall failed to guide any of his clients to the summit in 1995, and his co-founder, Gary Ball, had died of altitude sickness in the Himalayas in 1993. Yet, Hall's company placed ads in American mountaineering magazines claiming "100 per cent Everest success."[15] Rob Hall's cockiness could be attributed to his ability to successfully guide 39 climbers of various abilities to the top in the past and his ability to save all his clients' lives under the worst of circumstances in 1995. His extraordinary success in the past seemed to have led him to believe, "there was little he couldn't handle on the mountain."[16] Yet, on May 10, 1996, Hall died on the mountain, along with two of his clients and one of his guides.

⊠ The Deadly Decisions

Were the deaths of Fischer, Hall and others just natural events due to unpredictable weather and bad luck, or did other human factors play a role? Ironically, it was Fischer who told a reporter before his 1996 expedition, "I am going to make all the right choices. When accidents happen, I think it's always human error. . . . You come up with lots of reasons,

---

[11]B. Coburn, *Everest: Mountain Without Mercy*, National Geographic Society, New York, 1997.

[12]Jon Krakauer, *Into Thin Air: A Personal Account of the Mt. Everest Disaster*, Anchor Books, New York, 1997.

[13]Ibid.

[14]Ibid., p. 263.

[15]J. Adler, and R. Nordland, "High Risk," *Newsweek*, Society Section, May 27, 1996, p. 50.

[16]Jon Krakauer, *Into Thin Air: A Personal Account of the Mt. Everest Disaster*, Anchor Books, New York 1997, p. 84.

but ultimately it's human error."[17] One accomplished guide put it rather bluntly: "The events of May 10 were not an accident, nor an act of God. They were the end result of people who were making decisions about how and whether to proceed."[18] Coburn concluded, "lives were lost as a result of compounding factors."[19] However, even he pre-qualified his statement, "But if one or two decisions, out of many hadn't been made . . . the outcome may have been very different."[20] Can we learn anything from this extreme case for climbing our own mountains in the workplace and guiding/leading others to the desired peaks of performance?

Everest is considered the toughest mountain to climb because the altitude makes even simple mountaineering exceptionally difficult. It took 101 years since its discovery before Hillary and Tenzing successfully reached the summit and returned alive to tell the story in May 1953. However, Mount Everest's popularity has been steadily increasing. With its popularity has come its commercialization. In 1996, 16 expeditions paid $70,000 a team plus an additional $10,000 a member if the expedition had more than seven members. Another 14 expeditions paid $15,000 a team to China to climb the mountain from the Tibetan side. There were five Web sites posting daily dispatches from the base camp including NOVA's Web site which received as many as 10,000 visits a day following the news of disaster on the mountain. A number of reporters were part of these expeditions to write stories for their respective publishers, including Jon Krakauer, who was to write about the commercialization of the mountain for *Outside* magazine. The IMAX team spent $5.5 million dollars to film the climb of Everest. Guided climbs to the summit became a subject

of controversy world-wide. There were commercial expedition leaders who themselves had never climbed Everest. Krakauer quotes Rob Hall, "With so many incompetent people on the mountain, I think it is pretty unlikely that we will get through the season without something bad happening up high."[21] Obviously, Hall was not thinking of anything bad happening to him or his clients.

Hall had the reputation of being a very methodical, organized and caring person. He was known to pay close attention to all the details, including the health and well-being of team members and their equipment. He paid his staff well and even had a paid doctor on staff. He was the epitome of an efficient operator, and his clients felt they were with the best commercial guide on the mountain. No wonder he had little trouble finding clients for the last seven years, even if he charged $65,000 a person. He was well-respected by his guides, clients, Sherpas and even other teams. He mediated labor disputes, co-ordinated equipment sharing responsibilities among expeditions and even tried to establish agreements on summit climbing dates to avoid crowding on the treacherous route at the top. He used the traditional five-week acclimatization process to get his clients accustomed to the thin air of the mountain, as the Everest summit has only one-third the oxygen of air at sea level. If climbers were dropped off on the summit from sea level, they would die within minutes from altitude-related illnesses. Like most other guides, Hall gathered his team in Nepal in March and took them to the base camp, at a height of 17,600 feet, in the beginning of April. From there, over a period of a month, the teams made grueling climbs back and forth to

[17]Ibid., p. 84.

[18]B. Coburn, *Everest: Mountain Without Mercy*, National Geographic Society, New York, 1997, p. 192.

[19]Ibid., p. 193.

[20]Ibid., p. 193.

[21]Jon Krakauer, *Into Thin Air: A Personal Account of the Mt. Everest Disaster*, Anchor Books, New York 1997, p. 182.

a series of four camps established higher up on the mountain at different heights in order to steadily acclimate their bodies to increasingly low levels of oxygen. Unlike many other commercial guides, Hall personally escorted his entire team up and down those climbs. He was always there when any of his clients suffered altitude illnesses or injuries related to mountaineering. His tactics might have been efficient, but they created and reinforced the clients' dependence on him.

Scott Fischer had a different strategy for his team. He had given his clients free rein in going up and down the mountain for acclimatization. His main guide, who was from Russia, had a different philosophy about client service. He did not share Fischer's western perspective of meeting all the needs of his clients. One of Fischer's clients said, "I doubted that I'll be able to count on him when it really mattered."[22] The Russian guide believed in the survival of the fittest, and many of these clients were not fit for such a demanding environment. Many of Hall's and Fischer's clients were well-to-do professionals with busy careers who had little time for real mountaineering on a regular basis. They used gym equipment to get ready for the climb. This is not to say they did not have any previous mountain climbing experience. Actually, their previous mountain successes might have given them a dangerous sense of confidence. Fischer personally had to do a lot of hurried and unscheduled running back and forth between the camps to help his clients in trouble. His team doctor was inexperienced and was there only on a voluntary basis. His most experienced Sherpa, who had climbed Everest three times previously without bottled oxygen, was poorly acclimatized for the summit this year and probably would not be there to support Fischer during the acclimatization of the team. Almost the entire month of April, the Sherpa was busy with the rescue of another Sherpa on the Mountain Madness

team who had to be brought down to the base camp and later evacuated to Kathmandu before he died in late April. Fischer, an energetic and charismatic person by nature, was described to be "extremely wasted" during his ascent to the summit.

Mountain Madness, Scott Fischer's company, had been a fiscally marginal enterprise since its launch in 1984. In 1995, Fischer's income was $12,000. His family had been supported mostly by his wife's income as a pilot for Alaskan Airlines. During the past year, however, she had been involved in a sexual harassment law suit with her employer. This was Fischer's chance to enter the Everest market and emulate Rob Hall. The competition between Fischer's Mountain Madness and Hall's Adventure Consultants for the high end of the market was obvious. Hall had failed to take any clients to the summit in 1995. If he failed again this year, Fischer was likely to become a formidable threat. He already had the strategic advantage of being based in the United States as more than 80 per cent of clients came from the United States. The need for market advantage was the reason Rob Hall had significantly undercut Fischer in his negotiations with *Outside* magazine to get Jon Krakauer on his team. He bartered for magazine space, in exchange for $55,000. Scott Fischer's cash-strapped enterprise probably was unable to match the deal. Fischer, however, did manage to have Sandy Pittman, a New York socialite and freelance reporter for multiple national papers magazines and television networks, on his team.

The Pressure to Perform

The presence of reporters among the teams was a double-edged sword. They provided visibility and notoriety world-wide through their reporting, much of which was posted on the Internet on a daily basis. Their presence also,

---

however, created pressure for performance among the team members and leaders. One of the clients on Rob Hall's team, Beck Weathers, commented on the presence of reporters among the teams, "I was concerned that it might drive people further than they wanted to go. And it might even for the guides . . . they want to get people on top of the mountain because . . . they're going to be written about, and they're going to be judged."[23] This thinking bears credence in light of Scott Fischer's comments, "If I can get Sandy to the summit, I'll bet she'll be on TV talk shows. Do you think she will include me in her fame and fanfare?"[24] The pressure to push beyond the limits was not all external. After investing a significant amount of money and an inordinate amount of time and effort in the ordeal, few would have had the courage to turn their back on the summit less than two vertical miles and a few days away. Jon Krakauer reported, "Doug was hell bent on joining the summit push even though . . . his strength seemed to be at a low ebb. 'I have put too much of myself into this mountain to quit now, without giving it everything I've got.'"[25] Doug Hansen was a 46-year-old postal worker from Seattle who had paid for this trip by working the night shift and doing construction work during the day. This was his second attempt to reach the summit with Rob Hall. In 1995, he had been turned around by Hall only 300 feet away from the summit because of their late arrival at the peak. Hansen died on his way down from the summit on May 10, 1996.

Hansen's sentiments were shared by others regardless of their physical condition. Beck Weathers, a pathologist from Dallas, insisted on attempting the summit on May 8 and 9, even though he was suffering from near blindness because of the impact of altitude on his vision correction eye surgery and his feet had

been badly wounded by his brand new boots. He survived miraculously after he had been left for dead on the mountain and his family had been notified of his demise.

The expedition leaders were not blind to these dangers; they were very cognizant of them. Hall had expressed concerns about his clients' inability to turn around on their own by impressing upon them how important it was for them to unconditionally obey him and his guides on the mountain during their final push to the summit. On their ascent on May 6, Hall had drawn their attention to another climber whom they encountered on his way down. The climber had turned around at 2 p.m. only 300 feet and an hour away from the summit. Hall said, "To turn around *that* close to the summit . . . *that* showed incredibly good judgment . . . I am impressed—considerably more impressed, actually, than if he'd continued climbing and made the top."[26] In the month of April, Hall repeatedly underscored the importance of having a predetermined turnaround time, either 1 p.m. or 2 p.m., and abiding by it no matter how close people were to the top. Unfortunately, he did not establish a specific time on the day they reached the summit and did not himself abide by the generally understood principle of turning around no later than 2 p.m.

⊠ Who Is the Leader of the Team?

The need for clear instructions and leadership was critical for these teams. In comparison to traditional mountain climbing teams, these teams were large and consisted of strangers with a wide range of abilities and experiences. This created a worrisome situation because the actions of a single member—bad knots, improper hooking-up or a fall—can jeopardize

---

[23]Ibid., pp. 177–178.

[24]Ibid., p. 221.

[25]Ibid., p. 191.

[26]Ibid., p. 190.

the safety of the entire team. No wonder Jon Krakauer "hoped fervently that Hall had been careful to weed out clients of dubious ability." He was not reassured by the actions of his teammates who brought unbroken, new boots or were seen not knowing how to hook the crampons on their boots for climbing the glacier. Under such circumstances, no wonder Hall and Fischer felt the need to establish their authority over their team members, including the guides, as unquestionable. Immediately prior to the departure for the summit from the base camp, Hall was reported to say, "I will tolerate no dissension up there. . . . My word will be absolute law beyond appeal."[27] The clients were obedient because dependence upon leaders, guides, Sherpas and passivity had been encouraged from the beginning.[28] Even the guides knew their place in the pecking order. One guide in Fischer's team later reported, "I was definitely considered the third guide. . . . So I didn't always speak up."[29] There were pay differences. Senior guides were paid twice as much as the junior guides. In addition, they were the only ones with radios for two-way communication on the day of summit—an error that is considered to have contributed to the tragedy.

For the summit push, Hall had instructed the team to "climb in close proximity . . . within a hundred metres of each other." The result was that on May 10, the team performed at the level of the slowest member of the team on the final summit day when they were to climb from Camp Four to the summit and return in a grueling race against time and elements. The stronger members of the team had to stop and wait periodically for the slower members to catch up for periods that added up to more than four hours just on their way up. In addition, these waits created crowding on narrow, treacherous pathways and bottlenecks, which added at least another four hours of delays for the stronger members. The

result was that no one reached the summit before 1 p.m. on May 10. In the absence of a clear directive from Fischer or Hall about when to turn around, the members kept ascending. Only six members from the two teams (three guides and three clients from the two teams) reached the top by 2 p.m. Doug Hansen and Rob Hall were the last ones to arrive at 4 p.m.—fully two hours behind the generally understood turnaround time of 2 p.m. Not every member of the team, however, succumbed to the temptation. Four members of Hall's team did turn around when they were caught in a bottleneck and realized they would not reach the top by 1 or even 2 p.m. Hall seemed disappointed in their decision, perhaps because Fischer's clients were continuing to push forward at that time and the weather still looked good.

⧄ Communication in Times of Crisis

The weather turned deadly very quickly in the evening during the teams' descent on May 10. The availability of only two radios on each team made communication scarce, chaotic and unreliable, right when precise communication and leadership mattered most to the members who were socialized to be passive and dependent. The 3,000-foot climb (less than one vertical mile) to the summit from Camp Four is a 16- to 18-hour race under the best of circumstances. These were not the best of circumstances. Even the strongest members had taken 14 hours on their way up because of wasted time waiting for the slower members and the bottlenecks. Most of the climbers on the two teams, as a result, were running out of canned oxygen. During their acclimatization, many were seen using oxygen at altitudes lower than where it is considered essential.

---

[27]Ibid., p. 216.

[28]Ibid.

[29]Ibid., p. 260.

Almost no one was coping well with wind chill factors near 100 degrees below zero, whiteout conditions, little canned oxygen to support their bodies or brains, and no leaders for moral support or physical guidance. Only two clients, Krakauer and Adams, barely managed to make it down to Camp Four before the conditions became utterly hopeless. Twenty-seven individuals were lost on the mountain that night.[30] The climbers were disoriented and suffering from hallucinations and exhaustion. Some of them huddled only 200 feet away from Camp Four for hours waiting to be rescued. Through combined heroic acts of some Sherpas, guides and the clients in Camp Four, most of them eventually were brought down to the sparse safety of Camp Four. Scott Fischer and Rob Hall were not among them. They were caught in the storm too high up, and were beyond help. Scott Fischer's poor physical health and possible illness had slowed down his descent to a crawl. His image of invincibility led others to ignore his condition.

They focused their energies on saving themselves or the other "weaker" climbers. Doug Hansen had used all he had to reach the summit. Rob Hall took 10 hours to negotiate a descent with Hansen that others would negotiate in a half-hour. Even when his friends at the lower levels urged him to save himself, Hall refused to abandon Hansen. Some have suggested that Hall was in an impossible situation. Leaving a live client on the mountain certain to die in order to save himself would have ruined his credibility as a guide. At the same time, staying with the client under deadly conditions was certainly going to kill him.[31] Also, Hansen told teammates Hall had called him a dozen times urging him to give the summit a second chance and offering him a reduced rate to come back. Neither Hansen nor Hall made it down. By the time the storm cleared, 11 climbers had died, and one died later from his injuries. Of the dead, four were from Adventure Consultants and three from Mountain Madness.

Chuck MacKinnon

Prepared by Kate Hall-Merenda under the supervision of Jane Howell

The day after his group's 1994 Christmas party, Chuck MacKinnon, a managing director with the Merchant Bank of Canada (MBC) in New York, wondered how both his group and his career had become so seriously derailed. The night before, he had witnessed the virtual disintegration of a group that he had worked diligently to mould into a fully functioning team. Chuck knew his career and his personal life, as well as the group's survival, depended on how he addressed the multitude of people problems which he thought had been resolved, but which he now knew had only been lying in wait, just below the surface. As he pondered the previous night's events as a denouement of 18 months dedicated to trying to bring his group up to speed for the changing marketplace of the 1990s, he wondered not only what he should do, but if he was the right person to do it.

                   Version: (A) 2002-09-30

[30]G. Rummler, "Everest Strikes Back", *Milwaukee Journal Sentinel*, Lifestyle Section, Sunday, June 23, 1996, p. 1.

[31]B. Coburn, *Everest: Mountain Without Mercy*, National Geographic Society, New York, 1997.

◥ Chuck MacKinnon

After graduating from Georgetown University with his Bachelor of Science in Foreign Service, Chuck MacKinnon immediately went to work for Corporate Bank International (CBI), partially because CBI offered him the opportunity to work and earn his MBA in Corporate Finance, which he received in 1980. From 1980 to 1991, he held progressively more responsible positions within CBI, including a stint in Hong Kong. Then, in 1992, following CBI's merger with the Merchant Bank of Canada, MacKinnon was offered and accepted a position managing a full service branch of MBC in Saudi Arabia.

The Saudi Arabian months, Chuck's first exposure to the MBC, were fraught with difficulties. Managing a matrix organization with many units having dotted line reporting relationships to other areas around the globe was a challenge, but the larger challenge was solving a myriad of people problems that had been left unresolved by the previous manager.

Not long after his arrival in Saudi Arabia, Chuck discovered that the senior expatriate manager in the branch frequently left the bank to lunch in a bar in the American compound and did not return, and that his predecessor had allowed it. Chuck called Pete Dimarco, his boss in the United States, advised him of the situation and wondered aloud why it had been permitted to go on for so long. He could not have anticipated that he would receive a call from Bill Perkins, yet another MBC senior manager with interests in Asia, who "went ballistic" about Chuck not calling him first. As he reflected on the situation, Chuck noted:

> Immediately I was put off by how the Bank was not dealing with these problems, seemingly allowing them to happen, and accepting it; and then even getting angry with it being surfaced.... From the beginning I was never on solid ground on how we

wanted to deal with this kind of stuff. We say the right things, but the messages once you get below the surface are not the same.

And there were other problems. Chuck caught some of his staff bribing government officials; having tax refunds directed into their personal accounts; cheating on credit cards; putting foreign exchange tickets in their personal desks; and having outside business interests that were in conflict with their jobs at the Bank. He resolved many of these problems by "firing a lot of people"; then he had union problems, but he persevered, trying to resolve the problems in the branch. His perseverance lasted until he started receiving death threats from a client who had bribed a Bank employee in order to get money out of the country illegally and whom Chuck had subsequently reported to the Bank of Saudi Arabia. According to Chuck:

> I thought that I had cleaned it up, that I had gotten the right people in place and that things were running fine and that maybe, after all this pain, given the cultural issues, it was time for somebody else to come in and take it to the next step.

Chuck was looking for a new lease on life when a phone call came from Eldon Frost in Montreal offering him a corporate banking job in New York City with the Merchant Bank of Canada. Eldon portrayed the New York group as "working wonderfully, making money." In fact, he said, "it's a great business, you'll have a lot of fun." Chuck, thinking of his wife and two-year-old child, jumped at the offer.

◥ One Job, Two Mandates

In August 1993, Chuck stepped into his new position as Managing Director, Financial Institutions, with MBC in New York, looking for a fresh start. His job was to manage MBC's relationships with a multitude of financial institution clients as well as to lead a team in marketing MBC's and CBI's corporate financial services and products. His first few weeks on the job were sufficient to convince Chuck that his group had a number of people problems as well as an outdated business strategy. Yet, when he broached the subjects of adopting a new strategy to deal with changing business conditions or making changes within the group with Eldon, Eldon's mantra was "this group is great. Hey, your group is making 10 million bucks a year; it's working wonderfully!"

Although he did support Chuck's idea of a new strategy, Eldon was unwilling to let go of the group's traditional products. He did not see the market the same way as Chuck did; he had a different perspective. Eldon's market was the world, where a shortfall in revenues in one country could be made up by strengthening revenues in another. Chuck's world, the United States, was very different; there was no "contingency" location for making up revenue shortfalls. In spite of these differences, or because of them, Eldon could not see any reason for change; he believed "our group is different, we don't need to change, we're happy, we're separate, don't worry about it."

Eldon was driven by the concept of keeping everyone happy. He had survived a major corporate downsizing and had adapted by keeping his head down and making no noise. Perhaps, Chuck speculated, that was why Eldon's attitude was, "Don't rock the boat, I'm a survivor." It did not help that Eldon had expected to be promoted into his boss's position, had been passed over, and consequently, harbored a great deal of resentment toward Margaret, who had been appointed executive vice president instead.

Margaret Mattson was two levels above Chuck in the corporate hierarchy (see Exhibit 1 for the organization chart) and Chuck met her only after he had taken up his position in New York. Unlike Eldon, Margaret was not satisfied with the Financial Institutions group or its performance. She had held Chuck's position open for a considerable length of time looking for the right person and was sure that Chuck was the person to carry out her "fix it" mandate.

In their very first face-to-face meeting, Margaret told Chuck that she was unsure if it had been the right decision to send Patrick Kinnard, one of the directors, from Montreal to New York. She was also critical of many of the staff that remained in Montreal and she wanted Chuck to fix the group by "getting rid of the weak staff." Margaret was sure that the group's current skills were not sufficient to meet the looming competitive challenges.

In their next meeting, Chuck convinced Margaret that there were also problems with the products the group had to offer, and that new ones were badly needed. "That clicked for her" when Chuck showed her the numbers on price concessions the group was making on traditional products and, from that moment on, Margaret fully supported Chuck in driving the group toward a new strategy. Unlike Eldon, Margaret had worked for another investment bank during the major downsizing at MBC. Possibly because of this, Chuck speculated, "she did not have the survivor mind set," and consequently, pushed hard for him to make major changes quickly.

Chuck informed both Eldon and Margaret of their conflicting expectations of him, but it appeared to have very little impact on either of his bosses. Eldon did tell Chuck that he and Margaret had a "you leave me alone, I'll leave you alone and we'll just work together but keep our distance as best we can" type of arrangement and implied that he would have to live with it. Chuck, himself, had seen that they were like "oil and water" and that they worked very hard not ever to be present in the same room. He wondered how he could possibly fulfill both mandates.

Exhibit 1 Financial Institutions Group Organization Chart

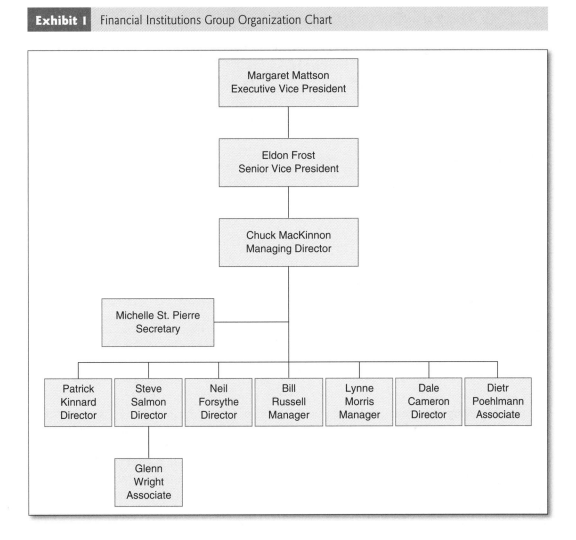

⌧ Getting to Know the Group

When Chuck arrived in New York, his first order of business was to get to know his group (see Exhibit 2 for a profile of the group). He travelled to Los Angeles and Montreal, meeting members of his team and assessing their skills and prospects. In Los Angeles, he found a high-performing team of 50 under the deft leadership of Bruce Wilson. In Montreal, he discovered a group that felt that Patrick Kinnard, one of their number who had recently transferred to New York, "had cut a deal for himself and deserted them to get paid in U.S. dollars." Practically all of the Montreal people wanted to join Patrick in New York. Chuck knew that Patrick's parting words to the Montreal group were that their much desired relocation would happen.

Chuck was well aware that the Financial Institutions banking business required that banking professionals be within easy access of their customers, not a lengthy flight away. He decided that the Montreal group had to stay in Montreal. While the group struggled with the

Exhibit 2	A Profile of the Financial Institutions Group

Name	Age	Years in Bank	Years in Position	PPR 1992	PPR 1993	PPR 1994
Chuck MacKinnon	39	3	1	EC	EC	QP
Patrick Kinnard	52	17	7	EC	EC	EC
Neil Forsythe	53	15	5	EC	EC	QP
Dale Cameron	40	18	1	EC	EC	QP
Glenn Wright	35	10	3	QP	QP	QP
Deitr Poehlmann	35	12	3	QP	QP	QP
Steve Salmon	50	20	7	QP	QP	QP
Lynne Morris	52	25	10	EC	EC	EC
Bill Russell	45	20	12	EC	EC	EC

NOTE: EC = exceptional contribution; PPR = performance planning and review; QP = quality performer.

prospect of staying in Canada (and being paid in Canadian dollars), Chuck investigated means by which they could successfully operate as a team across two countries and a continent. Technology and travel both offered solutions.

Travel was the easier of the two solutions. Chuck flew to Montreal on a varying schedule, never less than once a month, sometimes twice a week, to travel with his directors and senior relationship managers as they visited their clients. In an attempt to keep the lines of communication open, he augmented those personal visits with conference and groups calls. But, it was not enough; additional technology was required.

The Montreal group was not up to date technology wise. They didn't use e-mail or notebook computers in Canada. Chuck reflected, "possibly because of the technology lag, in Montreal they didn't see the vision" of a continent-spanning team. Chuck tried to correct the technology problem by supplying the Montreal group with notebook computers and cellular phones, primarily for use when they were travelling; but some members of the group could not, or would not, use them.

Chuck's frustration level grew. It took two days to track down one member of the group who was travelling in Europe when a client needed him; "nobody in Montreal even had an itinerary for him!" Why, he wondered, would they not use the scheduling package that he provided on their desk and laptop computers? Why did they view it as "big brother," or use it to check up on what Chuck was doing, instead of just acknowledging that it was merely a tool to make them accessible in times of need? Chuck felt that technology made it okay to have distant groups, while some of the group members said that it destroyed the camaraderie of face-to-face conversation. There was apparently not going to be a meeting of the minds.

Chuck had to admit that technology and travel could not furnish all of the answers to the group's problems. He discovered tremendous frictions within the group: Glenn Wright only worked with, and supported, Neil Forsyth, even though he was supposed to support the whole group; there was conflict between Steve Salmon, Neil and Glenn; and all of this was exacerbated when a demoted Patrick Kinnard moved to New York and began to notice that Glenn was not supporting him either. The fact that Chuck himself was an unknown to the group, except for Dale Cameron and Patrick, added to the overall tension levels. Even though the "sales people got along with everybody and they were great," they were not enough to salvage the team.

Chuck knew that something had to be done to turn his disparate and geographically dispersed group into a team and he thought maybe skill-enhancing courses might be part of the answer. He enrolled the entire group in courses to improve organizational and sales skills and to introduce them to the use of technology in sales, figuring that if they went as a group and developed skills together, it would help to build camaraderie and team spirit. In keeping with that theme, in May, Chuck and the group attended a team-building and high performance team work course that, according to Chuck, went well.

> People came out good friends. I thought there was commitment and I was positive about the whole thing.

Then, in July, Chuck hired the team-building course instructor to work as a consultant to the group.

⬛ The Strategy

Chuck had another reason for providing the group members with a minimum of 10 training days per year, even though that number exceeded the average for the Bank. His first few months in New York and Montreal convinced him that the group's business strategy was hopelessly out-of-date with the needs of the Financial Institutions sector and that something had to change. When he arrived, the strategy had been very much cash management-driven, dealing mostly with cash letters and lock box type accounts. There were two problems with that strategy. First, with all the U.S. mergers, the group had lost business over time because their customers were taken over and they had not always been successful in gaining the acquirer's business. Second, the trend line in the cash management and lending business was downwards, and pricing pressures had been enormous. Even though volume had been increasing, prices were declining and the revenue line had been flat. Chuck knew that "if we had just stayed doing that, there would be no bonuses, no incentive, nothing. It would have been barely treading water . . . we needed to do something else."

Something else was a new strategy that involved expanding into other product lines such as Treasury, derivative products, stock transfer, lending and trust. The group had "never talked any of those other product lines to any U.S. financial institutions." Lack of familiarity bred resistance, even though Chuck worked hard to get and keep the group involved in designing and implementing the new strategy. His people, after all, knew their customers and presumably knew what their customers needed. In Chuck's words:

> That was part of the change that I was trying to get some of these people to deal with; to get up to speed with those products and go out and market them. And that was where I ran into resistance. They would say, why these products, what we're doing now is fine. Why change? And my feeling was that business was being commoditized and going to go away and that, in the long run, we were not going to be able to succeed with that.

He hoped by adding to their skill base and teaching them to perform as a team, their resistance to the new strategy would wither and die.

⊠ The Group as Individuals

Neil Forsyth, Director

Located in Montreal, and in his mid-50s, Neil Forsyth was the first person to cause real friction for Chuck. He would say, "Why change, we cannot do this, I can't do it because I don't know how, I'm afraid, I don't see the need, I like the traditional thing and I'm good at it and it works." He was angry about the new strategy and kept agitating Chuck about it, making statements like, "You're nuts, it just won't work," while Chuck was trying to build a team. Although previously an exceptional performer, Neil received a quality contributor rating on his 1994 performance appraisal. While Neil believed that his performance ratings fell because of a personality conflict between himself and Chuck, Chuck noted that Neil's "ratings fell because he did not adopt the new strategy or provide that exceptional performance." Given the tension and disagreement between them, by late 1994, Chuck knew that he had to move Neil out of the group and he had started looking seriously for other opportunities for him within the Bank.

Glenn Wright, Associate

Also based in Montreal, during his first meeting with Chuck, Glenn told his new boss "what a great guy he was, how he was better than anyone else, and that he had been promised a directorship." Chuck, taking him at his word, promised to look into that directorship. What he discovered was that Glenn was not always delivering exceptional service. Indeed, Chuck was receiving mixed messages about Glenn's performance from Steve Salmon and Neil; evidently, Glenn had decided he would support Neil but not Steve. Chuck decided that he would not pursue the directorship for Glenn; in fact, he told Glenn that the only way to get promoted was through exceptional performance and that he had seen no sign of such performance.

Glenn felt that he could not deliver the expected exceptional performance in a strictly support role and asked Chuck to allow him to prove himself with his own clients. Trying to be fair, Chuck gave Glenn his own portfolio. Glenn liked having his own clients and did really well with some of them; others he alienated. According to Chuck, "if he needed you, you were his best buddy; if he did not need you, he ignored you; and if you pushed him, you were an !!!!!!!!!" Many of his client relationships were strained.

Glenn displayed very poor work habits and many Monday/Friday absences. Chuck started to get "a lot of heat" about Glenn from both Margaret and Eldon. Margaret, who had initially been critical of Glenn, became even more so after she saw him playing solitaire on his computer in the office. One day Eldon saw Glenn playing solitaire and called Chuck in wonderment, asking "how can an employee play solitaire right out in the open in the office?" Glenn, for his part, did not demonstrate that he wanted to work harder or support the new strategy. His attitude was, "I think you're wrong, I don't buy into any of this, I come in at nine and I'm leaving at 4:30." The chip on his shoulder just got larger and larger.

Deitr Poehlmann, Associate

Based in New York, Deitr's initial relationship with Chuck was a good one. Chuck saw from the beginning that, for some unknown reasons, Deitr was being "grossly underpaid" and undertook to make up a $20,000 annual shortfall over a period of time. As time went on, however, Chuck noted that "Deitr's work was spotty, sometimes okay and sometimes poor," particularly when it came to verbal and written communications in English. Deitr's first language was German, and that, to him, was sufficient reason not to do anything about his English. He believed people would make allowances for his language, even though Chuck spoke with him repeatedly on the matter and told him that they would not. At one point, Deitr went so far as to find an English-speaking trainer of operational staff to attest to his fluency in the English language.

Deitr also had "tremendous problems communicating internally; he would call people liars on e-mail and send copies of the e-mail to everyone, including their bosses" (see Exhibit 3). Such behavior created seemingly endless problems for Chuck, who was called upon time and again to smooth ruffled feathers of colleagues and clients who had been offended by Deitr's rather abrupt manner of communicating

---

Exhibit 3 Deitr Poehlmann's Correspondence

From: Deitr Poehlmann
To: Chuck MacKinnon
CC: Bob Grange; Joe Peoples; Stan Mantrop
Chuck,

Usually people that feel threatened, weak, try to hide their weaknesses, or try to ruin one's reputation will send e-mail as Joe did (the one below). I do not know what Joe has against me. I never create conference calls unless all parties know about it and agree to it.

I spoke with Bob Grange this morning. First, he still says that he was not aware of Cory's participation. Since this view is different from mine, I suggest that we call Cory and find out his view. Bob suggested (and I agreed) that we should not have our clients get involved in this. Bob and I decided that from now on, our phone conversations will not include third parties in order to avoid one's not knowing who else is on the phone. Bob also said that Boston Mutual's situation introduced to him is very clear.

I tried to call Joe but he is already in Hong Kong. I wanted to see what was so convoluted to him as, I hope, obviously you understood my e-mail. Obviously, Joe did not. Since it is so difficult to have this thing done with Joe, I think we should just drop it and let Boston Mutual do its thing on its own (which they are as we speak).

From: Deitr Poehlmann
To: Chuck MacKinnon

Chuck, as we agreed and you asked me to do so, I am sending you this e-mail to friendly remind you that as of August 1, you were to consider giving me a merit increase in my salary. I hope that you will be generous and take into consideration all my contribution to growing revenue at International Portfolio. I hope that I am exceeding your expectations from working on reducing backlog, bringing new business, and cross-selling business to existing clients. I want to thank you for your prior recognition in the form of increases and bonus and hope that you see me as a productive member of your team. Also, as you know, my salary, in my view, is below average, although I must say that you kept your word to me about increasing it 'over time' to higher level.

(Continued)

| **Exhibit 3** | (Continued) |

From: Steve Salmon
To: Chuck MacKinnon
CC: Deitr Poehlmann

Yes, and I think we'll find Lansing were unhappy as to HOW we dialogued with them, and that also had an influence. While I'm sure it was misinterpreted, I'm told Deitr Poehlmann didn't come across very well in his conversations with them.

From: Deitr Poehlmann
To: Chuck MacKinnon; Steve Salmon

Steve, if they told you that I am not surprised about the statement. There was only one person that I spoke at Lansing. She herself was rude, imposing and cancelled our (Chuck and myself) meeting with them day before we were to go to Atlanta. Their point was that we were 'demanding' reciprocity business (custody) from them. I did what I was told by Chuck and Brett Davies. We did not extend the lines as they wanted and I am sorry if they did not like that. I have been dealing with them for the past 3 years without any problem until not all of their demands were met. At that point, I guess, I fell into disfavor. The only bad thing is that right now we are out of $40,000 + revenue.

Dear Merridith,
As you know, after closing USD account, Corporate Bank International still maintains Canadian Dollar account with your fine bank. With our ongoing process of reviewing all of our account relationships in an effort to process our business more efficiently and cost effectively, it has become apparent that we need to close the Canadian Dollar account that we maintain with you, as well. Therefore, we decided to close it effective May 15. The account by that time should have no balances left, however, should there be any money left on that day, please have it sent to:

Sincerely,
Deitr Poehlmann

and by his tactless language. Chuck attempted to counsel Deitr on both his use of English and the English he used, but to no avail. Indeed, it seemed to have the opposite effect; Deitr had, for many years, believed that the world was prejudiced against the Germans and eventually he directed those sentiments towards Chuck.

Dale Cameron, Director

Dale Cameron originally came from Corporate Bank International and started in the New York group following the 1992 merger between CBI and MBC. He had had a long standing and positive relationship with Chuck when the latter arrived in August 1993. Although Chuck did not push him, indeed, he let him slide because of more pressing issues with others, he did notice that Dale had problems with erratic work. Some of Dale's memos were totally unintelligible, while others were cogent and well written. Chuck suspected a drug or alcohol problem and suggested that Dale access the Employee Assistance Program, but Dale claimed that there was no problem. In retrospect, Chuck admitted that "I ended up protecting him a little bit, became a little co-dependent," and, in November 1994, he gave Dale a quality contribution rating on his performance appraisal, noting that Dale had both accepted, and attempted to implement, the new strategy.

Patrick Kinnard, Director

Patrick Kinnard was Chuck's predecessor, a very capable individual in the cash management business. He had developed some new product lines that were interesting and Eldon had moved him to New York from Montreal in the summer of 1993 to give him a fresh start in a new location after his demotion. Eldon publicly said that, in spite of the demotion, he thought Patrick was great at everything he did and he told Chuck that "Patrick's nose will be out of joint since you got his job, but he will come around." In the beginning, it seemed as if that might be true. Their early relationship was fine and, although Chuck had heard numerous stories about Patrick's serious drinking problem, he did not mention those stories to Patrick. Chuck had decided to reserve judgment and give Patrick a chance to prove otherwise.

Six months later, coinciding with the initiation of the new strategy, Patrick and Chuck's relationship started to deteriorate. Patrick had agreed to follow the new strategy, but felt that Chuck did not respect the traditional cash management business sufficiently. At one point, Patrick went to Eldon, complaining about the strategy and saying that they were heading for disaster. He even brought Dale along to say the

same thing. Eldon's reaction was to call Chuck immediately, questioning him about what was going on in New York and demanding that they find a way to work together. Chuck's subsequent interviews with both Patrick and Dale got all of the issues out on the table and he did what could be done to address the doubts both men had about the new strategy.

Then, in the summer of 1994, Chuck received a call from Margaret inquiring about Patrick's random sick days; to her, the absences looked suspicious. Having had some experience with alcoholics and their habits and patterns, Chuck sat down with Patrick, asked him if he had a drinking problem and offered to work with him through the Alcoholics Anonymous steps. Patrick's response was that "he was dealing with it" (see Exhibit 4 for a synopsis of Patrick's absences). Chuck, who was not sure Patrick was dealing with it or that any alcoholic could deal with their alcoholism by *drinking moderately* or *keeping it under control*, suggested the Bank's Employee Assistance Program but Patrick did not take advantage of the offer. Chuck felt that he had done all that he could insofar as Patrick was concerned.

The 1994 Christmas Party

Thinking he could bring the group together and really cement the team spirit and acceptance of the new strategy that he thought was taking hold in the group, Chuck decided to hold the Christmas party in Montreal. He brought in all of the people from the New York office and some from the Los Angeles unit to join the festivities. The party was held in a fancy restaurant and they were seated out in the open. For a while, all went well, but as the evening advanced and people got progressively more "toasted," the illusion of camaraderie began to disintegrate.

The worst part came when group members rose to their feet and began to give speeches. Patrick and Glenn each gave 10-minute speeches putting down the new business direction, asking

| **Exhibit 4** | Patrick Kinnard's Absences |

From: Eldon Frost
To: Patrick Kinnard

I am writing to register my concern on your performance on June 17 as reported to me and Margaret Mattson by Peter Delottinville, VP Employee/Industrial Relations, and as related to him by the two lawyers who spoke with you by phone on Friday June 17 on matters related to a criminal court case against the Bank and where your input was requested.

As advised to me your behavior was such that you were not making sense of the information provided you, nor were you able to answer the questions posed in a coherent and understandable manner. As a result, counsel for the Bank and for Elections Canada have had to prepare a list of questions for you to answer in written form.

In addition, I understand Margaret Mattson also spoke with you by phone the morning of Friday June 17, at approximately 10 a.m., and she was of the impression you had been on calls earlier that morning with Neil Forsythe and Bill Russell. In this regard I have been informed by Neil Forsythe that neither he nor Bill Russell called on customers with you that day and that in fact you advised them that morning that you were ill and could not attend the planned meetings.

Patrick, I am very much concerned with what happened on Friday as this is not the customary behavior expected of you.
In this regard your input on the above events would be appreciated so that we may work together to overcome whatever problems may exist. Eldon Frost.

Chuck MacKinnon's log of events:

12/9   Patrick at the last minute called in to take a vacation day.

1/23   Patrick arrived at 12:00 p.m. "Drove his brother-in-law to the airport."

4/26   Sick day.

6/12   Patrick arrived at 10:00 a.m., said a cab did not show up to take him to the train, so had to drive in.

7/7   Sick Day—back was out.

7/12   Sick Day—back was out.

9/1   Vacation day, family flight delayed in returning from holidays. Called Friday morning.

9/6   Sick day, called at 8:30 a.m. with the flu.

9/25   Had lunch with Patrick today to discuss some of the concerns that he has raised previously. At the same time we discussed some of the administrative problems he has had (the audit, problems with expense claims, not getting back to Redboard on time on information he needed for a board presentation, last minute absences and vacation days, etc.). I indicated that I did not think I should be put in a position of having to cover for him on these problems. I indicated that I thought they were a possible indication of the drinking problem we had previously discussed but Patrick indicated this was not the case. He said he was just sloppy on some things and tended to procrastinate but would work on cleaning this up in the future.

9/27   Sick Day, supposed to be in Montreal after calls in Pittsburgh the prior day, had the flu, was dizzy and sick to his stomach.. Had dinner with PNC the night before.

9/28   Sick day, supposed to be in New York, had the flu.

9/28   Had conversation with Eldon this afternoon. Eldon was wondering where Patrick was on Wednesday as he had an appointment to see him. I told him he was sick and Eldon wondered if he was drinking again. I don't know whether Patrick was drinking on this occasion as I did not speak to him but this is not the first time that Patrick has missed a day in Montreal after travelling and having dinner with clients the night before. I did clarify for Eldon that I had had several conversations with Patrick as a friend about the drinking and cautioned him that he could not have any repetitions of past events. When Eldon heard that Patrick continues to drink (he regularly does so with and without clients although I have never seen him drunk again) and believes that he can handle it, he was very concerned as his deal with Ken is that there can be no drinking at all. If there is, their understanding is that Patrick will no longer be allowed to be in a client marketing position as his history in Montreal indicates he cannot control his drinking. Eldon referred to this as his 'smoking gun.'

"where are we going with this strategy?" They also could not resist harping on the bitter relationships in the group. Bill Russell then gave a speech about how "we should all be getting along better." Chuck, who had been trying to sit near those individuals who had major issues, was both embarrassed, "everyone in the place was paying attention," and angry "at the group and at individuals, for rehashing old stuff. It had been a year and a half and they weren't suggesting anything new to replace what they didn't like."

Having had enough, Chuck decided it was time for the party to break up. Passing Lynne Morris on the way out of the restaurant, Chuck could see that she was as appalled as he was and as uncomprehending of what was going on. Although he only wanted to go to sleep, the evening was not over for Chuck. In order to stop Patrick from hitting on Michelle St. Pierre, his executive secretary, he bundled Dale and Patrick into a taxi and got them to the hotel bar. In the bar, Patrick first picked a fight with Dale, and, after Chuck broke up that fight, he picked a fight with Chuck. The whole miserable evening only

ended, Chuck reflected, when he finally gave up and went up to bed.

The next day Patrick was nowhere to be seen. Chuck spoke with Bill Russell to see if he could make sense out of Bill's behavior the previous evening. Bill did not really remember making the speech about everyone working together as a team, but he was embarrassed and fully apologetic and vowed it would never happen again. Chuck, for his part, was able to overlook one slip from a stellar performer—it was, after all, Christmas—but he would not overlook another one.

As Chuck reflected on the previous evening's disaster, he found some things to be thankful for. His group was not completely dysfunctional.

The Functional Group

Steve Salmon, Director

Steve Salmon was based in Montreal. He was "a good guy, an average performer, one who would never be a superstar but he supported the strategy and did his best to implement it." He was very good at his job, well liked by his clients in a portfolio that he had handled for five years and he produced consistently good results. Steve was a "solid member of the team and a pleasure to work with. He is well liked by everyone on the team."

Lynne Morris, Manager

An exceptional performer and team player, Lynne was well liked and respected by clients and team members alike. She was a delightful individual who supported the new strategy, who had made the transition into new products fairly successfully, and "she was rewarded that way with big bonuses." Chuck counted on her for fielding calls on traditional cash management issues as well as for implementing the new strategy.

Bill Russell, Manager

Bill Russell was an exceptional performer who had increased his role in the identification of sales opportunities and was taking the necessary steps to close sales. Bill was a committed team member who supported the changes taking place, who willingly brought ideas and opinions to the table, who did a lot of cross-selling of products and who had made the transition to the new products well. Like Lynne Morris, Bill was a high performer and rewarded that way and, again like Lynne, Chuck counted on him for traditional cash management inquires and problems.

Bruce Wilson

A very high performer based in Los Angeles with 50 people reporting to him, Bruce Wilson managed a quality operation with a very thin staff that dealt with a wide range of responsibilities including systems and marketing. His service levels were high and his clients were both very loyal and supportive; his employee morale was high. Bruce emerged from the

1994 Christmas party saying, "Holy God, what the heck is going on here? Good luck to you!"

◾ Chuck's Dilemma

The previous 18 months had not been easy for Chuck. He had always been an exceptional performer but had received only a "quality contributor" rating from Eldon on his 1994 performance appraisal. Although he had tried, he could not get Eldon to explain why he considered him only "quality" and what it would take to become "exceptional" again. Eldon had only suggested that maybe the problem with the group's dynamics was partly due to Chuck's management style. At his wits end, Chuck thought maybe Eldon was right. Perhaps he "just did not get it." He thought, "This is it, I don't know what is going on around here, this isn't working" (see Exhibit 5 for an example of team conflict). But he did not have other avenues in the Bank to pursue. He had talked to people at CBI, but it was tough to get back in once you had left, and he had no network within MBC that he could tap. He felt stuck.

Chuck's growing self-doubts were reinforced by the messages he was getting from Margaret. Although he was convinced that he was pursuing the right business strategy, he wondered about his management style. Margaret's "fix it mandate" had changed; she openly wondered if Chuck's management style had been too severe, too hard. Chuck wondered if, and what, he could be doing better, if he had misunderstood the degree to which the bank was willing to change. "After all," he confessed, "when you have that many dysfunctionalities and a boss persistently saying everything is fine, the result is self-doubt."

On top of the erosion of his self-confidence in his management style, Chuck was beginning to see himself as a co-dependent in protecting Patrick and Dale. He had helped both of them with their work, redone their work and covered for them by writing memos addressing what were major problems and making light of

Exhibit 5 Team Conflict

From: Dale Cameron
To: Glenn Wright
Cc: Chuck MacKinnon

Thank you for your quick turnaround and I believe that your presentation was done well. I would add, however, that we should be careful about using words (in letters and our presentations) which tend to undermine the 'relationship team' concept. Specifically and despite our clearly being more capable of answering their questions, it might have been nice to say that they could also call myself. Finally, I called Linda and Jennifer yesterday and asked for feedback. Had I known you had done so, we could have avoided the extra call and the potential of appearing that we are not coordinating with one another. I will, likewise, endeavor to do the same. I assume the reports and letters are in the centrepoint file, and will copy you on the ones for the other three visits.

From: Glenn Wright
To: Dale Cameron
Cc: Chuck MacKinnon

Dale, this is one relationship you should leave to me. I have an excellent rapport with them and I think we are starting to confuse them. They have also asked several times that the relationship be managed by me through Linda, Homer and now Jennifer, something Linda reiterated in the meeting, if you remember, and in subsequent conversations. In the end, through PPR, we will all share any rewards to be had.

Glenn

From: Dale Cameron
To: Glenn Wright
Cc: Chuck MacKinnon

I could care less about 'rewards' and PPR, other than as it relates to doing the job we are expected to do in a fashion that places professionalism and client service first. For that matter, you can have 100 per cent of all the credit on anything that is done with this client. We should always do, within reason, what the client wants and as global R/M you are responsible. If you recall, I specifically said that in my intro. I do not ever remember hearing Linda say anything about this, it was never expressed that way to me by Mike or Linda on the intro call, and I would like to know what conversation you are referring to where Jennifer said this. She's your contact anyway. Finally, I haven't even heard about this request from you until today.

Chuck, your decision is needed and perhaps you should call Homer or Jennifer and ask them outright. In the meantime, as long as I am 'responsible' for this specific entity, I expect to be kept appraised of what is being discussed, done and acted upon, as you would expect of me. I have done so and will continue to do so. For that matter, all other entities for which I have responsibility. Rewards—absolutely misses the point.

From: Chuck MacKinnon
To: Dale Cameron; Glenn Wright

P.S. Sounds like there is some friction here. Let's talk about this on Monday between the three of us but the client's interests must be foremost.

them. Had he been mistaken in his attempts to give everyone a fair chance to adjust to the new regime before taking action? Could some of the problems have been avoided if he had been, not softer, but tougher?

Then there was his personal life. He had been short-tempered with both his wife and children and had been feeling guilty about allowing his work stresses to spill over into his personal life. Normally, he had been adept in separating the two, but in this case, he had failed.

The day after the 1994 Christmas party found Chuck wondering what was going on. Should he be looking for work elsewhere? The messages from his boss and his boss's boss were clear: it might be his management style. Had he done something wrong? What could he, or anyone else, do to fix it now?

X-Teams

New Ways of Leading in a New World

By Deborah Ancona, Elaine Backman, and Henrik Bresman

There's nothing really wrong with the way organizational teams work—except for the fact that they are inward looking. This exception is critical, since the connections that enable the firm to seize market opportunities and leverage technological breakthroughs are on the outside. X-teams are externally oriented, and enabling them will lead the organization to step up the pace of change and innovation.

Business pundits tell us that we live in a new world—a world that's flat, global, diverse, and networked.[32] In this world, information flows freely across organizational, geographic, and cultural borders. The result is a hyper-drive environment where innovation is the name of the game, rules are invented on the fly, and the challenge always is to do it better and faster or fall prey to some unknown competitor who just arrived on the playing field.

This article examines how three very different enterprises are dealing with this new reality. In doing so, the article will explore the application of two key concepts. The first is the idea of distributed leadership—a way of harnessing, aligning, and leveraging the leadership capabilities that exist all across an organization to make it more agile, responsive, and creative. The second concept is that of X-teams—teams that enable companies to practice distributed leadership and to reach beyond internal and external boundaries to accelerate the process of innovation and change.

⊠ Responding to a New World

Let's take a look at some of the ways people have reacted to the new world. Some have focused on building virtual enterprises—nimble networks of ad hoc teams leveraging new information technologies to accelerate innovation. Others have created more stable organizational structures and cultures designed for consistent and steady innovation over time. Still others have focused on strategic partnerships to spur innovative practices.

---

[32]Thomas Friedman, *The World Is Flat.*

One example of the nimble-network approach is the Vehicle Design Summit, an MIT student-led international consortium formed to design a two-hundred mile per gallon car for sale in India. With over thirty-six teams on six continents, funding from major corporations, input from the best universities on the planet, the consortium has already created a working prototype. Each team works on its own part of the design and gets its own funding, while coordinating with other teams and outside individuals and companies. Coordinators—like the logistics people working on how to keep the value chain as green as possible—create rules and tools that enable the teams to reach specific targets. A management team energizes the effort, brokers conflicts, and arranges meetings where teams bring their respective parts of the car together. This is not your typical student project.

A different example is W. L. Gore,[33] best known for Gore-Tex®, and which operates on a very different scale from the Vehicle Design Summit. The company has been in business for 50 years, has operations in forty-five countries, and generates $2.1 billion in annual revenues. In dealing with the change sweeping across today's corporate environment, Gore has taken the approach of designing more formal organizational structures and cultures that foster innovation and change.

While the traditional role of top-level leadership is to set strategy—including choosing key products, markets, and development priorities—W. L. Gore has turned this process on its head. At Gore, employees get to spend "dabble time" on projects they see as particularly interesting and promising. They elect their own project leaders who then engage in a peer-review process to determine which projects will eventually get funded and become part of the corporate portfolio.

One of the company's engineers working on cardiac implants chose to use his "dabble time" to develop a more tone-resilient guitar string, using the polymer prominent in Gore-Tex fabric. Over a three-year period the engineer assembled a small team of volunteers to develop the new string and explore the market demand. The peer-review committee awarded the resources to bring the project to scale, and today the company's Elixir strings outsell their closest competitor by a two-to-one ratio.

Multiply this process many times over, add a lattice-type flat organizational structure and an elected top leadership team, and you will get an innovation hot house. Gore has leveraged its knowledge of polymers to develop thousands of products, and step out of its original textiles market into areas such as medical devices, high-tech cables, and new energy technologies.

The new world we live in has spurred even the largest firms to become more agile. One such success story is Procter & Gamble. Historically, this Fortune 50 giant relied on internal capabilities and a small set of suppliers to invent and deliver new products and services to the market. By 2000, however, the company realized that this invent-it-yourself model was not cutting it in today's more competitive environment. The result was a shift from R&D (research and development) to C&D (connect and develop)—from "7,500 individuals inside to 7,500 plus one and a half million innovators outside the company with a permeable boundary between them".[34]

In this new C&D environment, P&G cast a broad global net to find a solution to allow it write on a Pringle's potato chip. Instead of taking months to put together a product development team and charge it with creating a new technology, it found a baker in Italy who could write on a cookie. It used that technology on Pringle's. The same collaborative approach, in this case between P&G and a Japanese competitor, led to the highly successful Swiffer dusters product line.

[33]Elaine's case.

[34]P&G.

A New Form of Leadership for a New World

Despite this shifting organizational terrain that includes everything from virtual enterprises to multi-billion-dollar global giants struggling to become "elephants that dance",[35] we cling to our old notions of leadership. We still think of leaders as those within our own organizational boundaries. We still look to the omniscient leader at the top to come up with an inspiring vision, the right strategic direction, exciting new ideas, and the answers to our most pressing problems. Leadership research and training still focuses on the individual leader—his or her traits, behaviors, charisma, character, values, and political savvy.

But the single leaders alone at the top or our organizational units cannot understand the complexity of our interdependent, information-driven world. One leader cannot manage the ever increasing levels of interconnectivity within and outside the organization. Nor can organizations afford to wait for information to be passed up to the top for decisions to be made.

In today's new world, there is a greater than ever need for leadership at all levels of the organization—what we call "distributed leadership".[36] Leadership needs to be distributed across many players, both within and across organizations, up and down the hierarchy, wherever information, expertise, vision, and new ways of working together reside. The result is a whole network of leaders who are aligned to move the organization in new directions based on market opportunities and technological breakthroughs. In this environment, influence does not just flow downward, but moves up, down, and laterally, empowering those who are best able to lead at any given time. Equally important, leadership is shared with those outside the firm who can help bring in new ideas, more efficient processes, and stronger links to outside markets and distribution channels.

But how do organizations move in this direction? How do they create the culture and structures that enable distributed leadership? How do they innovate, adapt, and execute rapidly while developing networks of leaders aligned to carry their organizations in new directions? One solution is X-teams.

A New Team for a New World

X-teams are *externally* oriented teams in which team members reach across their boundaries from day one, forging dense networks of contacts inside and outside the firm. These connections enable members to keep pace with shifts in markets, technologies, cultures, and competitors. They enable team members to learn about complex problems and find innovative solutions. They help the team link upper and lower levels of the firm, so that those with the knowledge of markets and potential new products and services can align with those forging new strategic directions and change. These connections can also enable players inside and outside the firm to share expertise and create new synergies that take advantage of emergent opportunities. These external connections enable innovation and adaptation.

X-teams[37] not only reach out across their boundaries to become networked teams (see Figure 1), they also enable rapid execution by moving through three phases: explore, exploit, and export. During exploration, X-Team members act like scouts making sense of their new terrain. They try to understand their task or

---

[35]Lou Gerstner.

[36]Ancona, Malone, Orlikowski, Senge, In Praise of the Incomplete Leader. *Harvard Business Review*, February, 2007.

[37]Ancona and Bresman. *X-team: how to build teams that lead, innovate, and succeed*. Boston: Harvard Business School Press, 2007.

Figure 1 X-Teams Build External Networks

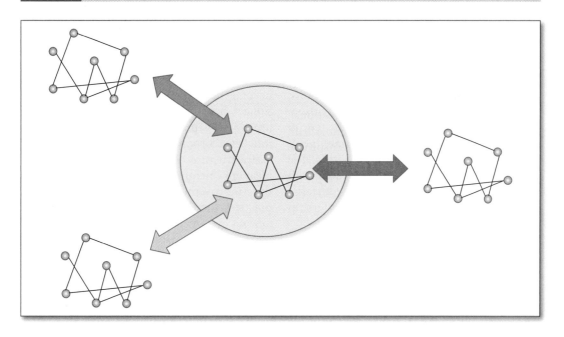

challenge with new eyes and new ideas—generating as many potential insights and possibilities as possible. Then, during exploitation, they shift gears and envision the one product they wish to create and move from possibilities to reality, doing rapid prototyping along the way. Finally, during exportation, they find ways to move their product, knowledge, and excitement to the rest of the organization or marketplace, assuring that their work is diffused into the broader environment.

Take a product design team at IDEO,[38] a product design firm headquartered in Palo Alto California. Asked to design a new emergency room, team members first *explored* emergency rooms from multiple perspectives. To capture the experience of the patients they placed a camera on the head of a patient.

After watching ten hours of different views of the ceiling, they *exploited* this information and decided to create a new design for the emergency room that included writing that was projected on the ceiling. They tested the new design with actual patients, doctors, and hospital staff, made some additional changes, and then *exported* their design to a real hospital setting.

X-teams at VDS, W.L. Gore, and P&G are bringing to life the concept of distributed leadership in each of those very different enterprises. For example, each of the thirty-six teams of the VDS initiative operates as an X-team. The teams reach out to get expertise from surrounding companies and universities, and to secure funding from a variety of external sources. They collaborate closely

---

[38]Taken from a talk given at the MIT Sloan School by IDEO CEO Tom Brown.

with other teams, whether those teams exist within the VDS consortium or outside of it. They coordinate with the leadership team to ensure that their work is in sync with the overall plan.

Thus, each of the VDS X-teams has a rich network of connections inside and outside the consortium. Through these connections, leadership is distributed across the consortium to more effectively move the entire organization closer to its ultimate goal. Leadership is also distributed within the teams themselves: as the teams move through the phases of explore, exploit, and export, the specific individuals taking on leadership responsibility changes.

When multiple X-teams are aligned they can be a powerful driver of change. At BP, for example, senior project leaders have been tasked with improving the company's project management capabilities. With billions spent each year on major oil and gas projects around the world, making such improvements could result in huge cost savings and strategic advantage.

Set up as X-teams, these leaders go through a BP/MIT executive program in groups of about thirty (a cadre). Melding six weeks of classroom work with their X-team work, the leaders spend a year moving through explore, exploit, and export. They reach out to benchmark other companies within the industry and those outside of it. They pull together expertise wherever they can find it. They collect data to better understand where there are problems and where there are new solutions. They communicate with top management to gain support and align with strategic goals. They invent and test new ways of managing projects, including new management systems, new modes of

contracting with suppliers, and new methods of project evaluation and staffing. And then they present their ideas to top management, inspiring a whole new set of organizational initiatives that spread new programs throughout the projects community.

BP's gains as a result of this process go beyond the specific projects—although the projects have generated financial gain. More broadly, the process of embedding X-teams into the corporate mindset has created an "infrastructure of innovation" in which new ideas are emerging, knowledge is building, and the improvement in project management practices increases with each year and each new set of X-teams.

In BP's new project management model, there is no one omniscient leader at the top. Instead, multiple leaders work within a team structure. This team creates a network of connections (see Figure 2) that carry out the leadership functions of making sense of a changing environment, creating a web of relationships that foster commitment to change, establishing a vision of what is possible in the future, and inventing new structures and processes that make the vision a reality.[39] Major change occurs as multiple teams work together over time, pulling in top-level leaders, as well as leaders outside the firm.

At organizations such as BP, VDS, W. L. Gore, P&G, and at many others, the X-Team model is an engine of distributed leadership, institutional change, and on-going innovation. As a new corporate landscape evolves, x-teams and distributed leadership will be needed to create the connectivity among these new organizational forms and to create value for employees, customers, partners, and stakeholders alike.

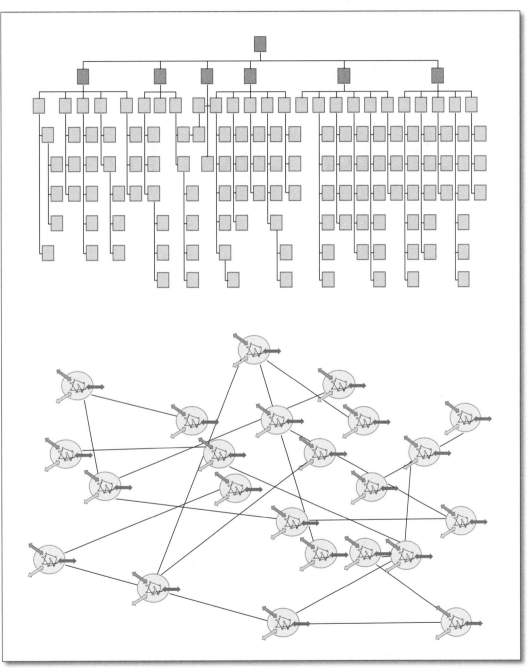

[39]Ancona, Malone, Orlikowski, and Senge.

Strategic Leadership

Natalie Slawinski

The University of Western Ontario

Positional power may still matter, and "because I said so" can still compel action from employees lower in the pyramid, but when ideas and directives support a vision that people—peers, partners, even those over whom the leader has no direct authority—believe in, they will be inspired rather than compelled.

—Goldsmith, Greenberg, Robertson, and
Hu-Chan (2003, p. 115)

I n the past 20 years, researchers have begun to pay more attention to the study of strategic leadership, which has come to be viewed by many as a critical aspect of firm success (Daft, 2005). Broadly speaking, strategic leadership refers to the study of executives who have overall responsibility for the firm and how their decisions affect organizational outcomes (Finkelstein, Hambrick, & Cannella, 2009). The focus is on top managers because they usually have decision-making responsibilities that affect the whole organization—including the other organizational members—and its overall performance (Daft, 2005).

Strategic leaders create a sense of purpose and direction, which guides strategy formulation and implementation within the firm (Daft, 2005; Hosmer, 1982; Shrivastava & Nachman, 1989). They also interact with key stakeholders, such as customers, government agencies, and unions, especially when these relationships are critical to firm performance (House & Aditya, 1997). Organizations and the environments in which they operate are increasingly complex and ambiguous. Therefore, strategic leaders must navigate through these complexities and develop strategies that will allow their organizations to be successful, whether they are for-profit or nonprofit.

Another perspective of strategic leadership focuses on the specific activities and behaviors of strategic leaders that can improve the success of the firm (Ireland & Hitt, 1999; Rowe, 2001). This perspective argues that in an ever-changing complex business environment, strategic leaders may be a source of competitive advantage. Ireland and Hitt (1999) define strategic leadership as the "ability to anticipate, envision, maintain flexibility, think strategically, and work with others to initiate changes that will create a viable future for the organization" (p. 43). Given the challenges that firms face in an often turbulent and unpredictable global environment, Ireland and Hitt have identified six components of strategic leadership that will lead to enhanced organizational performance: determining the firm's purpose or vision, exploiting and maintaining core competencies, developing human capital, sustaining an effective organizational culture, emphasizing ethical practices, and establishing balanced organizational controls.

Determining the Firm's Purpose or Vision

The first component of strategic leadership consists of determining the firm's purpose or vision. This means that strategic leaders must articulate a clear and realistic statement about why the firm exists and what is distinctive about it. This statement will then empower members of the organization to develop and execute strategies that are in line with the vision of the firm.

Exploiting and Maintaining Core Competencies

Strategic leaders exploit and maintain core competencies. Core competencies are resources and capabilities that give firms an edge over their rivals. Strategic leaders need to understand which combinations of resources and capabilities are valuable, rare, costly to imitate, and difficult to substitute for, as these will allow the firm to gain a competitive advantage.

Developing Human Capital

Strategic leaders are effective at developing human capital. Human capital refers to the knowledge, skills, and abilities of the firm's employees. Because these employees are critical to the success of the organization, strategic leaders invest in them through training and mentoring.

Sustaining an Effective Organizational Culture

Strategic leaders sustain an effective organizational culture. An organization's culture is a complex combination of ideologies, symbols, and values that are shared by employees of the firm. Strategic leaders learn how to shape a firm's shared values and symbols in ways that allow the firm to be more competitive.

Emphasizing Ethical Practices

Strategic leadership involves the emphasis of ethical practices. Top managers who use honesty, trust, and integrity in their decision making are able to inspire their employees and create an organizational culture that encourages the use of ethical practices in day-to-day organizational activities.

Establishing Balanced Organizational Controls

Organizational controls refer to the formal procedures that are used in organizations to influence and guide work. These controls act as limits on what employees can and cannot do. There are two types of internal controls: strategic and financial. Strategic controls are accomplished through information exchanges that help to develop strategies, whereas financial controls are accomplished through setting objective criteria such as performance targets. Strategic controls emphasize actions, whereas financial controls emphasize outcomes. Financial controls can be especially constraining and can stifle creativity in organizations. Strategic leaders must establish balanced organizational controls by incorporating the two types in order to allow employees to remain flexible and innovative.

In addition to accomplishing the above activities, strategic leaders must balance the short-term needs of their organizations while ensuring a future competitive position. Rowe (2001) defines strategic leadership as "the ability to influence others to voluntarily make day-to-day decisions that enhance the long-term viability of the organization, while at the same time maintaining its short-term financial stability" (pp. 82–83). This type of leadership is a synergistic combination of visionary leadership, which emphasizes investing in the future, and managerial leadership, which emphasizes preserving the existing order. Strategic leaders focus on both the day-to-day operations and the long-term strategic orientation of the firm, recognizing that neither can be ignored if a firm is to be successful.

Importantly, strategic leaders have strong positive expectations of the performance they expect from their superiors, peers, subordinates, and themselves (Rowe, 2001). These expectations encourage organizational members to voluntarily make decisions that contribute to short-term stability and long-term viability of the organization. As such, strategic leaders do not have to expend as much effort on monitoring and controlling employees. It is also important that those leaders who already exhibit strategic leadership abilities encourage their development in other organizational members. In this way, strategic leadership can exist at all levels of the organization. Strategic leaders also select the next generation of leaders to ensure that the organization will continue to have strategic leadership in the long term (Boal & Hooijberg, 2000).

Strategic Leadership Versus Leadership

In Chapter 1 of this casebook, leadership was defined as the process of influencing others in order to accomplish a goal. The focus was on the relationship between the leader and follower in a group context and on the process of leading in order to achieve a goal. So how is strategic leadership different from leadership? The main difference is that leadership can be accomplished at any level of the organization and can have an impact on different types of organizational goals, such as increasing the sales of a particular product line or reducing the turnover of employees.

Strategic leadership, on the other hand, is mainly concerned with, but not necessarily restricted to, the higher levels of the organization, given that executives are in a unique position to influence the direction and vision of the organization (Finkelstein, Hambrick, & Cannella, 2009). Strategic leadership has an impact on organization-wide outcomes, such as the financial performance of a small manufacturing company or the strategic change of a large multinational company. The difference can also be thought of as leadership "in" organizations versus leadership "of" organizations (Boal & Hooijberg, 2001). The leadership approaches discussed throughout this book are mainly concerned with how leaders affect followers "in" the organization, whereas strategic leadership is primarily concerned with the leadership "of" organization by top managers. But as we saw earlier, leaders at all levels of the organization can have an impact on organizational performance. The focus of strategic leadership is often on top-level executives such as CEOs because they tend to have more power and are given responsibility for the overall performance of the firm. They are also held accountable by shareholders for the success of the firm, and poor performance can lead to their dismissal.

Positional Versus Behavioral

In contrast to some of the other theories within the realm of leadership, such as the trait approach and the skills approach, the strategic leadership perspective is not as well developed. Furthermore, there is a lack of agreement regarding what strategic leadership is. As we have seen, strategic leadership has come to have several different, but often complementary, meanings. Some (e.g., Finkelstein, Hambrick, & Cannella, 2009) view it as having to do with one's position in a company, while others (e.g., Ireland & Hitt, 1999) view it as a set of behaviors that lead to superior performance.

The positional view argues that anyone holding the position of CEO or another top executive position is a strategic leader because of his or her decision-making power and level of responsibility. This perspective looks at the differences in psychological characteristics of strategic leaders to examine how these differences affect their organizations (Finkelstein & Hambrick, 1996). Others view strategic leadership as a set of activities that leaders must perform if they are to enhance organizational performance. For example, strategic leaders are those who sustain an effective corporate culture (Ireland & Hitt, 1999). A related perspective (Rowe, 2001) on strategic leadership views it as a leadership style that individuals may possess at any level of the organization. Rowe (2001) argues that organizations that have CEOs who are strategic leaders will create more value than those who have visionary or managerial leaders.

As we saw in the definitions above, there is no consensus on exactly what strategic leadership is, but certain themes do emerge. For instance, most of the definitions or conceptualizations of strategic leadership mention the importance of studying CEOs and other top managers to better understand why some firms outperform others. Whether it is viewed as a style of leadership, a set of activities, or a broad area of study, strategic leadership is viewed by many as critical to firm success, especially given our complex, global business environment.

Several themes emerge in the literature concerning what strategic leaders do to increase firm performance. They look after both the short-term operational side of their organization and the long-term directional aspects, such as defining the firm's purpose (Phillips & Hunt, 1992; Rowe, 2001). Strategic leaders select and develop other organizational members to ensure that these successful strategic leader abilities will exist throughout the organization, not just at the top. They influence others by behaving ethically and transparently. Strategic leaders who have overall responsibility for the firm (such as a CEO) articulate a vision that will provide the organization's members with meaning and guidance. They are also in a position to influence external constituents, such as suppliers, unions, and government agencies. Strategic leaders who incorporate these important activities can help ensure the future competitiveness of the firm.

References

Boal, K. B., & Hooijberg, R. (2001). Strategic leadership research: Moving on. *Leadership Quarterly, 11,* 515–549.

Daft, R. L. (2005). *The leadership experience* (3rd ed.). Mason, OH: Thomson, South-Western.

Finkelstein, S., & Hambrick, D. C. (1996). *Strategic leadership: Top executives and their effects on organizations.* St. Paul, MN: West.

Finkelstein, S., Hambrick, D. C., & Cannella, A. A., Jr. (2009). *Strategic leadership: Theory and research on executives, top management teams, and boards.* New York: Oxford University Press.

Goldsmith, M., Greenberg, C. L., Robertson, A., & Hu-Chan, M. (2003). *Global leadership: The next generation.* Upper Saddle River, NJ: Financial Times Prentice Hall.

Hosmer, L. T. (1982). The importance of strategic leadership. *Journal of Business Strategy, 3,* 47–57.

House, R. J., & Aditya, R. N. (1997). The social scientific study of leadership: Quo vadis? *Journal of Management, 2*(23), 409–473.

Ireland, R. D., & Hitt, M. A. (1999). Achieving and maintaining strategic competitiveness in the 21st century: The role of strategic leadership. *Academy of Management Executive, 13,* 43–57.

Phillips, R. L., & Hunt, J. G. (1992). *Strategic leadership: A multi-organizational-level perspective.* London: Quorum Books.

Rowe, W. G. (2001). Creating wealth in organizations: The role of strategic leadership. *Academy of Management Executive, 15,* 81–94.

Shrivastava, P., & Nachman, S. A. (1989). Strategic leadership patterns. *Strategic Management Journal, 10,* 51–66.

The Cases

Strategic Leadership at Coca-Cola: The Real Thing

Muhtar Kent had just been promoted to the CEO position in Coca-Cola. He was reflecting upon the past leadership of the company, in particular the success that Coca-Cola enjoyed during Robert Goizueta's leadership. The CEOs that had followed Goizueta were not able to have as positive an impact on the stock value. When his promotion was announced, Kent mentioned that he did not have immediate plans to change any management roles but that some fine-tuning might be necessary.

Compassion Canada

Compassion Canada is a nonprofit ministry focusing on the holistic development of poor children in developing countries. Over the past 10 years, the organization has only doubled its sponsorships. The chief executive officer must analyze the organization's performance and develop a strategic plan that will enable Compassion Canada to reach its goal of fivefold growth over the next 10 years.

▧ The Reading

You're an Entrepreneur: But Do You Exercise Strategic Leadership?

This brief article describes the differences among the concepts of strategic leadership, visionary leadership, and managerial leadership. In addition, it defines strategic leadership. It describes two entrepreneurs who developed large organizations that created wealth for their owners.

Strategic Leadership at Coca-Cola

The Real Thing

Prepared by Suhaib Riaz under the supervision of W. Glenn Rowe

In recent years, The Coca-Cola Company (Coca-Cola) has seen a much lower rise in its stock price compared with the exceptional 5,800 per cent rise during the 16-year tenure of its well-known chief executive officer (CEO), Robert Goizueta. After Goizueta's untimely death from cancer in October 1997, the company witnessed some tumultuous times, and Goizueta's three immediate successors have not lasted for even half as long as his total tenure (see Exhibit 1). Coca-Cola's CEO succession process was widely regarded as being ad hoc, and

Exhibit 1 CEO Succession Timeline and Stock Price Performance at Coca-Cola

CEO	Period of Tenure	Adjusted Monthly Closing Stock Price at Beginning Month of Tenure*	Adjusted Monthly Closing Stock Price at Ending Month of Tenure*
Robert Goizueta	March 1981 to October 1997	$00.78	$46.23
Douglas Ivester	October 1997 to February 2000	$46.23	$40.54
Douglas Daft	February 2000 to February 2004	$40.54	$44.25
E. Neville Isdell	May 2004 to June 2008	$45.71	$51.61**
Muhtar Kent	July 2008 to present		

* Closing price adjusted for dividends and stock splits.
** As of June 30, 2008.

AUTHOR'S NOTE: This case has been written on the basis of published sources only. Consequently, the interpretation and perspectives presented in this case are not necessarily those of The Coca-Cola Company or any of its employees.

each succession story had its own peculiarities and intrigues. The leadership styles of CEOs at Coca-Cola differed and were often a source of interest in the media and the investment community, where many speculated on the type of leadership that was needed at the helm.

In general, leadership styles can be described as managerial, visionary, or strategic.[1] In this categorization, *managerial leaders* are considered those who are risk averse, reactive and for whom goals are based on the past and on necessities, as opposed to goals arising from desires and dreams. Such leaders relate to people according to their roles in the decision-making process, see themselves as conservators and regulators of the existing order, and involve themselves in situations and contexts characteristic of day-to-day activities. They are concerned with, and are more comfortable in, functional areas of responsibility, ensuring compliance to standard operating procedures. These leaders exhibit linear thinking and are deterministic, i.e., they believe their choices are determined by their internal and external environments.

In contrast, *visionary leaders* are proactive; they shape ideas, and they change the way people think about what is desirable, possible, and necessary. They are given to risk taking. They bring fresh approaches to long-standing problems, concern themselves with ideas, and relate to people in intuitive and empathetic ways. They feel separate from their environment, working in, but not belonging to, their organizations. Such leaders are concerned with ensuring the future of the organization, especially through development and management of people. They engage in multifunctional and integrative tasks, they know less than their functional area experts, utilize non-linear thinking, and believe in strategic choice

i.e., their choices make a difference to their organizations and, through their organizations, to their environment.

Strategic leaders are a synergistic combination of managerial and visionary leadership. They oversee both operating (day-to-day) and strategic (long-term) responsibilities, apply both linear and non-linear thinking, and emphasize ethical behavior and value-based decisions. Strategic leadership is defined as the ability to influence those with whom you work to voluntarily make decisions on a day-to-day basis that enhance both the long-term viability of the organization and the organization's short-term financial stability.[2]

Goizueta Is It![3]

Background

Robert Goizueta was born in Havana, Cuba, in 1931, a scion of a major sugar industry family in Cuba. Goizueta's maternal grandfather immigrated to Cuba from Spain, and, despite a lack of education beyond high school, was able to save enough money to buy a sugar refining business and some real estate during the Cuban depression. His grandfather's focus on the importance of cash made an early impression on Goizueta. After attending a Jesuit school in Cuba, Goizueta moved to a private academy in Connecticut for a year to improve his English. His outstanding performance and connections at the academy helped him gain admission to Yale University, where he majored in chemical engineering with an eye to a possible future in the family business.

When he returned to Cuba, he chose not to join the family business. Instead he answered a blind advertisement in a newspaper that led to a job as an entry-level chemist at

---

[1]W. Glenn Rowe, "Creating Wealth in Organizations: The Role of Strategic Leadership, Academy of Management Executive, February 2001, pp. 81–94.

[2]Ibid.

[3]Slogans used in titles retrieved from The Coca-Cola Company website, Heritage section, http://www.thecoca-colacompany.com/heritage/ourheritage.html on March 22, 2008.

The Coca-Cola Company in Havana. "It was going to be a temporary thing for me, $500 a month—my friends thought I was absolutely crazy," he recalled. However, he soon rose to become chief technical director of five Cuban bottling plants. Then, in 1959, Fid el Castro came to power and Coca-Cola's Cuban operations came under a strong threat of takeover.

The family escaped to Miami, where Goizueta, his wife, three children, and a nursemaid shared a motel room for a month. Fortunately, Goizueta landed a job with Coca-Cola in a new Miami office. His only possessions of value were 100 shares of Coca-Cola stock in a New York bank and US$40. He later recalled the importance of that experience:

> You cannot explain that experience to any person. That was ten times more important than anything else in my life. It was a shocker. All of a sudden you don't own anything, except the stock. One hundred shares! That's the only thing I had. It brings a sense of humility. It builds a feeling of not much regard for material things.[4]

After working in the Miami office, he worked as a chemist in the Bahamas for Coca-Cola's Caribbean region and later moved back to headquarters in Atlanta, Georgia. At age 35, he was promoted to vice-president, Technical Research and Development, the youngest person to hold this position. He was then promoted to head the Legal and External Affairs department in 1975 and became vice chairman in 1979.

Goizueta as CEO of Coca-Cola

Robert Woodruff, widely regarded as Coke's main power broker because he revitalized the company after taking over as CEO in 1923 and served in that position for decades, befriended Goizueta. Aided by a close relationship with Robert Woodruff, Goizueta moved up through the technical operations and became president in 1980 after J. Lucian Smith's resignation. When the chairman, J. Paul Austin retired in 1981, Goizueta became chairman and CEO. At the time, the transition was seen as messy, because Woodruff (despite being retired) used his position as the company's 90-year-old patriarch to overrule Austin's choice for successor, Donald R. Keough. Woodruff's pick, the chemical engineer from Cuba, was regarded as the darkest horse in the succession process. However, Woodruff and others on the board saw Goizueta as the person needed to introduce change and improve performance.

Goizueta generously asked Keough to be his chief operating officer (COO) and president, sending the broader message that

> The day of the one-man band is gone. It would be a crime for me to try to lead the bottlers the way Don Keough can. I would look like a phony. . . . My job is to pick the people, then give them the responsibility and authority to get the job done.

Goizueta created a two-page, double-spaced document, "The Job of the Chief Executive Officer," which delineated what he could and couldn't delegate.[5] For 12 years, Goizueta and Keough complemented each other. Goizueta was known as the business philosopher, whereas Keough did more of the footwork—traveling to bottlers, meeting customers and ensuring overall operations were in shape.[6]

Goizueta stated that he had viewed Coca-Cola as having become "too conservative" and revealed his desire for major changes: "It took us a little bit longer to change than it should

---

[4]Betsy Morris, "Roberto Goizueta and Jack Welch: The Wealth Builders," *Fortune*, December 11, 1995, p. 80–94.

[5]Betsy Morris, "Roberto Goizueta and Jack Welch: The Wealth Builders," *Fortune*, December 11, 1995, pp. 80–94.

[6]Betsy Morris, "The Real Story," *Fortune*, May 31, 2004, pp. 84–98.

have. The world was changing, and we were not changing with the world." At a retreat for company executives, he unveiled a "Strategy for the 80's" and emphasized that "We're going to take risks."[7]

When Goizueta took over, the company was in multiple businesses: soft drinks, wine, coffee, tea, plastics, shrimp farming, orange groves, steam generators, industrial boilers, desalting plants, and industrial water treatment. Goizueta subjected each business to a standard financial formula: Is our return on capital greater than our cost of capital? He then divested non-core businesses that did not measure up until the only business left by the late 1980s was the selling of bottled carbonated soft drinks (CSDs)—predominantly Coca-Cola and minor quantities of Sprite and Tab (a diet soft drink)—and one non-CSD beverage (i.e., Minute Maid). He stated his rule of investment: "You borrow money at a certain rate and invest it at a higher rate and pocket the difference. It's simple." He was a pioneer in promoting the idea of economic profit (i.e. after-tax operating profits in excess of capital costs) and wrote to Wall Street analysts personally about it. Today, the concept has gained ground as economic value added (EVA), a well-regarded tool for increasing shareholder wealth.

Goizueta's style was less hands-on and more intellectual. Despite the fact that Coca-Cola earned up to 80 per cent of its profits abroad, Goizueta visited only about a half-dozen countries a year and remained most comfortable defining "the character of the company" from his office at Coca-Cola's headquarters. Goizueta used rewards based on economic profit targets to motivate his management team to perform.[8] A contemporary CEO characterized Goizueta's style in the following manner: "A lot of executives can intellectualize the process, but [Goizueta] can follow through."[9]

Although Coca-Cola had never borrowed money, under Goizueta, it borrowed billions and bought out independent bottlers around the world to upgrade its own distribution systems. With Douglas Ivester as chief financial officer (CFO), the "49 per cent solution" was devised. This involved Coca-Cola buying out U.S. bottlers that were not doing well and combining them with its own bottling network. The new creation was called Coca-Cola Enterprises (CCE) and was spun off to the public, with Coca-Cola retaining a strategic 49 per cent of the stock. This arrangement helped Coca-Cola reduce its debt and divest itself of a low-return, capital intensive business.[10]

Looking back at that time, Goizueta later commented during an interview:

> We really lost focus on who our customer was. We felt our customer was the bottler as opposed to McDonald's and Wal-Mart. So consequently, we were being either cheerleaders or critics of our bottlers. But hands off; we didn't have anything to do with it—that was their job. I think the worst thing we ever had to do was to establish a sense of direction . . . so that they know where they're going. Then you can let them have a lot of freedom.[11]

During this same interview, Goizueta emphasized the need for leaders to establish a

[7]"Coke CEO Roberto C. Goizueta Dies at 65," *CNN Interactive News*, October 18, 1997, http://www.cnn.com/US/9710/18/goizueta.obit.9am, retrieved April 18, 2008.

[8]Patricia Sellers, "Where Coke Goes from Here," *Fortune*, October 13, 1997, pp. 88–91.

[9]Betsy Morris, "Roberto Goizueta and Jack Welch: The Wealth Builders," *Fortune*, December 11, 1995, pp. 80–94.

[10]Patricia Sellers, "How Coke Is Kicking Pepsi's Can," *Fortune*, October 28, 1996, pp. 70–84.

[11]Betsy Morris, "Roberto Goizueta and Jack Welch: The Wealth Builders," *Fortune*, December 11, 1995, pp. 80–94.

sense of direction, so people both knew where they are going and had a lot of freedom to get there. He added that if people did not know where they were going, you do not want them to get there too fast. Finally, he encouraged people to create what can be, as opposed to what is.

Goizueta emphasized the importance of relationships. He enticed the Cisneroses (Pepsi's most venerable bottlers in Venezuela) away from Pepsi and signed the deal in the presence of three generations of the Cisneroses at Coca-Cola headquarters. "It was a very family-like gathering, to symbolize that this was to be a long-term relationship," Gustavo Cisneros recalled. "This is a people-relations business," Goizueta later said.[12]

These moves were also in line with Goizueta's overall approach of developing senior managers' intimate strategic knowledge of, and engagement in, the core business. Whereas CCE and other bottlers carried out the operational details on the ground, Goizueta focused his own role and that of other senior managers on brand building, making deals, and selling concentrate. Coca-Cola did not rotate its successful managers through jobs rapidly, in contrast to its main rival Pepsi. "If you do that, you can never see how good the people really are," Goizueta explained.

Goizueta encouraged calculated risk-taking, epitomized by his decision to put the Coca-Cola trademark on a new product, Diet Coke, in 1982, which turned into the most successful product launch of the 1980s. Traditionally, the company had never put the Coca-Cola trademark on other products. Goizueta invested outside the core business only on one occasion, to buy Columbia Pictures in 1982, after it went bust. He later sold it to Sony in 1989 for a large profit. He stated that this investment was not to hedge

his bets, but to pile up earnings until he could sort out issues with the soft drinks business.

The new moves included launching New Coke. Based on a sweeter formula, it was a departure from the traditional Coke formula and was developed to counter Pepsi, which was doing better on taste tests. In Goizueta's words, the launch of New Coke was "the boldest single marketing move in the history of the consumer goods business." However, when New Coke bombed in 1985 and loyal customers demanded a return of the old formula, the old Coke was re-launched as "Classic Coke," and over time "New Coke" was allowed to die out. Coca-Cola learned a valuable lesson: its brand and marketing, not the taste of the sugar water, was its asset, and Coca-Cola marketing was consequently overhauled. "I realized what I should have before," he recalled. "That this was a most unique company with a most unique product. We have a product that people have an unusual attachment to. I had never felt so bullish about it."[13]

Goizueta encouraged speedier decision-making and kept encouraging risk-taking. At a worldwide gathering of Coca-Cola's quality assurance staff, in response to a concern about all the changes taking place, Goizueta said:

> Don't wrap the flag of Coca-Cola around you to prevent change from taking place. It is extremely important that you show some insensitivity to your past in order to show the proper respect for the future.[14]

During Goizueta's reign, the company expanded both domestically and internationally, backed by the new slogan, "Coke Is It!" Goizueta turned Coca-Cola around financially, organizationally and culturally, making it America's most admired company, against all

[12]Patricia Sellers, "How Coke Is Kicking Pepsi's Can," *Fortune*, October 28, 1996, pp. 70–84.

[13]Ibid.

[14]Ibid.

expectations. Coca-Cola's stock price increased 5829 percent during Goizueta's tenure (see Exhibits 1 and 2). Its market value grew 34 times, from $4.3 billion to $147 billion during Goizueta's 16-year tenure. In addition, in a *Fortune* story on Goizueta in October, 1997 describing "The Goizueta Effect" it was reported that revenues had increased from $4.8 billion to $18.5 billion, net income from $0.5 billion to $3.5 billion, and return on equity from 20 per cent to 60 per cent from 1981 to 1996 (see Exhibit 3).[15]

When asked what he looked for in a future successor, Goizueta agreed with his fellow interviewee, Jack Welch, General Electric's CEO, that his successor needed incredible energy, the ability to excite others, a defined vision, the capacity to find change fun, and the facility to be as comfortable in New Delhi as in Denver. Goizueta added that while energy is the number-one quality, two other qualities were also important—integrity and the intellectual courage to take a risk, a leap of faith, whether the leap was big or small.

Roberto Goizueta died of cancer at the age of 65 in October 1997. The 100 shares he had when he arrived in Miami were worth more than $3 million. He was a billionaire by 1997 and his belief in Coca-Cola was evidenced by the fact that in 1995 more than 99 per cent of his personal wealth was tied up in Coca-Cola stock.[16] He was replaced by heir apparent

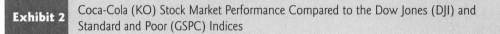

| **Exhibit 2** | Coca-Cola (KO) Stock Market Performance Compared to the Dow Jones (DJI) and Standard and Poor (GSPC) Indices |

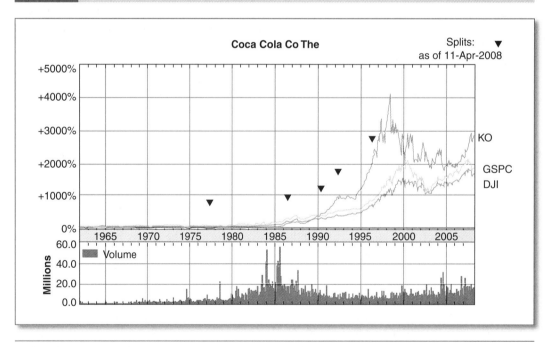

SOURCE: Yahoo Finance website, accessed April 11, 2008. Copyright © Yahoo! Inc. 2008. Reproduced with permission of Yahoo! Inc. YAHOO! and the YAHOO! logo are trademarks of Yahoo! Inc.

[15]Patricia Sellers, "Where Coke Goes from Here," *Fortune*, October 13, 1997, pp. 88–91.

[16]Patricia Sellers, "Where Coke Goes from Here," *Fortune*, October 13, 1997, pp. 88–91; Betsy Morris, "Roberto Goizueta and Jack Welch: The Wealth Builders," *Fortune*, December 11, 1995, pp. 80–94.

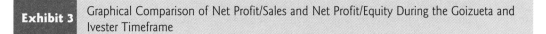

Exhibit 3 Graphical Comparison of Net Profit/Sales and Net Profit/Equity During the Goizueta and Ivester Timeframe

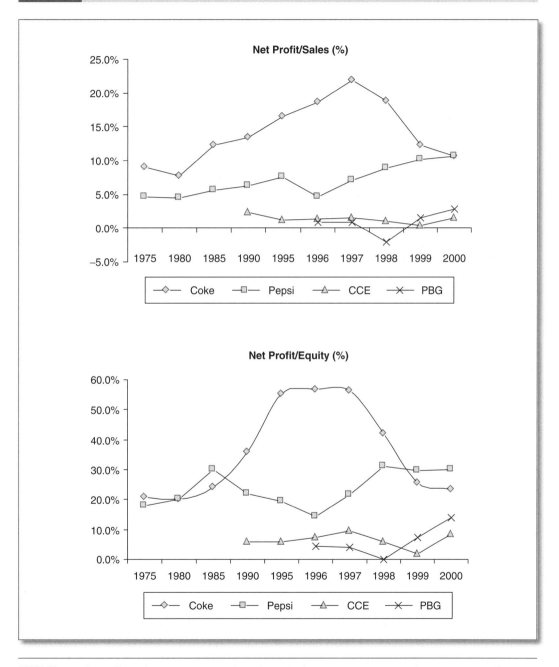

SOURCE: David B. Yoffie, *Cola Wars Continue: Coke and Pepsi in the Twenty-First Century*, July 30, 2002, Harvard Business School, Exhibit 4, pp. 19.

NOTE: CCE: Coca-Cola enterprise; PBG: Pepsi Bottling Group.

Douglas Ivester. Some said that Goizueta's strategic planning showed in his leaving behind a solid management team. Herbert Allen, a director at Coca-Cola since 1982 stated, "Roberto has filled in behind him so well. He established at least four people who can run the company . . . and behind them are ten more people who could fill their jobs."

✉ Always Douglas Ivester

Background

In a few ways, Ivester was comparable to Goizueta. He had his own rags-to-riches story and was regarded as a dark horse who came from corporate backwaters. Ivester was the only child of conservative Southern Baptist factory workers raised with discipline and rigidity in the Georgia mill village of New Holland, 60 miles north of Atlanta. He described his parents as "strong savers, [with] very strong religious values," partly due to their being children of the Depression. They had very high expectations of him. When he got an A in school, his father would remark, "They give A-pluses, don't they?" As a child, Ivester worked after school doing odd jobs. He hardly had time for any extra-curricular activities or team sports.

"One thing I learned in Gainesville was to never let my memories be greater than my dreams," Ivester recalled. He graduated from the University of Georgia with an accounting major and worked as an accountant at Ernst & Whinney. Ivester headed the audit team for Coca-Cola and was recruited by Coca-Cola as assistant controller in 1979. Six years later, CEO Goizueta, impressed with Ivester's solutions to complex financial problems that helped maximize returns on investment, made him CFO.[17]

As CFO, Ivester was the brains behind getting Coca-Cola's low-return bottling operations and its debt off the company's books. Under Goizueta's leadership, Ivester helped create a separate bottling company, Coca-Cola Enterprises (CCE), and spun it off to shareholders while keeping 49 per cent equity for Coca-Cola to control the business. Goizueta groomed Ivester and provided opportunities for varied experiences in marketing and international operations. Ivester's first operations job was as president of Coca-Cola's European operations in mid-1989. When the Berlin Wall came down later that year, Ivester cut deals with bottling plants across Eastern Europe, and his opportunism saw Coca-Cola seizing control of the region that had long been dominated by Pepsi.

As president of Coca-Cola in 1990, Ivester visited overseas markets and sent out a new message. Instead of setting goals in the traditional style, he asked executives to think about what kind of growth would be possible in a market, and to figure out how to knock down the barriers to attain that growth. He also stated that, like Goizueta, he would remain focused on one business—non-alcoholic beverages. During his time as president of Coca-Cola USA, he spent every Saturday morning for a year learning marketing from Sergio Zyman, who went on to become Coca-Cola's global marketing boss. He added the position of chief learning officer and encouraged its first incumbent, Judith A. Rosenblum, to turn the company into "a learning organization." His goal was to capture all of the growth in Coca-Cola's markets.

Upon Goizueta's unexpected death due to cancer in 1997, Doug Ivester was the heir apparent and became CEO. However, it was rumored that his appointment was not supported by Don Keough.[18]

Douglas Ivester as CEO of Coca-Cola

As CEO, Ivester made some important changes in positions. His competitor for the CEO

---

[17]Patricia Sellers, "Where Coke Goes from Here," *Fortune*, October 13, 1997, pp. 88–91.

[18]Betsy Morris, "The Real Story," *Fortune*, May 31, 2004, pp. 84–98.

position, E. Neville Isdell, was moved to head a bottler in Britain. Carl Ware, a senior vice-president was demoted. Don Keough, who, after his retirement, had continued attending Coca-Cola board meetings as Goizueta's consultant, lost his consulting contract and his place at the boardroom table.

Ivester's personality, like Goizueta's, was seen as reserved on the surface. Yet, despite wide recognition for being brilliant, Ivester seemed to lack some of Goizueta's characteristics. Ivester was known for an obsession with a rational and orderly way of operating. He was considered arrogant and insecure, blind to his own weaknesses and not forthcoming in soliciting advice. He placed less emphasis on Goizueta's tradition of having almost daily chats with directors. During his reign, Coca-Cola alienated European regulators and several executives at major customers, such as Disney and Wal-Mart. Some major bottlers, including Coca-Cola Enterprises, were also alienated. In time, he became more and more obsessed with controlling the most minor details of every operation. To make matters worse, the Asian currency crisis occurred during his reign and affected Coca-Cola's business. The U.S. dollar, which had remained weak for a long time and had contributed to Coca-Cola's earnings, strengthened during Ivester's tenure.[19]

As CEO, continuing on in his earlier approach, Douglas Ivester was known for working seven days a week and nearly all the time. On visiting Shanghai as CEO, he was known to have walked out on the streets while the "World of Coca-Cola" traveling multimedia exhibit was going on. Ivester walked into little stores and asked why Coke was not prominently displayed on shelves and noted where fountain machines were turned off. He was known to have done similar walks as

president of Coca-Cola USA, going from store to store and even identifying the hairdressing salons and laundromats where Coke couldn't be found. On one Saturday morning, he drove from Atlanta to Rome, Georgia, with a video crew to identify missed opportunities along the way.[20] He encouraged people to avoid doing things sequentially and pushed for "viral growth." As an example, he suggested if you opened offices in China, not to open them one at a time but to have each new office assist in opening several more.[21]

Ivester was known to be a CEO who communicated with people at all levels and ignored hierarchy. He wanted employees to think of themselves as knowledge workers, to think of their office as the information they carried with them, supported by technology that would allow them to work anywhere. With Ivester, business planning was not done annually, but became an ongoing discussion involving top executives. Ivester focused on getting lots of information, aided by technology, which he believed was necessary for real-time decision making. Although past CEOs had focused on letting executives find their own solutions, Ivester involve himself in finding solutions for them. Ivester explained his involvement by stating that in such a fast and complicated world, a CEO could not run a business by sitting in an office. To many, this approach sounded like micromanaging.[22]

Jack Stahl, senior vice-president and president of Coca-Cola's North America group, reported that he often got six or seven notes a day from Ivester. And Ivester expected prompt replies to all his communications, including his voice mails. Ivester went without a number-two person for about a year, working instead with a flat structure that had 14 senior vice-presidents, including six operating heads,

[19]Ibid.

[20]Betsy Morris, "Doug Is It," *Fortune*, May 25, 1998, pp. 71–84.

[21]Ibid.

[22]Ibid.

reporting to him directly. Ivester took less naturally to the ceremonial nature of his job, remarking to the mayor of Shanghai, "Nice place you have here," on visiting the mayor's opulent meeting room. While he delivered a message to all officials about helping China, he was known to enjoy his time most with his troops in the trenches.[23]

Ivester's thirst for information was rarely satiated and he continued delving into every little detail of the company's worldwide operations. When an executive from Coca-Cola's biggest Mexican bottler talked about tens of thousands of mom-and-pop stores, Ivester jumped in and asked, "So which are they—moms or pops?" The bottler's COO could only muster a weak response, "I think it's more moms than pops, Doug, but I'm not sure."[24]

The downturn in overseas markets, where Coca-Cola derived about three-quarters of its profits, was met head on as an opportunity to buy bottlers, distribution, and rival brands at bargain prices. Ivester was betting that the investments would help fuel growth in the future. Whereas Goizueta had handled international operations from a distance, Ivester worked 14-hour days and stayed in contact with executives worldwide through email, voicemail, and pagers even as the business grew in size and complexity around the world.

Under Ivester, the era of exclusive contracts in the soft drink industry became very aggressive. Coca-Cola and Pepsi pursued such contracts not only in restaurant chains but in other locations, such as schools and convenience stores. A marketing consultant for Cadbury Schweppes remarked, "Coke is the No. 1 icon in the world; it has to be a good corporate citizen. They are not in a situation where they can create shareholder value by being a bully."

Whereas Goizueta had focused on stockholders, Ivester spent his energies on customers, "If you focus on the customer, the business will prosper, and if the business prospers, the stock will eventually be priced right."[25] However, when dozens of Belgian school children fell sick after drinking Coca-Cola products, Ivester maintained silence for a week before going to Belgium to apologize. Coca-Cola ultimately recalled 65 million cans due to this incident. When he failed to promote Carl Ware, senior vice-president for African operations and Coca-Cola's top African-American executive, the doors opened for four past and current employees to sue Coca-Cola for racial discrimination.

Ivester took much of the credit for improvements in the bottler system, including the creation of CCE and technological improvements across the company. Some of these claims served to isolate Don Keough, Goizueta's erstwhile president and COO, who was also connected to two powerful Coca-Cola board members, Herbert Allen and Warren Buffet. Keough became the person all constituents, including customers, bottlers and employees, gradually started complaining to.[26]

Commenting on his earlier successes under Goizueta, Ivester had stated, "I look at the business like a chessboard. You always need to be seeing three, four, five moves ahead. Otherwise, your first move can prove fatal." His methodical approach extended to all areas, "I learned that marketing is not a black box," he stated, "Marketing can be even more logical than finance. If you ask enough questions and listen closely, you find that people are very logical."[27] He was also reported to have once said, "I know how all the levers work, and I could generate so much cash I could make

[23]Ibid.

[24]"Man on the Spot," *BusinessWeek*, May 3, 1999, pp. 142–151.

[25]Ibid.

[26]Betsy Morris, "The Real Story," *Fortune*, May 31, 2004, pp. 84–98.

[27]Patricia Sellers, "How Coke Is Kicking Pepsi's Can," *Fortune*, October 28, 1996, pp. 70–84.

everybody's head spin." However, after Ivester's more than two years as CEO, Coca-Cola's market value remained stuck at $148 billion compared with the $147 billion market value when Goizueta had left the helm.[28]

In early December 1999, Ivester flew to Chicago for a regular meeting with McDonald's executives and during the same trip also had a private meeting with Coca-Cola's two most powerful directors, Warren Buffet and Herbert Allen. The two directors informed Ivester that they had lost faith in his leadership, and it was time for a change. Don Keough, who had been Goizueta's number-two person for 12 years as COO and president was said to have played a role in this meeting. Upon retirement in 1993, Keough had remained involved in Coca-Cola as a consultant and later rejoined as a director when Coca-Cola abolished its 74-year age limit for board membership. Keough was chairman at Allen & Co., Herbert Allen's small investment firm housed in Coca-Cola's building in New York.

At only age 52 and after just more than two years as the chairman and CEO, Ivester was pushed to retire from the position. On returning from the meeting in Chicago, Ivester publicly announced his departure from Coca-Cola, "After extensive reflection and thought, I have concluded that it is time for me to move on to the next stage of my life and, therefore, to put into place an orderly transition for this great company."[29] In reaction to the news, Coca-Cola's share price, which had already lagged the American stock market by 30 per cent over the previous two years, fell 12 per cent in two days. This drop was quite a contrast for investors who had seen the stock

price rise over 5800 per cent during Goizueta's 16-year tenure.[30] During Ivester's tenure the stock price had dropped 12.3 per cent (see Exhibits 1and 2).

Douglas Daft. Enjoy.

Background

The next CEO of Coca-Cola, Douglas Daft, was born in 1943, in Cessnock, New South Wales, Australia. He received a bachelor of arts degree with a major in mathematics from the University of New England in Armidale, New South Wales. He later received a post-graduate degree in administration from the University of New South Wales.

Daft was a first-generation college student, being the first in his family to attend university. He later recalled that the opportunity had led him to develop a passion for lifelong learning about the world and different cultures. In an interview, he mentioned his profound respect for the differences and similarities of people and his experiences of cultural and intellectual diversity across Singapore, Tokyo, and Beijing, which shaped him for leadership roles at Coca-Cola, one of the most international companies in the world.[31]

Daft started at Coca-Cola as a planning officer in the Sydney (Australia) office in 1969. He progressed through the company, holding positions of increasing responsibility, and became vice-president of Coca-Cola Far East Ltd. in 1982. Daft was named president of the North Pacific Division and president of Coca-Cola (Japan) Co., Ltd. in 1988. In 1991, he moved to Coca-Cola's Atlanta headquarters as

---

[28]Betsy Morris and Patricia Sellers, "What Really Happened at Coke—Doug Ivester Was a Demon for Information," *Fortune*, January 10, 2000, pp. 114–116.

[29]"Coke CEO Stepping Down after Difficult Tenure," *CBC News*, December 6, 1999, http://www.cbc.ca/money/story/1999/12/06/coke991206.html, retrieved April 19, 2008.

[30]"New Doug, Old Tricks," *The Economist*, December 11, 1999, p. 55.

[31]Interview with Doug Daft, Institute of International Education, IIENetwork.org http://iienetwork.org/?p=29253, accessed on June 21, 2008.

president of the Pacific Group with responsibilities including the Africa Group, the Middle and Far East Group, and the Schweppes Beverage Division. He was elected president and COO in December 1999.

Douglas Daft as CEO of Coca-Cola

Daft was preparing for retirement in Australia when he was brought in to replace Ivester. It was said that Daft neither aspired to, nor was groomed for, the CEO job and was "an accidental CEO."[32] Daft had spent most of his 30 years with the company in Asia, and had succeeded as president of Coca-Cola in Japan, one of the company's most difficult and largest markets outside the United States.

Daft's personality was described as low-key, unassuming, media-shy, and not communication friendly. He was known for a consensus-driven style and for avoiding conflict. He began by making changes that were seen as culturally new, such as removing flags that had traditionally flown at Atlanta headquarters: the American flag, the Georgia flag, the Coca-Cola flag, and a flag to honor the visitor of the day, generally a bottler or customer. He called upon a feng shui consultant to make interior decoration changes and to rearrange telephones so that the cords would not coil in the wrong direction. Life-sized ceramic roosters were installed in the offices of Daft and two senior executives.[33]

In his first few weeks, Daft started the process of cutting 5,200 jobs to reduce costs. However these cuts were not seen as steering the company in a clear strategic direction. Whereas Ivester's mantra had been "Think global—act local," Daft's vision leaned more toward "Think local—act local." This mindset reflected his experience away from headquarters where he had developed the idea that bureaucracy at headquarters was a problem. Daft challenged Coca-Cola's matrix system, which, created and nurtured by Goizueta, had ensured that the finance, marketing, technical, law and quality control departments at headquarters networked with and controlled the corresponding departments in other countries. Daft's approach was to get rid of corporate bureaucracy and give more decision-making power to the field managers.

Under Daft's tenure, Don Keough's advice and attendance at board meetings was again welcomed. Under Daft's leadership and Keough's approval, several key executives who had served under Ivester were ousted. Turnover among senior managers during Daft's tenure was severe. In just more than four years, Coca-Cola had two new marketing heads, two new European operations heads and new management in the company's human resources departments and in the North America, Asia and Latin America divisions.[34]

Daft also built the company's forays into the fast-growing area of non-carbonated drinks, including bottled water and juices,[35] exemplified by Daft's attempts to buy Quaker Oats, maker of Gatorade in 2000. Although Quaker Oats broke off talks with Pepsi and Danone, in the end the Coca-Cola board did not pass the deal. Reportedly, directors Warren Buffet and Peter Ueberroth objected, seeing the exchange of Coca-Cola's 10 per cent stock for Quaker Oats as too risky. A joint venture with Procter & Gamble Co. (P&G) was created to develop synergies between Coca-Cola's Minute Maid juices and distribution prowess with P&G's potato chip and juice brands. Ideas included developing a half-size can of P&G's Pringle's potato chips for distribution through Coca-Cola's machines and other channels. A

---

[32]Patricia Sellers, "Who's in Charge Here?" *Fortune*, December 24, 2001, pp. 76–80, 83, 86.

[33]Betsy Morris, "The Real Story," *Fortune*, May 31, 2004, pp. 84–98.

[34]Ibid.

[35]"Repairing the Coke Machine," *BusinessWeek*, March 19, 2001, p. 86.

similar deal with Nestlé was crafted to develop tea and coffee drinks using Nestlé's research and development labs. Historically, Coca-Cola had not succeeded in using its distribution and marketing to develop a presence in the high-margin premium beverage market dominated by Snapple, AriZona, SoBe and Gatorade.

These changes epitomized Daft's approach as a passionate, idea-a-minute manager, building upon intuitions from his Asia-Pacific experience. His approach contrasted sharply with Ivester's numbers-based accountant's approach to decision making. At a retreat in San Francisco, Daft asked for new ideas from two dozen Coca-Cola executives and, on the spot, funded four of the ideas with $250,000 each. Under Daft's tenure, scientists and marketers united to build new products ranging from calcium-fortified waters to vitamin-enriched drinks bearing Disney characters' names.

Coca-Cola's advertising was also overhauled, because the "Always" campaign had "lost people, lost humanity and become clinical," according to Coca-Cola's Marketing Director, Stephen C. Jones. In a new move, Coca-Cola began to allow bottlers to customize promotions to local events. Although Ivester had opposed tie-ins with movies, Daft made a deal with Warner Bros. Entertainment Inc. to co-market movies such as the *Harry Potter* series around the world.[36]

Daft announced another major step in his restructuring when he let go president and COO, Jack L. Stahl. Steve Heyer, formerly president and COO at Turner Broadcasting, was brought in as the new president. Subsequently, Daft used this time to be out in the field to improve relations with bottlers. However, Daft remained known for making quick decisions and sometimes being unsure about them later. Coca-Cola's bottlers in Colombia had faced violence, and Daft announced at an awards dinner in Washington that he would have

general counsel Deval Patrick investigate. However, the decision was abruptly reversed four months later and an announcement about Patrick's resignation leaked out. At an annual meeting, stockholders were distributed leaflets by demonstrators who shouted, "Coca-Cola, killer Cola, toxic Cola, racist Cola." None of the directors faced the crowd, and Daft, seemingly losing control, unwittingly urged a child questioner to "Drink Coke, Sam," later amending the line by saying "That is, if your parents let you."[37]

At the same meeting, Keough commented on Coca-Cola's succession plan saying that the company would find the best candidate for the job. A very public search was launched, which included talks with Jim Kilts, CEO of Gillette, and Jack Welch, the retired CEO of GE. During Daft's tenure as CEO, Coke's stock price increased 9.15 per cent (see Exhibits 1 and 2).

The Isdell Side of Life

Background

Coca-Cola's next CEO, Edward Neville Isdell, was born in Downpatrick, Northern Ireland, in 1943. He moved to Zambia in childhood and later completed a bachelor's degree in social science at the University of Capetown, South Africa. In 1966, Isdell joined Coca-Cola through the local bottling company in Zambia. Moving up on the bottling side of operations, in 1972 he became general manager of the Johannesburg bottler, the largest Coca-Cola bottler in Africa. In 1980, he became the regional manager for Australia, and the following year became the president of the bottling joint venture between Coca-Cola and San Miguel Corporation in the Philippines. Isdell was subsequently credited with turning around and renewing the entire Coca-Cola business in the Philippines.

[36]Ibid.

[37]Betsy Morris, "The Real Story," *Fortune*, May 31, 2004, pp. 84–98.

Isdell's international career continued with a stint in Germany, starting in 1985 as president of the company's Central European division. He moved up the ranks of the company in 1989, when he was elected senior vice president, and concurrently became president of the Northeast Europe/Africa Group (later to become the Northeast Europe/Middle East group in 1992). During this phase, Isdell oversaw the company's expansion into new markets, such as India, Middle East, Eastern Europe and the Soviet Union. He became president of the Greater Europe Group in 1995.

Isdell subsequently moved to Great Britain in 1998 as CEO of Coca-Cola Beverages Plc in Great Britain. Under his watch, that company merged with Hellenic Bottling and resulted in the largest Coca-Cola bottler of that time, Coca-Cola Hellenic Bottling Company (HBC). He left Coca-Cola in 2001 to form his own investment company in Barbados.[38]

Isdell as CEO of Coca-Cola

Doug Daft's retirement announcement in February 2004 was followed by two months of speculation regarding his successor. Some wondered whether an outsider such as Gillette's president and CEO, James M. Kilts, might be the likely candidate. Instead, E. Neville Isdell was named the new chairman and CEO. Interestingly, Isdell had been passed over for the top job in 1997 (in favor of Douglas Ivester), despite having been Keough's preference at the time.

On accepting the position, Isdell said:

I am both proud and humbled to be given the opportunity to help write the next chapter in this illustrious company's history. I appreciate the importance of this position and the trust placed in me by the board of directors. We are all grateful to Doug Daft for his enormous contributions and look forward to building upon the tremendous foundation he and his team have built. I am excited to get started and help shape our future.[39]

During Isdell's CEO tenure, Coca-Cola's profits rose steadily, in particular from international operations. Right at the start, Isdell had laid out his plans, based on his belief in significant future growth for the Coca-Cola brand. Some growth was expected to come from new markets, such as China and India, while further growth was still possible in the United States and Europe. Keough let his confidence in Isdell be known, mentioning that it was the first time in 119 years that the company would have a CEO who had worked on both sides of the system, referring to Isdell's experience of being involved both as a bottler and concentrate person and his experience on working on five continents.[40] Under Isdell's leadership Coke's stock price increased 12.9 percent. Overall, the three CEOs who had served after Goizueta's untimely death in 1997 had increased Coke's stock price 11.6 per cent.

✂ Epilogue

In December 2007, Isdell announced that he would step down from the CEO position in July 2008 to be replaced by Muhtar Kent, the company's COO. However, Isdell would remain chairman of the board until the company's annual meeting in 2009, splitting the position of CEO and chairman at Coca-Cola for the first time. To questions on why Isdell chose this time to announce his departure, he

---

[38]The Coca-Cola Company website, http://www.thecoca-colacompany.com/ourcompany/board.html, accessed February 15, 2008.

[39]The Coca-Cola Co. 8-K report filed with SEC on 5/5/04. http://www.secinfo.com/dkrf.12f.d.htm, accessed on June 21, 2008.

[40]Betsy Morris, "The Real Story," *Fortune*, May 31, 2004, pp. 84–98.

said, "Because it's the right time. I've been working on succession since Day 1". Although a national search had been launched when Doug Daft left, there would be no doubt as to who the next CEO would be this time.

Commenting on the news, John Sicher, a beverage industry expert remarked, "Kent understands the company and the system literally as well as anybody in the world and better than most." Deutsche Bank analyst Marc Greenberg said, "Kent has played a formative role in shaping the current course—'steady as she goes' is likely the mantra." In the position of COO, Kent saw major strategic initiatives undertaken, such as the $4.1 billion acquisition of glacéau in 2007, strengthening Coca-Cola's position with new brands, such as vitaminwater.

At the time of this announcement, Kent mentioned that he had no immediate plans to change any leadership roles but that some scope was available for fine-tuning management. He pointed out that he knew he faced challenges: "We have confidence the United States has growth left in it," he said. Regarding the bottling issues, he added, "We were at each other's throats with our bottlers a year ago—we are aligned now."[41]

As the plane headed toward Atlanta and Coca-Cola's corporate headquarters, Kent looked out at the Atlantic ocean and thought about the company's previous illustrious leaders, their times and strategies, and wondered how he would take charge and lead the company into the future.

Compassion Canada

Prepared by Hari Bapuji under the supervision of Glenn Rowe

Barry Slauenwhite, chief executive officer (CEO) of Compassion Canada, had reason to be happy when he reviewed the figures of sponsorship growth in 2002. Compassion Canada had grown from 18,684 sponsorships in 2001 to over 21,886 in 2002, a growth of 17 per cent against the 11 per cent projected for the year. However, Slauenwhite needed to turn his attention to the target of reaching 100,000 sponsorships by 2013. In the last 10 years, Compassion Canada had only doubled its sponsorships. Now, the goal was to achieve a five fold growth in the same amount of time. He needed a strategic plan that was based on a comprehensive analysis of the competitive landscape and resources and capabilities of Compassion Canada.

Compassion International Incorporated

Compassion Canada was associated with Compassion International Incorporated, a Christian non-profit ministry dedicated to the long-term holistic development of poor children, particularly those in developing nations. Everett Swanson, an American evangelist, established the ministry in 1952 in the basement of his house in Chicago. During the early 1950s, Swanson went to South Korea to preach to soldiers. In Korea, he witnessed the conditions in which many orphaned and abandoned children lived. He was moved by their condition and established the Everett Swanson

Version: (A) 2006-10-13

[41]"Coca-Cola's CEO Isdell to step down," Associated Press, MSNBC, December 6, 2007; http://www.msnbc.msn.com/id/22127700/, accessed June 22, 2008.

Evangelist Association (ESEA). He appealed to American sponsors to help the needy Korean children with their schooling, clothing, food and health care. In his words:

> Christians have a responsibility to share with those in need. Surely our homes are the finest in the world, and our children are well clothed and happy. Our tables are spread with good things, and we enjoy many luxuries. Our babies do not need to cry for food or milk. We ought to thank God for His great goodness to America. But while God is good to us, in Korea there are thousands of boys who walk the street carrying a little tin can or pail, begging for a little morsel of bread. Americans put more in their garbage can every day than Koreans have to eat.

Soon ESEA grew and attracted a large number of supporters who were willing to sponsor the costs of providing food, education and health care to the needy children. In 1963, ESEA changed its name to Compassion International Incorporated. It worked solely in South Korea until it expanded its operations to Indonesia and India in 1968. As of June 2002, its operations spanned over 22 countries in Africa, Asia, the Caribbean, Central America, and South America, helping a total of 350,484 children in these countries with food, shelter, health care, and education. ESEA consisted of eight entities: Compassion International Incorporated, the founding entity in the Compassion International Incorporated (United States), Compassion Canada; TEAR Fund Great Britain (Compassion United Kingdom); Compassion Australia; TEAR Fund New Zealand; SEL France; Compassion Netherlands; and Compassion Italia. A brief sketch of Compassion organization is presented in Exhibit 1.

Compassion Canada

Compassion Canada was established in 1963. It began its operations in the basement of a home in Blenheim, Ontario, and moved to its own office suite in London, Ontario, in 1972, shifting to a bigger office space in 1986. Compassion Canada's activities, as reflected in its mission and purpose, revolved around helping needy children in developing countries in the areas of education, food, health care and overall development.

Mission

In response to the Great Commission, Compassion Canada exists as an advocate for children, to release them from their spiritual, economic, social and physical poverty and enable them to become responsible and fulfilled Christian adults.

Purpose

Assisting children to be:

- Christian in faith and deed
- Responsible members of their family, church and community
- Self-supporting
- Able to maintain their health

In pursuit of its mission and purpose, Compassion Canada found individuals who were willing to sponsor the expenses for children, linked individual sponsors with individual children and helped them maintain that link. Compassion Canada believed that most people cared enough to help needy children, if they could find a dependable and reliable mechanism through which to do so. Compassion Canada aimed to provide that mechanism in an efficient manner so that most of the money collected from the sponsors was spent on the children. In addition, it implemented projects aimed at

| **Exhibit 1** | Schematic Diagram of Compassion Activities |

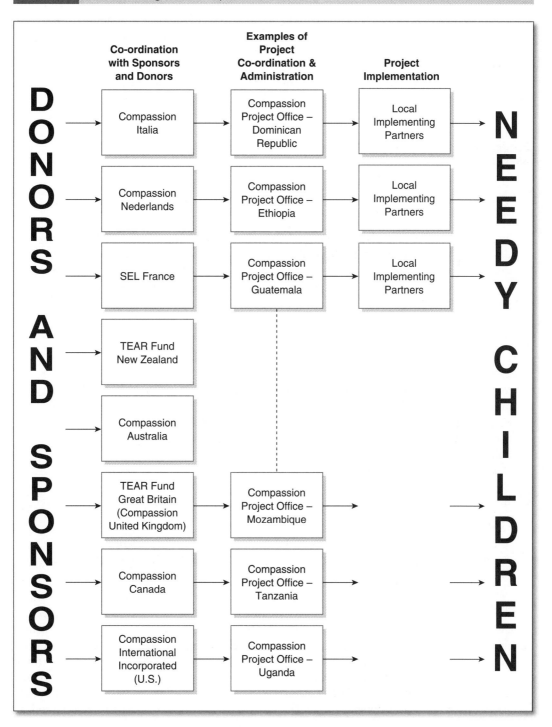

child development through partnerships with local churches and community members who approached Compassion Canada and were approved through a stringent screening process.

"The child is the absolute key to whatever we do," said Slauenwhite. The activities of Compassion Canada aptly reflected that. As mentioned, it found sponsors who would support one or more children. In addition, Compassion Canada found donors who would support larger projects aimed at developing the communities in which the sponsored children lived. A list of current community projects of Compassion Canada is presented in Exhibit 2.

Exhibit 2 Community Project Types

Education
Vocational and Primary Education

These projects focus on skills development for young people. Compassion Canada's primary education efforts are presently related to programs with children that fall outside of standard child development work (e.g., street children). Vocational training involves essential life trade skills for teens in areas such as carpentry, metal-work, hairdressing, tailoring and other clothing pattern work.

Current Projects

Bujora Children's Home Vocational Training Centre—Tanzania
Casa de Plastilina Children's Education—Mexico
Community Leaders Educated AIDS Response (CLEAR) Phase II—Kenya
Kumi Staff Training—Uganda
Meals for Children Program: Day Love Children's Project 2001–2002—Kenya
Meals for Children Program: Mathare Street Children Rescue Centre 2001–2002—Kenya
Mukura Technical School Expansion—Uganda
Ukuru Community Development—Uganda

Health
Primary Health Care

Compassion Canada's primary health-care partnerships focus on important preventative measures—like immunization, personal hygiene, nutrition, and health training for mothers with children under five years of age.

Current Projects

Children's Medical Program: House of Hope—Haiti
Children's Medical Program: Kiwoko Hospital Community Health Care—Uganda
Community Leaders Educated AIDS Response (CLEAR) Phase II—Kenya
Dessalines Community Health Program—Haiti
Rubirizi Gravity Flow Water Project—Uganda
Ukuru Community Development—Uganda

Clean Water
Clean-Water Supply

Compassion Canada supports initiatives aimed at supplying clean water to families. This may take the form of gravity-fed water systems in mountainous areas, well drilling or spring capping. Often the projects also include a sanitation component, such as the building of pit latrines, as uncontaminated water and effective waste management measures need to be in harmony.

Current Projects

Agwata Water and Sanitation—Uganda
Rubirizi Gravity Flow Water Project—Uganda

Micro-Finance
Small-Business Microenterprise Development (MED)

MED helps poor people by giving them access to capital and training so they can launch and grow small businesses. It is highly effective in lifting people from the lowest ranks of poverty and does so in a way that provides dignity and a sense of self-respect. Compassion Canada supports microcredit loan projects, including programming that can involve the parents and guardians of Compassion-sponsored children.

Current Projects

Dominican Trust Bank—Dominican Republic
Faulu Microfinance Expansion—Uganda
Ukuru Community Development—Uganda

Agriculture
Agriculture

Compassion Canada supports community-based efforts that concentrate on objectives such as experimental crops, reforestation activities to conserve water and prevent soil erosion, vaccinations for livestock, the use of organic fertilizers and the developing of small farmers' co-operatives. The co-operatives help farmers to bring their produce to larger markets, while avoiding stiff profit charges from market middle-men.

Current Projects

Bujora Children's Home Vocational Training Centre—Tanzania
Casa de Plastilina Children's Education—Mexico
Comitancillo Fruit Growers Association—Guatemala
Ukuru Community Development—Uganda

SOURCE: http://www.compassioncanada.ca/ca_communityprojects/project_types.html.

⊠ Child Sponsorship

An individual willing to sponsor a child was required to make a tax-deductible donation of Cdn$31 per month to Compassion Canada. Sponsors could choose the child of their choice or request Compassion Canada to randomly select one. The child so sponsored would be enrolled in the project of Compassion Canada and provided education, food and health care. When Compassion Canada enrolled a child in any of its projects, the funds were committed to help the child through to graduation from school (usually until attaining the age of about 16 or 17 years, depending on the education system of the country in which the child lived). However, it was not binding on the sponsor to continue to sponsor a child until this age. Sponsorship could be discontinued anytime.

Compassion Canada facilitated the interaction between sponsor and child. The sponsor was encouraged to write to the child regularly and was allowed to send monetary gifts two times in a year. Compassion Canada suggested that such gifts be in the range of $15 to $40. Implementation agencies helped the child in writing to his/her sponsor three times in a year. Compassion Canada sent the sponsor periodic updates on the progress of the child. In addition, it sent a biannual publication (*Compassion Today*) that featured Compassion Canada's work worldwide and a newsletter about Compassion Canada's work in the country where the child lived. If a sponsor decided to visit his/her child, Compassion Canada provided translators and gave out necessary information to the sponsor. The customer service centre of Compassion Canada handled the interaction with all sponsors.

Compassion Canada was very particular about emphasizing its belief in Christianity and its philosophy of using the Christian message to help develop each child and that child's family. It believed that church was a reliable and dependable infrastructure in most parts of the world. Therefore, it partnered only with churches and Christian agencies to support each child and to implement community projects. It focused on obtaining sponsorships from Christians, particularly the Evangelical Christians, because Christians have a '*biblical obligation*' to help the poor. Of Compassion Canada's over 20,000 sponsor-base, 60 per cent were Evangelical Christians while 37 per cent

were other Christians. The remaining three per cent were non-Christians who shared the philosophy of Compassion Canada in its entirety.

It is not simply child sponsorship that we are interested in but child development in a Christian way. If we have a large number of non-Christian sponsors, it would be difficult for them as well as for us. There were occasions when we turned down offers of huge money from some donors because they did not share our philosophy. They would either ask us to work on areas that we were not interested in or ask us to be secular. In fact, we even stopped actively approaching the Canadian government for financial support because it expected agencies that received government aid to maintain a secular nature in their activities. In addition, government aid had the potential of diverting a large part of our energies towards interfacing with them.

—Barry Slauenwhite, CEO

In the past, Compassion Canada targeted all segments of the population, including young and high school-age sponsors who were more ready to lend a helping hand. However, over time, the focus has been refined to target young married couples and post high school sponsors who tended to remain sponsors for a longer time. Compassion Canada enlisted the support of sponsors largely through promotion and advertising. It adopted a multipronged approach to promotional campaigning. First, it deployed Christian speakers and artists who supported Compassion Canada and were willing to promote its cause as part of their speaking or singing engagement. These artists became the ambassadors of Compassion Canada's cause. Second, it advertised on a growing network of 15 Christian radio stations throughout Canada. Third, it requested sponsors to promote its cause, in what was termed 'Awareness to Advocacy.' Sponsors were encouraged to approach pastors to promote Compassion Canada one Sunday each year (the last Sunday in May). Further, sponsors were encouraged to enrol new sponsors and volunteer their own time and effort to promote the cause of Compassion Canada.

Compassion Canada acquired sponsors through many ways. It participated in Christian events such as Kingdom Bound, Creation West, Teen Mania, Missions Fest Edmonton, and YC Edmonton. It helped sponsor these events and used them to promote the concept of child sponsorship and enrol new sponsors. It received sponsorships as a result of the Compassion Sunday that was held in churches. Speakers and artists who promoted the cause of Compassion Canada often persuaded their audience members to sponsor children. Compassion Canada's own staff, volunteers, existing sponsors, Internet and the *Compassion Today* magazine were other sources through which new sponsors were acquired. Acquisition of sponsorships through each of these sources is presented in Exhibit 3.

Exhibit 3 Sponsorships by Source (July 2000 to June 2001)

Source	Number
Christian events	766
Canadian office (from another sponsor/donor, Web, etc.)	749
Campaigns (such as Compassion Sunday)	529
Speakers	310
Staff	302
Volunteers	213
U.S. office (from other sponsors, Web, etc.)	116
Artists	46
Advertising (*Compassion Today* magazine)	31
Other	303

SOURCE: Company files.

Acquiring sponsors was not an easy task and required investment of resources in advertising and marketing. Compassion Canada believed that it was important to be cost-effective, not only in sponsor management but in the sponsor acquisition as well. Accordingly, the ministry strived to bring down these costs continuously each year. In 2001, Compassion Canada spent an average of $103 to acquire a sponsor, whereas in the years 1999 and 2000, the costs were $121 and $130, respectively.

Compassion Canada strived to ensure that overhead costs (cost of raising funds and administration costs) were less than 20 per cent and program costs (costs towards child support, grants and services, field services, sponsor ministry and gifts in kind) were over 80 per cent. A breakdown of the costs over the last five years is presented along with a pictorial representation of how sponsorship money was spent in Exhibit 4.

Compassion Canada consisted of 27 full-time employees. Besides the full-time employees,

Exhibit 4	Usage of Sponsorship Income (1997 to 2002)					

Activity	2002	2001	2000	1999	1998	1997
Raising funds	838,367	722,639	676,558	660,881	646,761	601,032
Administration	522,267	495,512	430,420	438,813	335,638	328,519
Child support	6,311,438	5,407,600	4,842,005	4,498,724	3,482,028	3,215,897
Sponsor ministry	431,236	442,808	315,630	266,564	294,198	273,411

NOTES: All amounts given in dollars. *Child support* component reflects the money used to provide learning opportunities for registered and sponsored children. *Sponsor ministry* supports letter translation, pays cost of child photographs and other incidental expenses related to strengthening the relationship of child and sponsor.

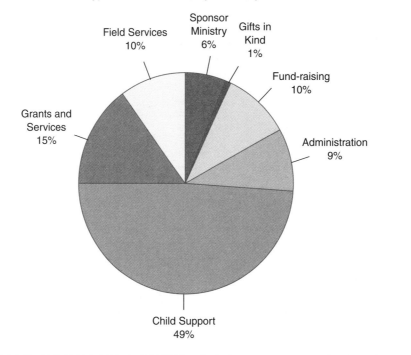

Typical Distribution of Sponsorship Income

SOURCE: Company files.

many individuals who shared its cause volunteered their services. These volunteers attended the office as per a prearranged work schedule and performed activities such as mailing, reading letters, sending letters, etc. About 40 volunteers performed the work of three full-time staff members in 2002. Availability of staff was reviewed every quarter to ensure that an appropriate number of employees were available to smoothly manage the operations. An additional employee was hired for every 1,000 new sponsorships expected. When a new employee was hired, besides the qualifications, their sense of commitment to Compassion Canada's cause and philosophy was evaluated. Typically, Compassion Canada employees were over-qualified for their jobs but joined because they had '*a sense of calling*' and decided to do something that was intrinsically satisfying. Each employee was trained in Compassion Canada's systems department for a period of six months before being given a formal responsibility. Compassion Canada had not laid off any employee in its 40-year history although some were asked to leave for reasons of under-performance.

When an employee had served Compassion Canada for a period of five years, that person was sent to visit one of the overseas projects to meet with sponsored children and to witness in person the real impact of their work. Major events and achievements were celebrated within Compassion Canada. Fo r example, when Compassion Canada crossed the 20,000 sponsorships mark, Slauenwhite organized a huge dinner for the employees because crossing that mark meant that Compassion Canada had '*changed the lives of 20,000 children.*'

Compassion International Incorporated, with which Compassion Canada was associated, relied heavily on planning and co-ordination. Consequently, Compassion Canada was required to send monthly projections of its growth to Compassion International Incorporated. These projections were made one year in advance and were based on sound planning. Each of the projections was supported by the campaign events planned, number of people expected to attend and the number of people likely to become sponsors. When an individual became a sponsor, their profile was prepared and added to the sponsor database. These profiles were periodically analysed to understand the characteristics so that persons with similar profiles could be targeted in the future for child sponsorships. Although the growth in

Compassion Canada was high, it was controlled growth.

Child Development Strategy

Compassion Canada's approach to child development was different than the approach of other similar organizations. The organization believed that to develop a child, one must help the child directly by providing food, education, health care, shelter and spiritual development in a Christian way. Accordingly, Compassion Canada focused most of its energies on child sponsorship. Other agencies followed a somewhat different strategy. They focused their energies on helping the communities and families to become self-sufficient. Focus on children was, therefore, not as visible in their projects and activities, although their mission was 'child development.'

Most of the child sponsorship agencies followed a community-based approach to child development, while Compassion Canada employed a direct approach in which the child sponsorship money was spent exclusively on child development by linking the sponsor and the child on a one-to-one basis. Compassion Canada's other programs ran parallel to child sponsorship and supported child development in an indirect manner. The organization raised money for community projects through a separate stream, and utilized them and accounted for them under a separate heading. On the other hand, the money raised by the organizations that followed the community-based approach was pooled together and centrally allocated for various projects aimed at child development, including direct benefits to children in the form of education, food and health care. Among the child sponsorship agencies in Canada, World Vision Canada, Foster Parents Plan and Christian Children's Fund of Canada were prominent competitors for the sponsorship revenue that Compassion Canada needed to fulfil its mission. Financial and other details of these organizations and Compassion Canada are presented in Exhibit 5.

Exhibit 5	Financial and Operational Details of Compassion Canada and Other Organizations (as of 2001)

Item	Compassion Canada	Foster Parents Plan	World Vision Canada	Christian Children's Fund of Canada
Revenue				
Child Sponsorship Income	7,065,231	36,892,048	131,082,000	9,960,794
Government Grants	185,391	2,507,319	21,292,000	317,568
Investment Income	161,160	577,698	274,000	n.a.
Other Income[1]	890,045	2,294,478	43,074,000	16,962,304
Total Income	8,301,827	42,271,543	195,722,000	27,240,666
Expenses				
Program Expenses[2]	6,690,790	33,575,328	157,002,000	22,633,973
Fundraising[3]	1,026,443	5,233,845	27,675,000	2,296,944
Administration	559,143	3,463,798	8,463,000	1,610,020
Total Expenses	8,276,376	42,272,971	193,240,000	26,540,937
Surplus	25,451	(1,428)	2,482,000	699,729
Number of Children Sponsored[4]	18,684	110,000	272,186	n.a.
Number of Sponsors	15,945	n.a.	223,995	n.a.
Sponsorship Cost in Cdn$ (per month per child)	31	31	31	29

SOURCE: Company files.

NOTE: All amounts in U.S. dollars except where noted.

1. Other income includes income in the form bequeaths, value of goods donated, and grants and donations for one or more specified or non-specified causes.
2. Expenses on all programs except in the case of Compassion Canada (where they pertain only to the expenses on child sponsorship).
3. Compassion Canada costs mentioned under two heads: marketing and community development.
4. Foster Parents Plan figure based on the information on the Web whereas figures of other agencies are taken from their annual reports.

World Vision Canada

World Vision Canada (WVC) was 'a Christian humanitarian organization that reached out to the World's poor.' It was established in 1950 to care for orphans in Asia. WVC worked to 'create a positive and permanent change in the lives of people suffering under the oppression of poverty and justice through long-term sustainable development.' WVC's approach to child development was based on its community-based strategy, i.e., to initiate projects that were aimed at community development so that the community itself became self-sufficient over time and took care of its children. It developed an area development program (ADP) model to help communities achieve sustainable development. Activities included emergency relief (in cases of natural calamities such as drought, floods, earthquake, etc.), health related projects (such as tuberculosis, AIDS and nutritional health projects), and long-term development projects (such as sanitation, irrigation, vocational training and farming).

Almost 80 per cent of WVC's funding came from private sources, including individuals, corporations and foundations. The remainder came from governments and multilateral agencies. Besides the cash contributions, WVC accepted 'gifts in kind,' typically food commodities, medicine and clothing donated through corporations or government agencies.

Approximately half of WVC's programs were funded through child sponsorship. In 2001, more than 207,000 Canadians supported its child sponsorship program. The money so received from Canada and other countries across the world was pooled together and centrally allocated to projects that were designed to support 1.6 million children in 40 countries.

Foster Parents Plan

Foster Parents Plan (FPP) of Canada was a member of Plan International, which was founded in 1937, as "Foster Parents Plan for Children in Spain" to help children whose lives were disrupted by the Spanish Civil War. With the outbreak of the Second World War, Plan International extended its work to include displaced children within war-torn Europe in the 1940s. Gradually, its operations expanded to other countries and as of 2001, it was organized into 16 national organizations, of which Canada was one (also known as donor countries), an international headquarters and over 40 program countries.

FPP implemented projects in health, education, water, sanitation, income-generation and cross-cultural communication. Most of the funds for its community projects came from individual sponsors. FPP actively involved local communities in setting up and implementing projects, including families and children. Its motto was 'sustainable development: a better world for children now and in the long-term future.' FPP believed that to help a child in a lasting way, the organization must also help that child's family and the local community to become self-sufficient.

FFP identified the countries in need of development work with the help of a number of criteria, such as infant mortality rates (more than 25 deaths per 1,000 live births), per capita gross national product (less than US\$1,700), and physical quality of life index (less than 80). As of 2001, about 111,000 children were sponsored by Canadians, and more than 1.3 million children were sponsored throughout Plan International worldwide.

After identifying the need, FPP worked in partnership with local non-government organizations and communities to effectively reach its goals. It aimed to work with them as long as was necessary to strengthen their capacity to provide their children with stability, protection and security in a sustainable way. Each community project took at least 10 to 12 years to achieve sustainable development.

In 2001, when Canadian contributions were combined with those of other supporters around the world, over \$365 million went to program implementation. Of this amount, over 24 per cent was spent on habitat projects, roughly 20 per cent on education, over 11 per cent on health, 12 per cent on building relationships and six per cent on livelihood.

Christian Children's Fund of Canada

Christian Children's Fund wa s founded in 1938 by Dr. J. Calvitt Clarke, a Virginia missionary, to care for Chinese-Japanese war orphans. He called it the China Children's Fund. It expanded into Europe during the Second World War and became Christian Children's Fund. CCF Canada (CCFC) was formed in 1960. As of 2001, more than 600,000 children were supported by CCFC and its International Co-operative of Christian Children's Fund around the world.

CCFC believed in making the communities self-sufficient so that children were taken care of by the community in the long run. The sponsorship amount received each month was spent on 'providing food, clothing, shelter, medical care, education, school supplies and love to the sponsored' child. It was also spent to provide food, health care, vocational training, and agricultural expertise to the sponsored child's family and to the child's community. CCFC's projects included clean water wells, immunization programs and micro-enterprise training.

The organization derived its revenue mainly from monthly sponsorship support for children, families and communities. Other sources of support were: donated goods and contributions, general contributions and bequests from public, and restricted or specific contributions that were donated for a particular purpose or project.

⊠ Compassion Canada's Target of 100,000 by 2013

Barry Slauenwhite, the chief executive officer of Compassion Canada, believed in taking a professional approach to the management of non-profit organizations. With experience in industry and pastoral service and the sense of God's calling in his heart, he was in a perfect position to professionalize and grow the activities of Compassion Canada.

Compassion Canada had set itself a target of 100,000 child sponsorships by 2013. To achieve that target, the organization needed to reach its projected figure of 26,150 for 2003 and then grow at the rate of 15 per cent per year. Projections and growth in child sponsorships over the past few years are presented in Exhibit 6. Reaching the figure of 100,000 in 2013 would be a great achievement for Compassion Canada for it would mark two milestones: 50 years of operations and 100,000 children.

Exhibit 6	Growth in Compassion Canada—Projected Versus Actual							
Number of Children Sponsored	**2002**	**2001**	**2000**	**1999**	**1998**	**1997**	**1996**	**1995**
Projected	20,775	17,800	16,473	15,732	14,898	14,196	13,330	12,310
Actual	21,886	18,684	16,659	15,377	14,505	13,556	12,818	12,088

SOURCE: Company files.

You're an Entrepreneur

But Do You Exercise Strategic Leadership?

Prepared by W. Glenn Rowe

If you are an entrepreneur, you are already in a leadership position. An important question you need to ask is: what type of leadership do I exercise? Answering this question may determine how your business will perform in the future. This article describes three types of leadership (Managerial Leadership, Visionary Leadership, and Strategic Leadership) and the expected consequences of each on future business performance.

⬚ Managerial Leadership

Some entrepreneurs exercise managerial leadership. As managerial leaders they influence only the actions/decisions of those with whom they work and are involved in situations and contexts characteristic of day-to-day activities.

They may make decisions that are not subject to value-based constraints. This does not mean that they are not moral or ethical people, but that as entrepreneurs they may not include values in their decision making because of certain pressures such as enhancing profitability.

These leaders are driven by bottom-line agendas that affect financial performance in the short-term. They want to maintain stability and to preserve the existing order. They are more comfortable handling the day-to-day activities, and are short-term oriented.

Managers will, at best, maintain wealth that has already been created and may even be a source for future wealth destruction as they are generally unwilling to invest in long-term investments such as human resource training and development, promotion, marketing, capital investment, and capital renewal.

Table 1 summarizes characteristics of managerial leaders, visionary leaders, and strategic leaders.

Table 1	Strategic, Visionary, or Managerial—What Kind of Leader Are You?

Strategic Leaders

- Display a synergistic combination of managerial and visionary leadership. Emphasize ethical behaviour and value-based decision making.
- Oversee operating (day-to-day) and strategic (long-term) responsibilities.
- Formulate and implement strategies for immediate impact and preservation of long-term goals to enhance organizational survival, growth, and long-term viability.
- Have strong, positive expectations of the performance they expect from superiors, peers, subordinates, and themselves.
- Believe in strategic choice, i.e., their choices make a difference in their organization and environment.

(Continued)

(...inued)

...y Leaders	Managerial Leaders
Are proactive, shape ideas, change the way people think about what is desirable, possible, and necessary.	Are reactive; adopt passive attitudes towards goals. Goals arise out of necessities, not desires and dreams; goals are based on past.
Work to develop choices, fresh approaches to long standing problems; work from high-risk positions.	View work as enabling process involving some combination of ideas and people interacting to establish strategies.
Are concerned with ideas; relate to people in intuitive and empathetic ways.	Relate to people according to their roles in the decision-making process.
Feel separate from their environment; work in, but do not belong to, their organization.	See themselves as conservators and regulators of existing order; sense of who they are depends on their role in the organization.
Influence the attitudes and opinions of others within the organization.	Influence actions and decisions of those with whom they work.
Know less than their functional area experts.	Are experts in their functional area.
More likely to make decisions based on values.	Are less likely to make value-based decisions.
Are more willing to invest in innovation, human capital, and creating and maintaining an effective culture to ensure long-term viability.	Are more likely to engage in, and support, short-term, least-cost behaviour to enhance financial performance figures.
Believe their choices make a difference in their organizations and environment.	Believe their choices are determined by their internal and external environments.

▧ Visionary Leadership

Most entrepreneurs are visionary leaders who influence the opinions and attitudes of others within the organization. They are concerned with insuring the future of an organization through the development and management of people.

Their task is multi-functional, more complex and integrative. Visionaries are more likely to make value-based decisions and are more willing to invest in innovation, human capital, and creating/maintaining an effective culture to ensure an organization's long-term viability.

Not only is visionary leadership future-oriented, but it is concerned with risk-taking. Furthermore, visionary leaders are not dependent on their organizations for their sense of who they are. Under these leaders, organizational control is maintained through socialization and the sharing of, and compliance with, a commonly held set of norms, values, and beliefs.

It is imperative that entrepreneurs exercise visionary leadership to ensure the long-term viability of the organizations they lead. However, organizations that are led by visionaries without the constraining influence of managerial leaders are probably more in danger of failing in the short-term than those led by managerial leaders. Since visionary leaders are willing to risk all, they may inadvertently destroy the organization and destroy wealth.

⬚ Strategic Leadership

Strategic leadership presumes that entrepreneurs and their employees have a shared vision of what your organization is to be.

There are three categories of people— the person who goes into the office, puts his feet up on his desk, and dreams for 12 hours; the person who arrives at 5 a.m. and works for 16 hours, never once stopping to dream; and the person who puts his feet up, dreams for one hour, then does something about those dreams.

—Steven J. Ross,
Former Chairman and
Co-CEO of Time-Warner

Strategic leadership is defined as the ability to influence your employees to voluntarily make decisions on a day-to-day basis that enhance the long-term viability of the organization while at the same time maintaining the short-term financial stability of the organization.

Entrepreneurs and employees make decisions every day as they interact with their firm's stakeholders, customers, suppliers, the communities in which they operate, and each other. What needs to be addressed is: are these decisions in accordance with the strategic direction of the organization? Will these decisions enhance the future viability of the organization, as well as the short-term financial stability? The answer is *absolutely*.

It makes sense to suggest that if you can count on employees to voluntarily make decisions that benefit the organization, entrepreneurs will not have to expend as much effort on monitoring and controlling their employees. Further, entrepreneurs will have more capacity to examine what the organization needs to do, both in the short and long term.

On the other hand, if employees do not know the strategic direction of the organization they may inadvertently make decisions that damage it. Influencing subordinates to voluntarily make decisions that enhance the organization is the most important part of strategic leadership.

Noel Tichy argues that "When you can't control, dictate or monitor, the only thing you can do is trust. And that means leaders have to be sure that the people they are trusting have values that are going to elicit the decisions and actions they want."

As presented above, the definition of strategic leadership presumes an ability to influence one's employees. It further presumes that the entrepreneur understands the emergent strategy process given that it has a greater impact on performance than the intended strategic planning process. This is related to understanding the importance of voluntary decision making.

The decisions voluntarily made and the actions voluntarily taken by employees on a day-to-day basis eventually determine what strategy will emerge. Entrepreneurs who are strategic leaders understand and utilize this emergent process to ensure the future viability of their organizations.

Strategic leadership presumes that entrepreneurs and their employees have a shared vision of what the organization is to be so that day-to-day decision making, or emergent strategy process, is consistent with this vision. It presumes agreement between entrepreneurs and their employees on the opportunities that can be taken advantage of, and the threats that can be neutralized, given the resources and capabilities of their organization.

Entrepreneurs need to develop the skills and abilities that are required to exercise strategic leadership. Those few that are managerial in nature need to develop their visionary side and those who are visionary need to develop their managerial side. To demonstrate that entrepreneurs need to exercise strategic leadership two entrepreneurs who made a difference to their firms and to their industries will be discussed next.

> Without effective strategic leadership, the probability that a firm can achieve superior or even satisfactory performance when confronting the challenges of the global economy will be greatly reduced.
>
> —R. Duane Ireland
> and Michael A. Hitt

Two Entrepreneurs Who Were Strategic Leaders

Konosuke Matsushita is the founder and former CEO of Matsushita Electric. At $49.5 billion, his revenue growth was the highest of any 20th century entrepreneur. The next closest were Soichiro Honda at $35.5 billion and Sam Walton at $35.0 billion. Matsushita was an incredible visionary who demanded revenue growth but with even more dramatic profit growth. One story describes how he told his senior managers that within five years he wanted revenue growth to quadruple and profit to more than quadruple. This goal was achieved in four years. How did he do this? Matsushita concentrated on creating products for his customers that created value in their minds that was greater than what they expected. However, he always wanted it done at a profit for his company. Matsushita's long-term vision was for the products his companies sold to create worldwide prosperity in such a way that in several hundred years there would be world peace.

The second entrepreneur is Bob Kierlin. Kierlin is the CEO of Fastenal, a company that sells nuts and bolts. His leadership style is characterized by employee empowerment, participation, wage compression (he pays himself $120,000 US per year) and promotion from within. However, he strongly encourages profitable revenue growth. This has been very beneficial for his employees, customers, and shareholders. In 1998, Fastenal's market value added was $0.077B—it was $1.609B in 1996—an increase of $1.53 billion. Kierlin started Fastenal in 1967 because he was unhappy with the bureaucracy at IBM.

These strategic leaders believed that their decisions would affect their companies' environments. They put great emphasis on achieving their visions by influencing the attitudes as well as behaviours of their employees. Moreover, they also ensured that their visions were achieved in a manner that was best for their employees, customers, and shareholders. In essence, these leaders were able to manage the paradox of investing strategically in their employees, in promotion through advertising, in research and development, and in capital equipment while still ensuring that their organizations were financially stable in the short term.

The Paradox of Leading and Managing

A recent Statistics Canada study found that the two most important reasons for the bankruptcies of small-to-medium-size firms were (1) poor overall management skills, such as lack of knowledge, lack of vision, and poor use of outside advisers, and (2) imperfect capital structures due to either institutional constraints or managerial inexperience.

The authors argue that managers in small firms need to be trained in general management and financial management skills. It is interesting that this study found a need for visionary and managerial leadership in small-to-medium-size firms just as it is needed in large firms such as General Motors and IBM.

Being a strategic leader is exciting as you create chaos, make mistakes, get occasionally rapped on the knuckles by your employees, and even occasionally have to apologize to your employees for creating too much disorder before they were ready for it. But the rewards are worth it as those with whom you work become energized and more productive—they accomplish more in less time and do not have to work dreadfully long days away from their families. Employees come to enjoy work more, as they become more creative and innovative, and more prone to taking risks because they know this enhances long-term viability.

Working through the paradox of leading and managing is an exciting challenge, one that is demanding and difficult, but one that is achievable for entrepreneurs. Entrepreneurs should start thinking of themselves as strategic leaders who have to accept and merge the visionaries and managerial leaders in their organizations. Fight against the constraining influence of financial controls and fight for the exercise of strategic and financial controls with the emphasis on strategic controls. The reward will be wealth creation and the achievement of above normal performance.

Women and Leadership

Laura Guerrero

The University of Texas at El Paso

We talk a lot today about the importance of mentoring and coaching, and they can be vital in helping novices learn the rules of the game. But it is very important that men should not always be mentored by men and women by women. Mentoring based on interests, not gender, can help to change the culture because it can lead to greater understanding of the perspective of the "Other."

—Sandra Dawson[1]

cademic researchers began to study gender and leadership in the 1970s. Early research asked, "Can women lead?" However, more recent research asks, "What are the differences in leadership style and effectiveness between men and women?" and "Why are women so underrepresented in executive leadership roles?" (Hoyt, 2007). This chapter looks at the differences in leadership style and effectiveness between men and women (Daft, 2005; Dubrin, 2007). It then looks at explanations for the underrepresentation of women in higher leadership positions. Finally, it discusses approaches to promoting women in leadership.

---

[1]Sandra Dawson is the nonexecutive director and trustee of Oxfam and chairman of the executive steering committee of the Advanced Institute of Management.

Gender: Examining Leadership Style and Effectiveness

Academic researchers have not agreed on whether there are gender differences in leadership style and effectiveness. Some findings seem to indicate there are no differences, while others find small but robust differences. Eagly and Johnson (1990) found that, contrary to expectations, women were not more likely to lead in a more interpersonally oriented manner and less task-oriented manner than men. However, women were found to be more likely to lead in a participative (democratic) manner than men. Other studies have found that women are undervalued compared to men when they occupy a typically masculine leadership role and when the evaluators are men (Bartol & Butterfield, 1976). It has been suggested that women may use a more democratic leadership style to obtain more favorable evaluations (Hoyt, 2007).

Recent research has found that women's leadership style tends to be more transformational than that of men (Daft, 2005; Eagly, Johannesen-Schmidt, & van Engen, 2003). Transformational leadership includes four components: idealized influence, inspirational motivation, intellectual stimulation, and individualized consideration. All are positively related to leadership effectiveness (Lowe, Kroeck, & Sivasubramaniam, 1996). This may be one of the sources of the modern popular view that women are better leaders.

Researchers have also studied the effectiveness of female and male leaders (Yukl, 2006). A review of published research showed that men and women were equally effective overall, but women and men were more effective in leadership roles that were seen to be congruent with their gender (Eagly, Karau, & Makhijani, 1995).

The Glass Ceiling Turned Labyrinth

Women occupy nearly half of the labor force in many countries, but they are still underrepresented in top positions in business and government. Women are only 15% of managers and legislators in countries such as Iran and Iraq and as many as 46% in the United States, 39% in Russia, and 35% in Canada (*The World's Women*, 2005). While these figures may suggest adequate representation in some countries, looking at top leadership positions, such as women's share of parliamentary or congressional seats, U.S. women have only 14% of the seats, Russian women 10%, and Canadian women 21%. In contrast, countries such as Cuba, Denmark, Finland, Norway, and others have more than 35% of the legislative seats filled by women (*The World's Women*, 2005).

The invisible barrier that prevents women from moving into top leadership positions is called the glass ceiling (Daft, 2005; Yukl, 2006). The glass ceiling can also be a barrier to other minorities. Women who are part of a racial or ethnic minority face additional challenges in the workplace. Removing barriers to advancement for women and other minorities has several benefits. First, it offers equal opportunity and, consequently, benefits society and more individuals. Second, it benefits businesses, governments, and their stakeholders by increasing the talent pool of candidates for leadership positions, which results in the availability of more qualified leaders. Third, having a more diverse profile of leaders makes institutions more representative of society. Finally, research shows that diversity is linked to group productivity (Forsyth, 2006), and gender diversity is linked to better organizational financial performance (Catalyst, 2004). Eagly and Carli (2007) have recently identified limitations with the glass ceiling metaphor. One of the limitations is that it implies that there is equal access to lower positions until all women hit this single, invisible, and impassable barrier. They propose an alternative image of a leadership labyrinth conveying the image of a journey filled with challenges along the way that can and has been successfully navigated by some women.

Explaining the Labyrinth

Human Capital Differences

One explanation for the labyrinth is that women have less human capital invested in education and work experience than men (Eagly & Carli, 2004). But women are obtaining undergraduate and master's degrees at a higher rate than men (Hoyt, 2007; National Center for Educational Statistics, 2003). Women are 44% of law degree graduates, but only 18% of law firm partners are women (National Association for Law Placement, 2006).

Another explanation is that women have less work experience and employment stability because they may have had to interrupt their careers to take care of their child-caring and domestic responsibilities, which are distributed unequally between genders. This explanation has some merit since it has been found that women with children are more likely to work fewer hours than women without children. In contrast, men with children are likely to work more hours than men without children (Kaufman & Uhlenberg, 2000).

Women respond to work–home challenges differentially. Some choose to attempt to excel in every role, others choose not to marry or have children, while others choose part-time employment in order to meet work and family commitments. Often, women who take time off from their careers have to reenter at lower positions than the ones they had when they left. This makes it more difficult to be promoted to higher leadership positions.

Another explanation for the existence of the leadership gap is that women choose not to pursue leadership positions for cultural reasons and instead choose to focus on raising a family. However, this argument has not found support in research (Eagly & Carli, 2004). Other explanations for the lack of representation of women in the top levels of management include women having fewer developmental opportunities, having less responsibility in the same jobs as men, having less access to mentors, and being in jobs that do not lead to top leadership positions.

Gender Differences

Other attempts to explain the leadership gap suggest that there are differences in leadership style and effectiveness between men and women. However, as mentioned earlier, research has not found evidence that women leaders are less effective or that their leadership style is a disadvantage for them. On the contrary, women are more likely to use transformational leadership, which has been positively linked to performance. Another attempt to explain the leadership gap is the alleged difference between genders in commitment and motivation to achieve leadership roles. However, research has shown that women and men show equal levels of commitment to paid employment. Both men and women view their role as workers as secondary to their roles as parents and partners (Bielby & Bielby, 1988; Thoits, 1992).

One difference researchers have found is that women are less likely than men to promote themselves for leadership positions (Bowles & McGinn, 2005). One other difference is that women are less likely than men to ask for what they want and negotiate (Babcock

& Laschever, 2003). These findings may be interpreted as reluctance on the part of women to take these roles or engage in such behavior due to the social backlash that they may face if they do promote themselves or negotiate aggressively.

Prejudice

Another explanation for the leadership gap is gender bias resulting from stereotypes (or cognitive shortcuts) such as that of men as leaders and women as nurturers. These cognitive shortcuts suggest to people ways to characterize groups or group members despite different characteristics among group members (Hamilton, Stroessner, & Driscoll, 1994; Hoyt, 2007). Stereotypes are not necessarily used intentionally to harm others. However, stereotypes can lead to discrimination in the selection and promotion of women to leadership positions and, therefore, can be very harmful. Women of color face prejudice not only as a result of their gender but also because of their ethnicity or race.

Another source of bias and prejudice is the tendency of people to report more positive evaluations of those who are more similar to them. This has the potential of putting women at a disadvantage when male leaders are in charge of promoting someone to a leadership position. Research has found that women respond in one of two ways to female leadership stereotypes. They either conform to the stereotype or engage in stereotype-countering behaviors. Women who are confident are more likely to engage in stereotype resistance, and those who are less confident are more likely to assimilate to the stereotype.

Navigating the Labyrinth

While there are still barriers for women in political and business leadership roles, there has been improvement in the past 20 to 30 years. Changes in organizations and in society are making it somewhat easier for women to reach top leadership positions. More organizations are starting to value flexible workers and diversity at all levels. Organizations can use career development, networking and mentoring, and work–life support programs to help ensure that women have equal opportunity to achieve top leadership roles in the workplace. There is evidence that society is also changing and that there is increasing parity in the involvement of men and women in child care and housework (Eagly & Carli, 2004). In response to the obstacles in the labyrinth, some women have opted for starting their own ventures, which allow them to have leadership positions and flexibility, rather than waiting for the business organizations to change to adapt to their needs.

References

Babcock, L., & Laschever, S. (2003). *Women don't ask: Negotiation and the gender divide.* Princeton, NJ: Princeton University Press.

Bartol, K. M., & Butterfield, D. A. (1976). Sex effects in evaluating leaders. *Journal of Applied Psychology, 61,* 446–454.

Bielby, D. D., & Bielby, W. T. (1988). She works hard for the money: Household responsibilities and the allocation of work effort. *American Journal of Sociology, 93,* 1031–1059.

Bowles, H. R., & McGinn, K. L. (2005). Claiming authority: Negotiating challenges for women leaders. In D. M. Messick & R. M. Kramer (Eds.), *The psychology of leadership: New perspectives and research* (pp. 191–208). Mahwah, NJ: Lawrence Erlbaum.

Catalyst. (2004). *The bottom line: Connecting corporate performance and gender diversity.* New York: Author.

Daft, R. L. (2005). *The leadership experience* (3rd ed.). Mason, OH: Thomson, South-Western.

Dubrin, A. (2007). *Leadership: Research findings, practice, and skills.* New York: Houghton Mifflin.

Eagly, A. H., & Carli, L. L. (2004). Women and men as leaders. In J. Antonakis, R. J. Stenberg, & A. T. Cianciolo (Eds.), *The nature of leadership* (pp. 279–301). Thousand Oaks, CA: Sage.

Eagly, A. H., & Carli, L. L. (2007). *Through the labyrinth: The truth about how women become leaders.* Boston: Harvard Business School Press.

Eagly, A. H., Johannesen-Schmidt, M. C., & van Engen, M. (2003). Transformational, transactional, and laissez-faire leadership styles: A meta-analysis comparing women and men. *Psychological Bulletin, 129,* 569–591.

Eagly, A. H., & Johnson, B. T. (1990). Gender and leadership style: A meta-analysis. *Psychological Bulletin, 108*(2), 233–256.

Eagly, A. H., Karau, S. J., & Makhijani, M. G. (1995). Gender and the effectiveness of leaders: A meta-analysis. *Psychological Bulletin, 117,* 125–145.

Forsyth, D. R. (2006). *Group dynamics* (4th ed.). Pacific Grove, CA: Brooks/Cole.

Hamilton, D. L., Stroessner, S. J., & Driscoll, D. M. (1994). Social cognition and the study of stereotyping. In P. G. Devine, D. L. Hamilton, & T. M. Ostrom (Eds.), *Social cognition: Impact on social psychology* (pp. 291–321). New York: Academic Press.

Hoyt, C. L. (2007). Women and leadership. In P. G. Northouse (Ed.), *Leadership: Theory and practice* (4th ed.). Thousand Oaks, CA: Sage.

Kaufman, G., & Uhlenberg, P. (2000). The influence of parenthood on work effort of married men and women. *Social Forces, 78*(3), 931–947.

Lowe, K. B., Kroeck, K. G., & Sivasubramaniam, N. (1996). Effectiveness correlates of transformational and transactional leadership: A meta-analytic review of the MLQ literature. *Leadership Quarterly, 7,* 385–425.

Meaney, M. C. (2008). Seeing beyond the woman: An interview with a pioneering academic and board member. McKinsey Quarterly, 4, 51–57.

National Association for Law Placement. (2006). *Percentage of women and minority lawyers up slightly for 2006—Minority women lag behind in partnership ranks.* Retrieved November 28, 2009, from http://www.nalp.org/2006octpercentageofwomenandminorities?s=women%20partners

National Center for Educational Statistics. (2003). *Digest of education statistics, 2002–2003.* Retrieved April 12, 2006, from http://nces.ed.gov/programs/digest/d04/lt3.asp#c3a_5

Thoits, P. A. (1992). Identity structures and psychological well-being: Gender and marital status comparisons. *Social Psychology Quarterly, 55,* 236–256.

The world's women 2005: Progress in statistics (Publication No. E.05.XVII.7). (2005). Progress in Statistics (ST/ESA/STAT/SER.K/17), United Nations Publication, Sales No. E.05.XVII.7. New York: United Nations.

Yukl, G. (2006). *Leadership in organizations* (6th ed.). Upper Saddle River, NJ: Pearson/Prentice Hall.

◤ The Cases

Anita Jairam at Metropole Services

The senior project manager at Metropole Services is getting the sense that her business relationship with her software development group is taking a turn for the worse. According to her, she was their project manager, and it seemed strange that her team members—all subordinates—were excluding her from an important client meeting. She must figure out what is wrong and take the appropriate steps to correct it immediately.

Marimekko

Kirsti Paakkanen has achieved a celebrity status in Finland for her enigmatic leadership of the Finnish design company Marimekko. Purchasing the company in a state of near bankruptcy in 1991, Paakkanen took several actions to restore profitability and realize growth. As of 2006, the company has sales of €64 million (of which 80% are from Finland) and net profits of €8.4 million. Over the last few years, Paakkanen and her team have focused on growing international sales. Recently, the company has opened concept shops owned by foreign partners in Japan, United Arab Emirates, Iceland, Sweden, and the United States. In light of the international expansion, Paakkanen is wondering if any changes to Marimekko's personnel policies and/or organization structure are necessary.

The Reading

Leveraging Diversity to Maximum Advantage:
The Business Case for Appointing More Women to Boards

Women bring a different perspective than do men to decision making. Yet where that perspective is, arguably, needed most—on boards—women are noticeably underrepresented. In this article, Ivey's Dean Carol Stephenson, who sits on several boards, makes a strong and compelling case for why there should be more women on more boards and what companies can do to identify and help more women to become board members. The case for why there are so few women on boards has become stale and easily refutable, which is why directors must read this compelling business case.

Anita Jairam at Metropole Services

Prepared by Ken Mark under the supervision of Alison Konrad

Introduction

"I cannot wait to see how pleased our client will be when we deliver this IT project to them one week ahead of schedule," beamed Anita Jairam, senior project manager at Metropole Services. Based in Newark, New Jersey, Metropole Services was a software development firm focusing on the U.S. health-care industry.

Metropole Services

Metropole provided information systems integration support for the many software applications that were being adopted in healthcare. For example, after a health-care centre decided to implement patient monitoring software and hardware, Metropole would work with the centre's current IT staff to integrate the software into the centre's IT network. This involved a

Version: (A) 2009-09-15

high degree of collaboration between client and service provider. Jairam met her counterpart at the centre at least once a week and communicated by e-mail or telephone at least once a day.

Internally, Jairam had to interpret her client's instructions and provide guidance for her team of eight software developers stationed in Newark. In addition, Jairam had scheduled weekly meetings with her supervisor, company founder Chandra Mishra, over video conference. As this was a rapidly growing startup with 30 people in total, Mishra handled a variety of roles including business development, human resources and strategy. During the past three months, Mishra had been stationed in Hyderabad, India, where he was working to set up an offshore location for software development. While Mishra had promised meetings with Jairam every week, more often than not, they were postponed or cancelled. Jairam estimated that she may have spoken to Mishra a total of four times in the past quarter.

⬛ Anita Jairam

Jairam had graduated from a prestigious East Coast business school and had finished her undergraduate studies at the Chennai campus India's Indian Institute of Technology. She had always been in the top 25 per cent in her class and was very ambitious. In her first job after her undergraduate degree, she had worked for a large consumer packaged goods manufacturer in India. There, she was part of a team of account executives whose goal was to sell new products to Indian retailers. She recalled her experience at this first job to be quite enjoyable— though she added that she had nothing to compare it to. The hours were long, nine to 10 hours per day, and everyone was preoccupied with executing sales plans. Jairam could not remember any instances of employee training other than the two-day orientation and introduction she was given at the start of her contract. Her team was a mix of male and female employees, and everyone seemed to be eager

to prove to management that they were candidates for promotion. Because of her above average performance, Jairam was part of the 20 per cent of account executives promoted to the account manager during the first round of promotions. (There were promotion rounds every six to 12 months.)

Promotions had been based solely on sales results. Jairam had the good fortune to be selling into a fast-growing group of retail outlets whose purchases of packaged goods grew rapidly every year. But by no means was Jairam merely fortunate that her accounts were growing: because she was able to sell additional non-food product lines to her accounts, she beat out another male account executive on her team and was promoted six months ahead of him. Understandably, she was very proud of her work ethic and achievements.

In her new role, Jairam was in charge of six account executives selling health and beauty care products. At the start of the fiscal year, she met with all six and set sales targets for the first quarter. During the first quarter, delivery disruptions threatened the business, but Jairam was able to find an unorthodox solution by using a third-party logistics provider to deliver the goods. Working around the clock, Jairam multi-tasked between answering sales-related questions from her team and tracking shipping progress on her laptop computer. For the rest of that first year as an account manager, there always seemed to be one external crisis or another that demanded her attention. Fortunately for Jairam, she had a motivated team of account executives working on her team who were able to conduct their business largely independently. After that first year, Jairam was identified as one of the top five candidates for promotion. But opportunity, in the form of a job offer from a start-up, came calling.

⬛ Joining Metropole

When he heard about Jairam's success in problem-solving, Mishra was convinced that she was the right person to help him grow his small company. Mishra had been a medical doctor in the Eastern United States for the past 20 years before he started Metropole. Concerned at the slow pace of IT adoption in the health-care sector, Mishra was convinced that someone like him, who knew the health-care system, could make a significant contribution to health care productivity and earn a decent living doing it. Relying on his network of contacts in India, Mishra had started Metropole three years ago to help health-care providers integrate IT into their workplace. But while he had no shortage of talented software developers, firm growth had been slow as Mishra lacked project management expertise.

Through his network, Mishra arranged a meeting with Jairam and was so impressed with her success that he offered her a job, including generous stock options, the same day. Jairam seized this opportunity and, within a month, had moved to Newark. She entered an organization that was operating very quickly and had limited systems in place. Managers seemed to be constantly overwhelmed with either client requests or software issues to fix, there were no set meetings or set targets for the year, and, although each person had a different business title, there seemed to be significant overlap in operating roles.

After providing a quick overview of the firm, Mishra immediately handed to Jairam her first assignment: working with a team of eight software developers to integrate a new patient monitoring system. With tight deadlines to manage and being new to the organization, Jairam believed that she had a lot to prove as she settled into the organization. Her first agenda item was to meet with all eight developers over lunch. As all eight were located in the same office building, she scheduled a meeting for Monday afternoon, a day least likely to conflict with client meetings.

She noticed that three of the eight developers showed up 10 minutes late for the luncheon. Wanting to start off on pleasant terms, Jairam said nothing to them, cheerfully greeting them

at the door. As she introduced herself and explained what she intended to do for the year, she was interrupted by one of the eight, Vivek. Vivek was the team's unofficial leader, since the team had been without a project manager for the past two months. Vivek commented:

We're very happy to meet you and we want to work with you to deliver this project. But as you know, we're already way behind schedule and, if possible, we should get back to work now and resume our introductions when the project has been delivered. I want to know if this is okay with you.

Pleased to know that her team was eager to get going with work, Jairam agreed to cut short her introductory lunch by half an hour and allow her team to return to their desks. In a converted conference room, all eight members worked alongside each other, sharing advice in an ad-hoc manner. Jairam listened enthusiastically as she met each team member in turn and asked them to explain their role to her. Every member of the team seemed to be extremely committed to the project and indicated that they were glad that she was coming on board. Jairam could not help noticing that she was the only woman in the room.

She left to go back to her office in order to attend her first client meeting. The client explained the urgency of the project, and Jairam reassured him that the team would do all in its power to get the project back on schedule. At 8 p.m. that evening, Jairam returned to the conference room to switch off the lights before leaving. She was surprised to see that her entire team was still present, still working on the project. One member greeted her and assured her that they were staying later by choice. Jairam was very impressed by their dedication and asked whether she could help with anything. When the group said they had been about to go for takeout, Jairam offered to pick it up for them.

When she returned with food, she sat down with the entire team for a 20-minute break and talked to them about their work. She was not surprised to hear that all eight had been working with the company from the very start. They spoke enthusiastically about the future value of their stock options in the company and kept repeating that they were proud to be owner-operators and that this was a once-in-a-career opportunity. Jairam had never met such dedicated workers.

For the rest of that week, on-site meetings with the client kept Jairam out of Newark. She kept in touch with her team by e-mail and was pleased to hear that their progress was faster as a result of having her as the key client contact.

When she returned the next Monday, Jairam spoke to Mishra briefly and proudly indicated that progress had been made. On her lunch break, which she took in her office in order to read the latest news on CNN.com, Jairam was interrupted by a team member who wanted to know whether she could help them get tea from the local Dunkin' Donuts. Of course, said Jairam, she would be glad to.

Over the next two weeks, Jairam seemed to thrive in her new role. When she reported to the client that the time deficit had been eliminated (they would deliver the project on time), the client was ecstatic. He indicated that there would be a lot more work for Metropole to bid on if the project were delivered on time. To give Jairam a sense for the variety of projects available, he arranged for her to tour the facility, meeting with eight to 10 different IT managers. Jairam conservatively estimated that up to four times Metropole's entire firm revenues was available, if she could just manage the execution of the current plan and gain credibility.

When she returned to the office after an absence of a (productive) week and half, her team casually chided her about her absence and the fact that they had to send out a member to get their regular order of tea and food. Jairam apologized for her absence and eagerly recounted her client meetings and the opportunity that lay before them. Her team spontaneously erupted in applause, and they celebrated by going to a nearby restaurant for a meal.

As the deadline approached, Jairam's days in the office included a combination of client meetings and e-mail missives to her team members. At 11 a.m. and 4 p.m. each day, she promptly headed out the door to Dunkin' Donuts to bring back drinks for her team. At 6 p.m., she would take dinner orders and bring them back. This arrangement worked nicely, except for one or two instances when she mixed up an order or two. When she saw the dissatisfied look on her team members' faces, she immediately offered to return to the donut shop or restaurant to get the correct order, which she did.

Two weeks before the deadline, Jairam knew that her project was in superb shape. She anticipated delivering the project a week early and indicated to Mishra (on only their fourth telephone meeting since she started at the company), that much more work was available. Mishra's enthusiasm was evident in the tone of his voice and he congratulated Jairam on a job well done.

Returning to check on her team, Jairam asked them to take a five-minute break to discuss follow-on work. As she began talking about another upcoming project, she was interrupted by Vivek, who said that he had to get back to his coding. Jairam excused him from the meeting.

One of the remaining team members was surprised to hear about future projects. "We assumed you'd be heading back to India to get married," he laughed. "How old are you? You must be no older than our daughters, who are all happily married now."

Jairam was caught off guard. But she recovered and replied, saying that she had no intention of starting a family in the next few years. She was very excited about her prospects at Metropole, she offered, and she wished to be able to lead the company's North American expansion. She indicated that she wanted to take on greater management responsibilities in the near future. At this point, Vivek returned to the room and conversation shifted to another topic. Jairam, wishing to leave them to their work, took their dinner orders and left to drive to the restaurant.

The next day, Jairam returned to the office to hear that there was a minor issue: a section of code written for the project was not working out as expected. As the code was written in a software language familiar to her, Jairam asked to take a look at it. Immediately, she noticed the error and informed the team member how to correct it. Her team member appeared skeptical and, in front of Jairam, turned to his colleague for advice. His colleague looked over the section of code and confirmed that Jairam was correct. Jairam, pleased that her judgment was correct, smiled and walked away.

The client was visiting Metropole's Newark site that day, and Jairam had planned a meeting and a facility tour. She assembled her entire team in a meeting room and was preparing to start her introduction when Vivek started speaking directly to the client. Vivek proudly indicated that the team was on-track to deliver the project a week ahead of schedule and that everyone had contributed greatly to the effort. Not wanting to interrupt the flow, Jairam remained silent, interjecting now and then to provide missing information. At the end of the client meeting, and as they were leaving to start the tour, Vivek turned to Jairam. He said, "I hope you don't mind that I started that meeting. I was very pleased at my team's effort and wanted to congratulate them in front of the client for the work they've put in thus far."

Jairam assured him that it was no problem, that she was glad that he took the initiative. As they turned to rejoin the group, Vivek turned to her: "Would you mind going to fetch us our teas? I'll meet with the client and get us started on the next project. Remember, I like my tea extra hot."

It dawned on Jairam that her relationship with her team might not be what she had assumed it to be. She was their project leader, and it did not seem right that she would not be present for the client meeting. As he hurried back to the group, Vivek added, "And by the way, when we met yesterday night, the team and I agreed that it would be helpful for me to resume my client contact duties. Let's sit down later to see how you can refocus your efforts to target future clients." Jairam was stunned. She had been unaware that the team had met the night before to discuss this. Did they even have the authority?

It was 11:30 a.m. in the morning, a half hour since the client had left on a facility tour with the team. Jairam had been standing in the same spot in the conference room, thinking about her reaction to what she believed was a sudden shift of events in the past few days. Although it was not clear what the issue was, she knew that something was wrong and had to be corrected immediately.

Marimekko

Prepared by Jordan Mitchell under the supervision of Alison Konrad

Business could be called life: A good and ethical corporate culture embodies the same values as our everyday life.

—Kirsti Paakkanen, president and chief executive officer, Marimekko

◪ Introduction

Early in the morning on May 19, 2006, Kirsti Paakkanen walked into Marimekko's head office at Puusepänkatu Road in Helsinki, Finland. The smell of coffee and blueberry cake was familiar, but today would be different. After 15 years at the helm of the legendary

    Version: (A) 2009-09-16

Finnish design firm Marimekko, Paakkanen was about to receive an honorary doctorate from the Helsinki School of Economics for her achievements in promoting Finnish design on a worldwide stage.

As Paakkanen walked to her large glass-topped desk, she thought back over the past 15 years and what she would tell the crowd about how she had restored Marimekko from a loss-making company on the verge of bankruptcy to the pride of Finnish design. As she stated:

> I feel I'm quite humble, and I feel rather inadequate in many respects. From Marimekko, there's a lot to learn. Starting with the founder, Armi Ratia, this company is a good example of being boldly different. In order to do big deeds, Marimekko had the courage to be very different.

Not wanting to rest on her past successes, Paakkanen's mind quickly moved to the future. The company was in an exciting phase of expanding internationally through exports and working with retail partners to open Marimekko-concept shops. Recently, Marimekko-concept shops had opened in Japan, the United Arab Emirates, Iceland, Sweden and the United States. Just as Marimekko had become a household name in Finland, Paakkanen was certain that its style would capture the hearts and minds of foreign customers as it had in the 1960s. At the same time, she wondered whether any changes were required to the company's personnel policies for the future. As the personnel section of Marimekko's 2005 annual report stated:

Going international ushers in mounting challenges for Marimekko's business operations, requiring personnel to have new kinds of capabilities and to adapt themselves to changing circumstances. On the other hand, the greater diversity of tasks and operating in the international market provide employees with excellent opportunities to expand their expertise and knowledge of other cultures.[2]

Kirsti Paakkanen

Born in 1929,[3] Paakkanen grew up in the small town of Saarijärvi in the middle of Finland's forested countryside. Her early days were said to have had a profound impact on how nature was at the forefront of her values. During high school, Paakkanen worked two jobs to support herself. She entered university and earned degrees in Finnish studies and advertising and marketing. She began her professional career at an advertising agency in Helsinki, before breaking out on her own and establishing Womena in 1969. Paakkanen's concept was to hire only women for her advertising agency, something unheard of at the time in Finland. The name itself, aside from the overt English-language connection to the word "Women," had a poetic "Adam and Eve" connotation, as "omena" means apple in Finnish.[4] Paakkanen quipped: "The first sales speech by a woman was made in the Garden of Eden when Eve persuaded Adam to eat the apple!"[5]

Paakkanen wanted to create a substantially different agency. She hired four female advertising professionals, rented a space in central Helsinki, made the office furniture herself and

[2]Marimekko Annual Report 2005, December 31, 2005, p. 22.

[3]Wikipedia, http://fi.wikipedia.org/wiki/Kirsti_Paakkanen, accessed July 28, 2006.

[4]Hannah Booth, "Women: Flower power," *The Guardian*, September 5, 2005, http://www.guardian.co.uk/g2/story/0,,1562697,00.html. accessed May 18, 2006.

[5]Profile on Kirsti Paakkanen, Internal Marimekko Publication, 2006, p. 1.

ensured that the scent in the office resembled that of a forest. To introduce her new agency to potential Finnish advertisers, she and her staff packaged up 600 green apples in elegant white boxes with the tag line: "Today 'omena' (apple), tomorrow 'Womena.'" Immediately, she attracted 35 customers. All business operations were financed directly through revenues.

Throughout the next 20 years, Paakkanen led the agency to become one of the most recognized names in the Finnish advertising industry. Womena was known for its all-female staff, no hierarchy among the employees and flexible job descriptions. In addition, Womena's results were often heeded by the industry—the company won over 30 national advertising awards from 1969 to 1988. As well, the agency posted profits every year. It exceeded the average European advertising agency since its operating profit before depreciation was 32.2 per cent versus the industry average of 12.8 per cent.[6] In building Womena to great acclaim, Paakkanen commented on the female-male divide and how she overcame the predominantly male culture at the time:

> At that time, women were not at all respected, and I wanted to respond in the same way to people that believed I could not do it. When men were reacting poorly to me, instead of acting poorly towards them, I acted conversely like a weak woman and threw myself at them begging for their help. It always worked—100 per cent of the time!

In 1988, Paakkanen sold Womena to The Interpublic Group of Companies, Inc./ McCann Worldwide (USA). Part of the agreement was that Paakkanen would work for the group for a period of three years. When she had fulfilled that part of the deal, in March 1991, Paakkanen announced her retirement and moved to Nice in southern

France. After just a couple of months, she received a phone call from Amer Group, the owners of Marimekko, to take the position of chief executive officer in the loss-making Marimekko. She turned down the offer, only to receive a counter offer to purchase the business at a nominal fee. Paakkanen agreed. She reflected back on her decision:

> First off, I'm always inspired by a strong brand. I saw that the management of Marimekko was bad, but no matter how much they abandoned it, it could not be killed off—the strength of the brand lived on. I was living in the south of France, and I suppose I was a little homesick. I have a strong sense of being Finnish, and I'm quite patriotic. I could see that Finland was going through one of its worst recessions in 1990–1991, and I had this mission of doing my own share to save Finland. But, more than that, it was also saving a pearl within the country. To me, there's nothing more important than inspiration in the heart—I knew that it would be a tough job to turn Marimekko around, but I knew I would not and could not fail if I had inspiration in my heart.

Exhibit 1 shows some of Paakkanen's well-known quotes.

The Building of a Finnish Icon: Marimekko's History

The first step in building Marimekko was taken in 1949, when Viljo Ratia purchased Printex Oy, a company producing oilcloth and printed fabrics. Viljo's wife, Armi Ratia, an adwoman and trained textile designer, encouraged her husband not to produce common floral prints, stating: "You must print something else. You

[6]Ibid., p. 2.

| **Exhibit 1** | Kirsti Paakkanen Quotes |

"My mother's advice: 'Each day one should work a wonder.'"

"Marimekko is so Finnish an enterprise that anything more Finnish would be difficult to find."

"Marimekko may be everyday, but it is never conventional."

"Feelings are the world's greatest natural resource."

"Whatever you're doing, be an example. Your actions speak louder than your words."

"No reward is greater than you saying to me: Thank you! Beautiful! Without pride and gratitude we would not be Marimekko."[a]

"Everyone, nearly everyone, has been imbued at birth with an extravagant force called the will to live. It moves us to go on struggling in seemingly hopeless situations and to discover in even the most trifling chaff the blossoming cherry tree. Fortunately, we know how to dream. . . . Without dreams there is no life."[b]

"Marimekko has been, and remains, a way of life. . . . We must create visions, see at one and the same time both near and far. Interpreting time is our most important task."[c]

On the difference between men and women in business: "Men in business start at the top, they create positions for themselves then work down. Women work from the bottom up and value their workers."[d]

On one of her mentors: "One of the people I admire the most is Coco Chanel. She built her dynasty up when she was 70 years old. Her story has been very inspiring, and I see a lot of commonalities in her approach. I respect the way that Chanel brought a great deal of discipline to a concept—all of the Chanel stores in the world are very consistent, and each season, a new story is told maintaining the consistency of the brand."

a. Tommy Tabermann and Tuija Wuori-Tabermann, "Spirit & Life: Marimekko," Porvoo: WS Bookwell Oy, 2001, pp. 151.

b. Ibid., pp. 22–25.

c. Ibid., pp. 217.

d. Hannah Booth, "Women: Flower power," *The Guardian*, September 5, 2005, http://www.guardian.co.uk/g2/story/0,,1562697,00 .html, Accessed May 18, 2006.

have to be different."[7] She commissioned aspiring young designers to generate prints for the company, one of which was Maija Isola, who went on to create many of the company's hallmark patterns. While the fabrics were well received by the public, many asked how they could be put to use. Armi and Viljo Ratia responded by setting up a separate company, Marimekko, in

[7]Judith Gura, "Marimekko: Resurgence of a Finnish Phenomenon," *Scandinavian Review*, Spring 2004.

1951. Marimekko was an amalgamation of the common female name "Mary" (spelt "Mari" in Finnish) with "mekko," meaning "dress." The concept of Marimekko was to create something radically different with beauty and longevity to give hope to the grey mood in post-war Finland. One writer described the motivation for the company in this way: "With full confidence, one can say that in its first years, Marimekko was driven forward by an idealism that involved taking personal risks and being completely indifferent to economic success."[8]

The company's dresses were known for their loose-fitting silhouettes akin to an artist's smock.[9] The garments were often described as "clothing for women who didn't want to think about clothes."[10] The company made its products available internationally in the late 1950s, in both Sweden and through the cutting-edge, Boston-based retail shop Design Research. Marimekko received a major push in 1960, when Jacqueline Kennedy, the wife of U.S. presidential candidate John F. Kennedy, purchased seven Marimekko garments from the company's U.S. distributor. She then appeared in her Marimekko dress for the cover shot of Sports Illustrated. During that time, the Kennedy-Nixon presidential campaign was in high gear, and when journalists criticized Jacqueline Kennedy for her expensive Paris-bought fashions, she quickly responded that they were inexpensive ready-to-wear garments from Finland.[11] The story spread quickly throughout the United States, and the small, relatively unknown Marimekko name was thrust into the international spotlight.

With this increased profile, press from around the world began focusing on Marimekko. However, Armi Ratia insisted that her name not be mentioned, and she encouraged the press to focus on the individual designers of each garment or design. Eventually, the press began focusing on Armi Ratia. Viljo stated:

When we were creating our corporate image, I had the idea of an "entrepreneurial couple," Armi on the artistic side, me on manufacturing and management side. Once Armi had stepped into the limelight, there was no holding her back. From then on it was a solo performance. Armi was a perfect pro. Her Finnish was so original, often downright shocking, that she was much sought-after for interviews, which, at the beginning, were about Marimekko, but later about quite other subjects.... Interest had spread abroad and Marimekko's newly created image showed that it was not just a business but a kind of cultural phenomenon. There was a constant stream of visitors, [including] cultural personalities from Finland and abroad.[12]

Armi Ratia refused to follow Paris haute couture and avoided the word "fashion." Instead, the company talked about "dressing Finnish women or the production of functional garments."[13] Later, the company began producing men's clothing beginning with the striped "Jokapoika" (the "Everyboy" shirt) in 1956 (see Exhibit 2). The company's product,

---

[8]Edited by Pekka Suhonen, "Phenomenon Marimekko," Porvoo: WS Bookwell Oy, 2004, p. 8.

[9]Judith Gura, "Marimekko: Resurgence of a Finnish Phenomenon," *Scandinavian Review*, Spring 2004.

[10]Ibid.

[11]Edited by Pekka Suhonen, "Phenomenon Marimekko," Porvoo: WS Bookwell Oy, 2004, p. 23.

[12]Ibid. p. 24.

[13]Ibid. p. 28.

Exhibit 2   Images of Marimekko

Maija Isola—
"Kivet" 1956

Maija Isola—
"Unikko" 1964

Fujiwo Ishimoto

"Tasaraita"—Created
1968
by Annika Rimala

Jokapoika "Everyboy" shirt
Created 1956 by Vuokko
Nurmesniemi

Mari-essu—Created
by Vuokko
Nurmesniemi

"Doggy" Bag from
Continuing Collection
2006/07

Fall/Winter 2006/07
Women's by Ritva Falla

Fall/Winter
2006/07 Men's by
Matti Seppänen

SOURCE: Company files.

known affectionately as "marimekkos," were seen to be completely egalitarian. Armi Ratia stated:

> I don't believe in national frontiers in dressing. Dresses are often quite recklessly bold and demand an unbourgeois wearer. The purpose of a dress is to permit freedom of movement and to do justice to its wearer as an individual. Therefore, there aren't any special models as such. They are dresses that have style. They are Finnish in the same way as are a burlap dress, a farmhorse's ear and a grey barnwall.[14]

Armi was also known for taking risks on purchasing decisions; she was guided by the principle to never say to a customer, "Sorry, we haven't got it." This led to excessive stocks and products and fabrics that needed to later be liquidated at a lower price. At the same time, designers and machinists were given freedom to make decisions, even if these decisions turned out to be unprofitable. As one designer stated: "We were encouraged to speak out like

owners. Armi's order was: You have to have your own opinion!"[15]

In the late 1960s, Armi developed a plan to create the Mari village—an idyllic village community for 3,500 inhabitants. The project garnered interest from a Helsinki-based building company, but before full construction began, the building company pulled out. Marimekko was going to continue the project on its own, but, in 1967, due to a shortage of cash, the concept was terminated by the board of directors. The cash crisis forced the company to embark on a restructuring process, which took over three years and involved culling office staff by nearly 50 per cent (from 191 to 100) and factory workers by 32 per cent (from 247 to 167).[16]

From the restructuring, a new Marimekko was born. The company abandoned its plans of producing diverse products such as shippable, full-sized modern saunas, opting to focus solely on clothing and textile home products. The company contracted freelance designers including two Japanese-born individuals—Katsuji Wakisaka and Fujiwo Ishimoto—during the 1970s. See Exhibit 3 for a list of select Marimekko designers.

Exhibit 3 List of Select Historical Marimekko Designers

Maija Isola (1927–2001): School of Applied Art, textile department 1946–1949. Maija Isola joined Printex in 1949. In 1953, she began working on printed textiles for frocks (previously she was devoted to interior textiles only). In 1979, she began designing with her daughter Kristina Isola. Her textiles were said to form the foundation for the Marimekko style, as they featured oversized geometric patterns and bright colors.

Vuokko Eskolin-Nurmesniemi (1930–): School of Applied Art, ceramics, 1948–1952. She was the chief designer for Marimekko's clothing and dress fabrics from 1953 to 1960, before she established her own firm in 1964. She was most well known for the "Piccolo" brushstroke patter and the "Everyboy" shirts (1956), one of Marimekko's best selling products as of 2006.

(Continued)

[14]Ibid. p. 49.

[15]Ibid. p. 75.

[16]Edited by Pekka Suhonen, "Phenomenon Marimekko," Porvoo: WS Bookwell Oy, 2004, p. 10.

Exhibit 3   (Continued)

Annika Rimala (1936–): School of Applied Art, graphics. Annika Rimala was Marimekko's dress designer from 1959 to 1982. In 1982, she founded her own shop. She designed the "Even Stripe" cotton jersey t-shirt that became a symbol of the new unisex trends in fashion.

Liisa Suvanto (1910–1983): Central School of Applied Art, 1937. Designer with Marimekko from 1963 to 1975. She was known for developing woolen garments and adding a new type of flowing line to Marimekko dresses.

Fujiwo Ishimoto (1941–): Studied design and graphics in Tokyo, Japan. Designer at Marimekko's subsidiary Decembre from 1970 to 1974. He has worked as a designer at Marimekko since 1974.

Katsuji Wakisaka (1944–): Kyoto School of Art and Design. Marimekko textile designer from 1968 to 1976. He was known for the use of bright colors and the melding of Japanese sensibilities into Marimekko. One of his most successful Marimekko designs was the Bo Boo in 1975 (a pattern with colorful cars and trucks).

Pentti Rinta (1946–): School of Applied Art, dress design, 1964–1969. Joined Marimekko as a designer in 1969. He was known for Marimekko's shirt-dresses and was the first to design Marimekko's first full men's outfit (the Kuski).

Marja Suna (1934–): School of Applied Art, 1951-1954. Joined Marimekko as head designer in 1979, after having worked in the industry for 25 years. She designed a wide range of blouses, gowns and tunics with a specialty in knit wear.

Ristomatti Ratia (1941–): Businessmen's Commercial College, 1961–1964, Leicester Polytechnic, interior decorating 1964–1967. He worked as a designer at Marimekko from 1973 to 1977 and led Marimekko Inc. in the United States from 1977 to 1984. He was known for developing families of products.

SOURCE: Compiled from "Phenomenon Marimekko," edited by Pekka Suhonen, Porvoo, WS Bookwell Oy, 2004, pp. 118–138.

The company expanded its printing and production capabilities in Finland with the inauguration of new plants, and it went public on the Helsinki Stock Exchange in 1974. In 1979, Armi Ratia passed away. The ownership of the company passed on to Armi Ratia's heirs. Risto Takala began as the chief executive officer (CEO) of Marimekko in 1980, and Kari Mattson led Marimekko from 1982 for a couple of years. One design historian commented:

Ristomatti Ratia (Armi's son) remained the company's chief image-builder, but the company never regained its lost lustre. Its image was maintained, to some degree, in licensed linen collections, and loyal retailers continued to sell the ready-to-wear to a coterie of devoted customers, but the firm generally fell "beneath the radar" of the design community, where it remained for more than a decade.[17]

---

[17]Judith Gura, "Marimekko: Resurgence of a Finnish Phenomenon," *Scandinavian Review*, Spring 2004.

In 1985, the company was suffering losses, and Amer Group, a diversified conglomerate that owned brands in sporting, plastics and other industries, purchased the company's shares. Being part of a big group, Marimekko was now managed in a centralized manner as a subsidiary through Amer Group's administration. The activities of the subsidiaries were followed mainly through reports, and special characteristics for the subsidiaries' individual business development needs were not taken into consideration. During this time, Marimekko's international sales practically disappeared, losing money every year from 1985 to 1991.

The Turnaround: Enter Kirsti Paakkanen

Paakkanen invested her own funds (generated from the sale of Womena) and took out a bank loan to finance the purchase and working capital necessary to operate Marimekko. On September 27, 1991, Paakkanen acquired Marimekko. Paakkanen commented on the business environment, "Finland was in a deep recession, the deepest Finnish business had ever experienced. Unemployment soared, and Finland's mental state was at rock bottom." Within the first few days of taking over the ownership of Marimekko, Paakkanen said to the employee base: "You possess creativity, expertise and are seasoned professionals. You have long been creating products that bear the Marimekko name. I am a newcomer to Marimekko, and to succeed in my work, I'll need every single one of you. Together we'll show them what we are made of."

Paakkanen started by eliminating hierarchy in the organization to quash bureaucratic processes. She stated:

When I came to the organization, I found that the company had all of

these boxes, and people were not communicating effectively. We had to start by bulldozing bureaucracy and turning it into a vibrant environment conducive to creativity. We had to restore the mental well-being of the employees, instill in them a belief in the future, self-confidence and enthusiasm for regeneration. We had to draw up new business strategies and write new rules of play.

In co-ordination with breaking down the bureaucratic structure, Paakkanen boosted the role of the individual designers by giving them profit responsibility on their designs. Paakkanen retrained the designers, emphasizing the profitability of their designs. She reflected: "The designers evidently found the training a novelty. But also motivating and inspiring."[18]

Paakkanen clearly stated to Marimekko's employees: "Design is now paramount throughout the organization. The entire organization serves top design." In orienting the entire company around the design function, she built state-of-the-art working facilities for the designers and gave them complete creative freedom. However, there was one condition: the designs had to be profitable. The name of each designer was placed on the inside hangtag of all garments and home products. Throughout its history, Marimekko had used a combination of in-house and freelance designers. When Paakkanen joined, there were very few in-house designers. Paakkanen opted for the freelance designer model. She sought new designers by hosting internal design competitions and working closely with both Finnish and international art and design institutes.

Paakkanen gathered existing staff to define the market position of Marimekko

---

[18]Kirsti Paakkanen speech, 2004, Marimekko company documents.

and determine what products to focus on. The team reached back into Marimekko's rich archives and began reproducing prints. This was before the major 'retro' fashion movement in the late 1990s and before the introduction of industrial design companies. One of the first retro designs was the "Fandango" group of prints developed by Maija Isola in 1962. When the reissue sold well, Paakkanen sent a cheque to the then-retired Isola, who immediately sent it back stating in a note, "Thank you for the beautiful thought. I think you will have better use for this money than I do."[19]

The company expanded into new areas. In the early 1990s, Paakkanen put more emphasis on the development of the home interiors market, using both archived and new patterns for products such as bed comforters, curtains, tablecloths and towels (these categories had also thrived during Armi Ratia's time but had been culled in the 1980s). In the mid-1990s, the company contracted freelance designer, Ritva Falla, to design a new line of women's business wear clothing. As Falla stated:

> When I came to work here at Marimekko, I didn't come to produce the "standard Marimekko" but a business range based on a concept of Kirsti Paakkanen's. Times had changed. My task was to create products that fit the spirit of the times. It hasn't been easy to convince the sales staff that the woman who typically wears Marimekko is not your '60s housewife but a busy '90s business-woman whose wardrobe contents are determined by the demands and desires of the era.[20]

The success in Marimekko's women's business wear division caused the company to begin a men's businesswear line in 2000. Matti Seppänen was contracted as a freelance designer to lead the development of the men's line. He stated: "When I design a collection for Finnish men, I picture a guy who is a classy, quality-conscious, courageous intellectual who asserts his Finnishness and knows how to play it safe with his wardrobe."[21]

In 2003, the company extended its assortment of children's wear and began expanding into more licensing agreements. One of the most notable was a deal inked with mobile phone manufacturer Nokia to license Marimekko patterns for mobile phone covers.

The expansion into new product lines was complemented by new store openings. In addition, the company set up subsidiaries in Sweden and Germany and signed a number of international distribution agreements in over 15 countries. To support the business expansion, the company went public on the Helsinki Stock Exchange in 1999 and moved to the exchange's main list in 2002. The company's financial situation improved year on year, from a loss of over 8 million in 1991 to a profit of 8.4 million in 2005 (see Exhibit 4).

The Marimekko Organization as of 2006

Guiding Paakkanen's management approach was her self-developed thesis, which included

---

[19]Hannah Booth, "Women: Flower power," *The Guardian*, September 5, 2005, http://www.guardian.co.uk/g2/story/0,,1562697,00.html, accessed May 18, 2006.

[20]Tommy Tabermann, Tuija Wuori-Tabermann, "Marimekko: Spirit & Life," Porvoo: WS Bookwell Oy, 2001, p. 180.

[21]Ibid, p. 199.

Exhibit 4 Key Indicators

in EUR 000s	2001	2002	2003	2004	2005
Net Sales	42,003	49,318	56,587	64,592	67,219
Change in Net Sales	27.1%	17.4%	14.7%	14.1%	4.1%
Operating Profit	4,720	6,450	8,849	9,129	11,413
% of Net Sales	11.2%	13.1%	15.6%	14.1%	17.0%
Financial Income	51	66	67	51	87
Financial expenses	(380)	(356)	(379)	(228)	(153)
Profit before taxes	4,391	6,160	8,537	8,952	11,347
% of Net Sales	10.4%	12.5%	15.1%	13.9%	16.9%
Taxes	1,303	1,771	2,492	2,957	2,923
Profit after taxes	3,088	4,389	6,045	5,995	8,424
Balance Sheet Total	26,119	29,271	33,592	32,735	36,302
Internet-bearing liabilities	5,238	5,515	6,004	4,912	3,738
Shareholders' equity and reserves	15,239	17,887	21,653	19,733	24,137
Return on equity (ROE) %	21.5%	26.5%	30.6%	28.9%	38.4%
Return on investment (ROI) %	23.8%	29.5%	34.6%	35.0%	43.9%
Equity ratio %	58.3%	61.1%	64.5%	60.3%	66.5%
Gearing %	25.5%	11.2%	−11.8%	−13.9%	−15.6%
Gross investments	546	626	893	2,234	1,361
% of Net Sales	1.3%	1.3%	1.6%	3.5%	2.0%
Average personnel	317	333	356	375	371
Personnel at the end of the financial year	324	344	365	355	377

SOURCE: Marimekko Annual Report, December 31, 2005, p. 62.

NOTE: Operating profit in 2004 includes a non-recurring capital loss of EUR 1.235 million on the sale of shares of Grünstein Product Oy. 2004–2005 reflects a change in accounting standard to International Financial Reporting Standards (IFRS).

(Continued)

Exhibit 4 (Continued)

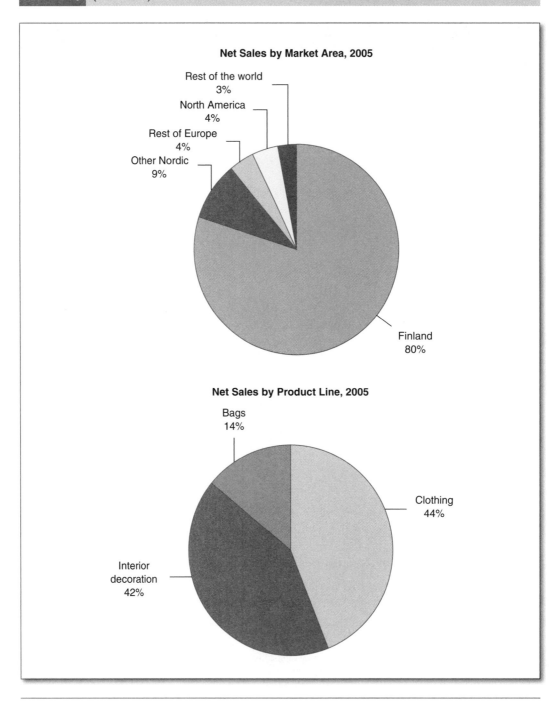

Net Sales by Market Area, 2005

Rest of the world
3%

North America
4%

Rest of Europe
4%

Other Nordic
9%

Finland
80%

Net Sales by Product Line, 2005

Bags
14%

Clothing
44%

Interior
decoration
42%

SOURCE: Company Documents.

11 key terms: feelings, respect, truth, enthusiasm, discipline, reward, team spirit, total responsibility, caring, fairness and social responsibility. Along with her thesis, Paakkanen openly promoted the following three components: management by emotion, doing things together, and creativity cannot be delegated. Management by emotion was based on respect for everyone in the company and the belief that all staff members were considered to have unique talents, creativity and skills. Doing things together addressed the concept that teamwork was necessary for success. Creativity cannot be delegated was a notion that permitted artistic freedom as long as it was accompanied by responsibility. See Exhibit 5 for more

Exhibit 5	Marimekko Company Principles

Company Principles

- Doing things together has been the most important.
- Employees are the most important capital of the company.
- Friendship has been more important than power in the working atmosphere.
- Creativity has been given the freedom, but it is also always followed by responsibility.
- One of our most important goals has been the everyday happiness of our personnel.

Kirsti Paakkanen's Management Principles

- *Marimekko is an example:* Whatever you do, act as an example. All your activities are followed. Your actions speak louder than your words. Today we also act as a trendsetter for our customers' consumer behavior. This is a great responsibility.
- *Inspire:* You must be the most enthusiastic "player" of your team. To be able to set an example to others, we need a team that pulls together. When such an exemplary group completes a project, all of its individual members and their achievements are evaluated and rewarded on the basis of the total result.
- *Develop:* Delegate decision making to that organizational level which has the best knowledge and expertise required for the project. Managers need to define the direction. Trust in the team's work is necessary, but support and control are as important.
- *Ascertain:* It is your duty to make sure that each task that you delegate gets done. It is an excellent idea to have a team as broad as possible around you, but you always need to ascertain who is responsible for the realization of the task and make sure that it continues to move in the right direction.
- *Commit yourself:* When an issue is decided, stand behind it, even if you had originally been against it.
- *Search:* We shall look for innovation. We shall create a play with a script for every season. The script has to work from design to the retail store. The script needs to be known by everyone.
- *Identify:* Identify, locate and eliminate the sources of problems. Do not only cure the symptoms.
- *Find out:* Make sure that everybody knows where we are going. Make sure that you understand and that others understand and know at which point of the play we are proceeding.

SOURCE: Company files.

information on Marimekko's company principles and Paakkanen's management principles.

Marimekko's senior management team was made up of nine individuals, including Paakkanen. All of the top management was Finnish and all were female, with the exception of the recently recruited Thomas Ekst röm as the company's chief financial officer (CFO) (see Exhibit 6). Marimekko did not publish an organizational chart and did not have strict job definitions. Tiina Alahuhta, Marimekko's public relations manager, explained:

Exhibit 6 Board and Key Executives

Board of Directors

Kari Miettinen, Born 1951, B.Sc. (Econ), Authorized Public Accountant, Chairman of the Board since 1991.

Matti Kavetvuo, Born 1944, M. Sc. (Eng), B. Sc. (Econ), Member since 1997.

Kirsti Paakkanen, Born 1929, B. Sc. (Advertising/Marketing and Finnish Studies), Member since 1991.

Management Group

Kirsti Paakkanen, CEO/President. Since 1991.

Riitta Kojonen, Product Information. Employed by the company since 1986

Sirpa Loukamo, Product Development, Clothing. Employed by the company since 1973.

Piia Rossi, Retail Sales. Employed by the company since 1988.

Merja Puntila, Domestic wholesale. Employed by the company since 1970.

Päivi Lonka, Export and Licensing Sales. Employed by the company since 2004.

Helinä Uotila, Production and Purchases. Employed by the company since 1972.

Ritva Schoultz, Personnel Affairs. Employed by the company since 1982.

Marja Korkeela, Corporate Communications and Investor Relations. Employed by the company since 1999.

Thomas Ekström, Finance and Administration. Employed by the company since 2006.

SOURCE: Company files.

For example, I'm the public relations manager, but there is no real strict job description. I also work on a number of other projects such as export and investor relations. For nearly all projects, there is a project leader and they must take responsibility and it must be clear what the objective is. We have to have good internal communication to make it work.

As of the end of 2005, the company had 377 people in total, of whom 90.9 per cent were women and 9.1 per cent were men. Approximately 90 per cent of the staff was from Finland. Staff turnover was six per cent and was attributed to retirements. The average age of the employee base was 42.

The Design Function

At the heart of Marimekko's organization was the relationship with the company's approximately 18 freelance designers. Marimekko had three main product lines— clothing, interiors and bags—each with its own product development teams. Each team was responsible for developing the context of the new line. For example, in clothing, the freelance designers worked with Marimekko's product development team, which was led by Kirsti Paakkanen and Sirpa Loukamo. In interior decoration, the product development team thoroughly examined the 'soul' of a pattern after it had been created to see which types of products it could be applied to and what the pattern or product would communicate. The designers were not given any direct instructions or limitations, but they were encouraged to create their own ideas into the patterns and/or garments. When asked how this worked in practice, Paakkanen responded:

> Marimekko is principally a design house. All of the personnel are organized around the design function. Everyone in the company knows this, and everyone in the company is aware of what we're aiming at from a design standpoint—we develop and explain this constantly. In managing designers, we have to make the controls to ensure that they are well briefed about what we want. The briefing process is one of the most vital parts of what we do. And then the designers' link up into other areas of the organization and work very closely with everyone, including marketing, sales and production.

For the designer to translate the concepts into producible designs, they would work with Marimekko's internal production team to test how the designs would be manufactured. After running tests in the printing machines for color and quality, the designer would meet with Marimekko's product and retail teams to finalize the designs. Production would determine whether or not the product would be made in Marimekko's Finnish facilities or outsourced in Finland or offshore. The retail team would begin planning how the new collection would be adapted into the Marimekko shop environment. Paakkanen was a part of the discussions, offering feedback and suggestions before the goods went into production.

The rationale for having freelance designers was to access highly talented individuals who had already made or who were seeking to make their name well known in the design community. Designers were often attracted to Marimekko, not only for the aesthetic, but also due to the creative freedom and the fact that they could build their own name under the umbrella of the company. Paakkanen explained:

> We are the only company that really stresses that every product displays the name of the designer. This goes not only for apparel, but for bags and fabrics as well. By putting the names on the products, it gives the designer responsibility and it makes them proud when the items are selling well. For the designers, I tell them they have to fight for their place in the sun. By being independent from Marimekko, their sole focus is on design, and they are given free reign to be creative.

Marimekko was constantly scanning the landscape for new design talent. As Paakkanen explained: "There's a large pool of designers who want to work here. We do, however, take a proactive approach by looking at all of the design schools, and we see who are some of the best designers. We also organize our own competitions and stay abreast of what's going on with other design competitions." Marimekko typically signed contracts with new designers for a specific season or particular task. With established designers, such as the 30-year plus relationship with Fujiwo Ishimoto, Marimekko had general agreements involving stipulations on the work to be performed and on confidentiality and remuneration. Designers were paid either for an individual design, a group of designs or a complete collection. Some designer contracts included an additional financial incentive in the form of a royalty payment if the products exceeded Marimekko's internally developed targets. As Ritva Schoultz, head of personnel affairs, stated:

> The freelance contracts vary by case. Some are paid for the product that we purchase; some for a collection that we decide to buy. The basic rule of thumb is that the freelance designers present us several alternatives from which we choose the ones that we wish to purchase. The freelance contracts do not have a fixed rate. Some designers have a contract to receive royalties.

Most of the designers currently working for Marimekko were Finnish. Only Fujiwo Ishimoto (Japan), Anna Danielsson (Sweden) and Katsuji Wakisaka (Japan) were foreign. Also, American designers, such as Robert Segal and Alicia Rosauer had created some items that Marimekko still had in production. Most designers split their working time between their own studios and the Marimekko head office.

Domestic Sales

Three individuals led the sales function: Piia Rossi for Marimekko-owned retail locations; Merja Puntila for domestic wholesale; and Päivi Lonka for exports.

As of mid-2006, the company owned 24 stores in Finland, one in Stockholm, Sweden, and one in Frankfurt, Germany. Rossi's internal team was responsible for the display and training of all in-store staff. Company-owned shops were seen to be the manifestation of the Marimekko brand experience. The stores were anywhere from 150 square metres to 600 square metres in size and featured bright colors, combining raw fabric prints with men's and women's apparel, home products, bags and other licensed accessories. All staff was adorned in seasonal Marimekko co-ordinates and strove to create an energetic and spirited shop environment (see Exhibit 7).

All new staff took part in intensive training sessions, which involved presentations from Marimekko's retail and product team as well as external philosophers, psychologists and creative experts. In addition, Paakkanen herself attended a portion of each training session and spoke one-on-one with each new employee. She explained:

> A lot of people in Finland already know a little bit about Marimekko before joining. When we opened our last shop, we had over 300 applicants for 10 positions. In the first training session, I talk about being a creative company instead of being a bunch of bureaucrats. I then talk to everyone and I ask them about their dreams, their home life, what they want to do and what they like. I want to feel who the people are, and I want to explain my thesis to them directly. I explain

Exhibit 7 Marimekko Shop

Store Interior

SOURCE: Company files.

Store Exterior

how they can make the thesis their own. My intention is to set the expectations for being an employee. The purpose of this is to really explain the corporate culture as this molds the attitude of people right from the beginning.

Marimekko's domestic wholesale division was responsible for selling to approximately 140 retailers in Finland, just under one-quarter of which were Marimekko concept shops; the rest were multi-label retailers.

International Sales

Marimekko sold to approximately 1,000 shops on a worldwide basis. Since 2004, the company had been actively pursuing the Marimekko-concept shop, which were retail venues that were owned by third parties and that had Marimekko branding. In 2005, the company had opened up four new Marimekko-concept shops in the United Arab Emirates, Iceland, Sweden and the United States. Marimekko had also signed agreements with Mitsubishi and Look Inc. to open 15 Marimekko-concept shops in Japan over the next few years. Additionally, for 2006, Marimekko was planning to open concept or shop-in-shop retail points in Belgium, Portugal and Sweden to name but a few. Päivi Lonka, head of export and licensing sales, talked about selling Marimekko outside of Finland:

> Marimekko's major strength is its unique, original design. Behind each Marimekko product is a designer whose creation has earned its place in the collection. Furthermore, during its entire 50-year history Marimekko, has always represented the most innovative designs and has managed its image within the spirit of the times.
>
> The key challenges for Marimekko's international expansion include the control of the distribution and managing a consistent brand image to maintain steady growth. [Because] the Marimekko design is unique, one of our major challenges has included examining whether there is enough demand for this kind of design in a new market. The second challenge concerns introducing and increasing the awareness of a new brand with limited marketing resources. There is also a challenge in maintaining a consistent brand image—without restricting the entrepreneur's freedom too much—that can still be adapted to different cultural environments. [A third

challenge] is the careful examination of the products' and product ranges' ability to meet the needs of each country market.

Marimekko provided training to all third-party retail venues, although sometimes the training was done outside of Finland due to logistics and costs in transporting shop owners to Helsinki. As of 2006, the company was in the early stages of developing a training package for the concept shops located outside of Finland. Paakkanen commented on the challenge of communicating the Marimekko philosophy to all third-party operations: "I meet with all of the shop owners and explain them to the Marimekko concept. We need to carefully choose new shop owners who understand the philosophy. However, it becomes more difficult describing this to all of their employees."

Production

Production was led by Helinä Uotila and included 118 staff. Most of the company's production needs were fulfilled within the European Union (EU), which was in direct contrast to the majority of textile companies in Western Europe and North America, who opted to produce the majority of textile goods in the Far East and Latin America. Marimekko preferred to produce in Finland and the EU for reasons of control, response time and integration with the rest of the company. The company produced goods in offshore locations for reasons of expertise, such as the manufacturing of knit shirts in India and China. Helinä Uotila talked about the rationale for keeping a large portion of the production in Finland:

> We feel that the Marimekko designs in printed fabrics are so special that

the best results are achieved with the co-operation of nearby designers and experienced technical personnel. This is why we think it is important to have our own textile printing factory. We intend to keep it that way.

For the Finnish market, the origin [label] "Made in Finland" is very important. It is the same as the guarantee of good quality, and it also allows a higher price level. Moreover, Finns are very patriotic, and they want to support Finnish labor.

Marimekko's EU production was split among its own three facilities (approximately 40 per cent of domestic production) and independent contractors (the remaining 60 per cent). The company's three facilities were all located in Finland and included: a textile printing factory in Helsinki (48 employees), a clothing factory in Kitee (50 employees), and a bag factory in Sulkava (20 employees). In 2004, the company purchased a state-of-the-art printing machine for increased capabilities at the Helsinki textile printing factory. Uotila talked about Marimekko's production capacity:

In fabrics we still have extra printing capacity. Subcontracting and sourcing from lower cost countries are also very important. In clothing and bags, we do not have any plans to increase our own production. All the growth will come from subcontracting and, at the moment, mainly from Baltic countries.

The company was constantly striving to exceed environmental regulations in its owned facilities. For example, in 2005, Marimekko began a series of studies to better utilize heat, thereby saving on energy consumption. The warehouse was located at the Helsinki complex, which housed the company's head offices.

The Future

As Paakkanen reflected on Marimekko's current strength and growth prospects, she thought about the question that had often been posed by members of the press, investment analysts and other observers: "When is your retirement date?" Paakkanen responded:

I don't have a successor right now because there's no acute need. I have no doubt that there will be the appropriate person, and I'm always keeping my eyes open. However, when I look at the future of this company, I don't see any real threats. We're fortunate to not be in a country with earthquakes and natural catastrophes. There's nothing else that would be a threat. Originally, post-war Finland didn't have anything, and Marimekko started when the country was in a very poor state—it filled a void and it answered this need by giving beauty to everyday life. Companies that respond with genuineness to this need in the future with will be the ones that make a difference.

I don't fear big changes to anything. Together we have accepted the way we work, and I see no reason why that shouldn't continue into the future. I don't have any doubt that it will. We have great talent and a lot of new young people with great language skills who are able to deal effectively in foreign markets. In the future, the only thing I see is opportunity.

Leveraging Diversity to Maximum Advantage

The Business Case for Appointing More Women to Boards

Prepared by Carol Stephenson

Women bring a different perspective to decision making. Yet where that perspective is, arguably, needed most, on boards, women are noticeably under-represented. In this article, Ivey's Dean, who sits on several boards, makes a strong and compelling case for why there should be more women on more boards and what companies can do to identify and help more women to become board members.

The poet Ezra Pound once said that: "When two men in business always agree, one of them is unnecessary." Many companies appear to recognize this truism and the fact that diversity fosters ideas and learning. Some have established comprehensive strategies to recruit and retain employees from different cultures and backgrounds. Others promote diversity and its benefits in their corporate vision statements. And many carefully portray diversity in their annual reports and advertising campaigns.

Unfortunately, however, few Canadian companies have boards with a range of people with different interests and backgrounds. Still fewer have plans in place to address diversity at the board level. The majority continue to be governed by all male, all white board members who share largely the same backgrounds, circles of influence and views.

William Donaldson, chairman of the U.S. Securities and Exchange Commission, recently wrote: "Just as we strive for diversity in our workforce, we should strive for diversity of thought and experience on our boards. Monolithic backgrounds are destined to foster monolithic thinking." And I believe that monolithic thinking leads to missed opportunities, unresolved issues and potentially unworkable solutions.

However, as research on the impact of women on leadership teams demonstrates, diversity often eliminates this stagnation. Gender diversity, in particular, brings a number of other vital benefits to the boardroom as well. So, if a company is serious about cultivating a dynamic and diverse leadership team, then having more women on the board is a great way to begin.

This article first presents some of the compelling evidence for why companies need more women at the board level. Second, it elaborates on why women are not progressing as quickly as they should. Third, it prescribes some preliminary actions to address these issues. Essentially, this article underscores the fact that women merit a place at the board table—not simply for equity reasons, but because it makes sound business sense.

Why More Women Should Be on More Boards

Let's look at some of the reports and studies that substantiate the valuable contributions women make in positions of executive and board power.

In January 2004, the New York research group Catalyst released a study which examined the financial performance of 353 companies for four out of five years between 1996 and 2000. Catalyst found that the group of companies with the highest representation of women in their senior management teams had a 35 percent higher return on equity (ROE) and a 34 percent higher total return to shareholders (TRS) than companies with the lowest women's representation.

This mirrors the results of a longer-term study led by Roy Adler, a marketing professor at Pepperdine University in Malibu, California and executive director of the Glass Ceiling Research Centre. This study tracked the number of women in high-ranking positions at 215 Fortune 500 companies between 1980 and 1998.

The 25 companies with the best record for promoting women to senior positions, including the board, posted returns 18 percent higher and returns on investment 69 percent higher than the Fortune 500 median of their industry.

Similarly, the Conference Board of Canada tracked the progress of Canadian corporations with two or more women on the board from 1995 to 2001. The Conference Board found that these companies "were far more likely to be industry leaders in revenues and profits six years later."

Interestingly, this 2002 Conference Board report also refutes some of the most common myths about the impact of women on corporate boards. These myths include widely held misconceptions such as: women only care about the "soft" issues; women don't have the financial or strategic acumen needed at the board level; and women will hamper board unity.

To the contrary, the Conference Board concludes that: "Far from focusing on traditionally 'soft' areas, boards with more women surpass all-male boards in their attention to audit and

risk oversight and control." Specifically, its research shows that:

- 74 percent of boards with three or more women explicitly identify criteria for measuring strategy; only 45 percent of all-male boards do; and
- 94 percent of boards with three or more women explicitly monitor the implementation of corporate strategy; 66 percent of all-male boards do.

The Conference Board further concludes that the diversity that women bring enriches "the leadership palette with different perspectives" and that this "diversity enables constructive dissent that leads to board unity."

The Conference Board's research points to other critical benefits. For instance, gender diversity on the board and senior management team helps organizations to attract and retain valuable female talent. Also, "CEOs report that having women on boards contributes to positive attitudes among female employees."

In addition, the advantages that women bring in terms of ethical conduct are clearly significant:

- 94 percent of boards with three or more women ensure conflict of interest guidelines, compared with 68 percent of all-male boards, and
- 86 percent of boards with three or more women ensure a code of conduct for the organization, compared with 66 percent of all-male boards.

Women apparently broaden the focus of a board as well. When more women are on the board, the Conference Board found a major increase in the use of non-financial performance measures—such as innovation and social and community responsibility. As the Conference Board believes, "the factors that appear to be influenced by more women on boards are precisely those that have the most impact on corporate results."

Another important consideration is the fact that women have a deep and intimate knowledge of consumer markets and customers. Women, for example, control 80 percent of household spending, and using their own resources, make up 47 percent of investors. They buy more than three quarters of all products and services in North America.

The influence of women in business-to-business markets is also growing, especially here in Canada. There are more women entrepreneurs per capita in Canada than in any industrialized country. According to the Prime Minister's Task Force on Women Entrepreneurs, more than 821,000 Canadian women entrepreneurs annually contribute in excess of $18 billion to Canada's economy. Their numbers have increased more than 200 percent over the past 20 years and they represent the fastest growing demographic in our economy today.

Sadly, the progress of women in advancing to the board level is not as impressive. According to the 2003 Catalyst Census of Women Board Directors of Canada, women hold 11.2 percent of board positions in the Financial Post 500, up from 9.8 percent in 2001. That's less than a two percent gain.

And the proportion of companies with no women directors has remained the same since 2001, 51.4 percent. What's more, women chair only three of the 243 publicly traded companies on the Financial Post 500.

◼ Why Aren't More Women on Boards?

The most common reason given for why more women are not occupying positions of corporate leadership is that they do not have the operational experience required. Catalyst, for example, blames the gap on the fact that women often choose staff jobs, such as marketing and

human resources, while most senior executives and board positions are filled from the ranks of line managers with critical profit-and-loss responsibility.

Recently, several business researchers and observers have also speculated that women are not advancing because they do not have the ambition and competitive drive of men. New York psychiatrist, Anna Fels, author of *Necessary Dreams: Ambition in Women's Changing Lives*, believes that women are conditioned to be "selflessly unambitious." From an early age, they learn that in order to be liked, they must play down their accomplishments. Consequently when they join the corporate world, they fail to push for raises and promotions.

Similarly, Linda Babcock and Sandra Laschever, co-authors of *Women Don't Ask: Negotiation and the Gender Divide*, say that girls are taught to be "communal," to make relationships a priority and to focus on the needs of others instead of their own needs. This makes them hesitant to negotiate for more pay or greater responsibility on the job.

A third common reason given for why women don't advance is that business—and society in general—still doesn't adequately compensate women for shouldering more family responsibilities. Consequently, women are paid less and don't advance as quickly or as far up the corporate ladder as men do.

For example, economist Stephen J. Rose and Heidi I. Hartmann, President of the Institute for Women's Policy Research in Washington, released a report earlier this year that compares the earnings of the average woman with those of the average man in the United States. Based on Bureau of Labour Statistics, the report shows that the average American woman earns less than half—about 44 percent—of what the average man earns over the course of his career.

Why? Outright discrimination is part of the reason. Another reason is that the majority of women and men still work in largely sex-segregated occupations, leaving women stuck in lower-paying jobs. However, a third reason is that few companies have found ways to help women blend their family responsibilities with the demands of the job. Rose and Hartmann found that women are sometimes treated equally, mostly when they behave like traditional men and leave their family responsibilities at home.

On the other hand, some experts dispute the belief that women are not as ambitious as men. Catalyst, for example, polled more than 950 Fortune 1000 executives within two to three reporting levels of the CEO and conducted in-depth interviews with more than 30 female and male executives. Women and men reported "equal aspirations to reach the corner office, and women who have children living with them are just as likely to aspire to the CEO job as those who do not."

These survey results also refuted the contention that only women care about achieving a balance between their working and personal lives. For example, both women and men reported that they employ similar advancement strategies and have experienced similar barriers during their rise to the top.

Catalyst further uncovered "striking similarities between men and women regarding work/life balance management: 51 percent of women and 43 percent of men reported difficulty in achieving a balance between work and personal lives, and women and men participants equally desire a variety of informal and formal flexible work arrangements." Nevertheless, as women advanced to senior levels, Catalyst reported that they have made more trade-offs than men between work and their personal lives.

From my experience, women are just as committed as men to achieving corporate success and career excellence. I have also found that men and women often express the same desire for balance between their work and personal lives. And I know that women can and do make powerful contributions to their organization's success, even though they are less likely to brag about their accomplishments.

What's more, so what if women prefer marketing or human resources as career paths? Are these functions any less important than operations or finance to the success of a company? Should these "softer" considerations be absent from discussions of corporate direction and strategy? And in an era where corporate social responsibility, trust and caring are the hallmarks of enduring corporate success, are not the tendencies of women to be more attuned and attentive to the interests of others invaluable to companies?

What Should Companies and Women Do?

To benefit from the increasingly important assets that women bring to companies, I believe that corporate boards must not only recognize those assets, but also develop a plan to ensure that their boards become more gender diverse. This plan should stem from a careful analysis of the current skills and experiences of board members, thus identifying any existing gaps.

Then, boards should actively seek out potential female candidates who could address these gaps. This means expanding the scope and depth of the search for new directors. For example, board recruiters could approach women's business groups or solicit the recommendations of female executives, both within and outside the company.

Contacting universities and business schools are other excellent ways to find out about potential leadership talent. At Ivey, for example, most of our students in the regular MBA program have at least five years of management experience. Our executive MBA program attracts business leaders with established credentials in a wide variety of industries, and in both the public and private sectors.

There is also the "Women in the Lead/ Femmes de Tete" Directory, co-sponsored by Ivey and HSBC Bank Canada. Developed by Doreen McKenzie-Sanders, it compiles the credentials and experience of more 568 Canadian women with impressive achievements in a range of industries.

In addition to improved recruiting, effective diversity plans should include programs to assist women to succeed in their new responsibilities, such as mentoring, corporate orientation and in-depth briefings on core business and industry issues. These programs ultimately benefit all new board members.

Overall, the board's diversity plan should be specific and measurable, with clear accountabilities. But, this is not about establishing quotas. Rather, an effective diversity initiative examines and evaluates results, not just numbers.

Nevertheless, I don't believe that boards are solely responsible for the poor representation of women on corporate boards. Women must also actively seek out potential opportunities to serve at the board level. No one can sit back and expect board appointments to come their way.

To attract board invitations, women must promote their accomplishments, build and leverage their connections, and seek opportunities to enhance their qualifications. And when they join a board, they must be willing to invest their time and talent toward learning and contributing to a healthy discussion of the issues. Once more women take charge of their own future, the fruits of their efforts will blossom, grow and spread the seeds for future opportunities.

Fully Leveraging Diversity

There is a powerful business case for why corporate boards should bring more women around the board table. As the research proves, companies with female board members can expect significantly higher returns and better overall financial performance.

More female representation also translates into improved risk management and audit control, increased ethical oversight and a broader, more accurate assessment of the company's success.

Equally important, with more female leadership, companies are better able to attract more female talent. They send a powerful message to the women who already work for their organizations that their contributions are valuable—that their voices are heard. They demonstrate to employees, investors and other stakeholders that diversity truly matters to their corporate success.

Indeed it does. When companies bring together a diversity of people—especially at the board level—ideas flow and innovation soars. Improved strategies emerge. Better decisions are made. A virtuous circle of continuous learning is created and sustained. In an economy where knowledge drives results, diversity is a precious asset.

Culture and Leadership

Laura Guerrero

The University of Texas at El Paso

When we sit together as Germans, Swiss, Americans, and Swedes, with many of us living, working, and travelling in different places, the insights can be remarkable. But you have to force people into these situations. Mixing nationalities doesn't just happen. You also have to acknowledge cultural differences without becoming paralyzed by them.

—Percy Barnevik[1]

Although there are no formal theories of global leadership, there are several ways in which culture affects leadership. As the trend toward globalization continues, there is increased frequency of contact between people of different cultures (Daft, 2005; Dubrin, 2007; Yukl, 2006).

Adler and Bartholomew (1992) suggest that global leaders need to develop the following cross-cultural competencies. First, leaders need to understand the business, political, and cultural environments worldwide. Second, leaders should learn to understand perspectives, tastes, trends, and technologies of many other cultures. Third, they need to learn to work with people from other cultures. Fourth, they should be able to adapt to living and communicating in other cultures. Fifth, leaders need to learn to relate to people from other cultures from a position of equality rather than a position of cultural superiority.

---

[1]Percy Barnevik is the president and CEO of ABB (Asea Brown Boveri).

Culture, Diversity, Ethnocentrism, and Prejudice

Culture can be defined in several ways. Northouse (2010) defines *culture* as "the learned beliefs, values, rules, norms, symbols, and traditions that are common to a group of people."

Related to culture are terms such as *multicultural* and *diversity*. *Multicultural* refers to a way of seeing or doing things that takes into account more than one culture. A multicultural leader is one with the attitudes and skills to build relationships with and motivate followers who are diverse across lifestyles, social attitudes, race, ethnic background, gender, age, and education (Dubrin, 2007). *Diversity* refers to the existence of different cultures, ethnicities, socioeconomic levels, sexual orientations, or races within a group or organization (Yukl, 2006). Some people now use the term *inclusion* instead of *diversity* to highlight that organizations need to include as many diverse people as possible in organizations (Dubrin, 2007).

Related to leadership and culture are the concepts of ethnocentrism and prejudice. *Ethnocentrism* is "the tendency for individuals to place their own group (ethnic, racial, or cultural) at the center of their observations of others and the world" (Northouse, 2010). Although ethnocentrism is a natural tendency, it can act as an obstacle to effective leadership because it prevents leaders from understanding and respecting the views of others. Ethnocentrism creates challenges for minority leaders and subordinates (Daft, 2005).

Another natural tendency is that of holding prejudices. *Prejudice* can be a pejorative "attitude, belief, or emotion held by an individual about another individual or group that is based on faulty or unsubstantiated data" (Northouse, 2010). Prejudice is often held against people or groups of people based on their race, gender, age, sexual preference, or other characteristics. Like ethnocentrism, prejudice prevents the leader from understanding and appreciating other people. Successful global leaders need to be able to recognize and minimize their own ethnocentrism and prejudice toward others, as well as manage others who may be ethnocentric or prejudiced.

Cultural Dimensions

Many studies have addressed the issue of identifying the different dimensions of culture. One of the best-known studies is Hofstede's (1980, 2001). Hofstede identified five major cultural dimensions: power distance, uncertainty avoidance, individualism–collectivism, masculinity–femininity, and long-term/short-term orientation.

A more recent and comprehensive study by House and his colleagues (2004), known as the GLOBE study, has identified nine cultural dimensions. The word *GLOBE* stands for Global Leadership and Organizational Behavior Effectiveness. These are the cultural dimensions identified by GLOBE researchers (Northouse, 2010; Yukl 2006):

- *Uncertainty avoidance* refers to the degree to which a society depends on established social norms, rituals, rules, and procedures to avoid uncertainty.
- *Power distance* describes the extent to which members of society expect and are comfortable with power and wealth being distributed unequally.
- *Institutional collectivism* refers to the extent to which society encourages institutional or societal collective action as opposed to individual action.
- *In-group collectivism* refers to the extent to which individuals express pride, loyalty, and cohesiveness toward their organizations or families.

- *Gender egalitarianism* refers to the degree to which a society deemphasizes gender differences and supports gender equality.
- *Assertiveness* refers to the degree to which individuals in a society are assertive, confrontational, and aggressive in their interaction with others.
- *Future orientation* describes the extent to which individuals in a culture participate in future-oriented behaviors such as planning, investing, and delaying gratification.
- *Performance orientation* refers to the extent to which a society encourages and rewards individuals for superior performance.
- *Humane orientation* refers to the extent to which a society encourages and rewards individuals for being fair, philanthropic, generous, and kind to others.

The GLOBE study grouped the 62 countries into 10 clusters that share language, geography, religion, and historical connections. The regional clusters are as follows: Anglo, Latin Europe, Nordic Europe, Germanic Europe, Eastern Europe, Latin America, Middle East, Sub-Saharan Africa, Southern Asia, and Confucian Asia. The results of the study indicate that although scores *within a cluster* were correlated, they were unrelated to the scores in *different clusters.*

Leadership Behavior and Culture Clusters

The general purpose of the GLOBE study was to determine whether cultural differences were related to different leadership views (Yukl, 2006). GLOBE researchers used the implicit leadership theory (Lord & Maher, 1991), which states that people have implicit beliefs about the attributes and characteristics that distinguish leaders from nonleaders and effective leaders from ineffective ones. GLOBE researchers identified six global leadership behaviors (Northouse, 2010):

- Charismatic/value-based leadership is the ability to inspire, motivate, and expect superior performance from followers based on strongly held core values. This type of leadership would result in being visionary, inspirational, self-sacrificing, trustworthy, and performance oriented.
- Team-oriented leadership places emphasis on team building and having a common purpose among members of the team. This leadership type is collaborative, integrative, diplomatic, compassionate, and administratively competent.
- Participative leadership emphasizes the involvement of others in making and implementing decisions. Participative leaders are democratic.
- Humane-oriented leadership places emphasis on being supportive, considerate, compassionate, generous, and sensitive to other people.
- Autonomous leadership requires an independent and individualistic leadership style, which includes being self-directed and unique.
- Self-protective leadership refers to a leadership style that focuses on ensuring the safety and security of the leader and the group. This type of leadership is self-centered and interested in preserving the status of the group and the leader, even if it causes conflict with others.

The GLOBE researchers used these six global leadership behaviors to determine what leadership view each culture cluster held. Not surprisingly, it was found that different culture clusters had different leadership profiles. However, it was also found that certain leadership characteristics were valued across cultures, and some leadership attributes were found to be universally undesirable.

The universally desirable characteristics of an outstanding leader are trustworthiness, fairness, honesty, optimism, dynamism, dependability, intelligence, decisiveness, administrative skill, having foresight, planning ahead, being encouraging, building confidence, being motivational, being effective at bargaining, being a win–win problem solver, having communication skills, being informed, coordinating, being a team builder, and being excellence oriented (House et al., 2004).

The attributes that were found to be universally viewed as obstacles to effective leadership are were noncooperativeness, irritability, ruthlessness, as well as being a loner, asocial, inexplicit, egocentric, and dictatorial (House et al., 2004).

The importance of considering culture in leadership is growing due to globalization and our increased interdependence with people of other cultures. Being aware that cultural differences affect the way people view the world and the way they act and communicate with others helps leaders be more effective. Leaders who understand culture and its impact can adjust their leadership styles to be more effective with people of different cultural backgrounds (Daft, 2005; Dubrin, 2007; Yukl, 2006).

▧ References

Adler, N. J., & Bartholomew, S. (1992). Managing globally competent people. *Academy of Management Executive, 6,* 52–65.

Daft, R. L. (2005). *The leadership experience* (3rd ed.). Mason, OH: Thomson, South-Western.

Dubrin, A. (2007). *Leadership: Research findings, practice, and skills.* New York: Houghton Mifflin.

Hofstede, G. (1980). *Culture's consequences: International differences in work-related values.* Beverly Hills, CA: Sage.

Hofstede, G. (2001). *Culture's consequences: Comparing values, behaviors, institutions, and organizations across nations.* Thousand Oaks, CA: Sage.

House, R. J., Hanges, P. J., Javidan, M., Dorfman, P. W., Gupta, V., & Associates. (2004). *Leadership, culture, and organizations: The GLOBE study of 62 societies.* Thousand Oaks, CA: Sage.

Lord, R., & Maher, K. J. (1991). *Leadership and information processing: Linking perceptions and performance.* Boston: Unwin-Everyman.

Northouse, P. G. (2010). *Leadership: Theory and practice* (5th ed.). Thousand Oaks, CA: Sage.

Taylor, W. (1992). The logic of global business: An interview with ABB's Percy Barnevik. In W. Bennis (Ed.), *Leaders on leadership: Interviews with top executives* (pp. 67–89). Boston, MA: Harvard Business Review.

Yukl, G. (2006). *Leadership in organizations* (6th ed.). Upper Saddle River, NJ: Pearson/Prentice Hall.

▧ The Cases

Intel in China

The newly appointed division head must examine organizational or communication problems within a division of a billion-dollar semiconductor manufacturer. The manager made a decision to which an employee responded emotionally, creating the potential for conflict within the department. Cross-cultural issues come into play given that the manager, although originally from China, was educated and gathered extensive experience in the West and was thus considered an expatriate by his employees. The manager must also examine the effect of organizational culture on an employee's behavior.

Grupo Financiero Inverlat

A small team of Canadian managers from a large financial institution is faced with the challenges of managing a recently acquired Mexican operation. Managers must cope with a language barrier and cultural differences as they try to restructure the overstaffed Mexican financial institution.

The Reading

Global Fatalities: When International Executives Derail

Developing global executives is an expensive proposition that can produce a significant return—provided that the corporation uses the knowledge and expertise it gained from earlier experiences effectively. These coauthors interviewed 101 individuals who succeeded in their international postings and concluded that poor management of three factors contributes to the failure of international executives: the individual, the cultural context, and organizational mistakes. Based on their book, *Developing Global Executives: The Lessons of International Experience,* the authors outline and discuss the steps an organization can take to ensure that executives posted abroad will be successful.

Intel in China

Prepared by Donna Everatt under the supervision of Kathleen Slaughter and Xiaojun Qian

In October 1999, Charles Tang, newly appointed manager of marketing programs of Intel China in Beijing, had just emerged from an emotionally charged meeting with Yong Li, an account manager in Tang's division. The meeting, attended by Li's direct supervisor, Qing Chen, was convened by Tang to discuss Li's feelings regarding a decision Tang had made to discontinue a project that had been assigned to Li by his previous supervisor. Despite what Tang considered to be sound business logic supporting his decision, Li's resistance left Tang wondering whether there were extenuating factors he needed to consider. Tang also wondered whether the blow-up with Li was an isolated incident, or whether it signalled deeper organizational or communication problems in his newly acquired division.

AUTHOR'S NOTE: The Richard Ivey School of Business gratefully acknowledges the generous support of The Richard and Jean Ivey Fund in the development of this case as part of the Richard and Jean Ivey Fund Asian Case Series.

Version: (B) 2009-09-10

⬛ Intel

In the mid-1960s, Intel introduced the world's first microprocessor, sparking a revolution in the technological industry. Intel was an unequivocal success story—its strategy of "driving new technology, serving global markets, and increasing customer preference for the Intel brand, while delivering excellent financial results to our stockholders" had served them well over the years. By 1996, driven by strong sales of the Pentium® processor, Intel was on their seventh consecutive year of record earnings of both sales and revenue, and had reached the US$20 billion in revenues milestone. 1997 was another year of record revenues (an increase of 20 per cent) and record net income of almost US$7 billion, up 35 per cent over 1996. However, 1998 brought weaker than anticipated demand for personal computer (PC) products, which lead to lower first quarter revenue and earnings. Dr. Andy Grove, the founder and enigmatic leader of Intel referred to first quarter 1998 results as "disappointing," and stated that the "PC industry seems to have gotten ahead of itself, building more product than customers wanted." First quarter 1998 revenue of US$6 billion fell seven per cent, net income and earnings per share declined 36 per cent from the first quarter of 1997. The company widely expected revenue for the second quarter of 1998 to be flat, and year-to-date performance during the year had reflected this expectation.

Intel's global mission was nothing short of being the "pre-eminent building block supplier to the new computing industry worldwide." Thus, a major part of Intel's strategy was their commitment to creating microprocessors that the software of the next millennium could tap into. Concurrently, Intel followed a strategy of encouraging the developments of software engineers so they could push the envelope in software design to ensure that users would receive the benefits of the most advanced hardware Intel was developing. To help strengthen the Pentium® brand name, Intel focused on emerging markets with programs that stimulated demand for Intel products. Intel had succeeded tremendously in their branding campaign, and was considered one of the world's top 10 brands. Indeed, in 1997, over half (56 per cent) of Intel's revenue was generated outside of the United States, with the Asia-Pacific region and Japan accounting for almost a third of Intel's revenue. In 1999, Intel considered China to be their single most important market.

⬛ Intel People's Republic of China (PRC)

Intel PRC Corporation established a representative office in China as early as 1985; however, it was not until 1993 that Intel felt the time was right to more fully enter the Chinese market with the establishment of two wholly owned foreign enterprises. The first, Intel Architecture Development Co., Ltd. (IADL) was responsible for the sales, marketing and development of Intel's products and services in China. IADL's 250 employees were located in 13 offices throughout China; however, the Shanghai office with 100 employees and the Beijing office with 80 were the largest. The second, Intel (China) Technology Co. Ltd., was the entity of Intel's assembly and testing plant operations.

IADL employed more than 80 engineers who worked with local and multinational software vendors to develop innovative consumer and business applications to PC users in China. IADL's charter was to "accelerate technology adoption in the PRC by providing technical and marketing support to local software developers." Initiatives included a developer support program, which included seminars, matchmaking events, training and conferences for Chinese software engineers and a donation of more than RMB$1.5 million of Pentium II processor-based development systems to assist leading Chinese software developers in bringing advanced software to local and international markets.

IADL's mandate was critical to Intel's growth, as senior management was aware that regardless of their research and development (R&D) expenditures, without software applications that could take advantage of the latest hardware developments, the user would not receive the advantage from that innovation. Thus, according to Tang, Intel's role in China was to act as a matchmaker, bringing all pieces of technology together to help China's PC users to understand how computing could help them in a comprehensive way. Tang explained that Intel looked at technology from a 'total solution standpoint.'

> By the time we start developing a new chip, we're already looking at what applications it will support and what solution it provides to the user. Thus, by the time the chip is ready to go into market, the platforms, the solutions are all ready so it is co-ordinated. This way, we're all moving forward and everybody wins.

By 1999, Intel had become involved in "just about every operation in the IT industry in China" and were aggressively marketing Intel-branded products throughout the country. Though still at its early stage of development, China's computer market had been growing twice as fast as the world average, and was poised to become the second largest computer market in the world by the end of the century. With its large population and fast economic growth, China's potential was extremely attractive to multinationals. As a global leader, Intel was well-positioned to capitalize on this opportunity and Charles Tang was one of the most important players in advancing Intel's presence in China.

◪ Charles Tang

Tang had not returned to China since his departure eight years prior and his home country had changed dramatically during that time. Beijing had undergone a rapid period of extensive growth and the ubiquity of shiny modern buildings and presence of so many foreign firms was a shock to Tang. However, despite the changes in Beijing that he saw, Tang had the advantage of being previously exposed to the reality of life in Beijing, which could overwhelm many expatriates—the crowded streets, the pungent aromas emanating from the street markets, traffic congestion, punishing heat, and air quality for example. Tang commented that he had known of other Chinese nationals who had returned to the mainland, and despite the fact several months had elapsed, they still did not feel comfortable being in China and never really could adjust to life there after having lived in the United States or Europe. Though he initially felt "like a tourist," after having spent just one weekend wandering through the street markets, alleyways and pathways through the heart of Beijing, he was convinced he had made the right decision and had not looked back since.

Tang was one of the first three employees who were transferred to China from other Intel sites in 1993 to more firmly establish Intel's operations in the mainland. Tang gained experience in many areas, including a two-year stint in Shanghai to help establish Intel Architecture Laboratory there. During his time there, Tang established Intel's software developer support program—an integral part of Intel's China strategy. The account managers (AMs) in Tang's department played a critical role in this support effort. Their prime mandate was to forge and nurture relationships with prestigious Chinese software developers and vendors. By 1999, Tang reported directly to the president of Intel PRC and oversaw critical areas such as government relations, as well as industry and community programs, which included donations to many of the top universities in China to support research and teaching activities, as well as donations of equipment, upgraded on an annual basis.

The scope of Tang's development projects ranged from the grassroots community level such as a program that would sponsor Chinese high school students to attend a popular international science and technology fair in the United States, to investigating strategic investment opportunities. Tang also played a leading role on Intel's corporate advisory board, a body that was comprised of some of the most prominent Chinese influencers, both from the IT industry and academia. The board's broad mandate was to "spearhead industry programs by working with trade associations and industry leaders to influence the development of programs throughout the region to promote indigenous development of the industry by transferring Intel's acquired experience and expertise locally."

Yong Li

Yong Li was one of four AMs, each of whom had individual projects in addition to their primary responsibility. According to Tang, an AM's required skill set included the ability to interact as an Intel ambassador with senior managers and owners of the software firms with whom Intel was developing relationships. This involved effectively communicating Intel's IT strategy, "not from a technical viewpoint but rather from a strategic perspective," while ensuring full customer satisfaction on a daily basis. Another critical strategic component of the AM's responsibilities lay in their ability to consistently recognize the possibilities of advancing the mutual interests of IADL and their clients—a key part of Intel's strategy in China. An AM's ability to exceed his clients' expectations was determined by his effectiveness in mobilizing Intel's internal resources, which involved extremely strong people skills and the ability to consistently demonstrate a mature, professional and diplomatic manner.

The Issue

When Tang took over Intel's Beijing division, he was eager to familiarize himself with the operation of each department, and to aid him in this, he reviewed the files of all employees to understand their roles. Using his best judgment, Tang reassigned work as he deemed necessary, to ensure that each employee was working, both individually and within a team,

toward advancing the strategic goals of the department and thus Intel in China. The same rationale was behind a reassignment of various departmental managers, and in the process, Tang reassigned the AMs under Qing Chen, a Beijing native. Though she had worked for a multinational before joining Intel, this was her first managerial position.

Tang's attention was drawn to Li's project upon reviewing Li's employee file. Though Tang felt the basic concept behind the project to be sound, he felt that it had expanded to such an extent from that which was initially proposed that it was not reasonable to expect that Li could realize the project's goals without it interfering with his primary duties of servicing his account base. The scope of the project had mushroomed in part due to the perspective of Li's previous supervisor who, according to Tang, was a very ambitious person who "approached everything on a grand scale with massive goals."

Initially, the project assigned to Li was the creation of a manual providing local software vendors with tips on running their enterprise, such as marketing various software products or how to manage or set up distribution channels, for example. However, Li approached the project with such unchecked zeal that it quickly transformed from a manual to a book form, with a chapter dedicated to comprehensive business planning issues, beginning with such basics as how to incorporate a business in China, sourcing venture capital, and the development of a comprehensive marketing plan tailored for software products.

Tang described the project as a "portable MBA-type book, covering essentially every topic a software company would need to know to do business in China." This was such an ambitious project, and Tang estimated it could take up to one year to complete, not including the two months of research Li had already conducted. Upon review of the file, Tang concluded that Li, a new and relatively young employee, without significant exposure to the business world or the software industry, did not have the background or expertise for this type of book.

Tang felt that the project would be better suited to a writer who specialized in issues in the software industry. Given that there were many other projects that could be assigned to Li, which were of a more appropriate scope and focus, Tang instructed Chen to inform Li that work on the project was to be halted immediately, and that Li should be assigned a new project.

When Chen informed Li of Tang's decision to cancel the project, Li "totally rejected her," and he was not willing to even listen to the rationale behind the decision. Chen turned to Tang for assistance as she was at a loss as to how to reconcile Tang's demand with Li's desire to continue with the project and his agitated state that it had been cancelled. Tang decided that given Li's reaction, the best course of action was to bring them all together, and he scheduled a meeting as soon as he could to resolve the issue. Tang was conscious of handling the situation in such a way that did not undermine Chen's authority, as he felt that the empowerment of direct supervisors was critical. On the other hand, Chen confessed she was confounded by Li's reaction.

Li's Perspective

During his brief history with Intel, Li had dedicated himself to exceeding his clients' service expectations. Indeed, Tang readily acknowledged that Li had excelled at developing relationships with senior management in the companies in his assigned account base. Tang agreed that this was no small feat, as Tang's client base included some of China's most influential software firms, and in some cases had been so successful that he had created strong 'guanxi' with senior management at those firms. Guanxi was the basis on which business in a Chinese context thrived. Loosely translated as 'relationships,' guanxi was such an integral part of doing business in China, that it was essentially impossible to do without it. Thus, when guanxi was established, it was protected at great cost, as it was widely considered to be the single most important factor in a successful business

transaction. Its value in a Chinese business context could not be underestimated.

Li's success, therefore, in the realm of his primary duties was indisputable; however, he also applied himself equally to conducting research for his project and took ownership of it very seriously. Upon hearing that Tang had cancelled his project, he voiced his opinion immediately to Chen, saying that the two months of work he had conducted on his project were "wasted." Moreover, it was Li's strong contention that Tang altered not only one of his projects, but the essence of his responsibilities in one broad stroke, without due consideration, thereby undermining his efforts to date. Li continued:

> This is typical of expat managers—they come along and don't really care about what the workers are doing. They don't show respect and change the workplace according to their whim without providing explanation, and without warning.

Li felt that Tang had caused him to 'lose face.' Causing another to 'lose face,' could result in irreparable damage to the interpersonal relations between those two parties.

Tang's Perspective

Though he had heard through Chen that Li was very upset, Tang was previously unaware of the extent to which Li felt he had 'lost face.' Tang was thus largely unsure of how his actions could have affected Li at such an emotional level, and he took a few moments to consider his perspective of the situation. Tang acknowledged that Li was successful in establishing strong relationships with his clients. However, Li won various concessions for his clients through a demanding style toward his colleagues and a single-mindedness of purpose. Another talent that Tang acknowledged Li brought to his AM position was his ability to "think big." However, Li's assertive manner was not commonly found in traditional Chinese workplaces, and some of his colleagues, both within his department and throughout other departments which Li relied upon, were uncomfortable with Li's level of zeal. Complicating the situation was Tang's assumption that Li had not been formally indoctrinated to the Intel culture.

To demonstrate the Intel culture, Tang explained that Intel's employees throughout the world were characterized by their energy and youth, and thrived in a dynamic and creative environment. Tang further explained that in order to sustain intense levels of innovation, a degree of dissension and constructive criticism was encouraged; however, policies that helped advance Intel's 64,000 employees globally in the same direction were required. Tang explained a crucial part of Intel's culture—which was in place to achieve this end—the "disagree and commit" philosophy.

> If a consensus has been established that a particular course of action or a decision is appropriate, any individual employee would not only have to commit to that decision, but if he or she were responsible in any way in implementing it, this concept would dictate that they act as if they were in 100 per cent agreement with the decision. This means that once the course of action had been decided, it should not be discernible who was for, and who was against the decision before it was made. This is a condition of employment at Intel. It is the professional code on which I was brought up on at Intel.

Given Li's reaction, Tang wondered whether he had communicated to Li, and potentially his other employees, the quintessential role that this philosophy played in Intel's culture.

Tang reflected upon what other factors he should consider in analysing Li's behavior

beyond his inexperience and apparent ignorance of Intel doctrine and considered potential underlying cross-cultural issues that might help to explain Li's behavior, while at the same time increase his understanding of all his employees. Although Tang had grown up in China and pursued his undergraduate degree in China, he had received a graduate degree from study in the United States as well as almost a decade of Western experience. Thus, he found himself in a precarious balance between two cultures. This created a rather unique situation for Tang—internally, he was perceived as a expatriate, yet because of his precise fluency in Mandarin and obvious comfort in Chinese culture, Tang felt he was perceived externally as a local Chinese.

✄ Tang—An Expatriate or a Local?

When Tang first returned to China, when meeting with local government officials, he had a difficult time in persuading them that he was directly authorized to make decisions. First, at 33, he was significantly younger than most senior managers at multinationals in Beijing. Second, most often local Chinese did not hold positions of such power in multinationals.

To establish his credibility externally, Tang used a clever and effective technique. When Tang first met with the officials, he noticed that when he proffered his opinions directly, many of the local officials did not have confidence that Tang was empowered to make decisions. After trying a more direct approach, when a decision was consequently required, Tang told the officials that "I should check with my boss" but offered his decision in the interim. In subsequent meetings, it became clear to the local officials that Tang's "boss'" decision correlated precisely with Tang's personal decisions, time and time again. Thus, in time, he succeeded in establishing his credibility.

On other occasions, when he encountered a reticence among senior external managers or officials, he used another technique, equally effective. Tang would say, "I'll see if I can set up a meeting with my boss to discuss this issue, but may I have some background information to impart to him on which he can base his decision." This would allow Tang to obtain the required information on which to base his decision, which he would disclose at the following meeting. In these ways, Tang artfully managed his credibility as a local Chinese with external stakeholders. However, internally, Tang was perceived as an expatriate.

Tang was aware that being perceived as an 'outsider' could undermine his ability to persuade his department that they were all part of the same team. Complicating the issue was not only Tang's expatriate status (one of few at the time), but as an expatriate, Tang received a superior pay and benefit package than local (Chinese) employees. Tang saw where he had advanced in relation to his employees as "just going through a different process to get to where we are, but now we're all at the same place—part of the Intel team." According to Tang:

> Work really doesn't have anything to do whether you're an expatriate or local Chinese—it has to do with your ideas, how you understand strategy, technology and marketing—that's work. As long as you focus on that, and once your employees begin to focus on that, perceived differences really become a non-issue.

Tang dealt with the potential for conflict because of his rank or his experience in the United States by largely ignoring it, but Tang did not view this as an abdication of his responsibilities. On the contrary, Tang believed that by working hard and proving himself trustworthy, his employees would come to see that "we're all working together." According to Tang:

> How people look at you and how they feel about you has everything to do with how you make them feel about you. If you want to be seen as different, and if you want them to see you as different, they will. If you want to distance yourself from them you can. However, if you want them to see you as one of them, they will.

Tang was cognizant of some basic tenets on which the foundation of organizational behavioral differences as generally found between Chinese and Western firms were based, and acknowledged that both his Western education and experience as well as his exposure to Eastern business cultures affected his interpretation of the situation he was facing with Li. What challenged Tang also, with regard to managing Li, was how much of a departure Li's behavior was from what Tang considered to be a traditional Chinese business culture. Tang wondered whether he should question some of his beliefs about Chinese communication patterns and organizational behavior. Had things changed drastically since he had been away or was Li's behavior out of the ordinary?

◪ Organizational Differences

Differences in Communication Patterns Between the East and the West

Generally speaking, Chinese organizational structures were more vertically layered than Western firms, resulting in dense reporting lines and bureaucratic administrative mechanisms. Moreover, Chinese organizations were most often led by a strong autocratic figure who took an active role in daily operations as well as the strategic direction of the firm. Whereas in some Western firms the organizational structure, supported by cultural influences, encouraged a degree of dissension and dis-agreement to advance the firm's organizational effectiveness and strategic direction, generally speaking Chinese firms operated on a princi-ple of unquestioning adherence to the direc-tion as dictated by senior management.

In contrast to Eastern management style, in Tang's opinion, Western organizational and communication systems promoted a more open discussion between managers and their employees. Tang's management experi-ence suggested to him that employees in the West had a higher propensity to be more open and possessed a greater willingness to listen to their bosses if they had established a proven track record of being reasonable and open-minded. In contrast, Tang felt there seemed to be more suspicion among employ-ees toward their supervisors in an Asian busi-ness context, as they managed with a much more closed style.

Though Tang considered his management style to be a mixture of Eastern and Western characteristics, he felt that many Western man-agement principles manifested themselves more strongly. For example, he considered being open with his employees an integral part of managing, and indeed had succeeded in encouraging many of his employees to treat him as a confidant. On several occasions, he had been approached by members of his team and had held closed-door, one-on-one discus-sions regarding various aspects of their per-sonal and professional lives. Tang was proud of the role he was able to take in acting in this capacity for his employees. On a broader level, Tang did his best to ensure that his employees' needs and concerns were addressed. For exam-ple, Tang ensured that his employees' salaries were commensurate with their responsibilities, and competitive as compared to other multina-tionals for employees working in a similar capacity. Tang considered actions such as this to be critical in establishing his employees' trust in him. It was actions such as this that rein-forced Tang's belief that his employees were more comfortable approaching him than they may have been with an expatriate manager from North America or Europe.

The Decision

In this context, Tang was confounded by Li's reactions. Why did he respond so emotion-ally, and what could he now do about it? Li was otherwise a promising employee who had forged valuable 'guanxi' with his accounts. Tang did not want to risk losing him. Moreover, on a personal level, Tang cared about the welfare of his employees and, thus, it was upsetting to him that he may have caused his employee some distress. Tang considered whether in light of Li's emotional attachment to the project he should allow him to continue with it, as in the scheme of things it was a relatively short-term project. Or was there a way to modify the project, finding a compromise between his needs and Li's desire to continue with the project? Tang was eager to have his employees contribute in such a way that would advance the strategic direction of his department, and felt strongly that whatever decision he made should be guided by that general principle. Tang knew that perhaps the easiest means to achieve this end would be to coerce Li to follow the "dis-agree and commit" philosophy at Intel and redirect Li's attention altogether to a more appropriate project. However, he was con-cerned about Li's reaction to this move, given his emotional state.

Tang also considered the idea that perhaps this issue pointed to a larger one. Were the sys-tems that facilitated vertical communication sufficient or should he consider implementing a more effective, more formal internal com-munications strategy? But Tang did not have time to consider this issue at the present moment—he glanced at his watch, jumped up and hurriedly placed his laptop in his briefcase to rush to a meeting.

Grupo Financiero Inverlat

Prepared by Daniel D. Campbell under the supervision
of Kathleen Slaughter and Henry W. Lane

By October 1996, it had been four months since management at the Bank of Nova Scotia (BNS) increased its stake in the Mexican bank, Grupo Financiero Inverlat (Inverlat), from 8.1 per cent, to an equity and convertible debt package that represented 54 per cent ownership of the bank. A team of Canadian managers had been sent to Mexico to assume management of the ailing financial institution immediately after the deal was struck. Jim O'Donnell, now Director General Adjunto (DGA)[2] of the retail bank at Inverlat, had been there from the beginning.

Jim was a member of the original group that performed the due diligence to analyze Inverlat's finances before negotiations could begin. Later, he and his wife Anne-Marie (also an executive with the bank) were the first Canadians to arrive in Mexico in May 1996. Since then, 14 additional Canadian managers had arrived, and restructured the four most senior levels within Inverlat. The pace of change had been overwhelming. Jim now wondered how successful his early efforts had been and what could be done to facilitate the remaining restructuring.

⬛ A Brief Inverlat History

In 1982, in his last days as leader of the Mexican Republic, President Lopez Portillo announced the nationalization of Mexico's banks. They would remain government institutions for the next eight to 10 years. Managers characterized the years under government control as a period of stagnation in which the structure of the Mexican financial institutions remained constant despite substantial innovations in technology and practice in the banking industry internationally.

Many Inverlat managers claimed that their bank had generally deteriorated more than the rest of the banking sector in Mexico. Managers believed that there was no overall strategy or leadership. Lacking a strong central management structure, each of the bank's geographic regions began to function independently, resulting in a system of control one manager described as "feudal." The eight regions developed such a level of autonomy that managers commonly referred to Inverlat not as a bank, but as eight small banks. The fragmented structure made new product development almost impossible. When the central corporate offices developed a new product, they had no guarantee that it would be implemented in the regions and ultimately, the branches. The power struggle within the regions demanded such loyalty that employees often had to say: "I cannot support you (in some initiative) because my boss told me not to."

In 1990, an amendment to the Mexican constitution allowed majority private sector ownership of Mexican commercial banks. Between 1990 and 1992, 18 banks were privatized by the Mexican government, including Inverlat. BNS, looking to expand its interests in Latin America, purchased eight per cent of the company in 1992 for Cdn$154 million.

Under the structure of the newly privatized bank, there were three corporate cultures: that of the original bank; that of the Casa de Bolsa, the bank's brokerage house; and that of the new

Version: (A) 2002-10-23

[2]Director General Adjunto is the Mexican equivalent of an Executive Vice President.

chair of the bank, an executive from Banamex, Mexico's largest financial institution. Many senior Banamex executives were invited to join Inverlat; some even came out of retirement to do so. The Banamex culture soon dominated the organization, as senior management tried to create a "Little Banamex." Inverlat managers without a history in Banamex said that the strategy could never function because Inverlat did not have the clients, technology, or financial resources of Banamex.

Inverlat's leaders did recognize, however, that the years of stagnation under nationalization had created a bank that had failed to create a new generation of bankers to reflect the changing times. They realized that the bank required a rejuvenation, but the managers did not have the knowledge or the capacity to effect the change.

Nowhere was the lack of development more prominent, and ultimately more devastating, than in the credit assessment function. The banks pursued a growth strategy dependent on increased lending but, unfamiliar with the challenges of lending to the private sector, failed to collateralize their loans properly or to ensure that covenants were being maintained. In early 1995, following a severe devaluation of the Mexican peso, Mexico's credit environment collapsed; so did the bank. The Mexican government assumed responsibility for the bank, and BNS was forced to write down its original investment by almost 95 per cent to Cdn$10 million.

Negotiations With BNS

Management at BNS chose to view the loss in value of their investment as a further buying opportunity and, in early 1996, they began negotiations with the Mexican government. BNS contributed Cdn$50 million for 16 per cent of new stock in the bank and Cdn$125 million in bonds convertible on March 31, in the year 2000 for an additional 39 per cent of equity. If, in the year 2000, BNS decided not to assume ownership of the bank, they could walk away without converting the debt and retain a much smaller portion of ownership.

As the majority shareholder until the year 2000, the Mexican government contracted BNS to manage the bank. A maximum of 20 BNS managers would be paid by the Mexican government to manage Inverlat on the government's behalf. If BNS wanted more Canadian managers to work in the bank, BNS would have to pay for them. It was intended that the Canadian managers would remain at Inverlat only until the Mexican managers developed the skills to manage the bank effectively on their own.

With the exception of a handful of the most senior officers in the bank, employees at Inverlat had no direct means of receiving information about the progression of the negotiations with BNS. Instead, they were forced to rely on often inaccurate reports from the Mexican media. As the negotiation progressed, support among Inverlat employees for a deal with BNS was very strong. Inverlat employees did not want to become government bureaucrats and viewed BNS as a savior that would bring money, technology and expertise.

Employee Expectations

Soon after the deal was completed with BNS, however, the general euphoria was gradually replaced by the fear of actions the Canadians were likely to take as they assumed their management role. Senior managers were worried that they would be replaced by someone younger, who spoke English and had an MBA. Rumors, supported by inaccurate reports in local newspapers, ran rampant. One newspaper reported that as many as 180 senior level managers would be imported to Inverlat from BNS in Canada.

Anxiety mounted as speculation increased about the magnitude of downsizing that BNS would implement as it restructured the bank in its turnaround. Although BNS had purchased banks in other Latin American countries, few Inverlat employees, including the most senior management, had any knowledge about the strategies that BNS management had used.

Inverlat managers felt that their employees viewed BNS as a "gringo" corporation, and expected them to take the same actions other U.S. companies had taken as they restructured companies they had purchased in Mexico. Most believed that if any foreign bank purchased Inverlat, most of the senior management team would be displaced and up to half of the bank staff would be let go. Similarly, very few managers knew the details of the contract that limited the number of managers that could come to the bank from Canada.

Very few of the Mexican employees had had any significant contact with Canadian managers, but the majority expected behavior similar to that of U.S. managers. Only a handful of senior level managers had been in contact during the due diligence and the Canadians realized that they required greater insight into the Mexican culture if they were to manage effectively. As a result, the members of the senior team that were going to manage the Mexican bank arrived in Mexico one month in advance to study Spanish. The Canadian managers studied in an intensive program in Cuernavaca, a small city 80 kilometres southwest of Mexico City. During the three-week course, lectures were available on the Mexican culture. Mexican managers were extremely impressed by this attempt by the Canadians to gain a better understanding of the situation they were entering and thought the consideration was very respectful. One manager commented that:

> At the first meeting, the Canadians apologized because it would be in English, but promised that the next would be in Spanish. The fact is, some are still in English, but the approach and the attempt were very important.

Four months later, the Canadian team was still undergoing intense tutorial sessions in Spanish on a daily basis with varying levels of success.

Canadian managers said they were trying to guard against putting people into positions simply because they were bilingual. A Canadian manager, expressing his commitment to function in Spanish, commented that:

> There are 16 Canadians down here and 10,000 Mexicans. Surely to God, the 16 Canadians can learn Spanish rather than trying to teach the 10,000 Mexicans English or having people feel that they are being left out of promotions or opportunities just because they don't speak English. This is a Spanish-speaking country and the customers speak Spanish.

Inverlat and BNS Cultures

In Canada, BNS was considered the bank with the most stringent financial control systems of the country's largest banks. Stringent, not only in deciding not to spend money in non-essential areas, but also in maintaining a tough system of policies and controls that ensured that managers held to their budgets.

Inverlat executives, on the other hand, were accustomed to almost complete autonomy with little or no control imposed on their spending. Very little analysis was done to allocate resources to a project, and adherence to budget was not monitored. Mexican managers believed that greater controls such as the ones used by BNS should be implemented in Inverlat, but they also felt that conflicts would arise.

An early example experienced in the bank was a new policy implemented by BNS management to control gifts received by managers from clients. BNS managers imposed a limit of 500 pesos[3] for the maximum value of a gift that could be received by an executive. Gifts of larger value could be accepted, but were then raffled off to all employees of the bank at Christmas. Some Mexican managers took offence at the imposition of an arbitrary limit. They felt that it was an

---

[3] In late 1996, one Mexican peso was valued at approximately US$0.0128.

indication that BNS did not trust their judgment. Managers thought that it would be better if the bank communicated the need for the use of good judgment when accepting gifts and then trusted their managers to act appropriately.

⚑ Mandate of BNS

Two months after the arrival of the Canadian executive team, the new bank chairman, Bill Sutton, gave an address to 175 senior executives within Inverlat. The purpose of the address was threefold: to outline management's main objectives in the short term; to unveil the new organizational structure of senior level managers; and to reassure employees that no staff reductions would be undertaken for the first year.

The primary objectives, later printed in a special companywide bulletin, were the following:

1. Identify all non-performing loans of the bank.

2. Develop an organization focussed on the client.

3. Improve the productivity and efficiency of all operations and activities.

4. Improve the profitability of the 315 branches.

5. Develop a liability strategy.

6. Improve the integrity of the financial information.

These objectives were generally well received by the Mexican managers. Some criticized them as being too intangible and difficult to measure. Most, however, believed that the general nature of the objectives was more practical, given the type of changes that were being made in the first year. They did agree that the goals would need to be adjusted as planning became more focussed during the 1997 budget planning process.

The new management structure differed sharply from the existing structure of the bank. The original eight geographic regions were reduced to four. Managers were pleased to see that the head of each of these divisions was Mexican and it was generally viewed as a promotion for the managers.

The second change was the nature in which the Canadians were added to the management structure. The senior Canadian managers became "Directores Generales Adjuntos (DGAs)" or senior vice presidents of several key areas, displacing Mexican managers. The Mexican DGAs not directly replaced by Canadians would now report to one or more of the Canadian DGAs, but this was not reflected in the organization chart (see Exhibit 1). Mexican DGAs retained their titles and formally remained at the same level as their Canadian counterparts.

Mexican managers later reported mixed feelings by employees about whether or not they worked under a Canadian or Mexican DGA. Many felt that a Mexican DGA and his (there were no female DGAs working within the bank) employees were more "vulnerable" than a Canadian; however, senior managers also felt that they had an opportunity to ascend to the DGA position when it was being held by a Mexican. Many felt that Canadian managers would always hold the key positions in the bank and that certain authority would never be relinquished to a Mexican. This was not the message that BNS management wanted to convey. One of Jim O'Donnell's first comments to his employees was that he would only be in Mexico until one of them felt confident that they could fill his shoes.

The last message was the new management's commitment not to reduce staff levels. A policy of "no hires, no fires" was put in place. Employees were able to breathe a sigh of relief. Many had expected the Canadian management team to reduce staff by 3,000 to 5,000 employees during the first several months after their arrival.

Exhibit 1 Grupo Financiero Inverlat Organizational Chart (post-reorganization)

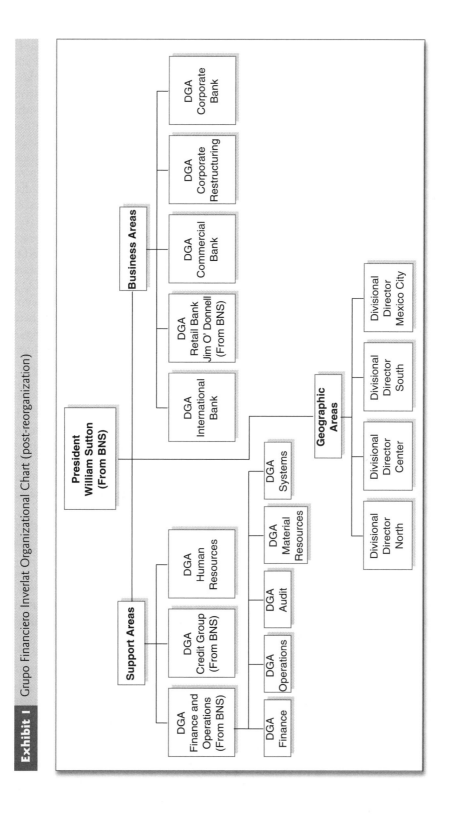

⬚ The Communication Challenge

Canadian and Mexican managers already experienced many of the difficulties that the two different languages could present. Many of the most senior Mexican managers spoke English, but the remaining managers required translators when speaking with the Canadians. Even when managers reporting directly to them spoke English, Canadians felt frustration at not being able to speak directly to the next level below. One manager commented that "sometimes, I feel like a bloody dictator" referring to the need to communicate decisions to his department via his most senior officers.

Meetings

Even when all managers at a meeting spoke English, the risk of miscommunication was high. A Mexican manager recalled one of the early meetings in English attended by several Mexicans. Each of the Mexican managers left the meeting with little doubt about what had been decided during the meeting. It was only later, when the Mexicans spoke of the proceedings in Spanish, that they realized they each had a different interpretation about what had transpired. What they found even more alarming was that each manager had heard what he had wanted to hear, clearly demonstrating to themselves the effect of their biases on their perception of events.

This problem might have been exacerbated by the way some of the Canadians chose to conduct meetings. Mexican managers were accustomed to a flexible atmosphere in which they were free to leave the room or carry on side-conversations as they saw fit. Canadian managers became frustrated and changed the meeting style to a more structured, controlled atmosphere similar to what they used in Canada. The Mexican managers were told that breaks would be scheduled every two hours and that only then should they get up from the table or leave the room.

Canadian managers believed that the original conduct of the Mexican managers during meetings was due to a lack of discipline and that the new conduct would lead to higher productivity. The Canadians did not recognize the negative impact that could result from the elimination of the informal interactions that had occurred in the original style.

Beyond Language

Despite the cross cultural training received in Cuernavaca, some Canadians still felt they had a lot to learn about the cultural nuances that could create major pitfalls. Jim O'Donnell recalled a meeting at which he and several Mexican managers were having difficulty with some material developed by another Mexican not present at the meeting. Jim requested that this manager join them to provide further explanation. Several minutes later, as this person entered the room, Jim said jokingly, "OK, *here*'s the guy that screwed it all up." The manager was noticeably upset. It was not until later, after some explaining, that Jim's comment was understood to be a joke. Jim said it brought home the fact that, in the Mexican culture, it was unacceptable, even in jest, to be critical of someone in front of other people.

This was easier said than done. Often, what the Canadians considered a minor difference of opinion could appear as criticism that Mexican managers would prefer be made behind closed doors when coming from a more senior manager. One Mexican manager commented on the risks of disagreeing with an employee when others were present:

> When someone's boss is not in agreement, or critical of actions taken by an employee and says something during a meeting with other employees present, other managers will use it as an opportunity to also say bad things about the manager. Instead, when a disagreement arises

in an open meeting, the senior manager should say 'see me later, and we will discuss it.'

On the contrary, the Canadian managers were trying to encourage an environment in which all managers participated in meetings and positive criticism was offered and accepted.

Mexican Communication Style

On verbal communication, one of the original Inverlat managers commented:

> In Mexico, interactions between individuals are extremely polite. Because Mexicans will make every effort not to offend the person they are dealing with, they are careful to 'sugar-coat' almost everything they say. Requests are always accompanied by 'por favor,' no matter how insignificant the request.

Mexicans often use the diminutive form. For example: *Esperame* means *Wait for me. Esperame un rato* means *Wait for me a moment.* A Mexican would more often say *Esperame un ratito.* 'Ratito' is the diminutive form meaning 'a very short moment.' It is not as direct.

This politeness is extended into other interactions. Every time a Mexican meets a coworker or subordinate, a greeting such as 'Hello, how are you?' is appropriate, even if it is the fourth or fifth time that day that they have met. If you don't do this, the other person will think you are angry with him or her or that you are poorly educated.

One Canadian manager explained that some of the Mexican managers he dealt with went to great lengths to avoid confrontation. He was frustrated when the Mexicans would "tell him what he wanted to hear." Often these managers would consent to something that they could or would not do, simply to avoid a confrontation at the time.

Other Messages: Intended or Otherwise

Due to the high level of anxiety, Mexican managers were very sensitive to messages they read into the actions taken by the Canadians. This process began before the Canadians made any significant changes.

As the Canadians began to plan the new organizational structure, they conducted a series of interviews with the senior Mexican managers. The Canadians decided who they would talk to based on areas where they believed they required more information. Unfortunately, many managers believed that if they were not spoken to, then they were not considered of importance to the Canadians and should fear for their positions. Even after the organizational structure was revealed and many Mexican managers found themselves in good positions, they still retained hard feelings, believing that they had not been considered important enough to provide input into the new structure.

Similarly, at lower levels in the bank, because of the lack of activity in the economy as a whole, many employees were left with time on their hands. Because many employees feared staff reductions at some point, they believed that those with the most work or those being offered new work were the ones that would retain their jobs.

Communications as an Ongoing Process

When Jim held his first meeting with the nine senior managers reporting to him, he began by saying that none of them would have their jobs in two months. Realizing the level of anxiety at that point, he quickly added that he meant they would all be shuffled around to other areas of the retail bank. Jim explained that this would give them an opportunity to learn about other areas of the bank and the interdependencies that needed to be considered when making decisions.

Jim stuck to his word, and within two months, all but one of the managers had been moved. Some, however, had experienced anxiety about the method by which they were moved. Typically, Jim would meet with an employee and tell him that in two or three days he would report to a new area (generally, Mexican managers gave at least a month's notice). When that day arrived, Jim would talk to them for 30 to 45 minutes about their new responsibilities and goals, and then he would send them on their way.

For many of the Mexicans, this means of communication was too abrupt. Many wondered if they had been moved from their past jobs because of poor performance. More senior Mexican managers explained that often these managers would come to them and ask why Jim had decided to move them. Most of the Mexicans felt that more communication was required about why things were happening the way they were.

Accountability

Early on, the Canadian managers identified an almost complete lack of accountability within the bank. Senior managers had rarely made decisions outside the anonymity of a committee, and when resources were committed to a project, it was equally rare for someone to check back to see what results were attained. As a result, very little analysis was done before a new project was approved and undertaken.

The first initiative taken by the Canadians to improve the level of analysis, and later implementation, was the use of what they called the "business case." The case represented a cost-benefit analysis that would be approved and reviewed by senior managers. Initially, it was difficult to explain to the Mexican managers how to provide the elements of analysis that the Canadians required. The Mexicans were given a framework, but they initially returned cases that adhered too rigidly to the outline. Similarly, managers would submit business cases of 140 pages for a $35,000 project.

Cases required multiple revisions to a point of frustration on both sides, but it was only when an analysis could be prepared that satisfied the Canadians and was understood by both parties that it could be certain they all had the same perception of what they were talking about.

Some of the Mexican managers found the business case method overly cumbersome and felt that many good ideas would be missed because of the disincentive created by the business case. One manager commented that "It is a bit discouraging. Some people around here feel like you need to do a business case to go to the bathroom."

Most agreed that a positive element of the business case was the need it created to talk with other areas of the bank. To do a complete analysis, it was often necessary to contact other branches of the bank for information because their business would be affected. This was the first time that efforts across functional areas of the bank would be coordinated. To reinforce this notion, often Canadian managers required that senior managers from several areas of the bank grant their approval before a project in a business case could move forward.

Matrix Responsibility

Changes in the organizational structure further complicated the implementation of a system of accountability. Senior management had recognized a duplication of services across the different functional areas of the bank. For example, each product group had its own marketing and systems departments. These functions were stripped away and consolidated into central groups that would service all areas of the organization.

Similarly, product groups had been responsible for the development and delivery of their products. Performance was evaluated based on the sales levels each product group could attain. Under the initial restructuring, the product groups would no longer be responsible for the sale of their products, only for their design. Instead, the branches would become a delivery network that would be responsible for almost all contact with the client. As a result, managers in product groups, who were still responsible for ensuring the sales levels, felt that they were now being measured against criteria over which they had no direct control. The Canadian management team was finding it very difficult to explain to the Mexicans that they now had to "influence" instead of "control." Product managers were being given the role of "coaches" who would help the branch delivery network to offer their product most effectively.

As adjustments were made to the structure, the Mexican manager's perception of his status also had to be considered. In the management hierarchy, the Mexican manager's relationships were with the people in the various positions that they dealt with, not with the positions themselves. When a person was moved, subordinates felt loyalty to that individual. As a result, Mexican managers moving within an organization (or even to another organization) often did so with a small entourage of employees who accompanied them.

⊠ Staff Reductions

As services within the bank were consolidated, it was obvious that staff reductions would be required. Inverlat staff were comforted by the bank's commitment to retain all staff for the first year, particularly when considering the poor state of the economy and the banking sector; but, even at lower levels of the organization, the need for reductions was apparent. Some managers complained that the restructuring process was being slowed considerably by the need to find places for personnel who were clearly no longer required.

Motivations for retaining staffing levels were twofold. First, BNS did not want to tarnish the image of its foreign investment in Mexico with massive reductions at the outset. When the Spanish bank, Banco Bilbao Viscaya (BBV), purchased Banca Cremi the previous year, they began the restructuring process with a staff reduction of over 2,000 employees. BNS executives thought that this action had not been well received by the Mexican government or marketplace.

The second reason BNS management felt compelled to wait for staff reductions was that they wanted adequate time to identify which employees were productive and fit into the new organizational culture, and which employees would not add significant value. The problem was, quality employees were not sure if they would have a job in a year, and many managers thought that employees would begin to look for secure positions in other organizations. One Canadian manager commented that even some employees who were performing well in their current positions would ultimately lose their jobs. Many thought action needed to be taken sooner than later. A senior Mexican manager explained the situation:

> Take the worst-case scenario, blind guessing. At least then you will be correct 50 per cent of the time and retain some good people. If you wait, people within the organization will begin to look for other jobs and the market will choose who it wants. But as the market hires away your people, it will be correct 90 per cent of the time, and you will be left with the rest.

Until that point, not many managers had been hired away from the bank. Many felt that this was due to the poor condition of the banking sector. As the economy improved, however, many believed that the talented managers would begin to leave the bank if job security could not be improved.

Jim felt that something was needed to communicate a sense of security to the talented managers they could already identify, but he was not certain how to proceed.

⊠ Conclusion

Jim felt that the Canadian team had been relatively successful in the early months. Many managers referred to the period as the "Honeymoon Stage." It was generally felt that the situation would intensify as managers looked for results from the restructured organization and as staff reductions became a reality. Jim then wondered how he could best prepare for the months ahead.

Much of the communication with employees to date had been on an ad hoc basis. Jim did not feel they could take the risk of starting reductions without laying out a plan. The negative rumors would cause the bank to lose many of its most valued Mexican managers.

Global Fatalities

When International Executives Derail

By Morgan W. McCall, Jr., and George P. Hollenbeck

Take a quick look at why global executives fail and you'll likely see personality flaws. However, the reasons for failure are deeper and more complex.

Developing global executives is an expensive proposition, especially when expatriate assignments are involved. But the investment can produce a significant return—provided that the corporation uses the knowledge and expertise gained from the experience effectively. When things go wrong, the investment is lost, and usually, so too is a person who was judged to be quite talented. Can these losses be prevented? Maybe, but the answer to that question depends on what causes such derailments. If the complexity and ambiguity of international work makes selection errors unavoidable, then the derailment of executives is just another cost of doing business. However, if derailments occur because of something that can be corrected or prevented, then a significant payoff is possible.

To shed some light on the dynamics underlying the derailment of global executives, we interviewed 101 individuals who were successful in their international postings. With an average of nine years experience abroad, they were in a unique position to observe other global executives come and go. The 121 tales they told are the basis for the conclusions we have developed about the underlying causes of international executive failures.

Three factors contribute to the failure of international executives:

1. The individual
2. The cultural context
3. Organizational mistakes

⊠ I. The Individual

Executives contributed to their failure in two ways. Some personal attributes and types of behaviours just don't play in international settings. However, more often, it wasn't simply a personal flaw that prevented an individual from succeeding. Rather, it was the complex interaction of a person's strengths or weaknesses with a change in the situation. We will consider both causes.

Fatal flaws

The successful executives we interviewed described over 300 flaws in the behaviour and management skills of the executives they had

AUTHOR'S NOTE: This article was adapted with permission of the Harvard Business School Press. Source: *Developing Global Executives: The Lessons of International Experience*, by Morgan W. McCall, Jr., and George P. Hollenbeck. Copyright © 2002 by Harvard Business School Publishing Corporation.

observed. A few of these flaws were factors regardless of the situation or context.

Foremost among them was a failure to adapt to change. What needed to be adapted to varied considerably—bosses, business strategy, leadership philosophy, changes in markets and technology. For many of those ill-fated executives, their inability or unwillingness to change was rooted in a career spent in a silo, or in a single function, which gave them a narrow perspective and made them unable to see the big picture. Unwilling to appreciate another point of view, some executives either refused to accept change or would not put energy into their effort to change.

Another flaw or set of flaws in the "clearly lethal" category resulted in bungled relationships with key people—customers, partners, senior management or peers. The bungling was especially toxic when it occurred in conjunction with a decline in performance or some significant mistake. In a global environment, quality relationships are crucial in certain countries and business situations (such as sensitive negotiations, joint ventures and cross-cultural alliances). Although a lack of people skills is annoying in any environment, the consequences are particularly severe in an international setting.

Other flaws led some executives to hesitate when action was needed, to default on promises made to senior management, and, when things subsequently went wrong, not to ask for (or accept) outside help. Powerful and successful executives in trouble may try to deal with matters on their own, viewing offers of assistance or advice as interference from the outside. This can be a fatal mistake, made all the more likely whenever, as an expatriate, the executive has lost contact with the rest of the company.

Complex Interaction

But just having flaws is too simplistic an explanation for the derailments that were described to us. As we have all observed, there are people who have glaring flaws who don't derail, while some with overpowering strengths actually do. Still others with no apparent flaws early in their

careers seem to develop them later on. And for still others, there is no apparent cause for the flameout. Moreover, the international executives in this derailed group were unusually talented to begin with. They were often described as having multiple strengths, rarely found together, such as brilliant and interpersonally skilled, technically skilled and shrewd about people, or people and results oriented. How could such gifted and successful people derail?

The paradoxes can be resolved if derailment is considered as a dynamic process rather than the inevitable result of some personality flaw. Indeed, if one assumes that there are no unqualified strengths and few universally fatal flaws, the data begin to make sense. We identified four patterns that describe the dynamics of many of the derailment scenarios.

1. **Early strengths that led to success became weaknesses later on.** Most often, this took the form of exceptional technical, functional or market expertise that resulted in early successes and promotions, but later on blinded the executive to the bigger picture or the need for different skills essential to a higher-level job.

2. **Long-standing flaws that became salient when something changed in an executive's situation.** Some leaders, for example, had always been abrasive and arrogant, but because they got great business results, they were never damaged by their flaws. Their sins were forgiven in light of their bottom-line performance. When the results weren't as good as expected or when the situation changed so that relationships (and not single-handed bravado) were critical to meeting the bottom line, the flaws "suddenly" emerged and the executive derailed.

3. **An executive's constant success.** Some executives began to believe that they were as good as they seemed and, like the Greek tragic heroes, their hubris led to their demise.

4. Some executives appeared to be just unlucky, ending up in the wrong place at the wrong time or running afoul of the wrong person. What happened, at least on the surface, was not the person's fault. But while ill fortune appeared to cause these derailments, other factors usually contributed to the fall. It was frequently suggested that the same events might not have derailed someone else—that there was something about the way the executive handled the situation, or about bridges burned in the past, that contributed to the outcome. In short, one of the other dynamics—not bad luck—may have been the real culprit.

While some flaws were uniformly problematic (e.g., failing to adapt to changed situations or an "appalling lack of people skills"), and others emerged when an executive's immediate situation changed, the vast majority of international derailments were anchored in the cultural context itself.

2. The Cultural Context

It was rarely sufficient to say that an executive's traits or flaws "caused" him or her to derail—most of these executives were extraordinarily talented individuals—unless one could place that trait or action in a larger context. For global executives, that context was almost always cultural.

Working abroad increases stress through its isolation, family pressures, and the broader job responsibilities it often entails. International executives may find themselves dealing with political issues, government corruption, bribery and a variety of contextual issues without the help that would be available in the home country. Contributing to the stress, but demanding in their own right, are the difficulties of understanding and being understood in one or more foreign languages, and the often subtle differences in values, norms, beliefs, religions, economic systems, and group and community identities.

The natural reluctance of people in organizations to be candid with each other can be magnified by cultural norms, as well as by the inability of outsiders to read the subtle cues. One executive, quite successful in a series of functional assignments, was promoted to a general manager's job outside of his own country. He did well initially, probably because of his functional expertise, but when things started to go wrong, he did not realize it. When he realized it, he didn't have the ability or business knowledge to diagnose the problem and figure out what was wrong. One can't help but wonder if he could have drawn on the expertise of others had this happened in his home country.

Different economic, religious, government and social systems in some countries have direct effects on how business is carried out. Here, complexity again takes several forms, including the potentially lethal—or at least convoluted—web of relationships and the presence of different business models and practices. As we interviewed executives, we saw how the web of relationships can grow more and more complex: from subordinates from a different culture who don't speak the executive's first language, to subordinates from multiple cultures speaking multiple languages in one region, to subordinates from multiple cultures speaking multiple languages and physically dispersed around the globe. To thicken the mix, add a boss from a different country who speaks a different language or multiple bosses from different countries in a matrix structure, and so on, through suppliers, customers, partners, shareholders, peers, consultants and others. As if that weren't complicated enough, different countries may have different business models, different definitions of ethical behaviour and different business approaches and systems.

All these complexities and others too numerous to recount, create a fertile context for derailment. The more relationships an executive has to cultivate, and the more varied they are, the greater the chances that some of them will go wrong. The greater the differences in how business operates in the countries involved, the greater the likelihood that an executive will make erroneous assumptions or commit errors without even knowing that anything is amiss. The more diverse and culturally different the countries, the greater the likelihood that seemingly extraneous factors—or what would be extraneous factors in the home country—will affect business results, the outcomes of deals and negotiations, and other activities for which the executive is accountable. In other words, not only are the executive's actions more likely to be ineffective or even counterproductive, but more circumstances will be beyond the executive's control and more likely to affect outcomes, regardless of the executive's actions. And for all the reasons we pointed out above, the executive may not get timely feedback or pick up the clues that anything is wrong in time to do anything about it.

Although cultural and business differences create a complex and sometimes treacherous context for executive action, international assignments also come with particular seductions that can lure executives onto the path to derailment. Being on their own, often far from direct supervision and with tremendous authority over local operations, global executives can come to believe that they are all-powerful, even above the law. Feeding self-aggrandizement were the perks of foreign duty, which might include servants, cars and drivers, luxurious homes, impressive expense accounts, invitations to galas and state affairs, and other special treatment that, over time, some executives began to view as entitlements.

Even if an executive completes an expatriate assignment successfully, he or she still faces a final risk that may cause derailment—repatriation. Though it is tempting to view coming home as an easy transition, it turns out to be anything but. Executives may return to find that they have lost their business networks and their friends, that their home country is not the same as it was when they left, and—perhaps the unkindest cut of all—that no one cares. Their living conditions may actually be worse, with no servants, drivers, luxurious homes, access to exciting events, or relationships with top business and government leaders. They may come back to less important jobs and reduced responsibility, they may find themselves outside the mainstream, and they may feel that their organization does not take advantage of or appreciate what they have learned. In such circumstances, the skids are greased for derailment.

✉ 3. Organizational Mistakes

Neither individual attributes and behaviour, nor the cultural context, were sufficient to explain all of the derailments. The organizations for which the derailed executives worked made numerous mistakes that contributed to, or in some cases directly caused, their derailment. The fall of one executive provides an example: "The company contributed [to the derailment] when they led him to believe they would back him up no matter what. But they didn't. They backed him when things went right, but they deserted him when things went wrong."

Absence of honest feedback was pervasive, as were mixed messages or unclear expectations from "back home." Companies picked people who were obviously wrong for the assignment, promoted people too fast (they were "untested"), or kept them out too long. Frequently, expatriate executives did not have access to the kinds of technical or other support that domestic executives could call upon.

The complexity of the global context increases the odds that the organization will make various mistakes that contribute to derailments, most of which are avoidable: giving little or no feedback, little monitoring, tolerating existing flaws and lack of support. Because organizations can influence these and similar factors, we fault them for being lazy, or worse, negligent. Although we don't absolve executives from being responsible for their actions, the organizations' lapses increase the probability that flaws and inappropriate or ineffective behaviour will go unnoticed and uncorrected until it is too late.

Some cases of global derailment resulted from poor selection decisions, usually made for technical or political reasons without considering the potential consequences. Organizations chose people who obviously would not fit in the environment, failed to prepare them properly for the challenges ahead, and/or failed to communicate their expectations or changes in expectations. In still other cases, organizations made decisions that directly affected the executive's operation without considering the situation "on the ground." At times, an organization made strategy or design changes without consulting, or even informing, the local executive.

Derailment risk is high for foreign nationals coming to headquarters and for other executives returning home. Organizations seem to botch their part in both events consistently, contributing to an already difficult situation for the executive.

Finally, we were told of derailments in which an executive's career was exploited for short-term gain. In these circumstances, the organization, purposely or not, knew that the situation was not viable—the executive was assigned an impossible job, or one that would almost certainly create an aftermath so intolerable that the executive could not survive.

Preventing Derailments

A single intervention or a smattering of human resource programs for international executives will not prevent events as complex as those leading to global derailments. Like global executive development itself, preventing derailment requires an integrated approach that connects strategic intent with the systems and practices that affect the selection, development and movement of global executives.

To begin with, solutions must address all three culprits in derailment: the executives' strengths and weaknesses, the global context in which the executives are placed, and the organizational practices that surround the whole process. All three depend on the fundamental strategic issues facing a global business. Only the strategy can determine how many and what kinds of global executive jobs are required, and how many and what kinds of executives are needed to fill them. Only the strategy can determine how many truly global executives are needed (if any), how many foreign nationals are necessary, how the international jobs will be structured and positioned, the extent and nature of alliances, how business will be done internationally, and so on.

There are important differences in the development of local nationals, host-country nationals and third-country nationals, and for this reason lock-step or undifferentiated development programs are likely to be ineffective for many in the international pool.

Further, global executive jobs, whatever the home country of the executive, are fraught with dangers, not the least of which is the increased probability of derailment associated with poorly designed and poorly managed assignments. Much can be done to improve the ways these jobs are structured, the processes by which performance is monitored, and the feedback processes associated with them.

To emphasize the strategic and structural aspects of developing international executive talent is not to say that individual development should be ignored. There is no question that many of the essential skills needed in global careers can be learned, and that very few individuals are so naturally gifted that they need no further development. While there are limits to what an organization can do to make someone grow, there is a lot they can do to help people who want to grow. These include providing opportunities, early in a career, to work with people from other countries and to be part of activities that cross borders, to work under competent bosses with international experience and perspective, and to live and work as an expatriate. These kinds of experiences, combined with effective assessment and feedback, seem to be essential ingredients in developing global talent.

CHAPTER

15

Ethical Leadership

Ethical behavior is a key characteristic of the global leader of the future. Young leaders place great value on ethics, think they are sorely lacking in current leaders, and feel that ethical behavior will become the most important characteristic of future leaders. This is not surprising in a time when shredding documents, creative accounting, and ruthless tactics come to light in the media on a fairly regular basis.

—Goldsmith, Greenberg, Robertson, and Hu-Chan (2003, p. 217)

This chapter presents a guide to ethical decision making in situations that will confront you as a leader and discusses several ethical perspectives that should help you make ethical decisions. There is constant debate as to where a chapter on ethics should appear in any book (e.g., textbooks, casebooks). In this book, we decided to place it last. We do this for one very specific reason. We want ethics and its intersection with leadership to be the last thing you read and consider as you finish your course on leadership. In our own teaching and research, we are struck by the number of times that what seem to be innocuous decisions can turn into very dicey ethical situations. In the first author's previous life as an officer in the Canadian Navy, he was often presented with situations that required him to think through several ethical dimensions before making a decision. Consequently, we hope and expect that this chapter will be one you return to many times as you develop as a leader in the organization you join after you finish your current degree.

Concern regarding leaders and their ethics has been central to everyday life throughout our history. Unfortunately, it is also a very messy topic to research. Consequently, research regarding leaders and their ethics is very sparse (Yukl, 2006). Recent research (Ciulla, 1998; Phillips, 2006) has begun to delve into these issues. Ciulla (1998) discusses how leadership theory and practices may lead to a more just and caring society. Phillips (2006) defines CEO moral capital and presents a more formal definition of moral capital.

> *CEO moral capital* is the belief that the CEO justly balances the disparate interests of individual and group stakeholders to achieve positive returns that benefit the firm, its stakeholders, and the CEO.

> *Moral capital* is the belief that an individual, organization, or cause justly balances the disparate interests of stakeholders to achieve positive returns that benefit their collective and individual purposes.

These definitions describe how CEOs and other individuals are viewed by their followers, peers, and superiors and, as Phillips (2006) argues, are based on their perception of the CEO's (or an individual's) character and behavior.

A Definition of Ethics

In the Western world, the definition of ethics dates back to Plato and Aristotle. Ethics comes from *ethos,* a Greek word meaning character, conduct, and/or customs. It is about what morals and values are found appropriate by members of society and individuals themselves. Ethics helps us decide what is right and good or wrong and bad in any given situation. With respect to leadership, ethics is about who leaders are—their character and what they do, their actions and behaviors.

Ethical Theories

As suggested above, ethical theories fall into two broad categories: those theories related to leaders' conduct, actions, and/or behavior and those related to leaders' character. For those theories related to conduct, there are two types: those that relate to leaders' conduct and their consequences and those that relate to the rules or duty that prescribe leaders' conduct.

Those theories related to consequences are called *teleological theories* (*telos* being a Greek word for purposes or ends). These theories emphasize whether a leader's actions, behavior, and/or conduct have positive outcomes. This means that the outcomes related to a person's behavior establish whether the behavior was ethical or unethical.

Those theories related to duty or rules are called *deontological theories* (*deos* being a Greek word for duty). These theories focus on the actions that lead to consequences and whether the actions are good or bad. Those theories related to character are described as virtue-based approaches.

Teleological Approaches

There are three approaches to assessing outcomes and whether they are viewed as ethical. First, *ethical egoism* describes the actions of a leader designed to obtain the greatest good for the leader. Second, *utilitarianism* refers to the actions of leaders that obtain the greatest good for the largest number of people. Third, *altruism* is a perspective that argues that a leader's conduct is ethical if he or she demonstrates concern for others' interests, even if these interests are contrary to the leader's self-interests.

Deontological Approach

This approach is derived from *deos,* a Greek word meaning duty. It argues that whether or not an action is ethical depends not only on its outcome but also on whether the action, behavior, or conduct is itself inherently good. Examples of actions and behaviors that are intrinsically good, irrespective of the outcomes, are "telling the truth, keeping promises, being fair, and respecting others" (Northouse, 2010). This approach emphasizes the actions of leaders *and* their ethical responsibility to do what is right.

Virtue-Based Approach

Virtue-based theories are related to leaders and who they are and are grounded in the leader's heart and character. In addition, these virtues can be learned and retained through experience and practice. This learning occurs in an individual's family and the various communities with which an individual interacts throughout his or her lifetime. This perspective can be traced back to Plato and Aristotle. Aristotle believed that individuals could be helped to become more virtuous and that more attention should be given to telling individuals what to be as opposed to telling them what to do (Velasquez, 1992). Aristotle suggested the following virtues as exemplars of an ethical person: generosity, courage, temperance, sociability, self-control, honesty, fairness, modesty, and justice (Velasquez, 1992). Velasquez (1992) argued that organizational managers should learn and retain virtues "such as perseverance, public-spiritedness, integrity, truthfulness, fidelity, benevolence, and humility" (Northouse, 2010).

The Centrality of Ethics to Leadership

Ethics is central to leadership because of the nature of the relationship between leaders and followers. Leaders influence followers—this means they affect followers' lives either negatively or positively (Yukl, 2006). The nature of the influence depends on the leaders' character and behavior (particularly the nature and outcome of behaviors). Leaders have more power—interpersonal and/or formal hierarchical power—and therefore have a greater responsibility with respect to their impact on their followers. Leaders influence followers in the pursuit and achievement of common goals. It is in these situations that leaders need to respect their followers and treat them with dignity—in other words, as individuals with distinctive identities. Finally, leaders are instrumental in developing and establishing organizational values. Their own personal values determine what kind of ethical climate will develop in their organizations.

Ethical Leadership: The Perspectives of Several Leadership Scholars

In this section, we review the perspectives of three prominent leadership scholars as these perspectives relate to leadership and ethics. We focus on Heifetz (1994), Burns (1978), and Greenleaf (1970, 1977).

Heifetz and Ethical Leadership

Heifetz (1994) emphasized conflict and the responsibility of leaders to assist followers in dealing with conflict and effecting changes that come from conflict. He focused on the values of followers, the values of the organizations in which they work, and the values of the communities in which they live. For Heifetz (1994), the paramount responsibility of leaders is to create a work atmosphere characterized by empathy, trust, and nurturance and to help followers to change and grow when faced with difficult situations (Northouse, 2010; Yukl, 2006).

Burns and Ethical Leadership

Like Heifetz (1994), Burns (1978) argued that leadership (especially transformational leadership, as described in Chapter 9) is about helping followers achieve higher ethical standards when differing values conflict—especially when conflict is confronted during difficult situations. He argued that the interaction of leaders and followers should raise the ethical behavior and character of both. Leaders would do this by assisting followers to emphasize values such as equality, justice, and liberty (Burns, 1978; Ciulla, 1998).

Greenleaf and Ethical Leadership

Greenleaf (1970, 1977) espoused servant leadership. This perspective comes closest to altruism, described earlier. The underlying tenants of servant leadership are as follows: Leaders need to be aware of followers' concerns and needs, attend to followers' needs and concerns, empathize with followers, nurture and support followers, and look after followers. Servant leaders make others better by their presence. Through serving their followers, servant leaders encourage followers to gain more knowledge, freedom, and autonomy and to develop as servant leaders themselves. In addition, Greenleaf believed that servant leaders have a broader responsibility to society to accept the "have-nots" and to set right inequalities and social injustices (Graham, 1991; Northouse, 2010; Yukl, 2006).

All three perspectives emphasize the relationship between leaders and followers and argue that this relationship is at the heart of ethical leadership. The ideas presented by these three scholars are similar to and in agreement with Gilligan's (1982) ethic of caring. This has become a central principle in ethical leadership research and is considered of paramount importance to organizations because it is of critical importance in developing collaboration and trust among leaders and followers (Brady, 1999).

Ethical Leadership Principles

In this section, we present five principles that are believed to lead to the development of ethical leadership. These are respect for others, service to others, justice for others, honesty toward others, and building community with others (Dubrin, 2007; Northouse, 2010).

Respect for Others

Ethical leaders treat others with dignity and respect. This means that we treat people as ends in themselves rather than as means to our own ends. This form of respect recognizes that followers have goals and ambitions and confirms followers as human beings who have worth and value to the organization. In addition, it leads to empathy, active listening, and tolerance for conflicting viewpoints.

Service to Others

Ethical leaders serve others. They behave in an altruistic fashion as opposed to behaving in a way that is based on ethical egoism. These leaders put followers first—their prime reason for being is to support and nurture subordinates. Service to others is exemplified through behaviors such as mentoring, building teams, and empowering (Kanungo & Mendonca, 1996).

Justice for Others

Ethical leaders ensure that justice and fairness are central parts of their decision making. This means treating all subordinates in very similar ways, except when there is a very clear need for differential treatment and there is transparency about why this need exists. In addition to being transparent, the logic for differential treatment should be morally sound and reasonable.

Honesty Toward Others

Ethical leadership requires honesty. Dishonesty destroys trust—a critical characteristic of any leader–follower relationship. On the other hand, honesty increases trust and builds the leader–follower relationship. Honesty means openness with others in that we express our thinking and our reality as fully as we can. This means balancing openness with disclosing only what is appropriate in a given scenario. Dalla Costa (1998) says that honesty for leaders means the following:

> Do not promise what you can't deliver, do not misrepresent, do not hide behind spin-doctored evasions, do not suppress obligations, do not evade accountability, do not accept that the "survival of the fittest" pressures of business release any of us from the responsibility to respect another's dignity and humanity. (p. 164)

We would argue that leaders need to ensure that *what they believe, what they think, what they say,* and *what they do* are internally consistent. This internal consistency, along with openness, will build trust among followers toward the leader.

Building Community With Others

Ethical leaders build community with others. This is crucial because leadership is about influencing others to achieve a communal goal. This means that leaders develop organizational or team goals that are appropriate for the leader and his or her followers. These goals need to excite as many people as possible, and ethical leaders achieve this by taking into account the goals of everyone in the team or organization.

How Does Ethical Leadership Work?

We are hoping that this chapter will enable you to better understand yourself as you develop your leadership skills, knowledge, and abilities. Use the thinking on ethical leadership in this chapter as a guide in making your decisions. Remember that the relationship between you and your followers is at the heart of ethical leadership and requires that you show sensitivity to others' needs, treat others in a just manner, and have a caring attitude toward others. Being an ethical leader will be easier if you entrench the following questions into your thinking (Northouse, 2010):

- Is this the right and fair thing to do?
- Is this what a good person would do?

- Am I respectful to others?
- Do I treat others generously?
- Am I honest toward others?
- Am I serving the community?

Ethical leaders must be concerned with more than running their businesses. They must be concerned with their employees, their customers, their suppliers, their communities, their shareholders, and themselves. Leadership is influencing people to achieve communal goals; ethical leadership is achieving those goals in a way that is fair and just to your employees, your customers, your suppliers, your communities, your shareholders, and yourselves (Daft, 2005; Phillips, 2006).

References

Brady, F. N. (1999). A systematic approach to teaching ethics in business. *Journal of Business Ethics, 19*(3), 309–319.

Burns, J. M. (1978). *Leadership.* New York: Harper & Row.

Ciulla, J. B. (1998). *Ethics, the heart of leadership.* Westport, CT: Greenwood.

Daft, R. L. (2005). *The leadership experience* (3rd ed.). Mason, OH: Thomson, South-Western.

Dalla Costa, J. (1998). *The ethical imperative: Why moral leadership is good business.* Reading, MA: Addison-Wesley.

Dubrin, A. (2007). *Leadership: Research findings, practice, and skills.* New York: Houghton Mifflin.

Gilligan, C. (1982). *In a different voice: Psychological theory and women's development.* Cambridge, MA: Harvard University Press.

Goldsmith, M., Greenberg, C. L., Robertson, A., & Hu-Chan, M. (2003). *Global leadership: The next generation.* Upper Saddle River, NJ: Financial Times Prentice Hall.

Graham, J. W. (1991). Servant-leadership in organizations: Inspirational and moral. *Leadership Quarterly, 2*(2), 105–119.

Greenleaf, R. K. (1970). *The servant as leader.* Newton Centre, MA: Robert K. Greenleaf Center.

Greenleaf, R. K. (1977). *Servant leadership: A journey into the nature of legitimate power and greatness.* New York: Paulist.

Heifetz, R. A. (1994). *Leadership without easy answers.* Cambridge, MA: Harvard University Press.

Kanungo, R. N., & Mendonca, M. (1996). *Ethical dimensions of leadership.* Thousand Oaks, CA: Sage.

Northouse, P. G. (2010). *Leadership: Theory and practice* (5th ed.). Thousand Oaks, CA: Sage.

Phillips, J. R. (2006). *CEO moral capital.* Unpublished doctoral manuscript, University of Western Ontario.

Velasquez, M. G. (1992). *Business ethics: Concepts and cases* (3rd ed.). Englewood Cliffs, NJ: Prentice Hall.

Yukl, G. (2006). *Leadership in organizations* (6th ed.). Upper Saddle River, NJ: Pearson/Prentice Hall.

The Cases

Lee and Li, Attorneys-at-Law, and the Embezzlement of NT$3 Billion by Eddie Liu (A)

Dr. C. V. Chen received news that one of Lee and Li's senior assistants had found a loophole in a power of attorney from one of the firm's clients, SanDisk Corporation (SanDisk), that had allowed him to illegally sell the client's shares in a Taiwanese company and to sneak out of Taiwan with more than NT$3 billion. Unfortunately, Lee and Li had no insurance to cover this embezzlement. Chen knew that the three senior partners needed to develop a plan of action to save the law firm, take care of the lawyers and other employees, maintain the reputation of the firm within Taiwan and abroad, do what was best for SanDisk and Lee and Li, and keep the more than 12,000 clients from deserting the firm.

Pembina Pipeline Corporation

Pembina Pipeline Corporation transports light crude oil and natural gas liquids in Western Canada. The president of the company is abruptly awakened one night by a phone call from his operations manager. He is informed that one of Pembina's pipelines has burst and is spilling thousands of barrels of crude oil into a nearby river. Emergency crews have responded to the disaster, but more help is needed. The president has to decide the best way to handle this situation with the media and plan a strategy for the company in containing the spill.

▧ The Reading

Principled Leadership: Taking the Hard Right

What makes a leader the most principled is a certain solidity at the core, a solidity founded on principles that are, essentially, points on a moral compass. Those principles are visible in the actions of some leaders, while other leaders act according to convenience. These authors lay down a blueprint that will allow a leader to be guided by principles.

Lee and Li, Attorneys-at-Law, and the Embezzlement of NT$3 Billion by Eddie Liu (A)

Prepared by Yeong-Yuh Chiang and W. Glenn Rowe

Dr. C.V. Chen was shocked and speechless. Paul Hsu, one of Lee and Li's most senior partners, had just briefed him and Kwan-Tao Li about the actions of Eddie Liu, one of the firm's senior assistants. Liu had found a loophole in a power of attorney from one of the firm's clients that had allowed him to illegally sell the client's shares in a Taiwanese company and to sneak out of Taiwan with NT$3.09 billion (approximately US$92 million).

Unfortunately, Lee and Li had no insurance to cover this embezzlement.

Many questions raced through Chen's mind: What about the firm? How would this action affect the more than 550 lawyers and employees? How would other clients react to the news of this crime? Would this breach of trust ruin the firm's reputation in Taiwan and abroad? Would the firm survive and remain financially stable? What should the firm do for

AUTHORS' NOTE: This case has been written on the basis of public sources. Consequently, the interpretation and perspectives presented in this case are not necessarily those of Lee and Li or any of its partners and employees.

the client whose shares had been used to perpetuate the fraud and theft by Liu?

Chen knew that action had to be taken quickly. The questions whirled in his head as he considered what he, Hsu and Kwan-Tao Li, the three most senior partners at Lee and Li, needed to do today, tomorrow, next week and over the next several months.

October 13, 2003 would forever be seared into Chen's memory.

☒ The Firm: Lee and Li, Attorneys-at-Law

The firm that later became Lee and Li had been founded in Shanghai, China, in the mid-1940s. James Lee, one of the two founders, had commenced practicing law with Allman and Kopps, and, in 1948, the firm was named Allman, Kopps and Lee. Dr. C. N. Li, the other founding partner, had also practiced in Shanghai during the 1940s. Both James Lee and C. N. Li were specialists in international legal matters.

In 1953, James Lee established his own law office in Taipei, Taiwan, and, in 1965, he was joined by C. N. Li. James Lee died in 1970, and Li renamed the firm Lee and Li. After C. N. Li died in 1973, Paul Hsu, Kwan-Tao Li (C. N. Li's son) and C. V. Chen, together with other senior partners, led the firm through extraordinary growth to become one of the largest law firms in Asia and the largest in Taiwan. Considered by many to be the top law firm in that country,[1] Lee and Li had offices in the cities of Taipei, Taichung, Hsinchu, Tainan and Kaohsiung.

Lee and Li's core values encompassed three principles: caring for people, excellence in quality and client service. A core goal was "doing well by doing good." The firm's motto "we care, we serve, we excel" was prominently displayed at the entrance to the firm's head office in Taipei. The partners and staff believed that adherence to these principles had made the firm a leader in each of its 28 practice areas. The firm was involved in the development of public policies and in promoting the rule of law in Taiwan and elsewhere, particularly in China. The firm had advised Taiwan's government on vital social and economic policies, and several firm members had helped draft new governmental legislation. Lee and Li lawyers had been involved in judicial reform and constitutional litigation work that were considered landmarks. Their work on pro bono cases had won them a reputation for "being a leader in public interest work in Taiwan." In 1999, the firm established the Lee and Li Foundation, a not-for-profit organization dedicated to promoting education and rule of law.

Lee and Li had several thousand clients, many of whom had been with the firm for decades. One-third of these clients were headquartered in Taiwan, and the rest were foreign firms. Companies from the United States, Europe and Japan had utilized Lee and Li's services. The firm's client list included internationally well-known firms, such as General Electric, Ford, 3M, Bank of America, City Bank, IBM, Sony, McDonald's and Siemens. Over the years, Lee and Li had represented almost all of the Fortune 500 firms and the multinational banks that were doing business in Taiwan.

Lee and Li's attorneys were globally connected, and several were fluent in English or Japanese in addition to their native tongue, Chinese. They were graduates of top law schools in countries such as Taiwan, the United States, and Japan (see Exhibit 1 for brief résumés for Chen and Li). Lee and Li's attorneys enjoyed long-standing relationships with law firms in North America, Asia and Europe. Collaboration on cross-border deals with other law firms was routine for Lee and Li attorneys. To better serve clients operating in the Greater China region, Lee and Li had established strategic alliances with Lee and Li Business Consultants (Shanghai) Ltd. and Lee and Li—Leaven IPR Agency Ltd. in Beijing.

---

[1] "Plugging the Loopholes," editorial, *Taipei Times*, October 18, 2003, p. 8; Jimmy Chuang, "Fugitive Liu Wanted in Hong Kong, *Taipei Times*, June 24, 2004, p. 1.

Exhibit 1	Brief Résumés for C. V. Chen and Kwan-Tao Li

C. V. Chen

Place of Birth: Yunan, China.
Nationality: Republic of China (on Taiwan).

Education

S.J.D., Harvard (1972); LL.M., Harvard (1970); LL.M., University of British Columbia (1969); LL.B., National Taiwan University (1967).

Experience

Professional: Chairman and Managing Partner, Lee and Li Attorneys-at-Law, Taipei, Taiwan; Adjunct Professor of Law, National Chengchi University Graduate School of Law, Taiwan, (1972–present); Lecture Professor of Law, Guanghua School of Management, Peking University, China; Lecture Professor of Law, School of Law, Tsinghua University, China; Chairman of Guanghua Law School Council, Zhejiang University, China; Lecturer, the Training Institute for Judges and Prosecutors, the Ministry of Justice of the Republic of China.

Pro Bono: President, The Red Cross Society of the Republic of China (April 2000–present); Chairman, Taipei European School Foundation, Taiwan, the Republic of China (1994–present); Director, Lee and Li Foundation; Managing Director, Chinese (Taiwan) Society of International Law (Jan. 2004–present).

Honors

Honorary President, Harvard Club of Republic of China on Taiwan (1989–present); Recipient of the Order of Resplendent Banner with Special Cravat from the President of the Republic of China in 1989 for contribution to the upgrading of legal education and establishment of procurement system in the armed forces; Recipient of other medals and awards from the government of the Republic of China on Taiwan.

Publications

Numerous articles on transnational legal problems

Kwan-Tao Li

Place of Birth: Shanghai, China.
Nationality: Republic of China (on Taiwan).

Education

MBA, Kellogg-HKUST; LL.M., New York University Law School, Graduate Division; LL.B., National Taiwan University.

Experience

Chief Counsellor, Lee and Li, Attorneys-at-law; Chairman, Lee and Li Foundation; Chairman, Lee and Li Business Consultants (Shanghai), Ltd; Director, Far Eastern Medical Foundation;

(Continued)

| **Exhibit 1** | (Continued) |

Director, Yen Tjing Ling Medical Foundation; Director, Far Eastern Y.Z. Hsu Science and Technology Memorial Foundation; Director, Asia Cement Corporation; Director, Far Eastern Textile Ltd; Director, Tai Yuen Textile Co., Ltd.; Supervisor, Yulon Nissan Motor Co., Ltd.; Associate Professor of Law, Chinese Culture University (1985–1998); Lecturer of Law, Soochow University Law School (1969–1999); Lecturer of Law, Soochow University Graduate Law School (1972–1985); Lecturer of Law, National Taiwan Institute of Technology (1975–1979); Lecturer of Law, Fu Jen Catholic University (1969–1971); Director, Yuan Ze University (1987–1999).

Member

Member, State Bar of New York.

Languages

Mandarin, English, Cantonese, Shanghainese

Practice Area

Corporate; Entertainment; Fair Trade; Intellectual Property Rights; International Mergers and Acquisitions; Labour; Maritime; Trademarks.

Coauthor

Coauthor of "A Study on Economic Contract Law of Mainland China," published by Chinese Culture University; Contributor to *Trade and Investment in Taiwan: The Legal and Economic Environment in the R.O.C.*, Published by University of Washington.

SOURCE: http://www.leeandli.com/web/e/default.htm, accessed June 8, 2008.

Lee and Li had achieved a stellar reputation and received many awards for its outstanding work in the areas other than intellectual property. The firm had received several awards for its work in "managing intellectual property" (see Exhibit 2 for a list of awards, honors and recognition for Lee and Li from 1998 to 2002).

| **Exhibit 2** | Awards, Honors, and Recognition for Lee and Li |

Managing Intellectual Property	
1998	Voted No.1 Firm for Non-patent Work in Taiwan 1997
1999	Voted No.1 Firm for Trade Mark and Copyright Work in Taiwan 1998
2000	Voted No.1 Firm for Patent in Taiwan 1999
2000	Voted No.1 Firm for Trade Mark/Copyright in Taiwan 1999

2001	Voted No.1 Firm for Patent in Taiwan 2000
2001	Voted No.1 Firm for Trade Mark/Copyright in Taiwan 2000
2002	Voted No.2 Firm for Patent in Taiwan 2001
2002	Voted No.2 Firm for Trade Mark/Copyright in Taiwan 2001
2003	Voted No.2 Firm for Patent in Taiwan 2002
2003	Voted No.1 Firm for Trade Mark/Copyright in Taiwan 2002
International Financial Law Review	
2001	Law Firm of the Year
2001	Pro Bono Award
2002	Regional Law Firm of the Year
2003	National Law Firm of the Year
Global Competition Review	
2002	The GCR 100: A Survey of the World's Leading Competition Law Practices and Economists

SOURCE: http://www.leeandli.com/web/e/default.htm, accessed June 8, 2008.

From its beginnings, the firm had developed the largest intellectual property practice in Taiwan, and, in the 1970s, had been extensively involved in foreign direct investment growth into Taiwan. The firm pioneered the development of the banking and capital markets practice in the 1980s and had been pivotal in the establishment of the technology and law practice in the 1990s. Lee and Li was structured into four departments (corporate, banking and capital markets, trademark and copyright, and patent and technology) with Hsu, Chen and Li jointly managing the operations. Although the associate partners and staff worked almost exclusively for one of the four departments, they would, as a rule, engage in cross-fertilization with their colleagues in the other departments.

The Client: SanDisk Corporation (NASDAQ: SNDK)

SanDisk Corporation (SanDisk) was founded in 1988 by Dr. Eli Harari, a world-renowned authority on non-volatile memory technology. Based in Sunnyvale, California, the company was the world's largest supplier of flash memory data storage card products. It designed, manufactured and marketed "industry-standard, solid-state data, digital imaging and audio storage products using its patented, high density flash memory and controller technology."[2] SanDisk was the only company that had the rights to manufacture and sell every major flash card format, including CF, SD, miniSD,

---

[2]"SanDisk . . . Its Taiwan Law Firm," *Business Wire*, November 15, 2003, p. 1.

SmartMedia, FlashDisk, MMC, MemoryStick Pro, xD-Picture cards and USB flash drives. The company did not operate fabrication facilities, but used a multiple-sources strategy to fluctuate its supply with changes in demand. SanDisk controlled a significant portion of its flash memory wafer manufacturing through its joint venture, FlashVision, and many other strategic arrangements with fabrication facility owners. These strategic and contractual partners included Toshiba, Samsung, Renasas Technology, United Microelectronic Inc. (UMC) and Tower Semiconductor Ltd. Such a multiple-sources strategy enabled SanDisk to concentrate on product designs and development of its core competency. SanDisk received a majority of its revenue from direct sales to retailers.

On September 30, 2003, SanDisk owned 147.8 million shares in UMC, one of its contractual partners in Taiwan. Twenty million of these shares were held by SanDisk with the remaining 127.8 million shares under the control of Lee and Li. SanDisk had sold 35 million UMC shares during the month of September for approximately US$30 million. The 127.8 million UMC shares controlled by Lee and Li were valued at US$83.3 million, based on cost, and were worth US$106.6 million based on trading price on the Taiwan Stock Exchange on September 30, 2003.

At SanDisk's previous fiscal year end on December 29, 2002, it reported revenues of US$541,273,000 with net income of US$36,240,000. Its diluted net income per share was US$0.26. SanDisk had working capital of US$584,450,000, total assets of US$973,579,000, long-term debt of US$150,000,000 and stockholders' equity of US$627,720,000. The company was doing well financially and was on an upward trajectory (see Exhibit 3 for the quarterly financial data as of September 28, 2003).

Exhibit 3 SanDisk Corporation 2003 Supplementary Quarterly Data (in thousands, except per share data)

	Quarters Ended		
	March 30	June 29	September 28
Revenues			
Product	$155,448	$214,044	$259,446
License and royalty	$19,032	$20,582	$21,954
Total revenues	$174,480	$234,626	$281,400
Gross profits	$71,591	$88,772	$113,635
Operating income	$34,686	$46,659	$66,803
Net income	$24,925	$41,326	$14,770
Net income per share			
Basic %	$0.18	$0.30	$0.11
Diluted %	$0.17	$0.26	$0.09

SOURCE: 2003, SanDisk Corporation's Annual Report on Form 10-K, 20.

The Senior Partners: Hsu, Chen, and Li

Paul Hsu, C. V. Chen, and Kwan-Tao Li, together with other senior partners who had retired before the turn of the century, had led the firm since the deaths of the founders, James Lee and C. N. Li. Kwan-Tao Li joined the firm in August 1969. In addition, he started teaching at Soochow University Law School and Fu Jen Catholic University that same year. Li had graduated from New York University Law School with his master's degree of law and had a master's of business administration from Kellogg/Hong Kong University of Science and Technology. Hsu had joined the firm in September 1969, preceding Chen by about four years. Chen joined in 1973 after having received his SJD (doctorate in law) from the Harvard Law School in 1972 and having taught at National Chengchi University Graduate School of Law. Together, Hsu, Chen and Li had been with Lee and Li for a combined 98 years.

The Perpetrator: Eddie Liu

Liu had graduated from National Chunghsing University with his bachelor's of law degree. He joined Lee and Li in December 1989 as a legal assistant. Liu handled non-litigation cases in the firm's corporate and investing department and was responsible for investing and mergers and acquisitions. He performed well and was considered a capable assistant. Although he was a law school graduate and a capable assistant, Liu had failed to pass the Taiwanese bar exam. On August 1, 2003, he approached the management of the firm and asked for a 12 month's leave without pay to prepare for the bar exam. Management approved his request on October 1 because the 41-year-old Liu was a trusted employee.

The Embezzlement: NT$3 Billion[3]

In 2002, SanDisk authorized Lee and Li to file an investment application with the Taiwanese government. This application was required to allow the remittance of the return on investment (the dividend) and the principle in the case of divestment to SanDisk because of the Taiwanese government's foreign exchange control. This arrangement required that SanDisk give Lee and Li a power of attorney. The power of attorney should have empowered Lee and Li only to interact with the government on SanDisk's behalf. However, it contained a clause that allowed Lee and Li to deal with the brokerage house holding SanDisk's shares in UMC. This clause meant that Lee and Li's representative could talk to the brokerage house on behalf of SanDisk. For this clause to have been included in the power of attorney was very unusual. The inclusion of the clause should have been noted by Lee and Li and deleted. The power of attorney authorized Lee and Li to make chops (signets) for SanDisk, and any transaction involving SanDisk required both these chops and those containing the name of Hsu, all of which were secured in a vault at Lee and Li.

In July 2002, Lee and Li, in its role representing SanDisk, opened a trading account in the investment firm KGI and a deposit account in Chang Hwa Bank. The proceeds from the sale of any shares acquired by SanDisk in Taiwanese firms were to be used to invest in mainland China and in Taiwan. Because of the flawed clause in the power of attorney and because of his position in the firm, Liu gained unauthorized access to the passbooks and chops for both accounts and could transact business through both accounts without any "actual" permission and/or supervision. He was not legally authorized to make

---

[3]Sheree Shiow-Ru Ma and Mei-Cyue Lee, "Internal Control and Employee's Fraudulent Behaviors," *Accounting Research Monthly*, No. 218, January 1, 2004.

any transactions but he had access to the tools that allowed him to do so.

In July 2003, SanDisk deposited 183 million UMC shares in the KGI account. Liu applied for a leave of absence on August 1 to prepare for his bar examination and immediately moved into a five-star hotel, having left his Peitou District residence in Taipei. During August, he privately opened several accounts for SanDisk at Asia Securities, United World Chinese Commercial Bank (a branch in Taiwan and a branch in Hong Kong), Taipei Bank, Hwatai Bank, Shanghai Commercial and Savings Bank, and Chang Hwa Bank. All accounts were under the name of SanDisk Corporation except for the bank account in the Hong Kong branch of the United World Chinese Commercial Bank, which was opened in the name of "SanDisk Investing Corporation."

From August 2 to 9, Liu, having forged the authorization document required, had transferred 120.3 million UMC shares from the KGI account to the Asia Securities account. He then conspired with private investment consulting firms to bid up the price of the UMC stock. From August 6 to 28, he sold the shares and obtained NT$3.09 billion (US$92 million). During August and September, to eliminate any trace of the NT$3.09 billion, he laundered the money by buying diamonds and travelers' checks with the money he had remitted to the Hong Kong account.

During September, the Money Laundering Prevention Center (MLPC) of the Taiwanese government was informed of the huge amount of funds transfers but the information indicated that it was a routine notification of a "huge amount transfer" in excess of NT$1 million. The transaction did not appear to be illegal for two reasons: First, the information MLPC received said that "SanDisk Corporation" had transferred earnings from the sale of UMC's stock to "SanDisk Investing Corporation" in Hong Kong, not to another company or individual; second, it appeared that Liu was fully authorized by both SanDisk and Lee and Li to sell the shares and transfer the earnings.

Therefore, the transaction was judged a legal transfer by the MLPC.

Around the end of September and beginning of October, Liu handed over his files to his colleagues, ostensibly in preparation for his leave without pay, and he intentionally withheld any files related to SanDisk. On October 1, Liu's leave without pay was approved; however, he continued to go to the office until Thursday, October 9. At 2:00 p.m. on October 9, Liu left Lee and Li and proceeded directly to the airport. He bought his ticket at the airline counter using as his travel documents both his roommate's passport and his Tai Bao Zheng (a travel document required for people from Taiwan to legally enter mainland China). He then flew to Hong Kong from where it was much easier to transfer the diamonds and travelers' checks to a bank in a city within mainland China, such as Shanghai.

⊠ Lee and Li's Dilemma: What to Do?

Chen was informed of Liu's embezzlement on Monday, October 13. October 10 had been a national holiday and October 11 and 12 was the weekend. Liu's colleagues had reconciled his files early on Monday and noticed the discrepancy. This finding led to the discovery of Liu's malfeasance, which was reported to Paul Hsu, who immediately briefed C.V. Chen and Kwan-Tao Li. The embezzlement left all of the partners in jeopardy because Lee and Li had no insurance to cover the NT$3 billion. In Taiwan, the partners in law firms shared unlimited liability, which meant that all of Lee and Li's partners faced the possibility of losing all of their personal possessions as well as their professional livelihood and standing.

Chen knew that, as the senior partners, the three of them needed to develop a plan of action that would save Lee and Li; take care of the lawyers and other employees, as well as their families; keep Lee and Li's reputation within Taiwan and abroad intact; do what was best for SanDisk and Lee and Li; and keep the more than 12,000 clients from deserting the firm. Chen knew that he, Hsu and Li had to act quickly and decisively. Liu's embezzlement would become public knowledge within hours, or the next day at the latest.

Pembina Pipeline Corporation

Prepared by Ken Mark under the supervision of Alexandra Hurst

▧ Introduction

Patrick Walsh, president of Pembina Pipeline Corporation, was abruptly awakened by a telephone call from Jim Thomas, his operations manager. It was 4:30 a.m. on August 2, 2000, in downtown Calgary, Alberta, and Thomas had no time for pleasantries:

> Walsh, I just heard from one of our pipeline operators that our new Taylor-Prince Georg e pipeline burst open this morning! Get up! We're leaking thousands of barrels of crude into a pristine salmon river. Our emergency response crews have started containment efforts but we're going to need much more help. What are we going to do next?

A wave of panic shook Walsh awake. Grabbing his car keys and the cellular phone, he scrambled into his Ford Explorer and began driving to Pembina's Calgary head office. Negotiating corners with one hand on the steering wheel, Walsh kept Thomas on the line:

> I want to know all the details of the spill now! Our first concern will be to contain the oil! I'll join you in a few minutes at the office and we'd better come

up with something. Damn it, Thomas, we don't even have media relations people, much less a PR agency!

▧ Pembina Pipeline Corporation

Involved in the transportation of light crude oil, condensate and natural gas liquids in western Canada, Pembina Pipeline Corporation owned the Pembina Pipeline Income Fund (the Fund), a publicly traded Canadian income fund. This fund was established in 1997 to give the investing public the opportunity to participate in a stable, well-managed pipeline transportation entity that had provided high quality, reliable service to the Canadian oil and gas industry since the mid-1950s. The Fund was intended to provide unitholders with attractive long-term returns through its investment in Pembina, which had a mandate to efficiently operate its pipeline systems and actively seek expansion opportunities. The Fund paid cash distributions to unitholders on a monthly basis. The trust units traded on the Toronto Stock Exchange under the symbol PIF.UN.

Pembina's pipeline systems served a large geographic area with 7,500 kilometres of pipeline and related pumping and storage facilities. The systems were well positioned in the heart of

---

AUTHOR'S NOTE: This case was written with public sources and the permission of Pembina Pipeline Corporation. Some facts have been altered.

Version: (A) 2001-07-06

western Canada's oil and natural gas production areas. There were four systems in total:

- Peace Pipeline System—Central Northwest Alberta
- Pembina Pipeline System—Central Southwest Alberta
- Bonnie Glen Pipeline System—Central South Alberta
- Wabasca Pipeline System—Northern Alberta

Collectively, Pembina's pipeline systems transported over 40 per cent of conventional light crude oil production in Western Canada.

⬚ Operations

Pembina's pipeline systems were maintained and operated by a dedicated group of field employees located in 10 field offices. Pembina's corporate head office was located in Calgary, Alberta where technical and administrative staff supported the pipeline operations. Through its pipeline, Pembina transported light crude oil, condensate and natural gas liquids. Virtually no heavy oil was transported on any of the Pembina systems, nor was Pembina a natural gas carrier. The company did not own the product it transported but, similar to a trucking company, it took custody of the product from when it entered the pipeline until it was delivered to the owners.

Pipelines and the materials used in them were designed, built and tested to high standards. When pipelines were properly maintained failures due to pipe breakdown were rare. Pembina had several maintenance programs in place to ensure line integrity. These were:

Internal Inspection Program

Internal inspection tools were designed to allow pipeline operators to measure the wall thickness along the pipe so that areas of metal loss could be located and repaired. These tools had been incorporated into Pembina's monitoring program, and pipeline systems were inspected on a rotating seven-to-eight-year-cycle. Pembina's pipeline systems, with the exception of the recently purchased Federated system, were last checked in 1998.

Hydrostatic Testing

Government regulations required new pipelines be filled with water and pressure tested to 125 per cent of their licensed maximum operating pressure before the lines could be put into service. The hydrotest was designed to reveal any structural weakness in the pipe or welds. Although not a regulatory requirement, all of the major pipelines in the Peace and Pembina System (built prior to 1970) had been hydrostatically retested. The first two phases of hydrostatic testing of the 16-inch mainline had been completed and confirmed the strength and quality of the pipe tested.

Bacterial Monitoring and Treatment

Pembina's pipeline systems employed programs of regular product sampling and testing for bacteria. Producers with excessive bacteria were required to treat their tanks with a biocide to kill the bacteria. Similarly, biocide was periodically shipped through pipelines to control and kill bacteria.

Cathodic Protection

Cathodic protection systems were used on steel pipelines to impress a small voltage on the pipe to help protect it from external corrosion. Every month, readings were taken on Pembina's pipelines to ensure that these systems were operating at effective levels. A complete cathodic protection survey was done annually in compliance with regulatory requirements and any necessary repairs or adjustments to the systems were made. Evaluation of the survey results provided important information on the condition of the pipeline coatings.

✑ Expansion

Pembina intended to continue to expand its service through new battery and facilities connections, tie-ins to third-party pipelines, and expansion of Pembina's existing systems to service new oil- and gas-producing areas. Ongoing exploration and development activity by the producer community was expected to continue to fuel demand for pipeline service in the regions served by Pembina's pipeline systems, particularly on the Continental System operating in northwestern Oregon and northeastern Washington.

The most significant increase in throughputs on the Pembina System could potentially come from technology developments to improve the recovery of crude oil in the oil fields. It was estimated that only 21 per cent of initial crude oil in place was recoverable using present technology.

Pembina's management was actively reviewing potential acquisitions and believed that Pembina was very well positioned to take advantage of any favorable opportunities to acquire or otherwise expand Pembina's business.

✑ Incident Control Mechanisms

While environmental incidents had never occurred on Pembina's pipeline systems, Pembina maintained insurance to provide coverage in relation to the ownership and operation of its pipeline assets. Property insurance coverage provided coverage on the property and equipment that was above-ground or that facilitated river crossings, with recovery based upon replacement costs. Business interruption

insurance covered loss of income arising from specific property damage. The comprehensive general liability coverage provided coverage in actions by third parties. The latter coverage included Pembina's sudden and accidental pollution coverage, which specifically insured against certain claims for damage from pipeline leaks or spills.

✑ The Pipeline Break

Thomas continued to feed more information to Walsh:

> At about 1:20 this morning, the pipeline break and subsequent spill of crude oil occurred at mile post 102.5 of the Federated Western Pipeline— the same pipeline company that we bought 12 hours ago.[4] The break released crude oil into the Pine River just upstream of Chetwynd, B.C.
>
> Our emergency response field team set up a control site half a mile downstream from the spill. A second control site was set further downstream at the creek's entry into the Pine as a precautionary measure, and a third control site beyond the town of Chetwynd is to be set up today.

When he heard that the spill had occurred near a small town and could threaten its water supply, Walsh knew that there was no stopping immediate media coverage. He let Thomas continue uninterrupted.

> We've set up vacuum facilities at each control site which are being manned right now, removing oil from the river. My guys are telling me that we'll lose as much as 6,300 barrels.[5] In the next hour, I'm going to set up a mobile lab to

---

[4]The deal to purchase Federated was completed on July 31, 2000—see Exhibit 1.

[5]This amount (6,300 barrels) was equivalent to one million cubic metres of oil.

Exhibit I	The Purchase of Federated Western Pipelines

NEWS RELEASE

Attention Business Editors:

Pembina Pipeline Corporation Completes Purchase of Federated Pipe Lines Ltd.

Not for distribution to United States Newswire Services or dissemination in the United States.

CALGARY, July 31/CNW/—Pembina Pipeline Income Fund (TSE-PIF.UN) announced today that its wholly owned subsidiary Pembina Pipeline Corporation has successfully completed its purchase of 100% of the shares of Federated Pipe Lines Ltd. from Anderson Exploration Ltd.'s subsidiary, Home Oil Company Limited, and Imperial Oil Limited. In a related transaction, Pembina closed the purchase of the Cynthia Pipeline from Imperial on the same date.

Following the completion of this transaction, Pembina's combined pipeline network comprises roughly 7,000 kilometres of pipeline and related pumping and storage facilities and in 1999 transported 548,400 barrels per day of crude oil, condensate and natural gas liquids. The Federated acquisition entrenches Pembina's position as Canada's leading feeder pipeline transportation business. Total consideration paid by Pembina for the Federated shares was $340-million, including the assumption of Federated debt. A further $9-million was paid for the Cynthia pipeline. The transactions were financed utilizing a new $420-million syndicated credit facility arranged with a Canadian chartered bank.

Pembina is working toward the timely and orderly integration of the Pembina and Federated pipeline networks, and expects a seamless transition during the consolidation process. The combination of these considerable pipeline operations is expected to produce significant synergies and operating efficiencies which will provide substantial value for Pembina's customers and Unitholders of the Fund. Incremental cash flow generated by the acquired assets is expected to be sufficient to service the acquisition debt as well as fund an increase in the distribution payments to Unitholders of the Fund once the pipelines have been successfully integrated.

Pembina's purchase of the pipeline assets of the Western Facilities Fund for $40.3 million is scheduled to close in late August 2000 following approval by the Unitholders of Western.

The Pembina Pipeline Income Fund is a Canadian income fund engaged, through its wholly owned subsidiary Pembina Pipeline Corporation, in the transportation of crude oil, condensate and natural gas liquids in Western Canada. Trust Units of the Fund trade on the Toronto Stock Exchange under the symbol PIF.UN.

This news release contains forward-looking statements that involve risks and uncertainties. Such information, although considered reasonable by Pembina at the time of preparation, may prove to be incorrect and actual results may differ materially from those anticipated in the statements made. For this purpose, any statements that are contained herein that are not statements of historical fact may be deemed to be forward-looking statements.

Such risks and uncertainties include, but are not limited to risks associated with operations, such as loss of market, regulatory matters, environmental risks, industry competition, and ability to access sufficient capital from internal and external sources.

This news release shall not constitute an offer to sell or the solicitation of an offer to buy securities in any jurisdiction. No securities of Pembina Pipeline Income Fund have been registered under the United States Securities Act of 1933, as amended, and such securities may not be offered or sold in the United States absent registration, or an applicable exemption from the registration requirements of such Act.

SOURCE: www.pembina.com, December 29, 2000.

continuously test the water upstream from Chetwynd. I'll also contact district officials to inform residents along the Pine River of the situation and to put in guidelines to restrict their water usage.

⬛ At Pembina's Head Office

Walsh parked his car and ran up two flights of stairs to the office. Thomas and the crew of pipeline monitors were hovering over a computer screen detailing Pembina's network of pipelines. Walsh knew that he would need help in dealing with the media. Even if he were able to contact and retain a media relations firm, he realized that the initial press release would be his responsibility. Thomas exclaimed:

We still do not know what caused the pipeline break, but I can tell you that we have between 70 to 80 people already onsite, beginning clean-up activities. They're using oil booms to stop the flow of oil and sponges to soak up what they can.

A map of the area was laid out on the table. Walsh could now clearly see the proximity of the town of Chetwynd to the spill. He knew that the health of the town and surrounding area would have to be his first priority. First, Pembina had to contain the oil spill.

It was 5 a.m., and daylight would break within the next two hours.

Principled Leadership

Taking the Hard Right

By Gerard H. Seijts and Hon. David Kilgour

What makes a leader the most is a certain solidity at the core, a solidity founded on principles that are, essentially, points on a moral compass. Those principles are visible in the actions of some leaders, while other leaders act according to convenience. These authors lay down a blueprint that will allow a leader to be guided by principles.

On August 30, 2004, former New York City mayor Rudolph Giuliani delivered a riveting speech at the Republican National Convention. "They [the media] ridiculed Winston Churchill. They belittled Ronald Reagan," Giuliani said. "But like President Bush, they were optimists, and leaders must be optimists. Their vision was beyond the present and set on a future of real peace and true freedom. Some call it stubbornness. I call it principled leadership."

Unfortunately, in the recent (and not so recent) past, we have seen too many leadership failures—too many examples of individuals in leadership positions who were unable to deal with the "great responsibility" that they were given. More specifically, too many so-called "leaders" did not exercise principled leadership. For example:

Harry Stonecipher came out of retirement in 2003 to help restore Boeing's reputation after an ethics scandal. Stonecipher helped write a new code of conduct that, he indicated, would apply to all people in the Boeing organization. Yet Stonecipher violated that very code when he began an affair with a female Boeing executive. The board asked him to resign.

WestJet Airlines admitted that its "highest management levels" were behind an elaborate scheme to steal commercially sensitive information from arch-rival Air Canada. A court case resulted in which WestJet admitted to wrongdoing and agreed to pay $5.5 million in investigation and legal bills, plus a $10 million donation to charity. On its web site, WestJet identifies 9 "legendary values," among them: "we are honest, open, and keep our commitments," and "we treat everyone with respect." Did the actions of the senior leadership put a dent in the values on which WestJet was built?

Several members of Hewlett-Packard's executive team employed a series of "disturbing" tactics (e.g., obtaining private phone record using false pretenses) in an effort to trace those board leaks. This led to the resignation of Chairman Patricia Dunn, and state and federal investigations. CEO Mark Hurd stated that the "tactics do not reflect the values of H-P." Hewlett-Packard's core values include "we conduct our business with uncompromising integrity" and "we have trust and respect for individuals."

Leadership today is about winning the trust and respect of constituents, including citizens, shareholders, employees, and customers. But should these constituents place their trust (and money) in a leader's hands? Constituents take the time to evaluate the character, competence and commitment of those that are (or aspire to be) in leadership positions. And anytime there is a gap between what the leader says and does the credibility of that leader will suffer. Therefore, it is no surprise that individuals get disillusioned when their leaders prove themselves to be only mere images of the values that they espouse. It is under such conditions that people believe that their "leaders" do not show principled leadership. As a result, the dynamic currency of leadership depreciates, compromising the leader's ability to lead. In this article, we describe principled leadership and how it keeps leaders on the right course.

⊠ What Is Principled Leadership?

Alan Yuspah, senior Vice President, Ethics, Compliance and Corporate Responsibility, the Hospital Corporation of America Inc., identified three essential elements of principled leadership.

1. *The articulation of certain principles or values.* Leaders need to decide what their personal or organizational values are and provide leadership consistent with these espoused or internalized values. Does the leader "live" the values in the business decisions that he or she has to make? Does the leader stick with his or her stated values no matter how difficult the business challenges prove to be? Consider the challenge that Ed Clark, the President and CEO, TD Bank Financial Group, recalled in a recent presentation to MBAs. To paraphrase him: We

are trying to be an inclusive workplace, and we believe in diversity of all kinds: women, visible minorities, gays, and so forth. We are supportive of the gay community; we sponsor the Pride parade. However, I get letters from customers, that state: If you want to defy God's will then I don't want to bank with you. Clark and the TD Bank Financial Group remain committed to their diversity initiatives.

2. *The principled leader is able to make tough decisions.* Principled leaders make a conscientious effort to get all the relevant information to make an informed decision and to see that their decisions are consistent with their values and those of the organization. The leadership of Flight Director Eugene Kranz during the Apollo 13 crisis is a compelling example. For years, he had championed a strong set of values: discipline, morale or confidence, toughness, competence, commitment, and teamwork. Observers of the space program have said that it was these characteristics that formed the culture that would keep Kranz's team together both in good times and, in particular, in bad times. In business settings, good leaders must be principled but also pragmatic—their principles cannot paralyze them from taking action. The principled person nearly always feels guilty that s/he cannot live up to his/her finest aspirations.

3. *Principled leadership is reflected in how leaders deal with other people.* Those individuals in leadership positions should never forget that the "how" is as important as the "what." For example, humility and integrity should be part of a principled leader's behavioral repertoire. Manuel London, a management scholar and practitioner, and Director of the Center of Human Resource Management, at the State University of New York, indicates that principled leaders always try to understand the various points of view and reach common ground without hostility, and without working over, around, or through other people. This is a key message that leaders such as Ed Clark, George

Cope (President and COO, Bell Canada), Michael McCain (President and CEO, Maple Leaf Foods), and Lt.-Gen. (ret.) Romeo Dallaire keep telling our MBA students. But, as London explained, principled leaders do not ignore the tough realities of business; they have mastered the art of business diplomacy. In his words, "They work together to enhance interpersonal work relationships and are particularly valuable in making tough decisions, resolving emotional conflicts, and negotiating sensitive issues."

The 16th President of the United States, Abraham Lincoln, can inspire all of us in our own careers. For example, in *Team of Rivals: The Political Genius of Abraham Lincoln,* author Doris Kearns Goodwin writes that Lincoln was able to defeat more privileged and accomplished rivals for the Republican nomination in 1860 because his life experience had forged a character that allowed him to put himself in the place of other persons, to know what they were feeling and to understand their fears, motives and desires. This same character allowed him to bring his rivals into his cabinet and marshal their talents to preserve the Union and win the war. Goodwin wrote that Lincoln was "plain and complex, shrewd and transparent, tender and iron-willed. . . . His success in dealing with the strong egos of the men in his cabinet suggests that in the hands of a truly great politician the qualities we generally associate with decency—kindness, sensitivity, compassion, honesty and empathy—can also be impressive political resources."

⊠ How to "Get" Principled Leadership

It is foolish to believe that there is a single most important determinant of principled leadership. There are actually four determinants, and they come in to play at the individual, group, and organizational levels. We list examples in this particular order. We do not assume that our list is complete.

1. Upbringing and Life Experiences

Retired Lieutenant-General Romeo Dallaire is the former head of the United Nations Peacekeeping Force in Rwanda. He witnessed genocide. Dallaire shared the following anecdote with a group of MBAs enrolled in a leadership course. A young lieutenant and his platoon enter a small village which had been the scene of a massacre. The troops notice a ditch with women and children, several who are hacked to pieces; others are bleeding to death. There is no doubt that these people are going to die. It is hard for the soldiers to just stand by and be a witness to these people dying. What should they do? The reader should know that, before the war, over 30 per cent of Rwandans were infected with HIV or had AIDS. Soldiers do not run around with protective gear, such as rubber gloves, and have scrapes, cuts, bruises, and wounds due to the nature of their business. What should the young lieutenant order the soldiers to do? Should he order the troops not to help and to march on because of the risk of contracting the devastating disease? Or should he order the troops to console and help the women and children? The Lieutenant figures that people are dying and that the soldiers have a moral or ethical duty to assist these people in any possible way. Dallaire went to his 26 commanders and explained the dilemma. He found out that 23 commanders would order the troops *not* to go in and help; three would assist, including the Canadians. The question then is, "For what reasons do some troops get in the ditch and assist the women and children, even with the risk involved, whereas others do not?" Dallaire believes that training has something to do with this. But perhaps more important, he articulated, it is the upbringing and the fundamental beliefs or values that Canadians espouse. Two of these beliefs are that human rights are important, and that every human is human . . . one person is not more human than the other.

2. Reflection

The development of one's leadership skills requires actual leadership actions, followed by reflection or debriefing. As a principled leader, do we take the time to pause and think about how we are doing in terms of the goals we have set for ourselves? Leaders are often under intense pressure to produce results. This is a plus when the leader has mastered important skills or performance routines. But what about those behaviors that require our continued attention because the objective is to develop these behaviors? Sometimes we need to be in a learning mode. For example, leaders can focus on several questions or "tests," including a hypothetical Globe and Mail headline. Would they like to see the action they were contemplating on tomorrow's front page? Could they live with the headline? Could they explain their actions to their 10-year old child? Seeking the advice of an executive coach who can help develop skills is becoming increasingly common for business executives.

3. Role Models

Gandhi considered modeling the moral example as the prime duty of a ruler, including the head of a family or the owner of a business. Studies have shown that people's behavior is shaped, in part, by their observation of others. For example, Albert Bandura, the David Starr Jordan Professor of Social Science in Psychology at Stanford University, and famous for his work on social learning, wrote:

> Learning would be exceedingly laborious, not to mention hazardous, if people had to rely solely on the effects of their own actions to inform them what to do. Fortunately, most human behavior is learned through modeling: from observing others one forms an idea of how new behaviors are manifested and perform; on later occasions this coded information serves as a guide for action.

Mentoring is consistent with Bandura's social learning theory; it involves learning in a social situation whereby a person models the behavior of a more experienced teacher or colleague. Seymour Schulich, a successful Canadian businessman and philanthropist, recently observed that, "I live the axiom that 100 years from now, it won't matter how much money you had, how big a house you lived in or what kind of car you drove. But if you are important in the life of a young person, you might make a difference. So I make time for young people and try to act as a mentor." We know that without the modeling of leadership behaviors, standards of principled leadership will be more difficult to achieve. This is because leaders help to set the tone of behavioral norms and organizational culture.

4. Code of Ethics and Communication

Organizations should have a code of ethics or a set of guiding values. Leaders should assess decisions or actions against that code. This is how the Johnson & Johnson organization was so successful in dealing with the Tylenol crisis. This is why organizations such as General Electric, Maple Leaf Foods, and TD Bank Financial Group are spending a lot of time on defining their core values and how to "live" those values. The events at Boeing discussed earlier show that a code of ethics can be effective. But a willingness to act on the code is required. One of the main purposes of a code of ethics is to provide guidelines that help people decide what actions to take from an ethical or organizational culture point of view. The importance of values and a code of ethics must be conveyed from the top of the organization—the CEO and his or her leadership team. The leader should make values a salient aspect of the leadership agenda so that the significance of these values does in fact reach those individuals in lower-level positions.

For example, leaders can explain how a set of values guided the decision making process. Consider the following actual event. Roy Vagelos, a former senior vice-president of research at Merck, and CEO, decided to give away a drug that prevented river blindness to all those who need it and who could not afford it. Former chairman of Merck, George W. Merck, explained, "We try never to forget that medicine is for the people. It is not for the profits. . . . The profits follow, and if we have remembered that, they have never failed to appear. The better we have remembered it, the larger they have been." The message? Values or guiding principles are important in making tough business decisions. Vagelos was later asked whether he would have committed his company to the costly program even without the benefits of strengthening its reputation, bolstering its recruiting, and the creation of shareholder value. He explained that he had no choice as his whole life had been dedicated to helping people.

The Challenges of Principled Leadership

There can be challenges to "living the values" and a leader's principled approach to decision making. For example, an activist group went after Ford Motor Co. and Walt Disney Co. because it believed the two companies were destroying traditional American values by supporting gay and lesbian rights. In his 2002 book *Leadership*, Giuliani recounts the events that took place in October 1995, the year in which the United Nations celebrated its 50th anniversary. The New York City Host Committee had raised money to sponsor several events, including a concert at Lincoln Center's Avery Fisher Hall. Who showed up? Yasser Arafat. Giuliani had specifically excluded the Palestinian delegation, as well as delegations from Cuba, Iraq, Iran, Libya, North Korea, Somalia, and Yugoslavia. Giuliani had special contempt for Arafat and so he had him thrown out. An international scandal was born. *The New York Times* and the Clinton administration condemned Giuliani's action. But Giuliani was convinced that he was on the right side; his core set of principles, and Arafat's ongoing terrorist activities, drove his behavior. In his words, "Some Americans are unable to face up to the fact that there really are evil people."

Sooner or later, therefore, leaders face the challenge of how to remain true to their principles, in particular, when other people put pressure on them. Most leaders operate in a fast-paced and complex world, where principles often collide. It is sometimes very difficult to do "the right thing" for both employees and shareholders, for customers and employees, for taxpayers and clients of the social welfare system. We conclude this article with five prescriptions that, we believe, will make people more receptive to principled leadership. These are the things that leaders can do to continue to "walk on water" as opposed to swimming or sinking.

1. Executives Should Be Model Citizens

John Edward Poole of Edmonton, who died recently at the age of ninety, is a hard-to-beat exemplar. On retiring as CEO of Poole Construction Ltd. (now PCL Construction Ltd.) in 1977, he and his brother George sold their majority stake to the organization's employees rather than accept the highest offer. (Today, the organization remains 100 percent owned by employees.) During the next three decades, he and his wife, Barbara, gave tens of millions of dollars, often on a sustained endowment basis, to a host of cultural, educational, social and environmental institutions in their city. The couple also led fund-raising campaigns for many good causes. *Edmonton Journal* columnist, Paula Simons, noted in a tribute, "[John Poole] believed that every man owed a duty to his fellow citizens. He understood that living in a city isn't just about occupying space—it's about participating in the life of a community. It's about taking responsibility for the future."

2. Stick to What You're Good At

How many businesses in Canada and elsewhere have been harmed or ruined by a senior leadership team that ventures into new activities or markets without enough advance study of conditions or an inadequate understanding of its own circle of competence? For example, Southwest Airlines' returns to shareholders over three decades have outdone even those of Warren Buffett's legendary Berkshire Hathaway. Southwest has no hotels, no travel businesses or real estate speculations. Both management and employees know what the airline is good at and stick to it: low-cost reliable air transportation. In an industry where profits rarely seem to last more than a year or two, Southwest continues to flourish. Contrast this approach with organizations such as K-Mart, ASDA, and Nortel that at some point struggled with strategic drift, unable to provide a clear direction in their activities. The implications for personal leadership? It is important to have a core set of convictions, or focus; without it, leaders yield to all kinds of pressures, and little gets achieved. Senator and former Democratic nominee for U.S. President John F. Kerry was seen as a mess of contradictions on various issues important to the American public. People perceived him as a flip-flopper; he lacked a clear focus. Bush won re-election in part because Americans wanted clear and consistent leadership.

3. An Inclusive Corporate Culture

Nucor Corporation, the out-performer in the American steel industry for many years, and one of America's most-admired organizations, is a good case study here. Its former CEO, F. Kenneth Iverson, is quoted in Jeremy J. Siegal's excellent book *The Future for Investors* as attributing most of the company's success to "the consistency of our company and our ability to project its philosophies throughout the whole organization, enabled by our lack of layers and bureaucracy." The philosophy of "no favourites" among all members of the corporate team is demonstrated in myriad ways. Distinctions between executives and other employees are even difficult to detect. For example, there is no executive dining room at Nucor's head office. All employees of the company are listed alphabetically in the annual report, with no distinctions for titles. There are no company vehicles or aircraft and no assigned parking places. All employees receive the same amount of vacation time and insurance coverage. Ideas won't get buried in bureaucracy; the freedom to try out ideas gives Nucor a distinct advantage over other companies: a creative, get-it-done workforce. Every employee is a member of the same winning team.

4. Have Sound Whistleblower Protection or Processes for Information Flow

Sherron Watkins, the ex-Enron executive who first confronted former CEO Kenneth Lay about her suspicions of accounting improprieties, became a national "hero" when her memos to Lay were leaked to the American media. She had attempted, without success, to protest Enron's accounting practices to other executives as early as 1996, but got nowhere. The then-CFO of Enron, Andrew Fastow, wanted her fired, but senior management could find no reasonable cause.

Every organization should have policies in place to protect the Sherron Watkinses of the world and to ensure that valid concerns are acted upon with deliberate speed. "Information patriots", as Canadian whistleblowers now often prefer to be called, are still usually forced to give up their careers in the offices where they encountered and confronted wrongdoing. Consider, for example, the fate of Joseph Darby, the U.S. Army Specialist who turned in the pictures of prisoner abuse at Abu Ghraib. He was a hero to some; Caroline Kennedy and Senator Ted Kennedy gave him a Profile In Courage award in honor of

President John F. Kennedy. But Darby could not return to his home because he had been threatened. Darby was supposed to remain anonymous, but former Secretary of Defense Donald Rumsfeld identified him without warning on national television, a gesture that some say was more about payback than an attempt to honor the whistleblower. There are scores of whistleblowers or information patriots that have paid a steep price for their courage to speak up. Responsible CEOs should ensure that people like Watkins and Darby are regarded as role models for all employees.

CEOs should appreciate the eyes and ears of their employees. Transparency is important; some even consider it an outright competitive weapon. Former U.S. Supreme Court Justice Louis Brandeis once said, "Sunlight is the best disinfectant." The quote refers to the benefits of openness and transparency. Some well-known organizations have made it their objective to operate in an atmosphere of avowed openness. Their leadership opines that individuals who feel a discomfort under the bright light of scrutiny may have something to hide. Those in leadership positions cannot solve problems if they don't know about them. Leaders are well-advised to create routes for their employees to express their views, so that maximum, not minimum, information is used in their decision making.

5. Boards of Directors Should Encourage CEOs to Speak Out Responsibly on Public Issues

How many of our business leaders have had the courage to speak out from a responsible perspective against income trusts? Or take climate change, the very inconvenient and doubtless most important issue facing humanity today. Recently, the Intergovernmental Panel on Climate Change, drawing on the work of thousands of scientists around the world, reported that all of us on the planet have only a decade to reverse surging greenhouse gas emissions or risk severe climate change that would render numerous regions of the world uninhabitable. A cover story in a recent *Economist*, "The Greening of America", indicated that corporate America is now among the loudest voices calling for emission controls and other measures designed to reduce the output of carbon dioxide and greenhouse gasses. For example, the CEO of Duke Energy, James Rogers, said about reductions, "It must be mandatory, so that there is no doubt about our actions. . . . The science of global warming is clear. We know enough to act now. We must act now." Not enough business voices appear yet have joined the parade on the issue in our own country. And for CEOs and the senior leadership team to do so effectively, they need the support of their board of directors; organizations should speak with one voice.

In her 2006 memoir titled *Tough Choices*, former Hewlett-Packard CEO Carly Fiorina writes about success and the importance of character. "Character was everything, and character was defined as candour, integrity, and authenticity. Candour was about speaking the truth, and about speaking up and speaking out. Integrity was about preserving your principles and action on them. Authenticity was about knowing what you believed, being who you were, and standing up for both." Fiorina explains that leaders can always choose to become something more. We suggest they can (and should) choose to work on their principled leadership, as it appears there is considerable room for improvement. A recent poll of 1,000 Canadians found that 93 per cent of respondents rated firefighters as trustworthy. In contrast, CEOs were considered trustworthy by just 21 per cent of the adult Canadians who were polled by Ipsos Reid; this number is virtually unchanged since 2002. Only union leaders (19 per cent), local politicians (12 per cent), national politicians and car salespeople (both at 7 per cent) ranked below CEOs in the "whom do we trust" survey. When asked what criteria they considered in rating the trustworthiness of people, the respondents indicated they used factors such as integrity, reliability, and commitment to promises in their ratings. These factors, of course, characterize the principled leader. But we also note that principled people sometimes cross the barrier between being right and being righteous. The first is admirable the second just alienates people.

About the Editors

W. Glenn Rowe served in the Canadian Navy for 22 years. While still in the navy, he completed his master of business administration degree at Memorial University of Newfoundland part-time (1983–1986) and taught on a part-time basis for 2 years (1986–1988) in Memorial's Faculty of Business Administration. In 1990, he retired from the navy and became a full-time lecturer in the Faculty of Business Administration at Memorial. In 1992, he began studying leadership within the context of strategic management at Texas A&M University, where he completed his PhD in 1996. He rejoined the Faculty of Business Administration at Memorial in September 1995, where he taught strategic management and strategic leadership. Professor Rowe joined the Richard Ivey School of Business as a faculty member on July 1, 2001. He served as the faculty adviser for the PhD program in general management/strategy from January 2002 to July 2009 and teaches strategy and strategic leadership to undergraduate business students, MBAs, EMBAs, and doctoral students. On July 1, 2009, he became the director of Ivey's Executive MBA Program. He serves as a reviewer for several academic journals and is active in the community. He has facilitated strategic-thinking sessions for several organizations such as the Alliance for the Control of Tobacco (Newfoundland and Labrador), the Newfoundland and Labrador Medical Association, Fishery Products International, Gros Morne National Park, and Sir Wilfred Grenfell College. He is the coauthor of a strategic management textbook and its associated casebook, both of which are in their third edition. His research is published in journals such as the *Strategic Management Journal,* the *Journal of Management,* and the *Leadership Quarterly.*

Laura Guerrero worked in retail management for 10 years in Canada, the United States, and Mexico. She has an undergraduate degree in economics from the University of Texas at El Paso. Later, she completed a masters of business administration with a concentration on management and organizational studies at Simon Fraser University in British Columbia, Canada. In 2009, she completed a PhD in organizational behavior at the Richard Ivey School of Business at The University of Western Ontario. In addition to her interest in gender and culture as they relate to leadership, her research has focused on careers of expatriates and immigrants. In September 2009, she joined the Faculty of Business Administration at the University of Texas at El Paso as an assistant professor of management.

Supporting researchers for more than 40 years

Research methods have always been at the core of SAGE's publishing program. Founder Sara Miller McCune published SAGE's first methods book, *Public Policy Evaluation*, in 1970. Soon after, she launched the *Quantitative Applications in the Social Sciences* series—affectionately known as the "little green books."

Always at the forefront of developing and supporting new approaches in methods, SAGE published early groundbreaking texts and journals in the fields of qualitative methods and evaluation.

Today, more than 40 years and two million little green books later, SAGE continues to push the boundaries with a growing list of more than 1,200 research methods books, journals, and reference works across the social, behavioral, and health sciences. Its imprints—Pine Forge Press, home of innovative textbooks in sociology, and Corwin, publisher of PreK–12 resources for teachers and administrators—broaden SAGE's range of offerings in methods. SAGE further extended its impact in 2008 when it acquired CQ Press and its best-selling and highly respected political science research methods list.

From qualitative, quantitative, and mixed methods to evaluation, SAGE is the essential resource for academics and practitioners looking for the latest methods by leading scholars.

For more information, visit **www.sagepub.com**.

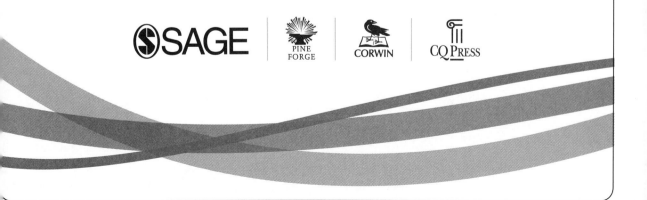